22.11.89

GW00546350

The Austrian Party System

The Austrian Party System

EDITED BY

Anton Pelinka and Fritz Plasser

Westview Press
BOULDER, SAN FRANCISCO, & LONDON

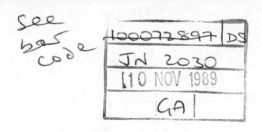

Westview Special Studies in West European Politics and Society

This Westview softcover edition is printed on acid-free paper and bound in library-quality, coated covers that carry the highest rating of the National Association of State Textbook Administrators, in consultation with the Association of American Publishers and the Book Manufacturers' Institute.

A somewhat larger edition of this work was published in German in 1988 by Böhlau Verlag Gesellschaft m. b. H. and Co. KG., Vienna.

Published in 1989 in the United States of America by Westview Press, Inc., 5500 Central Avenue, Boulder, Colorado 80301, and in the United Kingdom by Westview Press, Inc., 13 Brunswick Centre, London, WC1N 1AF, England

Library of Congress Cataloging-in-Publication Data
The Austrian party system / edited by Anton Pelinka and Fritz Plasser.
    p. cm.—(Westview special studies in West
European politics and society)
  Includes bibliographies and index.
  ISBN 0-8133-7755-2
  1. Political parties—Austria. 2. Austria—Politics and
government—1945-   . I. Pelinka, Anton, 1941-   . II. Plasser,
Fritz, 1948- .
JN2030.A97 1989
324.2436—dc20   89-32835
                                              CIP

Printed and bound in the United States of America

The paper used in this publication meets the requirements of the American National Standard for Permanence of Paper for Printed Library Materials Z39.48-1984.

10   9   8   7   6   5   4   3   2   1

Contents

List of Tables and Figures   viii

Abbreviations   xvii

Preface   xix

1   *Pelinka/Plasser*
    Compared to What?
    The Austrian Party System in an International Comparison   1

2   *Pelinka*
    Decline of the Party State and the Rise of Parliamentarianism:
    Change within the Austrian Party System   21

3   *Plasser*
    The Austrian Party System between Erosion and Innovation:
    An Empirical Long-term Analysis   41

4   *Plasser/Ulram*
    Major Parties on the Defensive:
    The Austrian Party- and Electoral Landscape after the
    1986 National Council Election   69

5   *Gehmacher/Birk/Ogris*
    1986—The Year of Election Surprises:
    From the Perspective of the Electoral Behavior Theory   93

6   *Traar/Birk*
    Factors of Voting Behavior:
    Why Do Austrian Voters Vote the Way They Do?   117

7   *Gehmacher/Haerpfer*
    Voting Behavior and the Party System:
    The Internal Structure of the SPÖ, ÖVP and FPÖ Electorates   145

8   *Dachs*
    Citizen Lists and Green-Alternative Parties in Austria   173

9   *Ulram*
    Changing Issues in the Austrian Party System   197

10 *Gerlich*
    National Consciousness and National Identity:
    A Contribution to the Political Culture of the
    Austrian Party System   223

11 *Bubendorfer*
    Between Alternative and Established Forms of Political
    Participation: Young Austrians and the Austrian Party System
    between 1960 and 1987   259

12 *Mantl*
    Reform Tendencies in the Austrian Party System   279

13 *Kofler*
    Between Old Symbolic Worlds and New Challenges:
    A Glance at the Internal Life of the Parties   297

14 *Nick*
    The States and the Austrian Party System   309

15 *Müller*
    Party Patronage in Austria:
    Theoretical Considerations and Empirical Findings   327

16 *Wicha*
    Party Funding in Austria   357

17 *Raschauer*
    The Legal Status of Political Parties   389

18 *Stirnemann*
    Recruitment and Recruitment Strategies   401

19 *Sully*
   The Austrian Way?   429

Documentation of Austrian Election Results, 1945–1986   447

List of Contributors   452

Index   454

Tables and Figures

Tables

2.1   Concentration of the Austrian party system from
1949 to 1986   29

2.2   Criticism of the claim to general representation
(poor distinguishability) of the parties   30

2.3a   The generation conflict exemplified by Zwentendorf, Hainburg
and Green-Alternative sympathizers   32

2.3b   Attitude to the Danube power station at Hainburg according
to age, education and residence (in %)   32

2.3c   Election of a Green or Alternative List at the national level
basically imaginable (in %)   33

3.1   Employed persons according to sectors (1951-1981)   46

3.2   Social voter basis of the major Austrian parties (1955-1985)   46

3.3   Decrease of the traditional social core voter groups of the major
Austrian parties (1961-1985)   47

3.4   Secularization (or de-confessionalization) in the Austrian party
system (1955-1985)   48

3.5   Party-political consonance of social networks (1972-1984)   49

3.6   Party identification in Austria (1954-1987)   50

3.7   Decomposition of the electorates of the major Austrian parties
(1954-1985)   51

3.8   Decision-making certainty, the time of decision and percentage
of party-shifters (1956-1986)   52

3.9	Decline of party ties in Austria (1969-1986)	53
3.10	The electoral foundation of the Austrian parties (1985/86)	54
3.11	Electoral-statistical cross-sectional analysis of National Council elections from 1971 to 1986	58
3.12	Statistical cross-sectional analysis of the 1971-1986 National Council elections based on prevailing socio-structural dynamics of change	59
3.13	Party ties and election behavior in the 1986 National Council election according to age and educational level	60
4.1	Changes in voting behavior (1983-1986)	73
4.2	Voting behavior according to socio-demographic groups (1986)	74
4.3	Structure of party electorates (1986)	75
4.4	Determinants of the 1986 National Council election referring to the individual parties	77
4.5	The percentage of party-shifters in selected voter groups (1979-1986) (NCE = National Council election)	78
4.6	The time of voting decision in selected voter groups (1979-1986)	79
4.7	The time of decision of the party-shifters (1986)	79
4.8	Negative voting in Austria (1986)	81
4.9	The political structure of the electorate of the FPÖ and the Greens (1986)	81
4.10	Proportional party representation in Parliament after the 1986 National Council election	83
4.11	Assessment of the problem-solving capacity of the coalition government in the spring of 1987	84
4.12	The largest voter potential of the FPÖ and the Greens (1988)	85
4.13	Party loyalty of Austrian voters (1977-1987)	87
4.14	Party identification in the spring of 1987	87
4.15	Satisfaction with the work of the coalition government (1987/88)	88
5.1	The 1986 Federal Presidential election and National Council election	96

5.2	Monthly IFES multi-theme surveys (mean values)	96
5.3	Intended voting behavior, compared over time— direct election	97
5.4	The November 23, 1986, election results	97
5.5	Party loyalty in Austria	99
5.6	Lack of trust in politics	100
5.7a	Political-strategic indicators (1969-1986)	101
5.7b	Annual mean values: voter sympathies: SPÖ, ÖVP, FPÖ, VGÖ, ALÖ	102
5.7c	Annual mean values: voter sympathies for top politicians	102
5.8	Political cycles (1984-1986)	104
5.9	Willingness to become politically involved	105
5.10	IFES: factors determining 1986 electoral behavior	106
5.11	Regressions—the influence of the media	107
5.12	Self-categorization on a right to left scale	108
5.13	IFES—voter trend analysis of the 1983/1986 National Council elections	109
5.14	IFES—voter trend analysis of the May 4, 1986, Federal Presidential election and the 1986 National Council election	110
5.15	Desired form of government (1966-1986)	111
5.16	Government preferences (1966-1986)	112
5.17	Party images	114
5.18	Party preference as a percent of all eligible voters	115
6.1	Changes in voting intention in favor of the SPÖ in the next National Council election in temporal comparison	119
6.2	Changes of voting intention in favor of the ÖVP for the next National Council election in temporal comparison	121
6.3	Distribution of the three types—post-materialists, mixed type, materialists—among the various age groups for 1979 and 1986	121
6.4	Voting intentions of eligible voters with college degrees for the National Council election	123
6.5	Generation-specific influence on voting behavior	128

6.6   Significant correlation coefficients between value dimensions
      and the intended voting behavior with regard to the National
      Council election and the June 1986 Presidential election in
      favor of Dr. Kurt Waldheim   129
6.7   Strong discontent with the SPÖ regarding its behavior in certain
      political issues—classified according to groups of voters   130
6.8   Variance explained by the model of voting factors in the form
      of a table—and the individual size of these factors   132
6.9   Voting intention for the next National Council election and
      social determinants   133
6.10 Which party represents the interests of ...?   134
6.11 Voting intention in the next National Council election and
      structure of the voters according to their personal basic
      conservative disposition   134
6.12 Structure of the voters according to their conservative
      disposition   134
6.13 Acceptance of the political system, the established parties,
      and satisfaction with the federal government and the ÖVP
      as opposition party   135
6.14 Trust in political parties and politicians   135
6.15 Structure of eligible voters according to the degree
      of their political resignation   136
6.16 The Austrians' expectations of the future   136
6.17 Structure of eligible voters according to their degree of
      pessimism regarding the future   136
6.18 The Austrians' tendency to believe in authority   137
6.19 The Austrians' tendency to believe in authority and their
      voting intention for the next National Council election   137
6.20 Acceptance of materialistic-realistic aims and the voting
      intention for the next National Council election and changes
      regarding the previous one   138
6.21 Strong discontent with the SPÖ regarding its attitudes to
      certain political issues—classified according to groups
      of voters   138

6.22   Voting behavior of interviewed eligible voters in the next
       National Council election who give high grades of sympathy   139
6.23   Voting intention for the next National Council election   139

7.1   Occupation and electorate structure, 1971-1983   146
7.2   Social structure of the ÖVP and SPÖ electorates, 1976-1983   147
7.3   Occupation and voting behavior, 1982-1983   148
7.4   Social structure of party membership, SPÖ, ÖVP, 1983   149
7.5   SPÖ and ÖVP party memberships according to occupation
       and sex, 1983   149
7.6   Party membership, occupation and sex   150
7.7   Social class and party preference, 1982   150
7.8   Occupational structure, social class and party preference, 1982   152
7.9   SPÖ voters: sex, age and social class, 1982   153
7.10   SPÖ voters: education, household income and social class, 1982   155
7.11   SPÖ voters: size of community, region and social class, 1982   156
7.12   ÖVP voters: sex, age and social class, 1982   158
7.13   ÖVP voters: education, household income and social class, 1982   160
7.14   ÖVP voters: community size, region and social class, 1982   162
7.15   FPÖ voters: sex, age and party preference, 1982   163
7.16   FPÖ voters: education, household income and party preference,
       1982   164
7.17   FPÖ voters: community size, region and party preference, 1982   165
7.18   Social structure and the Austrian party system, 1986   168

8.1   Electoral success of selected citizens' initiatives and
       Green-Alternative parties   182
8.2   Social profile of party supporters in Austria (1983)   183
8.3   Political origin of Green voters in Austria (1983)   184
8.4   Green-Alternative electoral potential in Austria   184
8.5   Reasons for voting GAL in the 1984 Vorarlberg diet election
       in the population's opinion   185
8.6   Opinion on expanding the Austrian party spectrum as seen
       over several years (1976-1984)   186

8.7   Votes cast for the Green-Alternatives in the 1986
        National Council election according to state—change as
        compared to the 1983 National Council election   187

9.1   Scale of attractiveness of political concepts (1976)   199
9.2   Placement of Austrians on the left-right continuum (1973-1985) 200
9.3   The decrease in the proportion of respondents on the "right"
        or "left" of the ideological self-placement scale by groups
        (1976-1985)   201
9.4   Austrians' political priorities, 1980-1987   205
9.5   Problems Austrians would like political parties to deal with
        (1981-1987)   206
9.6   Judgement of environmental protection activities (1982-1984) 207
9.7   Environmental protection and jobs (1982-1985)   208
9.8   Attitudes toward taxes (the tax burden), 1980-1985   209
9.9   Judging the use of taxpayers' money, 1980-1985   210
9.10   Loss of faith and criticism of subsidies   210
9.11   Insufficient consideration given to problems by political parties
        (1981-1987)   212
9.12   The image of politicians (1980/81-1984/85)   213
9.13   The social profile of issue voters (1985)   215

10.1   Concepts associated with Austria   239
10.2   National consciousness   241
10.3   Development of national consciousness   242
10.4   Judgement of the anschluss   243
10.5   Anticipation of another anschluss   244
10.6   Orientation of reporting on foreign events   244
10.7   Attractiveness of various nations   245
10.8   State consciousness   245
10.9   National characteristics   247
10.10   Austrians' talents   248
10.11   National pride   248
10.12   Nostalgia for Austria in a foreign country   249

10.13	Patriotic pride	250
10.14	Uplifting feeling of pride in Austria	250
10.15	Defending the flag	251

11.1	The degree of severity of the detachment from politics	261
11.2	Agreement with parents on political issues	262
11.3	Young people's interest in politics	263
11.4	Membership in a political party	264
11.5	Party disenchantment: the attitude of the younger generation toward the political parties	264
11.6	Differentiating between the parliamentary parties	265
11.7	The demands made of the political parties by the younger generation	266
11.8	The problem-handling deficits of the parties	267
11.9	Potential Green voters among those under 30	268
11.10	The 1986 National Council elections	269
11.11	The attributes of the ideal politician	269
11.12	The image of Austrian politicians in the eyes of the younger generation	270
11.13	Values of personal importance to the younger generation	271
11.14	Degree of satisfaction with the political parties	272
11.15	Satisfaction with the political system	273
11.16	The importance of the democratic instruments	274
11.17	The potential political participation of 16- to 24-year-olds	274
11.18	Personal involvement in political actions	275

| 13.1 | Types of party membership | 301 |
| 13.2 | Subjective influence on political events (1977 - 1985) | 304 |

14.1	The heterogeneity of the states	312
14.2	Margin between strongest and second-strongest party in state diet elections from 1949 to 1986	313
14.3	Church attendance according to state and town size	318
14.4	Chances for a regional party	321

15.1 Ministerial patronage 337
15.2 Motives for joining a party, 1969-70 338
15.3 Motives for party membership, 1980 339
15.4 Motives for party membership, 1985 340
15.5 Own and others' motives for party membership, 1980 342

16.1 Party funding: fund-raising 360
16.2 Direct funding for parties as per Article 2a and b of the parties' law between 1978 and 1986 368
16.3 Income received by the parliamentary parties according to the 1983 and 1984 statements of accounts (in absolute figures) 383
16.4 Income received by the parliamentary parties according to the 1983 and 1984 statements of accounts (in percent) 384
16.5 Expenditures by the parliamentary parties according to the 1983 and 1984 statements of accounts 385

18.1 Candidates elected by "ranking and striking" 405
18.2 The five candidates with the most preference votes (1983) 407
18.3 Interrelationship of parties and interest groups (%) 412
18.4 The ÖVP ticket in Election District 11 (Viertel unterm Manhartsberg), 1956-1966, shown according to league membership 414
18.5 Advancement of SPÖ candidates in Election District 07 (Vienna West) 414
18.6 ÖVP basic seat in Vienna (1959-1966) 416
18.7 Deputies leaving and moving up the party list 420
18.8 Crucial National Council seats that were actually decided on election day 421

19.1 Styrian LTW (Sept. 1986) 434
19.2 Age profile of voters, 1986 436
19.3 Voting patterns in general elections since 1979 for the SPÖ (%) 438
19.4 Distribution of seats in the Nationalrat (%) for the SPÖ/ÖVP compared with other parties, 1945-86 439

20.1   National Council elections, 1945-1986   448
20.2   Federal presidential elections in Austria   449
20.3   The popular referendum on 5 November 1978 concerning
       a federal law about the peaceful use of nuclear energy in Austria   450
20.4   Petitions for parliamentary decisions in Austria (1964-1987)   451

Figures

3.1   Hegemony and erosion in the Austrian party system (1966-1989)   56
3.2   Erosion, decomposition and turbulence in the Austrian party
       system (1974-1989)   57

6.1   Factors of voting behavior   140

9.1   Sociopolitical orientations—Austria in 1976 and 1987   203
9.2   Sociopolitical orientations—selected groups (1987)   204

13.1   Proportion of votes of the two major and the small parties
       in elections since 1945   298
13.2   Membership density of the major Austrian parties   300

16.1   Distribution of the individual types of income among the
       parliamentary parties in 1984   361
16.2   The developments of direct public funding as foreseen
       in the parties' law from 1975 to 1986   378
16.3   Total "grants to political parties"   378

19.1   Electoral profile of the parties since 1949   439
19.2   Percentage of votes for the SPÖ/ÖVP compared with other
       parties (1949-1986)   440

Abbreviations

AL	Alternative Liste Alternative List
ALG	Alternative Liste Graz Alternative List Graz
ALI	Alternative Liste Innsbruck Alternative List Innsbruck
ALNÖ	Alternative Liste Niederösterreich Alternative List of Lower Austria
ALÖ	Alternative Liste Österreichs Alternative List of Austria
ALV	Alternative Liste Vorarlberg Alternative List Vorarlberg
ALW	Alternative Liste Wien Alternative Liste Vienna
AT	Anderes Tirol Other Tirol
AUS	Ausländer Halt Bewegung Stop Foreigners Movement
BIP	Bürgerinitiative Parlament Citizens' Initiative for Parliament
BL	Bürgerliste Citizens' List
CV	Cartellverband Confederation of Catholic University Fraternities
DFP	Demokratisch-fortschrittliche Partei Democratic Progressive Party

DGÖ	Die Grünen Österreichs The Greens of Austria
DÖW	Dokumentationsarchiv des österreichischen Widerstands Documentation Archive of the Austrian Resistance
FMB	Freda Meissner-Blau
FPÖ	Freiheitliche Partei Österreichs Freedom Party of Austria
GABL	Grün-Alternative Bürgerliste Green-Alternative Citizens' List
GAL	Grün-Alternative (Demokratische) Liste Green-Alternative (Democratic) List
GfK	Gesellschaft für Konsum-, Markt- und Absatzforschung Association for Consumer and Market Research
GRAS	Grün-Alternative Sammlung Green-Alternative Collective
IFD	Institut für Demoskopie Allensbach Institute for Demoscopy Allensbach
IFES	Institut für Empirische Sozialforschung Institute for Empirical Social Research

IMAS	Institut für Markt- und Sozialanalyse Institute for Market- and Social Analysis	ÖVP	Österreichische Volkspartei Austrian People's Party
		ÖWB	Österreichischer Wirtschaftsbund Austrian Business League
JN	Jurisdictionsnorm Austrian Court Organization Act		
		ORF	Österreichischer Rundfunk
KLS	Kommunist- und Linkssozialisten Communist and Leftist Socialists		Austrian Broadcasting Company
		SPD	Sozialdemokratische Partei
KPÖ	Kommunistische Partei Österreichs Communist Party of Austria		Social Democratic Party
		SPÖ	Sozialistische Partei Österreichs
MB	Meissner-Blau		Socialist Party of Austria

Mir reichts's! - I've had enough!

		VdU	Verband der Unabhängigen
NCE	National Council election		Union of Independents
NDP	Nationaldemokratische Partei National Democratic Party	VG	Vereinte Grüne United Greens
NRW	Nationalratswahl National Council election (NCE)	VGÖ	Vereinte Grüne Österreichs United Greens of Austria
NRWO	Nationalratswahlordnung National Council Election Regulations	VÖGA	Vereinte Österreichische Grün-Alternativen United Austrian Green-Alternatives
NSDAP	Nationalsozialistische Deutsche Arbeiterpartei National Socialist German Workers' Party		
		VSM	Verband Sozialistische Mittelschüler Union of Socialist High School Students
ÖAAB	Österreichischer Arbeiter- und Angestelltenbund Austrian League of Workers and Employees	VSSTÖ	Verband Sozialistischer Studenten Österreichs Union of Socialist University Students of Austria
ÖBB	Österreichischer Bauernbund Austrian Farmers' League	WBU	Wahlgemeinschaft für Bürger-initiativen und Umweltschutz Election Collective for Citizens' Initiatives and Environmental Protection
ÖP	Österreich Partei Austria Party		
ÖSTZ	Österreichisches Statistisches Zentralamt Austrian Central Office of Statistics	WdU	Wahlpartei der Unabhängigen League of Independents (Steiner)

Preface

Political science in Austria is a relatively young discipline. It began to gradually establish itself in the 60's and only as recently as 1971 was it anchored in the curriculum of Austrian universities as a separate field of study. From the very beginning, however, questions regarding the parties and the party system have played a prominent role in the sphere of activities of Austrian political science. The great significance which originally was and still is attributed to the parties and the party system with respect to the development and concretization of the Austrian party system was an important reason for the relatively intensive occupation with such questions.

Impulses came at the same time from outside the country. Political scientists in other countries occupied themselves with Austria and with Austrian parties. The present collection of articles, translated from German into English, is intended as the further development of these beginnings; in particular, however, it seeks to present a representative survey of the field of political science in Austria. With only few regrettable exceptions the editors were successful in their attempt to publish articles from all the political scientists who have concentrated themselves over the years on questions dealing with the parties and the party system.

Within the course of the last years and decades Austria has gained importance as the object of sociological research. Questions about the stability of the political system, questions about the development of national consciousness and the quality of democracy, questions about coming to terms with past experiences, of political resocialization and political participation— the literature of international political science has an abundance of contributions treating Austria specifically and making references to it. With the present book in English the editors hope to stimulate the interest of international social scientists in Austria, to overcome language barriers, and to make the topical problems and developments of Austrian democracy accessible to an international reading public.

The book is intended to reflect the current state of a discipline—political science. However, it is also to be a contribution to the further development of this discipline. It should stimulate further, intensive and critical occupation with the theme "parties and the party system in Austria."

Innsbruck and Vienna, May 1989

Anton Pelinka   Fritz Plasser

1

Compared to What?

The Austrian Party System
in an International Comparison

ANTON PELINKA and FRITZ PLASSER

1. In-depth structure

The Austrian party system, in the consolidated form it showed toward the end of the 19th century and which it retained with only minor changes up to the last third of the 20th century, is characterized by the formation of only a few significant parties. In 19th and 20th century Europe 10 lines of conflict can be recognized which had a significant influence on the development of parties. Of those only a few had a party-founding effect in Austria.[1]

— The field of tension between liberal and conservative parties typical of the attitude toward the "Ancien regime" had, in any case from 1880 onwards, no significance in Austria.
— The contrast between agrarian interests and industrial society never took on party-founding dimensions in Austria.
— The resistance of petty bourgeois currents against the modern welfare state had no constitutive effect on parties in Austria either.

Other lines of conflict had a constitutive significance for the party system only to a limited extent:

— The field of tension between regional and centralistic interests is constitutive only as an exception (as for example the Tyrolean People's Party between 1918 and 1934).[2]

— The separate formation of a Communist party out of the integrative "old" social democracy influenced the Austrian party system only to a relatively minor extent.[3]
— In Austrian party history the principal difference between Fascist parties and a democratic system is less conspicuous because Fascism was integrated to a certain degree into the traditional parties.

The following fields of tension had a constitutive effect on the Austrian party system:

— labor parties and a "bourgeois system," as seen in the emergence and the rise of the Social Democratic Workers' Party, or the SPÖ, respectively.[4]
— parties based on religious denomination in a field of tension with laical parties—in Austria through the emergence and development of the Christian-Social Party, or the ÖVP, respectively.[5]
— ecological (and radical democratic) movements in protest against growth-oriented politics—a contrast which gradually took on party-founding character perhaps from 1980 onwards.

The formation of different Austrian parties is therefore characterized by the concentration on a few main conflict areas—initially class and religion, later also ecology. The Social Democratic Workers' Party, the socialist camp, originally saw itself as an organized form of protest of the working class against the capitalistic social system with its feudal remnants. The Christian-Social Party, the Christian-conservative camp, regarded itself in the first decades of its existence as a political organization of Catholicism in constant conflict with the laicism particularly of the socialist kind. Added to these forms of differentiation of parties, which could basically be identified all over Europe, was an Austrian particularity, the conflict between different interpretations of national identity. The third of the three traditional political-ideological camps, the German-national camp, saw itself as the political arm of the anschluss idea, to which also the two parties of the large camps agreed from time to time, but which—in particular between 1918 and 1934—was advocated most strongly by both German-national parties, the Pan-Germanic People's Party and the Country Party.[6]

The prevention of the development of separate Fascist parties is proof of the dominance of the three camps and of the lines of conflict behind them—class, religion and national identity. Fascist currents in Austria were partially integrated by the Christian-conservative camp (the majority of the various currents of the Austrian militia movement and various other paramilitary associations—like the "Ostmärkische Sturmscharen"—and finally carried on to the "Vaterländische Front," an incomplete single party in an incomplete system of an incomplete Fascism.[7]

Although National Socialism originated in Austria as a movement competing with the traditional party formations of the German-national camp, it finally overshadowed the Pan-Germanic People's Party and the Country Party, entered upon their inheritance, and became the single party of the German-national camp while simultaneously having the power to integrate parts of the two other camps.[8] The two main forms of Fascism in Austria—authoritarian, Catholic-influenced "Austro-fascism" and totalitarian, German-national National Socialism—were definite historical forms of expression of the traditional political-ideological camps in a definite historical phase.

The reduction of the social lines of conflict which in Europe are known to be constitutive for the founding of parties has increased in the Second Republic. With the de facto end of the anschluss idea in 1945 the German nationalism of the German-national camp reduced itself to general declarations of loyalty to a German cultural community. They were less and less clearly and definitively able to establish the identity of the Association of Independents, and the Freedom Party (FPÖ), i.e. those parties originating as successors of the Pan-Germanic People's Party, Country Party and the National Socialist Party.[9] The lines of conflict constitutive for the party system were in the final analysis mainly concentrated on social class and religion—paradoxically in a period in which the politically motive force of these two factors clearly seemed to weaken. The "class question" in the Marxian sense was reflected in any case less and less in the SPO's conception of itself, and political Catholicism in its integrative form could be observed in the development of the ÖVP only in residual amounts:

— An indicator of the receding importance of the "class" factor is the softening of the property question, which was formulated originally by social democracy itself as a crucial point of conflict.[10]

— An indicator of the softening of the factor "religion" is the modification, by the ÖVP of all parties, of the typical issues like marriage law and the school question.[11]

Reduction at first and later modification prepared the ground for the extensive concentration of the party system in the direction of a two-party system, and both major parties very clearly took on the character of catch-all parties. In the fourth decade of the Second Republic, this development was finally challenged by the emergence of parties identifying with a new line of conflict—the tension between a (growth-oriented) economy and (growth-sceptical) ecology.

According to the typology of Jean Blondel, the party system of the Second Republic was a two-party system.[12] The electoral law of proportional representation attributes an at least potential key function to the third party, the FPÖ. This would allow—beyond Blondel's quantitative features—a characterization of this party system, which was unbroken up until about 1979, as a two-and-a-half-party system.[13] According to the typology of Giovanni Sartori, the party system of the Second Republic was characterized by a "simple" or "moderate" pluralism, not, however, by an "extreme" pluralism. This pluralism was basically bipolar, dominated by the SPÖ and ÖVP, distinguished by a low polarity, and centripetal, i.e. oriented to the center.[14]

From about 1980 onwards, due to the development of the party system, and in particular due to its deconcentration, these characteristics were no longer so self-evident. The decrease in concentration, in particular the gradual emergence of fourth parties in combination with new lines of conflict (ecology—economy) as well as new, politically constitutive elements (post-materialism, new social movements) allow recognition of a trend which could go in the direction of an "extreme" pluralism. It would be characterized by multi-polarity, i.e. by the presence of more than two poles dominating the party system, by a general polarization with regard to issues, and by centrifugal tendencies.

It is for just this reason that Arend Lijphart's qualitative classification of the Austrian political system and the Austrian political culture of the Second Republic seems less and less self-evident:[15] the fragmentation of the social basis into political camps is challenged by a certain permeability; the bipolar basic consensus between the elitist groups appears to be endangered by the emergence of new developments which are no longer completely controllable by the traditional elite. The "consociational democracy" ascertained by Lijphart for the Second Republic, which is also and especially the result of learning based on experience with the "centrifugal democracy" of the period from 1918 to 1934, seems gradually softened—be it toward a "centrifugal democracy" (for which there are really no indicators which can be taken seriously), or be it toward a competitive democracy; for this tendency there are actually numerous indicators.

In an analysis of the 70's John Clayton Thomas stated that the convergence of the major parties in Austria had progressed farther than in the party systems it was compared with, those of France, Italy, the Federal Republic of Germany, Great Britain and the United States. What is striking about this comparison, which included the standpoints of the parties regarding central political issues, was the rapid decrease in the programmatic controversies between the major Austrian parties. This was characterized prior to World War I by an already noticeable centrifugal development which became moderated to some extent after World War II. The Austrian party system became the vanguard of the general convergence trend during the Second Republic:[16] "The convergence process appeared almost completed in Austria. In the 1970's the Socialist party and the People's party no longer differed on such traditional sources of controversy as to how much control government should have over industry, what government should do about the distribution of wealth, and what government should provide in the way of social welfare programs. The only vestige of traditional ideological divisions was a slim one point difference between the two parties on the economic planning issues."

In the course of the 20th century these developments caused the Austrian party system to become an extremely centripetally oriented system of competition. A high point was reached about 1980. Parallel to the end of the "Kreisky era" pluralism advanced once again—certainly not in the sense of a revival of the old fragmentation according to the fields of conflict of class and religion, but indeed according to new fields of conflict such as ecology, education, sex, peace, and the generation gap.[17] This turnabout of the development can also be interpreted as normalization—the Austrian party system loses its particularly noticeable attributes; it becomes "normal" in the sense of a (Western) European averageness.

2. Political culture

Above-average integration, concentration, penetration and legitimation are viewed in the literature of international political science as the most conspicuous characteristics of the Austrian party system. Indicators such as the high degree of voter turnout and density of organization initially seem to support the thesis of the extraordinary hyperstability of the Austrian party system.

— With regard to the average voter turnout for national ballots, Austria leads the field of Western democracies. In an average of several years Austrian voter turnout is bested only by Australia and Belgium. These two countries have a general duty to vote, while in Austria only one fourth of all qualified voters fall under a duty to vote—as required by individual Federal States. For the period 1970-87 the average voter turnout in Austria is 92.1%. In the Federal Republic of Germany the average for the same period is 88.8%, in Great Britain 74.6% and in Switzerland 50.5%.

— Also characteristic of the Austrian party system is its above-average degree of concentration. During the period of 1956-66, 89.6% of the cast, valid votes went to the two major parties; between 1970 and 1983 the degree of concentration amounted to 92.7%. In 1986 the degree of concentration was still 84.4%. In the 1980 Bundestag elections of the Federal Republic of Germany 87.4% of the valid votes went to the two major parties. Statistics for 1983 showed 87% and for 1987 81.5%.

— The above-average concentration of votes corresponded over a number of decades to an above-average degree of parliamentary concentration. The mean number of parliamentary parties in the period from 1966 to

1983 was 3.0. In comparison, this was 3.2 for the Federal Republic of Germany, 10.8 for Switzerland, 10.0 for Italy, 7.4 for Belgium, and 12.5 for the Netherlands (Nohlen 1986, p. 225).[18]

— When regarded by themselves, however, voter turnout percentages and degrees of concentration are not very significant as indicators of a comparison of political cultures (Crewe 1981). It is only in connection with qualitative subindicators that conclusions can be drawn regarding the actual integrative capacity of a party system.[19]

— Hidden behind such above-average turnout figures is a high percentage of democratic ritualists who view participation in elections as a pure exercise of duty devoid of any great motivation. This extraordinary election discipline is therefore supported by a normative conception of democracy which regards periodic voting in elections as sufficient proof of democratic involvement. This seems to apply as well to the comparatively high voter turnout in the Federal Republic of Germany, which "expresses no specific attitude toward the political system, but shows rather a neutral social habit without motivation" (Klages/Herbert 1983, p. 44). Therefore, for 28% of the eligible voters in Austria and 31% in the German Federal Republic it is enough to participate regularly in elections because in a democracy one supposedly need not do more (Plasser 1987, p. 112).

— In Austria the high voter participation is encouraged as well by a restricted understanding of democracy which views the act of voting as the only means available in order to have a little influence on politics.[20] In the mid-1980's about 80% of all eligible Austrian voters were seen to have such a restricted notion of democracy. Comparatively, the proportion of voters in the Federal Republic of Germany with a restricted view of their chances and possibilities of exerting democratic influence is 62%, in the United States 58% (Plasser 1987, p. 110).

— The integrative capacity of the Austrian party system is relativized, however, not only by a remarkable number of democratic ritualists and a restricted notion of democracy. Also noteworthy is an exceptionally pessimistic evaluation of the relevancy of the act of voting, one bordering on impotent tolerance. 72% of the eligible Austrian voters are convinced that the political parties are concerned only about getting votes, but not about what voters think. Similarly high reservations toward such election tactics by parties are found only in Italy (77%). The comparative figure for the United States is 59%, for the Federal Republic of Germany and Holland 48% each (Plasser 1987, p. 112).

— Hence pronounced qualitative deficiencies oppose the formal integrative capacity of the Austrian party system. Routine democratic actions in many cases tend to cover up political lethargy, inactivity and alienation. The political infrastructure of the Austrian party system has an inhibiting effect on participation.[21] The candor and accessibility so declamatorily evoked by the party elite stands in contradiction to an exceptionally low consciousness of political efficacy on the part of the population.[22]

— While for example in the Federal Republic of Germany the citizens' consciousness of political efficacy has continually risen in the last few decades—although it was clearly under the figures for the United States at the beginning of the 1980's—the findings of the Political Action Study of 1974 are still valid for Austria. According to this study, the comparative data from the United States, Great Britain, Holland and West Germany show that feelings of political inefficacy are strongest in Austria (Barnes/Kaase 1979; Rosenmayr 1980, p. 47).

— As regards the feeling of political efficacy of its citizens and deficient political self-assurance, the Austrian party system occupies a dubious leading position within Western party democracies. Its high formal integrative capacity—as for example indicated by the voter turnout—is opposed by considerable qualitative deficiencies of integration. The predominant majority of eligible Austrian voters has a distinct feeling of personal helplessness and lack of influence regarding a political decision-making process experienced as elitist and unapproachable. In 1984 76% of the eligible Austrian voters believed they had no influence whatsoever on the actions of politicians in office. In 1980 in the Federal Republic of Germany 61% of the voters interviewed expressed doubt as to their power of asserting their political opinion; for the Netherlands in 1981 this was 47%, and for the United States in 1984 only 33% (Plasser 1987).[23]

— Regarding the feeling of political impotence of Austrian citizens and a highly ritualized and restricted notion of democracy, the not so pleasing results of the Political Action Study of the 1970's continue to apply to the political culture of the Austrian party system. While, for example, Gabriel (1987) states that in the Federal Republic of Germany the political attitudes are drawing closer and closer to the model of a "civic culture"—even though the "input component is just as weak as before and only a small minority lives up to democratic-participative ideals" (p. 211)—the political culture of the Austrian party system continues to persist in a servile mentality oriented towards bureaucracy and authoritarianism. Deficient political self-assurance and a resigned estimation of the possibilities of political influence extending past the (formal) act of voting and evading the discipline and control of a strong party machine continue to determine the atmosphere of the day-to-day existence of the Austrian party system. Far from the normative ideal of a civic culture, however, a kind of voter protest culture seems to be spreading out within the Austrian party system, one which—in terms of an international comparison—is also to be understood as a reaction to the excessive organizational control of the Austrian party system.

— An extraordinarily high number of party members is characteristic of the Austrian party system.[24] 23% of all eligible voters in Austria are registered members of a political party. In the Federal Republic of Germany the organisational density (the number of party members divided by the total number of eligible voters) is 4.5%, in Switzerland 8.5%, in Italy and Holland 9.5%, in Belgium 10% and in Sweden 15% (Plasser 1987). A Western European average shows about 5% as members of a political party. The organizational hypertrophy of the Austrian party system becomes even clearer through an absolute numerical comparison: the total number of eligible voters in the Federal Republic of Germany is about 45 million; in 1985 1.9 million voters were recorded as members in official party statistics. In 1986 in Austria there were about 5.5 million eligible voters; 1.4 million of them were registered as party members.

— Hidden behind the unusually high organizational density of the Austrian party system, however, is an organizational paradox relativizing the strength and efficiency of the Austrian parties. The organizational penetration of all areas of life, in some cases repressive practices of member recruitment and the omnipresence of the big parties in the governmental and semi-governmental sector of the working world, changed the original function of party membership by turning the membership card in many cases into an allotment certificate for the procurement of a publicly financed dwelling, employment in Civil Service, or chances of a career or advancement, respectively. Opportunistic motives, forced party-political good conduct, undisguised expectations of protection and patronage as well as thinking oriented toward pragmatic election tactics therefore overshadow participation, tradition and loyalty as motives for joining a party in Austria (Pelinka 1982).

— Just as the criticism of a "party-book system" has burdened the public image of the political parties for decades, the "party book" is definitely among the most disagreeable terms in the language of politics.

— The predominantly formal character of party membership therefore lowers the mobilization capacity of the Austrian party system and does not meet those expectations which the unusually high organizational density appears at first glance to suggest.[25] Using a minimal definition of the personal activity for a political party, it becomes apparent that in an average of a number of years only every fourth party member is active in some way for his party. Hence at least sporadic work for a political party can be assumed for only about 7% of the eligible voters. In the Federal Republic of Germany the proportion of party activists—with a significantly lower number of party members—is comparably high. Even in the United States—which does not have party membership in the European sense—between 4 and 7% of the eligible voters are active for their candidates or their party in some form during election periods. The degree of activity in the Austrian party system therefore corresponds in no way to the exceptionally high degree of organization. There is a remarkable disparity in Austria between party membership and active party work. The (idealized) role of party membership as a catalyst of political penetration of Austrian society has proved to be increasingly dysfunctional, inhibiting the development of participative involvement instead of promoting it, and undermines the repute and credibility of the political parties with the majority of the non-organized population which is, nonetheless, subject to attempts of party political influence.

The low degree of the Austrian population's consciousness of political efficacy relativizes the formal integrative capacity of the party system, and opportunistic expectations of patronage and repressive recruitment practices weaken the significance of the unusually high number of party members. The same situation applies to the intensity of affective party ties.[26] The majority of Austrian voters regard the political parties with only dampened emotions. As concerns the degree and intensity of party identification, the Austrian party system ranks in the middle ground of Western party democracies; meanwhile also "strong" parties like the Austrian ones have to contend with a weakening of their power to attract and permanently hold party members.[27]

— The "hard" core of party partisans, i.e. those eligible voters strongly leaning toward a particular political party, was about 23% in 1986. For the same year the Federal Republic of Germany—with a comparable set of questions—had 25%. Great Britain had 26% in 1983, Sweden 36% in 1979, Denmark 32% in 1979, Holland 20% in 1981, and Norway about 28% in 1981.[28] In the United States in 1984 about 30% were classified as strong partisans (Plasser 1987, p. 156).

— A comparison of long-term party ties has in the meantime also relativized the special position which the literature of international political science attributes to the Austrian party system with regard to historical camp mentalities, segmentation and pillarization.[29] In 1986 50% of the eligible voters leaned basically toward one particular political party. For the same year the comparable figure for the Federal Republic of Germany was 49%. In 1983 in Great Britain 46% of the voters considered themselves to be "supporters of one of the political parties"; in 1982 in the United States 48% indicated habitualized party ties (Plasser 1987). Regarding its basis of support, the Austrian party system hence lies within the average of Western party democracies and its structural and institutional characteristic features do not generate any particularly distinctive affective party ties.

Alongside a high degree of integration, concentration and penetration, a high degree of legitimation is also an indicator of the exceptional stability of the Austrian party system. Compared internationally, already in the mid-1960's an exceptional degree of contentment with the political system was demonstrated by the data of the Political Action Study. Its index of political trust, however, was focussed more strongly on specific support based on concrete output and performance expectations.

— The results of comparative studies in the mid-1980's also indicate a high degree of contentment with the system.[30] In 1986 about 77% of the eligible voters were more or less content with the political parties and with the entire political system. For the Federal Republic of Germany the comparable figure was about 90%. Compared with Austria, the party system of West Germany therefore has a slight lead in terms of acceptance, one which is reflected not only by general satisfaction with the system, but also by strong emotional ties to the party system.

— While in 1986 about 65% of the German voters favored one particular party rather than other parties, Austria had just short of 60% and Switzerland only about 42% (Longchamp 1987, p. 63).

— While the degree of contentment with the political system in West Germany became stabilized at an average of about 90%, available Austrian time studies indicate a receding tendency. Whereas in 1984, 84% were more or less content with the political parties and with the entire political system, in 1986 the figure had dropped to only 77%.

— The findings on hand should not, however, be interpreted as signs of a beginning crisis of legitimation in the Austrian party system.[31] On the contrary, hidden behind such findings is a distinct disillusionment and anger with regard to the actions of the major parties—which vented themselves in the protest election of the year 1986, causing both major parties heavy losses in favor of 3rd and 4th parties. Signs of deeper lying disgruntlement, increasing disillusionment and an obvious uneasiness within the Austrian party state had already been recognizable over a longer period of time (Plasser/Ulram 1982). Burdening the atmosphere within the Austrian party system for some time has been criticism of the petrified structures of an over-controlled and over-organized party system, of the orientation of both the party elite and the middle level of functionaries to feudal obligation, of the proneness to corruption and of the undisguised practices involving patronage and privileges.[32]

— Characteristic of the turbulence in the Austrian party system is an unusual increase of undifferentiated anger and displeasure aimed at the political parties. Whereas in 1982 43% of the persons questioned admitted being irritated about the political parties, in 1986 this feeling rose to 68%.

— Comparative studies have offered further indications of an above-average degree of criticism of the members of the "political class" and the political parties on the whole. In the course of a representative cross section study 80% of the persons interviewed in Austria agreed to the statement: "The politicians are much too concerned about preserving their power instead of thinking about the real needs of the population"; in West Germany the comparative figure was 65%. The marked displeasure of Austrian voters regarding the "classe politica" finds its counterpart only in Italy, where in 1985 81% agreed to the statement "I politici non si preoccupano de quello che pensa la gente come me" (Sani/Mannheimer 1987, p. 16).

— Even more pronounced are differences in the assessment of the openness and accessibility of the political parties. In 1984 in Austria the statement "the parties today lead a life of their own which no longer interests the citizens" found the agreement of 72% of those surveyed; in comparison, in West Germany 50% agreed. Such empirical findings are to be interpreted only with great caution, since already the "loaded wording" of the questions and statements used suggestively evokes latent attitudes of disillusionment, and since, moreover, a specific "response culture" has to be taken into consideration. Still, a critical and reserved attitude toward political parties in Austria appears to be presently more prevalent than, say, in neighboring West Germany. If according to available data an increasing lack of enthusiasm for or disillusionment with political parties does not apply to West Germany (Klingemann 1986, p. 392), relevant findings show an ambivalent picture for the Austrian party system, one in which a high degree of trust in a democratic system and its procedures can be seen as much as an obvious displeasure with disturbing side effects of the Austrian party society.

Within the framework of a political cultural comparison, which can rely on only a few empirical indicators due to lack of data, the "exotic" position of Austria within international party studies has become doubtful. At the same time, some of the drawbacks of a party world which is still "pre-modern" in many ways are moved into the field of vision of the observer. The social structures and the behavior of voters are increasingly approaching the Western European average standard, thus subjecting the deep structure of the Austrian party system to a permanent process of modernization; simultaneously, however, the party elite and functionary cadres still orient themselves to a great extent on, comparatively speaking, easily surveyable social sectors, homogeneous milieus, encapsulated interests and traditional clientele relations which in the meantime have largely become outmoded.[33]

3. Factors challenging the parties

Social modernization confronts the Austrian party system with three challenges, the overcoming of which will decisively influence its future development: change with respect to structure, values and issues.[34]

— Societal and generative change in the coming years will bring about a progressive weakening or perhaps loosening of existing party ties. Processes of erosion and dealignment (Dalton/Flanagan/Beck 1985) will not only undermine the cohesion between existing voter coalitions, but also presumably make the voter landscape more flexible and more unpredictable (Crewe/Denver 1985). The increasing flexibility of the electorate, faced with constantly lower socio-structural barriers and sociopsychological conversion thresholds, will cause mainly the two major parties considerable strategic problems.[35] Their heightened electoral-political vulnerability could reinforce the wish for defensive strategies to preserve their electorate. As a retreat into the milieu, into the security of their (shrinking) traditional and core voter groups, this strategy would be connected with the attempt at a (dogmatic) reindoctrination of ideology, encapsulation and a stronger orientation on traditional clientele relations.[36] Such an attempt at stabilization would be at the same time, however, the renunciation of the search for a voter coalition capable of attaining a majority and could—projected negatively—even lead to a development in which the major parties gradually draw closer to the electoral-political status of middle-sized parties. The defensive strategy of preserving the existing electorate would force the major parties to abandon the growing potential of non-party-affiliated, younger, more mobile voters with above-average qualifications to new party groupings like the Greens or the new populism of the FPÖ. As a result, the political and strategic pressure brought to bear on a government with a grand coalition could strengthen existing encapsulation tendencies or lead to a reciprocal obstruction of timid attempts to gain status.[37] Contrary to the defensive strategy of maintaining the electorate are offensive strategies which accept the challenges of structural change, consciously take on electoral-political risks, and adapt party structures to the structure of the electorate.[38] Such a strategy of becoming more receptive and more modern will encounter the resistance of the interests of intra-party groups and individuals at least in the first phase, and trigger the delaying reactions of traditionalistic party- and functionary cadres, since an adaptation to social reality would also be connected with far-reaching shifts in intra-party power relationships. The search for more open, receptive, and more flexible forms of integration and mobilization could therefore initially strengthen latent disintegration processes within the core of the major parties, cause intra-party conflicts, and effect temporary turbulence and heated debates on strategy. Subsequent to the completion of the process of structural and organizational transformation, however, the major Austrian parties would presumably be once again in the position of presenting heterogeneous, mobile and discriminating voter groups with an attractive and future-oriented platform. Which strategic option the major parties will accept, and which middle-term path of development they will take, cannot be predicted at the moment. It will finally depend on the disposition of the traditional major parties toward reform and risk-taking whether the current fragmentation tendencies in the Austrian party system are further strengthened and whether new, respectively regenerated, party groupings occupy niches in the electoral market which the major parties can no longer integrate due to lethargy, incapability and/or the fear of taking risks (Plasser 1987, p. 270f.).

— The dissolution of the traditional socio-economic, socio-structural and religious milieus, and their decoupling from voting behavior (Traar/Birk 1987), is accompanied by a change of social values oriented increasingly on ways and styles of living. Lines of tension between materialism and post-materialism (Inglehart 1983), between realism and idealism (Bürklin 1984), and between an industrial rear guard and a post-industrial vanguard leave their traces in the deep structure of the Austrian party system too. Becoming visible also in Austria are the contours of a "post-industrial" voter segment which evades the integrative efforts of the traditional parties and shows reactions of reservation and even rejection toward conventional attempts at incorporation. Between 10 and 15% of all eligible Austrian voters can presently be considered members of a "post-materialistic avant-garde" within the party system (Plasser 1987). However, whereas the post-materialistic voter segment in the West German party system indicates characteristics of a "new" left which has settled within the ideological spectrum to the left of the SPD (Social Democratic Party), the majority of which formed the Green Party, the Austrian post-materialists tend more strongly toward the center. On the one hand, the Austrian Greens can hardly be classified as a clearly defined left-wing party—as regards the orientation of their voters. On the other hand, one can also find post-materialistic and post-industrial voter segments among the voters of the traditional Austrian parties, which cause latent intra-party tension and unrest. In contrast to the pronounced left-wing post-materialism in the Federal Republic of Germany there is a moderate form of post-materialism in Austria which, logically enough, represents a strategical irritation factor for both major parties and which restricts their maneuverability when dealing with touchy controversial issues. With questions regarding the choice of locations for power plants, those regarding other environmental issues, e.g. political decisions regarding industrial growth and production, both major Austrian parties hence stand not only in the crossover of criticism by the Greens—who as the fourth faction now also command possibilities of representation and influence in parliament—but also under the pressure of post-materialistic intra-party wings. The challenge for the Austrian party elite consists in cautiously balancing opposing intra-party interests and in augmenting their mainly materialistically oriented catalog of objectives with qualitative post-materialistic objectives. Along with a reform of party structures this prerequires, above all, a reform of the content of their political platform.

— Coming to grips with changing issues is hence the real test for the future of the Austrian parties. At present, even though economic measures for recuperation and consolidation are on the agenda, and the battle against increasing unemployment, reduction of the budgetary deficit and the decrease of the national debt represent the priorities of governmental policy, the value of other issues should not be underestimated, for example questions regarding the quality of the environment and living, the development of personality, social fairness and justice. It remains to be seen whether the political parties will adequately cover the broad spectrum of issues in the coming years and offer attractive future-oriented goals and solutions for discussion. Their success, or failure, respectively, will ultimately decide whether the Austrian party system—in the face of the increasing differentiation of the electorate, increasing strain and intensified conditions of competition—will be regarded also in the 1990's internationally as one of the most stable Western party democracies.

Notes

1. Beyme 1982, pp. 26-40; Lane/Ersson 1987, pp. 39-93.
2. Pelinka/Reischenböck 1988.
3. For the history of the KPÖ see especially Gärtner 1979; Spira 1979.
4. For the early history of Austrian social democracy see in particular Brügel, 1922-1925; for an overall treatment see Kaufmann 1978, and Sully 1982. For an international discussion see also Rabinbach 1985.
5. For the early history of the Christian-conservative camp see particularly Boyer 1981; Knoll 1973; for the history of the ÖVP see Reichhold 1975. As an attempt at an overall treatment of the ÖVP: Schwarz-bunter Vogel. Studien zu Programm, Politik und Struktur der ÖVP (1985).
6. For the social background to the anschluss idea see Schausberger 1978.
7. Bärnthaler 1979; Talos/Neugebauer 1985.
8. Pauley 1981.
9. Riedlsperger 1978; Reimann 1980; Reiter 1982.
10. Pelinka 1979, p. 65f.
11. Pelinka 1979, p. 69f.

12. Blondel 1968, pp. 180-203; 1969, pp. 153-176.

13. For an overall treatment of the party system up into the 80's see the various contributions in Gerlich/Müller 1983.

14. Sartori 1966, pp. 137-176; Daalder/Mair 1983.

15. Lijphart 1977, pp. 104-141.

16. Cited after Thomas 1980, pp. 348-366, in particular p. 354.

17. For the first comprehensive systematic treatment of these changes see Plasser/Ulram 1982.

18. In 1986 the Greens achieved 4.8% and were able to enter the Austrian parliament as the fourth faction.

19. Source citations for the following quoted data can be found in Plasser 1987 (where the wording of the various questions used is documented in the appendix).

20. The cited data is oriented on the internationally common "measures of political efficacy."

21. This refers to the quality of democracy from the view of the population. As regards institutional possibilities of participation, the Austrian constitution offers plebiscitary instruments which are, for instance, not provided for in the constitution of the Federal Republic of Germany (e.g. the instrument of a nationwide plebiscite, petition for a referendum, etc.) In addition, presently under discussion are an electoral reform in the direction of stronger personalization as well as ways of facilitating proposals for referendum petitions.

22. "Consciousness of political efficacy" is to be understood as one's feeling of subjective political competence, i.e. the feeling of being able to influence political decisions and processes. "Responsiveness," on the other hand, refers to the perceived readiness of representatives and institutions of the political system to comply with the concerns of citizens, to open up decision-making processes and make them more accessible.

23. Since the classic work by Almond/Verba efficacy scales have been used for the classification of the specific political culture of a country. On an (idealized) scale a low degree of consciousness of political efficacy is interpreted as a sign of a "servile culture," as compared with a high degree of consciousness of efficacy, which goes in the direction of a democratic "civic culture."

24. Results of demoscopic investigations had to be used for Austria because the official membership statistics do homage to an unmistakable numerical magic (Kofler 1985). For the situation in Western Europe see the pertinent contributions in Daalder 1987 and Katz 1987.

25. The number of permanent party activists and functionaries of the political parties is estimated in Austria—as in the Federal Republic of Germany—at about only 10% of the registered party members. The two major Austrian parties each have about 50,000 to 60,000 active members, or persons of confidence, respectively, who represent the organizational backbone of the party machine.

26. An affective party tie is to be understood as the readiness to identify with a particular party. In international comparative party research the degree of party identification is an indicator of the emotional cohesiveness of a party system.

27. The structural and generative changes in Austrian society lead to obvious manifestations of dealignment in the sense of a dissolution of traditional party ties and a progressive decoupling of social structure and electoral behavior.

28. Different versions of questions obstruct the transnational comparability of the cited findings, which are to be interpreted only with utmost caution.

29. The interest of international political scientists in the Austrian party system is—which is not very astonishing—very small. The few contributions in English, hence internationally accessible, mostly describe the state of the Austrian party system in the 1960's. With the exception of the Political Action Study, points of intersection regarding international multi-country studies are lacking. In terms of international empirical-analytical comparative studies Austria has as yet hardly been studied.

30. The required distinctiveness in the operationalization of "specific" and "diffuse" readiness to offer support is in the case of the selected question ensured only to a limited extent. As regards the basis of trust within the Common Market countries, cf. the comparative analysis by Schmitt 1983.

31. For an empirical refutation of alarming assertions and speculations as to crises, cf. Plasser 1987.

32. The reproach of the Austrian "party-book system" has become a standard criticism of Austrian parties without having induced the major parties to adopt any appreciable measures of reform and correction.

33. Tension between an increasingly "post-modern" electorate and "pre-modern" organizational structures persisting defensively will strain the day-to-day activities of the Austrian party system at least for a medium-term period of time.

34. The challenges referred to above are found—in varying importance and intensity—in all highly industrialized party systems. Historically strongly segmented party systems like the Austrian one, however, seem to find the necessary processes of adaptation particularly difficult.

35. Structural processes of erosion weaken, as a consequence, first and foremost those parties which owe their identity to grown structures, traditional lines of interest and identifiable blocks of voters.

36. For strategic perspectives and scenarios regarding the future development of the Austrian party system, cf. Plasser 1987, p. 263f.

37. In terms of electoral strategy the grand coalition between the SPÖ and ÖVP is approaching a situation in which neither can win since every offensive effort by one coalition partner to gain status is more or less at the cost of the other partner.

38. Both the SPÖ and the ÖVP are aware of the necessity of structural and organizational reforms. As experience shows, however, party reform efforts have tended for the most part in the direction of the smallest common reform denominator without changing the core of party reality.

Bibliography

Bärnthaler, Irmgard, Die Vaterländische Front. Geschichte und Organisation. Wien 1979 (Bärnthaler, 1979)

Beyme, Klaus von, Parteien in westlichen Demokratien. München 1982 (Beyme, 1982)

Blondel, Jean, Party Systems and Patterns of Government in Western Democracies. In: Canadian Journal of Political Science. I/2, Juni 1968 (Blondel, 1968)

Blondel, Jean, Introduction to Comparative Government. London 1969 (Blondel, 1969)

Boyer, John W., Political Radicalism in Late Imperial Vienna. Origins of the Christians Social Movement 1848-1887. Chicago 1981 (Boyer, 1981)

Brügel, Ludwig, *Geschichte der österreichischen Sozialdemokratie.* 5 Bände, Wien (1922-1925) (Brügel, 1922-25)

Bürklin, Wilhelm P., *Grüne Politik. Ideologische Zyklen, Wähler und Parteiensystem.* Opladen 1984 (Bürklin, 1984)

Crewe, Ivor, *Electoral Participation.* In: David Butler/Howard R. Penniman/Austin Ranney (eds.), *Democracy at the Polls. A Comparative Study of Competitive National Election.* Washington 1981 (Crewe, 1981)

Crewe, Ivor/Denver, David (eds.), *Electoral Change in Western Democracies. Patterns and Sources of Electoral Volatility.* London/Sidney 1985 (Crewe/Denver, 1985)

Daalder, Hans (ed.), *Party Systems in Denmark, Austria, Switzerland, The Netherlands and Belgium*, London 1987 (Daalder, 1987)

Dalton, Russel J./Flanagan, Scott C./Beck, Allen (eds.), *Electoral Change in Advanced Industrial Democracies. Realignment or Dealignment?* Princeton 1984 (Dalton/Flanagan/Beck, 1984)

Dalton, Russel J., *Citizen Politics in Western Democracies*, Chatham 1988 (Dalton 1988)

Gabriel, Oscar W., *Politische Kultur, Postmaterialismus und Materialismus in der Bundesrepublik Deutschland.* Opladen 1987 (Gabriel, 1987)

Gärtner, Heinz, *Zwischen Moskau und Österreich. Die KPÖ-Analyse einer sowjetabhängigen Partei*, Wien 1979 (Gärtner, 1979)

Gerlich, Peter, *Consociationalism to Competition: The Austrian Party System since 1945*, in: Hans Daalder (ed.), *The Party Systems in Denmark, Austria, Switzerland, The Netherlands and Belgium.* London 1987 (Gerlich, 1987)

Gerlich, Peter/Müller, Wolfgang C. (Hg.), *Zwischen Koalition und Konkurrenz. Österreichs Parteien seit 1945.* Wien 1983 (Gerlich/Müller, 1983)

Inglehart, Ronald, *Traditionelle, politische Trennungslinien und die Entwicklung der neuen Politik in westlichen Gesellschaften.* In: *Politische Vierteljahresschrift* 2/1983 (Inglehart, 1983)

Kaufmann, Fritz, *Sozialdemokratie in Österreich. Ideen und Geschichte einer Partei. Von 1889 bis zur Gegenwart.* Wien 1978 (Kaufmann, 1978)

Katz, Richard S. (ed.), *Party Governments: European and American Experiences.* Berlin/New York 1987 (Katz, 1987)

Klingemann, Hans-Dieter, *Der vorsichtig abwägende Wähler. Einstellungen zu den politischen Parteien und Wahlabsicht.* In: Hans-Dieter Klingemann/Max Kaase (Hg.), *Wahlen und politischer Prozeß. Analysen aus Anlaß der Bundestagswahl 1983*, Opladen 1986 (Klingemann, 1986)

Knoll, Reinhold, *Zur Tradition der Christlichsozialen Partei. Ihre Früh- und Entwicklungsgeschichte bis zu den Reichsratswahlen 1907.* Wien 1973 (Knoll, 1973)

Lane, Jan-Erik/Ersson, Svante O., *Politics and Society in Western Europe.* London/Beverly Hills/Newbury Park/New Delhi 1987 (Lane/Ersson, 1987)

Longchamp, Claude, *Die neue Instabilität als Kennzeichen des heutigen Wahlverhaltens.* In: *Schweizerisches Jahrbuch für Politische Wissenschaft* 27/1987 (Longchamp 1987)

Nohlen, Dieter, *Wahlrecht und Parteiensystem*. Leverkusen 1986 (Nohlen, 1986)

Pauley, Bruce F., *Hitler and the Forgotten Nazis. A History of Austrian National Socialism*, Chapel Hill 1981 (Pauley, 1981)

Pelinka, Anton, *Die Entwicklungslinien der Grundsatzprogramme*. In: Albert Kadan/Anton Pelinka, *Die Grundsatzprogramme der österreichischen Parteien. Dokumentation und Analyse*. St. Pölten 1979 (Pelinka, 1979)

Pelinka, Anton, *Struktur und Funktion der politischen Parteien*. In: Heinz Fischer (Hg.), *Das politische System Österreichs* (dritte überarbeitete Auflage) Wien 1982 (Pelinka, 1982)

Pelinka, Anton/Reischenböck, Helmut, *Das politische System Nordtirols 1918-1938*, in: Andreas Maislinger/Anton Pelinka (Hg.), *Zeitgeschichte*, Band 4 des *Handbuches zur Geschichte Tirols*, hg. von Helmut Reinalter (erscheint 1988) (Pelinka/Reischenböck, 1988))

Plasser, Fritz, *Parteien unter Streß. Zur Dynamik der Parteiensysteme in Österreich, der Bundesrepublik Deutschland und den Vereinigten Staaten*. Wien/Köln/Graz 1987 (Plasser, 1987)

Plasser, Fritz/Ulram, Peter A., *Unbehagen im Parteienstaat*. Wien/Köln/Graz 1982 (Plasser/Ulram, 1982)

Plasser, Fritz/Ulram, Peter A., *From Stability to Diffusion. Dealignment in the Austrian Party System*, Paper delivered at the Annual Meeting of the American Political Science Association, New Orleans 1985 (Plasser/Ulram, 1985)

Rabinbach, Anson (ed.), *The Austrian Socialist experiment. Social Democracy and Austrian Marxism, 1918-1934*. Boulder 1985 (Rabinbach, 1985)

Reichhold, Ludwig, *Geschichte der ÖVP*. Graz 1975 (Reichhold, 1975)

Reimann, Viktor, *Die Dritte Kraft in Österreich*. Wien 1980 (Reimann, 1980)

Reiter, Erich, *Programm und Programmentwicklung der FPÖ*. Wien 1982 (Reiter, 1982)

Reiter, Erich, *Technikskepsis und neue Parteien*. Wien 1987 (Reiter, 1987)

Riedlsperger, Max E., *The Lingering Shadow of Nazism: The Austrian Independent Party Movement since 1945*. New York 1978 (Riedlsperger, 1978)

Sani, Giacomo/Mannheimer, Renato, *Il Mercato Elettorale. Identikit dell' elettore italiano*. Bologna 1987 (Sani/Mannheimer, 1987)

Schausberger, Norbert, *Der Griff nach Österreich. Der Anschluß*, Wien 1978 (Schausberger, 1978)

Schmitt, Hermann, *Party Government in Public Opinion: A European Cross-National Comparison*. In: *European Journal of Political Research* 4/1983 (Schmitt, 1983)

Spira, Leopold, *Ein gescheiterter Versuch. Der Austro-Eurokommunismus*, Wien 1979 (Spira, 1979)

Sully, Melanie A., *Continuity and Change in Austrian Socialism. The Eternal Quest for the Third Way*. New York 1982 (Sully, 1982)

Talos, Emmerich/Neugebauer, Wolfgang (Hg.), *"Austrofaschismus"*. *Beiträge über Politik, Ökonomie und Kultur 1934-1938*. 3. Auflage, Wien 1985 (Talos/Neugebauer, 1985)

Traar, Kurt/Birk, Franz, *Der durchleuchtete Wähler—in den achtziger Jahren*. In: *Journal für Sozialforschung* 1/1987 (Traar/Birk, 1987)

2

The Decline of the Party State

The Rise of Parliamentarianism: Change within the Austrian Party System

ANTON PELINKA

1. Introduction

The Austrian party system indicates a number of striking features which make it stand out in a comparison of European party systems.[1] The following features are particularly noteworthy:

— Concentration. In no other European multi-party system have the voters, on an average of many years, concentrated themselves on so few parties as in Austria.[2] This concentration is all the more striking because in Austria the principle of election by proportional representation is anchored in the Federal Constitutional Law and because this principle was additionally perfected through the election law reform of 1971.

— Organization. In no other European multi-party system is such a high percentage of voters organized as members in political parties.[3] Depending on the method of counting and on consideration of the associated organizations, the degree of organization in Austria is between 30 and 40%.

— Participation. Above and beyond the degree of organization, formal participation in the political process in Austria is strikingly high.[4] The degree of voter participation particularly in Austria is among the highest of the European multi-party systems.

Concentration, organization and participation are closely associated with the tradition of the Austrian parties. And this tradition is also responsible for the development of a particularly close interrelationship between parties and society, between parties and the state—for the Austrian party state.

The Austrian parties are relatively old and have a relatively unbroken tradition.[5] Their history goes back to the time of the expansion of the elitist election law of the curia system in the direction of a general and equal suffrage. Through the gradual extension of the right to vote in favor of the participation of the majority of the population the old-style notable parties, for which in Austria to a great extent the term "liberal" or "conservative" has become adopted, were replaced by modern mass parties. These mass parties, which originated between 1880 and 1900, continue to form the basis of today's Austrian parties. In principle, therefore, they can look back on a century of unbroken history.

To be sure, these parties—the Social Democratic Workers' Party, the Christian-Social Party and (indeed as the most important representative of the less homogeneous German national camp) the Pan-German Party—were more than just parties in the sense of the party theory prevalent for multiparty systems. These parties formed the center of social sub-systems in which the most significant societal tasks, especially the function of political socialization and the formation of a political culture, were carried out by a division of labor. The parties were the centers of the political-ideological camps, the "pillars."[6]

The existence of these camps, or "pillars," was an expression of a multiple fragmentation of Austrian society. Whereas the foundation of political parties in the Europe of the 19th century was in most countries the expression of social conflicts, at times also national or religious ones, the coexistence of all three was reflected in the establishment of the Austrian parties—the social conflict, expressed mainly in the tension between the bourgeoisie and the working class; the national conflict, expressed above all in the tension between German domination and non-German protest; and the religious conflict, expressed for the most part in the confrontation between political Catholicism and secular tendencies. Social democracy was not simply the Workers' Party; as a secularized party it was also opposed to political Catholicism, which then predominated. And, contrary to its international pretensions, it became the battlefield of national differences.[7] The Christian-Social Party was not only a bourgeois party; it also represented political Catholicism and initially, in its beginnings, the Austro-German claim to cultural predominance.[8] The Pan-German Party concentrated on just this claim, questioned—in addition—the sovereignty of Austria, and opposed, as a bourgeois party, political Catholicism.[9]

While this spectrum of parties determined by social, national and religious factors was enriched by the development in the last years of the Monarchy, it was, however, not changed. The essential elements of the German-speaking, mainly Catholic farmer population were integrated into this spectrum through the assimilation of the Conservatives into the Christian-Social Party, and the Social Democratic Workers' Party forfeited its supranational claim—at the end of the Monarchy it was split up into various national social democratic groupings.

This complex party system, the expression of a far-reaching and multiple fragmentation of society, determined also the history of the First Republic. And in spite of the authoritarian break with Parliamentarianism, in spite of civil war, in spite of the authoritarian corporate state, in spite of the "anschluss" to the Pan-Germanic Empire, in spite of the 7-year oppression of Austrians by Austrians, and in spite of the exclusion of the (former) National Socialists between 1945 and 1949 from the right to vote by the revived democratic republic of Austria, from 1949 on it appeared as if nothing had changed: the Austrian party system was once again a two-party system with, firstly, two major parties representing the two major camps; secondly the VDU, and later the FPÖ, representing the German-national camp, which of course now no longer advocated the idea of anschluss;[10] and finally fourth parties, especially the KPÖ (Austrian Communist Party)[11], which participated substantially in the foundation of the new state in 1945, had no chances at all. It was above all the stable voter behavior in the first decades of the Second Republic that showed that not only the structure of the two-and-a-half-party system remained unchanged, that the parties continued to be not only organized machinery for the legitimation of the political system and for the recruiting of the political elite, and that they were rather, as before, the expression of political-ideological camps and their specific camp mentality. With voter turnout regularly over 90% there were minor margins of fluctuation, the process of concentration continued in favor of the two major parties, and fourth parties remained more and more clearly excluded.

The development of the party state was closely connected with this situation, which reached a peak and a turning point in the 1970's. The parties were twice the founders of the Austrian republic, they gave the republic its constitution, and they also determined for this republic the informal rules of allocation, control and transfer of power. In 1918 the parties represented in the hitherto basically powerless Reichsrat took over as a "reserve power" the place of the old powers, which had been brought down through the outcome of the World War. They founded the republic, gave it form, determined its constitution and logically felt themselves placed historically and politically at the head of the state.[12] In 1945 this same situation repeated itself: the declaration of independence of 27 April 1945 was signed, definitely more than merely a symbolic act, by the representatives of the parties—the three "anti-Fascist parties," the ÖVP, SPÖ, and KPÖ.

2. The flexibility of the suprastructure—the stability of the infrastructure

What did change after 1945 was the behavior of the political elite. Although the leading functionaries of the ÖVP and SPÖ were to a great extent identical with those of the Christian-Social Party (or the Vaterländische Front) and the Social Democratic Workers' Party, and although this continuity of personnel was particularly emphasized through the person of the chancellor of the provisional government from 1918 to 1929, Karl Renner, the leaders of the parties now acted simply antithetically: they developed a system of compromise and integrated it into a comprehensive network of institutions. The most important of these institutions was initially the Grand Coalition, increasingly augmented by social partnership.

The flexibility of the suprastructure guaranteed the transition from a "centrifugal democracy" to a "consociational democracy." This transition was and still is rated by political scientists as a typical example of the fact that the political elite are indeed able to learn from history.[13] In any case, the top functionaries of the ÖVP and the SPÖ have altered their behavior considerably on the basis of experience in and with the authoritative corporate state, and in and with National Socialism.

This elitist flexibility, however, changed nothing of the rigid fragmentation at the basis of the society. As earlier, Austrian society was divided into sub-systems—that of the Christian-conservative camp, at whose center the ÖVP now stood; that of the socialist camp, with the SPÖ as its center; and finally that of the German-national camp, in which, however, the VDU and then the FPÖ were not able to hinder a process of shrinkage of both their party and their camp in favor of the two major parties.

In spite of the altered behavior of the elite, the image of the enemy within inter-party competition remained initially the same, camp loyalty was stipulated and controlled by the party leaders, and especially contacts between the basis of one camp and the basis of the other camp remained forbidden. That too is a characteristic feature of Austrian consociational democracy: the concerns between the elite changed the effects of societal fragmentation, but at the same time it laid the foundation for an indirect interest of the same elite in the preservation of fragmentation. It was possible for the elite to turn to making compromises because on account of the pronounced loyalty of their respective basis they did not have to fear any appreciable losses.

The stability of the infrastructure was guaranteed, however, not only by the continuance of traditional loyalties, of the "camp mentality." The party state developed as well, which allowed the parties the function of being the lockkeeper for all branches of society.[14] As was the case in other Western liberal political systems, the parties recruited "leadership personnel" for both government and parliament. In addition to this, it became more and more the task of the parties to recruit top-level leaders for spheres outside the political system in a more restricted sense—for example for the economic sector, which—through the high number of public-interest enterprises as a consequence of the two nationalization laws of 1946 and 1947—was subject to the influence of the federal state and hence the parties controlling the federal state.[15] This also applies to the educational sector, whose personnel decisions were determined by the parties according to the system of proportional representation. This procedure was based on informal, as well as formal, regulations, e.g. the school laws of 1962.[16]

The role of the parties in Austria's consociational democracy increasingly assumed the role of the feudal lord who passed on gratuities to his retainers in return for trust and loyalty—here a job position, there economic intervention, and finally also special social services, as for example the procurement of a publicly assisted apartment.

The connection of the motive of tradition, which lies based in loyalty and in the transmission of exactly this loyalty, with the motive of protection, which was the case in the party state after 1945, also explains the extremely high degree of organization of the Austrian parties.[17]

The combination of a stable infrastructure and flexible suprastructure was weakened for the first time by the breaking apart of the Grand Coalition in 1966. To be sure, the transition to one-party governments by no means meant the end of the consociational democracy—also after 1966 a clear majority of all laws were and still are passed unanimously in the National Council, hence a climate of agreement has prevailed;[18] also after 1966 the Grand Coalition continued to exist in most federal states as well as in most large communities; and also after 1966 social partnership remained in existence, even enjoying a rise in popularity as the continuation of the Grand Coalition with other means even after the end of the ÖVP-SPÖ governments.

In retrospect, however, the end of the Grand Coalition can be assessed as the catalyst of a gradual turning away from consociational democracy—the stability of the infrastructure as expressed in the behavior of the voters and the party members, and the flexibility of the suprastructure as expressed in the pragmatic behavior of the party leaders, were challenged by a gradually changed and still changing framework.[19] In particular, the triad of the social, religious and national lines of conflict appeared less and less convincing after 1966.

— The social conflict, which was particularly the driving force behind the development of the Social Democratic Workers' Party and the workers' movement, was diminished—at least in the consciousness of the persons affected—by the Grand Coalition and social partnership, by economic growth and (relative) mass prosperity.

— The religious conflict was mitigated more and more also in the consciousness of the individual voters by various agreements—as they form, for example, the basis of the Concordat of 1960 and the school laws of 1962.

— The national conflict lost significance to the extent to which the concept of an Austrian nation became self-evident for a further increasing majority;[20] as a result it lost its party-founding power increasingly.

3. Changes in party typology

The political-ideological character of the parties, explainable by the fragmentation of Austrian society, had to change radically due to the shift of conflict lines. The parties, which controlled the three traditional camps of the Austrian party system, were "Weltanschauung parties" and (or) class parties during the first fifty years of their existence.[21] As a consequence of the fragmenting conflict lines constituting the system of camps and parties, these parties did not raise a claim to a general right of representation, but to a special one. As phenomena of pillarization, as representatives of sub-systems, the parties generally claimed the right to speak for only a particular class or a particular ideology, but not for the population on the whole; or, if this was the case, then only by equating general interest and party interest.

The Social Democratic Workers' Party was mainly a class party. Based on a Marxist notion of society, a long-term identity was posited between the interests of the working class and the overwhelming majority of the total population, but nevertheless the party's notion of itself was one which postulated distinctions based on excluding other socio-economic groups. In the "Linz Program" of 1926 social democracy formulated a party concept typical of a class party:[22]

> To unite and to organize ... the entire working class ... is the objective of the Social Democratic Workers' Party ... the entire bourgeoisie—that is to say: the big capitalists and the bourgeois middle-class in the cities, the big landowners and the big farmers in the country—join forces against the working class.

An analogous example of exclusion, even though reflecting the religious line of conflict, characterized also the party concept of the Christian-Social Party. As the representative of political Catholicism it claimed to speak for the interests of the Christians—in Austria meaning especially the Catholics. The party concept of the Christian-Socialists corresponded to a methodic integralism,[23] an explicit combination of ideology and politics. The parts of the population which could not or did not want to comply with this ideological claim were implicitly excluded from the program of the Christian-Social Party—for example from that of 1926:

> The Christian-Social Party saw the highest goal of the state in the promotion of the well-being of the population to the fullest extent. Convinced that this goal can only be achieved if the underlying principles of Christianity are observed, it sees its task as giving politics the direction which corresponds to these principles.[24]

The parties of the German national camp, as regards their claim to special representation, postulated exclusions along national and racial lines; the (German) national concept of exclusion was more extreme than the basic German nationalism represented by the two major parties of this time, and (anti-semitic) racist segregation was harsher than the contemporary anti-semitism of the Christian-Socialists.[25] In the "Salzburg Program" of 1920 the Pan-German Peoples' Party, for example, stated:

> The concept of a community of people also has a negative side: Within it lies the precept of warding off foreign, damaging influences and the need for protection against foreign elements dangerous to the communal organism. Such a foreign element is Judaism.[26]

This claim to the right of exclusion, which separated and—in the concept of the party—simultaneously unified the three camps and their parties, was already questioned due to the events from 1933 on. The civil wars, the tensions similar to a civil war, the dictatorial acts of suppression and the political terror of the authoritarian corporate state and especially of National Socialism created a consciousness of new common factors, but also of new differences. The "spirit of 1945," the consciousness which formed the basis of the consociational democracy of the Second Republic, was certainly first and foremost a matter of the political elite. And this elite, on the basis of their party concept, by no means explicitly renounced the old policies of exclusion—only in this way was the political loyalty within one's own camp to be upheld. Only gradually, only as a hesitant, lagging consequence of the coalition climate and the willingness to seek agreement in the spirit of social partnership was the concept of the party expanded.

The expansion of the party concept expressed itself in the transition from a claim of special to general representation. Emerging step by step out of the class and Weltanschauung parties were the popular parties, which asserted for themselves the right to represent the general interest. The equating of this general interest with a specific interest regarding class and Weltanschauung was taken back more and more, and the references to the social and religious lines of conflict became weaker. References to the (German) national line of conflict disappeared completely in the party concept of the two major parties; in the concept of the German national camp, of the VDU and FPÖ these references reflected a non-obligatory, general, and vague adherence to the German people and its culture.[27]

The claim to general representation dominated practical politics, penetrated campaign and election programs, and finally found expression in the basic programs of the parties. Already in 1958 the "new party program" of the SPÖ read as follows: "The socialists want to reach their goal through the political integration of all workers. Supported by the knowledge of scientific socialism, their party developed itself from a party of wage earners ... to a party of all employed persons."[28] And the ÖVP wrote in its "Klagenfurt Manifesto" of 1964: "The Austrian People's Party is the political body uniting all Austrians who acknowledge the structuring of society on the basis of the solidary bonds of all social classes."[29]

It is true that references to the tendency toward the discriminatory tradition of the class and weltanschauung parties can also be seen in the later basic programs of the parties (ÖVP:1972; SPÖ:1978; FPÖ:1985). Yet they conflict increasingly with the parties' claim to general representation, as practiced in day-to-day politics and is also increasingly integrated into the party programs. In general, the parties want to speak for everyone, not only for specific segments of the electorate.

This change from class and weltanschauung parties to popular parties is not the product of simple reorientation; it is, most of all, the expression of societal change. The shrinking of the traditional core voter groups, the decline of a class consciousness shaping political behavioral patterns, the loss of meaning of an ideological integralism wanting to determine policy, the banning of explicitly advocated German nationalism—all that was not programmatically formulated—or at least not primarily—all that developed within social reality and was later integrated into the programs.

The change of the old weltanschauung parties and class parties to popular parties, to "catch-all parties,"[30] which basically sought to appeal to all voters, initially paralleled an increasing concentration of the party system. Fewer and fewer Austrians voted for fourth parties, and more and more Austrians preferred the two major parties within the framework of the three traditional parties. In any case, up until 1975 one can speak of a functional parallelism between a claim to general representation and increasing party concentration (see Table 2.1).

The first signs of a retrogression of party concentration are bound to be all the more conspicuous. Party concentration dropped back at the federal level for the first time in favor of the two major parties in 1979—yet in 1979 only the FPÖ was to enjoy the benefits of this development and so the counter-trend still remained within the framework of the traditional parties. In 1983, however, a significant increase of the proportion of fourth party votes became clear for the first time. Since this increase was accompanied by much stronger analogous indicators at the community and state level, it is very likely that this phenomenon is more of a long-term than a short-term nature. In 1986, for the first time since 1956, a fourth party made the breakthrough into the National Council.

Table 2.1
Concentration of the Austrian party system from 1949 to 1986[31]

national Council elections	common proportion of votes: SPÖ, ÖVP	proportion of votes: VDU, FPÖ	proportion of votes: fourth parties
1949	82.7	11.7	5.6 [1]
1953	83.3	11.0	5.6 [1]
1956	88.9	6.5	4.6 [1]
1959	89.0	7.7	3.3 [1]
1962	89.4	7.1	3.5 [1]
1966	91.0	5.4	3.6 [2]
1970	93.0	5.5	1.5
1971	93.1	5.5	1.4
1975	93.4	5.4	1.2
1979	92.9	6.1	1.0
1983	90.9	5.0	4.1 [3]
1986	84.4	9.7	5.9 [4]

1: mainly KPÖ (1949: 5.1; 1953: 5.3; 1956: 4.4; 1959: 3.3; 1962: 3.3)
2: mainly DFP (3.3)
3: mainly VGÖ and ALÖ (3.5)
4: mainly the Greens (4.8%)

The decreasing concentration of the party system indicates at this point a no longer functional parallelism between the claim to representation and party concentration. That the parties, that especially the SPÖ and ÖVP want to speak for all Austrians on principle, can now no longer hinder a growing minority of Austrians from disassociating itself from the traditional party system.

4. New lines of conflict—new parties?

The development of the party system indicates a further change in party typology. The popular party character of the parties, especially of the two major parties, is really working toward an integration of particular voter segments. This can be inferred from the criticism made by particular voter groups with regard to—in their opinion—the poor distinguishability between the traditional parties (see Table 2.2).

The popular party character is evidently now exaggerated for a growing minority; it essentially produces a turning away from the traditional parties. This of course does not mean a resurgence of the traditional lines of conflict which were responsible for the development of the camps and the parties in the 19th century. For the trend away from the traditional parties does not favor the parties which criticize the traditional parties for abandoning the claim to special representation—the trend, for example, does not go in the direction of the KPÖ, which wants to gain status against the SPÖ as a class-conscious workers' party;[32] Neither does it go in the direction of markedly German national groupings, as for example the NDP, which reproaches the FPÖ for "betrayal" of a (German) "national" policy and which consciously continues the programmatic traditions of the German national camp of the past.[33]

Table 2.2
Criticism of the claim to general representation (poor distinguishability) of the parties[34]

In the opinion of the interviewees the political parties differ from one another...(in %)	1975 a)	1977 b)	1981 c)		1985 d)		1987 e)	
very strongly	} (36)	} (38)	11	} 40	11	} 36	8	} 28
rather strongly			29		25		20	
rather little	} (54)	} (55)	44	} 54	47	} 61	48	} 64
very little			10		14		16	

Source:
a+b) Institut für Markt- and Sozialanalyse (IMAS), Das politische Verhalten der Österreicher (1975, 1977)
c) Dr. Fessel + GfK, Parteienverdrossenheit (1981)
d) Dr. Fessel + GfK, Innen- und Außenperspektive des österreichischen Parteiensystems (1985)
e) Dr. Fessel + GfK, Thematische Determinanten der Wahlentscheidung (1987)
() = scale 1975/77 (strong, somewhat, very similar)

The parties which profit from the change in voter behavior and which enjoy the benefits of an increasingly critical attitude toward the exaggerated claim to general representation of the traditional parties rather represent a new line of conflict—the issues of the new social movements, the value change from "materialism" to "post-materialism"[35], and an increasing insight into the significance of generation and sex as political factors.

What is paradoxical about this situation is that the traditional parties change with just the voters in view whom they repel with this change. The end of the class and Weltanschauung parties was brought about in the final analysis by the turn—one stipulated by election strategy and unavoidable within the framework of the system—to the "new middle classes" consisting of voters more likely to be younger, better earning, and better educated.[36] The SPÖ could never have been so successful between 1970 and 1983 as a "workers' party" in the sense of a class party; it was successful because it was able, in part, to appeal to these middle classes. To be able to compete with the SPÖ, the ÖVP also had to develop out of a party with an active Catholic element with a middle-class and rural background into a party which, freed from the integralism of the traditional type, knew how to appeal to secularized, flexible voters. But from just these flexible voters, who are solicited by the major parties, come the groupings which bring about the already beginning change and expansion of the party system.[37] The logic of party competition has led to a turn to just these voters, who now—fully aware of their increased significance—have already initiated the decomposition of the traditional party system.

In the battle for voter segments no longer fitting into the old patterns the parties became "catch-all parties"; and now, from just these same voter segments, they must face the criticism that—for lack of differentiation—the old traditional kind of politics can only give rise to withdrawal from the traditional party system.

The changes presently taking place within the party system can be paraphrased with the term "ideological re-indoctrination"—certainly not in the sense of a new consolidation of old lines of conflict, but in the sense of consolidating new conflict lines and establishing them theoretically. These new conflict lines are:

— ecology, a political field that, unlike for example "social security" or "economic performance," is not "occupied" by the traditional parties and camps.[38]

— social equality between men and women; a political field that, although belonging to the classic repertoire of social democracy, proves to be an explosive problem in view of the inconsistency between egalitarian theory and non-egalitarian reality.[39]

— peace and a policy of peace, which of course in Austria, with its status of permanent neutrality, have another significance than in aligned countries—which nevertheless, also as a result of the contradictions arising from for example Austria's production and export of arms, also produce a peace movement with respect to Austria.[40]

These lines of conflict lead to a processual line of conflict as yet unknown in the party system of the Second Republic—to a conflict between the generations. Since younger (and better educated) voters show an above-average concern with these lines of conflict, the changes in party typology and the new lines of conflict go hand in hand with a step-by-step polarization between the generations. This is apparent not only through the concrete disputes for example about the energy policy (Zwentendorf, Hainburg), but also through the readiness to vote for the parties of the Green-Alternative spectrum.

Table 2.3a
The generation conflict exemplified by Zwentendorf, Hainburg and Green-Alternative sympathizers[41]
Voter behavior on 5 November 1978: For or against Zwentendorf?

Occupation	yes	no	abstention	(no answer)	Σ in %
white-collar employees	31	34	20	(15)	100
skilled workers	38	25	25	(12)	100
unskilled workers	32	15	33	(20)	100
self-employed persons	14	48	28	(10)	100
professionals	22	45	27	(6)	100
farmers	10	51	29	(10)	100
no employment (housewives)	35	31	27	(7)	100
retired persons	34	27	26	(13)	100
age groups					
19-29	25	32	31	(12)	100
30-49	33	35	24	(8)	100
50+	36	31	24	(9)	100

(N = 2000)

Table 2.3b
Attitude to the Danube power station at Hainburg according to age, education and residence (in %)

	should be built at the planned location			at another location			should not be built		
	XI/84	III/85	swing	XI/84	III/85	swing	XI/84	III/85	swing
eligible voters	39	43	+4	20	30	+10	32	23	-9
first-time voters	37	36	-1	24	29	+5	35	32	-3
voters under the age of 30	32	37	+5	23	23	0	37	37	0
compulsory education	40	47	+7	17	26	+9	31	22	-9
technical education	41	45	+4	21	28	+7	30	25	-5
high-school graduates university graduates	29	29	0	28	47	+19	39	23	-16
from Vienna	25	29	+4	23	41	+18	48	29	-19
from Lower Austria	54	51	-3	15	27	+12	21	19	-2

(N = 1500)

Table 2.3c
Election of a Green or Alternative List at the national level basically imaginable (in %)

	March 1982a)	July 1982b)	Feb. 1983c)	24 Apr. 1983d) (NCE)	July 1983e)	Nov. 1984f)	March 1985g)	July 1985h)	23 Nov. 1986j) (NCE)	March 1987k)	March 1988l)
electoral population (total)	11	18	13	(3.3)	17	29	26	19	(4.8)	16	12
those preferring the SPÖ	7	14	4		14	18	15	12		8	8
those preferring the ÖVP	8	15	8		13	20	19	15		8	7
voters willing to switch	*	23	25		25	41	69	55		43	30
first-time voters	*	36	31		43	40	44	37		20	12
voters under the age of 30	14	31	22		32	39	39	29		25	20
white-collar workers	16	30	23		24	36	34	24		27	19
high-school/university graduates	21	28	27		41	55	41	36		34	30
Regarding the preference question, those declaring the intention to vote for a Green or Alternative List...	2	5	6	(3.3)	2	7	8	3	(4.8)	5	3

Sources:
a) Institut für Demoskopie Allensbach (IFD), Das politische Meinungsklima in Österreich (1982)
b) Institut für Empirische Sozialforschung (IFES) + Dr. Fessel + GfK, Die Grünen (1982)
c) Dr. Fessel + GfK, Politische Umfrage (1983)
d) Proportion of votes of VGÖ and ALÖ in the National Council election of 1983
e) Dr. Fessel + Co., Grüne Parteien (1983)
f) Dr. Fessel + Co., Politische Umfrage (1984)
g) Dr. Fessel + GfK, Innen- und Außenperspektive des österreichischen Parteiensystems (1985)
h) Dr. Fessel + GfK, Politische Umfrage (1985)
j) Proportion of votes of the Green-Alternative parties in the National Council election of 1983
k) Dr. Fessel + GfK, Thematische Determinanten der Wahlentscheidung (1987)
l) Dr. Fessel + GfK, Politische Umfrage (1988)

5. Loss of functionality as a "healthful shrinking process"

In liberal systems an articulation-, recruiting- and (extensive) legitimation function is attributed to parties.[42] In the past the Austrian parties have made maximum use of primarily the latter two:

— The parties and the party system have recruited not only the political elite of the political system in the restricted sense, i.e. the decision-makers in the government and parliament at the national, state and municipal level; they have, as a consequence of the party state, also recruited economic elitists in the economic sub-system and educational elitists in the educational system.

— The Austrian parties have legitimated their power not only within the framework of the political system; they have legitimated the political system in its entirety. In no other European country is the political system to this extent the product of the multi-party system, the result of the cooperation of political parties which—older than the state—have created a state for themselves.

The carrying out of both functions, extensively exercised over a number of decades, has been receding for some time. For several years, in the social economic sector for example, the distribution of seats on a board of directors and supervisory board has no longer been exclusively based on "proportional party representation"; on the contrary, a demonstrative break with this practice can be observed, for example as a reaction to the VÖEST crisis at the end of 1985. The parties have made a retreat from their function as "lock-keepers" in the social economy.

This can be explained only in connection with the fact that the parties no longer continue to carry out their legitimation function as extensively as before. For the parties do not on their own accord relinquish the recruiting function for example in the social economic sector; they relinquish it as a result of public pressure. This pressure is caused by a competition between the parties which they can no longer fully control. Just as in the decision-making process with regard to the Zwentendorf atomic power plant, in 1978 and later, and with regard to the building of the dam near Hainburg, in 1984 and later, the parties were less the pursuers and more the pursued[43]—less the ones making the decisions and more those subordinating themselves to certain factors determining events, to certain forces inherent in party competition.

The loss of significance of the recruiting and legitimation function is equivalent to a loss of significance of the party state. The political system emancipates itself partially from the dominance of the parties and the associations interlinked with them; the state is no longer to the same extent the product of the parties and their actions; the democratic republic is no longer to the same extent as before the "property" of the parties.

This does not mean, however, that the parties cease to be transmission belts between citizens and interests on the one hand, and the political system on the other. Rather, the parties as the founders of the Republic, as those giving it its constitution, allow—late, but nevertheless—this same Republic more independence. And therefore there is also the possibility that the function of articulation gains significance in comparison with the legitimation and recruiting functions. As soon as political events are no longer determined by the parties to the same extent as earlier, they are more strongly forced to consider certain fluctuations of interests in the electorate—especially to react to minority interests organized so well that they must be reckoned with. But such are not necessarily socially weak; they can also represent the socially strong. They are even probably without direct organization, hence without any direct ties to parties and associations more capable of achieving their objectives than socially weak minorities. The decline of the party state is therefore also connected at the same time with the possibility, even to the probability, that certain special interests can articulate and realize themselves.

The decline of the party state means an increase in the importance of Parliamentarian in the Western sense. The receding legitimation and recruiting function is certainly also the consequence of the progressive emergence of political conflicts and of the decrease of political cartels, as for example stable coalitions or neocorporatistic agreements which in broad subsections of the political system prevent competition for votes. The party state is declining—the consequence is a freer intra-party competition within the framework of Parliamentarian, a competition of the parties for votes with a view to parliament and the formation of a majority in parliament.[44]

In part, the party state has made itself superfluous. It created the prerequisites for its own decline—prerequisites such as a republic and a constitution, the consociationalism of the elite and stabilization, national consciousness and a fundamental societal consensus. The extremely pronounced party state has made itself superfluous through its own success. What remains is a reduced, shrunken party state; what remains is an Austrian Parliamentarian which has normalized itself in the Western sense—with all its advantages and disadvantages.

Notes

1. Cf. in general Daalder 1983.
2. Haerpfer 1985.
3. Beyme 1982, pp. 203-230.
4. Powell 1980.
5. For the development of the parties and of the party system in Austria in general, cf. Sully 1981; Gerlich/Müller 1983.
6. Regarding the term "camp," cf. Wandruszka 1945, in particular pp. 291-300. Regarding the term "pillars," cf. Lijphart 1977, particularly pp. 41-44.
7. For the early history of Austrian social democracy, cf. Brügel 1925. For an overall treatment reaching (almost) into the present, cf. Kaufmann 1978; Sully 1982.
8. Knoll 1973; Boyer 1981.
9. Wandruszka 1954. pp. 369-421.
10. Riedlsperger 1978.
11. Gärtner 1979; Spira 1979.

36   *Pelinka*

12. Stadler 1983; Ableitinger 1983.

13. Lehmbruch 1967. Lijphart 1977, particularly pp. 99-103. Steininger 1975.

14. Regarding the concept of the party state, cf. Plasser/Ulram 1982, particularly pp. 11-60.

15. Nassmacher 1975; Müller 1981.

16. Dermutz 1983.

17. Deiser/Winkler 1982, particularly pp. 94-98. Kofler 1985, in particular pp. 46-49.

18. Nick/Pelinka 1984, pp. 45-51 and p. 73.

19. Regarding the "stability of the infrastructure" with a community as an example, cf. Powell 1970. For a comparison of this "stable infrastructure" with a "flexible suprastructure," cf. Pelinka 1984.

20. Bluhm 1973; Kreissler 1984.

21. Regarding party typology in general, cf. Duverger 1951. Lenk/Neumann, in particular pp. 313-367. Oberreuter 1984, particularly pp. 33-44.

22. Kadan/Pelinka 1979, p. 77f.

23. Regarding the term "integralism," cf. Knoll 1962 and Knoll 1966, particularly pp. 69-73.

24. Kadan/Pelinka 1979, p. 115.

25. Regarding the historical function of anti-semitism in Austria, cf. Bunzl/Marin 1983, in particular pp. 9-88; Spira 1981.

26. Berchtold 1967, p. 478.

27. Reiter 1982.

28. Kadan/Pelinka 1979, p. 96.

29. Kadan/Pelinka 1979, p. 135.

30. Kirchheimer 1968.

31. Compiled according to official election results.

32. Cf. for example the position of the KPÖ on social partnership. Wimmer 1979.

33. DÖW (Dokumentationsarchiv = Documentation Archive of the Austrian Resistance) 1981, in particular pp. 146-149.

34. Plasser 1986, p. 379.

35. Barnes/Kaase 1979, particularly pp. 203-380. Rosenmayr 1980.

36. Ulram 1985.

37. Plasser 1986, pp. 376-435.

38. Gerlich 1985.

39. Cf. the various themes treated in the österreichische Zeitschrift für Politikwissenschaft, so 4/1978, 4/1984. Cf. also Rosenberger 1987.

40. Schneider 1984; Maislinger 1984.

41. Pelinka 1983; Pelinka 1986; Plasser 1986, p. 352.

42. Regarding the function of the parties, cf. generally Beyme 1982, pp. 22-40.

43. Pelinka 1986; Natter 1987.

44. The term "Parliamentarian" used here signifies neither a parliamentary system nor the assumption of a dominant position of the parliamentary decision-making process itself. Parliamentarian is a comprehensive term in which competition for votes aimed at the parliament and parliamentary majority conditions is central. This concept of Parliamentarian corresponds to the notion of democracy of "empirical" or "economic" democracy theory and hence disassociates itself more strongly from the notion of democracy of for example consociational democracy, but as well from a po-

litical system which focuses on neocorporatism. For the point of view of democratic theory, cf. also Schediwy (1980).

Bibliography

Ableitinger, Alfred, *Grundlegung der Verfassung*, in: Erika Weinzierl/Kurt Skalnik: *Österreich 1918-1938. Geschichte der ersten Republik*. Zwei Bände, Graz/ Wien/Köln 1983 (Ableitinger, 1983)

Barnes, Samuel H./Kaase, Max et al., *Political Action. Mass Participation in five Western Democracies*, Beverly Hills/London 1979 (Barnes/Kaase, 1979)

Berchtold, Klaus (Hg.), *Österreichische Parteiprogramme 1868-1966*, Wien 1967 (Berchtold, 1967)

Beyme, Klaus von, *Parteien in westlichen Demokratien*, München 1982 (Beyme, 1982)

Bluhm, William T., *Building an Austrian Nation. The Political Integration of a Western State*, New Haven/London 1973 (Bluhm, 1973)

Boyer, John W., *Political Radicalism in Late Emperial Vienna. Origins of the Christian Social Movement 1848-1897*, Chicago/London 1981 (Boyer, 1981)

Brügel, Ludwig, *Geschichte der österreichischen Sozialdemokratie*, 5 Bände, Wien 1922-1925 (Brügel, 1925)

Bunzl, John/Marin, Bernd, *Antisemitismus in Österreich. Sozialhistorische und soziologische Studien*, Innsbruck 1983 (Bunzl/Marin, 1983)

Daalder, Hans/Mair, Peter (eds.), *Western European Party System. Continuity and Change*, Beverly Hills/London 1983 (Daalder/Mair, 1983)

Deiser, Roland/Winkler, Norbert, *Das politische Handeln der Österreicher*, Wien 1982 (Deiser/Winkler, 1982)

Dermutz, Susanne, *Der österreichische Weg. Schulreform und Bildungspolitik in der Zweiten Republik*, Wien 1983 (Dermutz, 1983)

Dokumentationsarchiv des österr. Widerstandes, Dokumentationsarchiv (Hg.), *Rechtsextremismus in Österreich nach 1945*, fünfte Auflage, Wien 1981 (Dokumentationsarchiv, 1981)

Duverger, Maurice, *Les Parties Politiques*, Paris 1951 (Duverger, 1951)

Gärtner, Heinz, *Zwischen Moskau und Österreich. Die KPÖ—Analyse einer sowjetabhängigen Partei*, Wien 1979 (Gärtner, 1979)

Gerlich, Peter, *Ernstnehmen oder Augenzwinkern. Grün-alternative Herausforderungen der traditionellen Politik*, in: Fritz Plasser/Peter A. Ulram/Manfried Welan (Hg.), *Demokratierituale*, Wien 1985 (Gerlich, 1985)

Gerlich, Peter/Müller, Wolfgang C., *Zwischen Koalition und Konkurrenz. Österreichs Parteien seit 1945*, Wien 1983 (Gerlich/Müller, 1983)

Gerlich, Peter, *Consociationalism to Competition. The Austrian Party System since 1945*, in: Hans Daalder (ed.), *Party System in Denmark, Austria, Switzerland, the Netherlands and Belgium*, New York 1987 (Gerlich, 1987)

Haerpfer, Christian, *Austria*, in: Ivor Crewe/David Denver (eds.), *Electoral Change in Western Democracies. Patterns and Sources of Electoral Volatility*, London/ Sidney 1985 (Haerpfer, 1985)

Kadan, Albert/Pelinka, Anton, *Die Grundsatzprogramme der österreichischen Parteien. Dokumentation und Analyse*, St. Pölten 1979 (Kadan/Pelinka, 1979)

Kaufmann, Fritz, *Sozialdemokratie in Österreich*, München/Wien 1978 (Kaufmann, 1978)

Kirchheimer, Otto, *Der Weg zur Allerweltspartei*, in: Kurt Lenk/Franz Neumann (Hg.), *Theorie und Soziologie der politischen Parteien*, Neuwied/Berlin 1968 (Kirchheimer, 1968)

Knoll, August M., *Katholische Kirche und scholastisches Naturrecht*, Wien/Frankfurt/ Zürich 1962 (Knoll, 1962)

Knoll, August M., *Katholische Gesellschaftslehre. Zwischen Glaube und Wissenschaft*, Wien/Frankfurt/Zürich 1966 (Knoll, 1966)

Knoll, Reinhold, *Zur Tradition der christlichsozialen Partei. Ihre Früh- und Entwicklungsgeschichte bis zu den Reichsratswahlen 1907*, Wien/Köln/Graz 1973 (Knoll, 1973)

Kofler, Anton, *Parteiengesellschaft im Umbruch*, Wien 1985 (Kofler, 1985)

Kreissler, Felix, *Der Österreicher und seine Nation. Ein Lernprozeß mit Hindernissen*, Wien/Köln/Graz 1984 (Kreissler, 1984)

Lehmbruch, Gerhard, *Proporzdemokratie. Politisches System und politische Kultur in der Schweiz und in Österreich*, Tübingen 1967 (Lehmbruch, 1967)

Lenk, Kurt/Neumann, Franz (Hg.), *Theorie und Soziologie der politischen Parteien*, Neuwied/Berlin 1968 (Lenk/Neumann, 1968)

Lijphart, Arend, *Democracy in Plural Societies. A Comparative Exploration*, New Haven/London 1977 (Lijphart, 1977)

Maislinger, Andreas, *"Neue" österreichische Friedensbewegung(en)*, in: ÖJP 1983, Wien 1984 (Maislinger, 1984)

Müller, Wolfgang C., *Zur Genese des Verhältnisses von Politik und verstaatlichter Industrie in Österreich (1946-1981)*, in: ÖZP 4/1981 (Müller, 1981)

Naßmacher, Karl-Heinz, *Verstaatlichung in Österreich. Erfahrungen mit der Teilsozialisierung von Schlüsselindustrien*, in: Konegen, Norbert/Kracht, Gerhard (Hg.), *Sozialismus und Sozialisierung*, Kronberg 1975 (Naßmacher, 1975)

Natter, Bernhard, *Fallstudie Zwentendorf und Hainburg*, in: Anton Pelinka (Hg.), *Populismus in Österreich*, Wien 1987 (Natter, 1987)

Nick, Rainer/Pelinka, Anton, *Parlamentarismus in Österreich*, Wien/München 1984 (Nick/Pelinka, 1984)

Nowotny, Thomas, *Bleibende Werte—verblichene Dogmen. Die Zukunft der Sozialdemokratie*, Wien 1985 (Nowotny, 1985)

Oberreuter, Heinrich, *Parteien—zwischen Nestwärme und Funktionskälte*, zweite Auflage, Osnabrück 1984 (Oberreuter, 1984)

Pelinka, Anton, *The Nuclear Power Referendum in Austria*, in: *Electoral Studies* 3/1983 (Pelinka, 1983)

Pelinka, Anton, *Die Entwicklung der österreichischen Sozialdemokratie nach dem Zweiten Weltkrieg*, in: Francois-Georges Dreyfus (ed.), *Reformism et Revisionnisme dans les socialismes allmand, autrichien et francais*, Paris 1984 (Pelinka, 1984)

Pelinka, Anton, *Hainburg—mehr als nur ein Kraftwerk*, in: ÖJP 1985, München/Wien 1986 (Pelinka, 1986)

Plasser, Fritz/Ulram, Peter A., *Unbehagen im Parteienstaat. Jugend und Politik in Österreich*, Wien 1982 (Plasser/Ulram, 1982)

Plasser, Fritz, *Parteien unter Stress. Zur Dynamik der Parteiensysteme in Österreich, Deutschland und den Vereinigten Staaten*, Habilitationsschrift, Universität Innsbruck 1986 (Plasser, 1986)

Powell, Bingham G. jr., *Social Fragmentation and Political Hostility. An Austrian Case Study*, Stanford 1970 (Powell, 1970)

Powell, Bingham G. jr., *Voting Turnout in Thirty Democracies. Partisan, Legal and Socio-Economic Influences*, in: Richard Rose (ed.), *Electoral Participation. A Comparative Analysis*, London/Beverly Hills 1980 (Powell, 1980)

Reiter, Erich, *Programm und Programmentwicklung der FPÖ*, Wien 1982 (Reiter, 1982)

Riedlsperger, Max, *The Lingering Shadow of Nazism. The Austrian Independent Party Movement since 1945*, New York 1978 (Riedlsperger, 1978)

Rosenberger, Sieglinde, *Autonome Frauenbewegung*, in: Anton Pelinka (Hg.), *Populismus in Österreich*, Wien 1987 (Rosenberger, 1987)

Rosenmayr, Leopold (Hg.), *Politische Beteiligung und Wertwandel in Österreich*, München/Wien 1980 (Rosenmayr, 1980)

Schediwy, Robert, *Empirische Politik, Chancen und Grenzen einer demokratischen Gesellschaft.* Wien 1980 (Schediwy, 1980)

Schneider, Heinrich, *Zur Entwicklung der Friedensbewegung in Österreich*, in: ÖJP 1983, München/Wien 1984 (Schneider, 1984)

Spira, Leopold, *Ein gescheiterter Versuch. Der Austro-Eurokommunismus*, Wien/München 1979 (Spira, 1979)

Spira, Leopold, *Feindbild "Jud." 100 Jahre politischer Antisemitismus in Österreich*, Wien/München 1981 (Spira, 1981)

Stadler, Karl R., *Die Gründung der Republik*, in: Erika Weinzierl/Kurt Skalnik, *Österreich 1918-1938. Geschichte der ersten Republik.* Zwei Bände, Graz/Wien/Köln 1983 (Stadler, 1983)

Steininger, Rudolf, *Polarisierung und Integration. Eine vergleichende Untersuchung der strukturellen Versäulung der Gesellschaft in den Niederlanden und in Österreich*, Meisenheim am Glan 1975 (Steininger, 1975)

Sully, Melanie A., *Political Parties and Elections in Austria*, London 1981 (Sully, 1981)

Sully, Melanie A., *Continuity and Change in Austrian Socialims. The Eternal Quest for the Third Way*, New York 1982 (Sully, 1982)

Ulram, Peter A., *Um die Mehrheit der Mehrheit. Die neuen, angestellten Mittelschichten 1975-1984*, in: Fritz Plasser/Peter A. Ulram/Manfried Welan (Hg.), *Demokratierituale*, Wien 1985 (Ulram, 1985)

Wandruszka, Adam, *Österreichs politische Struktur. Die Entwicklung der Parteien und politischen Bewegungen*, in: Heinrich Benedikt (Hg.), *Geschichte der Republik Österreich*, Wien 1954 (Wandruszka, 1954)

Wimmer, Ernst, *Sozialpartnerschaft aus marxistischer Sicht*, Wien 1979 (Wimmer, 1979)

3

The Austrian Party System between Erosion and Innovation

An Empirical Long-term Analysis

FRITZ PLASSER

1. Parties in post-industrial democracy

In the literature of international political science the Austrian party system has the reputation of having a very high degree of stability. Characterized by structural "pillarization," a segmented "camp mentality," an extraordinarily high formal integrative capacity and an unusually low conflict level, the Austrian party system was regarded in the 50's and 60's to be "one of the most stable of the competitive systems" (Janda 1980, p. 318). In the meantime, however, latent signs of corrosion are stimulating doubt about its historical hyperstability. The "golden age" of the Austrian party system seems finally to be a thing of the past. Structural processes of erosion, an increase of voter protest and an intensification of intra-party conflicts indicate that the Austrian party system has entered a transitory stage which is a "crisis of phase transition" (Bühl 1984, p. 69) with increased conditions of tension, critical fluctuations and contradictory reactions.[1] In an attempt to divide the dynamics of change of the party systems into periods, Dalton/Flanagan/Beck (1984) differentiate between "three general types of electoral periods—stable alignments, realignments and dealignments" (p. 11), each period evincing a specific system behavior:

(1) In stationary periods (stable alignments) party systems are in a state of dynamic balance. The traditional voter coalitions forming the supporting pillars of the party system remain largely intact. In spite of occasional fluctuations in voter behavior, which follow an oscillating logic as a tem-

porary deviation from the "normal" voter behavior, the party system remains in a dynamic state of rest.

(2) In periods of innovation (partisan realignments) the handed-down basic structure of a party system changes.[2] The existent voter coalitions begin to stir. Internal tensions and dissonances increase. Voter behavior becomes unstable and unpredictable. The party system enters a transition phase which culminates via a "critical" election in a re-grouping or re-allocation of the party field.[3]

(3) In periods of erosion (partisan dealignments) handed-down loyalties and affective party ties become weaker.[4] The internal loosening processes shake the structural and affective foundation of the party system. Traditional lines of tension are overshadowed by lines of conflict reflecting new issues. The party system enters a turbulent phase culminating either in a "critical" election or going on into a continuous structural phase of decline characterized by weakness, exhaustion and critical signs of dissolution.[5]

Independent of modish diagnoses of crises, suggestive evocations of crises and speculative prognoses of change, empirical long-term findings indicate far-reaching transformation processes in the Austrian party system which subject its structural stability to severe tests:[6]

a) The continuous decrease in the number of traditional- and core voters has made the traditional parties more vulnerable. The historical camps, to which the Austrian party system owes its extraordinary "hyperstability," were undermined by socio-structural change, split up and overrun by the societal process of modernization.[7] Encapsulated social milieus, dense organizational networks and handed-down ties and loyalties were just as little able to cope with the socio-structural dynamics of change as identity-giving symbols, collective historical experiences and the myths of movement were to generative change. In the meantime, a highly differentiated network of heterogeneous—very often only indirectly experienceable—reference and status groups has developed out of a "politicalized social structure" in which primarily membership in a respective class, social stratum and social milieu determined voting behavior. The progressive disintegration of historical camps and traditional social milieus must not be equated with their disappearance. The political parties still continue to command the services of remaining handed-down loyalties, sub-cultural remnants and affiliated organizations. Remains of the "camp mentality" can still be found within the intimate cadre sections of the parties; emotional affiliation, inflexible doctrines and the readiness to render unconditional allegiance dominate the daily routine of the sections, local chapters and municipal party headquarters.[8] Just as before, the political parties command social and regional "strongholds," even though their foundations are becoming increasingly shaky; they continue to offer tens of thousands of activists sub-cultural security, identity and a sense of belonging, even though recruiting of cadres is becoming more difficult since a growing aversion to the organizational logic of the political parties can be observed on the part of the advancing generations of voters.[9]

On the other hand, in advanced sectors of society, in the congested areas, centers of the service sector and the suburbia of the large cities the political parties are increasingly confronted by a colder, sometimes even hostile environment. An above-average educational level, high occupational qualifications, orientation toward social advancement, secularization and pluralization of social environments characterize a new type of voter who evades the conventional integrative, incorporative strategies of the political parties.[10] Having outgrown handed-down loyalties and ties, he reacts on the whole more autonomously, more pragmatically and in a more critical way than the "bound" voter of past decades. Whether a personality- or an issue-voter, in any case this "floating vote" is an irritating factor for the traditional parties and forces them to adopt more and more differentiated strategies to handle potential party-shifters.

b) Increasing flexibility and selectivity in the behavior of the Austrian voter have clearly aggravated the orientation problems of the parties, intensified debates on strategy and made party-political competition more difficult.[11] Since already at the end of the 60's the number of "bound" traditional voters and milieu voters was no longer sufficient to maintain the customary electoral-political levels, the parties were forced to open up for purely tactical considerations. Strategies aiming at party-shifters and specific target groups took over the place of appellative mobilization efforts. A differentiated "strategy-mix" along with emotions and public opinions reinforced by mass media have become the benchmarks for strategic calculations.

c) The erosion of handed-down loyalties and emotional ties and a more and more pragmatic—soberly calculating—attitude toward the political parties led logically to far-reaching changes in the way the parties present themselves. Professionalization of staff work, excessive personalization and perfecting of the means of image politics suited for the TV-camera were the—tactical—answers to the continuous erosion of their social structures of integration and control.[12] Short-termed bursts of emotion, vague appeals to image and indistinct promises have overshadowed recognizable lines of interest and attributable areas of responsibility. Determining the actions of the parties is no longer the persistent representation of specific interests, but the pretension of being able to simultaneously satisfy as many societal interests as possible. Traditional weltanschauung and interest parties—rooted in historical currents—have

transformed themselves into political service enterprises and om-
nipresent—apparently omnipotent—problem-solving agencies, vehicles
for career advancement, and providers of apartments and jobs.[13]

d) In the meantime, economic slumps, an overstraining of the public budget, growing problems in financing the welfare state's security network,
the downfall of nationalized large-scale industry, and structural unemployment mark the borders of the material capability of the political
system and of a state interventionist crisis management. The gradual
transition from the policy of a general increase of prosperity to a "cut
back management" of a policy of distribution of burdens restricts the
maneuverability of the parties. Distribution conflicts—concealed by the
growth- and prosperity dynamics of the 60's and early 70's—began to
emerge. Conflicting intra-party interests put the integrative capacity of
the party elite to a severe test. Not only intensified economic and sociopolitical problems, but also environmental and energy issues cause intra-
party dissonances, far-reaching—and often unsolved—identity problems,
disgruntlement and frustration.

e) An increase of voter protest, latent secession tendencies, the expansion
of the party spectrum and a widespread displeasure and discontent with
the political parties indicate more serious structural problems within the
Austrian party system.[14] The widespread disillusionment with politicians
and parties offers new protest groups a broad field in which to maneuver, provided that they understand how to emotionally react to this latent
discontent, to openly expose the party book system and—utilizing the
intensifying effect of the mass media—to turn communal, regional and
national elections into protest- and "object-lesson" elections. The traditional major parties are to a great extent helpless against "classic" party
protest since their latitude for reform is in fact limited and reform attempts can be quite easily defamed as stratagems. If new protest parties
and their proponents are successful in articulating protest motives—which are deep-seated and can easily be evoked—they can force,
at least for a time, the traditional parties into the defensive—even
though the permanence of their success appears doubtful.[15]

The Austrian party system is steering unmistakably toward a phase of
radical structural change in which, however, a number of "critical" developments, when more closely analyzed, turn out to be the consequences of a
process of structural change and modernization within advanced industrial
societies. These developments logically affect the motives and interests of the
voter, his behavior and his relationship and attitudes to the political parties.[16]
Extensive changes of the social environment place the parties under an increasing strain which tests their capability to learn and adapt:[17]

— The decrease of traditional and core voter groups makes the parties more vulnerable.

— Increasing flexibility and selectivity in voter behavior intensify the orientation problems of the parties.

— Varying expectations and demands strain the integrative capacity of the parties and aggravate latent intra-party conflicts.

— The weakening of affective party ties increases the costs of integration and mobilization and leads to the increased employment of symbolic political forms.

— New issues pose challenges for which the political parties have been unable to find workable solutions and create lines of tension running through all the parties.

— Shifts in voter preferences regarding goals and values hinder political agreement and contribute to the irritation of the system of political goals.

— A quantitative and qualitative change of the need to participate in politics overstrains or competes with the conventional participation offers of the political parties (Plasser 1987, S.35).

— The expansion of the party spectrum and the formation of new party groups intensify the competition between the traditional parties. The "calm" in the Austrian party system (Pelinka 1985) has become a raw tail wind which causes turbulence and obvious course and orientation problems.

2. Erosion of the structural foundations

Within the last three decades Austrian society has developed from a partially "pre-modern" society to a mature industrial and service-oriented society. A rapid decrease of the agrarian sector, to which in 1951 still every third employed person belonged, is contrasted with a constant increase of the tertiary sector, to which in 1981 already every second Austrian employed person could be ascribed.[18]

Socio-structural change (a decrease in the number of independent farmers, tradespeople, self-employed persons and professionals; an increase in regional and occupational mobility (flexibility), industrialization and suburbanization of formerly rural regions) and the modernization of production structures (a decrease in the traditional industrial workforce, growth of the tertiary sector, of the public sector and of the new white-collar middle classes) have radically changed the social voter basis of the major parties.

Table 3.1
Employed persons according to sectors (1951-1981)

Sector in % of the employed population		1951	1961	1971	1981	change 1951/1981
I	agriculture and forestry	31.6	23.0	15.0	8.5	-24.1
II	mining, industry and trade	37.6	41.4	42.2	41.0	+3.4
III	services	29.8	35.6	42.8	50.5	+20.7

Source: ÖSTZ (Österreichisches Statistisches Zentralamt) (= Austrian Central Office of Statistics)
Results of official censuses (1951-1981)

Table 3.2
Social voter basis of the major Austrian parties (1955-1985)

declared party supporters (in %)	SPÖ				ÖVP			
	1955a)	1978b)	1985c)	change 1955-85	1955a)	1978b)	1985c)	change 1955-85
self-employed professionals tradespeople	4	3	2	-2	17	7	6	-11
white-collar workers/ civil servants	16	20	23	+7	13	21	25	+12
blue-collar workers	39	34	28	-11	13	17	17	+4
farmers	5	2	1	-4	26	20	10	-16
housewives	24	17	16	-8	20	13	16	-4
retired or non-employed persons	12	25	30	+18	11	21	26	+15
Σ in %	100	100	100		100	100	100	

Source:
a)   Österreichisches Institut für Markt- und Meinungsforschung, (Dr. Fessel-Institut); accumulated data from several representative opinion polls of the year 1955, cited after: Querschnitte der öffentlichen Meinung (März) 1956 (S.2)
b)   Data cited after: Plasser/Ulram (1984, p. 39)
c)   Dr. Fessel + GfK, Kumulierte Jahreszählung der Parteipräferenzen 1985 (N = 27,000)

The social profile of the major Austrian parties in the middle of the 80's differs fundamentally from the structure of the historical "camp parties" of the 50's. Milieu parties and firmly established voter blocks have meanwhile developed into highly sophisticated, heterogeneous voter coalitions. Whereas in 1955 the ÖVP electorate consisted of 43% self-employed persons, tradespeople and farmers and only 26% employed persons, in the meantime there are 16% self-employed and farmers and already 42% employed persons. The ÖVP has transformed itself from a party of tradespeople and farmers to a party of employed persons in which white-collar personnel and civil servants comprise the largest voter group. The SPÖ too has undergone a great deal of structural change within the last three decades. Whereas in 1955 39% blue-collar workers were contrasted with only 16% white-collar personnel and civil servants, in the meantime blue-collar and white-collar persons are represented equally strongly. Here a second thrust of modernization and change in the congested urban-industrial areas appears to be sweeping over the core of the industrial workforce like the tradespeople and farmer core sections of the ÖVP through the first thrust of modernization in the 60's.

Table 3.3
Decrease of the traditional social core voter groups of the major Austrian parties (1961-1985)

declared party supporters (in %)	SPÖ core section	ÖVP core section
1961a)	75	57
1969b)	68	48
1978c)	60	36
1985d)	53	30
Change 1961/1985	-22	-27

Source:
a)-c) Cited after: Plasser/Ulram (1984, p. 38)
d)   Dr. Fessel + GfK, Kumulierte Jahreszählung der Parteipräferenzen 1985 (N = 27,000), Vienna 1986
Note:
SPÖ core section = SPÖ supporters living in worker households
ÖVP core section = ÖVP supporters living in self-employed, tradespeople or farming households

The social process of modernization has undermined not only the social and sub-cultural binding power of the parties, but also weakened religious lines of tension. Above all within the ÖVP electorate during the last three decades church ties have become looser, church attendance has decreased, and the ÖVP has begun to break away voter generation by voter generation from its traditional religious milieu. Still basically intact in rural and village regions, the Catholic milieu is losing its clearly defined features in urbanized centers, the networks are breaking down, and its socio-political relevancy is diminishing.

Table 3.4
Secularization (or de-confessionalization) in the Austrian party system (1955-1985)

Declared party supporters in % go to church every Sunday or did so the previous Sunday	1955a)	1972b)	1985c)	change 1955/1985
ÖVP supporters	67	55	45	-22
SPÖ supporters	15	14	14	-1

Source:
a)   Dr. Fessel-Institut, Repräsentativumfrage (1955), cited after: Querschnitte der öffentlichen Meinung (Juni) 1956 (S.12)
b)   Dr. Fessel + GfK, Politische Umfrage (1972)
c)   Dr. Fessel + GfK, Innen- und Außenperspektive des österreichischen Parteiensystems (1985)

The weakening of social and religious lines of tension,[19] the splitting up of sub-cultural milieus and the dissemination of political information through the electronic "cultural revolution" (Plasser 1985a) in the form of the dominant medium of television have relativized also the capacity of informal networks and contact structures to convince and reinforce. While the weakening of the socio-structural "immune-system" of the major parties at the beginning of the 70's was compensated for by an informal "immune-system" of party-politically consonant networks in the daily routine of the voter, now even this integrative mechanism seems to show a tendency to fail. Whereas in 1972 still about 80% of the voters of the two major parties participated in a party-politically more or less consonant network of personal contacts and relationships, in the mid-80's only 60% receive consonant signals from their immediate social environment.[20] About one third of the supporters of both major parties exist in the meantime in a party-politically neutral daily routine. Their political attitudes are no longer reinforced by the immediate environment, they have to assimilate dissonant experiences individually, to cope alone with irritations and frustrations, and orient themselves increasingly on a mass-media-produced climate of opinions subject to hectic fluctuations.[21]

Table 3.5
Party-political consonance of social networks (1972-1984)

The respective party adherent (in %)	1972a)	1984b)	change
SPÖ adherents in a party-politically extensively consonant network	86	60	-26
SPÖ adherents in a party-politically extensively dissonant network	4	7	+3
SPÖ adherents in a party-politically neutral or unspecific network	10	33	+23
Σ in %	100	100	
ÖVP adherents in a party-politically extensively consonant network	78	60	-18
ÖVP adherents in a party-politically extensively dissonant network	10	10	+-0
ÖVP adherents in a party-politically neutral or unspecific network	12	30	+18
Σ in %	100	100	

Source:
a)   Dr. Fessel + GfK, Politische Umfrage (1972)
b)   Dr. Fessel + GfK, Politische Umfrage (1984)

3. Erosion of affective ties

The erosion of the structural foundation of the major Austrian parties was accompanied by an erosion of affective ties and loyalties. In comparison to the 50's and 60's affective ties to the political parties have become distinctly weaker. A growing number of Austrian voters has only dampened feelings toward the parties and party identification—i.e. the "long-term affective ties of the individual to a political party" (Falter 1984, p. 14)—have declined. Conversely, the number of voters not bound to any particular party is increasing.[22]

The present (sparse) data from time-series demonstrate initially the very strong (affective) ties of the Austrian party system in the 1950's and 60's. In the course of the 70's, however, a loosening of affective ties and loyalties can already be recognized. Covered up by the successful elections of the specific "Kreisky voter coalition" of the traditional industrial workhorse, parts of the new (white-collar) middle class and proponents of the intellectual and artistic elite of Austria, which succeeded in attaining the absolute majority of votes and seats in three successive National Council elections (1971, 1975, 1979), in the course of the 70's the Austrian party system was confronted by a "partisan dealignment with a concurrent stability of the vote" (Gehmacher/Haerpfer 1984, p. 43). The presumable extent of the erosion of affective ties becomes even clearer if one uses the percentage of voters declaring themselves in representative surveys as traditional voters for a specific party as an indicator of affective party ties.[23] While in the mid-70's about 80% of the supporters of both major parties could be classified as more or less firmly bound traditional voters, in the mid-80's the percentage of (subjectively) bound voters lies already under 50%. Every second voter of the two major parties has meanwhile become questionable for the parties because his unconditional loyalty and willingness to follow can no longer be totally reckoned with.

Table 3.6
Party identification in Austria (1954-1987)

the electoral population (in %)	1954a)	1957b)	1969c)	1974d)	1976e)	1984f)	1985g)	1986h)	1987i)
party identification (total)	73	71	75	65	63	61	60	60	58
strong identification	*	*	31	*	31	30	(21)	(23)	(23)
moderate or weak identification	*	*	44	*	32	31	(39)	(37)	(35)
no identification or no opinion	27	29	25	35	37	39	40	40	42

Source:
a)   Dr. Fessel-Institut, Untersuchung über die politische Einstellung der österreichischen Bevölkerung (1954, p. 10)
b)   Representative survey of the Dr. Fessel-Institut from May, 1957, cited after: Querschnitte der öffentlichen Meinung 36/1957 (pp. 4-5)
c)   Data cited after: Verba et al (1978, p. 98)
d)   Data cited after: Barnes/Kaase (1979, p. 580) and Rosenmayr (1980, p. 266)
e)   Dr. Fessel + GfK, Staat und Bürokratie (1976)
f)   Dr. Fessel + GfK, Politische Umfrage (1984)
g)   Dr. Fessel + GfK, Innen- und Außenperspektive des österreichischen Parteiensystems (1985)
h)   Dr. Fessel + GfK, Politische Umfrage (1986)
i)   Dr. Fessel + GfK, Thematische Determinanten der Wahlentscheidung (1987)
Note:
*   = no comparative data available
()   = data not directly comparable due to modified scaling
Versions of questions:
a)-b) in the course of a historical trend analysis only "soft" approximation indicators of affective ties
c)   the question version was not reconstructable
(Continued)

Source (Cont.)
d)-i) the questions correspond very much to the international standard versions for measure-
ment of affective party orientation or party identification (P.I.), respectively. See the
technical appendix in Plasser (1987)

Table 3.7
Decomposition of the electorates of the major Austrian parties (1954-1985)

adherents of a particular party (in %)	affective ties with "party identi- fication"			cognitive ties subjectively bound traditional voters		
	1954	1985	change	1984	1985	change
SPÖ adherents	89	76	-13	81	55	-26
ÖVP adherents	85	71	-14	82	49	-33

Source:
a) Data for 1954 according to: Dr. Fessel-Institut, Untersuchung über die politische Einstellung der österreichischen Bevölkerung (1954, p. 6 and p. 11)
b) Dr. Fessel + GfK, Innen- und Außenperspektive des österreichischen Parteiensystems
(1985) and Dr. Fessel + GfK, Kumulierte Jahreszählung der Parteipräferenzen 1985
(N = 27,000)

The erosion of structural and affective ties of the Austrian party system
has up to now, however, not led to any "critical" destabilization of voter behavior in National Council elections. The unmistakable loosening of internal
ties on the micro-level is contrasted by a predominantly unbroken stability on
the macro-level of the party system.[24] Voter behavior in national ballots up to
the last National Council election followed a more or less "conservative"
track. While an increase in volatility, i.e. strong voter shifting between the
parties, and an increase in insecurity in making the decision could be observed in the majority of West European party systems, no concrete signs of
increasing unpredictability of voter behavior could be seen in the Austrian
party system.[25] At the beginning of the 80's the number of "late deciders" still
corresponded to the figures for the 50's and 60's; about 90% had made their
voting decision well in advance of election day; stability and constancy were
the outstanding features of the Austrian party system.[26] The presidential
election in the spring of 1986 showed for the first time to what extent party
ties had weakened in the previous years and what potential flexibility and
willingness to shift parties had collected underneath a seemingly stable surface.[27] The National Council election in November 1986 marked to that point
the peak of such weighty weakening processes—the 16% figure for party-
shifters was spectacularly high for Austrian conditions.

Table 3.8
Decision-making certainty, the time of decision and percentage of party-shifters (1956-1986)

interviewees having made their personal voting decision ... (in %)	1956a)	1962b)	1966c)	1979d)	1983e)	1986f)	1986g)
shortly before the election or during the election campaign (late deciders)	11	7	10	9	8	(15)	16
well in advance of election day (early deciders) or non-voters	89	93	90	91	92	(84)	84
% of party-shifters	*	*	*	7	10	*	16

Source:
a)   Representative poll of the Dr. Fessel-Institut in the spring of 1956 cited after: Querschnitte der öffentlichen Meinung 13/1956 (p. 10)
b)   Dr. Fessel-Institut, Wähleranalyse 1962 (1962)
c)   Dr. Fessel-Institut, Wähleranalyse 1966 (1966)
d)   Dr. Fessel + GfK, Repräsentative Nachwahluntersuchung 1979 (1979)
e)   Dr. Fessel + GfK, Repräsentative Nachwahluntersuchung 1983 (1983)
f)   Dr. Fessel + GfK, Repräsentative Wahltagsbefragung Bundespräsidentenwahl 1986 (1986)
g)   Dr. Fessel + GfK, Repräsentative Wahltagsbefragung Nationalratswahl 1986 (1986)

If one follows newer theories of the dynamics of change in parties in highly industrialized societies, decomposition, the phenomenon of "weakening psychological ties between voters and parties" (Bürklin 1984, p. 24) opens up the option for a fundamental realignment of the party field.[28] The declining cohesive force of the Austrian party system shows, in fact, a considerable realignment potential that confronts a regrouping of the electorate with lower and lower thresholds and hindrances. During the 70's at the latest a structurally "pillarized," sub-culturally segmented and encapsulated party system became an increasingly more flexible, reactive and venturesome electorate in which ideological solidarity, emotional ties and handed-down loyalties gave way to a perceptibly removed and pragmatic attitude toward what the spectrum of existing parties had to offer.

The "weakening of internal ties in social systems" (Luhmann 1984, p. 543)—constitutive for advanced industrial societies—has in Austria also started to undermine the position of the political parties. In advanced industrial societies there is little room and even less demand for structurally firmly anchored, homogeneous weltanschauung- and camp parties which are based on handed-down group loyalties, which offer comprehensive perspectives of life, and which can provide a sense of belonging and social identity (Plasser 1987). The mass- and cadre parties of the past have developed into loose interest- and voter coalitions which have to react flexibly to the signals of the political market, to cope with the increasing vulnerability of their voter base, and who have to constantly win political trust by means of credible proof of performance and competence.

Table 3.9
Decline of party ties in Austria (1969-1986)

eligible voters (in %)	1969/70a)	1972b)	1974c)	1976d)	1984e)	1986f)	change in %
party identification *)	75	*	65	63	61	59	-16
traditional voters **) (cognitive party tie)	65	61	*	56	47	39	-26
negative attitude toward shifting parties ***)	*	59	56	*	39	*	-20
ideology as a determinant of the voting decision ****)	*	59	61	*	37	*	-22

Explanation:
*) = % of those interviewed who tend toward a particular party or who identify with a particular party.
**) = % of those interviewed who agree with the statement "I have decided on a party and cast my vote for it even when I am not 100% in agreement with what it does or plans to do."
***) = % of those interviewed who reject the development that there are more people today than earlier who don't always vote for the same party, but sometimes vote for one and sometimes for another.
****) = % of those interviewed who agree with the statement "if one has a particular ideology, one can vote for only one party and one also remains with it."
Source:
Party identification from 1969 to 1984 (see Table 9)
a)-f) Dr. Fessel + GfK, Politische Umfragen (1970-1986)

The retreat into the milieu, into the security of their core- and milieu electorates, uncritical loyalty and the unswerving willingness to follow the party, is—theoretically—possible for them at any time; however, this would be a retreat to the periphery of society or capitulation to a complexity one no longer feels equal to. Even though the increasing loss of ties in the Austrian party system and the resultant nervousness and hectic state of the party elite are obvious, the Austrian version of partisan dealignment is no cause for exaggerated diagnoses of crises. The traditional parties continue to control considerable identification reserves and associated organizations as resources, and their electoral foundation still appears able to weather many a storm and gusts of wind.

Table 3.10
The electoral foundation of the Austrian parties (1985/86)

in %	SPÖ voters	ÖVP voters	FPÖ voters	Green voters
strong party attachment a)	55	56	30	38
voted for their party in 1986 as in 1983a)	85	88	25	23
see themselves as traditional voters of their partya)	43	46	10	6
are registered members of their partyb)	33	30	6	1
are occasionally active for their partyb)	9	12	2	2

Source:
a)   Dr. Fessel + GfK, Repräsentative Wahltagsbefragung Nationalratswahl 1986 (1986)
b)   Dr. Fessel + GfK, Innen- und Außenperspektive des österreichischen Parteiensystems (1985)

About one third of the voters of both major parties is registered as members.[29] Approximately 55% tend to feel a strong attachment to their party. In the National Council election of 1986 both major parties succeeded in once again winning between 85 and 90% of their electorate. More than 40% of their voter potential can be classified as traditional voters. Every tenth voter of one of the two major parties is a member of the "hard" core of party activists and is active for his party in some way at least occasionally. In contrast, the electoral foundation of the FPÖ and the Greens is far more fragile. Whether as a catch basin for disillusioned protest voters or as a collecting tank for ecological sensitivity and post-materialistic desires—in comparison to the major parties there is in both cases a strong dependence on political climates and fluctuating levels of enthusiasm which make future election successes just as probable as slipping off into electoral-political insignificance.

4. Hegemony, erosion and turbulence

The National Council election of 1970, as a "critical" election, was the prelude to a hegemonic period of the Socialist Party which lasted 13 years and only came to an end in the National Council election of 1983.[30] Going into the elections as a reform-oriented voter coalition emphasizing change, characterized by a modernistic "frontier mentality," supported by the personal attractiveness of Bruno Kreisky's symbolic figure, the SPÖ embodied the "social democratic consensus," which most impressively tested its capability of attaining a majority in three successive National Council elections most impressively. The extremely strong foundation of this specific voter coalition is demonstrated by demoscopic streams of data showing the extent to which the SPÖ dominated the political opinion climate of the 70's. Although the streams of data present unweighted crude data from continuous measurements of party preferences, which have numerous technical and interpretive problems, they signal both the high-points of the "Kreisky voter coalition" and the electoral-political malaise of the opposition in view of a far-reaching "hegemonic" reformation of the electorate.[31]

Under the surface of socialist hegemony, which made the SPÖ the "dominant" party in the Austrian party system for over a decade, unmistakable erosion tendencies were recognizable already in the late 70's. The socialist voter coalition began to wear around the edges. At the beginning of the 80's at the latest, the Austrian party system was confronted with a "decompression effect."[32] The coinciding of a complex bundle of factors ranging from the exhaustion symptoms of the hegemonic elite—characteristic of the late and end phase of hegemonic alliances—the loss of capability to change and adapt, economic-structural crises, on to weakening and erosional processes within the system and climatic factors, and finally to value and issue changes, shook the cohesion of the "dominant" voter coalition.[33] The outcome of the 1983 National Council election was not able to halt latent erosional tendencies. Even though the formation of an SPÖ-FPÖ coalition government at parliamentary level brought about a new institutional arrangement which also rearranged the terms of party-political competition, the Austrian party system still maintained a transitory picture at the micro-level.

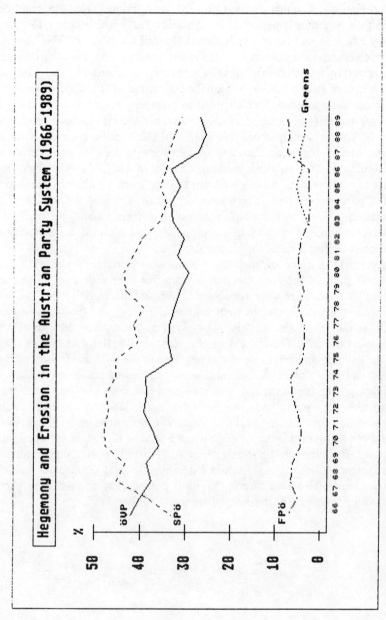

Graph 3.1: Hegemony and erosion in the Austrian party system (1966-1989)

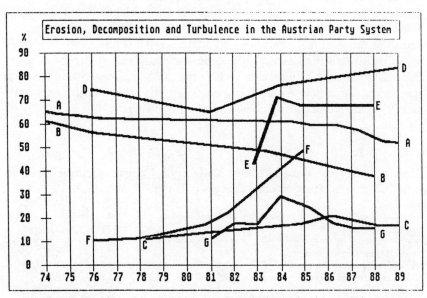

Graph 3.2: Erosion, decomposition and turbulence in the Austrian party
system (1974-1989)

Note:
a)   = development of affective party identification
b)   = cognitive party ties (proportion of declared traditional voters)
c)   = dissatisfaction with the political parties
d)   = subjective political alienation or a subjective feeling of political inefficacy
e)   = unspecific anger directed at the political parties
f)   = positive attitude toward an expansion of the Austrian party spectrum
g)   = broadest voter potential of new Green-Alternative party groupings.
Source: See graph 102 in (Plasser 1987)

5. Fragmentation or normalization?

The 1986 National Council election sealed the end of the hegemonic position of the SPÖ even though it continues to be the strongest party in terms of votes and seats and provides the Federal Chancellor in a grand coalition government. The outcome of the 1986 National Council election, on the other hand, temporarily ended the hopes of the ÖVP to advance to the position of the strongest party after 16 years of opposition. Whereas the SPÖ lost 4.5% in relation to 1983, the ÖVP lost only 1.9%. The SPÖ now lies 2.5% under its "normal" election results, the ÖVP 2.6% under its average performance in the National Council elections between 1949 and 1986.[34] Viewed according to structural aspects, the 1986 National Council election appears thoroughly "normal."[35] In relation to 1971 the ÖVP lost about 5% in the rural agrarian communities. Within the same time period the SPÖ lost between 7 and 8% in the municipal industrial and congested areas.

Table 3.11
Electoral-statistical cross-sectional analysis of National Council elections from 1971 to 1986 (proportional changes in %)

type of community	SPÖ	ÖVP	FPÖ	The Greens*
rural agrarian communities	-0.8	-5.1	+3.7	2.2
rural worker communities	-3.9	-3.2	+4.6	2.8
rural service communities	-4.5	-3.6	+5.2	3.2
urban industrial communities	-7.5	-1.2	+5.1	4.3
urban service communities	-7.4	-1.7	+5.0	4.9
congested areas	-8.1	-1.1	+2.8	6.2
federal territory (1971-1986)	-6.9	-1.8	+4.2	4.8

*   did not run in 1971

Just as modernization of rural areas destroys the traditional milieus of the ÖVP, so too does modernization of industrial production structures and the expansion of the tertiary sector weaken the traditional strongholds of the SPÖ. It is evident that both major parties are faced with the necessity of making their structures more accessible and of appealing to unbound voter groups, i.e. those not attributable to any traditional social milieu. In doing so, it is just as obvious that both major parties are confronted with tremendous identity problems, since the desired strategies aimed at potential party-

shifters come more frequently into conflict with the requirements of traditional voter strategies designed to preserve the electorate (Plasser 1987).

Table 3.12
Statistical cross-sectional analysis of the 1971-1986 National Council elections
based on prevailing socio-structural dynamics of change (proportional
changes in %)

socio-structural dynamics of change based on communities	SPÖ	ÖVP	FPÖ	The Greens*
primary structural change (prevailing dynamics of change = decline of the agrarian sector)	-0.9	-6.0	+4.1	2.4
secondary structural change (prevailing dynamics of change = decline of the industrial sector)	-8.1	-0.3	+3.9	5.5
federal territory (1971-1986)	-6.9	-1.8	+4.2	4.8

*   did not run in 1971

Added to the—still unsolved—structural problems of the major parties
are problems resulting from the generation-specific change of the electorate.
In Austria too the contours of two generation-specific party systems have begun to emerge. On the one hand there is the traditional highly concentrated,
bi-polar two-party system supported by voters of older age-groups, or members of the reconstruction generation respectively. On the other hand there
are indications of a broadly differentiated and flexible multi-party system
which is supported by younger, better qualified voters with only weakly developed party ties.

In the event that this is really a generation-specific polarization, the
Austrian party system faces troubled times in which the conflicts between the
two "party worlds" could become more and more critical, and the erosion of
the major parties almost pre-programmed. However, such a structure- and
generation-specific process of erosion does not necessarily have to cause a
critical destabilization of the party system. Perhaps the major parties have really passed their peak; perhaps a flexible multi-party system is more advantageous to desirable democratic competition than a voter market monopolized
and "frozen" to a great extent by two major parties. To join in in hasty speculations of crises and decline would mean in any case to have a low opinion of

the collective rationality of the voters, to mourn after a party world only apparently in order and to experience a fragmentation which in reality only represents long overdue normalization.

Table 3.13
Party ties and election behavior in the 1986 National Council election according to age and educational level

in %	rather strongly inclined to the party just voted for	voted for SPÖ or ÖVP	voted for FPÖ or the Greens	N =
up to 44 years old	42	76	20	1,110
over 44 years old	60	90	8	1,039
difference in %	+18	+14	-12	2,149
compulsory or technical education	53	85	12	1,642
high-school or university graduate	48	73	22	507
difference in %	-5	-12	+10	2,149

Source: Dr. Fessel + GfK, Repräsentative Wahltagsbefragung (exit poll), N = 2,149 voters interviewed after leaving the polling place

Notes

1. With regard to the dynamics of change of democratic party systems, cf. the theoretical survey by Plasser (1987). Regarding the state of discussion in international party and electoral research, see: (Flanagan/Dalton 1984; Dalton/Flanagan/Beck 1984; Crewe/Denver 1985; Dalton 1988).
2. By "basic structure of a party system" the "party-superstructure" is meant, i.e., "... the institutional profile of a party system—the number, relative strength and ideological position of the parties competing for votes" (Crewe 1985, p. 14).
3. Within the model of the "realignment perspective" the National Council election of 1970 presents itself, with limitations, as a "critical" election, because it was connected with a far-reaching thrust of innovation which substantially molded and influenced the hegemonic structure of the Austrian party system for more than a decade (Plasser/Ulram 1984).
4. "Partisan dealignment" is understood as the "loosening" decline and/or dissolution of structural and long-term stable ties of the electorate to the political parties based on the structure of society, milieus (primary and secondary environments) and party identification (Schulze 1985, p. 121f.).

5. Within the framework of theories of a cyclical re-grouping of party systems such transition phases are classified as "pre-alignment" or "inter-realignment periods." From the perspective of the "functional model of dealignment," however, structural erosion and decomposition tendencies in the party systems of advanced industrial societies indicate an increasing marginalization of the political parties, respectively to a developmental phase of "post-industrial" democracies in which the "focus of political action moves completely away from the arena of party competition" (Smith 1984, p. 17). Cf., among others, (Flanagan/Dalton 1984; Kaase 1984; Mair 1984).

6. Regarding transformation processes in the Austrian party system, see Müller 1984; Plasser/Ulram 1984; 1985; Gerlich 1987.

7. The "enclaves of loyalty" (Smith 1983, p. 12), which were still characteristic of the Austrian party system in the mid-1960's, have in the meantime become peripheral remnants. The "relative constancy and persistence of socio-economic structural characteristics and regionally-specific behavioral syndromes" (Mintzel 1984, p. 247), which once molded the political culture of Austria, can be found, significantly enough, only in structurally weak rural peripheral areas or in the old industrial regions, i.e. politico-economic crisis areas. Yet these remnants too have meanwhile been exposed to a constant process of erosion which has undermined both SPÖ and ÖVP bastions and transformed them into problem areas as regards electoral strategy.

8. The criticism in the direction of "desolation" of life in the sections has missed the essential point. The problem is really that the petrified and ceremonial daily routine of party life has estranged itself from social reality, i.e. the required degree of "faithfulness" and the willingness to follow the party can no longer be assumed for younger generations.

9. In spite of all the convergence theories, also in Austria the major political parties have continued to be "empirically demonstrable both ideologically and socio-structurally clearly identifiable and distinguishable tendency organizations." (Minzl 1984, pp. 321f.). In spite of rapid social and industrial structural change, societal reality is still quite distant from a "post-industrial" stage of development. "Pre-modern" structures continue to exist in peripheral niches and sectors, and "pre-materialistic" islands relativize a "post-materialistic" euphory.

10. The territorial organization principle of the classic party sections—the roots of which can be seen in the Paris of the Jacobins at the highpoint of the French Revolution—is in modern big cities with their social mixture, flexibility and anonymity just as dysfunctional as canvassing efforts are thwarted by the intercom-systems of modern apartment houses.

11. The end of the "Kreisky era," i.e. the SPO's loss of the absolute majority of seats in the National Council elections of 1983, and the formation of an SPÖ-FPÖ coalition have intensified inter-party competition. Through the entrance of the "little" opposition party, the FPÖ, into the coalition government, the ÖVP had the parliamentary opposition monopoly, but was not able to exploit it with the required consistency. The formation of a grand coalition government of SPÖ-ÖVP now offers the oppositional FPÖ and the Greens any number of chances of gaining status.

12. Personalization and image politics, professional public relations work and the employment of subtle, symbolic integration strategies are the attempts of the political parties to compensate for the erosion of their structural foundation. As regards the intricate problematic nature of excessive image- and communication politics see, among other, Plasser/Ulram 1982; Müller 1983; Plasser 1985a.

13. The spiral of increasing expectations which has been set into motion has in the meantime totally overtaxed the political parties and involved them in part in almost unbearable entanglements, situations of dependency and scandals which greatly burden the day-to-day climate within the Austrian party system. Between the "claim of totality and self-restraint" (Oberreuter 1985) the political parties are not attempting to steer for a "new" abstinence, a course with numerous pitfalls and barriers.

14. In this regard, see, among others, Gerlich 1985; Plasser 1985b, and the literature listed there.

15. The success of the FPÖ in the National Council election of 1986, which under its new leadership was able to almost double its number of votes, confirms the degree of disillusionment and anger which has been accumulated and dammed up in the Austrian party system over the years. According to the available data of a representative exit poll, 19 % of the interviewed voters admitted to being swayed by negative motives and to voting for the "lesser evil."

16. The following empirical sections are oriented on the scant amount of available data on long-term development tendencies in the Austrian party system. Just as data collection approaches being an "archaeological excavation," the same idea often applies as well to the quality of the data, which permits only soft operationalizations and cautious approximations.

17. For details with regard to stress see Plasser 1987.

18. Regarding change within Austrian society see the informative overview presented by Bodzenta/Seidel/Stiglbauer 1985. See also the results of the second processing phase of the 1981 census, which are now published continuously by the Central Office of Statistics (Statistisches Zentralamt).

19. Regarding the decline in "class-bound" voting in Austria, cf. the empirical long-term data of Haerpfer/Gehmacher 1984, Haerpfer 1985a, b. See also the contribution by Gehmacher/Haerpfer in this book.

20. The question read "If you consider your closest circle of friends, which party do most of them presently favor?"

21. Behavioral density is able to temporarily compensate for the orientation capacity of decreasing social density. If both orientation mechanisms fail, the only thing that actually remains as a measure of orientation is the diffuse opinion climate of mass-media news coverage. For the dynamics of social context factors see the theoretical survey by Huckfeldt 1983.

22. A decline of party identification is one of the most prominent indicators of "partisan dealignment." As a multifunctional concept, party identification provides for "diffuse support" at the system level and long-term stability of the party system. At the group- and individual level party identification reduces political complexity, offers symbolic orientation and structures and organizes political attitudes. A significant decline of party identification is seen as an indicator of strong destabilization tendencies within a party system.

23. Voters declaring themselves adherents of a specific party were classified as (subjectively) bound traditional voters if they agreed to the following statement: "I have decided on a particular party and vote for it even when I am not 100% in agreement with what it does and plans."

24. Whereby, however, an increase in the number of "party-shifters," i.e. those voters who shift back and forth between different parties, can be deduced from the continuous strategic opinion polls since the National Council election of 1983.

25. As regards volatility in the Austrian party system, see the long-term analysis in Haerpfer 1985, and Gerlich 1987.

26. The time the voting decision is made—established by retrospective questioning during post-election opinion polling—is often used in international party and election research—due to the well-known lack of comparable data reaching farther back in time—as a sub-indicator of latent destabilization processes. "In a stable, aligned system, we can expect voters to know considerably in advance of an actual election for which party they will cast their vote" (Irvin/Dittrich 1984, p. 286). If one accepts the empirical significance of the indicator "time of decision," the "stationary period" of the Austrian party system would have continued until 1983.

27. Apparently, latent destabilization processes at the micro-level of the party system can be covered up over a long period by aggregated) macro-stability. Regarding this aspect, cf. the summary by Mair 1983. Regarding volatility in an international comparison, see Crewe/Denver 1985.

28. According to the "fragmentation/realignment model" (Borre 1985) and the cyclical theories of an "electoral re-grouping" (Bürklin 1984), phenomena of erosion and dealignment are considered as a preliminary phase of a fundamental re-grouping/realignment of the party field.

29. Compared internationally, the relation between "registered" and "active" members stimulates justified doubts about the hypertrophic organizational density of the Austrian party system. Cf. the pertinent contributions by Kofler and Müller in this book.

30. In the 70's the SPÖ was clearly the most successful party within Western European social democracy.

31. The graphed values represent unweighted crude data of continuous measurements of party preferences. Through the remaining category, i.e. those refusing to answer, unweighted crude data are very hazy because certain social and habitual regularities in the behavior of the interviewee prevent a proportional allotment of those refusing to answer. The large opinion poll institutes attempt to solve the problem of the remaining category by employing subtle methods of recall, re-weighting, indication and segmentation or regression, respectively. Each of these methods has numerous methodic weaknesses which have until now, however, though application of all accumulated research experience, prevented serious false estimations.

32. The first signs of turbulence were already observable in situations focussing on the referendum for putting the Zwentendorf nuclear power plant into service in 1978. The majority of Austrian analysts regard the outcome of the referendum as a momentous turning point in the Austrian party system.

33. As concerns change in the Austrian party system with regard to issues, cf. the contribution by Ulram.

34. The mean score of National Council election results between 1949 and 1986 is 45.7% for the SPÖ, and 43.9% for the ÖVP. In 1986 the SPÖ attained 43.1% of all cast and valid votes, the ÖVP 41.3%.

35. For an analysis of the 1986 National Council elections, cf. the pertinent articles in this book by Plasser/Ulram and Gehmacher/Birk/Ogris.

Bibliography

Barnes, Samuel H./Kaase, Max et al., *Political Action. Mass Participation in Five Western Democracies*, Beverly Hills/London 1979 (Barnes/Kaase, 1979)

Bartolini, Stefano/Mair, Peter (eds.), *Party Politics in Contemporary Western Europe, West European Politics* (Special Issue) 4/1984 (Bartolini/Mair, 1984)

Bodzenta, Erich/Seidel, Hans/Stiglbauer, Karl, *Österreich im Wandel. Gesellschaft, Wirtschaft, Raum*, Wien/New York 1985 (Bodzenta/Seidel/Stiglbauer, 1985)

Borre, Ole, *Denmark*, in: Ivor Crewe/David Denver (eds.), *Electoral Change in Western Democracies. Patterns and Sources of Electoral Volatility*, London/Sidney 1985 (Borre, 1985)

Bühl, Walter L., *Krisentheorien. Politik, Wirtschaft und Gesellschaft im Übergang*, Darmstadt 1984 (Bühl, 1984)

Bürklin, Wilhelm P., *Grüne Politik. Ideologische Zyklen, Wähler und Parteiensystem*, Opladen 1984 (Bürklin, 1984)

Crewe, Ivor, *Introduction: Electoral Change in Western Democracies: A Framework for Analysis*, in: Ivor Crewe/David Denver (eds.), *Electoral Change in Western Democracies. Patterns and Sources of Electoral Volatility*, London/Sidney 1985 (Crewe, 1985)

Crewe, Ivor/Denver, David (eds.), *Electoral Change in Western Democracies. Patterns and Sources of Electoral Volatility*, London/Sidney 1985 (Crewe/Denver, 1985)

Daalder, Hans/Mair, Peter (eds.), *Western European Party Systems. Continuity and Change*, Beverly Hills/London 1983 (Daalder/Mair, 1983)

Daalder, Hans (ed.), *Party Systems in Denmark, Austria, Switzerland, The Netherlands and Belgium*, London 1987 (Daalder, 1987)

Dalton, Russell J./Flanagan, Scott C./Beck, Paul Allen (eds.), *Electoral Change in Advanced Industrial Democracies. Realignment or Dealignment?* Princeton, New Jersey 1984 (Dalton/Flanagan/Beck, 1984)

Dalton, Russell J., *Citizen Politics in Western Democracies*, Chatham 1988 (Dalton 1988)

Deiser, Roland/Winkler, Norbert, *Das politische Handeln der Österreicher*, Wien, 1982 (Deiser/Winkler, 1982)

Engelmann, Frederick C., *The Austrian Party System: Continuity and Change*, in: Steven B. Wolinetz (ed.): *Parties and Party System in Liberal Democracies*, London and New York 1988 (Engelmann, 1988)

Falter, Jürgen W., *Zur Übertragbarkeit des Konzepts der Parteiidentifikation auf deutsche Verhältnisse. Einige Ergebnisse*, in: Manfred J. Holler (Hg.), *Wahlanalyse. Hypothesen, Methoden und Ergebnisse*, München 1984 (Falter, 1984)

Flanagan, Scott C./Dalton, Russell J., *Parties Under Stress. Realignment and Dealignment in Advanced Industrial Societies*, in: *West European Politics* 1/1984 (Flanagan/Dalton, 1984)

Gerlich, Peter/Müller, Wolfgang C. (Hg.), *Zwischen Koalition und Konkurrenz. Österreichs Parteien seit 1945*, Wien 1983 (Gerlich/Müller, 1983)

Gerlich, Peter, *Ernstnehmen oder Augenzwinkern. Grün-alternative Herausforderungen der traditionellen Politik*, in: Fritz Plasser/Peter A. Ulram/Manfried Welan (Hg.), *Demokratierituale. Zur politischen Kultur der Informationsgesellschaft*, Wien 1985 (Gerlich, 1985)

Gerlich, Peter, *Consociationalism to Competition: The Austrian Party System since 1945*, in: Hans Daalder (ed.), *Party Systems in Denmark, Austria, Switzerland, The Netherlands, and Belgium*, London 1987 (Gerlich, 1987)

Haerpfer, Christian/Gehmacher, Ernst, *Social Structure and Voting in the Austrian Party System*, in: *Electoral Studies 1/1984* (Haerpfer/Gehmacher, 1984)

Haerpfer, Christian, *Abschied vom Loyalitätsritual. Langfristige Veränderungen im Wählerverhalten*, in: Fritz Plasser/Peter A. Ulram/Manfried Welan (Hg.), *Demokratierituale. Zur politischen Kultur der Informationsgesellschaft*, Wien 1985 (Haerpfer, 1985)

Haerpfer, Christian, *Electoral Volatility in Austria 1945-1983*, in: Ivor Crewe/David Denver (eds.), *Electoral Change in Western Democracies. Patterns and Sources of Electoral Volatility*, London/Sidney 1985 (Haerpfer, 1985)

Haerpfer, Christian, *Austria: The "United Greens" and the "Alternative List/Green Alternative,"* in: Ferdinand Müller-Rommel (ed.): *New Politics in Western Europe: The Rise and Success of Green Parties and Alternative Lists*, Boulder and London 1989 (Haerpfer, 1989)

Houska, Joseph J., *Influencing Mass Political Behavior: Elites and Political Subcultures in the Netherlands and Austria*, Berkeley 1985 (Houska, 1985)

Huckfeldt, Robert R., *The Social Context of Political Change: Durability, Volatility, and Social Influence*, in: *American Political Science Review 4/1983* (Huckfeldt, 1983)

Irwin, Galen/Dittrich, Karl, *And the Walls Came Tumbling Down: Party Dealignment in The Netherlands*, in: Russell J. Dalton/Scott C. Flanagan/Paul Allen Beck (eds.), *Electoral Change in Advanced Industrial Democracies. Realignment or Dealignment?* Princeton, New Jersey 1984 (Irwin/Dittrich, 1984)

Janda, Kenneth, *Political Parties. A Cross-National Survey*, New York/London 1980 (Janda, 1980)

Kaase, Max, *The Challenge of the "Participatory Revolution" in Pluralist Democracies*, in: Mattei Dogan (ed.), *Political Crises, International Political Science Review 3/1984* (Kaase, 1984)

Luhmann, Niklas, *Soziale Systeme. Grundriß einer allgemeinen Theorie*, Frankfurt 1984 (Luhmann, 1984)

Mair, Peter, *Adaption and Control: Towards an Understanding of Party and Party System Change*, in: Hans Daalder/Peter Mair (eds.), *Western European Party Systems. Continuity and Change*, Beverly Hills/London 1983 (Mair, 1983)

Mair, Peter, *Party Politics in Contemporary Europe, A Challenge To Party?* In: *West European Politics 4/1984* (Mair, 1984)

Mantl, Wolfgang, *Politik und Parteipolitik*, in: *Österreichische Monatshefte 4/1985* (Mantl, 1985)

Mintzel, Alf, *Die Volkspartei, Typus und Wirklichkeit*, Opladen 1984 (Mintzel, 1984)

Müller, Wolfgang C., *Parteien zwischen Öffentlichkeitsarbeit und Medienzwängen*, in: Peter Gerlich/Wolfgang C. Müller (Hg.), *Zwischen Koalition und Konkurrenz. Österreichs Parteien seit 1945*, Wien 1983 (Müller, 1983)

Müller, Wolfgang C., *Politische Kultur und Parteientransformation in Österreich*, in: *Österreichische Zeitschrift für Politikwissenschaft 1/1984* (Müller, 1984)

Nick, Rainer/Pelinka, Anton, *Bürgerkrieg–Sozialpartnerschaft. Das politische System Österreichs 1. und 2. Republik. Ein Vergleich*, Wien/München 1983 (Nick/Pelinka, 1983)

Oberreuter, Heinrich, *Parteien–zwischen Nestwärme und Funktionskälte*, Zürich 1983 (Oberreuter, 1983)

Oberreuter, Heinrich, *Parteienselbstverständnis zwischen Totalitätsanspruch und Selbstbeschränkung*, in: *Österreichische Monatshefte 4/1985* (Oberreuter, 1985)

Pelinka, Anton, *Struktur und Funktionen der politischen Parteien*, in: Heinz Fischer (Hg.), *Das politische System Österreichs* (dritte überarbeitete Auflage), Wien 1982 (Pelinka, 1982)

Pelinka, Anton, *Windstille. Klagen über Österreich*, Wien/München 1985 (Pelinka, 1985)

Plasser, Fritz/Ulram, Peter A., *Unbehagen im Parteienstaat*, Wien/Köln/Graz 1982 (Plasser/Ulram, 1982)

Plasser, Fritz/Ulram, Peter A., *Themenwechsel–Machtwechsel? Konturen einer neuen Mehrheit in Österreich*, in: Stephan Koren/Karl Pisa/Kurt Waldheim (Hg.), *Politik für die Zukunft*, Wien 1984 (Plasser/Ulram, 1984)

Plasser, Fritz, *Elektronische Politik und politische Technostruktur reifer Industriegesellschaften*, in: Fritz Plasser/Peter A. Ulram/Manfried Welan (Hg.), *Demokratierituale. Zur politischen Kultur der Informationsgesellschaft*, Wien 1985 (Plasser, 1985a)

Plasser, Fritz, *Die "unsichtbare" Fraktion. Struktur und Profil der Grün-Alternativen in Österreich*, in: Andreas Khol/Alfred Stirnemann (Hg.): *Österreichisches Jahrbuch für Politik 1984*, München/Wien 1985 (Plasser, 1985b)

Plasser, Fritz/Ulram, Peter A., *From Stability to Diffusion: Dealignment in the Austrian Party System*, Paper delivered at the Annual Meeting of The American Political Science Association, New Orleans 1985 (Plasser/Ulram, 1985)

Plasser, Fritz, *Parteien unter Streß. Zur Dynamik der Parteiensysteme in Österreich, der Bundesrepublik Deutschland und den Vereinigten Staaten*, Wien 1987 (Plasser, 1987)

Reiter, Erich, *Technikskepsis und neue Parteien*, Wien/Köln/Graz 1987 (Reiter, 1987)

Rose, Richard/Allister, Ian Mc, *Voters Begin to Choose*, London 1986 (Rose/Allister, 1986)

Rosenmayr, Leopold (Hg.), *Politische Beteiligung und Wertwandel in Österreich. Einstellungen zu Politik und Demokratieverständnis im internationalen Vergleich*, München/Wien 1980 (Rosenmayr, 1980)

Smith, Gordon, *Politics in Western Europe. A Comparative Analysis*, London 1983 (Smith, 1983)

Smith, Gordon, *Europäische Parteiensysteme—Stationen einer Entwicklung?* In: Jürgen W. Falter/Christian Fenner/Michael Th. Greven (Hg.), *Politische Willensbildung und Interessenvermittlung*, Opladen 1984 (Smith, 1984)

Schultze, Rainer-Olaf, *Dealignment*, in: Dieter Nohlen/Rainer-Olaf Schultze (Hg.), *Wörterbuch der Politikwissenschaft*, (Band I), München 1985 (Schultze, 1985)

Ulram, Peter A., *Um die Mehrheit der Mehrheit. Die neuen, angestellten Mittelschichten, 1975-1984*, in: Fritz Plasser/Peter A. Ulram/Manfried Welan (Hg.), *Demokratierituale. Zur politischen Kultur der Informationsgesellschaft*, Wien 1985 (Ulram, 1985)

Verba, Sidney/Nie, Norman H./Kim, Jae-On, *Participation and Political Equality. A Seven-Nation Comparison*, Cambridge 1978 (Verba/Nie/Kim, 1978)

Welan, Manfried, *Parteien und Verbände in Österreich*, Wien 1985 (Schriftenreihe: Politische Bildung 46), Wien 1985 (Welan, 1985)

4

Major Parties on the Defensive

The Austrian Party- and Electoral Landscape
after the 1986 National Council Election

FRITZ PLASSER and PETER A. ULRAM

The 1986 National Council election marks up to now the political high point of a development which has led to the end of the special position enjoyed for a great number of years by the Austrian party- and electoral landscape in Western Europe. "The end of Austrian exceptionality" hence applies not only to the economic, but to the political system as well. It is also the case for both areas that what the persons affected perceive at the moment as a (painful) break is actually only the appearance of long-termed changes of structure and overall climate.

1. The end of the camp (party)

In the course of decades, the Austrian party system of the Second Republic has reflected social, economic and cultural lines of conflict (primarily: class conflicts and the cleavage of religious vs. secular tendencies; within limits: German vs. Austrian nationalism), the origins of which reach back to the previous century. While this handing down of "frozen" cleavages can be shown to exist also in most Western European party systems (Lipset/Rokkan 1967), two specifics can be added—the comprehensive societal and cultural dominance of socio-structurally and ideologically rooted camp cultures (Wandruszka 1954) and camp mentalities (Powell 1974), as well as their political-organizational perpetuation and propagation through party-political colonization and the interrelationship between administration, education, the public sector of the economy, and organized representation of interests (Lehmbruch 1967; Steiner 1972; Pelinka 1974).

It is mainly the two major parties which presented themselves essentially as the political organization of the respective camp cultures; electoral behavior was determined mainly by socio-economic factors (and religious affiliation). The majority of the electorate showed stable party ties, a fact particularly true of informed and politically active groups (Kienzl 1964). Correspondingly small was political flexibility—fluctuations in electoral behavior had their origin to a great extent in first-time voters who were not yet fully integrated into the camps (Haerpfer 1983).[1]

This pattern was broken, albeit temporarily, by the ballots in 1966 and 1970/71, which evinced great shifts in the majority conditions; single-party governments (first the ÖVP, then the SPÖ) replaced the grand coalition, and the conflict-oriented components of party competition were strengthened (Gerlich 1982, 1983). The 70's, however, brought a new phase of electoral-political stability—the position of the SPÖ was reinforced, voter fluctuation was (in a European comparison) minimal, and the tendency toward concentration which began in the 60's consolidated itself into a de facto two-party system. In view of the political dominance of the social democratic coalition of voters, interests and values (Plasser/Ulram 1982), at the level of the electorate one can speak at best of "minor changes" (Gerlich 1987).[2]

Under this apparently so stable surface, however, the electorate and the structure of political motivation have been undergoing fundamental changes:

— socio-structural change leads to a constant shrinking of the traditional social basis of the (major) parties (Plasser/Ulram 1985; Traar/Birk 1987; Plasser 1987a);
— the camp cultures undergo a process of erosion which, among other things, can be attributed to a decreasing capability of the parties and their associated organizations with regard to socialization and establishing ties, to changes in the political value system of the population (Ulram 1988) and to changes in the behavioral forms and political-ideological self-representation of the parties;
— the population's system of political goals is altered;
— the beginnings of a "participatory revolution" become visible in Austria too;
— apparently more significant, however, is the increase in disillusionment with politicians and parties. This is initially diffuse, but is later more and more specific and tends to increasingly influence electoral behavior (Plasser/Ulram 1982, 1985).

Austria now follows a general tendency of development (Haerpfer 1987a): socio-economic (we add: and cultural) processes of change bring about an erosion of party ties on the individual level and an erosion of camp structures on the collective level. This increases potential voter flexibility and actual voter fluctuation. The fragmentation of the party system increases through a reduction of the number of votes for the major parties and the rise in significance of old and new small parties.[3]

2. The National Council election of 23 November 1986

In this historical context an analysis of the 1986 National Council election appears to be interesting for two reasons: on the one hand, the developments outlined above find their electoral-political expression as well for the first time; on the other hand, an examination of the way the election campaign was conducted also provides information about the willingness and/or ability of the individual politicians to adapt to changes in the electorate.

The campaign, which began in the fall of 1986, showed the parties in the following starting positions:[4]

— The SPÖ as the (large) government party was in a defensive position following a series of regional and national ballots. Particularly since the crisis of the nationalized industries in the winter of 1985/86, losses of political status in general and of competence in terms of certain issues (of all places the crucial area of job security became obvious). Only their top candidate (and Federal Chancellor) had a clear lead in popularity in comparison to the opposition leader. In contrast, the ÖVP started the election campaign from a leading position. In view of the victories made over the years in intermediate elections, increasing politico-economic gains in competence and a favorable climate of public emotions and opinion, success seemed to have come within easy reach.

— The Green-Alternatives had gotten their earlier internal conflicts under control to a great extent and presented themselves—disregarding regional splinter groups—as a unified election movement. On the other hand, the FPÖ, at this point still in the government, made a fundamental change of position after a series of grave election defeats and intra-party turbulence, and took a populist-oriented opposition course under a new party chairman.

Thus, the SPÖ organized its election campaign primarily around the person of the top candidate, but at the same time promised the former opposition a partnership in the future government for the "modernization of Austria." In contrast, the ÖVP initially waged an issue-oriented economic and "retribution" campaign. This offensive course, however, increasingly encountered:

— less and less open resonance in the mass media for disputes centered around political issues;
— intra-party resistance with regard to the "hard" consolidation- and economization line and the "risks" of an offensive issue-oriented election campaign;
— an intra-party tendency toward personalization of the election campaign also on the part of the ÖVP.

Finally, the ÖVP left the field of issue-oriented confrontation and put more emphasis on aspects of personnel and style.

The move away from issues and toward personalization of the election campaign by the mass media and the major parties gave the small parties, FPÖ and GAL, a wide range for action. While the Green-Alternatives were largely unrivalled in effectively getting across their commitment to environmental policy and hence (in the consciousness of the population) were able to cover an important problem area, the FPÖ consolidated its position in a number of respects:

— the person of the FPÖ's top candidate stood out optimally during the phase of the election centering on the candidates;
— the sphere of oppositional government criticism vacated de facto—but prepared earlier—by the ÖVP was taken over by the FPÖ;
— the strong increase in disillusionment with parties and politicians in recent years could—not least in view of the lack of issue-orientation on the part of the campaign of the SPÖ and ÖVP—be focussed on a populist direction of assault and strategically used to advantage in the election (Plasser 1987b).

Consequently, the ÖVP not only lost arguing strength, but also forfeited its leadership role in terms of the opinion climate and declared electoral intentions. While the SPÖ was able to gain a small advantage over the ÖVP, in the final analysis it was less able to influence the degree than the direction of votes lost (now also to the FPÖ). Conversely, the Green-Alternatives were successful in attracting a portion of the ecology-minded voters while the FPÖ—as a result of the progressing exhaustion of the major parties—became more attractive for voters disillusioned with the major parties.[5]

The intensity of voter shifting between the parties also led to considerable changes in the composition of the party electorates. The tendency of conformation, or levelling, of the voter profiles of the SPÖ and ÖVP progressed just like the weakening, or dissolution, of their traditional milieus and camp structures (see Table 4.2).

Table 4.1
Changes in voting behavior (1983-1986)

The % of the interviewed voters who voted for...	1986 SPÖ	1986 ÖVP	1986 FPÖ	1986 The Greens
1983 SPÖ	85	5	6	2
1983 ÖVP	3	88	7	2
1983 FPÖ	7	19	69	5
1983 The Greens	6	25	2	53

Source: Dr. Fessel + GfK, Repräsentative Wahltagsbefragung (exit poll), N = 2,149 voters interviewed after leaving the polling place (1986)

While the structure of the electorates of both major parties tended to become more similar, the electorates of the FPÖ and the Greens differed in part considerably. FPÖ voters were predominantly male, but Green voters predominantly female. In addition, both the FPÖ and the Greens had an above-average percentage of young voters: 31% of the FPÖ voters and even 58% of the Green voters were under the age of 30. Both parties were apparently successful in attracting a numerically growing class of younger voter generations which for any number of reasons had weak ties, or no ties at all, to the two major parties. The Greens had by far not only the youngest electorate, but also the best-educated one: 54% of the Green voters in 1986 had at least completed high-school.

If one analyzes the fundamental dimensions of the voting decision of 23 November, it can be seen that socio-structural factors are of secondary importance in comparison with factors pertaining to issues or motivation. Of all the traditional socio-structural determinants, the farmer/self-employed (pro-ÖVP, contra-SPÖ) and blue-collar worker (pro-SPÖ, contra-ÖVP) have the greatest statistical value—this, however, does not apply to the election of FPÖ and GAL. On the other hand, white-collar workers and officials indicate no significant preference distribution. A better school education is favorable for the ÖVP and the Greens and unfavorable for the SPÖ.

Table 4.2
Voting behavior according to socio-demographic groups (1986)

The % of interviewees who voted on 23 Nov 1986	SPÖ	ÖVP	FPÖ	KPÖ	The Greens	invalid
men	42	38	12	1	4	2
employed	41	38	13	1	4	2
not employed	44	37	11	1	5	2
women	43	43	7	1	5	1
employed	46	37	7	0	7	2
not employed	34	49	8	1	7	1
retired	49	44	5	1	0	1
first-time voters	37	35	14	1	12	1
- 29 years old	39	33	12	1	11	3
30-44 years old	43	37	11	1	5	2
45-59 years old	42	48	6	1	1	1
60-69 years old	44	45	8	1	1	1
70 and older	46	43	9	0	1	1
self-employed, professionals	14	60	15	0	6	5
officials, Civil Service	49	32	9	0	6	4
white collar workers						
skilled workers, master						
craftsmen, foremen	56	26	11	2	4	1
workers (unskilled,						
semiskilled)	59	28	8	1	3	1
farmers	1	93	5	0	1	0
retired	49	41	7	1	1	1
housewives	36	52	8	0	4	0
still in school	19	38	9	4	23	7
unemployed	38	34	8	0	13	7
compulsory education	47	43	6	0	2	2
technical education	45	38	11	1	3	2
high-school graduates	33	41	10	2	11	1
university graduates	19	52	14	0	10	2
voting decision made						
in the pre-election week	23	35	28	2	11	1
1 - 2 weeks before	31	23	34	3	8	0
much earlier	46	44	6	0	4	0
traditional voters	50	45	3	0	1	0
party-shifters	10	24	39	3	22	0
non-voters 1983	38	25	15	2	20	0

Source: Dr. Fessel + GfK, Repräsentative Wahltagsbefragung (exit poll), N = 2,149 voters interviewed after leaving the polling place, nationwide sample

On the basis of a multi-variance analysis[6] (of the representative post-election opinion poll), in the event of the election of the SPÖ more than half, of the ÖVP about one third, of the Greens two thirds and of the FPÖ about 85% of the explained variance can be accounted for by motives based on issues or the person of the candidate.[7] Protest orientation explains, above all, a voting decision in favor of the Green-Alternatives (more than half of the explained variance), and, together with a candidate-based orientation, also the election of the FPÖ.

Table 4.3
Structure of party electorates (1986)

The % of the respective party electorate	SPÖ	ÖVP	FPÖ	The Greens
men	46	44	61	40
women	54	56	39	60
Σ in %	100	100	100	100
- 29 years old	22	20	31	58
- 44 years old	28	25	32	32
- 59 years old	23	27	15	6
- 69 years old	12	13	10	2
70 and older	15	15	12	3
Σ in %	100	100	100	100
self-employed, professionals	2	7	7	6
officials	7	5	6	8
white-collar workers	18	17	27	29
blue-collar workers	30	14	22	17
farmers	0	9	2	1
retired	28	25	19	4
housewives12	18	12	12	
still in school	2	4	4	20
unemployed	1	1	1	3
Σ in %	100	100	100	100
compulsory education	32	30	18	15
technical education	52	45	56	31
high-school/university graduates	16	25	26	54
Σ in %	100	100	100	100

Source: Dr. Fessel + GfK, Repräsentative Wahltagsbefragung (exit poll), N = 2,149 voters interviewed after leaving the polling place, nationwide sample

Traditional voting based on camp loyalties hence remains primarily restricted to a shrinking core of both major parties; generally—and particularly in the case of the Greens and FPÖ—other motives for the voting decision are more influential. Increased flexibility (or a willingness to be flexible) is at the expense of the major parties. This is shown, among other things, by the positive significance of weak to no party ties in favor of a voting decision for the

Greens as well as one of a late time of decision or a shift away from the originally preferred party for the FPÖ. (See table 4.4)

Every sixth voter at the 1986 National Council election was a party-shifter. The willingness to shift parties was particularly pronounced among members of the younger voter generations and the new middle classes (white-collar workers/officials). Of the qualified workers (skilled workers/master craftsmen) 18% are party-shifters; of the segment of semi- and unskilled workers as many as 10% shifted parties in 1986. Farmers and members of the older voter generations continued to be in the comparatively stationary voter groups.

3. Trends in Austrian voting behavior

The weakening of existing party ties (electoral dealignment), increased willingness to shift parties, and signs of beginning voter protest can be empirically shown to exist at the latest since the mid-70's. Electoral-politically, these developments were first reflected in the 1983 National Council election. They ultimately vented themselves in the 1986 National Council election, which was, however, not a "critical" election in the sense of the classic election typology of V.O. Key. Nevertheless, they did change the structural power relationships to a great degree. More recent trends in Austrian voting behavior are:[8]

— an increasing number of party-shifters,[9]
— a rising number of late deciders, i.e. voters who decide to vote for a certain party only in the final phase of the election campaign,
— an increasing number of "wavering" voters (electoral wavering),
— an increasing number of protest voters (negative voters) who finally decide on the "lesser evil" and hence whose attitudes on the whole range from skepticism to disillusionment,
— an increasing number of non-voters: 9.5% of all eligible voters, which is still well under the percentages of neighboring countries (e.g. West Germany: 15.6%), as well as
— an increasing number of invalid votes (1986: 1.7% of all cast votes).

What is striking is the above-average number of party-shifters among those voters who make their definitive decision only in the final phase of the election campaign. 60% of the late deciders, by their own account, shifted parties in the 1986 election, another sign that the Austrian voter's certainty in making decisions has clearly decreased. Whereas the percentage of late deciders in the preceding National Council election fluctuated between 8 and maximally 10% (Plasser 1987b), it rose in 1986 to 16%.

Table 4.4

Determinants of the 1986 National Council election referring to the individual parties

explained variance of the vote for the...	33% SPÖ	22% ÖVP	28% FPÖ	31% Greens
1. socio-structural information:				
sex			-.06	.07
age				
-30	-	-	-	-
-40	-	-.05	-	.10
-50	.04	-	-	-
-60	-	.05	-	-.06
-70	-	-	-	-.05
>70	-	-	.05	-
education	-.09	.06	-	.05
occupational position:				
self-employed persons	-.13	.10	-	-
executive personnel/officials	-	-	-	-
lower-ranking personnel/officials	-	-	-	-
master craftsmen/skilled workers	.14	-.15	-	-
semi-skilled workers	.09	-.09	-	-
farmers	-.20	.19	-	-
permanent position:				
employed persons	-	-	-	-
retired persons	-	-	-	-
in a restricted activity period/ unemployed	-	-	-	-
household	-	.07	-	-
still in school	-.05	-	-.05	.13
size of locality of residence	.09	-.10	-	-
state:				
Vorarlberg	-	-	-	-
Tirol	-.08	.06	-	-
Salzburg	-.14	.09	.04	.05
Upper Austria	-.05	-	.10	-
Carinthia	-.05	-	.10	-
Styria	-	.07	-	-.04
Burgenland	-	-	-	-
Lower Austria	-	.05	-	-
Vienna	.13	-.15	-.07	-
2. "motives":				
candidate-oriented	.28	-.26	.24	-.13
issue voter	.21	.08	-.28	-
negative voter	-	.09	-	-.07
party ties	-	.09	-	-.07
party identification	.06	-	-	-.05
3. features of the voting decision				
time	.07	-	-.09	-
wavering	-	-	+.07	-

Univariant qualitative covariance analyses; standardized partial correlation coefficient P<0.05. For an interpretation, see footnote 6.

Although this percentage is still clearly under an international average, the factor "time of voting decision" tentatively indicates an increasing reactivity in the behavior of Austrian voters and short-term factors relevant to the election campaign which have a growing influence on the individual voting decision.

Table 4.5
The percentage of party-shifters in selected voter groups (1979-1986) (NCE = National Council election)

The percentage of party-shifters of the respective voter group	NCE 1979a)	NCE 1983b)	NCE 1986c)	Change 1979-1986
voters under the age of 30	7	13	28	+21
self-employed, tradespeople, professionals	16	29	16	+-0
white-collar workers/officials	10	15	23	+13
blue-collar workers	4	6	14	+10
farmers	2	6	7	+5
compulsory education	6	8	11	+5
technical education	7	10	15	+8
high-school/university graduates	13	19	24	+11
voters whose decision was made much earlier than election day	5	8	9	+4
voters who decided on a particular party during the election campaign	27	43	60	+33
voters (total)	7	10	16	+9

Source:
a)   Dr. Fessel + GfK, Repräsentative Nachwahlanalyse zur Nationalratswahl 1979, N = 1,746 voters
b)   Dr. Fessel + GfK, Repräsentative Nachwahlanalyse zur Nationalratswahl 1983, N = 1,661 voters
c)   Dr. Fessel + GfK, Repräsentative Wahltagsbefragung (exit poll) zur Nationalratswahl 1986, N = 2,149 voters interviewed after leaving the polling place (1986)

Whereas only every tenth voter in the previous National Council election made his definitive voting decision in the final phase of the campaign, in 1986 every sixth voter was a late decider. 16% of the voters, or every second party-shifter respectively, decided on a party only within the last two campaign weeks. The potential influence of political events in the campaign was hence greater than ever before. The extremely high number of wavering, or undecided, voters was also indicated in the data of the accompanying election campaign research (track polling). Only four days before the 23rd of November 11% of the interviewees were still rather uncertain and 5% by their own account were still fully uncertain as to which party they would vote for on the coming Sunday. The time series data showed that primarily the party-shifters tended to make their final voting decision only in the last weeks or even days of the campaign. The FPÖ profited first and foremost from the obvious exhaustion affecting the campaigns of both major parties in the final phase. About two thirds of the voters switching from the SPÖ and ÖVP to Jörg Haider's party decided only in the last two weeks.

Table 4.6
The time of voting decision in selected voter groups (1979-1986)

The percentage of the respective voter group making their definitive decision only within the last two election campaign weeks (late deciders)	NCE 1979a)	NCE 1983b)	NCE 1986c)	Change 1979-1986
voters under the age of 30	16	15	25	+9
self-employed, tradespeople, professionals	14	8	15	+1
white-collar workers/civil servants	13	13	19	+6
blue-collar workers	8	8	17	+9
farmers	7	7	5	-2
compulsory education	6	5	11	+5
technical education	10	8	16	+6
high-school/university graduates	17	11	20	+3
voters (total)	9	8	16	+7

Source:
a)   Dr. Fessel + GfK, Repräsentative Nachwahlanalyse zur Nationalratswahl 1979, N = 1,746 voters
b)   Dr. Fessel + GfK, Repräsentative Nachwahlanalyse zur Nationalratswahl 1983, N = 1,661 voters
c)   Dr. Fessel + GfK, Repräsentative Wahltagsbefragung (exit poll) zur Nationalratswahl 1986, N = 2,149 voters interviewed after leaving the polling place (1986)

Table 4.7
The time of decision of the party-shifters (1986)

Of the polled partyshifters the final voting decision was made	within the last two weeks prior to election day	a long time beforehand
shifters from SPÖ to ÖVP	39	61
shifters from ÖVP to SPÖ	49	51
shifters from SPÖ to FPÖ	64	36
shifters from ÖVP to FPÖ	69	31
party-shifters (total)	48	52

Source: Dr. Fessel + GfK, Repräsentative Wahltagsbefragung (exit poll) zur Nationalratswahl 1986

Every second FPÖ-voter made his final voting decision only within the last two weeks of the election campaign. While 90% of the voters of both major parties indicated that their final voting decision had been made long before election day, the number of such voters for the Greens was 69% and for the FPÖ only 49%. The swing-over of voters to the FPÖ, the intensity of which was underestimated also by political opinion polls, evidently took place only in the final phase of the election campaign. As regards the Greens, every third voter made his final decision only within the last 14 days.

Along with the high percentage of actual party-shifters (about 16%), and the tendency to decide on a particular party only in the final days of the election campaign (16% late deciders), a further indicator of the increasing unrest in Austrian voting behavior is the above-average percentage of electoral waverers, i.e. of voters who revise their original voting intention in the course of the election campaign. About 30% of the polled voters indicated having initially decided on voting for another party—but then changing their minds at a later point in the campaign. Whereas indicators such as an increasing number of party-shifters, increasing uncertainty regarding a voting decision, and a growing number of "wavering" voters show increasing unrest in Austrian voting behavior, the number of "negative" voters points to a voter protest culture which seems to be spreading increasingly in the Austrian party system. 19% of the Austrian voters in the 1986 National Council election can be classified as "negative voters"—mainly voters for the FPÖ and the Greens whose decisions were strongly guided by deep-seated reactions of disappointment, anger at the major parties, and an obvious willingness to teach the major parties an "object lesson." Even though the percentage of "negative voters" is still below average in an international comparison—in Great Britain for example the proportion of "negative voters" is estimated to be over 50%—the "golden age" of the Austrian party system seems to finally be over at least for the traditional major parties (Plasser/Ulram 1985). The reactivity of Austrian voters unquestionably evinces a rising tendency. At least in terms of Austrian voting behavior the signs point to renewal. It remains to be seen whether the elite of the major parties understand how to interpret these signs, or whether from now on third and fourth parties—such as the FPÖ and the Greens—increasingly become the pacemakers of the future development of the Austrian party- and electoral landscape.

On the 23rd of November both major parties lost crucial parts of their mobile voter groups to other parties. Both major parties were apparently not in the position of continuing to maintain the loyalties of such groups, which have only weak party ties. According to available data, those who shifted away from the ÖVP were primarily:

— voters of younger to medium age groups,
— voters of the white-collar, secretarial, and tertiary sector,

Table 4.8
Negative voting in Austria (1986)

in %	SPÖ voters	ÖVP voters	FPÖ voters	Green voters	Voters 1986 (total)
By the voter's own account, a particular party was finally decided on because in comparison to the other parties it was the "least" of all evils	17	21	19	27	19
By the voter's own account, the FPÖ (or the Greens) was finally decided on in order to teach both major parties an object-lesson	*		46	32	6

(brace grouping FPÖ: 65, Green: 59)

Source: Dr. Fessel + GfK, Repräsentative Wahltagsbefragung (exit poll) zur Nationalratswahl 1986, N = 2,149 voters interviewed after leaving the polling place, supported questions (presentation of a list of several voting motives)

Table 4.9
The political structure of the electorate of the FPÖ and the Greens (1986)

the respective party electorates (in %)	FPÖ	The Greens
1983 - voters for the SPÖ	28	19
1983 - voters for the ÖVP	26	16
1983 - voters for the FPÖ	25	4
1983 - voters for the Greens	0	23
first-time voters in 1986	11	20
non-voters in 1983	4	12
no answer	6	6
Σ in %	100	100

Source: Dr. Fessel + GfK, Repräsentative Wahltagsbefragung (exit poll) zur Nationalratswahl 1986, N = 2,149 voters interviewed after leaving the polling place

— voters with a higher school education (one third of those shifting away from the ÖVP had completed at least high-school),
— personality voters, i.e. voters for whom the personality of the respective top candidate was an important motive to vote this time for another party (two thirds of those shifting away from the ÖVP did so primarily on account of the image of the top candidate either personally or presented via mass media),
— voters who made their decision only in the final phase of the election campaign.

Those who shifted away from the SPÖ were:

— also primarily of younger to medium age groups,
— representatives of the new white-collar middle classes, but as well of the skilled work force,
— in comparison to those voters shifting away from the ÖVP, those leaving the SPÖ did so less on a basis of orientation on the personality of the top candidate and probably more as protest voters,
— those shifting away from both SPÖ and ÖVP made their voting decision only in the final phase of the election campaign.

Mainly the FPÖ and the Greens profited from the extraordinary mobility of voting behavior. Both parties were able to book a total of about 60% of the floating vote. In contrast, the ÖVP was able to appeal to only 25%, the SPÖ to only 10% of the party-shifters of the year 1986. The obvious strength of the shift away from the major parties in the direction of third and fourth parties not only accelerated latent deconcentration and fragmentation tendencies at the macro level of the party system, but also provoked considerable regrouping at the micro level of the structure of the electorate. 54% of the FPÖ voters in 1986 voted for one of the major parties in 1983. As regards the Greens, 35% voted formerly for one of the major parties. The FPÖ and the Greens have therefore developed into a catch-basin for voters disappointed with the major parties.

4. The formation of new proportions in the Austrian party system

The outcome of the National Council election on the 23rd of November 1986 radically changed the structure of the Austrian party system. In addition to the institutionalization of the Green-Alternatives as the fourth parliamentary faction and the doubling of the electorate of the FPÖ under their new populistic party leadership, the proportions of political forces in the Austrian party system have been restructured through the formation of an SPÖ-ÖVP coalition government.

Table 4.10

Proportional party representation in Parliament after the 1986 National Council election

Government parties (SPÖ + ÖVP)		Opposition parties (FPÖ + The Greens)	
% of votes	parliamentary seats	% of votes	parliamentary seats
84.4	80 + 77 = 157	14.6	18 + 8 = 26

Critical developments in the sphere of nationalized industry, a dramatic situation with regard to national finances, lack of growth-related structural factors, a threatening decline of the international competitiveness of the Austrian economy, unsolved financial problems of the social system, and the knowledge of the necessity of partially drastic corrective measures—all of these almost incapacitated the latitude for action of the major parties in the coalition.[10]

The formation of a grand coalition government therefore took place under the dictates of critical objective restraints and the necessity to give unavoidable and painful corrective and restructuring measures as broad a basis of legitimation as possible. The grand coalition form of government, moreover, suited a widespread need for concerns and harmony within the Austrian electorate and the obvious expectation that a government which can claim the support of 84% of Austrian voters would be in the position of carrying out also unpopular measures to solve urgent financial and economic problems.[11] In the joint work program representing the programmatic platform of the coalition government the newly formed federal government under the leadership of the socialist Federal Chancellor Vranitzky agreed upon an extensive catalog of measures with the goal of restoring national finances, reducing governmental interference and modernizing production structures to improve international competitiveness while simultaneously reducing environmental pollution. The principal features of the work program initially met with mainly positive resonance, even though exaggerated expectations regarding the problem-solving capacity of the coalition government quickly gave way to a sober to reserved and sceptical assessment.

Already the first six months of work of the grand coalition government indicate a number of conflict zones triggering off tensions, irritations and disputes in both major parties:

— The correction of national financial problems requires, logically enough, rigorous economizing measures, the reduction of subsidies and the abandonment of an expansionistic promotion policy concentrating on the satisfaction of well-organized clientele interests. Just as the withdrawal of guarantees of work-places and subsidies in the sphere of nationalized industry evokes an existential threat and to some extent highly emotional protest among the traditionally socialist oriented working classes, already the announcement of economizing measures in the area of civil service—which is primarily pro-ÖVP—elicits intra-party gestures of disapproval and intimidation from the union representatives. In addition, the ÖVP is pressured by its representatives of agrarian interests, who are ready to put their intra-party veto on any form of curtailment or reduction of governmental support. Both government parties therefore have to battle with serious intra-party tensions. Here the pragmatic restraints of governmental action are often diametrically opposed to the interests of their respective traditional voter clientele.[12]

— The marked irritation of traditional voter groups and the strain of (delicate) clientele relations led not only to intra-party protest reactions, but also brought about an obvious correction of intra-party power relationships. In both parties the militant functionaries aiming at a consistent representation of traditional voter interests seem to be getting the upper hand over pragmatic leadership groups oriented toward party-shifters. In both parties influential representatives of traditional clientele interests are joining forces for the purpose of intra-party resistance against government action which is beginning to encroach upon sacrosanct proprietary levels, vested rights and well-earned privileges.

Table 4.11

Assessment of the problem-solving capacity of the coalition government in the spring of 1987

Those interviewed (in %)	Assessment of the problem-solving capacity of the coalition government in the areas of			
	economy and national finances		environmental protection	
	+	-	+	-
eligible voters (total)	38	54	26	66
SPÖ adherents	49	44	37	59
ÖVP adherents	40	54	28	65
FPÖ adherents	23	70	15	80
Green adherents	20	79	8	92
voters willing to switch	41	57	27	72

Note:
+ = the coalition government will be able to solve respective problems
- = the coalition government will not be able to solve respective problems
Source: Dr. Fessel + GfK, Thematische Determinanten der Wahlentscheidung (March 1987)

— The shock of extensive voter losses in the 1986 National Council election has led to a distinct reduction of electoral-strategical perspectives. Ideological dogmatists and representatives of a "pure" doctrine, who had always followed offensive party-shifter strategies with disapproving scepticism, saw their opinions confirmed through the disappointing election results. They, who had always voiced warnings of the risks of opening up the programmatic platform—in their opinion one already carried too far—now attribute the election defeat to the fact that the wishes of traditional voters had been neglected, and see the salvation of their respective party in a return to traditional positions and doctrines. The degree of strategic latitude of the party elite is recognizably restricted with reference to the pressure of the basis. The preservation of the electoral status quo takes priority over offensive strategies aimed at expansion of existing voter coalitions.[13]

In contrast to the defensive strategies of both major parties is a newly formed spectrum of opposition which utilizes various methods in seeking to appeal to voters who are discontent with government policy, i.e. with the two major parties. Both the FPÖ and the Green-Alternatives presently reckon that they have a good chance of attracting protest voters who are ready to change parties, and of expanding their respective voter basis at the cost of the two major parties.[14]

Table 4.12
The largest voter potential of the FPÖ and the Greens (1988)

In the next National Council election the interviewees could imagine voting for (in %)	the FPÖ	the Greens
eligible voters (total)	25	12
SPÖ adherents	14	8
ÖVP adherents	21	7
party-shifters	61	30
SPÖ voters ready to shift	70	41
ÖVP voters ready to shift	87	28

Source: Dr. Fessel + GfK, Politische Umfrage (1988)

Both opposition parties have a theoretical voter potential which extends far past the real proportion of voters (the FPÖ in the summer of 1988 about 12%, the Green-Alternatives about 6%) and—on the condition of successful mobilization—which could weaken the position of both major parties for a long time:[15]

— Under its new party leadership, the FPÖ has swung around to a populistic course which, by renouncing to a great extent programmatic remnants, seeks to get control of existing protest attitudes, anger at the parties, disappointment and resentment. Supported by the attractiveness of its top candidate in the media, the FPÖ offers itself as a valve for diffuse disillusionment, overall dissatisfaction and a deep-seated object lesson mentality.

— In contrast, the Green-Alternatives are counting on the desire for alternative kinds of living and politics exactly on the part of the younger voter generations, and attempt to appeal to alternative groupings from the left wing of the SPÖ just as much as to ecology-minded conservationists, those opposing the building of new nuclear power plants, and activists of citizens' initiatives. Although still by no means consolidated as a party, confronted with internal disputes, group rivalries and permanent splinter tendencies, it already commands, nevertheless, a core electorate which appears likely to be able to guarantee its place in parliament at least for a medium-term period of time.

Whether both major parties can break out of their present defensive position and which intra-party power constellations will lead to which strategic decisions is just as unclear at the moment as the question whether the grand coalition government will fulfill the expectations placed in it. The number of strategic unknowns is too great, the space of time too brief to be able to make even vague assumptions about the future proportions of power in the Austrian party system. The grand coalition in the 50's and 60's showed voter mobility as being clearly limited by relatively rigid camp structures and emotionally reinforced party ties; stabilizing incentives were also present through an extensive convergence of social interests, political goals and socio-economic development. Now at the end of the 80's, in contrast, not only the political process of secularization is well advanced, but also the cleft between individual societal segments, organized politics and material possibilities has become wider.

Due to structural factors, party ties, and hence the willingness to maintain one's party-political loyalty, will certainly continue to loosen up and weaken in the coming years. Large parties which undogmatically preserve their historical identity as political movements, but are simultaneously prepared to modernize their structures and to become more accessible to society, will be able to exist successfully in an unsettled and unpredictable voter landscape. However, if they continue to adhere to petrified structures and antiquated routines, to neglect a renewal of their political substance, their political style and their symbolic self-representation, then the Austrian party system faces turbulent times characterized by dissolution, fragmentation and increasing diffusion.

Table 4.13
Party loyalty of Austrian voters (1977-1987)

A particular party was decided on and voted for even though one was not 100% in agreement with what this party did and planned (agreement in %)	1977	1987	Change
voters under 30	41	24	-17
self-employed, tradespeople, professionals	52	33	-19
white-collar workers/civil servants	48	30	-18
blue-collar workers	60	37	-23
farmers	61	57	-4
compulsory education	59	48	-11
technical education	49	37	-12
high-school/university graduates	41	35	-6
voters (total)	53	39	-14

Source:
Dr. Fessel + GfK, Politische Umfrage (1977)
Dr. Fessel + GfK, Thematische Determinanten der Wahlentscheidung (1987)

Table 4.14
Party identification in the spring of 1987

The interviewees tended emotionally toward (in %)...	SPÖ	ÖVP	FPÖ	The Greens	Other	No party	No answer
eligible voters (total)	28	21	5	3	1	27	15
first-time voters	14	14	2	8	0	40	22
under the age of 30	19	21	6	8	0	30	16
those contented with the work of the coalition government	36	23	2	2	1	23	13
those not contented with the work of the coalition government	17	20	10	5	1	33	14

Source: Dr. Fessel + GfK, Thematische Determinanten der Wahlentscheidung (1987/88)

Table 4.15
Satisfaction with the work of the coalition government (1987/88)

The work of the SPÖ + ÖVP government is considered to be	March 1987a)		July 1987b)		March 1988c)	
very satisfying	4	} 56	4	} 57	2	} 43
rather satisfying	52		53		41	
rather unsatisfying	28		32		41	
		} 36		} 39		} 52
not satisfying at all	8		7		11	
no answer given	9		4		5	

Source:
a)   Dr. Fessel + GfK, Thematische Determinanten der Wahlentscheidung (1987)
b)   Dr. Fessel + GfK, Politische Umfrage (1987)
c)   Dr. Fessel + GfK, Politische Umfrage (1988)

Notes

1. This applies, however, only from the end of the 50's and the beginning 60's onwards, when the re-establishment of the party system after 1945, respectively 1949, appears provisionally completed.

2. The cited paper is based on theses which Gerlich formulated already in the mid-60's. For a detailed representation of this development and its reflection in political-scientific research, cf. Plasser/Ulram/Grausgruber (1987).

3. The last-mentioned point should, however, be furnished with a question mark. While the appearance of certain small parties (e.g. the Greens) can be initially attributed to changes in social structure and value orientations, the chances of the major parties are presumably dependent on their ability to form new voter coalitions. It remains undisputed, however, that such voter coalitions basically differ from the stable traditional electorates of previous periods; maintaining large numbers of votes is hence clearly "more difficult."

4. For a detailed analysis cf. Plasser/Ulram (1987a), and Gehmacher/Birk/Ogris (1987), Plasser/Ulram (1987b).

5. Contrary to assumptions (mainly from journalists) that a flare up again of German national or even neo-Nazi emotions played an important role in the election victory of the FPÖ, all available studies clearly show that this was not the case. The FPÖ of the 1986 National Council election is, from the standpoint of the voters–those supporting it–"the party of party protest" or that of its top candidate, who personifies this attitude.

6. Explanation to Table 4.4: The interpretation of the symbols (+-) of the coefficients is dependent on the direction of coding. The following applies for the dummy variables occupation, permanent position, age, state, and "motive": positive/negative signs signify that the corresponding feature has a favorable/unfavorable effect on voting for a particular party. Positive signs for education, size of locality, time, wavering and sex signify higher education, larger localities, an early decision, etc., favored voting for a party, and vice versa.

7. For a detailed and more extensive presentation cf. Plasser/Ulram/ Grausgruber (1987). A multi-variance analysis from the year 1985 (Haerpfer 1987b) achieves similar results except for the fact that issue orientations play a stronger role for ÖVP voters. This can be explained basically by the loss of flexible voter groups—which shifted in 1985 from the SPÖ to the ÖVP—in the course of the election campaign. For its part, however, it is an indicator of the increased flexibility of the Austrian electorate.

8. See also: (Plasser/Ulram 1987a, b).

9. For an international comparison of volatility, see again: (Haerpfer 1987a).

10. The SPÖ had already committed itself in the election campaign to a government coalition with the ÖVP. In the ÖVP, however, a minority had broached the subject of a coalition with the FPÖ. In reality though, steps had also been initiated in the direction of a grand coalition.

11. The capability of carrying out unpopular measures as well—whereby each of the coalition partners is responsible for its own clientele—was the strongest argument for the formation of an SPÖ-ÖVP government. Here the disciplinary capability of the party leadership was apparently just as overrated as the egoism of organized groups was underrated.

12. Moreover, the leadership of the SPÖ is faced with the awkward task of having to explain the abandonment of an expansionistic, state-interventionistic crisis management to their party basis, and to find plausible arguments why the guarantees of job and employment security given in the past could no longer be fulfilled. On the other hand, the ÖVP is practically paralyzed by smouldering internal leadership discussions and is still trying to adjust to the change of roles from an opposition to a government party. Both factors hinder it from being able to exploit this politico-economic change of course as an improvement of programmatic and political status.

13. A more militant way of doing things within the major parties is, for example in the ÖVP, seen in the occupation of important intra-party key positions with proponents of a pronounced traditional and core voter strategy. On the other hand, in the SPÖ delegates at party conventions are unmistakably expressing the displeasure of the traditional party basis.

14. The parliamentary latitude of both opposition parties is very restricted due to the overwhelming preponderance of the two government par-

ties. Ingenious staging on the part of the mass media can, however, by all means compensate for actual institutional weaknesses.

15. The main point of attack of the FPÖ is the classic protest issue "the abuse of privileges and the party-book system," which in Austria has a mobilization potential not to be underestimated. On the other hand, the Green-Alternatives profit from politico-environmental grievances, controversial power-station projects, and the growing impression of a more and more critical endangerment of the natural foundations of life.

Bibliography

Gehmacher, E./Birk, F./Orgris, G., *Das Wahljahr 1986: Welche Theorien stimmen?*, in: *Journal für Sozialforschung 1987/2* (Gehmacher/Birk/Ogris, 1987)

Gerlich, P., *The Development of the Political System of Austria*, in: K. Steiner (ed.), *Tradition and Innovation in Contemporary Austria*, Palo Alto 1982 (Gerlich, 1982)

Gerlich, P., *Österreichs Parteien: Ergebnisse und Perspektiven*, in: P. Gerlich/W.C. Müller (Hg.), *Zwischen Koalition und Konkurrenz: Österreichs Parteien seit 1945*, Wien 1983 (Gerlich, 1983)

Gerlich, P., *Consociationalism to Competition: The Austrian Party System since 1945*, in: H. Daalder (ed.), *Party Systems in Denmark, Austria, Switzerland, the Netherlands and Belgium*, London 1987 (Gerlich, 1987)

Haerpfer, Ch., *Gesellschaft, Wählerverhalten und Parteiensystem: Wahlverhalten in Österreich, der BRD, Belgien und Großbritannien 1974-1987*, in: *Journal für Sozialforschung 1987/2* (Haerpfer, 1987a)

Haerpfer, Ch., *Lineare Modellierung von Wähler-Partei-Beziehungen in Österreich*, in: *Österreichische Zeitschrift für Politikwissenschaft 1987/3* (Haerpfer, 1987b)

Kienzl, H., *Die Struktur der österreichischen Wählerschaft*, in: K. Blecha et al., *Der durchleuchtete Wähler*, 1964 (Kienzl, 1964)

Lehmbruch, G., *Proporzdemokratie: Politisches System und politische Kultur in der Schweiz und in Österreich*, Tübingen 1967 (Lehmbruch, 1967)

Lipset, S.M./Rokkan, S. (eds.), *Party Systems and Voter Alignments*, New York 1967 (Lipset/Rokkan, 1967)

Pelinka, A., *Struktur und Funktion der politischen Parteien*, in: H. Fischer (Hg.): *Das politische System Österreichs*, Wien 1974 (1. Auflage) (Pelinka, 1974)

Plasser, F., *Parteien unter Streß. Zur Dynamik der Parteiensysteme in Österreich, der Bundesrepublik Deutschland und den Vereinigten Staaten*, Wien/Köln/Graz 1987 (Plasser 1987a)

Plasser, F., *Die populistische Arena: Massenmedien als Verstärker*, in: A. Pelinka (Hg.): *Populismus in Österreich*, Wien 1987 (Plasser, 1987b)

Plasser, F./Ulram, P.A., *Unbehagen im Parteienstaat: Jugend und Politik in Österreich*, Wien/Köln/Graz 1982 (Plasser/Ulram, 1982)

Plasser, F./Ulram, P.A., *From Stability to Diffusion: Dealignment in the Austrian Party System*, Paper delivered at the Annual Meeting of the American Political Science Association, New Orleans 1985 (Plasser/Ulram, 1985)

Plasser, F./Ulram, P.A., *Das Jahr der Wechselwähler—Wahlen und Neustrukturierung des österreichischen Parteiensystems 1986*, in: *Österreichisches Jahrbuch für Politik '86*, Wien 1987 (Plasser/Ulram, 1987a)

Plasser, F./Ulram, P.A., *Der reaktive Wähler: Zur Analyse der Nationalratswahl 1986*, in: *Journal für Sozialforschung 1987/2* (Plasser/Ulram, 1987b)

Plasser, F./Ulram, P.A./Grausgruber, A., *Vom Ende der Lagerparteien: Perspektivenwechsel in der österreichischen Parteien- und Wahlforschung*, in: *Österreichische Zeitschrift für Politikwissenschaft 1987/3* (Plasser/Ulram/Grausgruber, 1987)

Powell, G.B., *Social Fragmentation and Political Hostility: An Austrian Case Study*, Stanford 1970 (Powell, 1970)

Steiner, K., *Politics in Austria*, Boston 1972 (Steiner, 1972)

Traar, K./Birk, F., *Der durchleuchtete Wähler in den achtziger Jahren*, Sonderheft des *Journals für Sozialforschung 1987/1* (Traar/Birk, 1987)

Ulram, P.A., *Hegemonie und Erosion. Politischer Wandel in Österreich* (Habilitationsschrift in Vorbereitung) Wien 1988 (Ulram, 1988)

Wandruszka, A., *Österreichs politische Struktur*, in: H. Benedikt (Hg.): *Geschichte der Republik Österreich*, Wien 1954 (Wandruszka, 1954)

5

1986–The Year of Election Surprises

From the Perspective of the Electoral Behavior Theory

ERNST GEHMACHER, FRANZ BIRK and GÜNTHER OGRIS

Austria is characterized by a remarkably stable electoral behavior. Prevailing power relationships are only slow to change, if at all, and thus, public opinion research and interim elections can provide good insight. In 1986, however, both the Federal Presidential Election (May 4 and June 8) and the National Council Election (November 23), produced results which did not conform to the trend and which were therefore difficult to interpret:

— Since the end of the Second World War, the office of Federal President has always fallen to a candidate supported by the Socialist Party of Austria (SPÖ). The SPÖ was able to count on the bonus of this traditional trend in the 1986 elections, and from the beginning of the campaign on, wagered heavily on this factor until the entire campaign was escalated by drawing the Second World War past of the ÖVP's candidate into the picture, strongly altering the face of the election campaign. Dr. Kurt Waldheim won the Federal Presidential Election with a surprisingly strong majority, having received a significant number of votes from former SPÖ voters as well. Waldheim's victory was viewed as a signal to change political horses; the SPÖ seemed to have been weakened considerably. Judging from the results of polls taken subsequent to the Styrian State Diet election, it was possible for the ÖVP to move ahead of the SPÖ in voters' favor.

— The National Council Election held that November, however, did not bring the relative majority hoped for by the ÖVP. Instead, the number of FPÖ supporters doubled to 9.7% under the leadership of the Party Chairman, Jörg Haider; the Greens also received a voice in Parliament. Dr. Franz Vranitzky led the SPÖ into a coalition government with the

ÖVP, a form which he had declaredly pursued from the start. The results were viewed with surprise by larger sections of the electorate, since earlier, even the opinion polls had spoken too cautiously of a neck-and-neck race.

Numerous hypotheses were established in explanation of the unexpected results of the two elections, whereby two major, contradictory premises were formulated. One relates to the effectiveness and thus the quality of the campaign management, i.e., the efficiency of the large political parties' particular marketing machinery and the products they promote, namely the top politicians. This premise is popular, for it allows placing blame, an essential psychological mechanism in coping with frustration, while on the other hand, helps to build up a particular image, providing an inherent factor in the marketing of politicians as well.

The Ups and Downs of Voter Favor

Opinion poll research, applied to an ever increasing extent to vote counts and electoral behavior, and made available to the public, provides a good picture of the course of major developments. In November 1985, after the commencement of the campaign for the office of Federal President, the SPÖ candidate, Dr. Kurt Steyrer, began an intense race to catch up with Dr. Kurt Waldheim, who, being able to draw on a long-time familiarity bonus, had enjoyed a more advantageous position from the start. The SPÖ had a slight advantage over the ÖVP in voter favor, and the presidential race between the two candidates appeared to be a toss-up.

The events surrounding the VOEST, from the disclosure about oil speculations at the end of November 1985 to the replacement of the VOEST's management and organizational re-planning of the state-owned enterprise in early 1986, sent shockwaves through the SPÖ electorate. The ÖVP rose over the SPÖ in voter favor and Steyrer "took a dive" as well. At that point, in early March, accusations of Waldheim began from abroad, initiated by the Jewish World Congress. Issues became strongly emotionalized. A minority of sensitive antifascists joined in the accusations as well, and some the SPÖ-supporters hoped that the ÖVP candidate would be weakened. Instead, a substantial proportion of the voters, even deep into the ranks of the SPÖ, reacted to the "foreign" insinuations against Waldheim with patriotic outrage, which at times became colored with the manifestation of long-tabooed anti-Semitism. Waldheim won the runoff on June 8 with an impressive advantage, after having lost the the first ballot on May 4 by a very thin margin. Election analyses revealed that over 10 percent of former SPÖ supporters had voted for Waldheim in a mood of protest, which was primarily nurtured by the dis-

appointment over the SPÖ's backing down from job guarantees in nationalized industries, but also by a desire for strong leadership "in hard times"
(which Waldheim promised). Moreover, Waldheim received a large number
of votes from the FPÖ, whose Pan-German-nationalist wing presented a
united front to the Jewish incriminations of Waldheim.

The SPÖ and its Federal Chancellor, Dr. Fred Sinowatz, had reached an
all-time low in voter favor. The prospects of a change to an ÖVP-dominated
government seemed likely. Then Dr. Sinowatz turned over the office of Federal Chancellor to the very popular Minister of Finance, Dr. Franz Vranitzky.
The voters' mood reacted sluggishly, and a considerable number of undecided voters existed after the substantial voter migrations of the presidential
election. Again, the two large parties approached a neck-and-neck race,
though distinct signs of fatigue on the part of the still unsettled SPÖ voters
were evident. In contrast, the ranks of ÖVP supporters seemed united with a
high level of mobilization.

In October, a demogogically brilliant young politician, Dr. Jörg Haider,
"dethroned" Vice-Chancellor and FPÖ Party Chairman Dr. Steger at the
FPÖ National Convention in Innsbruck, whereupon Chancellor Vranitzky
dissolved the Coalition between the SPÖ and the FPÖ and moved the National Council Election planned for Spring, 1987, ahead to November 23,
1986.

Jörg Haider brought along considerable voter potential; he had not only
roused the united support of the nationalistic (Pan-German) lager, but had
also attracted a large number of protest voters, even from the SPÖ, though
certainly not those with leftist and/or antifascist sentiments. In the month
prior to the election, he was able to draw an additional 3% of the voters away
from the "old" parties (as he had labeled the large parties, whereby he also
presented himself with the image of newness and youth). The election on
November 23 was thus an overwhelming triumph for Jörg Haider and a disappointment for supporters of the ÖVP, who had strongly hoped that their
party be able to obtain a relative majority. This strong desire was not necessarily that for a transition to a more conservative-liberal course, but rather
the wish for the establishment of a "Grand Coalition" government. The latter
was accomplished under the leadership of Chancellor Franz Vranitzky, who
was the absolute majority's favored candidate in any case; every fifth ÖVP
voter supported him as well. The Greens were also able to enter Parliament,
despite the breaking away of their extreme left wing.

The consequences of the 1986 election year were thus:

— a distinctly altered party landscape, with the Greens at the center (subsequent to the breaking away of the small leftist group) and a strong
FPÖ-led right wing,

— a coalition of both large parties under SPÖ leadership, with strong representation of unions and state-regulatory forces in the government,
— a decided right shift of Austria's international image, afflicted with the accusation of "not coming to terms with its past."

Table 5.1
The 1986 Federal Presidential Election and National Council Election (party strengths indicated in percent of eligible voters).

| | | Pres.Elect. | | Nat.Council Elect. | |
		May 4	June 8	Nov. 23	
Left Wing	Steyrer	38.1 ⎫	38.8	KPÖ	0.6 ⎫
		⎬ 42.8			⎬ 42.1
	Meissner-Blau	4.7 ⎭		SPÖ	37.5
	Non-voters	12.9	15.9	Greens	4.0 ⎭
	Waldheim	43.3 ⎫	45.3	Non-voters	13.8
		⎬ 44.4			
Right Wing	Scrinzi	1.0 ⎭		ÖVP	35.7 ⎫
					⎬ 44.1
				FPÖ	8.4 ⎭

Table 5.2
Monthly IFES Multi-Theme Surveys (mean values)

	Likeability Values (Scale +5 to -5) Mean of Total Pop.			Fictitious Election % of elig.voters			
	SPÖ	ÖVP	FPÖ	SPÖ	ÖVP	FPÖ	Greens
1983	+1.6	+0.8	-0.3	43	37	4	-
1984	+1.4	+0.9	-0.4	38	38	4	3
1985	+1.3	+0.6	-0.8	40	38	2	4
Jan. to March, 1986	+0.9	+0.6	-0.9	37	38	2	3
April to June, 1986	+0.8	+0.6	-0.8	36	38	2	4
July, 1986	+1.1	+0.8	-0.7	36	37	2	4
September, 1986	+1.1	+1.0	-0.8	38	39	3	4
October, 1986	+1.3	+1.1	-0.8	39	38	4	4
November, 1986	+1.0	+0.9	-0.7	38	36	7	4

Table 5.3
Intended Voting Behavior, Compared over Time - Direct Election
(In percent, referring to all persons polled over the age of 19)

Question: "Please imagine that it would be possible to elect the Chancellor directly, as with the Federal President, and that you had the choice between Dr. Vranitzky and Dr. Mock. Who would you vote for?"

	Dr. Vranitzky	Dr. Mock	For neither/ No response
June, 1986	45	32	23
July, 1986	48	27	25
September, 1986	49	30	21
October, 1986	49	31	20
November, 1986	48	28	24

Source: IFES, Monatliche Mehrthemenumfrage, approx. 2000 persons polled, oral interviews.

Table 5.4
The November 23, 1986 Election Results (in percent)

	Electorate	Valid Votes
SPÖ	37.5	43.3
ÖVP	35.7	41.3
FPÖ	8.4	9.7
Greens	4.0	4.6

Electorate turnout: 90.5%
Valid votes: 4,851,913

This presentation of the developments, based on opinion poll results, partially include the major hypotheses of the popular short-term premises, or is not contradictory to these:

— the disappointment felt by the SPÖ supporters induced by the VOEST events,
— the desire to rapidly get the economy on its feet and activated again,
— the feeling of solidarity toward an "indicted" Waldheim
— the readiness of the Austrians to accept a turnaround in power relationships,
— finally, the fascination felt for with "young, cheeky" Jörg Haider by the "politically disenchanted" younger generation voters,

— the "shift to the right" toward Haider's FPÖ in the wake of politically mobilized "latent anti-Semitism," and
— the poor showing on the part of the "election campaign management," first in the SPÖ and then in the ÖVP.

The scientific analysis, however, presented the question as to whether this vaccilation of voter sympathies was not also the consequence of more far-reaching tendencies. Here, it is not only the political scientist who must search for such comprehensive patterns, but also those in the political arena who need guidelines for electoral decision-making as well.

The following major theories of change, which could contribute to finding an explanation of the two elections, are considered here:

1.   A change in electoral behavior norms—alternating vote, floating vote, wavering vote, protest vote, disenchantment with democracy, the departure from voting in accordance with set ideological orientation to "occasional, issue-dependent" voting, which in turn leads to spur-of-the moment vote decisions and lower election turnouts.
2.   Political-ideological shifts in the electorate—a conservative trend, a shift to the right, post-materialism, new middle classes, de-ideologization; deeply penetrating and long-lasting changes in the formation of interest groups, in fundamental values, in the electorate's view of humanity and society.
3.   A change in the party landscape—the establishment of the Greens as an independent party, the FPÖ as a right-wing party, the adaptation of the large parties to majority wishes, pragmatism and short-term holds on votes.

Such larger scale lines of development can only be viewed over longer periods of time (as already made available in part in opinion research). Where these are lacking, the differences between the generations permit cautious inferences in retrospect about the trend.

The Voters begin to Choose

In both elections (the Federal Presidential Election and the National Council Election), the surprising changes in electoral behavior which decided the outcome of the elections only took place in the course of the election campaigns. Is there an increasing tendency to make one's decision at the last moment? Do the electoral behavior norms here change systematically? Several results point in this direction. Basically, this type of vaccilation is also to be expected down to the last day when "lager ties" and "party loyalties" relax and instead, votes are cast more or less out of protest or in response to current issues. Nevertheless, the thought pattern proponing increasing "disenchantment with politics" and the "occasional, issue-dependent vote" could prove too superficial in its simplicity. Party loyalty will doubtlessly decrease, although at a very slow rate (Haerpfer, 1985). A shift in norms within the course of a modernization process does, however, seem to be well substantiated in this case.

Table 5.5
Party Loyalty in Austria

Question: "Some people are of the opinion that it is correct to remain loyal in future elections to the party for which one has already voted in the past. Others maintain that the modern citizen should alternate parties from election to election, when he feels that this is more advantageous. Please tell me your opinion. Are you loyal to a particular party or do you switch parties?"

In percent of the base figures in parentheses	Maintain Party Loyalty	Switch Parties
Total (1809)	65	35
Sex		
Male (840)	61	39
Female (969)	68	32
Age		
20 to 29 (306)	48	51
30 to 49 (654)	59	41
50 to 69 (582)	70	30
70 and older (267)	84	15
Education		
Compulsory, without further education (686)	77	23
Compulsory, with further education (863)	62	37
High school/university (258)	40	60

Source: IFES, 1986

The actual extent of voter mobility in the dissolution of psychological party loyalty remains to be seen. A considerable portion of the declaredly (thus conforming to their norm) so loyal older voters have also switched parties throughout their voting lives. There is no indication that a lower degree of party loyalty must be coupled with a lack of trust in the political system.

Table 5.6
Lack of Trust in Politics (in percent)

	Age in Years Total	< 19	< 29	< 44	< 59	> 60
Many politicians are dishonest Polticians waste tax-payers' money It does not matter which party wins the election, the man on the street doesn't count						
Agree	31	21	33	37	34	24
Disagree	42	28	33	45	47	46
No Comment	60	50	51	61	64	68

Source: IFES, Soziologische und psychologische Ursachen des Wertwandelphenomens (1985).

The opinion that the younger generation is disenchanted with politics is repeatedly challenged by opinion polls. The youth of the 1980s is more committed to the democratic ideal and has more, though certainly not blind, trust in politicians than is true of their parents. They also participate more avidly in political activities. It is even more difficult to establish a general decline in sympathies for political parties.

The Disenchantment with Politics—A Chimera

Since 1970, the IFES has been gathering information on the sympathies of eligible voters for political parties and leading candidates, and evaluating this data on an 11-point scale (from +5 to -5). It was shown that for the SPÖ, annual mean likeability fluctuated between +1.3 and +1.9. A trend of declining sympathies was only registered from 1983 on, namely following the SPÖ's loss of its absolute majority and Kreisky's resignation as Chancellor, and the establishment of the SPÖ-FPÖ coalition government. The nadir of SPÖ voter sympathies was reached in the first half of 1986. That year, the ÖVP was able to attain its best voter likeability level of +1.1; otherwise, the level had fluctuated between +0.4 and +0.9 from 1970 on, without a longer-lasting trend discernable. Due to its minority party position, the FPÖ has always shown negative values and a great deal of fluctuation, here between -0.9 and -0.1. There is not much trend shown here, except that toward the end, this governmental party continued to lose voter sympathies within the government. Under Haider's leadership, the FPÖ was able to regain a good position, though not as good as during the first two years of Dr. Steger's leadership of the opposition FPÖ.

Table 5.7a
Political-Strategic Indicators (1969-1986)

Annual Mean Values:
Voter Intentions: SPÖ, ÖVP, FPÖ, VGÖ, ALÖ, Non-Voters,
Undeclared:

	SPÖ	ÖVP	FPÖ	VGÖ	ALÖ	Non-Voters	Economic Index +)
1969/70	41*)	28*)	3*)			24*)	-6
1971	44*)	29*)	3*)			24*)	-0
1972	41*)	30*)	4*)			25*)	-7
1973	44	33	6			16	+1
1974	45	37	5			13	-16
1975	46	37	4			12	-11
1976	45	38	4			13	-16
1977	44	39	4			13	-11
1978	44	39	5			12	-10
1979	45	36	4			15	-6
1980	44	37	4			14	-13
1981	43	36	4			16	-24
1982	42	36	4			16	-23
1983	41	37	3	1	1	15	-18
1984	39	38	3	2	1	16	-24
1985	38	36	3	3	1	18	-19
1986							
-6/86)	37	38	2	3	1	19	-16
6/1986	37	38	1	4	1	19	-16
7/1986	36	37	2	3	1	21	-16
9/1986	38	39	3	3	1	16	-14
10/1986	39	38	4	3	*	16	-8
11/1986	38	36	7	4	*	15	-8
12/1986	38	31	9	5	-	18	-8
1-6/87	38	33	7	4		18	
7-12/87	37	32	7	4		20	
1-4/87	37	32	7	3		21	

Table 5.7b
Annual Mean Values:
Voter Sympathies: SPÖ, ÖVP, FPÖ, VGÖ, ALÖ

	SPÖ	ÖVP	FPÖ	VGÖ	ALÖ
1969/70	+1.9	+0.8	-0.4		
1971	+1.7	+0.5	-0.5		
1972	+1.3	+0.6	-0.4		
1973	+1.6	+0.6	-0.2		
1974	+1.3	+0.4	-0.4		
1975	+1.9	+0.5	-0.3		
1976	+1.7	+0.6	-0.2		
1977	+1.5	+0.6	-0.2		
1978	+1.6	+0.6	-0.2		
1979	+1.8	+0.7	-0.7		
1980	+1.8	+0.9	-0.3		
1981	+1.7	+0.8	-0.1		
1982	+1.6	+0.8	-0.2		
1983	+1.7	+0.9	-0.3	-2.0	-2.4
1984	+1.4	+0.9	-0.4	-1.5	-2.0
1985	+1.3	+0.6	-0.8	-1.5	-2.1
1986					
(-6/86)	+0.9	+0.7	-1.1	-1.4	-2.0
6/1986	+1.0	+0.9	-0.6	-0.8	-1.5
7/1986	+1.1	+0.8	-0.6	-0.8	-1.5
9/1986	+1.1	+1.0	-0.8	-1.0	-1.7
10/1986	+1.3	+1.1	-0.8	-0.8	-1.4
11/1986	+1.0	+0.9	-0.7	-1.2	-1.9
12/1986	+1.7	+1.1	-0.3	-0.7	-
1-6/87	+1.7	+1.1	-0.3		-1.1
7-12/87	+1.4	+0.8	-0.3		-1.5
1-4/88	+1.4	+0.9	-0.5		-1.7

Table 5.7c
Annual Mean Values:
Voter Sympathies for Top Politicians

	SPÖ		ÖVP		FPÖ	
1969/70	+2.1	Dr. Kreisky	+0.3	Dr. Klaus/		
1971	+1.9		+0.8	Dr. Widhalm		
1972	+1.6		+0.7	Dr. Schleinzer		
1973	+1.9		+0.4		0.0	Dr. Peter
1974	+1.8		+0.1		0.0	

(Continued)

Table 5.7c (Cont.)

	SPÖ		ÖVP		FPÖ	
1975	+2.3		+0.3	Dr. Taus	-0.1	
1976	+2.5		+0.4		+0.1	
1977	+2.4		+0.3		+0.2	
1978	+2.4		+0.2		+0.1	
1979	+2.7		+0.6	Dr. Mock	-0.6	DDr. Götz
1980	+3.1		+1.2		0.0	
1981	+2.9		+1.2		+0.3	Dr. Steger
1982	+2.5		+1.0		+0.1	
1983	+2.4	Dr. Sinowatz	+1.0		-0.1	
1984	+1.9		+0.9		-0.2	
1985	+1.8		+0.4		-0.5	
1986						
(-6/86)	+1.3		+0.5		-0.7	
6/1986	+2.4	Dr. Vranitzky	+0.7		-0.4	
7/1986	+2.8		+0.8		-0.6	
9/1986	+3.0		+0.9		-0.7	
10/1986	+2.8		+1.2		-0.7	
11/1986	+2.6		+1.2		+0.1	Dr. Haider
12/1986	+3.1		+1.2		+0.1	
1-6/87	+3.3		+1.3		+0.2	
7-12/87	+3.2		+0.8		+0.3	
1-4/88	+3.1		+1.1		0.0	

*) Until 1973, the question as to who one would vote for was asked directly; for this reason, there is a relatively high percentage of "undeclared voters." Thereafter, intended voter behavior was polled using a simulated ballot. Thus, the results attained at the beginning of the 1970s are not comparable with those gathered during later polls.

+) The economic climate index provides an indication of the general economic climate in the nation and is calculated as follows: portion of interviewed persons who were of the opinion that their economic situation had improved during the last year, minus the portion of interviewed persons who were of exactly the opposite opinion. A negative index signaled an increase in economic pessimism; a positive result spoke for economic optimism.

Source: IFES-Repraesentativeumfragen

Only the Greens showed a positive trend with regard to voter sympathy; they started from a position of total rejection (-2.0 and lower), and today still attain very low voter sympathy values.

Following the 1986 election and the SPÖ-ÖVP coalition government led by Chancellor Franz Vranitzky, the situation did not change significantly up to mid-1988. The government parties show typical "wear," though this cannot be said of the top politicians in office. This did not benefit the opposition, however, which also lost popularity. Even Haider, after initial victories with his often quite polemic criticisms, was unable to expand on his political attractivity—at least not at the national level; regionally, the FPÖ showed very divergent developments, as indicated by several local elections in 1987.

From this, one could conclude that, apparently, the parties had never been particularly likeable. The accusation of a society being run by party membership and political machines was already prevalent under the Grand Coalition. Even during the years of strong economic growth, the parties were not placed on a pedestal. This can also be seen in the fact that a more or less popular party leader is almost always more favorably received than his party itself.

On the other hand, this time series contradicts the hypothesis of a legitimation crisis in democracy, or perhaps only that of a massive loss of trust by the two large parties. The fluctuations in voter sympathies for the SPÖ, the ÖVP and the FPÖ cannot be traced to a single trend, though these plausibly follow the political events as they occur (or as they are presented by the media).

Table 5.8
Political Cycles (1984-1986)
Valuation (on a scale from +5 to -5)

Difference to the results of the 1983 Nat.Council Election in %
Intended Voter Behavior (+/- 1983 N.C.E.) in %

	Fed. Chanc.	Fed.. Govt.	SPÖ	ÖVP	SPÖ	ÖVP	FPÖ	Greens	
1-3/84	2.15	1.39	1.45	0.88	-2.7	+2.0	-0.7	+1.3	
4-7/84	1.76	1.25	1.32	0.89	-3.5	+3.0	-0.8	+1.3	Androsch affair
9-10/84	1.95	1.71	1.66	0.86	-2.5	+0.5	-0.0	+2.0	New government
11/84-2/85	1.87	1.40	1.39	0.70	-3.8	-2.0	-0.0	+5.8	Hainburg affair
3-5/85	1.72	1.21	1.22	0.49	-3.3	-0.0	-1.3	+5.0	Reder affair
6-10/85	1.91	1.52	1.46	0.71	-2.4	-0.4	-0.6	+3.5	
11/85-2/86	1.53	1.03	1.07	0.65	-2.7	-1.4	-0.7	+1.4	VOEST affair
3-5/86	0.76	0.65	0.70	0.72	-3.6	-2.1	-0.7	+2.1	Waldheim campaign
6/86	2.39	1.10	1.03	0.90	-2.9	-1.4	-0.6	+2.8	Vranitzky government
7/86	2.80	1.29	1.09	0.82	-2.8	-0.5	-0.3	+2.5	

Correlations:	Valuation of the Federal Government	and SPÖ valuation	0.98
		and election of SPÖ	0.48
		and election of FPÖ	0.47
		and election of Greens	0.17
	ÖVP valuation	and election of ÖVP	0.29
		and election of Greens	-0.45

Apparently, party sympathies are strongly influenced by public opinion in daily issues, without allowing the development of an obvious trend. The parties are neither able to make themselves especially popular nor do the constant oppositional criticisms or media chiding have the effect of ruining their reputations. It seems that these influences maintain a good balance. Nor has a smaller party as yet been able to even approach the "Big Two" in appealing to the voters.

Neither is it possible to speak of a general decline in political participation over the past few years; instead, mention could be made of a decrease in the traditional forms of political participation and of an increase in protest forms, while a steady level of interest in personal involvement with parties and "movements" is maintained.

Table 5.9
Willingness to Become Politically Involved (in percent)

	IFES-Omnibus Poll	
	12/82	12/85
Authorized political demonstration	22	14
Boycott	15	10
Occupation of factories, buildings	2	3
Winning over friends for one's own views	23	29
Refusal to pay rents/taxes	3	6
Blocking traffic	4	5
Attending political gatherings	59	45
Walkout strike	4	4
Participating in citizens' initiatives	47	46
Voting in a referendum	74	61
Taking action for other ways of life	48	52
Holding a party office	17	17
Slogans / unauthorized placards	*	1
Going along on a peace march	29	32

Source: IFES

The new self-realization philosophy of today's younger generation gives rise to a higher level of self-confidence toward politics. A young person does not feel powerless in any way toward the politicians and parties which he so loves to criticize.

One could express doubt as to the efficiency of the forms of political participation assumed by young people. The desire to participate, however, is certainly not lacking, at least in comparison to their parents' generation. Indeed, the historic process of modernization, characterized by a strong increase in education to rational thinking, inundation with information and ideological reactivation, has also consistantly modified the norms of electoral behavior—though not progressing as far as complete rejection.

Table 5.10
IFES: Factors Determining 1986 Electoral Behavior (in percent)

ITEMS: Very applicable to me, agree fully	Age in years				
	< 20	< 29	< 49	< 69	> 70
People like me have no influence on what the government does or does not do	43	41	46	58	58
The parties are only interested in winning votes; voters' views are insignificant	22	26	30	37	37

Source: IFES, 1986

Democracy is without doubt regaining recognition in Austria to an increasing extent. The more secure democracy and the social state appear and the more the norms of individual participation develop, the more elections will probably be viewed as separate electoral acts, each involving a new personal decision, as a conscious process of selecting between persons and single, current issues of interest. This, however, leads to a "selective" voting, to floating and to wavering votes, thereby giving the media more influence over the distribution of political power.

Media Power Increases

The influence of the media on the Federal Presidential Election is substantially documented in a study carried out at the Department of Journalism of the University of Vienna (Langenbucher, Gehmacher, Rust: seminar report, summer semester, 1986). A random survey of a small representative population was repeated four times (122 persons, surveys made at the beginning of April, end of April, mid-May and mid-June, 1986) and served to trace the development of public opinion which finally placed Waldheim in the presidential office.

From early April to the second ballot on June 8, Waldheim gained 15% new voters among those surveyed, while simultaneously losing 9%. This was a clear process of selection in an emotionalized struggle surrounding the conflict of "coming to terms with the past," which ultimately earned Waldheim a net increase of 6%. A multiple regression carried out using regular readings of the Austrian KURIER and KRONENZEITUNG newspapers and the news magazine PROFIL as independent variables, and taking into consideration the factors of sex, age and education, provided the following regressions of Waldheim's gain / loss.

Table 5.11
Regressions—The Influence of the Media

| | Dependent variable | |
| | Waldheim Gain | Waldheim Loss |
	Beta (T)	Beta (T)
Kurier	+.09(0.84)	-.12(1.17)
Kronenzeitung	+.28(2.70)	-.10(0.93)
Profil	+.12(1.21)	+.17(1.66)
Sex (female)	-.03(0.33)	-.19(1.80)
Age (three groups)	-.05(0.48)	-.12(1.04)
Education (high school grad.)	+.16(1.43)	+.11(0.98)

Statistically valid (despite the study's small survey population) and impressive in magnitude is the KRONENZEITUNG's pro-Waldheim influence and the PROFIL's contra-Waldheim's effectiveness, whereby, however, the differing circulations of the two publications (both within the survey population and during the election campaign, which brought with it a noticeable increase in newspaper readership: KURIER 31%, KRONENZEITUNG 56%, PROFIL 18%) weighted the outcome to an even greater extent. PROFIL proved an especially opinion-forming periodical.

The theory of election behavior norms outlined here lies far from the popular catchwords of "party disenchantment" and the "coming of age of democracy," but does not relieve the parties of the problem of having to continue constant "political marketing" in order to keep the now selective electorate in line, thus making them highly dependent on the information propagation activities of the media. Democracy seems to be less endangered by apathy or disenchantment on the part of the electorate than by attractive opportunists and political faddists. The positive side of this trend is that it should lead to a very active and participatory type of democracy, with a well-informed public and engaged political managers.

"Right" and "Left" are Easy to Confuse

In the political debate, several hypotheses of ideological shift have been employed to explain the results of the two elections. On the one hand, a neo-conservative trend which actually should have helped the ÖVP come to power, is postulated. On the other hand, one speaks of a shift to the right which manifested itself on Waldheim's election and was further utilized by Jörg Haider. The post-materialist change of values is somewhat less often cited subsequent to the weak showing of the Greens relative to the FPÖ. The limited amount of IFES data available does not support any of these theories in a very convincing manner.

Table 5.12
Self-Categorization on a Right to Left Scale (in percent)

| | All Voters | | | | SPÖ-Voters | | | ÖVP-Voters | | |
	1	2	3	4	1	2	3	1	2	3
4/1982	34	40	20	6						
5/1983	31	42	18	9	10	44	40	63	28	1
6/1986	27	51	18	4	8	52	37	56	38	4
12/1986	31	45	18	6	16	40	38	57	36	2

(1 = right, 2 = neither/nor, 3 = left, 4 = no response)

Source: IFES (1982-1986)

This time series, in which those surveyed categorized themselves on a right to left scale, shows no evidence substantiating a significant swing to the right in past years. The general trend is rather a gradual turning away from ideological lagers—an ever increasing number of people say that they are "neither right nor left."

In June 1986, during the final phase of the presidential campaign, it was probably especially unpopular to classify oneself as "right wing." Only after Haider's election did one again openly declare one's political color. The shift to the right can more or less be viewed as a turning of tides that Haider was able to convert into votes for himself due to the timing of the election. It also appears that the SPÖ, because of the change from Steger to Haider, was able to win back from the FPÖ several right-leaning voters who had rejected the ÖVP ("liberals," "anti-clerical voters").

Without doubt, occasional right-radical tones were to be heard during the excitement of the presidential campaign surrounding Waldheim and in the FPÖ's internal disagreements comprising the power struggle between Jörg Haider and Dr. Norbert Steger. This, however, says nothing about the propagation of right-wing political ideas and ideologies. It is equally difficult to prove an increase in anti-Semitic attitudes over the past few years—rather the opposite is true. The study conducted at the Department of Journalism mentioned above (W. Langenbucher, E. Gehmacher, H. Rust) also indicated an increase in Austrian Pan-German nationalism but no significant rise in anti-Semitism or general prejudicial tendencies during the campaign—it apparently takes more than politics to create prejudices.

Instead, one finds support for the hypothesis that a right-left political orientation is becoming increasingly meaningless for more and more citizens, and this not so much in favor of a new post-materialistic dimension of conflict between "green" (the environment) and "silver" (modern technology) than in favor of pluralistic conflicts of interest. One could derive from this that a tendency of drifting toward the middle of the road, i.e., in the direction of a harmonizing balance of political interests. According to the IFES voter trend analysis of the 1986 National Council Election, approximately 38% of the Haider voters came from the FPÖ, 27% from the ÖVP and 23% from the SPÖ, as compared to the preceding National Council Election. For many voters, the road to Haider was via Waldheim; about 51% of the votes came from that source, and only 17% had voted for Steyrer during the presidential election.

Table 5.13
IFES—Voter Trend Analysis of the 1983/1986 National Council Elections

| Absolute No. of Votes (in thousands) | Nov.23, 1986 National Council Election | | | | | |
	SPÖ	ÖVP	FPÖ F.M.-Blau	Greens	Non Voters	Total
1983 National Council Election						
SPÖ	1970	46	107	54	152	2329
ÖVP	39	1837	126	62	55	2119
FPÖ	7	10	174	16	37	244
Greens	25	22	26	72	36	181
Non-Voters	23	45	29	18	467	581
Sum	2064	1960	462	221	747	5454

Source: IFES 1986

Table 5.14

IFES - Voter Trend Analysis of the May 4, 1986 Fed. Presidential Election
and the 1986 National Council Election

Absolute No. of Votes (in thousands)	Nov.23, 1986 National Council Election					
	SPÖ	ÖVP	FPÖ F.M.	Greens Blau	Non Voters	Total
May 4, 1986 Fed.Pres. Election						
Steyrer	1844	17	79	25	92	2058
Waldheim	55	1822	235	63	165	2339
Scrinzi	4	4	34	1	12	56
Meissner-Blau	49	23	44	95	49	260
Non-Voters	100	90	69	36	425	720
Sum	2053	1956	461	220	742	5433

Source: IFES 1986

Multiple regression of the primary to final election results at the
city/town level, cumulative, from 9 regional analyses, using iterative fitting.

Ideological self-categorization represents an important political factor
since it determines to a considerable extent the election success of parties
and of declared political positions, and thus also practical politics (though
very watered down by major issues and traditions). It is, however, not to be
confused with the voter's perception of humanity, the value system and an
interpretation of society, all of which not need be identical with a label of
right- or left-wing.

The postulated right shift of voters' moods is more likely a conservative
"mood change" than an adoption of rightist ideologies. Right-wing funda-
mentalists have been rare in Austria up to this point but there is increasing
hope, particularly among the young, that more emphasis be placed on private
initiative and more freedom be given to the industrious, combined with a
"change in the ruling elites"—from socialist-state functionaries to upright
managers.

The Longing for Harmony

If one accepts the desire for a "Grand Coalition" government formed by
the SPÖ and the ÖVP, or one for a three-party government under the SPÖ,
the ÖVP and the FPÖ, as an indicator of the harmony ideology, a clear picture appears. The "Grand Coalition" first became less popular toward the end

of the 1966 campaign, i.e., during its final days; until that time, it had been held in esteem by a majority. Even during the SPÖ single-party government under Chancellor Dr. Bruno Kreisky, around one-third of the eligible voters supported such a pursuit of harmony. Only after the SPÖ's absolute majority had been lost and subsequent to Dr. Kreisky's resignation (May, 1983) did the desire for a large coalition re-awaken and grow to become that of the majority in 1986.

This time series barely allows establishing any sort of regularity. Perhaps it reflects only the fear of Austria's falling back into the historically so calamitous separation of lagers, the trauma of civil war and a dictatorship. A call for social partnership in the composition of one's government is heard when the fear of crisis arises. The extent to which the entire spectrum of political opinions will gradually shift can probably be diagnosed neither by means of right-left self-categorizations nor with the few survey questions that have remained constant over a period of years. Only extensive, repetitive studies can provide an adequate response, which must also take changing nuances (changing words rather than changing values) into account.

Table 5.15
Desired Form of Government (1966-1986) (in percent)

Time (existing government)	Single party government under the ÖVP would mean			under the SPÖ would mean		
	advant.	no chng.	disadvant.	advant.	no chng.	disadvant.
1966/2 (ÖVP-SPÖ coalition)	11	21	51	15	20	48
1966/8 (ÖVP-SPÖ coalition)	11	32	40	22	41	22

The best form of government is viewed as:

Time (existing government)	SPÖ	ÖVP	SPÖ-ÖVP	SPÖ-FPÖ	ÖVP-FPÖ	SPÖ-ÖVP-FPÖ
1975/3 (Solely SPÖ govt.)	36	15	22	3	2	9
1979/1 (SPÖ government)	37	12	21	1	4	17
1983/2 (SPÖ government)	30	17	29	2	4	11
1983/3 (SPÖ government)	37	13	21	5	4	10
1983/12 (SPÖ + FPÖ)	not polled		32	27	8	22

Time (existing government)	SPÖ+ÖVP	ÖVP+SPÖ	ÖVP+FPÖ	ÖVP+Green	SPÖ+Green	SPÖ+FPÖ
1986/7 (SPÖ + FPÖ)	21	31	5	2	1	9

Time (existing government)	SPÖ+ÖVP	ÖVP+SPÖ	ÖVP+FPÖ	SPÖ+FPÖ	SPÖ-ÖVP-FPÖ	SPÖ	ÖVP
1986/10 (SPÖ+FPÖ in process of dissolving Coalition)	24	21	3	3	11	17	11

Source: IFES-Mehrthemenumfrage (N = 1800)

Table 5.16
Government Preferences (1966-1986)(in percent)

	Grand Coalition	Preference	SPÖ-ÖVP-FPÖ
1966/2	50		
		41	41
1966/3	31		
1975/3	22	31	
1979/1	21	38	
1983/2	29		
		25	36
1983/3	21		
1983/12	32	54	
1986/7	52		
		48	56
1986/10	45		

Source: IFES (1966-1986)

More Flexible Parties Pursue the Voters

It is far less doubtful that the parties are learning to an ever increasing extent that they must adapt themselves to the ideological standpoints and opinions of the voters on the "vote market." According to this theory, de-ideologization does not emanate from the voters but rather from the parties themselves. Following the SPÖ's retreat from many of its former dogmas, the ÖVP's playing all sides of the field, from left (job guarantees), green (being against the construction of a nuclear power plant) and right (partially during the Waldheim campaign), and the FPÖ's teeter-tottering between liberal and nationalistic (Pan-German) courses, such an interpretation may not be that far-fetched. A survey carried out by the IFES on party images provides several helpful insights.

In response to the question as to how the individual parties' primary directions and areas of emphasis were viewed, it was seen that each party was defined in a less extreme light, i.e., as being more "middle-of-the-road," by its voters than by those who had not voted for that party. Does de-ideologization first affect a party's own voters, or are the parties only able to glean voters because they present themselves in a less ideological light? (See Table 5.17).

No mention, however, can be made of a complete aggregation of political standpoints. The SPÖ is still viewed as being left, representing the expansion of the state and modernization. The ÖVP wears a right-wing label and has the reputation of supporting the privatization of state-owned industries and maintaining the traditional value system. The distinction between tradition vs. modernization, however, becomes somewhat blurred when a party's own members are asked. Such a flexibility on the part of the parties in wooing shift voters may better serve to explain the political landscape than the assumption that the voters are driven back and forth in trends, fads and waves by the media. Value patterns and ideologies, as well as human prejudices, have proven extremely stable, even over a period of generations, especially as long as society is not confronted by a fundamental identity crisis. Political parties, however, can more easily change their standpoints by obtaining new leaders (for instance, the transfer from Steger to Haider in the FPÖ or from Sinowatz to Vranitzky in the SPÖ), or simply by changing tactics, (as, for instance, the ÖVP did in shifting to the right during the Waldheim campaign).

The Multiparty System—Nothing More than a Possibility

Is Austria on its way to adopting a pronounced multiparty system or is it only that the lager ties and the positions of the two large parties are loosening within the fundamental left-right spectrum of economic conflicts? A short digression in response to this question was made on the basis of the information provided by three IFES multitheme surveys carried out in January, July and November, 1986, whereby electoral structure corresponded almost entirely to that of 1983.

The monthly fluctuations partially reflect the 1986 political events. The percentage of workers voting ÖVP was highest in July, directly after Waldheim's (ÖVP candidate) election to president. The "class substructure" of the two large parties still seems to be quite firm, though in the case of the ÖVP, somewhat threatened by the FPÖ.

The question arises as to whether the constancy of the "class parties" in the 1980s can be interpreted as a general consolidation of the political lagers or whether 1986, with its political drama, caused a return to a stronger class consciousness.

The 1986 developments do not rule out the possibility that the two smaller parties gain more weight in the long-term as fixed elements of the party system. The modification of the two-party system has progressed much further in western and southern Austria than in the east. The two-party system is still completely intact in both Lower Austria and Burgenland, and electoral behavior is most stable there. Carinthia and Vorarlberg no longer have a strict two-party system. In the former, the FPÖ received over 21% of the valid votes at the National Council election, making this party almost as strong as the Carinthian ÖVP (27%). In Vorarlberg, the Greens received 13% at the State Diet Election and are thus counted as the second opposition party, almost half as strong as Vorarlberg's SPÖ. These events both represent considerable and probably long-lasting changes in the two-party system.

Table 5.17
Party Images

As a percent of all eligible voters (As a percent of the party's own voters)					
Which parties work to	SPÖ	ÖVP	FPÖ	Greens	
maintain tradition	29 (50)	45 (60)	9 (32)	3 (4)	
modernize society and the economy	42 (63)	29 (44)	7 (19)	5 (17)	
expand state power	60 (66)	15 (18)	4 (16)	2 (-)	
privatize businesses	5 (7)	68 (74)	7 (35)	1 (-)	
place business ahead of environmental protection	31 (29)	29 (30)	9 (6)	1 (4)	
place environmental protection ahead of business	8 (11)	6 (8)	3 (10)	57 (83)	
Which parties lean to the				Undecided	
Left	55 (56)	3 (2)	6 (6)	11 (28)	32
Right	5 (6)	58 (65)	20 (32)	3 (2)	33
Which party is most likely to solve ...				None + Undecided	
unemployment?	27 (52)	14 (29)	* (-)	1 (-)	59
destruction of nature and the environment?	13 (28)	11 (22)	1 (6)	21 (70)	54
corruption in business?	11 (24)	15 (28)	2 (16)	2 (7)	70
ineptness in economy?	10 (22)	19 (36)	1 (3)	1 (4)	70
corruption in government?	11 (23)	11 (23)	2 (6)	2 (26)	75
ineptness in government?	9 (22)	13 (28)	1 (10	2 (7)	76
the influence of the media?	9 (21)	9 (18)	1 (6)	2 (13)	79
Austria's image abroad?	18 (37)	14 (27)	* (-)	* (4)	68

Source: IFES Multithemenumfrage, 1986/7 (N = 1532)

A nation-wide change in the Austrian "party landscape" is, however, not certain by any means, for the two smaller parties lack definite "class substructures" as well as coherent party platforms—even the organization structures are less developed. A joining of the two smaller parties for the purpose of presenting a united oppositional front does not seem conceivable at this time, whereby such an alliance (similar to that of the Liberals and Social Democrats in England) would, however, be the only means for a "third power" to cross the party size threshold in the near future.

Table 5.18
Party Preference as a Percent of all Eligible Voters

IFES Omnibus Poll Months, 1986 (in percent)

	Farmers			Self-employed				Employees			
	SPÖ	ÖVP	FPÖ	Greens	SPÖ	ÖVP	FPÖ	Greens	SPÖ	ÖVP	FPÖ	Greens
1-3	4	78	1	*	16	51	3	3	34	32	2	4
5-7	5	76	2	1	12	55	2	3	33	33	2	6
9-11	5	72	3	1	13	54	3	3	35	32	3	6
12	4	69	8	2	25	38	11	3	34	28	7	7

IFES Omnibus Poll Months, 1986 (in percent)

	Civil Servants				Skilled Workers				Unskilled Workers			
	SPÖ	ÖVP	FPÖ	Greens	SPÖ	ÖVP	FPÖ	Greens	SPÖ	ÖVP	FPÖ	Greens
1-3	43	32	2	2	56	20	1	1	53	25	2	1
5-7	45	29	1	4	54	23	2	2	55	26	1	2
9-11	42	29	1	4	53	23	3	1	52	25	2	1
12	51	17	5	3	62	18	5	2	53	23	1	2

Source: IFES Multithemaumfragen, 1986

The likelihood that the power balance will be maintained by the two large parties is obviously still considerable at this point in Austria. The multiparty system is currently nothing more than a possibility which could, however, easily become reality should the two large parties prove failures. In any case, the 1986 election year brought with it for the two coalition parties, the SPÖ and the FPÖ, the problem that they must now reckon with two quite successful opposition parties, both of which, moreover, can build on an increasing number of selective protest voters.

In this first year of the new coalition government, the two big parties, the SPÖ and the ÖVP, have been able to maintain their dominant position. The opposition parties were unable to further build on the victories gained in the 1986 elections. Currents of opposition toward the government are manifested in an increasing tendency to refrain from voting and by inner-party controversies among the members of the governing parties.

Bibliography

Gehmacher, Ernst/Birk, Franz/Ogris, Günther, *Der durchleuchtete Wahlkampf. Analyse der Bundespräsidentenwahl vom 4. Mai an Hand von Umfragen und Wahlergebnissen*, in: *Zukunft* (Mai;) 1986 (Gehmacher/Birk/Ogris, 1986a)

Gehmacher, Ernst/Birk, Franz/Ogris, Günther, *Die Waldheim-Wahl. Eine erste Analyse*, in: *Journal für Sozialforschung 3/1986* (Gehmacher/Birk/Ogris, 1986b)

Gehmacher, Ernst/Birk, Franz/Ogris, Günther, *Nicht Wende, sondern Warnung. Erste Ergebnisse der Wahlanalyse 1986*, in: *Zukunft* (Dezember) 1986 (Gehmacher/Birk/Ogris, 1986c)

Gehmacher, Ernst/Birk, Franz/Ogris, Günther, *Das Wahljahr 1986: Welche Theorien stimmen*, in: *Journal für Sozialforschung 2/1987* (Gehmacher/Birk/Ogris, 1987)

Haerpfer, Christian, *Electoral Volatility in Austria, 1945-1983*, in: Crewe, Ivor/Denver, David (eds.): *Electoral Change in Western Democracies. Patterns and Sources of Electoral Volatility*, London/Sidney 1985 (Haerpfer, 1985)

Haerpfer, Christian, *Gesellschaft, Wählerverhalten und Parteiensystem. Wahlverhalten in Österreich, der BRD, Belgien und Großbritannien 1974-1987* (Haerpfer, 1987)

Plasser, Fritz et al., *Die Nationalratswahl 1986—Analyse und politische Konsequenzen*, in: *Österreichische Monatshefte* (Dezember) 1986 (Plasser, 1986)

Plasser, Fritz/Ulram, Peter A., *Der reaktive Wähler. Zur Analyse der Nationalratswahl 1986*, in: *Journal für Sozialforschung 2/1987* (Plasser/Ulram, 1987)

Traar, Kurt/Birk, Franz, *Der durchleuchtete Wähler—in den achtziger Jahren*, in: *Journal für Sozialforschung 1/1987* (Traar/Birk, 1987)

6

Factors of Voting Behavior
Why Do Austrian Voters Vote the Way They Do?

KURT TRAAR and FRANZ BIRK

1. Changes in structures and values alter the political landscape in Austria

In election times the citizen has to decide between political parties and candidates competing for seats. Voting in favor of a party does, however, not depend on just one factor of influence, but behind this decision complex patterns of mutually influencing factors are very often concealed. These can be psychological components just as much as rational decisions, or the influence of social structures.

In order to explain voting intentions, frequently two conflicting theories are employed: the voter embedded in social and economic structures versus the voter making the voting decision with regard to political issues (competence and efficiency of the parties).

The first theory offers a sociologically oriented explanation of voting behavior. On the ideological level the political parties reflect the interests of the classes they represent. This theory does, however, not suggest that group membership in a social class is the only factor that influences the voting decision; it rather represents the climate in which the voting decision is shaped.

The influence of "class-voting," i.e. the social structure, on voting behavior has become less important. In an empirically oriented study Christian Haerpfer has shown that in Austria it is increasingly more difficult to explain voting behavior by socio-cultural factors (membership in a social class, regional factor, and religious ties). While in 1969 34% of the voting behavior could still be explained by social structure, in 1972 this figure dropped to 30% and did not exceed 19% in 1977.

A. Marsh and M. Kaase arrived at similar results in their analyses of various Western European countries. Even when demographic factors were additionally taken into consideration, only 12 and 23 percent of the variance (R2) in the voting behavior could be explained.

The second theoretical approach, completely contrary to the first, rather socially deterministic one (primarily Paul Lazarsfeld who in his works draws on Simmel), stems fom A. Downs. He argues the hypothesis of the "rational" voter. Similar to consumer behavior the voter makes his voting decision by orienting himself on real or imagined needs and supports with his vote the campaigning group which shows the stongest likelihood of fulfilling these needs.

The prerequisite for such "rational" voting behavior is the dissolution of political camps.

The development of the overall social system in this direction is supported by two factors:

— the decline of political camps due to structural change:
   Between 1969 and 1985 the working-class decreased by seven percent; the group of self-employed people—predominantly farmers—also shrunk by six percent, while the middle-class increased by 13 percent. In the time period surveyed the decrease in the camp of the workers (the numer of people employed in industry alone has since 1973 decreased by approximately 100,000 people) led to a decline of votes for the SPÖ to the extent of 5.4 percent. This loss with regard to the working class is contrasted with an increase regarding votes from the new middle-class of only 3.6%.
   Without taking topical political events into consideration, the structural change alone which has taken place within the last fifteen years has effected SPÖ losses to the extent of 2 percent. Something that in this context could console the social democrats is the fact that the ÖVP had to face an equally high decrease of its traditional voters (decline of the group of self-employed people).
   This development, unfavorable for social democracy, is also expressed by J. Fourastie's well-known formula: 10% in the primary sector, 10% in the secondary sector and 80% in the service sector. At this point of time (survey: census of 1981) the proportion of primary, secondary, and tertiary sector is 1:4:5.
   Even if Fourastie's forecast shows only a trend, it still points in the direction of a further, quite considerable reduction in the sphere of production.

— decrease of camp ties:
   SPÖ losses among its own traditional voters, the workers, cannot merely be explained away by possible short-term discontent with the Socialist

party. Behind this fact one can also find long-term processes regarding voting opinion—a basic loosening of affective party ties. The SPÖ is therefore confronted by double strain in its own camp. On the one hand, there is a shrinkage of the working-class due to structural change, and on the other hand party ties become progressively looser. At this point the SPÖ is, however, unable to gain a stronger foothold among the new middle-class.

The following table, which also includes the proportion of SPÖ and ÖVP voters in other occupational groups, serves to illustrate these considerations.

Table 6.1
Changes in voting intention in favor of the SPÖ in the next National Council election in temporal comparison (in %)

Legislative period	Traditional SPÖ-voters		Middle-class		People with a distance to the SPÖ	
	1	2	3	4	5	6
1971-1975	64	60	40	46	17	8
1975-1979	65	59	42	46	18	10
1979-1983	62	60	40	46	18	11
1983 onwards	55	53	35	42	14	9

(1 = skilled worker, 2 = unskilled worker, 3 = white-collar worker, 4 = civil servant, 5 = freelancer/self-employed person, 6 = farmer)
Source: Continuous IFES surveys for the years 1971-1986, average number of interviewees: 2000 people

The dissolution of political camp mentality, a fact which can be proved, also leads to a weakening of ties and trust in bodies which represent specific interests (for instance a decrease in the degree of labor union organization).

From a sociological point of view such a development causes the drifting apart of individual groups in society, even among the working-class. For instance, new lines of conflict between the new middle-class and the workers, but also between employed people and those on the social fringe, i.e. the unemployed, can be assumed to exist. The same situation exists between blue and white-collar workers, as Daniel Bell already in 1973 established for the American society.

Structural change in society also leads to new needs and to their re-classification in terms of importance, to new political movements, and to the wish for new representatives and institutions claiming to react better to these overall changes than the established institutions.

For broad parts of the Austrian population it can be shown that hedonistic values in the sphere of environmentalism and health have augmented values referring to materialism and security (job security, regular income, law and order). In the short time span between 1979 and 1986, since research on post-materialism has also been conducted in Austria, the number of materialists has decreased from 38 to 10 percent.

This shift was predominantly effected in the sphere of environmental protection—the pursuit of both interests regarding material wealth, security, and environmental protection as post-materialistic objective is no longer seen to be a contradiction, but rather as an augmentation.

This is exemplified by the fact that 63% of the people surveyed who constitute this mixed type—no pure post-materialists and also no pure materialists (in total 82% of all elegible voters)—indicated environmental protection and at the same time materialistic aims as being important goals in their lives.

In the meanwhile the number of post-materialists has practically not changed: 5% in 1979 and 6% in 1986. This means that younger, post-materialistically oriented people abandon this attitude once they get older.

It contradicts Ingelhart's hypothesis of socialization when the group of post-materialists does not grow or when the age groups affiliated with post-materialism disappear in the course of time.

According to Ingelhardt, the best-known proponent of this theory, post-industrial value change is based on three central hypotheses: first of all scarcity, secondly the assumption of a hierarchy of needs, and the hypothesis of socialization.

The hypothesis of scarcity, based on Maslow's theory of motivation, argues that the utility of a good is indirectly proportional to the possibility of attaining this good—in economics this is known as the theory of marginal utility. The individual utility of a good decreases; the person questioned strives to attain the next good, which, according to Maslow, is embedded in a hierarchy of needs—ranging from material to idealistic-aesthetic ones. When one combines the hypothesis of scarcity and the hierarchy of needs with the hypothesis of socialization (the value orientation arrived at in one's youth is not given up in the course of a lifetime), a complete theory of value change manifests itself in three typical forms, materialists, mixed type, and post-materialists.

For the majority of the Austrian population the impact of generation-specific factors on post-materialism is less influential than factors depending on the life-cycle. The latter influence, however, disappears in the course of a lifetime.

For people with a higher educational level, however, such a generation-specific socialization can be shown to exist, even if in modified form. The proponents of an often alternative culture are primarily the young members of the educational elite—especially when they are both young and live in the city.

For instance, an IFES study conducted in 1985 shows that the proportion of post-materialists among interviewed teachers is almost five times higher than the average of the Austrian population, and almost two times higher than that of people with a higher educational level. The same tendency is confirmed by results regarding journalists, also investigated in this study.

Table 6.2[1]
Changes of voting intention in favor of the ÖVP for the next National Council election in temporal comparison (in %)

Legislative period	People with a distance to the ÖVP		Middle-class		Traditional ÖVP-voters	
1971-1975	16	20	32	31	51	72
1975-1979	20	25	38	36	58	75
1979-1983	20	22	35	33	56	73
from 1983 onwards	23	26	36	33	58	73

(1 = skilled worker, 2 = unskilled worker, 3 = white-collar worker, 4 = civil servant, 5 = professional/self-employed, 6 = farmer)
Source: continuous IFES surveys from 1971-1986, on the average N = 2,000

Table 6.3
Distribution of the three types—post-materialists, mixed type, materialists—among the various age groups for 1979 and 1986

(in %)						Age groups							
	16-21 Years		22-29 Years		30-39 Years		40-49 Years		50-59 Years		60 and older Years		total
	79	86	79	86	79	86	79	86	79	86	79	86	79 86
Post-materialists	10	5	9	12	7	8	4	6	4	2	4	3	5	6
Mixed type	68	82	57	81	57	77	55	85	54	90	45	80	51	82
Materialists	22	8	34	6	37	15	41	7	43	7	51	13	38	10

Sources:
IFES survey 1979, N = 1,479
IFES survey 1986, N = 1,809

2. Voter model: Which factors influence voting behavior?

The object of the following section is to describe factors that influence voting behavior.

The goal in this case was to develop a model of voting behavior. This should then answer the question as to how strongly individual factors such as affiliation with a political camp, value and issue orientation, and affective party ties influence a person's voting behavior.

However, the results of such a model analysis are not to be interpreted as unchangable and absolute; they should rather be regarded as hypotheses. The need for relativizing the statements results not only from the data that form the basis of this analysis—a single survey in 1986 with 1,809 eligible voters in the whole of Austria—but also from the immanent character of such a model analysis. Models are supposed to reflect a section of reality. It is true that such a claim is easily formulated on a theoretical basis, but it can only be corroborated empirically when one uses gross, often inadmissable simplifications.

The problem for this model analysis too was to determine the factors relevant for voting behavior, to recast them in the form of questions, and to establish their empirical significance (in %) by means of an opinion poll.

The selection of the voting factors followed the two voting theories sketched above, which are based on social and rational parameters.

Of course, the limitation to voting factors that are founded on social and rational parameters presents a gross simplification—whether this is admissable or not will be shown by the results of the model analysis.

The voting model did not take approaches into account that are biologically-motivationally based. These dimensions of the personality of a human being (for instance, whether extroverted or introverted) certainly do exert an influence on voting behavior. They seem, however, to be of an indirect nature and part of other voting factors such as affective party ties, or issue and value orientation.

It was also assumed that socio-demographic factors such as age, sex, and the level of school educational indirectly influence voting behavior. Demoscopic investigations frequently employ exactly these "objective" items in order to explain political attitudes. Here it is often overlooked that such factors are not necessarily causally connected with political attitudes, but that much more complex processes lie hidden behind them. For instance, two questions have to be answered regarding the correlation between age and political attitude: Are there, for example, specific attitudinal structures which are typical of a certain phase in a life cycle? And how strong is the influence of generation-specific socialization (basic political attitudes adopted in one's youth are preserved into one's old age)? However, it is very hard to empirically measure the concrete influence of generation-specific socialization on voting behavior, because it cannot clearly be isolated from influences that are dependent on the life-cycle.

An attempt in this direction is, however, the combination of the individual age groups into homogenous age groups based on politically decisive time periods in the youth of elegible voters. This approach reveals that the SPÖ is strongly represented among those age groups which were politically formed in the inter-war years and in the period of reconstruction after 1945. Then the years of Socialist governments since 1970 gave rise to opposition against the SPÖ.

The assumption of a modified generation-specific socialization with regard to politics is supported by the fact that the people today between 60 and 73-years-old who experienced their period of political socialization between 1931 and 1945 are still today more strongly oriented toward German nationalism and vote for the FPÖ (four percent declared FPÖ-voters in contrast to two percent for the federal average—date of survey: prior to the 1986 National Council election).

Table 6.4
Voting intentions of eligible voters with college degrees for the National Council election

Basis: all eligible voters

(in %)	SPÖ	ÖVP	FPÖ	VGÖ/ALÖ
Age groups				
- 24 years	28	46	3	13
25-30 years	17	35	1	27
31-40 years	20	44	2	16
41-50 years	15	50	3	10
51-60 years	20	46	1	10
60 years and older	12	50	7	5
Eligible voters with college degrees				
Total	17	46	3	13

Source: IFES cross sectional analyses of the years 1984 and 1985 (1,148 out of 38,952 interviewed eligible voters)

The voting model also took into account factors effective on a long, intermediate, and short-term basis.

Short description of the voting factors:
Long-term factors

1. Social origin, socialization, and milieu
    This complex of questions—empirically examined for Austrian election research—combined the most important social determinants of voting behavior: regional influence regarding the question of the party-political position of the governor in the state of the interviewed eligible voter, size and economic structure of the interviewee's location of residence—whether rural community, small city, industrial city, or big city—, as well as the social class and party-political orientation of his parents and the occupation of the head of the household. Also included were questions about influential political events in the interviewee's youth and his current communicative environment.

2. Basic socio-economic interests
    The current approach still reflects a strongly deterministic point of view with regard to voting behavior in which parties are postulated to be institutionalized forms of certain interests, namely those of groups, strata, or classes. In this case parties are mere representatives of group interests:
    The SPÖ is regarded as a genuine representative of worker interests, i.e. a party guaranteeing job security, while the ÖVP is seen to represent the interests of self-employed people.

3.-5. Value orientation
    In the last years the tendency has clearly developed to explain voting behavior by drawing on more basic attitudes which can no longer simply be interpreted as reflecting objective group or "class-interests" (ideologies). It is true that value orientation has shown to be a good indicator for voting behavior; its scope, however, is enormous: It ranges from values that refer to society as a whole (in this context one should recall the discussion of Ingelhardt's theories about post-materialism, a discussion which has not yet been finished) to the dimensions of personality. What makes the situation even more difficult is the problem of how these values can be operationalized for demoscopic surveys—a problem that, of course, does not exist with regard to socio-economic indicators.

    In our model analysis three value dimensions were taken into account:

    — acceptance of values regarding society as a whole analogous to the current discussion of value change;
    — categories of a voter's aims in life—job, spare time, and family;
    — the way in which the interviewee describes his own personality.

Intermediate and short-term factors
In addition to these factors, which influence voting behavior on a long-term basis, other factors, of an intermediate and short-term nature, are of importance:

6. Issue orientation
During election times the voter also forms his opinion about current political issues. These issues also include certain topical events, such as scandals, which influence voting behavior and/or voting intention. The survey itself differentiated between "position-issues" (topical questions where the various political parties assume different positions) and "valence-issues" (the parties have the same position, e.g. with regard to job-security, but offer different solutions). The first type of issues requires the voter's concrete knowledge about the individual questions, while the second asks him to decide whom he would rather trust to present a solution. "Valence-issues," such as job-security, environmental protection, and political morals, are not a question of knowledge but one of trust.

7. Image of the parties and candidates (party and candidate orientation)
The voters attribute certain qualities and characteristics to parties and politicians. This is the basis of the subsequent evaluation of political information. The image of parties and politicians can be established as a relatively stable pattern, which is very often changed only hesitantly. Frequently, the image of a party is personified by its top candidate.

8. Selected indicators of political behavior
It can be assumed that there are certain predispositions in political behavior which form preferences regarding the support of a campaigning party—for instance above-average interest in political events, the tendency to be an opinion leader in political discussions, or flexibility in one's political behavior (party shifters) lead to a voting decision in favor of protest parties.

3. Discussion of the results of the model analysis

As we know from numerous empirical studies, the voting factors described in the preceding pages influence voting behavior. This, however, raises the question of possible overlaps: Camp affiliation influences a voter's personal aims in life and also his value orientation, which in turn affect issue orientation and party ties—and all together play a more or less strong role in the voting decision.

The object of this model analysis was to describe these causal relationships on the basis of a closed model of voting behavior—and to determine how much they contribute, without any influence from other factors, to the explanation of voting behavior.[2]

(See graph 6.1: Factors of voting behavior, following the tables)

We want to examine how strong the explanatory power of the individual voting factors on voting behavior is. Beforehand, however, the example of voting decisions in favor of the SPÖ will be used to describe how the individual voting factors are causally interrelated, in order to illustrate the complex web of relationships governing voting decisions.[3]

The decision in favor of the SPÖ is to a high degree influenced by the social origin and social milieu of a voter (voting factor 1)—to exactly which degree will be discussed farther below.

Two of the variables which were included in this block of the model (regional influence, occupation of the voter and his parents, political socialization in his youth, the parents' political camp and the voter's communicative environment) influence the voting decision to a high degree:

a)   the political camp of the voter's parents, if they are affiliated with the SPÖ. This naturally applies also—with changed parameters—to a voting decision in favor of the ÖVP.

b)   the voter's communicative environment; discussions with fellow workers, family, and friends contribute to the shaping of the voting decision: discussion partners with Socialist orientation exert an influence in favor of the SPÖ, those oriented toward the ÖVP in favor of the ÖVP, and Green-Alternatives for the Greens.

The job milieu of the voter—for the SPÖ voter model it was the job of a blue collar worker ("objective class membership")—influences the voting behavior; compared to the two other social determinants, however, its direct influence is insignificant (voting factor 2). Concretely, this means that a worker does not necessarily vote for the SPÖ because it is the party representing the workers but because he comes from a socialist home (traditional reasons) and/or because his environment of family, job (predominantly!) and friends shows a socialist orientation.

The social determinants of voting factor 1 strengthen the opinion that the SPÖ is a workers' party (voting factor 2); they are also the reason for the attitude that the SPÖ is the one political group that can guarantee the realization of their—material—aims in life (voting factor 5); they influence party ties (voting factor 7), and ultimately a voting decision in favor of the SPÖ.

Another important complex of causes and effects derives from the voter's attitude toward his personal aims in life and their realization through the parties (voting factor 5): In this case satisfaction with the SPÖ leads to a high degree of civic orientation (acceptance of the established parties and the federal government) (voting factor 4), to a high degree of satisfaction with the federal government's day-to-day political work (voting factor 6), to strong party ties (voting factor 7), and to support of the SPÖ in elections.

The influence of values concerning the social system as a whole (voting factor 4) on voting behavior and also on the other voting factors is not linear, but highly contradictory. This is connected with the determination of value dimensions. Yet, values concerning the social system on the whole, such as a high degree of civic orientation, a small degree of pessimism regarding the future, and also a small degree of religiousness, are not only causally connected with the decision for the SPÖ, they also influence issue orientation (satisfaction with the work of the government), and the affective ties to the SPÖ.

The following table with the correlation coefficients between value dimensions and voting behavior should illustrate how the individual value dimensions combined in this model can influence voting behavior. Among other things this table shows that there is a positive correlation between strong religiousness and voting for the ÖVP, a negative one, however, for a decision in favor of the SPÖ. A high degree of civic orientation (with regard to the federal governement and also to the ÖVP as opposition party—date of survey: May 1986) leads to votes for the SPÖ and also for the ÖVP. Pessimism regarding the future and voting for the Greens are also closely connected, whereas optimistic attitudes can be found among SPÖ-voters. There is a statistic correlation between a strong tendency to believe in authority and voting behavior; it is, however, not very significant: positive with regard to ÖVP votes and negative regarding the intention to vote for Green-Alternative groupings.

Yet, according to this model analysis, one cannot say that during the presidential elections in May and June 1986 people with a strong tendency to believe in authority voted for the ÖVP candidate Dr. Kurt Waldheim because of this tendency. Apart from minor deviations, the voters' support for Dr. Waldheim can be explained by exactly the same voting factors (internal political issues) that in general also influence a decision for the ÖVP. (see table 6.5)

Toward the end of this analysis the following question will of course also be answered: To which degree can such an average voting decision be explained by the voting factors included in this model analysis, and how strong were the individual factors?

The voting decision of an average ÖVP and SPÖ voter is well described by the model of voting factors, as presented above—46 and 58 percent of explained variance.

A vote for the SPÖ or also one for the ÖVP primarily depends on the answer to the question whether or not one believes that the respective party can guarantee the realization of material aims in life (interests).

Compared to this, social voting factors are rather unimportant: They explain 11 percent of a pro-SPÖ decision (taking third place after party ties) and 12 percent of a decision in favor of the ÖVP.

Value orientation can explain four and six percent of a possible decision for one of the two major parties.

Issue orientation influences voting behavior only to a minor degree: Content or discontent with the achievements of the SPÖ in government is not really an independent voting factor but is controlled by other factors, such as social determinants, value orientation, and party ties.

Table 6.5
Generation-specific influence on voting behavior (in %)

AGE	Time period of political socialization in the interviewee's youth	Voting intention regarding the next NCE				Decline of SPÖ votes compared to the last NCE	Structure of age groups 1981-
		SPÖ	ÖVP	FPÖ	VGÖ /ALÖ		
19-23	The difficult 80's	32	37	3	8	first-time voters	9
24-28	Consolidation of the Kreisky era: 1976-1980	36	38	3	7	-4,4	9
29-35	Period of party-political changes and reforms: 1968-1975	35	38	3	6	-5,0	13
36-48	Economic upswing 1956-1967	38	39	3	3	-3,5	23
49-58	Reconstruction 1945-1955	41	37	2	1	-2,5	16
59-66	Period of National Socialism in Austria 1938-1945	40	35	4	2	-1,7	14
61-73	Period of authoritarianism: dissolution of parliament, civil war, Corporate State 1931-1937	41	34	4	1	-2,1	8
74-84	The first years of the First Republic, economic depression and political upheaval 1918-1930	41	34	3	1	-1,0	8
85 and older	Monarchy/WWI before 1918	39	36	1	-	-1,2	1
							100

Source: IFES surveys of the years 1984 and 1985, N=38,950

This does not mean, of course, that political issues are not attributed any importance. On the contrary: any political discussion centers around some kinds of events, most of all those considered negative. Most of the time, however, the voter only pretends to base his voting decision on political issues. Yet, what it is really based on is ties to a certain camp—perhaps not even admitted to—and also on the sympathy for a party and its top candidate, for which rational reasons cannot be given. Judgements about political questions therefore reflect less rational decisions, but are most often only the result of party propaganda and group opinion.

Table 6.6
Significant correlation coefficients between value dimensions and the intended voting behavior with regard to the National Council election and the June 1986 Presidential election in favor of Dr. Kurt Waldheim

	Next National Council election				Dr. Kurt Waldheim in the next Presidential election
	SPÖ	ÖVP	FPÖ	Greens	
Civic orientation					
- with regard to the political system	+0.08				
- with regard to the estalished parties	+0.09	+0.07		-0.18	
- with regard to the federal government	+0.43	-0.26		-0.13	-0.30
Trust in parties and politicians					
- political resignation	-0.06	+0.06	+0.07		
Expectations for the future					
- pessimism regarding the future	-0.13		+0.09	+0.11	
Strong tendency toward believing in authority and coming to terms with the past		+0.10		-0.07	-0.06
Strong religious ties	-0.30	+0.31			+0.29

Source: IFES study, May 1986, N=1,809

Intended voting support of the new Green-Alternative movement cannot satisfactorily be explained by this model (28 percent of Green-Alternative voting behavior).

Table 6.7
Strong discontent with the SPÖ regarding its behavior in certain political issues—classified according to groups of voters (weighted discontent[4])

Voters in the next National Council election (in %) Order of importance	all	SPÖ	ÖVP	FPÖ	VGÖ	ALÖ
1. "clean" politics	40	26	52	32	62	53
2. tax reform/taxes reduction	27	17	37	27	44	42
3. solution of the VOEST crisis	20	13	25	18	36	37
4. construction of new hydro-electric power plant	19	12	24	15	31	53
5. starting up the nuclear power plant at Zwentendorf	18	10	23	12	28	53
6. policy of evironmental protection	16	8	20	18	48	32
7. judicial scandals in the last months	16	10	21	9	26	26
8. job security	14	6	21	27	13	26
9. arms exports	12	8	13	-	32	50
10. wine scandal	12	5	19	21	13	-
11. expulsion of DDr. Nenning from the SPÖ	9	5	9	6	27	37
12. reduction of working hours/35-hour week	6	4	7	9	10	21
13. appointment of Dr. Androsch as chairman of the Credit-anstalt Bankverein	5	4	6	-	10	16

Source: IFES study, May 1986, N = 1,809

According to the voter model, support of one of the Green-Alternative
parties can be explained by three factors which influence voting intention and
by one factor characterizing political behavior:

1.   Green-Alternative groupings primarily stand for the realization of ideal-
     istic-democratic aims of life (more democracy, more honesty and morals
     in politics, and also more protection of the environment—often formu-
     lated in an alternative way). On the other hand, they are not expected to
     guarantee the materialistic-economic interests of the people. This might
     be because people who are secure in terms of their jobs, economic and
     social interests do not attribute as much importance to these aspects any
     more, but perhaps also because people realistically assume that the
     Green-Alternative parties are not at all capable of doing so.
2.   Green-Alternative votes are also controlled to a high degree by social
     determinants: social origin (if one comes from the new middle-class, i.e.
     civil servants, white-collar workers) and communicative environment
     (most friends and acquaintances also regard themselves as belonging to

the Green-Alternative camp), which influences and controls group opinion.
3.   An additional, important voting factor regarding Green votes consists of very general party ties and sympathy, which frequently cannot clearly be accounted for.
4.   Green-voters also differ strongly from supporters of the established parties in their political behavior: They are generally more interested in politics and also more frequently dominate political discussions (opinion leaders). It therefore seems to be the politically and intellectually more flexible people who have become associated with the new Green-Alternative movements.

The voting model we developed completely fails, however, to explain the voting behavior of an average FPÖ voter—only 10 percent explained variance.

In this case the strongest explanatory power can be attributed to the social determinants (if the eligible voter's parents are oriented toward German-nationalism) and the basic economic orientation (the FPÖ as respresentative of self-employed people and professionals, i.e. the old middle-class).

The reason why the voting model totally fails to explain the voting intention of the average FPÖ voter might first of all be connected with the fact that even in a sample of 2,000 people only a handful of declared FPÖ-voters were included, which could lead to considerable sampling fluctuations. Additionally, people who decide to vote for the FPÖ tend to conceal their voting intentions in interviews.

A further feature is that the party ties of an average FPÖ voter are weak. While the two major parties' proportion of traditional voters ranges between 80 and 90%, that of the FPÖ lies only at 50%. From that point of view the FPÖ has to be seen as a party of "the new type"; it has to continually fight for its votes and cannot count on party loyalty. If it did, the party might be in danger of being reduced to political meaninglessness.

The voting factors explain decisions in favor of the FPÖ and also of Green-Alternative parties only to a small degree. Even the voting decision of an average SPÖ-voter is controlled by party ties only up to 58%, that of an ÖVP voter up to 46%. The remainder in the variance regarding votes can be explained by sampling errors, by other factors of party ties unaccounted for within the model, or by totally different influencing factors—for example the effect of mass media.

If one follows this line of argumentation, then it can be predicted that also in Austria there will be a decline in party ties (the minor parties served in this case as pacemakers for the major ones) and an increase in the mobility of the electorate and its external control through mass media.

Table 6.8
Variance explained by the model of voting factors in the form of a table—and
the individual size of these factors (in %)

	SPÖ	ÖVP	FPÖ	The Greens (VGÖ+ALÖ)
Long-term factors				
Social determinants				
1. social origin, socialization, etc.	8	12	7	6
2. basic economic orientation	3	-	2	-
Value orientation				
3. personality traits (basic conservative attitude)	1	-	-	-
4. personal aims in life	20	21	-	11
5. acceptance of values regarding society as a whole	4	6	-	2
Intermediate and short-term factors				
6. issue orientation	2	1	-	-
7. party ties	18	6	1	6
8. selected indicators of political behavior	2	-	-	2
Total of variance as explained by the voting model	58	46	10	28

Source: IFES study, May 1986, N=1,809

Appendix of tables

Correlation between the voting factors included in the model analysis
and the voting intentions of eligible voters (IFES study, May 1986, N=1,809)

Long-term factors
1. Social origin, socialization, and milieu of the voter

Table 6.9
Voting intention for the next National Council election and social determinants
(basis: interviewees who openly declared their voting intention)

(in %)	SPÖ	ÖVP	FPÖ	The Greens (VGÖ/ALÖ)
Regional effect				
ÖVP governor in the respective state	41	51	2	6
SPÖ governor in the respective state	52	38	2	8
interviewee lives in a rural				
community/small city	39	53	3	4
medium-size city	49	40	2	10
big city	52	36	1	11
Occupational status and political camp				
Occupational status of the parents:				
self-employed	24	67	4	5
white-collar worker/civil servant	42	45	2	12
blue-collar worker	67	26	2	6
Occupational position of the head				
of the household:				
self-employed/freelance	10	84	4	3
employees and civil servants in				
middle or higher position	27	52	2	20
other employees and civil servants	69	27	-	4
worker	61	32	2	5
Political camp of the parents:				
(German-)national camp	37	41	15	8
Socialist camp	78	15	1	6
Christian-Socialist camp	14	78	1	6
no camp/don't know	49	41	2	8
Political affiliation of friends,				
fellow-workers				
SPÖ-oriented	72	20	1	6
ÖVP-oriented	16	74	3	7
Green-oriented	20	12	-	68
Political socialization				
confronted with major political				
events in one's youth	44	48	2	6
discussed politics a lot in				
one's youth	44	47	2	7

2. Representation of basic economic interests

Table 6.10
Which party represents the interests of ...?

(in %)	SPÖ	ÖVP
... blue-collar workers	61	9
... white-collar workers	35	27
... civil servants	25	31
... farmers	6	68
... businesspeople	6	60

3. - 5. Value orientation of the voters

3. How interviewees describe their own personality

Table 6.11
Voting intention in the next National Council election and structure of the voters according to their personal basic conservative disposition

(in %)	SPÖ	ÖVP	FPÖ	VGÖ/ALÖ
interviewees with a weak conservative disposition	37	47	3	12
interviewees with an average conservative disposition	45	49	3	4
interviewees with a strong conservative disposition	52	44	*	4

Table 6.12
Structure of the voters according to their conservative disposition

(in %)	SPÖ voters	ÖVP voters	FPÖ voters	VGÖ/ALÖ voters	all eligible voters
weak conservative disposition	29	34	52	100	35
average conservative disposition	41	43	29	-	41
strong conservative disposition	30	24	18	-	24
total	100	100	100	100	100

4. Acceptance of values regarding society as a whole analogous to the current discussion of value change—only referring to the conditions in Austria

4.1. Civic orientation

Table 6.13
Acceptance of the political system, the established parties, and satisfaction with the federal government and the ÖVP as opposition party

	Agreement expressed by 1 and 2 on a five-grade scale
Acceptance of the political system: Question: "Our democratic constitution certainly has its weaknesses; compared, however, with others it still presents the best political order imaginable."	70
Acceptance of the established parties: Question: "A new political party is not really necessary. If one doesn't agree with the government party, one can vote for the opposition."	64
Satisfaction with the federal government and the ÖVP as an opposition party in parliament: Question: "On the whole I am satisfied with the federal government."	31
Question: "On the whole I am satisfied with the behavior of the ÖVP as an opposition party."	31

Table 6.14
Trust in political parties and politicians (graded 1 to 5, in %)

Questions:	Agreement (1+2)	Neutral (3)	Disagreement (4+5)
"People like me don't have any influence on what the government does."	70	17	13
"I think that our politicians don't care much about what the people think."	63	21	14
"The parties only want votes; they are not interested in the opinions of the voters."	58	27	12
"There is no other way than elections to influence what the government does."	57	21	18

Table 6.15
Structure of eligible voters according to the degree of their political resignation (in %)

	all eligible voters	SPÖ voters	ÖVP voters	FPÖ voters	VGÖ voters	ALÖ voters
low degree of political resignation	23	26	20	15	21	41
average degree of political resignation	51	50	51	38	62	58
high degree of political resignation	26	24	29	47	17	-

Table 6.16
The Austrians' expectations of the future (in %)

Question:	Agreement (1+2)	Neutral (3)	Disagreement (4+5)
Pessimism regarding the future: "The future will bring problems that we can't even imagine today."	75	11	5
"We will have full employment again."	21	32	44
Skeptical attitudes regarding technology: "In the future technology and science will find solutions to all the problems."	25	30	41

Table 6.17
Structure of eligible voters according to their degree of pessimism regarding the future (in %)

	all eligible voters	SPÖ voters	ÖVP voters	FPÖ voters	VGÖ voters	ALÖ voters
low degree of pessimism regarding the future	46	56	42	27	33	11
average degree of pessimism regarding the future	33	29	35	27	33	47
high degree of pessimism regarding the future	21	15	22	47	34	42

Table 6.18
The Austrians' tendency to believe in authority (in %)

Question:	Agreement (1+2)	Neutral (3)	Disagreement (4+5)
Desire for social subordination: "Obedience and respect regarding authorities are the most important virtues a child should learn."	71	16	12
Acceptance of the community: "Employers and employees sit in the same boat."	54	21	23
Desire for clear leadership: "If a problem should be solved well, only one person can decide."	33	24	39
Transfiguration of the National Socialist past: "Today the Hitler era is presented in much too negative a light; it also had its good sides."	27	17	49
Antisemitism: "Because of their behavior the Jews were not totally innocent of their own persecution."	30	21	40
"It is certainly true that wrong things were done in the Third Reich, but it is not true that 6 million Jews were killed."	13	13	52

Table 6.19
The Austrians' tendency to believe in authority and their voting intention for the next National Council election (basis: voters who openly declared their voting intention)

(in %)	SPÖ	ÖVP	FPÖ	The Greens (VGÖ/ALÖ)
weak tendency to believe in authority	39	43	1	17
average tendency to believe in authority	48	46	2	4
strong tendency to believe in authority	41	55	2	1

Table 6.20
Acceptance of materialistic-realistic aims and the voting intention for the next National Council election and changes regarding the previous one (basis: voters who openly declared their voting intention)

(in %)	Voting intention for the next NCE				Changes between the previous and the next NCE			
	SPÖ	ÖVP	FPÖ	Greens (VGÖ+ ALÖ)	SPÖ	ÖVP	FPÖ	Greens (VGÖ+ ALÖ)
low degree of acceptance of materialistic values	33	50	1	15	-7	+2	-2	+7
average degree of acceptance of materialistic values	46	47	2	5	-4	+3	-2	+2
high degree of acceptance of materialistic values	50	45	1	4	-6	+4	0	+2

Table 6.21
Strong discontent with the SPÖ regarding its attitudes to certain political issues—classified according to groups of voters (in %)

			Voters in the next National Council election				
		all	SPÖ	ÖVP	FPÖ	VGÖ	ALÖ
1.	"clean" politics	40	26	52	32	62	53
2.	tax reform/taxes reduction	27	17	37	27	44	42
3.	solution of the VOEST crisis	20	13	25	18	36	37
4.	construction of new hydroelectric power plant	19	12	24	15	31	53
5.	starting up the nuclear power plant at Zwentendorf	18	10	23	12	28	53
6.	policy of evironmental protection	16	8	20	18	48	32
7.	judicial scandals in the last months	16	10	21	9	26	26
8.	job security	14	6	21	27	13	26
9.	arms exports	12	8	13	-	32	50
10.	wine scandal	12	5	19	21	13	-
11.	expulsion of DDr. Nenning from the SPÖ	9	5	9	6	27	37
12.	reduction of working hours/ 35-hour week	6	4	7	9	10	21
13.	appointment of Dr. Androsch as chairman of the Creditanstalt Bankverein	5	4	6	-	10	16

Table 6.22
Voting behavior of interviewed eligible voters in the next National Council election who give high grades of sympathy (+5, +4, +3 on a scale of +/- 5,0) to SPÖ, ÖVP, and FPÖ and their top candidates (in %)

	Proportion of inter-viewees who gave such high positive grades	Voting intention for the next National Council election			
		SPÖ	ÖVP	FPÖ	The Greens (VGÖ/ALÖ)
Socialist Party of Austria (SPÖ)					
... for the party	36	86	10	2	2
... for the top candidate	35	85	11	2	2
Austrian People's Party (ÖVP)					
... for the party	28	26	72	2	1
... for the top candidate	26	15	81	1	2
Austrian Freedom Party (FPÖ)					
... for the party	9	59	33	7	1
... for the top candidate	15	81	15	4	-
The new "Green-Alternative" parties					
... for the VGÖ	9	33	40	4	25
... for the ALÖ	5	33	30	3	35

Table 6.23
Voting intention for the next National Council election (basis: voters who openly declared their voting intention)

(in %)	SPÖ	ÖVP	FPÖ	VGÖ+ALÖ
Traditional voters (eligible voters who always voted for the same party in the last elections)	51	45	2	2
Voters who have already clearly decided (interviewees who already know exactly which party the are going to vote for in the next National Council election)	45	47	2	6
eligible voters with a high degree of interest in politics	42	47	2	9
interested readers of the political articles in daily newspapers and perio-dicals (very often or, in the case of daily newspapers, almost every day)	42	46	3	9
Opinion makers:				
* tried to convince somebody with regard to politics	41	41	3	15
* was recently asked for political advice	35	44	2	16

Graph 6.1: Factors of voting behavior

LONG-TERM VOTING FACTORS

SOCIAL DETERMINANTS

1. Social origin, socialization, and milieu of the voter
2. Representation of basic economic interests
3. Interviewee's assessment of his own personality traits (basic conservative attitude)
4. Acceptance of values regarding society as a whole

VALUE ORIENTATION

 * civic orientation
 * trust in political parties and politicians
 * expectations for the future
 * belief in authority and coming to terms with the past

5. Voter's personal aims in life - and their realization through the political parties
6. Issue orientation
7. Affective party ties (image of parties and their candidates)
8. Selected indicators of political behavior (included were: voting behavior of traditional and shifting voters, interest in politics, and opinion makers)

INTERMEDIATE AND SHORT-TERM VOTING FACTORS

VOTING INTENTION/ VOTING BEHAVIOR

Notes

1. The individual types were determined through the following question: "Here is a number of aims which people say our country should try to achieve. Maybe in one way or another all of theses aims are important for all of us; but which are the three most important ones for you?" The interviewee was given a list of the following aims: "economic growth," "preservation of strong national defenses," "preservation of a stable economy," and "fighting against crime" as materialistic aims and "more influence on decisions at the work place and concerning the community," "preserving the landscape and making the cities more attractive," "development in the direction of a more friendly and less impersonal society," and "development of a society in which ideas are more important than money."

Frequency of stating (post-)materialistic aims (in %)	post-materialistic	materialistic
three	6	10
aims		
two	35	47
one	47	35
aim		
none	13	8

Interviewees stating only post-materialistic aims (three or four) were registered as post-materialists. The same method applies to materialists. Interviewees with post-materialistic and materialistic aims were registered as a mixed type.

2. The chosen method was that of a path analysis, following the PLS (partial least squares) approach developed by WOLD in 1979 and extended by Lothmüller from the Hochschule der Bundeswehr in Munich.

This path model consists of 53 questions (manifest variables) and—behind them—eight latent variables, here also called voting factors.

The model used here is a combination of factor and path analysis: In a factor analysis the relationship between the individual questions and their respective latent variable, e.g. the social voting factor, value attitude, or issue orientation is determined; the path model proper analyzes the connection between the latent variables (voting factors).

The estimate parameters are, in contrast to LISREL (JÖRESKOG), not calculated according to the maximum-likelihood method, but according to the partial least squares method.

The prerequisite for the calculation was, however, the development of a voting model: the 53 questions included in the voting model were subdivided into blocks (eight latent variables), which were supposed to fulfil the requirements of a fully recursive model. The estimation of the parameters then resulted in the partial path coefficients, explaining the individual influence of each voting factor on voting behavior.

In a sample of 2,000 interviewees path coefficients of 0.06 and higher can be regarded as highly significant (99%) and no longer as random results.

The percentage to which a voting decision is explained by a certain voting factor is calculated by a simple multiplication of these path coefficients with the corresponding correlation coefficients.

The sum of the variance proportions for the individual voting factors results in a dimension figure which expresses the percentage of voting decisions explained by our voting model. For instance, if know from our path analysis that our model explains 58% of the variance of a voting decision in favor of the SPÖ, then this means that almost 60% of a pro-SPÖ vote have been explained. The remaining 40% can be attributed to sampling problems, other voting factors, or to random decisions.

3. The individual correlation between the examined voting factors und voting intentions can be found in a table in the appendix.

4. This table also refers to the importance of individual issues. This is because the dissatisfaction with an issue personally considered unimportant cannot be compared with one referring to an important question. The figures above therefore show the proportion of those interviewees who consider a political issue as personally important and in this respect are dissatisfied with the behavior of the SPÖ.

Bibliography

Bartl, Peter/Unverdorben, Karl/Lohmüller, Jan-Bernd, *Soziale Probleme im Grundwehrdienst. Eine Pfadanalyse zu Alkohol- und Suicidproblemen*, Forschungsbericht, Fachbereich Pädagogik der Hochschule der Bundeswehr in München 1981 (Bartl/Unverdorben/Lohmüller, 1981)

Berger, Herbert/Traar, Kurt, *Grundlegende Faktoren des Wahlverhaltens*, in: *ÖZP 3/1983* (Berger/Traar, 1983)

Blecha, Karl/Gmoser, Rupert/Kienzl, Heinz, *Der durchleuchtete Wähler. Beiträge zur politischen Soziologie in Österreich*, Wien 1964 (Blecha/Gmoser/Kienzl, 1964)

Bobek, H./Hofmayer, A., *Gliederung Österreichs in wirtschaftliche Strukturgebiete*, in: Kommission für Raumforschung der österreichischen Akademie der Wissenschaften (Hg.): *Beiträge zur Regionalforschung*, Band 3, Wien 1981 (Bobek/Hofmayer, 1981)

Bodzenta, Erich/Seidel, Hans/Stiglbauer, Karl, *Österreich im Wandel, Gesellschaft, Wirtschaft, Raum*, Wien/New York 1985 (Bodzenta/Seidel/Stiglbauer, 1985)

Bürklin, Wilhelm P., *Grüne Politik, Ideologische Zyklen, Wähler und Parteiensystem*, Opladen 1984 (Bürklin, 1984)

Capra, Fritjof/Spretnak, Charlene, *Green Politics. The Global Promise*, New York 1984 (Capra/Spretnak, 1984)

Danneberg, Robert, *Die Wiener Nationalratswahlen am 9. November 1930 im Lichte der Zahlen*, entnommen aus der Monatszeitschrift „Der Kampf" 1931 (Danneberg, 1931)

Fabris, Heinz/Luger, Kurt, *Das politische Starsystem Österreichs*, in: *ÖZP 4/1981* (Fabris/Luger, 1981)

Gehmacher, Ernst, *Faktoren des Wählerverhaltens*, in: Heinz Fischer (Hg.), *Das politische System Österreichs*, Wien 1977 (Gehmacher, 1977)

Müller, Wolfgang C., *Parteien zwischen Öffentlichkeitsarbeit und Medienzwängen*, in: Peter Gerlich/Wolfgang C. Müller (Hg.), *Zwischen Koalition und Konkurrenz*, Wien 1983 (Müller, 1983)

Noelle-Neumann, Elisabeth, *Die Schweigespirale*, München 1980 (Noelle-Neumann, 1980)

Norpoth, Helmut, *Wählerverhalten in der Bundesrepublik*, Arbeitsbücher zur sozialwissenschaftlichen Methodenlehre, Frankfurt/New York 1980 (Norpoth, 1980)

Nowotny, Thomas, *Bleibende Werte—verblichene Dogmen. Die Zukunft gehört der Sozialdemokratie*, Wien/Köln/Graz 1985 (Nowotny, 1985)

Ofner, Günther, *Wahlkampf und Parteiorganisation*, in: Fritz Plasser/Peter A. Ulram/Manfried Welan (Hg.), *Demokratierituale*, Wien 1985 (Ofner, 1985)

Plasser, Fritz, *Elektronische Politik und politische Technostruktur reifer Industriegesellschaften*, in: Fritz Plasser/Peter A. Ulram/Manfried Welan (Hg.), *Demokratierituale*, Wien 1985 (Plasser, 1985)

Plasser, Fritz, *Das österreichische Parteiensystem zwischen Erosion und Innovation. Eine empirische Langzeitstudie*, in: Pelinka, Anton/Plasser, Fritz (Hg.), *Das österreichische Parteiensystem*, Wien 1987 (Plasser, 1987)

Plasser, Fritz/Ulram, Peter A., *Unbehagen im Parteienstaat*, Wien 1982 (Plasser/Ulram, 1982)

Postman, Neil, *Wir amüsieren uns zu Tode. Urteilsbildung im Zeitalter der Unterhaltungsindustrie*, Frankfurt/Main 1985 (Postman, 1985)

Rosenmayr, Leopold, *Politische Beteiligung und Wertwandel in Österreich*, Wien 1980 (Rosenmayr, 1980)

Schwartz, Tony, *Media The Second God*, New York 1983 (Schwartz, 1983)

Schönbach, Klaus, *Werden Wahlen im Fernsehen entschieden?* Überarbeitetes Manuskript der Antrittsvorlesung an der Universität Münster, 1983 (Schönbach, 1983)

Sommer, Franz, *Medien zwischen Macht und Ohnmacht*, in: Fritz Plasser/Peter A. Ulram/Manfried Welan (Hg.), *Demokratierituale*, Wien 1985 (Sommer, 1983)

Taylor, J.P./Johnston, R.J., *Geography of Elections*, Penguin Books, 1979 (Taylor/Johnston, 1979)

Traar, Kurt/Birk, Franz, *Der durchleuchtete Wähler—in den achtziger Jahren*, in: *Journal für Sozialforschung* 1/1987 (Traar/Birk, 1987)

Ucakar, Karl, *Demokratie und Wahlrecht in Österreich*, Wien 1985 (Ucakar, 1985)

Ucakar, Karl/Gerlich, Peter, *Staatsbürger und Volksvertretung*, Salzburg 1981 (Ucakar/Gerlich, 1981)

Ulram, Peter A., *Thematischer Wandel im österreichischen Parteiensystem*, in: Pelinka Anton/Plasser Fritz (Hg.), *Das österreichische Parteiensystem*, Böhlau-Verlag, Wien-Köln-Graz, 1987 (Ulram, 1987)

7

Voting Behavior and the Party System

The Internal Structure of the SPÖ, ÖVP and FPÖ Electorates

ERNST GEHMACHER and CHRISTIAN HAERPFER

1. Introduction

The principal aim of this article is to present an empirical and quantitative analysis of the internal structures of the electorates of the three parliamentary parties, the SPÖ, ÖVP and FPÖ. Above all, breakdowns along sociostructural dimensions will be used to examine the internal structures of the Socialist, Catholic-Conservative and Freedom Party electorates.[1]

Developments over time will also be dealt with.

In addition, several wide-spread theories will be tested.

To what extent is it true that the structural changes with regard to education and occupation which earlier led to a decrease in the number of self-employed and a loss of support for the People's Party are now, during "de-industrialization", mostly affecting the core voters of the SPÖ, the workers? How quickly is the generally accepted "dissolution of the camps" of these two parties actually taking place? What effects will young people's "disillusionment with political parties", a concept often spoken of in Austria, have on voting their behavior?

The data this article is based on is cumulative data from random sample surveys carried out by the Institute for Empirical Social Research (IFES), chiefly in 1982-83. Although medium-term trends in the Austrian electorate are pointed out, this article mainly offers a systematic overview of the internal structures of the constituencies of the three parliamentary parties on the eve of the 1983 National Council elections.[2]

A general overview is presented in the form of a retrospective of the period between 1971 and 1982-83 based on previously published data.[3]

The strongest impression to be gathered from this overview covering more than a decade (which corresponds by and large to the "Kreisky era") is how consistent the Austrian electorate is. The character of the system with its two pronounced "class parties" had, in any case, not changed by 1983.[4]

Table 7.1
Occupation and electorate structure, 1971-1983 (in percent)

| Employed persons only | SPÖ | | | ÖVP | | |
	1971	1976	1982/83	1971	1976	1982/83
self-employed	7	6	8	50	45	35
salaried employees and civil servants	39	42	40	34	34	39
workers	54	52	52	16	21	26

Source: IFES archive

Among the Austrian working population, it still holds true that just a few percentage points more than half the SPÖ voters are workers (and this hasn't changed substantially), and even during 12 years of single-party Socialist governments, this party was not able to attract farmers or the self-employed.

The ÖVP, however, was able to induce voters to cross traditional voting lines—the loss of votes from the self-employed due to structural changes was apparently largely compensated for by an increase in votes from middle-class workers.

More detailed data (which are not, however, available for 1971) confirm Austrians' quite stable voting behavior (see table 7.2).

The increasing educational level of the Austrian electorate is providing the ÖVP with a continually growing number of middle-class voters, and this in turn ensures the continuity of the conservative camp. The SPÖ, on the other hand, is apparently more appealing to those with emancipatory goals (e.g. among women or the lower middle classes). These tendencies, however, no longer represent ideological fixations, but demonstrate, rather, that each party focuses on representing certain interests.

If the data from the years 1982 and 1983 are separated, the trend outlined here toward very stable voting behavior within the major social groups is confirmed for this one-year period as well. It has probably never been accurate to speak of pure "class parties", although the term is common in political rhetoric.

Table 7.2
Social structure of the ÖVP and SPÖ electorates, 1976-1983

| | SPÖ | | | ÖVP | | |
	1976 (5528)	1982 (9049)	1983 (11999)	1976 (2948)	1982 (7519)	1983 (10189)
sex						
men	47	45	46	44	48	45
women	53	55	54	56	52	55
education						
compulsory schooling only	45	42	40	48	38	38
compulsory schooling and apprenticeship technical or commercial school	49	52	52	40	44	46
high school graduates	5	5	6	9	13	11
university education	1	1	2	3	4	5
occupation						
self-employed (farmers, free lances and self-employed)	4	5	6	29	24	23
senior salaried employees and civil servants	2	3	2	4	5	5
other salaried employees and civil servants	22	22	23	18	21	23
workers	30	32	23	18	21	23
not employed						
retired, homemakers and those undergoing schooling or training	42	38	38	35	32	32

Source: IFES archive

The fact that the SPÖ as the "welfare party" is more appealing to retired persons than would correspond to occupational structure conforms with the democratic rules of representation of interests according to criteria which vary between social strata.

If voting behavior does not confirm the concept of "class parties", but instead the electorate rather resembles groups of people with similar economic and social interests, what is the situation with party membership structure?[5]

If it is assumed that the members of a party have a stronger influence on the policies of that party than do its voters, then the character of each of the major parties might be greatly shaped by the class structure of its membership. This would mean the middle classes would be clearly predominant in the SPÖ, and the self-employed would have a disproportionately large influence within the ÖVP–in both cases in relation to membership structure.

Table 7.3
Occupation and voting behavior, 1982-1983

| | SPÖ 1982 (9049) 1983 (11999) | | | | | | ÖVP 1982 (7519) 1983 (10189) | | | | | |
| | men | | women | | | | men | | women | | | |
	1982	1983	1982	1983	1982	1983	1982	1983	1982	1983	1982	1983
employed persons												
farmers	*	1	1	1			8	7	7	7		
self-employed	1	1	1	1	5	5	4	4	3	3	24	23
free lances	*	*	*	*			1	1	*	*		
senior salaried employees	1	1	*	*			3	2	1	*		
					3	2					5	5
senior civil servants	1	*	*	*			1	1	*	*		
other salaried employees	6	6	9	8			5	6	7	8		
					22	23					21	23
other civil servants	5	6	2	3			5	5	4	4		
workers in public service												
Workers	2	2	1	1			1	1	*	*		
skilled workers	10	11	1	1	32	32	6	5	1	1	18	17
unskilled workers	9	9	8	8			6	5	3	4		
housewives	-	-	21	20	21	20	-	-	18	18	18	18
retired persons	8	9	7	8	15	16	6	6	5	5	11	11
schooling or training					2	2					3	3

Source: IFES archive

Evidence supporting this point of view may be found readily in everyday politics. When this situation is examined in more detail, the importance of farming members in the ÖVP, and that of retired persons in the SPÖ becomes clear.

If the retired and civil servants are considered to be those who naturally have the greatest interest in the welfare state (with its large public sector), it becomes apparent that the propensity of public service employees, in particular, to actively participate in politics results in strong representation of the interests of the welfare state system in both major parties.

Table 7.4
Social structure of party membership, SPÖ, ÖVP, 1983

	self-employed and senior salaried employees	salaried employees and civil servants	workers	housewives and retired persons	total
SPÖ (700,000)	5.0	32.0	35.0	28.0	100
in 1000s of members	35	224	245	196	700
% of total membership	3.0	19.5	21.3	17.0	60.9
ÖVP (450,000)	39.0	26.0	17.0	18.0	100
in 1000s of members	176	117	76	81	450
% of total membership	15.3	10.2	6.6	7.0	39.1
voters					
SPÖ	7.0	23.0	32.0	38.0	100
ÖVP	23.0	28.0	17.0	32.0	100

Source: IFES archive

Table 7.5
SPÖ and ÖVP party memberships according to occupation and sex, 1983

employed persons (in percent)	SPÖ				ÖVP			
	men	women	total		men	women	total	
farmers	*	*	*	⎫	17	9	27	⎫
self-employed	1	*	1	⎬ 2	4	1	6	⎬ 34
free lances	*	*	1	⎭	*	*	1	⎭
senior salaried employees	1	*	1	⎫	3	*	3	⎫
				⎬ 3				⎬ 5
senior civil servants	1	*	2	⎭	2	*	2	⎭
other salaried employees	8	7	16	⎫	6	5	12	⎫
				⎬ 32				⎬ 26
other civil servants	12	4	16	⎭	8	6	14	⎭
workers in public service								
workers	4	1	5	⎫	2	*	2	⎫
skilled workers	13	1	15	⎬ 35	6	*	7	⎬ 17
unskilled workers	10	5	15	⎭	6	2	8	⎭
housewives	-	8	8		-	8	8	
retired persons	12	8	20		7	3	10	

Source: IFES archive

Table 7.6
Party membership, occupation and sex

(1 = SPÖ member, 2 = ÖVP member, 3 = both major parties, 4 = ÖVP of party members)							
	men				women		
	1	2	3	4	1	2	3	4
farmers	1	39	40	98	*	22	23	96
self-employed	6	15	21	71	2	4	6	67
free lances	6	8	14	57	5	*	6	83
senior salaried employees	12	13	25	52	6	13	19	68
senior civil servants	23	26	49	53	24	17	41	42
other salaried employees	18	7	25	28	10	5	15	33
other civil servants	31	13	44	30	17	14	31	45
workers in public service								
workers	36	9	45	20	24	6	30	20
skilled workers	19	6	25	24	7	3	10	30
unskilled workers	18	7	25	28	12	3	15	20
housewives	-	-	-	-	6	4	10	40
retired persons	22	8	30	27	14	4	18	22

Source: IFES archive

The internal structure of a "Green-Alternative" camp which began to emerge in 1983 on the occasion of the elections to the National Council will not be analyzed in this article, since in 1982 the question of the political organization of the new social movements was largely unresolved.[6] This made it difficult to describe the internal social structure of one or two Green-Alternative parties on the basis of the data available in 1982, since the lack of organizational stability in these parties made it impossible to clearly establish the voter potential of a–legitimate, so to speak–Green-Alternative party.

Table 7.7
Social class and party preference, 1982

in percent	SPÖ	ÖVP	FPÖ	independent
upper middle class	6	18	19	19
middle class	36	32	37	41
farmers	2	22	10	7
workers	57	28	34	34
Austria	44	29	3	25

The basis for the establishment of these general party preferences was the answer to the question: "In general, which party are you most attracted to?"
Source: IFES archive

If we break down Austrian society according to occupational criteria into four major strata, namely workers (skilled workers, unskilled workers, workers in public service), middle class (low- and medium-level salaried employees, low- and medium-level civil servants), upper middle class[7] (entrepreneurs, tradesmen, senior salaried employees, senior civil servants) and farmers, we can describe the sociostructural representativeness of the Austrian party system as follows: even in the early eighties, the SPÖ can still be called a "worker's party", since 59 percent of Austrian workers demonstrate a clear preference for the Socialist Party. By the same token, the ÖVP can be seen as a "farmer's party", since nearly 70 percent (69%) of farmers have ties to the ÖVP. Whereas there is thus a worker's party and a farmer's party—despite the increasing sociostructural dealignment in the Austrian party system—there is still no party in Austria that would be the "natural" choice of the middle class, although in national elections it does constitute the decisive social stratum.[8]

An interesting situation is that of independent voters—those with no party ties—who, in 1982, constituted approximately 25 percent—or one-fourth—of the Austrian electorate.[9] This group of independent voters which will definitely play an essential role in elections in the eighties has the largest proportion of middle-class voters. A majority of independent voters, namely 60 percent, belong to the cumulative middle class—41 percent to the new middle class and 19 percent to the upper middle class. This group constitutes a predominantly middle-class phenomenon—a fact which has become apparent since this survey with, among other things, the emergence of Green-Alternative parties, most of whose support is derived from the reservoir of independent voters. The proportion of independent voters belonging to the other occupational groups is approximately representative of their size. About one-third of independent voters are workers. The proportion of farmers—seven percent—is relatively low.

2. The Structure of the SPÖ Electorate

The greatest amount of support for the SPÖ comes from the working classes.[10] In 1982, workers constituted 57 percent of persons preferring the SPÖ. A further 42 percent of SPÖ supporters belong to the cumulative middle class, with the Socialists deriving 36 percent of their support from the "new" middle class and 6 percent from the upper middle class. Not surprisingly, the proportion of farmers in the SPÖ electorate hovers around 2 percent. A breakdown according to individual occupational groups (cf. table 7.8) shows that the two largest groups of core SPÖ voters are the unskilled workers (30%) and the skilled workers (21%), immediately followed by the large group of low- and medium-level salaried employees who constitute 21 percent of the Socialist electorate. The fourth-largest occupational group consists of Socialist-oriented low- and medium-level civil servants from whom the SPÖ derives 16 percent of its support. The other occupational groups are not as significant because of their small size. The fifth-largest group in the SPÖ electorate is made up of workers in public service (5%).

Table 7.8
Occupational structure, social class and party preference, 1982

in percent	SPÖ	ÖVP	FPÖ	independent
Upper middle class:				
entrepreneurs	1	1	1	3
tradesmen	2	9	9	9
senior salaried employees	2	5	6	4
senior civil servants	1	3	2	2
Middle class:				
other salaried employees	21	19	24	26
other civil servants	16	13	14	15
Farmers:	2	22	10	7
Workers:				
skilled workers	21	10	15	15
unskilled workers	30	15	16	15
workers in public service				
workers	5	3	4	4

Source: IFES archive

The internal structure of the SPÖ electorate corresponds by and large to the proportion of men and women in the Austrian population (cf. table 7.9). What is remarkable is that male workers (62 percent of SPÖ voters) demonstrate an above-average inclination to vote for the Socialist Party (around 5 percent above the proportion of all workers supporting the SPÖ). It can therefore be assumed that the Socialist Party is significantly more attractive to male workers than it is to female workers. This sex-specific bias is exactly the opposite among middle-class SPÖ voters—the proportion of female SPÖ supporters belonging to the middle class amounts to 41 percent of all female SPÖ voters and is thus distinctly higher than the proportion of middle-class SPÖ supporters which is 36 percent. The Socialist Party therefore seems significantly more attractive to middle-class women than to middle-class men.[11]

Table 7.9
SPÖ voters: sex, age and social class, 1982

in percent	female	male
upper middle class	5	7
middle class	41	30
farmers	3	1
workers	52	62
all SPÖ voters 1982	53	47
Austria 1982	54	46

age	16-25	25-39	40-59	60 and above
upper middle class	5	5	6	4
middle class	39	41	33	31
farmers	1	1	3	4
workers	56	53	59	58
all SPÖ voters 1982	16	28	38	18
Austria 1982	18	29	37	17

Source: IFES archive

If the electorate of the Socialist Party is analyzed in its age structure, we see that, here too, the SPÖ is representative of the Austrian population, although there are minor deviations. In the younger age groups up to 39 years of age, the SPÖ is between one and two percentage points below the proportion for Austria as a whole, whereas it is slightly above the average proportion in the older age groups. It is interesting to analyze the voting behavior of the middle class according to age groups. In the age groups of persons over 40, around one-third of SPÖ supporters belong to the middle class, whereas in the 25-39 year old age group, this proportion is 41 percent. In the 16-25 year old group of SPÖ supporters, 39 percent belong to the middle class. The structural change producing a growing percentage of middle-class voters is apparently being followed by a similar change in the SPÖ electorate.

As for the relationship between educational level and preference for the SPÖ, the following patterns can be perceived (cf. table 7.10): the greatest percentage of SPÖ voters has an intermediate level of education; exactly 50 percent of SPÖ supporters belong to the group of people who have completed compulsory schooling and, in addition, a technical school, an apprenticeship, or a commercial school, and this proportion is 7 percentage points above the Austrian average. A majority of SPÖ supporters with an intermediate level of education—53 percent—are workers, followed by members of the middle class with 42 percent. Members of the middle class having completed an apprenticeship or a technical or commercial school are presumably particularly attached to the SPÖ. Fourty-two percent of those preferring the SPÖ are voters with only compulsory schooling—this is about equal to the Austrian average. Seventy percent of SPÖ voters with only compulsory schooling are workers, and just under one-fourth of them are members of the middle class. Even in 1982, it remains a fact that high-school and university graduates are underrepresented in the SPÖ electorate (see table 7.10).

In an analysis according to income—at least as long as income is within the wide range of normal income taken into account by surveys—the structure of the Socialist Party electorate differs less from the structure of the total Austrian electorate than in an analysis according to education. Such rough measurements certainly do not allow us to say that economic determinants have less influence on a person's political identification than cultural determinants. At least in an analytical study, however, cultural and educational factors must be considered to be at least as important as economic ones.

A territorial breakdown of the SPÖ electorate shows a clear east-west cleavage. For this part of our analysis, the nine federal states were grouped into four regions—east (Vienna, Lower Austria and Burgenland), south (Styria, Carinthia), center (Upper Austria, Salzburg) and west (Tirol, Vorarlberg). The bulk of SPÖ voters live in the eastern region which provides 47 percent of the SPÖ electorate (cf. table 7.10). Exactly one-fourth of SPÖ voters are from Carinthia and Styria, and a further 22 percent of SPÖ support comes from Upper Austria and Salzburg. The remaining 7 percent of SPÖ voters live in Tirol and Vorarlberg.

The proportion of workers in the SPÖ electorates in the southern, central and western regions is around 60 percent. In contrast, this proportion in eastern Austria is just slightly over one-half, namely 52 percent. Directly related to this phenomenon is the fact that members of the middle class represent around 30 percent of the SPÖ electorate in the southern, central and western regions, whereas this proportion is considerably higher in the east, namely 41 percent. This can be interpreted as meaning that the SPÖ is more dependent on core voter groups in the western and southern states, whereas it is already developing strong support among the new middle class in Vienna.[12]

A breakdown of the SPÖ electorate along the urban-rural dimension presents a clear picture—precisely 25 percent of the Socialist electorate lives in Vienna, but this proportion of SPÖ voters from Vienna is just 3 percentage points above the proportion of Viennese in the total Austrian electorate. Similarly, the SPÖ is not dramatically underrepresented in predominantly farming communities with less than 5,000 inhabitants. Whereas, in 1982, approximately 44 percent of all Austrian voters lived in communities of this size, only 38 percent of SPÖ supporters came from these rural areas. On the basis of these data, it can be assumed that as urbanization progresses, the influence of the SPÖ in rural areas will increase.

Table 7.10
SPÖ voters: education, household income and social class, 1982

in percent (4375)	university high school graduates	apprenticeship technical school	compulsory schooling
upper middle class	22	5	3
middle class	68	42	23
farmers	0	1	4
workers	10	53	70
all SPÖ voters 1982	8	50	42
Austria 1982	14	46	40

	stratum A 18,000 schillings or more	stratum B 14,000-17,999 schillings	stratum C 10,000-13,999 schillings	stratum D 9,999 schillings or less
upper middle class	11	3	3	4
middle class	46	46	35	23
farmers	1	1	2	3
workers	42	50	60	71
all SPÖ voters 1982	22	21	27	30
Austria 1982	26	20	26	29

Source: IFES archive

3. The Structure of the ÖVP Electorate

The middle-class base of ÖVP voters provides exactly 50 percent of all ÖVP support, with 32 percent coming from the new middle class, and 18 percent from the upper middle class. At the beginning of the 1980s, the ÖVP can also be called the party of the farmers, since 70 percent of this group of traditional ÖVP voters do prefer this party. The second pillar of support for the ÖVP and the second core group in the party's electorate is thus the group of farmers who constitute 22 percent of all ÖVP voters. The proportion of workers in the ÖVP electorate is 28 percent. The next largest group of ÖVP voters consists of low- and medium-level salaried employees (19%), followed by unskilled workers (15%) and low- and medium-level civil servants (13%). The proportion of skilled workers voting for the ÖVP—10 percent—is the lowest of all three parliamentary parties. Nearly one in ten ÖVP voters is a tradesman (9%). In addition to these major groups in the ÖVP electorate, there are relatively high proportions of senior salaried workers (5%) and senior civil servants (3%). The smallest groups are made up of workers in public service (3%) on the one hand, and entrepreneurs (1%) on the other. An interesting fact is that the percentage of entrepreneurs in the ÖVP electorate is not higher than their proportion of the Austrian population. The only group in which entrepreneurs are overrepresented is the group of independent voters.[13]

Table 7.11
SPÖ voters, size of community, region and social class, 1982

in percent (4375)	Vienna	50,000- 250,000 inhabitants	5,000- 49,000 inhabitants	under 5,000 inhabitants
upper middle class	7	9	6	3
middle class	53	50	34	21
farmers	0	0	1	5
workers	40	41	58	72
all SPÖ voters 1982	25	13	24	38
Austria 1982	22	13	21	44

	East	South	Center	West
upper middle class	6	4	6	8
middle class	41	31	33	31
farmers	2	3	2	1
workers	52	62	59	60
all SPÖ voters 1982	47	25	22	7
Austria 1982	45	23	22	11

Source: IFES archive

The internal structure of the ÖVP electorate corresponds to the ratio of men to women in Austrian society—at least it did so in 1982 (cf. table 7.12). A majority—54%—of ÖVP voters are women (percentage of women in the Austrian population: 54%). This compares to the remaining 46 percent of the party's electorate who are men (percentage of men in the Austrian population: 46%). The lowest sex-specific differential is between female workers (27 percent of ÖVP voters) and male workers (28 percent of ÖVP voters). Slightly more than one in five ÖVP voters is a farmer, with male farmers providing 23 percent of male support for the People's Party, and female farmers and female members of farming families providing 21 percent of female support for this party. With regard to members of the upper middle class with a preference for the ÖVP, men (20%) demonstrate slightly stronger ties to this party than do women (17%). The only social class with a significant sex-specific differential is the middle class. The largest group of female ÖVP voters is made up of middle-class women, 36 percent of whom prefer the People's Party, so this group can justifiably be called a core voter group. The percentage of male ÖVP voters from the middle class, on the other hand, is just 28 percent, a proportion which is about equal to that of workers in the male ÖVP electorate.

In summary, it can be stated that the voting behavior of farming and working class men and women is quite similar; that a slight "male bias" can be ascertained in the upper middle class; and that, with regard to the ÖVP, the voting behavior of middle-class women differs greatly from that of middle-class men—the ÖVP can depend in particular upon support from female middle-class voters.

If the ÖVP electorate is broken down according to age, we see that the age structure of the People's Party corresponds more closely to the age structure of the total Austrian population than does that of the SPÖ (cf. table 7.12). Only among the young—persons under 25—is the proportion of ÖVP voters (16%) around 2 percentage points below this group's proportion of the total population. The largest age group of ÖVP supporters is the 40 to 59 year old group with 38 percent, followed by the group of ÖVP supporters aged 25 to 39 with 29 percent. Both the youngest and the oldest generation—persons 60 and above—provide 16 percent of ÖVP support. Two groups of traditional ÖVP voters, namely farmers and the upper middle class, demonstrate a clear generational differential—the proportion of these groups preferring the ÖVP rises as age increases. Among farmers, this proportion rises from 12 percent of the young generation under 25 to 29 percent of the oldest generation. The same pattern can be perceived in the upper middle class, with its proportion of the ÖVP electorate increasing from 12 percent among the youngest generation to about one in five among persons over 40. Among ÖVP voters from the working class, an interesting phenomenon can be perceived. The largest proportion of ÖVP supporters among young voters are workers (36%). The proportion of workers in the 60 and above age group of the ÖVP electorate, among the traditionally "conservative" workers, so to speak, is also clearly above average. In the two middle age groups, in contrast, workers provide merely one-fourth of the support for the ÖVP. In the two youngest generations of voters under 40, the ÖVP is a middle-class party—40 percent of ÖVP voters in both these age groups are from the middle class, a class which in the medium-term future will play such an important role in elections. The percentage of middle-class voters drops as age increases, and the proportion of middle-class voters in the oldest age group is just 24 percent. In general, it can be stated that as age increases, the ÖVP electorate increasingly reflects the suborganizational structure of the party. Directly related to this socio-demographic development is the fact that the relative membership strength of the individual party suborganizations changes significantly in the younger age groups.

Table 7.12
ÖVP voters, sex, age and social class, 1982

in percent	female	male
upper middle class	17	20
middle class	36	28
farmers	21	23
workers	27	28
all ÖVP voters 1982	54	46
Austria 1982	54	46

age	16-24	25-39	40-59	60 and above
upper middle class	12	17	22	18
middle class	40	40	27	24
farmers	12	18	26	29
workers	36	25	26	29
all ÖVP voters 1982	16	29	38	16
Austria 1982	18	29	37	17

Source: IFES archive

This process has been recognized by the ÖVP in the last few years, and efforts to reform the internal structure of the party must also be seen in the light of the changes in the internal structure of the ÖVP electorate outlined here.[14]

With regard to the relationship between educational level and voting behavior, it can be seen that both high school and university graduates, with a proportion of 17 percent of ÖVP voters, as well as persons with only compulsory schooling (42%) are overrepresented in the ÖVP electorate. The intermediate educational stratum provides 41 percent of ÖVP voters (cf. table 7.13). With regard to this dimension, two clear trends must be distinguished: as educational level rises, the percentage of ÖVP voters from the middle and upper middle classes increases; among ÖVP voters with only compulsory schooling, the proportion belonging to the upper middle class is 8 percent, and this proportion increases to 41 percent ÖVP supporters with high school or university education. The same by no means surprising trend can be perceived in the middle class—its proportion rises from 15 percent of ÖVP supporters with only compulsory education to 53 percent of those with a high school or university education. The reverse relationship exists among farmers and workers: the percentages of both groups decrease as educational level rises. The proportion of farmers drops from 39 percent of ÖVP voters with only compulsory education to 4 percent those with a high school or university education. An analogous trend can be perceived among workers—their proportion decreases from 38 percent of ÖVP supporters with only compulsory education to 2 percent of those in the highest educational stratum. The ÖVP can thus count primarily on support from voters with only compulsory education and from high school and university graduates, whereas support appears to be relatively weak in the intermediate educational stratum.

When we examine the relationship between household income and support for the ÖVP, it becomes apparent that the ÖVP has the characteristics of a "People's Party", since the distribution of support for the party among income groups largely corresponds to Austria as a whole. In general, the electorate of the ÖVP can be considered a reflection of the distribution of income in Austrian society. The only deviation is that of the top income category—stratum A (household income of 18,000 schillings or more)—to which 29 percent of ÖVP voters belong (Austria: 26%), but this group is overrepresented in the ÖVP electorate to a very limited degree—just 3 percent. The next largest income group is stratum D (household income of 9,999 schillings or less) which makes up 28 percent of the ÖVP electorate (Austria: 29%), followed by stratum C (household income of 10,000 to 13,999 schillings) with exactly one-fourth of ÖVP voters (Austria: 26%). A group which is somewhat underrepresented among ÖVP supporters is stratum B (household income of 14,000 to 17,999 schillings)—it provides only 18 percent of the party's electorate (Austria: 20%).

In strata C and D, on the one hand, the ÖVP is the party of farmers and workers, and in strata A and B, on the other, it is the party of the middle class. In the lowest income category, stratum D, three-fourths of ÖVP voters are either workers (40%) or farmers (35%), whereas only one-fourth of them belong to the middle class. In stratum C, the majority of farmers and workers drops from 75 percent to 52 percent—with workers representing 36 percent of this category and farmers 16 percent—whereas the proportion belonging to the middle class increases to 49 percent. In the second highest income category, stratum B, the middle-class character of the ÖVP is clearly visible—47 percent of stratum B belongs to the middle class and 17 percent to the upper middle class. The proportion of workers in this second highest income category amounts to just 28 percent, and the proportion of farmers in this group drops to 9 percent. Finally, in stratum A, the highest income category, the situation is the reverse of that in stratum D. In this highest income category, 73 percent of ÖVP voters are from the cumulative middle class, with 40 percent of them belonging to the new middle class, and 33 percent to the upper middle class. The remaining one-fourth of those in stratum A are from high-income working-class households (19%) or high-income farming households (7%).

Table 7.13
ÖVP voters: education, household income and social class, 1982

in percent (2479)	university high school	apprenticeship technical school	compulsory schooling
upper middle class	41	19	8
middle class	53	41	15
farmers	4	12	39
workers	2	28	38
all ÖVP voters 1982	17	41	42
Austria 1982	14	46	40

	stratum A 18,000 schillings or more	stratum B 14,000-17,999 schillings	stratum C 10,000-13,999 schillings	stratum D 9,999 schillings or less
upper middle class	33	17	9	10
middle class	40	47	40	15
farmers	7	9	16	35
workers	19	28	36	40
all ÖVP voters 1982	29	18	25	28
Austria 1982	26	20	26	29

Source: IFES archive

The relationship between size of community and support for the ÖVP can be considered to be quite close (cf. table 7.14). In all small and medium-sized towns as well as in regional centers in Austria, the percentages of ÖVP voters are below the Austrian averages—in other words, the ÖVP is under-represented in all community sizes between 5,000 and 1.5 million inhabitants. A majority of ÖVP voters, namely 57 percent, are from farming or mixed farming communities with a population of less than 5,000 (Austria: 44%). The second largest group of ÖVP voters, exactly 17 percent of the party's electorate (Austria: 21%), is the group of inhabitants of small and medium-sized towns with populations between 5,000 and 49,000. A further 10 percent of the ÖVP electorate comes from regional centers with populations between 50,000 and 250,000 (Austria: 13%), and just 16% of ÖVP voters live in Vienna (Austria: 22%). If measured along the rural-urban dimension, there-fore, the bastion of ÖVP support is clearly in Austria's farming and mixed farming communities, with less support in urban industrial areas.

With regard to middle-class support for the ÖVP, it can be hypothesized that there is a positive correlation between community size on the one hand and the proportion of ÖVP voters in the middle class on the other. The larger the community, the larger the proportion of the ÖVP electorate be-longing to the middle and upper middle classes. The middle class provides about one-third of ÖVP supporters in farming areas and just under one-half in small and medium-sized towns. In regional centers with a population be-tween 50,000 and 250,000 inhabitants, the proportion from the cumulative middle class increases dramatically to 78 percent, with 47 percent belonging to the middle class and 31 percent to the upper middle class. The character of the ÖVP is most clearly that of a middle-class party in Vienna, where the proportion of the ÖVP electorate belonging to the cumulative middle class is nearly 90 percent (87%). Workers and the minor group of farmers represent a mere 13 percent of ÖVP supporters in Vienna.

A breakdown of the electorate according to territorial distribution shows a clear influence of this factor on the proportion of ÖVP supporters in the population (cf. table 7.14). The farther west we go in Austria, the greater the support for the ÖVP. Forty-two percent of ÖVP voters live in the eastern re-gion (Vienna, Lower Austria, Burgenland) (Austria: 45%), one-fifth (21%) in the southern region (Styria, Carinthia) (Austria: 23%), and one-fifth (21%) in the central region as well (Austria: 22%). The western region is a bastion of support for the ÖVP, since this is where 16% of People's Party voters live (Austria: 11%).

In summary, it can be said that a majority of ÖVP voters in the western and eastern regions belong to the cumulative middle class, whereas in the central and southern regions this class represents merely a plurality of ÖVP supporters.

Table 7.14
ÖVP voters: community size, region and social class, 1982

in percent (2884)	Vienna	50,000-250,000 inhabitants	5,000-49,000 inhabitants	under 5,000 inhabitants
upper middle class	32	31	22	11
middle class	55	47	37	22
farmers	1	3	13	34
workers	12	19	28	33
all ÖVP voters 1982	16	10	17	57
Austria 1982	22	13	21	44

	East	South	Center	West
upper middle class	20	14	13	29
middle class	36	30	30	29
farmers	23	26	25	10
workers	22	31	33	32
all ÖVP voters 1982	42	21	21	16
Austria 1982	45	23	22	11

Source: IFES archive

4. The Structure of the FPÖ Electorate

The proportion of the FPÖ electorate belonging to the cumulative middle class is 56 percent and thus larger than in the ÖVP. This middle-class base consists of the 37 percent of Freedom Party voters who are from the middle class, and the 19 percent from the upper middle class. A further 10 percent of FPÖ voters are farmers, and the proportion of workers in the FPÖ electorate amounts to about one-third (34%). The core group of FPÖ voters is characterized by its heterogeneousness. Farmers appear to be slightly overrepresented in the FPÖ electorate, since their proportion is 10 percent. Tradesmen (9%) and senior salaried employees (6%) are also overrepresented among FPÖ supporters. The proportions of workers in public service (4%), senior civil servants (2%) and entrepreneurs in the FPÖ electorate correspond to their proportions in the Austrian electorate as a whole.[15]

Table 7.15
FPÖ voters: sex, age and party preference, 1982

in percent (N = 291)	male	female
FPÖ voters 1982	51	49
Austria 1982	54	46

age	16-24	25-39	40-59	60 and above
FPÖ voters 1982	17	26	38	19
Austria 1982	18	29	37	17

Source: IFES archive

An analysis of the FPÖ electorate according to the sex of the voters demonstrates that the proportion of male supporters is clearly greater than that of female supporters. During the 1970s, the FPÖ did not change the fact that it tends to be a "male" party. Women make up 51 percent of the Freedom Party electorate, a proportion which is three percentage points below their proportion of the Austrian population. A breakdown of the FPÖ electorate according to age demonstrates that the largest percentage of FPÖ supporters belong to the 40 to 59 year-old age group—38 percent of FPÖ voters fall into this generational group. The 25 to 39 year-old age group represents the second largest group of FPÖ voters, since its proportion is 26 percent. Just under one-fifth of FPÖ supporters (19%) belong to the oldest generation of those over 60, and the youngest generation of those under 25 makes up 17 percent of the Freedom Party electorate. These data offer no empirical basis for stating that the core FPÖ voters are slowly "dying out", a theory which some people support. The younger generation of voters is underrepresented in the FPÖ by around 2 percent, and the proportion of older FPÖ voters is above the Austrian average by about the same amount, so it would be incorrect to say that the age distribution of the FPÖ electorate is dramatically distorted by a greatly overrepresented older generation of FPÖ supporters.

There is a strong relationship between the factor of educational level and the tendency to vote for the FPÖ. The Freedom Party is clearly more attractive to persons with a higher educational level. One in every five FPÖ voters is a high school or university graduate, which means that this proportion in the FPÖ electorate is 6 percentage points above this group's proportion of the Austrian electorate as a whole.

Table 7.16
FPÖ voters: education, household income and party preference, 1982

in percent (N = 291)	university high school	apprenticeship technical school	compulsory schooling
FPÖ voters 1982	20	46	34
Austria 1982	14	46	40

in percent (N = 291)	stratum A 18,000 schillings or more	stratum B 14,000- 17,999- schillings	stratum C 10,000- 13.999 schillings	stratum D 9,999 schillings or less
FPÖ voters 1982	30	20	20	30
Austria 1982	26	20	26	29

Source: IFES archive

Examination of the relationship between household income and support for the FPÖ shows no clear evidence that income influences voting behavior–there is no clear evidence, for example, that the FPÖ is the party of members of high-income middle-class households. It is interesting to note that the FPÖ is overrepresented at both the upper and lower end of the income dimension, whereas the income groups in between are, in part, underrepresented in the FPÖ electorate. Income stratum A, whose proportion of the FPÖ electorate is 30 percent (Austria: 26%), is clearly overrepresented. In exact correspondence with the Austrian average, one in five FPÖ voters belongs to income stratum B, whereas stratum C with a proportion of 20 percent of FPÖ voters is somewhat underrepresented (Austria: 26%). Finally, 30 percent of FPÖ supporters belong to the lowest income stratum (Austria: 29%), with this group presumably consisting mostly of farmers and workers.

Table 7.17
FPÖ voters: community size, region and party preference, 1982

in percent (N = 291)	Vienna	50,000-250,000 inhabitants	5,000-49,000 inhabitants	under 5,000 inhabitants
FPÖ voters 1982	20	16	25	39
Austria 1982	22	13	21	44

	East	South	Center	West
FPÖ voters 1982	31	27	25	17
Austria 1982	45	23	22	11

Source: IFES archive

A breakdown of the Freedom Party electorate along the urban-rural dimension shows a clear relationship between community size and support for the FPÖ. We can classify small and medium-sized towns, on the one hand, and regional centers, on the other, as strongholds of FPÖ support. Exactly one-fourth of FPÖ voters are from small and medium-sized towns with between 5,000 and 49,000 inhabitants (Austria:21%). A further 16 percent of members of the Freedom Party electorate live in regional centers with populations between 50,000 and 250,000 inhabitants (Austria: 13%). The FPÖ is clearly underrepresented in rural areas, since just 39 percent of its electorate lives in communities with less than 5,000 inhabitants—a proportion which is 5 percentage points below the Austrian average.

5. Summary

On the basis of the main results of this article, a number of conclusions about the sociostructural composition of the electorates of the Socialist Party of Austria, the Austrian People's Party and the Freedom Party of Austria can be reached.

SPÖ electorate:
Conclusion 1:
Even in the early 1980s, the SPÖ has retained its character as a workers' party while continually adapting to structural changes.

Conclusion 2:
Male workers have stronger ties to the SPÖ than female workers; middle-class women have stronger ties to the SPÖ than middle-class men.
Conclusion 3:
People with a medium level of education form one core group of SPÖ voters, whereas the proportion of high school and university graduates in the SPÖ electorate can be said to be far below average.
Conclusion 4:
In farming communities and small and medium-sized towns with up to 50,000 inhabitants, the SPÖ is a workers' party; in regional centers and in Vienna, the SPÖ is a middle-class party. The larger the community, the greater the proportion of SPÖ voters belonging to the middle class; the smaller the community, the greater the proportion of workers.

ÖVP electorate:
Conclusion 1:
The primary core group of ÖVP voters is made up of the self-employed and the middle educational stratum.
Conclusion 2:
The second core voter group in the ÖVP electorate consists of farmers. In the early 1980s, the ÖVP can also be called the farmers' party, since 70 percent of the members this group support the ÖVP.
Conclusion 3:
The older the ÖVP voters, the more closely the party's electorate reflects the suborganizational structure of the party; the younger the ÖVP voters, the more the party suborganizations representing them are a distortion of their true strength.
Conclusion 4:
The ÖVP relies principally upon support from voters with only compulsory schooling and those belonging to the upper educational stratum.
Conclusion 5:
The middle class provides the majority of voters in the ÖVP electorate in the eastern and western regions, but merely a plurality of ÖVP voters in the southern and central regions.

FPÖ electorate:
Conclusion 1:
Of all Austian parliamentary parties, the FPÖ has the largest proportion of middle-class voters in its electorate.
Conclusion 2:
The FPÖ is the most "male" Austrian party.
Conclusion 3:

The age distribution of FPÖ voters corresponds to age distribution in the electorates of the two major parties; there is not a disproportionate number of older voters in the FPÖ electorate which would threaten the existence of the party.

Conclusion 4:

The FPÖ is most attractive to the upper educational stratum and is clearly underrepresented among persons with only compulsory schooling.

With regard to the stability and change of basic electoral patterns within the Austrian party system in the period from 1982 to 1986, there were no dramatic changes (table 7.18). In the mid-eighties, the Socialist Party is still the party of the working class—exactly 50 percent of the Austrian working class supported the SPÖ in 1986. Half the Socialist vote (48%) is provided by blue-collar workers. The traditional weakness of the SPÖ among persons with a university education remained stable—there are no indications that the group of Austrians with higher education will develop stronger affective ties to the Socialists in the late 1980s. As for the urban-rural cleavage, the Austrian capital of Vienna was still clearly a Socialist Party stronghold in 1986. With regard to the regional distribution of the Socialist vote, the eastern parts of Austria demonstrate higher levels of Socialist partisanship than do the western parts.

As for the Conservative Party—the ÖVP -, the basic pattern remained the same, with the upper middle class of employers and the higher strata of white collar employees and farmers forming the core group of Conservative voters. The ÖVP is still "the" party for farmers—75 percent of this social group regularly supported the ÖVP in 1986, and 57 percent of the upper middle class vote Conservative. This bias toward the upper middle class within the ÖVP is reflected by the fact that 20 percent of Conservative support is derived from persons with higher education. The ÖVP can therefore justifiably be called "the" party of persons with higher education, because 55 percent of this social group vote Conservative. With regard to the urban-rural cleavage, nearly 60 percent (59%) of ÖVP supporters live in rural areas.

The basic patterns of support for the Freedom Party also remained constant. More than 60 percent of the FPÖ vote is from the middle and upper middle classes. An interesting fact is that 39 percent of FPÖ supporters belong to the upper middle class. Hence, the FPÖ is the most "bourgeois" party within the Austrian party system. A new tendency is visible along the age dimension. The strongest support for the FPÖ is provided by the youngest and oldest age groups. This is partly due to the attractiveness of FPÖ party leader Haider—who took over the leadership of the party in 1986—to the younger generation, and partly to the traditional support for the Freedom Party among "nationalist" voters, some of whom are influenced by right-wing political attitudes. The generational distribution within the FPÖ electorate has changed somewhat since the early 1980s. Other strong supporters of the FPÖ are persons with secondary education (57 percent of FPÖ voters), income stratum B (39 percent of FPÖ voters), city dwellers and persons in the southern parts of Austria. With regard to the development of voting patterns in the Austrian party system between 1982 and 1986, we are entitled to speak of a remarkable stability of the internal distribution of support among the three Austrian parliamentary parties in the wake of emerging new parties, for example Green parties.

Table 7.18
Social structure and the Austrian party system, 1986

1986	SPÖ	ÖVP	FPÖ	total
Social Class				
upper middle class	11	22	39	17
middle class	32	26	23	29
farmers	9	31	7	19
workers	48	21	32	35
Sex				
female	54	57	55	55
male	46	43	45	45
Age				
16-24	4	4	9	4
25-39	27	27	17	28
40-59	39	37	32	37
60 and above	30	33	43	31
Education				
higher education	11	20	17	16
secondary education	51	38	57	45
compulsory schooling	38	41	26	39
Income				
stratum A	20	21	16	20
stratum B	24	27	39	26
stratum C	32	28	30	30
stratum D	24	24	16	24
Urban-Rural Cleavage				
Vienna	23	14	15	19
cities	13	11	17	12
small towns	18	17	17	17
villages	46	59	51	52
Region				
east	46	38	30	42
south	25	24	36	25
center	22	25	23	23
west	8	13	11	11

Source: Austrian Social Survey 1986 (IFK data archive)

The present article is primarily a quantitative and empirical attempt to analyze the structures of the electorates of Austria's three traditional parliamentary parties, the SPÖ, ÖVP and FPÖ, according to sociostructural dimensions. This type of synchronous cross-section is one further apparently necessary step in the authors' research program and it follows studies of Austrian voting behavior from 1969 to 1977 on the aggregate level of National Council elections. It is, however, merely preliminary to the systematic longitudinal analysis of voting behavior in the period from 1969 to 1985 which has yet to be carried out by the authors. Existing research on the dynamism of voting behavior and the party system carried out by Austrian political scientists, above all by Plasser and Ulram[16], demonstrate how fruitful this type of research approach is and are a contribution to the "modernization" of Austrian political science. What appears to be particularly important in this context of research strategies is the analysis of other factors influencing voting behavior which transcend the sociostructural dimension, for example the influence of political issues and their development on the Austrian voter[17] the influence of affective party ties or party identification, or that of the post-materialist change in values—all of these are factors which influence voting behavior and can presumably clearly increase the degree of explained variance.

Notes

1. Cf. Rose 1974 and Rose 1980 for the methodology of the research approach this study is based on.

2. An excellent long-term empirical analysis can be found in Plasser's contribution to this volume. The internal structure of the electorates of the Austrian parliamentary parties for the period from 1969 to 1974 is dealt with in Haerpfer/Gehmacher 1984

3. Cf. Gehmacher 1982.

4. An international comparison of the phenomenon of class parties can be found in Crewe/Denver 1985; Dalton/Flanagan/Beck 1984; Keeley/McAllister/Mughan 1985; Robertson 1984, and the most recent developments in research on this topic in Rose/McAllister 1986.

5. Cf. Nick/Pelinka 1983, pp. 49-56.

6. For an up-to-date analysis from the viewpoint of the political scientist of the new social movements and Green-Alternative political formations, see the contribution to this volume by Dachs.

7. In this article, "middle class" is used synonymously with "new middle class", and "upper middle class" is used synonymously with "older middle class". The sum of the middle class and the upper middle class is called the "cumulative middle class".

8. For the electoral-sociological meaning of this situation, cf. the fundamental contribution in Ulram 1985.

9. This figure results from—among other things—the fact that only crude data concerning declared party supporters were used in the analysis upon which this article is based. No method was utilized to classify undeclared persons in the crude data as supporters of one of the three parties in order to avoid distortions in this respect. Cf. Plasser's observations in this volume.

10. For the internal structures of Social-Democratic parties in Scandinavian party systems, see Sainsbury 1985. For the development of the membership structures of Social-Democratic parties in general between 1889 and 1978, see Bartolini 1983.

11. For an international comparison of sex-specific differences in voting behavior, see Bashevkin 1985a, Bashevkin 1985b; Siemienska 1985 and Miller 1986.

12. An exemplary representation of the territorial dimension with regard to the British party system can be found in McAllister/Rose 1984.

13. Interesting comparisons of the internal structure of the ÖVP with analogous electorate structures in other European conservative and Christian-Democrat parties can be found in Nick 1984, pp. 83-130 and Homer 1981, pp. 140-169.

14. With regard to the different types of changes in party structure and the adaption of party systems to changed framework conditions, cf. Mair 1983 and Mair 1984.

15. An interesting electoral-sociological analysis of the electorate structure of the Liberal—Social-Democratic alliance in Great Britain can be found in Curtice 1983 and Crewe 1985.

16. Cf., in particular, Plasser/Ulram 1982, Plasser/Ulram 1984 and the contributions to this volume by Plasser and Ulram.

17. Cf. the contribution by Ulram to this volume which deals systematically with this field of research.

Bibliography

Bartolini, Stefano, *The Membership of Mass Parties: The Social Democratic Experience. 1889-1978*, in: Hans Daalder/Peter Mair (eds.), *Western European Party Systems. Continuity and Change*, London/Beverly Hills 1983 (Bartolini, 1983)

Bashevkin, Silvia B., *Changing Patterns of Politicization and Partisanship among Women in France*, in: *British Journal of Political Science*, 15/1985 (Bashevkin, 1985a)

Bashevkin, Silvia B. (eds.), *Women and Politics in Western Europe, Special Issue—West European Politics* 8/1985 (Bashevkin, 1985b)

Birk, Franz/Gehmacher, Ernst/Traar, Kurt, *Eine veränderte politische Landschaft. Ergebnisse der Umfrageforschung zu den Nationalratswahlen 1983*, in: *Journal für Sozialforschung* 23/1983 (Birk/Gehmacher/Traar, 1983)

Birk, Franz/Traar, Kurt, *Das Ende einer Ära*, in: *ÖJP* 1983, München/Wien 1984 (Birk/Traar, 1984)

Chapman, Jenny, *Martial Status, Sex and the Formation of Political Attitudes in Adult Life*, in: *Political Studies* 33/1985 (Chapman, 1985)

Crewe, Ivor, *Great Britain*, in: Ivor Crewe/David Denver (eds.): *Electoral Change in Western Democracies. Patterns and Sources of Electoral Volatility*, London/Sidney/New York 1985 (Crewe, 1985)

Crewe, Ivor/Denver, David (eds.), *Electoral Change in Western Democracies. Patterns and Sources of Electoral Volatility*, London/Sidney/New York 1985 (Crewe/Denver, 1985)

Curtice, John, *Liberal Voters and the Alliance: Realignment or Protest*, in: Vernon Bogdanor (ed.), *Liberal Political Party Politics*, Oxford 1983 (Curtice, 1983)

Dalton, Russell J. et al. (eds.), *Electoral Change in Advanced Industrial Democracies. Realignment or Dealignment?* Princeton 1984 (Dalton, 1984)

Flanagan, Scott C./Dalton, Russel J., *Parties under Stress: Realignment and Dealignment in Advanced Industrial Societies*, in: *West European Politics*, 7/1984 (Flanagan/Dalton, 1984)

Gehmacher, Ernst, *Faktoren des Wählerverhaltens*, in: Heinz Fischer (ed.), *Das politische System Österreichs*, dritte Auflage, Wien 1982 (Gehmacher, 1982)

Gerlich, Peter/Müller, Wolfgang C. (eds.), *Zwischen Koalition und Konkurrenz. Österreichs Parteien seit 1945*, Wien 1983 (Gerlich/Müller, 1983)

Haerpfer, Christian, *Nationalratswahlen und Wahlverhalten 1945-1980*, in: Peter Gerlich/Wolfgang C. Müller (eds.), *Zwischen Koalition und Konkurrenz. Österreichs Parteien seit 1945*, Wien 1983 (Haerpfer, 1983)

Haerpfer, Christian, *Abschied vom Loyalitätsritual? Langfristige Veränderungen im Wählerverhalten*, in: Fritz Plasser/Peter A. Ulram/Manfried Welan (eds.), *Demokratierituale*, Wien 1985 (Haerpfer, 1985)

Haerpfer, Christian, *Electoral Volatility in Austria 1945-1983*, in: Ivor Crewe/David Denver (eds.), *Electoral Change in Western Democracies. Patterns and Sources of Electoral Volatility*, London/Sidney/New York 1985 (Haerpfer, 1985)

Haerpfer, Christian/Gehmacher, Ernst, *Social Structure and Voting in the Austrian Party System*, in: *Electoral Studies* 3/1984 (Haerpfer/Gehmacher, 1984)

Horner, Franz, *Konservative und christdemokratische Parteien in Europa*, Wien/München 1981 (Horner, 1981)

Kelley, Jonathan/McAllister, Ian/Mughan, Anthony, *The Decline of Class Revisited: Class and Party in England. 1964-1979*, in: *American Political Science Review* 79/1985 (Kelley/McAllister/Mughan, 1985)

LeDuc, Lawrence, *Partisan Change and Dealignment in Canada, Great Britain and the United States*, in: *Comparative Politics* 17/1985 (LeDuc, 1985)

Mair, Peter, *Party Politics in Contemporary Europe: A Challenge to Party?* in: *West European Politics* 7/1984 (Mair, 1984)

McAllister, Ian/Rose, Richard, *The Nationwide Competition for Votes*, London 1984 (McAllister/Rose, 1984)

Miller, Arthur H., *Gender Politics in the United States*, Occasional Papers Nr. 20, Laboratory for Political Research, University of Iowa 1986 (Miller, 1986)

Nick, Rainer, *Schwesterparteien. CDU, CSU und Österreichische Volkspartei. Ein Vergleich*, Innsbruck 1984 (Nick, 1984)

Nick, Rainer/Pelinka, Anton, *Bürgerkrieg—Sozialpartnerschaft. Das politische System Österreichs. 1. und 2. Republik. Ein Vergleich*. Wien/München 1983 (Nick/Pelinka, 1983)

Plasser, Fritz/Ulram, Peter A., *Unbehagen im Parteienstaat*, Wien 1982 (Plasser/Ulram, 1982)

Plasser, Fritz/Ulram, Peter A., *Themenwechsel—Machtwechsel? Konturen einer neuen Mehrheit in Österreich*, in: Stephan Koren/Karl Pisa/Kurt Waldheim (eds.), *Politik für die Zukunft*, Wien 1984 (Plasser/Ulram, 1984)

Robertson, David, *Class and the British Electorate*, Oxford 1984 (Robertson, 1984)

Rose, Richard, *Class Does Not Equal Party. The Decline of a Model of British Voting*, Studies in Public Policy Nr. 74, Centre for the Study of Public Policy, University of Strathclyde 1980 (Rose, 1980)

Rose, Richard (ed.), *Electoral Behavior. A Comparative Handbook*, New York/London 1974 (Rose, 1974)

Rose, Richard/McAllister, Ian, *Voters Begin to Choose. From Closed-Class to Open Elections in Britain*, London/Beverly Hills 1986 (Rose/McAllister, 1986)

Sainsbury, Diane, *The Electoral Difficulties of the Scandinavian Social Democrats in the 1970s: The Social Basis of the Parties and Structural Explanations of Party Decline*, in: *Comparative Politics* 18/1985 (Sainsbury, 1985)

Shamir, Michael, *Are Western Party Systems "Frozen"?*, in: *Comparative Political Studies* 17/1984 (Shamir, 1984)

Simienska, Renata (ed.), *Women in Politics, Special Issue—International Political Science Review* 6/1985 (Simienska, 1985)

Särlvik, Bo/Crewe, Ivor, *Decade of dealignment. The Conservative victory of 1979 and electoral trends in the 1970s*, Cambridge 1983 (Särlvik/Crewe, 1983)

Ulram, Peter A., *Um die Mehrheit der Mehrheit. Die neuen angestellten Mittelschichten 1975-1984*, in: Fritz Plasser/Peter A. Ulram/Manfried Welan (eds.), *Demokratierituale*, Wien 1985 (Ulram, 1985)

8

Citizen Lists and Green-Alternative Parties in Austria

HERBERT DACHS

1. Preliminary Remarks

For a long time the Austrian party system was regarded as a model of stability and continuity and was counted among the "rigid" party systems of Western Europe.[1] Since the end of the 1970s and fully since November 23, 1986 this judgment no longer holds. As far back as the early 1970s citizen lists sprang up in many places with the goal of fighting individual measures enacted by the political bureaucracy or of applying to government for action on specific issues. These lists worked against the political parties or bypassed them to make demands and raise issues that, they felt, had been given too little or no consideration until then. Local politics was the preferred sphere of activity of these new groups. The majority of the lists eventually disappeared from the political scene, but in several cities some groups formed alliances and then loosely organized parties that campaigned for a voice in local government. But this was not the end of the party system's development toward parliamentarism, because since the beginning of the 1980s the traditional parties have been increasingly challenged by new parties at the state and federal level. The extent to which the Austrian party system in general and the established parties in particular have evolved and changed in the face of these developments will be treated in other chapters of this book and will therefore receive only occasional mention here. The main interest of this chapter focuses on the green-alternatives and citizen protest parties, their genesis, platform, adherents, organizational structure and electoral success to date.

This study meets with several methodological obstacles, the largest of which is that these are not parties in a conventional sense with a transparent history, clear-cut organizational structure, platform and uninterrupted political practice, but rather more or less loosely organized quasi-parties and electoral platforms of heterogeneous groups, whose profile and politics are still far from maturity. All attempts to analyze these phenomena on a social science basis have thus been tentative and in many cases vague.

Notwithstanding the methodological problems, these new parties, precisely because they are so new, count among those occurrences followed with relative interest by the media, opinion analysts and social scientists, whereby numerous fundamental analyses of their platform and especially the motives and social make-up of their electorate receive repeated confirmation. The following will give a rough sketch of these movements and subsequently proceed to a discussion of their political category, the reasons for their emergence and their prospects for future development.

2. Social Framework

Before proceeding to these new parties in Austria, it is necessary to mention some of the important background factors that originally made it possible for such political groups to emerge at all and that then developed and strengthened them, whereby the following account is not to be construed as a chain of cause and effect nor does the order given reflect any priority.

Austrian society, too, has passed something like an ecopolitical turning point, i.e. the population increasingly realizes that in various respects the limits of growth have been reached, and the protection and rehabilitation of the environment have thus rapidly increased in significance for the voter. In Austria, too, postmaterialist attitude patterns took on added value. The social structure of Austrian society changed, the number of self-employed persons and wage earners is on the decline, and the percentage of persons primarily employed in the tertiary sector, who as the so-called "new middle class" cannot be ascribed to any one clear-cut category, is growing in scope and political weight. Both the level of education and the demands made of politics are on an overall increase. The lager borders, that for decades appeared unshakeable and insurmountable, are becoming less rigid. The borders blur and there is a subsequent decline in the percentage of traditional voters, while voter readiness to cross over party lines is on the increase. The exorbitant extent of party influence that is evidenced and felt in almost every sector of life in Austria is ultimately also responsible for a deep-seated listlessness toward political parties that is coupled with a wide-spread subjective feeling of powerlessness and lack of influence in political matters. Despite all its advantages, the social partnership ultimately cannot deny its character of being a political institution whose politics are formulated by those "on top" for those "on the bottom," and interests that run contrary or at a right angle to its politics have a relatively minor or at least a considerably reduced chance of being realized.

3. The Genesis of Alternative Parties in Austria

In the early 1970s numerous citizen lists arose in Austria, that, similar to those in West Germany, all had their origins in the problems of local government. The majority of these lists were formed to focus attention on specific, distinct issues and generally disbanded once the issue proved successful or unsuccessful (single-issue movements). Not least of all, it was the impact of the growth crisis and the anti-nuclear power debate that increasingly raised fundamental questions on what the origins of our means of production, our energy policy and the exercise of our political representation are and, most importantly, where they are headed. With the stage thus set, regular election groups formed and campaigned as quasi-parties for the voters' favor.

The first more sizeable group to summon the courage to take this step in Austria was the "Citizen List" (Bürgerliste, BL) in the city of Salzburg. An alliance of several citizen initiatives, in 1977 it already won two seats on the city council, then tripled its votes five years later to become the third strongest faction (with seven seats) on the city council. From 1982—1987 it even held one municipal portfolio.[2] To date, its activities have been confined to the city of Salzburg, but it will campaign in Salzburg's 1989 State Diet election.

The "Alternative List" in Graz (Alternative Liste Graz, AL Graz) went through similar stages in its formation. Here, too, there was an abundance of political problems on the municipal scene, and at times Graz was known as the stronghold of the citizen's list movement[3] with close to 200 lists. Here, again, a group of activists came to the conclusion that they would have to depart from single issues and find a means of exerting more comprehensive influence. AL Graz was then founded in November 1981 with the goal of campaigning in the city council elections and was also the driving force behind the ultimate founding of the "Alternative List of Austria" (Alternative Liste Österreichs, ALÖ) exactly one year later. This list ran for office in the 1983 National Council election.

Shortly before the ALÖ came into being, several leading nuclear power opponents founded the "United Greens of Austria" (Vereinte Grüne Österreichs, VGÖ) that also campaigned nationwide in the following year's National Council election.

With these three parties the most important groups in the green-alternative party spectrum have now been introduced. In addition to these, there were and still are a large number of party-like organizations and movements that, on the one hand, can only be termed "parties" in the formal legal sense of the Parties Law of 1975 but that otherwise evoke hardly any response worth mentioning or that, because of lacking support, have seldom been strong enough to run for office as yet.[4] Several of these were founded as a tactical maneuver aimed at the 1986 National Council election and the related attempts at unification (for example VÖGA, United Austrian Green-Alternatives; GRAS, Green-Alternative Collective etc.).

The three parties mentioned above will be profiled in the following. They have many things in common but at least as many distinguishing features.

3.1 Salzburg City's Citizen List (BL)[5]

Development to Date
Salzburg's BL, that had been formed from various citizen initiatives, won two seats in its maiden campaign for office in the 1977 city council election despite its last-minute decision to campaign. In the following years, its two councilmen (the baker Richard Hörl and the actor Herbert Fux) regularly kept the city council in uproar with their interpellations, criticism and attention-getting campaigns. In its efforts to get the greatest possible publicity for itself and its issues, the Citizen List did not restrict its activities to the city council arena. In letters to newspaper editors, flyers, open letters and spectacular actions it repeatedly unleashed movements and political controversies outside the municipal legislature that subsequently reverberated on the city council.

BL not only drew attention to itself through its unconventional style, but also through the explosive political issues it adopted. It concentrated on four major themes: preservation of the old city, grasslands protection, the privileged status of politicians (i.e. it demanded a separation of politics and private careers) and democratization or more political control in the hands of voters who know their own mind. All these were topics that later played a leading role in the 1982 city council election. While not much was achieved in the formulation of constructive election platforms, BL above all attempted to maintain and strengthen its image as an uncompromising party of political attack and control. BL campaigned, among other things, as a "democratic movement for reform and renewal ... an instrument of control and government participation for everyone ... an environmental movement" ("Die Bürgerliste informiert": brochure). The people of Salzburg, so it was claimed, were faced with the choice of being "free citizens or vassals."

This course met with an unexpectedly large response. In 1982 BL won 17.6% of the vote and seven seats on the city council (thereby relegating the FPÖ, traditionally strong in Salzburg, to fourth place) as well as one seat on the city council's five-member executive board. BL's new councilman Johannes Voggenhuber was assigned exactly those portfolios that had been the subject of BL's severest criticism (environmental protection, board of construction, urban planning, communications and roadworks). In the 1987 election BL's share of the vote dropped to 10.1% (four seats), and the municipal portfolio was lost.

Categorization and Evaluation

BL's 1982 voters were younger than average, better educated, had a relatively good income and, to a disproportionately large extent, were upper or middle class. In its own view of itself, the party stood almost exactly in the middle of the political road.[6] It is thus justifiable to term its electorate "liberal middle-of-the-road voters" or to speak of a citizens' protest party strongly oriented toward environmental issues, because BL and its voters have been seen to be very open to environmental issues. No fundamental changes in the system are strived for. Instead, the demand is made for an environmental policy of "peripheral intervention," according to which the existing production and distribution relationships should remain as they are but environmental protection laws be introduced. Strictly speaking, BL is thus to be regarded as a reform group. The system of representative democracy is accepted in essence, but the plebiscitary elements should be expanded and developed. Optimistic faith is held in the prevailing political instruments. It is not a new theory that is needed, but instead better political practice.

Its organizational structure is decidedly loose and purposely open, and to date little has been done to tighten it. BL's inner circle of activists probably never went further than 20 to 30 persons.

In type, BL has remained a media or voter party. Its almost complete lack of traditional voters as well as of suitable publishing avenues and a powerful party apparatus force it more than traditional parties to convey its content and ideas through the mass media.

It must be emphatically noted here that BL Salzburg evoked such a large response in 1982 not because of the platform it had barely conceived or its candidates, but because it was expected to exert a controlling and corrective influence. In other words, BL voter turnout "primarily reflected a large-scale need for protest on the part of the population together with the desire for more earnest environmental protection." For example, an IMAS survey showed that 42% of a survey group had voted for BL mainly "because many people were disappointed with the established parties," and 39% because BL was especially active for environmental protection, while only 8% and 4% respectively gave the compelling platform and the convincing candidates as their motive. "The fascination with BL as a corrective political instrument runs so high that it outweighs BL's lack of constructive programs for the future just as its likeable image."[7] BL, however, was only partly able to live up to these tremendously high expectations, and a large portion of those voters who had especially been motivated by protest turned away from BL in the 1987 elections.

3.2 United Greens of Austria (VGÖ)[8]

Development to Date

This party was founded by leading members of the "Study Group *No to Zwentendorf*" (Professor Alexander Tollman, Consul Alois Englander, retired) with the goal of campaigning nationwide in the 1983 National Council election. And that is what the party did.

Its then sparsely formulated fundamental platform focused on the themes "Citizen and State" and "Man and the Environment." VGÖ's aim is to "realize a united front or working partnership of all those groups that, on the one hand, are dedicated to the preservation of a healthy environment and environmental protection in its broadest sense including the protection of animals and, on the other hand, that stand up for the democratic rights of the country's citizens and for safeguarding and developing the democratic order of our nation."[9] The party explicitly distances itself from any type of left or right extremism (critics feel that, in practice, the left is more vehemently renounced than the right). Sociopolitical demands of a more far-reaching nature, those that transgress the existing constitution and ground rules of parliamentarism, are strictly rejected. Its statutes and organizational structure are similar to those of other, established parties. The party has a chairman at the provincial and federal levels, committees and a secretary-general.

The strong emphasis placed on the personal element has in the past often led to seemingly never ending squabbles. In the face of the 1983 National Council election VGÖ presented the picture of a party distorted by power struggles and personnel disputes, a circumstance that soon caused the tide of the initially very positive reports in most of the mass media to turn. The two main rivals Alexander Tollmann and Herbert Fux resigned after the election, and the party chairmanship went to the Deputy Mayor of Steyregg, Josef Buchner, while Wolfgang Pelikan became Secretary-General. The fact that this did not put an end to the party's struggles to decide its political orientation is seen, among other things, from VGÖ's turbulent special national convention in Salzburg at the end of February 1986, where, following several disputed party ousters, the Vienna chapter broke away from the national party.[10]

Categorization and Evaluation

VGÖ describes itself as a reforming protest party focusing on civil rights and environmental protection. It, too, can only rely on a comparatively small number of steady campaign workers, while until now, presumably because of the less radical nature of its platform, it has always polled clearly more votes than ALÖ. A. Gonner correctly views this party as an "ecologically oriented group of the middle class political center ... (with a somewhat ragged right edge)"[11]. In its concept of politics it does "not notably (differ) from the 'established' parties. Hierarchical leadership structure, strong emphasis on a publicity-effective presence in the mass media in place of steady grassroots work have VGÖ appear more a traditional election party led by distinguished persons. Celebrities and experts attract voters."[12]

For the rest, the prevailing political and economic system is fundamentally affirmed, and the belief is held that with the right reforms or after a moral renewal on the part of the actors the impending ecological disasters can be averted. As party founder Tollmann stated in this connection, "Working from the status quo we want the parties reformed, the privileged status of politicians reduced, our civil rights strengthened and the political and ecological grievances remedied."[13] In the meantime a number of programs have been aimed at the issues, conspicuous among them are radical demands in environmental matters and a tendency to statism.

3.3 Alternative List of Austria (ALÖ)

Development to Date

The initiative to found ALÖ in 1982 stemmed, as already mentioned, from AL Graz, that had been formed just one year earlier. Above all, it was the desire to not have VGÖ campaign as the only serious representative of the green-alternative lager that led to a somewhat over-hasty founding of the national party and brought on no small amount of criticism from its own ranks (especially from the Alternative List Vienna).

ALÖ sees itself as an alliance of nine regional alternative lists and as a spokesman for the ethnic minorities (having the status of Austria's "tenth state"). Its platform shows pronounced differences from those of other parties. It views itself as an instrument of the peace and alternative movement and orients its activities according to the four principles "ecology," "grassroots democracy," "solidarity" and "non-violent activities." ALÖ's manifesto goes into these principles in more detail. Here several catchwords:[14]

> "Ecology" is more than environmental protection—an ecological society is only possible after the displacement competition, the patriarchy and other forms of domination are eliminated.

"Grassroots democracy": People have to be responsible for their own lives and the people must have a voice in decisions.

"Solidarity": Labor and the economy must be reorganized—development of transparent, humanized ways of life—tolerance as the basis for social intercourse.

"Non-violent Activities": For less violence—against all types of war preparations, arms production—appeal for active resistance against injustice and life-threatening aggression.

These principles are developed still further in the manifesto, and political programs are aimed at other subjects.

ALÖ's organizational set-up is unique in Austria. It radically realized its demand for decentralization, i.e. the provincial organizations are autonomous. Its supreme decision-making body is the Federal Congress (with ten delegates for each of the provincial groups, and resolutions being passed with a two-thirds majority). Otherwise there is only a loosely coordinated party management based in Graz. Various provisions (rotation of offices, no accumulation of offices, remuneration based on actual work load, etc.) are intended to ensure that the demands for grassroots democracy are at least realized within the party itself.

Categorization and Evaluation

Politically, ALÖ is very heterogeneous, with individual provincial groups being markedly different in character. A large portion of its activists come from the antinuclear power movement and from ecological movements, while women's groups, the peace movement and third-world groups also play an important role. The complaint initially voiced before the 1983 National Council election, namely that ALÖ, too, is nothing different than an election party, is largely true for some states. Its personnel and organizational possibilities are too meager for it to be modestly present in daily politics other than preceding elections. The best substructure, the broadest support, is undoubtedly enjoyed by AL Graz that, as already mentioned, did not spring up overnight, but is ."..the product of a lengthy evolution. Its social structure shows it to be a middle-class group, predominantly made up of members of the middle class with a higher education including, above all, civil servants, students and teachers. Also conspicuous among its rank and file is the large number of non-employed persons (students, housewives)."[15]

Overall, ALÖ is also characterized by the tension between two wings, one interested in promoting fundamental social change and the other holding a more environmental ideology. As will be seen later, it too clearly shows signs of being a protest party, but "also contours of a party of the 'wage-earning, new middle class'."[16]

**4. Electoral Success and Voters of the Green-Alternative Parties:
Developments to Summer 1986**

Considering the votes cast for these three green-alternative parties over the past years with the exception of the 1986 National Council election, the results in all but one or two special cases, although not exactly exhilarating, were still downright good in the light of the Austrian party system's persistent high stability.

Electoral successes such as those in Salzburg City, Graz or Vorarlberg were of course accompanied by a large number of defeats (for example, in the latest state diet elections in Upper Austria). Nonetheless, the new parties were all given high grades for likeability. For instance, in 1983 11% of the voters (very much) wanted the greens to take the hurdle into Parliament, 21% said that it was "more likely what they wanted,"[17] and in Vorarlberg, two weeks before going into the 1984 state elections, the green-alternatives had a latent electoral potential of 30%.[18] Despite these figures that would seem to indicate a considerable margin of confidence and a great willingness to change on the part of the voter, it is not so easy, as hasty election forecasters would have it appear, to convert this basic goodwill into votes. There is no automatic conversion mechanism. Rather, election analysts have shown that electoral behavior is decided by a number of very important factors, for example social and regional structure of the electorate, party ties (in connection with ideologies and value systems), current political issues with a strong grip on public opinion, political celebrities serving almost like "mascots" for ideologies and platforms, as well as a campaign's effectiveness in getting the voter's attention and mobilizing him.[19] It would go into unnecessary detail here to evaluate according to these criteria every Austrian election since 1982 and particularly the performance of the green-alternative parties. A look into the available analyses of earlier elections, however, clearly shows that alternative parties have been successful in elections (Salzburg, Graz, Vorarlberg) where a majority of the mentioned factors were dealt with satisfactorily and convincingly.[20]

4.1 Social Profile and Political Recruitment

Table 8.2[21] gives the basic social profile of green-alternative voters. (Although the data are taken from the year 1983, the social profile of green voters has most likely not undergone significant change since then.) Green sympathizers are young, disproportionately well educated and belong to the non-selfemployed middle class, with ALÖ voters being quite a bit younger and having a better education than VGÖ voters.

182

Table 8.1
Electoral Success of Selected Citizens' Initiatives and Green-Alternative Parties

Year	Election	Party and Returns		Seats	Seats (hypothetical, in case of a joint candidacy)
Oct. 77	Salzburg City Council	BL	5.6%	2	-
Mar. 79	Salzburg Diet	BL	1.8%	-	
Oct. 82	Salzburg City Council	BL	17.0%	7	
				1	portfolio
Jan. 83	Graz City Council	ALG	7%	4	
		GMÖ	1.3%	-	
Apr. 83	National Council	VGÖ	1.9%	-	7
		ALÖ	1.4%	-	
Apr. 83	Vienna City Council	ALW	2.5%	-	-
		WBU	0.6%	-	
Sept. 83	Innsbruck City Council	ALI	2.9%	1	
Oct. 83	Lower Austrian Diet	VGÖ	1.0%		
		ALNÖ	0.6%	-	-
Mar. 84	Salzburg Diet	GABL	4.3%	-	2
		DGÖ	1.3%	-	
June 84	Tyrolian Diet	AT	3.6%	-	-
Sept. 84	Carinthian Diet	KELÖ	1.5%	-	
		VGÖ	1.1%	-	
		DGÖ	0.7%	-	
Oct. 84	Vorarlberg Diet	GAL	13.0%	4	-
Oct. 85	Upper Austrian Diet	VGÖ	2.2%	-	
		ALÖ	1.7%	-	1-2
		DGÖ	0.4%	-	
May 86	Federal President	Blau-Meissner	5.5%		
Sept. 86	Styrian Diet	VGÖ-AL	3.7%	2	
Nov. 86	National Council	GA-FMB	4.8%	8	9
		GAL	0.12%	-	
Oct. 87	Burgenland Diet	Greens	2.2%	-	
	Salzburg City Council	BL	10.1%	4	
Nov. 87	Vienna City Council	Greens	4.4%	-	
		VGÖ	0.8%	-	
Jan. 88	Graz City Council	ALG	4.9%	2	
		VGÖ-AL	1.0%		
		Greens	0.7%		

Table 8.2
Social Profile of Party Supporters in Austria (1983)
(in % of declared supporters)

	SPÖ	ÖVP	VGÖ	ALÖ
Age				
under 19 years	2	2	4	8
20 - 29 years	19	22	36	63
30 - 44 years	29	30	37	24
45 - 59 years	25	22	15	1
60 years and over	26	24	8	5
Education				
College	1	4	8	12
High School Graduate	5	12	25	48
Completed Compulsory Education	48	43	51	26
Uncompleted Compulsory Education	45	40	16	14
Occupational Environment				
Professional				
Business, Trades	3	12	14	10
White-/Blue-Collar Work	44	43	60	60
Labor/Skilled Work	50	24	23	14
Farmer	2	20	6	3
Occupation				
Professional				
Businessman, Tradesman	1	5	4	4
White-Collar Worker	17 ⎫	21 ⎫	36 ⎫	37 ⎫
	⎬ 24	⎬ 27	⎬ 45	⎬ 43
Blue-Collar Worker	7 ⎭	6 ⎭	9 ⎭	6 ⎭
Skilled Worker	12 ⎫	7 ⎫	9 ⎫	7 ⎫
	⎬ 27	⎬ 14	⎬ 14	⎬ 11
Other Worker	15 ⎭	7 ⎭	5 ⎭	4 ⎭
Farmer	1	12	2	1
Housewife	19 ⎫	15 ⎫	16 ⎫	7 ⎫
	⎬ 46	⎬ 38	⎬ 25	⎬ 11
Non-Employed (retired etc.)	27 ⎭	23 ⎭	9 ⎭	4 ⎭
In Training	1	3	12	31

Source: Dr. Fessel + GfK, Kumulierte Halbjahreszählung, 2. Hälfte 1983

As for the political origin of green voters, different voter streams can be read from the individual regional results. On average, the established parties lose ground, albeit in differing degrees, while there is also a strong tendency to self-recruitment (Table 8.3)[22].

Especially impressive is the analysis of first-time voters in the 1984 Vorarlberg Diet election. In urban areas, 50% of first-time voters supported the greens, 20% did not vote, 14.7% came out for the SPÖ, 11.1% for the ÖVP and only 0.1% for the FPÖ.[23]

Table 8.3
Political Origin of Green Voters in Austria (1983):
(in % of Declared Green Voters)

	Austria 1983 National Election	Vienna 1983 National Election	Graz 1983 City Election	Vorarlberg 1984 Diet
Former SPÖ Voters	35	35	20	20
Former ÖVP Voters	30	20	20	40
Former FPÖ Voters	10	10	25	10
First-Time and Former Nonvoters	25	35	35	30

Source: Political Survey by Dr. Fessel + GfK-Institut 1983/84 (values rounded off)

Opinion analysts remark that this development has not yet come to an end and that the electoral potential of the green-alternatives has only been partly exploited to date. Table 8.4 shows that the green-alternatives can presently reckon with the support of a steady 4% to 6% of the electorate. Over and above that there is an "electoral potential" of 15% to 20%.[24]

Table 8.4
Green-Alternative Electoral Potential in Austria (%)

	1982	Feb. 83	July 83	Nov. 84	Jan. 85*)	Mar. 85	June 85	Feb. 86	Mar. 87
Potential**) Green Voters	19	13	17	26	33	26	19	19	16
Declared Green Voters	5	6	2	9	15	8	4	4	6
Green Votes in National Elections		Nat. Coun. 83 3.3						Fed. Pres. 86 5.5	Nat. Coun. 86 5.0

Source: Dr. Fessel + GfK, Political Surveys (1982 to 1987)
Election Returns: National Council April 1983: VGÖ and ALÖ
Federal President May 1986: Liste Meissner-Blau
National Council Nov. 1986: GAL/MB, GAL, Kärntner Grüne
*)   Hainburg
**)   can basically imagine voting for a "green" party.

4.2 Electoral Motives: Environmental Concern and Party Protest

What is it that causes green sympathizers to cast their vote for one of the new parties? The answer was already mentioned briefly. There are two reasons: the general dissatisfaction with and protest against the traditional parties' actions as well as their candidates and, secondly, the concern and worry about the environmental future of our society. For example, the motives for voting for AL Graz in 1983 ranked its attractive environmental protection platform (for 87% of ALG voters) ahead of a general disenchantment with political parties (72%) and a special dissatisfaction with the traditional parties in Graz (69%).[25] These two elements also played a decisive role in the last Vorarlberg Diet election, as shown in Table 8.5.[26]

Table 8.5
Reasons for Voting GAL in the 1984 Vorarlberg Diet Election in the Population's Opinion (answers open, then coded) in Percent

Presumable Voting Motive in Percent of Those Polled	
general disenchantment with politicians	
dissatisfaction with the parties	62
environmental problems, dying forests	28
attractiveness for young voters	13
for a change, novelty	8
leading GAL candidate	7

Source: E. Berndt: Die Behandlung aktueller Themen der Vorarlberger Landespolitik sowie Analysen der Landtagswahlen 1984, Göfis 1985

The motivation among the Blau-Meissner voters in the 1986 presidential election was similar: 63% voted for the candidate as a "protest against the big parties," 60% "because she advocates alternative politics" and 48% "because of a disappointment with the big parties' candidates."[27]

Austrians' overall annoyance with the traditional political parties also seems to have grown considerably in recent years. While 43% of the population stated in 1981 that they had recently been annoyed with the political parties, in 1984 this figure had already climbed to 70%.[28] Parallel to this, the basic attitude toward expanding the Austrian party spectrum had changed considerably.[29]

Table 8.6
Opinion on Expanding the Austrian Party Spectrum as Seen Over Several
Years (1976-1984) (in % of the Electorate)

	1976a)	1978b)	1981c)	1982d)	1984e)
Are Basically in Favor of Expanding the Party Spectrum	10	11	17	22	39

Source:
a)   Dr. Fessel + GfK, Vorwahlen und Demokratie (1976)
b)   Dr. Fessel + GfK, Parteien und Demokratie (1978)
c)   Institut für Markt- und Sozialanalysen (IMAS), Politische Befragung (1981)
d)   Institut für Demoskopie Allensbach (IfD), Das politische Meinungsklima in Österreich (1982)
e)   Institut für Markt und Sozialanalysen (IMAS), Politische Befragung (1984)

5. The Joint Campaign for the National Council in 1986 and Election to Parliament

The brief history of Austria's green parties has often illustrated the ambivalence of the phrase "diversity in unity." In many cases the leaders of the
various green groups and parties felt it necessary to put so much energy into
preparing election platforms and candidate slates as well as into infighting
that often they were no longer able to muster the necessary vigor for the actual campaign offensive. These "frictional losses," that to a certain degree are
probably inevitable for a young political movement, were already visible before the 1983 National Council election and in many state diet elections. How
heterogeneous the green-alternative party landscape still was, at least until
recently, and how far apart the ideological positions as well as personal views,
expectations and ambitions of the leading actors were, was brought to light by
the tormentingly tedious so-called "process of integration" leading up to the
1986 National Council election, a process that was hard to judge for outsiders. The number of groups and factions involved was awesome in itself:
VGÖ, ALÖ, Meissner Election Movement, BIP (Citizens' Initiative for Parliament), GRAS, AL Vienna and VÖGA, to name only the most well
known.[30] Freda Meissner-Blau's candidacy in the presidential election put the
Green-Alternatives in a very good starting position for the parliamentary
race. A GALLUP survey in June of 1986 showed a 10.2%[31] voter preference
for the Greens, but the actual National Council election brought them a voter
turnout of less than half this figure. To blame for this rapid decline were pri-

marily the different groups in the green-alternative lager. All too often, personal ambition and tactical maneuvers appeared to take preference over a selfless loyalty to principles and an unswerving ideology. It was precisely these last qualities that had brought many protest voters to support the Greens during the preceding years, as already mentioned several times. The early praise of the greens now appeared to be premature, and a portion of the dissatisfied voters switched to someone who was seen to better fit the bill for protest or distance to the "old" parties, namely the new FPÖ Chairman with the smart populist arguments that appealed to young negative voters, Jörg Haider.

Table 8.7
Votes Cast for the Green-Alternatives in the 1986 National Council Election According to State—Change as Compared to the 1983 National Council Election (%)

	Votes Cast for Greens	Change from 1983 National Council Election
Vienna	6.1	+2.4
Lower Austria	3.6	+1.2
Burgenland	2.5	+0.6
Upper Austria	4.9	+1.2
Styria	4.1	+0.7
Carinthia	3.8	+0.2
Salzburg	5.9	+1.7
Tyrol	5.8	+3.1
Vorarlberg	8.8	+4.2
Austria	4.8	+1.5

Nonetheless, the election of the Green-Alternatives to the National Council with eight seats undeniably represents a definite turning point, since this is the first group elected to Parliament from outside the three traditional ideological camps. This success does nothing to mask the fact that this electoral alliance, and it is really nothing other than that, is highly heterogeneous (the political positions range from "conservative" to "desirous of social change"), was tediously put together and only superficially appears to be pacified. The motives for voting for green parties that had been observed in earlier elections were confirmed in the last National Council election. More than 80% of those who shifted to the Greens based this move on their expectation that the party would make a definite commitment to environmental protection. Some 50% of new Green voters favored this party to promote a "contrast to the set interchangeable party in the public self-portrait of the traditional parties," and, finally, the "teach-them-a-lesson and protest motive" also played a major role.[32]

All in all, the parliamentary election of November 23, 1986, in comparison to that of 1983, brought only modest gains for the green-alternatives (+1.5%) in the face of the otherwise major shifts among the other parties (SPÖ -4.5%, FPÖ +4.8%, ÖVP -1.9%).

Table 8.7 shows the Greens' share of the vote in the 1986 National Council election as well as the change from the preceding 1983 election, listed according to state.

As can be seen from Table 8.7, the green-alternatives made the clearest percentual gains in Vienna and in western Austria, while in Burgenland, Lower Austria, Upper Austria, Carinthia and Styria their increase in votes remained below the national average.

6. Conclusion

Despite the abundance of studies dealing with Austrian elections in recent years and despite the availability of no less demoscopic data, it remains difficult to draw a valid and balanced portrait of Austria's green-alternative parties except in a few relatively established basic aspects. More than ever before, things in the other parties toos have started to move. Aside from certain common factors, the political situation in general and for the green-alternatives in particular varies greatly from state to state. Political practice conceived solely by alternative parties is only found in individual cases, and the sorry personnel squabbles and ideological infighting repeatedly furnish the most surprising spectacles. Irrespective of these reservations, the attempt is made to summarize this chapter with a few final remarks and evaluations:

— Austria's green-alternative parties represent an attempt to institutionalize or parliamentarize the new social movements that until now have been working from outside the parliamentary arena, without covering their entire spectrum or being identical with them.

— The existence of green-alternative parties and their having joined in party competition for the voter's favor is now a fact of everyday-life in Austria. Their importance in quantitative terms, however, should not yet be overestimated despite their success in the 1986 National Council election. Although they will probably be able to reckon with relatively steady support from certain of the social strata for some time to come, it is, on the other hand, not their aim to be mass movements. In other words, they will not be able to dislodge the big traditional parties in the foreseeable future.

— In comparison to their purely numerical strength (or might the word be "weakness"?), their significance and influence in raising and defining public issues has been disproportionately large to date. In local politics they have even been temporarily able to discard their classic role of "exposing problems" (for example, in the city of Salzburg in 1982 to 1987).

— Austria's alternative parties are definitely phenomena of the cities and urbanized areas. They are mainly supported by the young, above-average educated population, that predominantly belongs to the non-selfemployed middle class, and by nonvoters.

— If the attempt is made to categorize the three parties discussed here and their electorate according to the traditional left-right scale, it could be said that (aside from state peculiarities) BL Salzburg occupies a place at the center of the scale with VGÖ to its right and ALÖ to its left. VGÖ sees itself as an environmental civil rights movement that strives to reform the existing political structures to produce a better, new political practice. Inasmuch as it campaigned on its own, VGÖ has until recently always come out more or less clearly ahead of ALÖ. BL Salzburg with an only local sphere of activity has no ideology of its own, but according to its basic aims can be placed near VGÖ, whereby here, too, there are signs of a certain wing formation (proximity to VGÖ, ALÖ). The concepts for change as held by ALÖ are the most pronounced. Relatively speaking, it is also the most emphatic advocate of analyzing social causes, but it does not yet have a solid, political platform or theory. Its sympathizers are mainly young (first-time) voters and nonvoters ("youth party"), while VGÖ is predominantly supported by voters who most recently voted for one of the traditional parties ("protest party").

— It can be said of the green-alternative parties and their protagonists that, contrary to the insinuations occasionally made by their political adversaries, as yet there is very little to indicate that they aim to do away with the democratic system in the sense of a fundamental opposition. On the contrary, in many cases they excel by doing just the opposite. They strive to take the democratic system's rules and values particularly serious. Abuses and inflexibilities, above all in representative practice, are criticized and pleas made for more opportunities to exert direct democratic influence.

— Other than in Salzburg, Austria's green-alternative parties have not yet had the opportunity and responsibility to shape political practice on their own or to at least have a decisive say in its formation. Preelection surveys now repeatedly show that the population takes a relatively poor view of the new parties' candidates and platforms or usually knows very little about them, but that the populace on the other hand hopes these new parties will energetically pursue environmental questions while controlling and shaking up the practices of the established party system that are allegedly outmoded and seriously in need of reform. To date, the green-alternative parties have enjoyed a major advance and credit in voter trust that stemmed from displeasure and disappointment just as much as from hope and expectation. The situation has not changed much since the 1986 National Council election although it was precisely in this election that the new parties realized they have no exclusive right to support from dissatisfied and critical voters. The days of advance praise and trust are coming to an end for the green parties, too.

— Seen in this light, the green-alternative parties were and still are a sort of bearer of hope for a none too small or qualitatively insignificant portion of the electorate. They carry the hopes of a large number of young voters (many of whom tend not to vote) and at times they were overwhelmingly successful in motivating former nonvoters to vote. It is precisely ALÖ's position and impact, somewhat on the fringe of the political system (half inside but also half outside), that produces the surprising result in which precisely the party that brings the most pronounced reservations to the traditional system of representation is also the party that ultimately makes a major contribution to the legitimation of just this system, in that it at least temporarily helps to reduce fundamental distance and apathy.

— The premise that the current green voters will sooner or later be disillusioned and return without exception to the familiar fold of the traditional parties will most likely prove improbable and illusory. This is sure to be the case for part of the greens' electorate. If, however, the green-alternative parties fail or the traditional parties do not credibly pick up their issues, other green voters could resort to radicalism or irrational protest, or find themselves standing out in the cold of defeatism and cynical apathy, and could increase the already significant nonvoter potential at certain levels (cities).

— Notwithstanding the aims and concepts for a fundamental change of our society and our economic system that were developed above all by AL in various campaign statements, only a very small portion of today's green-alternative voters and sympathizers can probably be counted on to support such fundamentalist positions. The very cautious voter behavior noted toward the GABL campaign in Salzburg State can certainly not be interpreted as a general trend, but many factors (most recently, the poor turnout for the further left-oriented GAL in Vienna with only 0.12% or 6,005 votes) indicate that similar reactions might be possible in other states.

— Therefore, the electoral success of Austria's green parties has until now been less dependent on their qualities and actual performance, but (and this is proved by the motives of green voters) above all on the behavior and reactions of the traditional parties, their shortcomings, omissions and mistakes and on the expectations of disenchanted voters. As a rule, the emergence of small parties is a response to integration deficits on the part of established parties, especially large parties, that in Austria possess many of the characteristics of people's parties (in the sense of Otto Kirchheimer). Only when these parties fail to give satisfactory consideration to important general or special interests, can suitable new parties form and evoke a noteworthy response. This premise also holds true for Austria because the issues attacked by the green-alternative parties in this connection are anything but minority problems: environmental destruction, world peace and political powerlessness are understood by large portions of the populace in existential terms (for example, 60% of the population advocate the peace movement, activation potential 5%; 35%-40% advocate the environmental movement, activation potential 15%[33]).

— Similar to the Federal Republic of Germany, the trend in the Austrian party system in recent years has been to greater deconcentration, differentiation and smaller entities. Thus, according to tendency, the various interests and value orientations can be better expressed than, for example, in a two-party system. "The organizational independence of adequately differentiated interest groups promotes the transparency of the party system and can increase its capacity for change, because alternatives are worked out more clearly than when there is excessive inner-party integration."[34]

This development toward a stronger differentiation of the party system is tantamount to criticism of the hitherto predominant "people's" type of political party and its dealings. Joachim Raschke concentrates this criticism around four deficits:

1. representation deficit (certain qualitative general interests and special issues shared by several parties are not given due consideration such as, for example, environmental policy and matters of postmaterialistic intelligence);
2. participation deficit (quasi-nationalization, oligarchization and bureaucratization of the parties make direct and effective participation impossible for citizens);
3. immobilism (people's parties appear as ponderous "tankers," citizen mobilization is reduced to the demands of "parliamentary ritual") and
4. autonomy deficit of society (the people's party views society above all as the object of steering and legitimation. This does not correspond to the image of society as the origin and proponent of the democratic process.)[35]

To put it roughly, green-alternative parties claim they will eliminate these deficits. They draw attention to them and attempt to provide remedies. Whether they will be successful in Austria is still undecided. No matter what, the expanded Austrian party system is expected to remain a fact for some time to come.

— Austria's green-alternative parties can be typified as "postindustrial frame-parties"[36]. "Postindustrial" because basic patterns and expectations of the same name play a role here, and "frame-parties" because these have only loose organizational frames that respect the autonomy of the different groups and movements. In a political system such parties can take on an important intervention role. "The frame-party intervenes in the industrial-social process, that it is not able to steer entirely or put on a completely new footing, ... by blocking the worst consequences of this development and striving for a reorientation within the system that attempts to reduce its aggressivity and its harmful effect on nature and society."[37]

These interventions will gain importance and be taken seriously if the green-alternative parties continue to strengthen their electoral support, because, conversely, a loss of voter support for the traditional parties is likely to make these more susceptible to voter opinion. As mentioned, developments could take several directions, including the direction in which the traditional parties resolutely take on the urgent shortcomings and remedy these.

— Whether the alternative parties VGÖ and ALÖ described in greater detail here still have a future as political parties (with regard to their organization but not their substance) currently appears very uncertain. As stated, a broad spectrum of green groups, including VGÖ and ALÖ, were able to agree on a common list of candidates for the 1986 National Council election. At that time its proponents founded a party conceived as a new collective movement under the name "The Green Alternative" (Die grüne Alternative). This party was intended to be a wide-spectrum unitary party that would unite as many of the then existing green parties, environmental initiatives etc. in one organization. How far this process of integration has already progressed from concept to reality, and thus also replaced VGÖ and ALÖ, and to what extent this development also finds acceptance in the state chapters cannot be accurately judged at this time because of the notorious lack of transparency in this segment of the political scene. The strongest reservations appear to come from parts of VGÖ. (This is also the reason for VGÖ Chairman Josef Buchner's resignation from the Green parliamentary club.) Many things, however, indicate that if the alternative groups' present organizational splintering and their sometimes ruinous habit of working against each other can at all be remedied or at least alleviated, then now by the organizationally quasi "improved" Green Alternative. It is clear that the days when the greens were able to reap advance praise and trust through the novelty of their newness are gone for good.[38] The green-alternative parliamentary club, upon whom the media naturally focus their spotlights, therefore seeks to get "out of the purely protest and exposé phase and on to one of platform and change."[39] Parallel thereto the manifold forms of "extra-parliamentary resistance," namely the political weight of the grassroots forces, are to be further strengthened, unified and thus integrated in the political process as a more lasting component.[40]

— In all the discussion and debate surrounding green-alternative parties and their role in the party system, the underlying fundamental problem should not be forgotten or reduced solely to questions of inter-party competition. Cause and effect must be considered separately. Parties and their representatives can change or come to pass, but there is nothing to indicate that the enormous problems of our endangered environment will solve themselves or simply go away. The task of rehabilitating the environment will not only put the legitimacy of our party system to the test but also our political system's capacity to act at all. Every change toward sensitizing relevant groups and increasing our parties' willingness and capacity to solve these problems can only be welcomed in the face of these vital challenges. Thus, the erosion of the traditional parties could in turn be a desirable step toward innovation.

Notes

1. Müller-Rommel, Ferdinand: "Parteien neuen Typs" in Westeuropa. Eine vergleichende Analyse, in: *Zeitschrift für Parlamentsfragen 13* (1982), 369.

2. cf. Dachs, Herbert: Eine Renaissance des "mündigen Bürgers"? Über den Aufstieg der Salzburger Bürgerliste, in: *Österreichische Zeitschrift für Politikwissenschaft*, (1983) 3, pp. 311-330.

3. Scheucher, Markus: AL Graz-Wahlkampf, Aktionen, Arbeit im Gemeinderat, in: *Umdenken. Analysen grüner Politik in Österreich*. Vienna 1984, p. 97; cf. also Marko, Joseph: Kommunale Reformpolitik in Graz - Entstehungsbedingungen alternativer Gruppen, in: *Österreiches Jahrbuch für Politik 1983*; Munich-Vienna 1984, pp. 277-293.

4. cf. Christian, Reinhold: Die Grünen—Momentaufnahme einer Bewegung in Österreich, in: *Österreichisches Jahrbuch für Politik* (ÖJP) 1982, Munich-Vienna 1983, pp. 75-81.

5. cf. on the following Dachs, Herbert, Renaissance, Note 2; Gutmann, Raimund/Pleschberger, Werner: Die Bürgerliste—grüne Mitte in Salzburg, in Umdenken, Note 3, pp. 106-124; Praschl, Bernhard: Kommunalpolitik in Österreich. Möglichkeiten einer alternativen Kommunalpolitik. Vier Fallstudien. Doctoral Thesis, Vienna 1984, pp. 89-113.

6. Salzburger Nachrichten of October 5, 1982, after a study by Institut für Grundlagenforschung.

7. Salzburg im zeitlichen Vorfeld der Nationalratswahl. IMAS Survey 1983, Typed Manuscript, pp. 9-10.

8. cf. among others: Gonner, Ali: VGÖ und ALÖ—grün-alternative Gruppierungen in Österreich, in: *Umdenken*, Note 3, pp. 79-96; Gerlich, Peter: Ernstnehmen oder Augenzwinkern. Grün-alternative Herausforderungen der traditionellen Politik, in: Plasser, F./Ulram, P./Welan, M. (eds.): *Demokratierituale*, Vienna-Graz-Cologne 1985, pp. 183-202. Christian, Reinhold/Ulram, Peter, Grün-Alternative Parteien in österreichischen Gemeinden, in: *Jahrbuch für Politik 1987*, Vienna-Munich 1988, pp. 509-539.

9. In: *Blätter der Vereinten Grünen Österreichs*, Nr. 1 (1983), quoted after Gonner, VGÖ und ALÖ, Note 8, p. 82.

10. cf. *Die Presse*, February 24, 1986, p. 5; February 25, 1986, p. 4; *Salzburger Nachrichten*, February 24, 1986, p. 2.

11. Gonner, VGÖ und ALÖ, Note 8, p. 86.

12. Ibid. p. 85.

13. Quoted after Ibid. p. 86.

14. Ibid. p. 88f.

15. Merli, Franz/Handstanger, Meinrad: Die Alternative Liste Graz als Erweiterung des kommunalpolitischen Systems, in: *ÖJP 1983*, Munich-Vienna, 1984, p. 317; cf. also Strobl, Helmut: Grazer Gemeinderatswahl 1983, in: *ÖJP 1983*, pp. 133-140.

16. Gonner, VGÖ und ALÖ, Note 8, p. 92.

17. Kienzl, Heinz: Eine Pyrrhusniederlage, in: *Die Zukunft*, June 1983, p. 18.

18. Plasser, Fritz/Sommer, Franz: Eine "grüne" Premiere. Analyse der Vorarlberger Landtagswahl 1984, in: *ÖJP 1984*, Munich-Vienna 1985, p. 62.

19. cf. Birk, Franz/Gehmacher, Ernst/Traar, Kurt: Der Wind weht uns ins Gesicht. Erste Ergebnisse einer quantitativen Analyse der Nationalratswahl, in: *Die Zukunft*, July/August 1983, p. 15.

20. cf. among others Dachs, Renaissance, Note 2; Dachs, Herbert, Die Salzburger Landtagswahl 1984, in: *ÖJP 1984*, Munich-Vienna 1985, pp. 93-112; Merli/Handstanger, Alternative Liste Graz, Note 15, pp. 295-318; Strobl, Gemeinderatswahl, Note 15; Plasser/Sommer, Premiere, Note 18, pp. 55-66; Rote Perspektiven. Eine gesellschaftspolitische Analyse nach der Landtagswahl 1984, edited by Sozialistische Fraktion des Vorarlberger Landtages (SPÖ-Information Nr. 18), Dornbirn.

21. Plasser, Fritz: Die unsichtbare Fraktion: Struktur und Profil der Grün-Alternativen in Österreich, in: *ÖJP 1984*, Munich-Vienna 1985, p. 139.

22. Ibid. p. 141; cf. also for Graz Merli/Handstanger, Alternative Liste, Note 20, p. 315 with somewhat other values.

23. Rote Perspektiven, Note 20, p. 30.

24. Christian/Ulram, Grün-alternative Parteien... Note 8, p. 519.

25. Merli/Handstanger, Alternative Liste, Note 20, p. 316.

26. Berndt, Edwin: Die Behandlung aktueller Themen der Vorarlberger Landespolitik sowie Analysierung der LT-Wahlen 1984, Typed Manuscript, GÖFIS 1985, p. 29.

27. Lenhardt, Dieter: Und unten das Sprungtuch alter Werte, in: *Die Presse*, May 10/11, 1986, p. 5.

28. Quoted after Plasser, Fraktion, Note 21, p. 136.
29. Ibid. p. 137.
30. cf. Vor einer "strahlenden" Grün-Einigung? Kandidatenliste für Nationalrat in Arbeit, in: *Die Presse*, May 21, 1986.
31. cf. *Wochenpresse*, Nr. 49, November 28, 1986, p. 23.
32. cf. Fritz Plasser, Die Nationalratswahl 1986: Analyse und politische Konsequenzen, in: *Österr. Monatshefte*, December 1986.
33. cf. Gehmacher, Ernst: Die neuen politischen Strömungen, in: *Die Zukunft*, July/August 1985, p. 19.
34. Raschke, Joachim: Soziale Konflikte und Parteiensystem in der Bundesrepublik, in: *aus Politik und Zeitgeschichte*, B 49/85, p. 36.
35. Ibid. p. 37f.
36. Ibid. p. 39.
37. Ibid.
38. "Eskalation des Widerstandes," in: *profil*, Nr. 21, May 24, 1988, p. 27.
39. Grüne werben um sozialistische Wählerschaft, *Salzburger Nachrichten*, July 13, 1988, p. 5.
40. "Eskalation des Widerstandes," Note 37, pp. 27-28.

Bibliography

Bernd, Edwin, *Die Behandlung aktueller Themen der Vorarlberger Landespolitik sowie Analysierung der LT-Wahlen 1984*, Typoskript, Göfis 1985 (Bernd, 1985)

Birk, Franz/Gehmacher, Ernst/Traar, Kurt, *Der Wind weht uns ins Gesicht. Erste Ergebnisse einer quantitativen Analyse der Nationalratswahl*, in: *Die Zukunft* Juli/August 1983 (Birk/Gehmacher/Traar, 1983)

Christian, Reinhold, *Die Grünen—Momentaufnahme einer Bewegung in Österreich*, in: *ÖJP 1982*, München/Wien 1983 (Christian, 1983)

Dachs, Herbert, *Eine Renaissance des "mündigen Bürgers"? Über den Aufstieg der Salzburger Bürgerliste*, in: *ÖZP 3/1983* (Dachs, 1983)

Dachs, Herbert, *Das Parteiensystem im Bundesland Salzburg*, in: derselbe (Hg.), *Das politische, soziale und wirtschaftliche System im Bundesland Salzburg*, Salzburg 1985 (Dachs, 1985)

Gehmacher, Ernst, *Die neuen politischen Strömungen*, in: *Die Zukunft* Juli/August 1985 (Gehmacher, 1985)

Gerlich, Peter, *Ernstnehmen oder Augenzwinkern. Grün-alternative Herausforderungen der traditionellen Politik*, in: Fritz Plasser/Peter A. Ulram/Manfried Welan (Hg.), *Demokratierituale*, Wien/Köln/Graz 1985 (Gerlich, 1985)

Gonner Ali, *VGÖ und ALÖ—grün-alternative Gruppierungen in Österreich*, in: *Umdenken. Analysen grüner Politik in Österreich*, Wien 1984 (Gonner, 1984)

Gutmann, Raimund/Pleschberger, Werner, *Die Bürgerliste—grüne Mitte in Salzburg*, in: *Umdenken. Analysen grüner Politik in Österreich*, Wien 1984 (Gutmann/ Pleschberger, 1984)

IMAS, *Salzburg im zeitlichen Vorfeld der Nationalratswahl. Umfrage 1983* (IMAS, 1983)

196   *Dachs*

Kienzl, Heinz, *Eine Pyrrhusniederlage,* in: *Die Zukunft,* Juni 1983 (Kienzl, 1983)

Lenhardt, Dieter, *Und unten das Sprungtuch alter Werte,* in: *Die Presse,* 10./11.5.1986 (Lenhardt, 1986)

Marko, Joseph, *Kommunale Reformpolitik in Graz—Entstehungsbedingungen alternativer Gruppen,* in: *ÖJP 1983,* München/Wien 1984 (Marko, 1984)

Merli, Franz/Handstanger, Meinrad, *Die Alternative Liste Graz als Erweiterung des kommunalpolitischen Systems,* in: *ÖJP 1983,* München/Wien 1984 (Merli/Handstanger, 1984)

Müller-Rommel, Ferdinand, *"Parteien neuen Typs" in Westeuropa. Eine vergleichende Analyse,* in: *Zeitschrift für Parlamentsfragen 3/1982* (Müller-Rommel, 1982)

Nick, Rainer, *Rahmenbedingungen und Entwicklung der grün-alternativen Szene in Vorarlberg,* in: *ÖZP 2/1986* (Nick, 1986)

Plasser, Fritz, *Die unsichtbare Fraktion: Struktur und Profil der Grün-Alternativen in Österreich,* in: *ÖJP 1984,* München/Wien 1985 (Plasser, 1985)

Plasser, Fritz/Sommer, Franz, *Eine "grüne" Premiere. Analyse der Vorarlberger Landtagswahl 1984,* in: *ÖJP 1984,* München/Wien 1985 (Plasser/Sommer, 1985)

Praschl, Bernhard, *Kommunalpolitik in Österreich. Möglichkeiten einer alternativen Kommunalpolitik.* Vier Fallstudien. Phil.Diss., Wien 1984 (Praschl, 1984)

Raschke, Joachim, *Soziale Konflikte und Parteiensystem in der Bundesrepublik,* in: *Aus Politik und Zeitgeschichte B49/1985* (Raschke, 1985)

Scheucher, Markus, *AL Graz-Wahlkampf, Aktionen, Arbeit im Gemeinderat,* in: *Umdenken. Analysen grüner Politik in Österreich,* Wien 1984 (Scheucher, 1984)

Strobl, Helmut, *Grazer Gemeinderatswahl 1983,* in: *ÖJP 1983,* München/Wien 1984 (Strobl, 1984)

9

Changing Issues in the Austrian Party System

PETER A. ULRAM

1. Changing Issues—Introduction

The changing of political issues and the resultant effects on the political system, in particular the party system, was long one of the questions in political science, not only in Austria, upon which little light was shed. Study and analysis were either limited:

— to the field of electoral and voter motivation research, which long seemed rather unproductive, particularly in Austria, due in no small measure to the highly stable voting behavior of the electorate over long periods of time, and the large proportion of traditional voters which prevailed until the end of the 1960s (Gehmacher 1982; Haerpfer 1983)[1]

— or to specific fields of research, such as research concentrating on the young, party platforms, parliamentarianism (Gerlich/Ucakar 1981), or participation (Deiser/Winkler 1982).

Not until interest in problems of political culture (Ulram 1982; Müller 1984) was rekindled and the international discussion of value changes (Kaase 1985) spread to Austria (Rosenmayr 1980), were questions relating to changing issues included to a greater degree in political discussion. In this discussion, the extent to which the supposed "postindustrial dynamics of change" have led to a modification, weakening, or even a tendency toward the replacement of traditional sociostructural and ideological cleavages (Lipset/ Rokkan 1967) by new lines of conflict based more on values (Inglehart 1983, 1984), or even to the forming of a new central axis of conflict (Milbrath 1984) appears to be particularly significant.[2]

In this context, the present article aims:

— to examine the development of the traditional ideological lines of conflict;
— to document the emergence of new political issues and potential lines of conflict—insofar as this can be expressed empirically; and, on the basis of this,
— to come to some initial conclusions for the Austrian party system and political culture; in this last aim we follow Fritz Plasser in his contribution to this volume.

2. Social-liberal Consensus and Social Democratic Hegemony

Two major phases in the political development of the Second Republic can be discerned. The consolidation of Austria's postwar democracy (Weil 1985) began with the "historical compromise" between the two major political and sociocultural camps. This included not only cooperation between elites, institutionalized in the Grand Coalition and Social Partnership, but also a broad consensus among a vast majority of the population as to the central political tasks and goals: economic reconstruction and modernization of the economy to make it resemble more closely those of Western industrialized societies; defusing the social conflicts over the distribution of wealth by achieving economic growth, full employment and the establishment of the welfare state (for a historical background, see Talos 1981). For politicians, the central objectives were regaining national sovereignty, creating an Austrian national consciousness and strengthening the country's democratic institutions.

Two decades later, signs of destabilization became increasingly apparent. This period saw a partisan dealignment (Schultze 1985) and the modification of established patterns of political behavior. The "critical election" in 1970 and its continuation in 1971 constitute the end of this transitional phase. A realignment of the electorate and the party landscape takes place; the Austrian party system enters a new period of stability—the period of social-liberal consensus or (at the level of institutionalized power structures) Social Democratic hegemony.

The main issues on which a social-liberal consensus was built were, firstly, economic expansion, full employment and the improvement of the social safety net; Austrian's attitudes on these issues were, however, no longer greatly determined by the reconstruction and (to a certain extent) restoration mentality of the postwar era. Approval of "social guaranteeism" (Plasser/Ulram 1982) becomes widespread. That is, individual citizens have a strong need for security (Hofstede 1980) and consider guaranteeing material security (job, income, social security) to be one of the central tasks of the political system. The "liberal element," in turn, is noticeable mainly in legal and educational policy (Kriechbaumer 1981; Mock 1984), as well as in citizens' demands for a larger say in government ("democratization"), calls for recognition of the changed role of women, and a liberalization of the intellectual and cultural climates (Pelinka 1985).

Unlike the "historical compromise" of consociational democracy during the Grand Coalition (Lehmbruch 1967), which was based on largely stable camps, a high degree of party identification and relatively low voter flexibility, the "Social Democratic hegemony" of the single-party socialist governments (1970-1983) had a less stable base. Although the shrinking of the camps' social bases and the continuing secularization of society (Zulehner 1981) has taken place primarily at the expense of the Austrian People's Party (Plasser/ Ulram 1984), the proportion of voters with emotional ties to the Socialist Party has declined to three-fourths of its electorate, and the proportion of traditional SPÖ voters to less than two-thirds (Plasser 1987).

The conversion of the social-liberal consensus on sociopolitical matters into the unchallenged supremacy of one political party was the result of a voter coalition between the (shrinking) Social Democratic core voter group and the (growing) new middle class. The SPÖ succeeded, in fact, not only in making this voter coalition a congenial political offer, but also in personifying this in the then party chairman and federal chancellor.[3] Compared to the "modern" and "open" Socialist Party, the People's Party seemed to a majority of Austrians in the 1970s to be not only more "incompetent" politically, but also "burdened by tradition" and "closed."[4]

Table 9.1
Scale of attractiveness of political concepts (1976)
Rankings and means on a scale of 1.00 (very attractive) to 5.00 (very unattractive).

	Ranking	Mean
Social Partnership	1	1.90
democratization	2	2.27
open party	3	2.34
Social Democratic	4	2.35
socialist	5	2.36
liberal	6	2.46
Christian-Social	7	2.49
Christian Democratic	8	2.54
nationalistic	9	2.58
progressive center	10	2.65

Source: Dr. Fessel + GfK, Grundlagenstudie (1976) (Excerpt from a list of concepts with a total of 25 items.)

3. The Fading of Old Ideologies

The (electoral and political) stability of the social-liberal coalition of values, interests and voters does, of course, conceal, in a way, the profound changes taking place at the foundations of the party system and, as a result, those of its hegemonic force as well (Gerlich 1987). In addition to the heightened mobility of the electorate and the waning strength of party ties (cf. F. Plasser's contribution to this volume), traditional ideological conceptualizations are in the process of fading. This change is taking place despite the fact that as early as the beginning of the 1970s, the population of Austria already showed a very low level of ideological self-anchoring in an international comparison.[5] The value of the classical "left-right continuum," for instance, as an expression of the (socio-) political placement of both individuals and parties is declining, with the "radical fringes" in particular ("far left/far right") becoming relatively insignificant.[6]

Table 9.2
Placement of Austrians on the left-right continuum (1973-1985)
(as a percentage of all Austrians)

	1973	1976	1980	1983[+)]	1985
far left		3			1
moderate left		16			10
"left"	16	19	13	14	11
center	44	40	52	51	49
"right"	23	26	18	19	20
moderate right		21			17
far right		5			3
no answer	17	15	17	16	21

+)   Year of elections to the National Council
Source:
Dr Fessel + GfK, Politische Studie (1973)
Dr Fessel + GfK, Grundlagenstudie (1976)
Gehmacher 1981 (IFES data from 1980)
Dr Fessel + GfK, Politische Kultur (1983)
Dr Fessel + GfK, Innen- und Außenperspektive des österreichischen Parteiensystems (1985)

The decline in the number of respondents placing themselves on the "right" or "left" of the ideological scale is particularly pronounced among the young (in 1985 only one in five, compared to one in three for the population as a whole) and core voter groups—workers (SPÖ) and tradesmen

(ÖVP)—all of whom still showed above-average polarization in 1976. Similarly, the most educated class becomes less right-leaning, and the less educated class less left-leaning (see table 9.3).

Thus it holds true for Austria too that traditional cleavages, loyalties and ideologies are losing ground, and new factors determining political attitudes and behavior are gaining prominence (Traar/Birk 1987). These range from the increase in personalism in politics to disillusionment with parties, to issue orientations.

Table 9.3
The decrease in the proportion of respondents on the "right" or "left" of the ideological self-placement scale by groups (1976-1985)

Decrease in percent between 1976 and 1985	"left"	"right"
All Austrians	-8	-6
aged 16-19	-11	-11
aged 20-29	-12	-8
University graduates	-2	-32
high school graduates	-8	-20
schooling completed	-8	-4
schooling not completed	-7	-4
tradesmen	-5	-14
workers	-12	-2
salaried employees/ civil servants	-8	-5

Source:
Dr Fessel + GfK, Grundlagenstudie (1976)
Dr Fessel + GfK, Innen- und Außenperspektive des österreichischen Parteiensystems (1985)

4. The Range of Issues in the 1980s

In comparison with the period of social-liberal consensus, the range of political issues in the 1980s has changed markedly. A few of the same issues continue to be stressed—this is above all true of issues concerning the quality of democracy and, to a lesser extent, the issue of "social guaranteeism"—but these have been modified and supplemented by new issues.

On the level of global sociopolitical orientations, for example, Austrians' approval of intervention in their lives by the social-welfare state (interventionism)[7] has clearly decreased, the law-and-order syndrome has weakened, and approval of aid to developing nations (globalism) has risen. The latter two developments can be seen as a widening of the area for which society is considered responsible (integration of marginalized groups, understanding of the Third World).

Simultaneously, a new ideological axis on the dimensions "jobs and standard of living" vs. "nature and the environment" is becoming apparent. Most significantly, it can no longer be taken for granted that increasing the standard of living is considered the ultimate political goal, as it now ranks in importance below the preservation of our natural environment.

Except for the "interventionism" and "egalitarianism" dimensions, where there are considerable differences between "Greens" (1985: VGÖ) and "Alternatives" (1985: ALÖ) (Dr Fessel + GfK, Innen- und Außenperspektive des österreichischen Parteiensystems 1985), the position of the "Green-Alternatives" as a whole diverges greatly from that of the average Austrian: they are especially reform-oriented and concerned for the environment, they show a high level of participation and are particularly open to the concerns of developing countries and marginalized groups in society. The young and the educated class are very environmentally-minded and reform-oriented; in addition, the young have an inclination towards increased participation; the educated class is more skeptical of interventionist and egalitarian tendencies.

The relatively stable issue of the quality of Austrian democracy is closely related to Austrians' growing detachment from their system of political and state institutions and the shifting importance of substantial political issues. Whereas in the mid 1970s two institutions, namely the school system and the health service, were at the top of the list of areas in which the population wanted more codetermination, the areas heading this list in 1985 are the natural and residential environments (Dr Fessel & Co., Bedingungen und Barrieren der Identifikation mit öffentlichen Institutionen 1986). In general, demands for more codetermination and a larger say in the system of institutions are abating, and calls for broad-based direct democracy and the desire for more participation on particular issues are becoming more common (see graph 9.2).

Our picture of the situation becomes sharper when we consider the development of several political issues in the 1980s. Whereas preserving jobs (and income level) remains about equally important, more emphasis is clearly placed on protecting the environment and preventing waste (of taxpayer's money). These issues are now given approximately the same priority as social guaranteeism. There is virtually a triad of political goals which a vast majority of the population believes the political institutions must achieve.[8]

Graph 9.1: Sociopolitical Orientations - Austria in 1976 and 1987
(Means on a scale of 1 to 5)

FESSEL + GFK

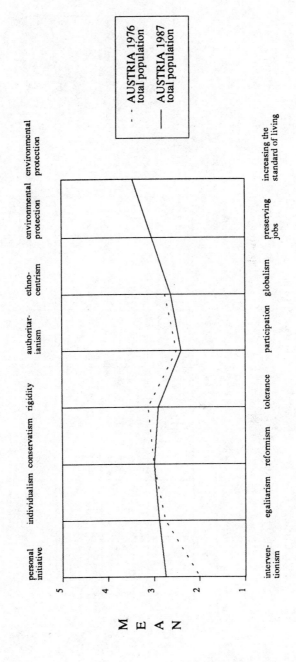

Graph 9.2: Sociopolitical Orientations - selected Groups (1987)
(Means on a scale of 1 to 5)

FESSEL + GFK

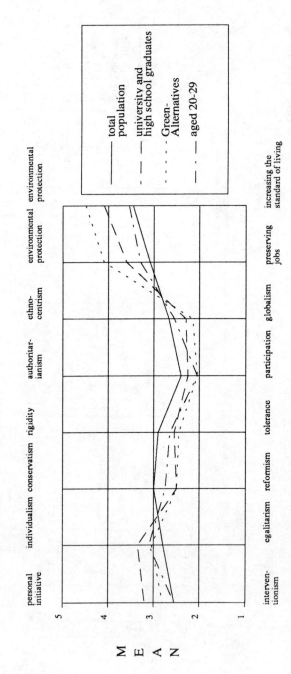

Table 9.4
Austrians' political priorities, 1980-1987
(as a percentage of all Austrians)

a) Rankings	1980	1981	1982	1983/1	1983/2	1984	1985	1987
preserving jobs	1	1	1	1	1	2	1	3
environmental protection	5	5	4	5	2	1	2	1
preventing waste in government	6	2	2	2	3	3	2	2
creating jobs	4	4	3	3	4	4	4	4

b) Percentages	1980	1981	1982	1983/1	1983/2	1984	1985	1987
preserving jobs	72	75	79	81	79	77	77	74
environmental protection	52	55	69	71	76	80	76	79
preventing waste in government	51	73	72	77	75	74	76	76
creating jobs	56	58	70	73	74	73	73	72

Source: Dr Fessel + GfK, Politische Umfragen (1980-1987)

Accordingly, improving environmental protection, maintaining full employment, fighting corruption and the abuse of privilege, and alleviating the tax burden are seen as the "most important problems" the political parties should deal with in 1987[9]. Employment and tax questions remain about as significant as in 1981, whereas consciousness of environmental protection and, to a lesser degree, corruption and the abuse of privilege as problems grew between 1981 and 1985/1987. The rising importance of the latter issue indicates a disillusionment with politicians and political parties, and this has likewise grown rapidly. This development, however, is only indirectly related to the change of substantial political issues (Plasser/Ulram 1985).

Preserving social peace, maintaining law and order (fighting crime), giving citizens a larger say in government, preserving the standard of living and eliminating social injustice are in the middle of the list of demands. Their importance hardly changes, except for that of the fight against crime, which is clearly given lower priority (cf. the related shift of sociopolitical preferences towards more liberal treatment of marginalized groups in society).

5. The "Greening" of Austria

The most important of the new issues is the environmental issue. As it was emerging, it was still a matter of concern for a minority only and struck a responsive chord mostly in traditional environmentalist circles and with committed intellectuals as well as Alternative and Green movements on the margin of established politics (Brand 1985). It has now, however, been taken up by all sections of the population, and even groups scarcely interested in politics and with very limited access to information are highly interested in environmental matters and follow the coverage of at least selected questions in the mass media (Dr. Fessel & Co., Umwelt und Wirtschaft in Österreich 1985).

Table 9.5
Problems Austrians would like political parties to deal with (1981-1987)

	ranking			percentage		
	81	85	87	81	85	87
improving environmental protection	5	3	1	35	49	64
maintaining full employment	1	1	2	60	61	62
fighting corruption and the abuse of privilege	4	2	3	36	53	45
alleviating the tax burden	2	4	4	44	44	37
preserving social peace	5	5	5	35	33	34
atomic power plant problem	10	10	6	21	21	28
preserving the standard of living	7	8	7	29	25	26
maintaining law and order (fighting crime)	3	5	7	41	33	26
eliminating injustice in society	9	9	9	22	22	18
giving citizens a larger say in government	8	7	10	24	27	17
preserving individual freedom	111	11	11	14	11	11
defending moral values	12	11	12	11	11	9
competition with other political parties to ensure that democracy continues to function	13	13	13	9	9	6

Source:
Dr. Fessel + GfK, Thematische Determinanten (1987)
Dr. Fessel + GfK, Innen- und Außenperspektive des österreichischen Parteiensystems (1985)
Dr. Fessel + GfK, Parteienverdrossenheit (1981)

In general, Austrians are extremely pessimistic about the state of the environment. The situation is perceived to have worsened since the beginning of the 1980s, with the areas "increasing damage to our forests," "environmental damage through waste products," "air pollution," "traffic noise," and "the extinction of animal and plant species" considered particularly worrisome. Citizens' opinions as to the urgency needed in taking measures to improve the state of the environment are subject to certain fluctuations (in 1982, in addition to air pollution, the health hazard posed by contaminants and chemicals in food products was perceived as predominant; due in no small measure to media coverage on the subject, 1984 was "the year of the dying forests"). Without taking these "details" into account, it can be stated, in any case, that in 1984 three-fourths of all Austrians were critical of failings in environmental policy, and only one-fourth considered the measures taken to be "sufficient" or "almost too much." Between 1982 and 1984, the percentage of respondents answering "sufficient" or "almost too much" was cut almost in half from 40 to 23 percent. Criticism of the lack of activity in protecting the environment is clearly greater as the level of education rises, and in the upper social classes. The young, white-collar workers (salaried employees and civil servants) and city dwellers (above all the Viennese) are particularly critical. The percentage of "severe critics" rises disproportionately in these groups—except in Vienna, where they already constituted a particularly high proportion in 1982.

In all Austria there is no section of the population which, in 1984, was more satisfied than in 1982 with the amount of environmental protection activity, or more critical of "exaggerated" environmental protection measures (see table 9.6).

Austrians are very deeply affected by this issue. Firstly, a general change in their relationship to their (natural) environment is becoming apparent, and it is increasingly seen as something valuable and worth protecting which should be subjected to external influence to a limited extent only. Secondly, it is increasingly understood how important the behavior of the individual is—this regards both his day-to-day treatment of nature and his economic behavior.

Table 9.6
Judgement of environmental protection activities (1982-1984) in percent

	far too little/ nothing really done at all			somewhat too little done			enough/almost too much done		
	82	84	82-84	82	84	82-84	82	84	82-84
Austria	18	22	+4	41	53	+12	40	23	-17
aged 20-29	18	30	+12	47	51	+4	36	18	-18
Vienna	28	33	+5	46	48	+2	26	17	-9
A/B classes	23	27	+4	44	54	+10	33	19	-14
C class	16	22	+6	41	54	+13	42	22	-20
D/E classes	14	17	+3	36	50	+14	45	28	-17
salaried employees/ civil servants	21	29	+8	56	54	-2	25	18	-7
workers	18	20	+2	41	57	+16	41	22	-19

Source: Dr. Fessel & Co., Umwelt und Wirtschaft in Österreich (1985)

At the same time, though, most Austrians denied that, in principle, a line of conflict ran between those concerned with protecting the environment and those concerned with preserving jobs. As consciousness of an existing problem grows, so does the (hopeful) belief that these two goals are compatible.

Table 9.7
Environmental protection and jobs (1982-1985)
(as a percentage of all Austrians)

	1982	1985	82-85
+ New jobs are created in many fields by introducing stringent environmental protection regulations (e.g. through the production of filters for sewage treatment and industrial plants). On the one hand, this protects the environment, and on the other, jobs are preserved in the long term because new products are made	69	79	+10
+ Of course environmental protection is important. But especially in times of economic difficulty, environmental protection measures should only be implemented in areas where they are not a financial burden on companies (e.g. industry), so that jobs are by no means endangered	27	18	-9
+ No response	3	4	-1

Source:
Dr. Fessel & Co., Umwelt und Wirtschaft in Österreich (1985)
Dr. Fessel & GfK, Angestelltenprojekt (1986)

6. The Tax State and Waste in Government

Unlike the environmental issue, the tax issue has a long history in politics. It was only recently, however, that it too became a central political question. One reason for this is that the tax burden has become heavier as a result of changed general economic and fiscal conditions—the income in real terms of wide segments of the population is either growing only slowly or is stagnant; the overall tax ratio has risen rapidly in the past decade; the specific effects the marginal tax rates have had. The other reason is that the tax issue is related to the issue of waste in government and to the loss of faith in the interventionist social-welfare state. The tax burden is increasingly considered "oppressive" and many parts of the tax system itself "unjust."[10] Accordingly, Austrians are increasingly understanding of those who evade or refuse to pay taxes, and they sympathize considerably with the thriving submerged economy (Hofbauer/Schüssel 1984).

Table 9.8
Attitudes toward taxes (the tax burden) 1980-1985:
(as a percentage of all Austrians)

		1980	1984	1985	80-85
+	"If the tax burden continues to increase, more and more people will try to avoid paying taxes"	73	*	82	+9
+	"If additional income is taxed, it is no longer worth working more"	61	*	68	+7
+	"Taxes in Austria are much higher or somewhat higher than in other countries"	30	*	66	+36
+	"For me personally the tax burden is high or very high"	*	55	*	*
+	"The amount of taxes I or my family have to pay is somewhat or completely unjust"	*	*	45	*

Source:
Dr. Fessel + GfK, Steuerwiderstand (1980)
Dr. Fessel + GfK, Politische Umfragen (1980, 1984, 1985)

The population is certainly even more dissatisfied with the way tax money is used than with the amount they pay. The impression that government "acts wastefully" is widespread. This is reinforced by the handling of various major construction projects which are often linked to corruption scandals (the construction of the new General Hospital and the International Convention Center in Vienna, various stretches of freeway) (see table 9.9).

At the same time, Austrians are losing faith at an absolutely dramatic rate in the government's capability of dealing with problems and in the positive effects of its interventionist activities. As for the social security system, it is doubted whether "the security system is secure," and faith in political promises guaranteeing security is wavering. In addition, support for policies which preserve jobs by subsidizing predominantly nationalized "sunset industries" producing deficits is disappearing.

Table 9.9

Judging the use of taxpayers' money 1980-1985:
(as a percentage of all Austrians)
(More than one answer possible)

	1980	1985	80-85
+ The state is often careless with taxpayers' money	41	61	+20
+ Taxes are often used for very different purposes than is originally planned	39	54	+15
+ The use of taxpayers' money is monitored very closely	16	8	-8
+ The state is very economical with taxpayers' money	5	1	-4

Source:
Dr. Fessel + GfK, Steuerwiderstand (1980)
Dr. Fessel + GfK, Politische Umfrage (1985)

Table 9.10

Loss of faith and criticism of subsidies
(as a percentage of all Austrians)

	1980	1981	1982	1983	1984	1985	1986
+ Retirement benefits will not be endangered for the next ten years	69	*	38	*	26	*	*
+ The state can be depended upon to always pay	55	*	36	*	30	28	*
+ Jobs in Austria are most endangered by the burden the state places on business	31	37	40	49	44	46	50
+ The nationalized industries should not be given billions of schillings to cover their losses	*	17	31	34	*	*	56

Source:
Dr. Fessel + GfK, Politische Umfragen (1980, 81, 82, 83, 86)
Dr. Fessel + Co., Einstellung der Österreicher zur sozialen Sicherheit (Ergänzung 1984)
Dr. Fessel + GfK, Angestelltenprojekt (1985)

7. Criticism of the Efficiency of Traditional Politics

The increase in consciousness of substantial political problems goes hand in hand with growing doubts about (among other things) the ability of traditional politics to deal with these problems. Whereas in 1981 three-fourths of those Austrians who criticized the parties for their inability to take problems into consideration could not spontaneously cite any concrete examples, this was true of only one in ten in 1985. The area most often spontaneously criticized was environmental policy, followed by labor market policy, political ethics/abuse of power/corruption and the related issues taxes/waste/national debt/reducing the budget deficit. More than three-fourths of all persons presented with a structured question[11] were dissatisfied with the amount of consideration given to "the fight against corruption and the abuse of privilege, alleviating the tax burden, eliminating social injustice, giving citizens a larger say in government, protecting the environment, and achieving full employment." The only areas witz which a majority was satisfied with were "preserving individual freedom, fighting crime and preserving social peace." Between 1981 and 1987, dissatisfaction increased in nearly all areas, with the largest growth in the areas "full employment, maintaining the standard of living, competition between the parties, and environmental protection." The only area with which Austrians were significantly more satisfied was "maintaining law and order"[12] (see table 9.11).

This deterioration of the balance of achievements of political parties corresponds to a deterioration of the image of politicians. As early as 1980/1981, Austrians did have grave doubts about certain moral qualities of politicians—they were accused above all of untruthfulness and pursuit of power and their own interests—but "the fact that politicians lacked credibility did not necessarily mean that citizens had a low opinion of their achievements" (Plasser/Ulram 1982, p. 162). A majority did believe their efforts were sincere and their work, on the whole, successful. Just five years later one-half of all Austrians no longer gave politicians passing marks and accused them of corruption and being open to bribery. This image is even more widespread among the young. Politicians are thus regarded as belonging to a privileged "political class," removed from the people, and their work is seen to have fewer and fewer positive effects. This too is a novel development in the Second Austrian Republic.

Table 9.11
Insufficient consideration given to problems by political parties (1981-1987)

	Index of insufficient problem consideration 1.00=sufficient, 2.00=insufficient, 3.00 none at all							problem given insufficient consideration/none at all in percent			problem given sufficient consideration in percent			importance		
	ranking			index value										ranking		
	81	85	87	81	85	87	81-87	81	87	81-87	81	87	81-87	81	85	87
+ fighting corruption and the abuse of privilege	2	2	1	2.08	2.18	2.23	neg.	79	84	+5	10	7	-3	4	2	3
+ alleviating tax burden	1	1	2	2.11	2.23	2.10	neg.	78	82	+4	13	10	-3	2	4	4
+ eliminating injustice in society	3	3	3	1.92	2.06	2.02	neg.	70	75	+5	20	17	-4	9	9	9
+ giving citizens a larger say in government	4	4	4	1.91	2.02	2.02	neg.	68	72	+4	23	19	-4	8	7	10
+ improving environmental protection	6	6	5	1.76	1.82	1.80	neg.	65	74	+9	29	18	-11	5	3	1
+ achieving full employment	10	8	6	1.42	1.78	1.86	neg.	36	71	+35	56	21	-35	1	1	2
+ atomic power plant problem	5	5	7	1.80	1.87	1.78		60	56	-4	29	34	+5	10	10	5
+ defending moral values	7	7	8	1.71	1.80	1.73		52	55	+3	35	35	+0	12	11	12
+ competition with other parties to ensure that democracy continues to function	9	9	9	1.52	1.73	1.66	neg.	41	51	+10	47	38	-9	13	13	13
+ preserving standard of living	10	10	10	1.42	1.66	1.64	neg.	36	53	+17	56	39	-17	7	8	7
+ preserving individual freedom	12	12	11	1.38	1.53	1.47	neg.	30	36	+6	59	54	-5	11	11	11
+ maintaining law and order (fighting crime)	8	11	11	1.68	1.60	1.47	pos.	55	40	-15	37	53	+16	3	5	7
+ preserving social peace	13	13	13	1.36	1.49	1.43	pos.	31	36	-5	50	56	-4	5	5	5

Source:
Dr. Fessel + GfK, Parteienverdrossenheit (1981)
Dr. Fessel + GfK, Innen- und Außenperspektive des Österreichischen Parteiensystems (1985)
Dr. Fessel + GfK, Thematische Determinanten der Wahlentscheidung (1987)

Table 9.12
The image of politicians (1980/81-1984/85)

as a percentage of	those aged 12-24			total population		
	1980	1984	80-84	1981	1985	81-85
+ Politicians are often untruthful, especially before elections.	74	88	+14	79	*	*
+ Politicians often argue in public, but are "good friends" again immediately afterwards.	72	76	+4	86	*	*
+ Politicians have mainly their own interests in mind.	55	72	+17	63	*	*
+ Politicians have mostly power in mind.	62	72	+10	70	*	*
+ Politicians are corrupt and open to bribery.	32	60	+28	38	49	+11
+ Rejection of the statement: "All in all, politicians do a pretty good job."	22	58	+36	30	45	+15
+ Rejection of the statement: "Politicians make a sincere effort on their voters' behalf."	33	55	+22	37	*	*
+ Politicians don't care about ordinary citizens.	36	52	+16	42	*	*

Source:
Plasser/Ulram 1982
Dr. Fessel & Co., Jugendstudie spezial (1984)
Dr. Fessel + GfK, Angestelltenprojekt (1985)

8. From Changing Issues to Changing Voters

If we attempt to summarize and interpret the changes in the ideological and political issues landscapes in Austria documented in this article, we reach the following conclusions:

1. The traditional conflict structures—particularly those linked to the conflicts of major segments of society over the distribution of material wealth and to ideological dividing lines such as "left-right," "liberal-conservative"—have not completely disappeared and been replaced by new conflicts of values, notably those along the "materialist-postmaterialist" dimension. Firstly, traditional ideological conceptualizations and conflicts over distribution of wealth continue to exist, and secondly, due in no small measure to the changed general economic situation, they have undergone certain modifications. This is true, for example, with regard to government intervention through social and economic policies.[13]

2. But these traditional axes of conflict and ideological conceptualizations in particular are fading in scope and intensity, and are thus becoming less dominant.[14] This is either due to the shrinking of the more or less unified political subcultures (political secularization), or because they must compete with other political-ideological conceptualizations.

3. These new conflict configurations should not be rashly interpreted as simply being a new "materialist-postmaterialist" dimension to complement the existing "right-left" dimension, that is, as the addition of a conflict of values to the structural conflict (Inglehart 1983). The issues of environmental protection and the quality of democracy, for example, are important to a far greater proportion of Austrians than just the "postmaterialists." Nor can the supporters and potential voters of Green-Alternative groups be equated with the group of postmaterialist protesters (Plasser 1985, 1987; Ulram 1985a; Gerlich 1985).

4. On the whole, a triangle of issues is ascertainable—"the environment"/"social guaranteeism"/"the tax state and waste in government." This describes the demands made by wide segments of society and also shows the areas where lines of conflict are present. Supplementary issues are "criticism of politicians and political parties" and "the search for new forms of expression of authentic politics."

5. These new configurations of issues, together with the growing mobility of the electorate, have subjected the traditional party system to considerable stress. They are one of the main factors contributing to the continuing erosion of the social-liberal consensus and the end of Social Democratic hegemony, but also have repercussions on the party system as a whole.[15]

6. In general, (groups of) specific issues are increasingly determining political behavior orientations. In Austria too, issue voters—i.e. those voters whose vote for a certain party essentially depends on its position regarding concrete questions and political issues—are becoming more numerous. In 1985, some 20 percent of all Austrians could be identified as environmental-issue voters, about 16 percent as tax-issue voters, and another 16 percent as job-security-issue voters. Although the individual groups of issue voters do vary with regard to social profile (the sections of society they are mainly based in), there is considerable overlapping between them. Approximately half the members of any group of issue voters can be considered members of one or both of the other issue voter groups. In addition, there is a statistically relevant number of issue voters from all three groups in all sections of Austrian society and with all political and value orientations.[16]

Table 9.13
The social profile of issue voters (1985)
Structural data in percent*

		environmental protection	tax reform	job security
age:	under 30	32	23	31
	30-59	46	52	45
	60 and over	23	25	25
education:	high school/ university graduates	27	19	16
	schooling completed	46	50	44
	schooling not completed	27	31	40
occupational group:	salaried employees/ civil servants	31	30	25
	skilled/unskilled workers	20	18	27
	self-employed (including farmers)	8	12	8
size of town:	less than 50,000 inhabitants	55	48	63
	50,000-100,000 inhabitants	18	16	15
	Vienna	27	26	23
party preference:	SPÖ	37	33	49
	ÖVP	26	37	22
	FPÖ	3	4	2
	VGÖ/	7	3	2
	ALÖ/ Greens	4 } 11	2 } 5	1 } 3
voter type:	traditional voters	34	37	41
	mobile voters	59	58	51
political integration:	high	17	17	21
	medium	25	26	22
	low	14	12	11
value preference:	postmaterialists	25	17	21
	intermediate group	55	58	22
	materialists	19	24	11
issue voters:	environment	100	56	60
	tax reform	49	100	51
	job security	46	51	100

*   This table should be read: 32% of respondents who stated that a party's commitment to environmental protection is very important for their voting decision are younger than 30, etc. In cases where the figures in one column (e.g. for educational group, party preference, etc.) do not total 100 percent, not all respondents could be included in one of the categories.

Source: Dr. Fessel + GfK, Angestelltenprojekt (1985)

7.   In the 1980s, the Austrian party system is in a phase of erosion and partial regrouping. The 1986 National Council elections (which brought heavy losses for the SPÖ and losses for the ÖVP) did electorally confirm the end of Social Democratic hegemony, but no new power center emerged.[17] Both major parties show "signs of structural exhaustion" (Plasser 1987), so that suitable reactions to the new challenges (Gerlich 1983, 1984) in the near future seem rather improbable.

8.   At the same time, the developments described above, namely political secularization, growing voter mobility, disillusionment with parties and politicians and changing issues, make clear what obstacles would have to be overcome to create a new hegemonic system (to follow the "historical compromise" and the "social-liberal consensus"). In order to surmount these difficulties, the traditional political actors would need to fundamentally reform the substance of their policies, their organizations, political behavior and self-portrayal. If they do not succeed in doing so—and at present they seem neither particularly able nor willing to carry out such a reorientation—the previous "hyperstability" of the system may be followed by a general destabilization of the Austrian party state. On the basis of developments thus far, a sudden crisis leading to a rupture appears less probable than a slowly developing crisis, that is, the continuing erosion of the party system, a "mobile" potential for protest, and the growing alienation of the rest of society from organized politics.

Notes

1. This was further aggravated by the difficulties, which are especially pronounced in Austria, that university political scientists encounter in achieving access to data.

2. For a summary of this discussion, see, above all, Dalton/Flanagan/Beck 1984, Sorauf 1984; Rommel 1983; Klages/Kmieciak 1979; Klages 1985, Oberndörfer/Rattinger/Schmitt 1985.

3. In 1976, 30 percent of all Austrians believed the SPÖ was an "open party," whereas only 16 percent believed this was true for the ÖVP. Among young voters and salaried employees/civil servants, the "groups of the future," the percentages were 32% (SPÖ) and 16% (ÖVP). (Dr. Fessel + GfK, Grundlagenstudie 1976). Table 9.1 shows that after the "neutral" concept of Social Partnership, the next five highest ranked concepts are ones which are considered to apply primarily to the SPÖ.

4. This is true despite the "modern" 1972 "Salzburg Plattform" and the "Plans on Quality of Life" (1972-1975) in which the Austrian People's Party portrayed itself as, among other things, open, modern, socially responsible, promoting participation to a certain extent, and "green" (although this expression had not yet been used in the political discussion). But this description, formulated mainly by leading party intellectuals, did not, in fact, correspond to the actual attitudes and behavior of a large majority of the party or its leaders. So, apart from certain exceptions, this platform was not put

into practice, and later on additions were made and both new versions and "popular versions" were written in attempts to make the contents of the party platform more conservative (cf. Ulram 1985b).

5. Among the countries examined in the 1973/74 Political Action Study—the United States, Great Britain, West Germany, Italy, the Netherlands, Finland, Switzerland and Austria—Austria showed the lowest level of ideological thinking with just 8% of the population demonstrating a medium or high level of ideological conceptualization of politics (Klingemann 1979; Rosenmayr 1980; Barnes 1985).

6. For a discussion of the meaningfulness of this indicator, see inter alia Pappi 1983; Klingemann 1979; Inglehart/Klingemann 1976. The figures in table 9.2 differ from those of the Political Action Study (Rosenmayr 1980; Barnes/Kaase 1979) which states that in a self-placement survey in 1974, 31 percent of Austrians placed themselves on the "right" (with 10% of this group belonging to the "far right").

7. See the appendix to this article for the definition of the concepts used and the exact formulation of the question. The two following graphs are based on the means of scales to be found in the source of graphs 5 and 6: Dr. Fessel + GfK, Grundlagenstudie (1976), Dr Fessel + GfK, Thematische Determinanten (1987).

8. This is a political "magical polygon," so to speak. A significant jump in the priority given to environmental protection between the spring and autumn of 1983 is ascertainable. The rise of this issue was apparently accelerated by its politicization and the extensive coverage it received in the media ("Electoral Chances of the Greens," cf. Sommer 1985) during the 1983 campaign for elections to the lower house of parliament (National Council).

9. The order differs from the ranking of Austrians' priorities listed above, since, firstly, the lists themselves differ, and secondly, defining an issue as a "problem" involves different cognitive and emotional connotations. For the relationship between the tax and waste issues, see below in section 6.

10. This latent discontent is activated on certain occasions and is then more significant than shown by the figures quoted in table 9.11. The government's package of tax "measures" (SPÖ)/"burdens" (ÖVP) passed in 1983, for example, is perceived by two-thirds of all Austrians to be socially unjust and it is believed to favor segments of society which are already "privileged" at the expense of "those earning lower salaries" and "workers" (Plasser/Ulram 1984).

11. Structured question—basis: all interviewees (four most important problems from a list presented them); open question—basis: respondents perceiving unsolved problems (59% of interviewees); of these problems, the three most important ones.

12. The decrease in dissatisfaction with the tax situation between 1985 and 1987 (after an increase from 1981 to 1985) is probably a result of the plans of the SPÖ and the ÖVP to carry out a tax reform—an issue which played an essential role in the 1986 election campaign; the decrease in dissatisfaction on the atomic power plant issue is presumably due to Austria's definitive decision to forgo the peaceful use of atomic energy after the accident in 1986 in the Chernobyl atomic power plant.

13. Cf. the discussion of reprivatization which began locally before spreading to a national level in the wake of the crisis in the nationalized industries.

14. In the Second Austrian Republic other "old" axes of conflict, such as political Catholicism-Anticlericalism/laicism, the question of an Austrian national identity, and centralism-regionalism have also continued to have an effect, although this is usually weaker.

15. In the list of reasons former SPÖ voters stated for not voting Socialist in the 1983 National Council elections—which caused the party to lose its absolute majority—the leading points were "greater commitment to economizing," "more economical use of tax money," "no more major construction projects," "the results of referenda and public opinion polls should be taken seriously," "containing the national debt," as well as the party's fundamental policies and the elimination of the abuse of privilege and the party-book system. The environmental issue was an additional motive for Green-Alternative voters (Ulram 1985b).

16. What is striking is the above-average percentage of postmaterialists in all issue groups. This too indicates that the change of values taking place in Austria is not principally one orientation replacing another, but, essentially, older orientations being supplemented by newer ones (cumulative change of values).

17. See the contribution to this volume by Plasser/Ulram.

Bibliography

Barnes, Samuel H., *Il Cittadino Italiano: un caso particolare?*, in: *Il Mulino 1985/6* (Barnes, 1985)

Barnes, Samuel H./Kaase, Max et al., *Political Action: Mass Participation in Five Western Democracies*, Beverly Hills/London 1979 (Barnes/Kaase, 1979)

Brand, Karl Werner (Hg.), *Neue soziale Bewegungen in Westeuropa und den USA*, Frankfurt/New York 1985 (Brand, 1985)

Dalton, Russel J./Flanagan, Scott C./Beck, Paul Allen, *Political Forces and Partisan Change*, in: Russel J. Dalton/Scott C. Flanagan/Paul Allen Beck (eds.), *Electoral Change in Advanced Industrial Democracies. Realignment or Dealignment?*, Princeton (N.J.), 1984 (Dalton/Flanagan/Beck, 1984)

Deiser, Roland/Winkler, Norbert, *Das politische Handeln der Österreicher*, Wien, 1982 (Deiser/Winkler, 1982)

Gehmacher, Ernst, *Faktoren des Wählerverhaltens*, in: Heinz Fischer (Hg.), *Das politische System Österreichs*, Wien/München/Zürich, 1982 (Gehmacher, 1982)

Gerlich, Peter, *Österreichs Parteien: Ergebnisse und Perspektiven*, in: Gerlich/Müller, 1983 (Gerlich, 1983)

Gerlich, Peter, *Die latente Krise der Traditionsparteien*, in: Koren/Pisa/Waldheim, 1984 (Gerlich, 1984)

Gerlich, Peter, *Ernstnehmen oder Augenzwinkern: Grün-alternative Herausforderungen der traditionellen Politik*, in: Plasser/Ulram/Welan, 1985 (Gerlich, 1985)

Gerlich, Peter, *Consocialism to Competition: The Austrian Party System since 1945*, in: Hans Daalder (ed.), *Party Systems in Denmark, Austria, Switzerland, the Netherlands and Belgium*, London 1987 (Gerlich, 1987)

Gerlich, Peter/Ucakar, Karl, *Staatsbürger und Volksvertretung: Das Alltagsverständnis von Parlament und Demokratie in Österreich*, Salzburg 1981 (Gerlich/Ucakar, 1981)

Gerlich, Peter/Müller, Wolfgang C. (Hg.), *Zwischen Koalition und Konkurrenz: Österreichs Parteien seit 1945*, Wien 1983 (Gerlich/Müller, 1983)

Haerpfer, Christian, *Nationalratswahlen und Wählerverhalten seit 1945*, in: Gerlich/ Müller, 1983 (Haerpfer, 1983)

Haerpfer, Christian, *Abschied vom Loyalitätsritual: Langfristige Veränderungen im Wählerverhalten*, in: Plasser/Ulram/Welan, 1985 (Haerpfer, 1985)

Hawlik, Johann/Schüssel, Wolfgang, *Staat laß nach. Vorschläge zur Begrenzung und Privatisierung öffentlicher Aufgaben*, Wien 1985 (Hawlik/Schüssel, 1985)

Hofbauer, Ernst/Schüssel, Wolfgang, *Schattenwirtschaft in Österreich: Ein ökonomisches Sittenbild*, Wien 1984 (Hofbauer/Schüssel, 1984)

Hofstede, Geert, *Culture's Consequences: International Differences in Work-Related Values*, Beverly Hills/London 1980 (Hofstede, 1980)

Inglehart, Roland, *Traditionelle politische Trennungslinien und die Entwicklung der neuen Politik in westlichen Gesellschaften*, in: *Politische Vierteljahresschrift 1983/2* (Inglehart, 1983)

Inglehart, Roland, *The Changing Structure of Political Cleavages in Western Society*, in: Dalton/Flanagan/Beck, 1984 (Inglehart, 1984)

Inglehart, Roland/Klingemann, Hans D., *Ideological Conceptualization and Value Priorities*, in: Barnes/Kaase 1979 (Inglehart/Klingemann, 1979)

Kaase, Max, *Wertwandel*, in: Dieter Nohlen (Hg.), *Pipers Wörterbuch zur Politik* (1, Nation Building—Zweiparteiensystem) München/Zürich 1985 (Kaase, 1985)

Klages, Herbert, *Wertorientierungen im Wandel: Rückblick, Gegenwartsanalyse, Prognosen*, Frankfurt/New York 1985 (Klages, 1985)

Klages, Helmut/Kmieciak, Peter (Hg.), *Wertwandel und gesellschaftlicher Wandel*, Frankfurt/New York 1979 (Klages/Kmieciak, 1979)

Klingemann, Hans D., *Measuring Ideological Conceptualizations*, in: Barnes/Kaase 1979 (Klingemann, 1979)

Koren, Stephan/Pisa, Karl/Waldheim, Kurt (Hg.), *Politik für die Zukunft, Festschrift für Alois Mock*, Wien/Köln/Graz 1984 (Koren/Pisa/Waldheim, 1984)

Kriechbaumer, Robert, *Österreichs Innenpolitik 1970-1975*, Wien 1981 (*Österreichisches Jahrbuch für Politik*, Sonderband 1) (Kriechbaumer, 1981)

Lehmbruch, Gerhard, *Proporzdemokratie: Politisches System und politische Kultur in der Schweiz und in Österreich*, Tübingen 1967 (Lehmbruch, 1967)

Lipset, Seymour Martin/Rokkan, Stein (eds.), *Party System and Voter Alignments*, New York 1967 (Lipset/Rokkan, 1967)

Milbrath, Lester W., *The Context of Public Opinion: How Our Belief Systems can Affect Poll Results*, in: L. John Martin (ed.), *Polling and the Democratic Consensus, The Annals of the Academy of Political and Social Science*, Vol. 472/ March 1984 (Milbrath, 1984)

Mock, Erhard, *Austria*, in: *Comparative Law Yearbook*, Vol. 7/1983 (Mock, 1984)

Müller, Wolfgang C., *Politische Kultur und Parteitransformation in Österreich*, in: *Österreichische Zeitschrift für Politikwissenschaft 1984/1* (Müller, 1984)

Müller-Rommel, Ferdinand, *Die Postmaterialismusdiskussion in der empirischen Sozialforschung: Politisch und wissenschaftlich überholt oder immer noch zukunftsweisend?*, in: *Politische Vierteljahresschrift* 1983/2 (Müller-Rommel, 1983)

Oberndörfer, Dieter/Rattinger, Hans/Schmitt, Karl (Hg.), *Wirtschaftlicher Wandel, religiöser Wandel und Wertwandel: Folgen für das politische Verhalten in der Bundesrepublik Deutschland*, Berlin 1985 (Oberndörfer/Rattinger/Schmitt, 1985)

Pappi, Franz Urban, *Die Links-Rechts-Dimension des deutschen Parteiensystems und die Parteipräferenz-Profile der Wählerschaft*, in: Max Kaase/Hans Dieter Klingemann (Hg.), *Wahlen und politisches System: Analysen aus Anlaß der Bundestagswahl 1980*, Opladen, 1983 (Pappi, 1983)

Pelinka, Anton, *Windstille: Klagen über Österreich*, Wien/München 1985 (Pelinka, 1985)

Plasser, Fritz, *Die "unsichtbare" Fraktion: Struktur und Profil der Grün-Alternativen in Österreich*, in: Andreas Khol/Alfred Stirnemann (Hg.), *Österreichisches Jahrbuch für Politik '84*, Wien, 1985 (Plasser, 1985)

Plasser, Fritz, *Parteien unter Streß: Zur Dynamik der Parteiensysteme in Österreich, der Bundesrepublik Deutschland und den Vereinigten Staaten*, Wien 1987 (Plasser, 1987)

Plasser, Fritz/Ulram, Peter A., *Unbehagen im Parteienstaat: Jugend und Politik in Österreich*, Wien/Köln/Graz, 1982 (Plasser/Ulram, 1982)

Plasser, Fritz/Ulram, Peter A., *Themenwechsel-Machtwechsel? Konturen einer neuen Mehrheit in Österreich*, in: Koren/Pisa/Waldheim 1984 (Plasser/Ulram, 1984)

Plasser, Fritz/Ulram, Peter A., *From Stability to Diffusion: Dealignment in the Austrian Party System*, Paper delivered at the Annual Meeting of the American Political Science Association, New Orleans 1985 (Plasser/Ulram, 1985)

Plasser, Fritz/Ulram, Peter A./Welan, Manfried (Hg.), *Demokratierituale: Zur politischen Kultur der Informationsgesellschaft*, Wien/Köln/Graz 1985 (Plasser/Ulram/Welan, 1985)

Rosenmayr, Leopold et al., *Politische Beteiligung und Wertwandel in Österreich*, Wien, 1980 (Rosenmayr, 1980)

Schultze, Rainer-Olaf, *Realigning elections/Realignment*, in: Dieter Nohlen (Hg.), *Pipers Wörterbuch zur Politik* (1, Nation-Building-Zweiparteiensystem), München/Zürich 1985 (Schultze, 1985)

Sommer, Franz, *Medien zwischen Macht und Ohnmacht: Empirische Ergebnisse zu den Phänomenen "Nachrichtenbonus", "agenda setting" und "Meinungsklima"*, in: Plasser/Ulram/Welan, 1985 (Sommer, 1985)

Sorauf, Frank J., *Party Politics in America*, Boston/Toronto 1984 (Sorauf, 1984)

Talos, Emmerich, *Staatliche Sozialpolitik in Österreich, Rekonstruktion und Analyse*, Wien 1981 (Talos, 1981)

Tieber, Herbert/Swoboda, Hannes (Hg.), *Privatisierung: Die falsche Alternative*, Wien 1984 (Tieber/Swoboda, 1984)

Traar, Kurt/Birk, Franz, *Der durchleuchtete Wähler in den achtziger Jahren*, in: *Journal für Sozialforschung, 1987/1* (Traar/Birk, 1987)

Ulram, Peter A., *Politische Kultur(forschung) im Wandel*, in: *Österreichische Zeitschrift für Politikwissenschaft 1982/2* (Ulram, 1982)

Ulram, Peter A., *Um die Mehrheit der Mehrheit: Die neuen angestellten Mittelschichten 1975-1985*, in: Plasser/Ulram/Welan 1985 (Ulram, 1985a)

Ulram, Peter A., *Umwelt- und Demokratiepolitik in der ÖVP*, in: *Schwarz-bunter Vogel: Studien zu Programm, Politik und Struktur der ÖVP* (Hg. vom Junius Verlag), Wien 1985 (Ulram, 1985b)

Weil, Frederick, *A Second Chance for Liberal Democracy: Popular Support in Post-Authoritarian European Regimes with Comparisons to Long-Term European and American Liberal Democracies*, Paper presented at the Annual Meeting of the American Political Science Association, New Orleans 1985 (Weil, 1985)

Zulehner, Paul Michael, *Religion im Leben der Österreicher: Dokumentation einer Umfrage*, Wien/Freiburg/Basel 1981 (Zulehner, 1981)

Appendix:

Question to graphs 9.1 and 9.2

On this chart you see several opinions and views with opposing views opposite one another. For each pair of opposing views, please tell me which side corresponds more to your personal view. "1" would mean that you are in complete agreement with the statement on the left. "5" would mean that you are in complete agreement with the statement on the right. You can also choose any value in between.

A- The state has an obligation to intervene whenever problems arise and people are having a hard time.

1...5 We already have far too much state. Individuals should make a greater effort to help themselves.

B- We need more equality and justice, even if this sometimes limits the freedom of the individual.

1...5 We need more individual freedom. There will always be social differences.

C- A lot still has to be improved in society. That is why reforms are constantly necessary.

1...5 We should at long last stop carrying out constant reforms. We now need stability and continuity in order to preserve what we have achieved.

D-   If someone goes astray he needs understanding and sometimes help to find his way back to good conduct.

1...5   We are much too lenient about everything nowadays. We should use the full force of the law to deal severely with criminals.

E-   What is important for the future is that as many people as possible have a say in all fields of public and economic life.

1...5   It is best if one person knows what must be done and gives clear instructions to all others who subordinate themselves.

F-   As Austrians we have an obligation to think of all other people in the world. That is why we should grant aid to developing countries.

1...5   Every people must think of itself first. Underdeveloped countries should above all help themselves.

G-   In order to preserve jobs we must continue to rely on economic growth, even if this occasionally has a detrimental effect on nature and the environment.

1...5   In order to protect nature and the environment we must abandon the policy of continued economic growth, even if this occasionally causes employment problems.

H-   The further increase in the standard of living of the population has priority over maintaining areas of unspoiled nature.

1...5   Maintaining areas of unspoiled nature has priority over a further increase in the standard of living of the population.

10

National Consciousness and National Identity

A Contribution to the Political Culture of the Austrian Party System[1]

PETER GERLICH

> "Es gibt kein geschichtliches Gebilde
> in Europa, dessen Existenz so sehr mit
> den Identitätsproblemen seiner Mitglieder
> verbunden ist wie Österreich."
>
> *(Friedrich Heer)*

1. Introduction

> "Ein Vorzug bleibt uns immer unverloren,
> Man preist ihn heut' als Nationalität.
> Er sagt, daß' irgendwo der Mensch geboren
> Was freilich sich von selbst versteht."
>
> *(Franz Grillparzer)*

Franz Grillparzer, who is, after all, considered to be Austria's greatest poet, wrote these lines as well as other bitter epigrams after the revolution in 1848 was defeated. They signalized the historical burdens on the concept of nationality in bourgeois German-speaking classes in the Hapsburg monarchy. Yet even after the multinational empire was broken up and an ethnically homogeneous republic established, these difficulties remained, particularly among the bourgeoisie. The "struggle for an Austrian identity," as Friedrich

Heer put it (Heer was, incidentally, also an artist and civil servant), seems by no means to have concluded today, far more than a century after Grillparzer composed this aphorism.

Since 1945, and, above all, since in the second attempt under more propitious framework conditions Austrians have improved their national self-image, the situation has, of course, changed. Yet at least compared with other countries whose national development has been continuous and uninterrupted, this self-image is less uniform and more fragile and is therefore presumably less suited to helping form a social identity (Bruckmüller 1984, p. 197). This became painfully manifest during the disputes in the course of the 1986 presidential election, but it was obviously latent prior to this date, for example when Austrian national consciousness was displayed just a trace too declaratively in the ceremonial of official representatives of the state or political parties. It is indirectly manifested in the essentially unimportant fact that unlike in countries with a long national tradition, the national holiday in Austria is not on the day the state was founded or refounded, that is, on the day a revolutionary mass movement was successful, but rather it commemorates a comparably dry legal event—the ratification of the Neutrality Law by the Austrian parliament. And finally, the latent fragility of the Austrian national self-image, which now superficially appears to be well established, can be detected in the depths of the "Austrian soul" (Ringel). In a country whose people appear to foreigners to be artistic, light-hearted and "gemütlich," the suicide rate and the frequency of psychosomatic disorders, alcoholism and other indicators of internalized conflicts are among the highest in the world (Ringel 1984, p. 32).

In addition, there is a political aspect to this subject, and although it has become somewhat less significant, it does occasionally become an acute matter at an official state level, at least since the Freedom Party of Austria was a member of a coalition government. In Austria, the people considered to be "nationalists" are not the ones who defend the national identity of their own country, but those who, on the contrary, deny its national identity and basically believe in one Pan-German linguistic and cultural nation. This attitude is a heritage from the nationalist conflicts in the Austro-Hungarian empire. It was reflected in the widespread desire for annexation by Germany after 1918, and this became a reality when Austria was unified with Nazi Germany under Hitler. A great majority of Austrians undoubtedly became aware of their distinctiveness during the anschluss period, and this contributed decisively to the resurrection of the Republic after 1945 and the development of a national self-image (Kreissler 1984, p. 189ff.). Nevertheless, attitudes from the period of occupation do still live on today. This is all the more so true since developments after the refounding of the Republic did not make it possible to deal with these problems or openly discuss Austrian participation in Nazism. Instead, thoughts of this period, like those of other dark periods of recent Austrian history, were collectively repressed for a very long time, not least of all by the governmental parties. What is worrisome is that these developments favored a considerable potential for antidemocratic political attitudes. Although only some 10% of the population reject the concept of an Austrian nation, as many as 25% consider "a strongman at the top" to be more desirable than the parliamentary system (cf. Gerlich/Ucakar 1981, p. 92). The parallels to "nationalist" attitudes are obvious.

The representatives of this "nationalist" attitude, in particular, generally had a static understanding of the concept of a nation. They believed a nation was predetermined, so to speak, by linguistic, cultural and historical facts. Thus, using a type of abstract logic, they rejected the concept of an Austrian nation—Austrians are Germans, they claimed, and as such they are obviously members of the German nation. In contrast with this attitude, it appears today both more realistic and more useful to assume that the concept of a nation is dynamic (cf. Stourzh 1980). If a community forming a state, no matter what its composition, recognizes subjectively as well as objectively its common existence as a state, this leads to a process of nation-building—a process in which existing similarities and differences are not seen as immutable, but rather are strengthened and reduced respectively.[2] This process, or, to express it more dramatically, this "struggle for an Austrian identity" began in full force at the latest after the World War II, and has led to a large majority of Austrians affirming the existence of an Austrian nation, although they still do have certain reservations.

The process of nation-building can be experienced subjectively by taking part in joint activities (Ernst Bruckmüller has proved convincingly using examples from Austrian history that the process in this case has a longer-lasting effect—Bruckmüller, 1984, p. 212), or passively, as it were, when it is decreed by political and other authorities. Thus, national consciousness is based on either traditions of collective participation or those of authoritarian manipulation. The fact that national identification can motivate the individual to work for what he perceives as common goals despite considerable personal disadvantages is exactly why it has been abused in the course of history by state and political authorities for their own interests (cf. Balfour 1953, p. 91ff.). There is therefore an ambivalent dialectic relationship between nationality and nationalism. Positive aspects—above all the possibility of aiding individuals in forming an identity and thus strengthening their egos—are opposed by negative aspects or dangers, i.e. the exploitation of national identification to attain political goals. Because this nation-building process began relatively late in Austria, the history of the country is largely free from examples of these dangers. Yet despite this fact we should remain vigilant for newly developing chauvinism in the exuberant emphasis of the newly developed national consciousness (cf. Leser 1971). On the other hand, however, there has been a great lack of truly participatory traditions in Austrian history. Revolutionary movements and spontaneous mass demonstrations were usually unsuccessful. The state, politics and not least of all national consciousness have been mandated from above—by the government, bureaucracy, party leaders and major interest groups (Pelinka/Welan 1971). This may be another reason why national consciousness in Austria is limited, and, incidentally, an explanation for the uncommon but nevertheless recurrent occasions on which the powerful in this country have suddenly been confronted with both spontaneous mass demonstrations they find inexplicable and difficult to control, and, more recently, alternative movements.[3]

Before concluding these introductory remarks with a number of hypotheses, a further decisive aspect must be pointed out, namely that it is difficult to comment upon questions of Austrian national consciousness with objective scientific detachment. Authors attitudes frequently influence their judgement in works on this subject, more so than in the analyses of other social questions. First of all there are the proponents who often paint a picture so optimistic it verges on the naive and who attempt to ignore the many blemishes and imperfections which quite simply are detectable. Then there are others, in particular representatives of influential currents in historiography, who follow Pan-German traditions—and although they are more restrained than earlier, they do continue to exist (cf. Kreissler 1984, p. 532). Finally, there are skeptical young scientists, seen with hostility by both sides, who consider the concept of national consciousness in this age of growing internationalism to be less relevant anyway, or who suspect it may just be an old concept in new clothing (cf. Falk 1980). This may be a generation problem to a certain extent, since the commitment of those who experienced firsthand the period of the anschluss, whichever side they were on, cannot be comprehended by those who have only experienced the reality of the successful Second Republic. If this commitment is not expended on superficial polemics, however, it can, I believe, definitely make a more open discussion possible and thus actively contribute to further strengthening Austrian national consciousness.

In summary, my observations below are based on five simply expressed hypotheses which may serve as an introduction to the analysis of the development and present state of the discussion about the Austrian nation.

(1) Disintegration and reintegration. Following a process of disintegration (the Hapsburg Empire) and considerable transitional difficulties and delays, Austrian national consciousness developed during a process of reintegration (the Second Republic).
(2) Dynamic, not static process. The process of nation-building upon which this development is based must be seen as a dynamic process of integration. This process cannot be understood if the concept "nation" is considered to be static.

(3) Distinctions, not uniformity. Due particularly to these historical experiences, Austrian national consciousness is not uniform, but rather varies according to social class, and there are still numerous remnants of anti-Austrian attitudes.

(4) Commitment and skepticism. Scientific analyses of this question are based on prejudices more so than analyses of other questions. This undoubtedly makes it more difficult to treat this very emotionalized subject objectively.

(5) Manipulation, not participation. Among wide sectors of the population in Austria, national consciousness is less the result of active participation or participatory traditions than in other countries. Instead, national consciousness is more the result of official announcements made by the authorities, which is why it has remained superficial. It can be presumed, therefore, that the (no doubt existent and empirically verifiable) national consciousness does not instill in Austrians as strong a sense of identity as does the sense of belonging to other areas or groups with greater participatory traditions and opportunities, namely the federal states and the camps. There is, of course, always a certain dialectic relationship between these units and a uniform sense of national identity. The federal states have stronger historical identities than the country; and despite the fact that Austrians are increasingly discontent with the camps—which I assume to include not only the political parties, but also their affiliated organizations—they do at least in principle offer the opportunity for active participation.

On the basis of this assumption and against a background of the problem as outlined in the introduction, an attempt will be made in the following to theoretically, historically and empirically examine the question of Austrian national consciousness, the conditions under which it developed, and the effects it has, as well as to reflect on the situation and come to some conclusions in the final section.

2. Theoretical Observations

"As the process of modernization transforms society, economy and politics, the interdependence between individuals and systems increases"

(Peter J. Katzenstein)

In those contemporary social sciences that are empirically oriented, what are called theories of modernization were developed in order to classify individual social phenomena from a historical and comparative point of view into larger categories. Another goal was not to establish laws of social science, but at least to permit conclusions which could be generalized. (cf. Wehler 1975, p. 18ff.) Although criticism of certain assumptions is due, since these are often too simple and sometimes naive, a number of conceptual frameworks, concepts and approaches were developed in both political science and history which can be applied to developments or present conditions in individual countries—in our case Austria—so we can come to new conclusions which surpass our traditional understanding.

What these approaches have in common is that in different ways they all bring together two different vantage points by comparing the system and the individual. They usually emphasize the perspective of the system. During the process of modernization of the system—which is seen as a fundamental necessity—a certain type of behavior on the part of individuals is considered useful. Because of his obligation to conform to the system, each individual has a role he must play, so to speak. There is an analogy here to the above-mentioned contrast between manipulation and participation in the concrete steps of nation-building, but on a theoretical level, so to speak. Since national identification is given a theoretical function, this theory—perhaps unconsciously—reflects actual political practice in which, as mentioned above, nationalist feelings are not uncommonly used as a means to achieve scarcely justifiable ends (cf. Balfour 1953, p. 91ff.). The political systems theory, in particular, explicitly complements this system perspective with a perspective based on the individual, which is, however, derived from the former. Accordingly to this theory, one of the functions of the system is to politically socialize the individual, that is, to convey to him those values and attitudes which represent what is called the political culture of the system, one of them being identification with the nation (cf. Steiner 1972, p. 189ff.).

First of all, several system-oriented approaches will be portrayed below. Then, on the basis of the hypothesis of socialization mentioned above, a model founded on the perspective of the individual will be developed to describe the formation and effects of national consciousness. In both cases, these theoretical observations will be followed by speculations on their relevance and meaningfulness with regard to conditions in Austria.

The political systems theory (cf. Gerlich 1972) assumes that politics as a relatively independent system stands out at least functionally from all other social systems and assumes certain tasks in society and the economy—above all that of control. On the one hand the political system can influence society and the economy, yet on the other hand it is also dependent upon and challenged by them. The first level of system functions is thus that of overcoming political problems—in a kind of feedback control system, the social fields influence the actual structures of the state through what are called inputs—for example (sometimes contradictory) demands or loyalty (resulting, for instance, from national consciousness)—and these state structures in turn react with outputs—above all decisions—and "symbolical" politics, for instance manipulation in the sense used above. What is implicit in this model is that a balance between inputs and outputs is achieved, and this helps in attaining the system's goal of stability or integration. On this second level of system functions, other goals such as achievement or improving the quality of democracy are sometimes postulated (cf. in particular Gerlich 1972). In addition to these functions, there are the system functions of preservation or adaptation on a third subordinated level which serve to integrate the individual into the system. One of the functions which serves this purpose is the above-mentioned function of political socialization during which "agents," such as family, school or occupational environment, assume the task of introducing the individual to the conditions of the system, its values, and his own role in it.

The real contribution of the systems theory to the discussion on modernization is what is called the theory of crises (cf. Wehler 1975, p. 34ff.). According to this theory, a system must solve above all four crises as it moves from a pre-modern to a modern society—state-building, nation-building, participation and distribution (cf. also Steiner 1972, p. 1ff.). Thus, central political institutions must first be set up and their effectiveness asserted over groups with traditional or regional power (penetration), and then the population must come to identify emotionally with the state as a whole (nation-building). Subsequently, according to the ideal-type model, new groups which emerge as a result of social developments must be given opportunities to participate (participation—particularly by the extension of voting rights), and finally, the policies of the state must also in substance take the interests of these new groups into account (distribution—transition from non-interventionist state to welfare state). The crises, therefore, on the one hand refer to both sides of the political process—input (nation-building and participation) and output (state-building and distribution)—and on the other hand pose challenges to the system to achieve its goals. Applying this theory to historical experience has shown that these crises are more likely to be solved if they occur consecutively; an accumulation of problems usually results in the collapse of the process of political modernization (cf. Steiner 1972, p. 46).

Whereas the question of national consciousness is an explicit part of the political crises theory, this is not necessarily true of the following historiographical approaches which deal more with the question of the emergence of certain structures of the state, in particular with the problem of the possibility of creating lasting parliamentary democracy. Unlike the abstract theoretical approach of the crises theory, they are used to attempt on the basis of comparative historical analyses of different countries to reach conclusions which can be generalized. The question of national consciousness plays an incidental role in these approaches as well. The development of structures of the state is attributed either to sociostructural, economic or foreign policy factors. The sociostructural approach emphasizes how important the experiences of social classes over long periods and their possibilities for development are for the future form of state institutions (Moore 1969). In his analysis of the emergence of the non-German nationalities in the Hapsburg monarchy, E. Bruckmüller demonstrated above all the roles the nobility, the bourgeoisie and the masses play in this process, and compared, for instance, the Czech developments with those in the German-speaking part of the empire (Bruckmüller 1984, p. 103ff.).The hypothesis of the historical approach emphasizing economic factors is of particular interest. According to this hypothesis, relative economic backwardness may result in special effort being made to catch up; in this context, authoritarian structures and nationalist ideologies are probable, the latter because of their great ability to motivate. Finally, foreign policy approaches emphasize the importance of the international position of a state for its development as a nation. On the one hand, a military threat leads to developments similar to those resulting from economic backwardness—it makes a larger defense effort, a stronger army and consequently a larger role for the state necessary, and also implies the development of nationalist tendencies (Hintze 1962). On the other hand, the approach of the communication theory presumes that international cooperation may lead to international integration and the development of national consciousness within the larger areas which are forming (Katzenstein 1976).

In what ways is it possible to apply to Austria, at least speculatively, these approaches which interpret national consciousness to be, in part, a product of certain developments, and on the other hand, a means to achieve the goals of the state? K. Steiner has applied the political crises theory to developments in Austria. Similar to W. Bluhm, who dealt with this question in a monograph, Steiner comes to the conclusion that the framework conditions necessary for the development of an Austrian national consciousness did not exist until after 1945 (Steiner 1972, p. 21; Bluhm 1973, p. 102). In this context E. Bruckmüller pointed out that this belated development, which is surprising to some, is particularly closely related to the fact that the output crises were solved either early (penetration) or relatively late, but that they were then finally permanently solved as a result of economic developments (distribution). On the input side, in contrast, there was long a considerable deficit, particularly with regard to the crisis of participation (cf. Bruckmüller 1984, p. 14). A look at Austrian social history helps us understand why essential groups identified insufficiently with the concept of an Austrian nation. This was true of both the bourgeoisie and, for a very long time, representatives of the workers. Both groups believed the chances of attaining their political goals were best in a Pan-German nation. This brings us back to the concepts of disintegration and reintegration, and, of course, it also makes it easier to understand the present non-uniformity of Austrian national consciousness. Economic and foreign policy challenges doubtlessly existed during the Hapsburg empire and they certainly contributed, among other things, to the development of strong state structures and a powerful bureaucracy. Yet in spite of a number of attempts, they never did lead to the development of a Pan-Austrian national consciousness—perhaps, in particular, because in both areas success was usually lacking. The hypothesis of the communication theory has been tested by P. Katzenstein using Austro-German relations as an example. In contrast to those who assume that integration has taken place, he comes to the conclusion that despite regular and finally complete interaction, both systems have remained autonomous, and that the two countries now exist side by side as disjoined partners. The changed international power constellations after 1945 did, of course, play an important role in this (Katzenstein 1976, p. 199ff.). It is interesting to note that F. Heer, too, strongly emphasizes foreign influence on developments in Austria (Heer 1981, p. 18).

From the point of view of the individual, national identity is imparted in a complex process influenced by various factors. Three types of these factors can be distinguished. First, it depends on the general framework conditions—the social and economic situations and the international position of a community. Another of these environmental factors is the collective historical experience, that is, the tradition of national unity or disunity. These factors have an indirect but lasting effect on the emergence of national identification, as is demonstrated by developments in Austria in particular. They were the source of the dynamic force which characterizes the process of nation-building in Austria. This process is, however, influenced more directly by numerous people, groups and institutions who could be called mediators of national consciousness. These mediators in turn make use of various means, forms and media to intentionally or unintentionally rouse, strengthen or weaken in the psyche of the individual a sense of belonging to a nation. Mediators and means may be divided into those which are everyday (private or cultural) on the one hand, and those which are official (governmental or institutional) on the other. In addition to the family, we must regard clubs, occupational and business associations and, at least partially, the mass media as belonging primarily to the private sphere; schools, churches and the numerous forms of bureaucracy belong primarily to the public sphere—consider, for instance, the socializing effect of the federal army or, in a very different area, of jurisdiction. I would call the local communities, federal states and camps primarily intermediary mediators and situate them between the official state level and the everyday private level, so to speak. All these institutions contribute to the process of national identification and intentionally or unintentionally employ various means to do so. Here too, we can differentiate between cultural and institutional means. All those phenomena ranging from everyday to classical culture which help to impart identity can be considered cultural means—these range from a common language, gastronomic culture, light music and folklore on the one hand to literature, theater, architectural style and last but not least what is called serious music on the other. As long as these activities are felt to belong to the environment of the community, they can contribute to the process of national identification. Institutional means are oriented toward participation on the one hand or manipulation on the other, to use a distinction suggested above. Active participation in political life, whether in local, state or camp (i.e. partisan) politics, rouses a far greater sense of belonging in the individual than when he is the object of official instructions and teaching during which his role is merely passive; examples of the latter are the presentation of symbols of the nation as such as well as of standardized signs and uniforms, the ceremonies of the state, the legal system which usually remains incomprehensible to the uninitiated, and the coverage of politics, crime and sports which in Austria in particular is largely ritualized. All of these can convey a sense of belonging, but they are less effective. Any teacher knows that students receive a longer-lasting impression when they participate in a lesson than when they merely listen to a lecture.

Each individual's national consciousness should be seen as the result of these mediating processes, and its effects can be at least twofold—on the one hand it can strengthen the personality of the individual since he knows where he belongs, and on the other it can make him inclined to be more loyal to representatives of the national system.

Using these assumptions as a model, what speculative statements can be made about the development of the processes of national identification in Austria? The importance of the framework conditions becomes quite clear when we compare the First and Second Republics. Even the most well-meant efforts made in the First Republic to mediate national consciousness remained unsuccessful, whereas the improved economic situation, the more balanced social structure and the secure international position of the Second Republic did definitely made it possible for an Austrian national consciousness to emerge (cf. Bluhm 1973, p. 102). What is no doubt most difficult even today is the relationship young Austrians in particular have with the history of their own country. In spite of all the good intentions, history in our schools in actual practice is still taught selectively and with omissions (Kreissler 1984, p. 527). With regard to modern history, however, some of the mass media are doing pioneering work. On the whole, events since 1986 have probably caused a positive process of reflection, for history can only develop its ability to increase national identity if it is revealed unreservedly—not only with its positive but also with its negative aspects, since these are part of the heritage of national identity. The changed framework conditions indirectly reflect the process of disintegration and reintegration which characterizes the development of Austrian national consciousness.

As for the mediation, or conveyance, of national identity, this has probably been done relatively seldom privately, and has been mostly manipulative in public. In the private sphere people probably still have some reservations, and parents or grandparents who remained silent on the subject were long scarcely able to correct the lack of discussion in schools about coming to terms with the past. Participatory mediation probably takes place most commonly at a local level, at the level of the federal states, which have their respective traditions of local consciousness, and in the political camps, that is, in the parties and their numerous affiliated organizations. In these areas too, however, there are traditions of subservience of the people to authority and these restrict the possibilities for meaningful participation (cf. for example Pelinka 1985). On the basis of these observations—which, as was mentioned above, are speculative—the general conclusion can be drawn that Austrian national consciousness must remain superficial, non-uniform and fragile in those areas where it is primarily learned and not experienced, taught and not worked for—and this presumably holds true for most of the mediators and means which contribute to its creation.[4]

These theoretical observations will be applied below to a concrete case by outlining the development of Austrian national consciousness and sketching its present state as it is seen in the results of opinion polls.

3. Historical Developments

"Preußenhaß eint"

(Ernst Bloch)

The year 1945 represents the most decisive point in the process of building an Austrian nation. During the Hapsburg monarchy, a Pan-Austrian national consciousness was never successfully developed despite many attempts to this effect. In the last few decades before its end, conflicts between the various nationalities raged—a process of disintegration had begun. After the founding of the Republic, this process continued in that, explicitly or implicitly, the desire for the anschluss was predominant. Not until Austrians had experienced actual unification with Nazi Germany did they have a change of heart. After 1945, the dynamic process of nation-building developed, although this reintegration was now confined to the territory of the smaller Republic of Austria.[5] The framework conditions, in particular the international situation and economic developments, greatly fostered this process. Not only social scientists but also Austrians themselves interpret developments in this way, as remains to be shown in the following section. It is nevertheless legitimate to study the long-lasting "struggle for an Austrian identity" which began much earlier, not least because collective historical experience is one of the framework conditions in which the Second Republic has developed, and, as has been explained above, certain aspects definitely continue to contribute to the non-uniformity of Austrian national consciousness. In this context, the fundamentally new analyses carried out by the historians Heer (1981), Kreissler (1984) and Bruckmüller (1984) can be pointed out. Only a few essential aspects will be dealt with here, above all from the viewpoint of the social sciences.

Although the name and idea of Austria can be traced back even further in time, as Bruckmüller has demonstrated (Bruckmüller 1984, p. 26ff.), it seems useful, in accordance with the theory of crises, to begin here with the solution to the problem of state-building which was solved in the late 18th century during the period of enlightened absolutism (Bruckmüller 1984, p. 66ff.). The problem of nation-building, however, was not solved. The integrative force of the central power apparatus was not strong enough to introduce a sense of Pan-Austrian national identity from above through manipulation. Despite the attempts to introduce a uniform central state under Joseph II (cf. Heer 1981, p. 145) and during the period of neo-absolutism after the suppression of the Revolution of 1848, this integration of the various peoples in the empire never took place. By way of comparison, we should not forget in this context that other states did succeed in uniting very heterogeneous regions and ethnic groups by conveying to them a uniform national consciousness—consider for example France or the United States. In comparison, it was possible to successfully solve the crises of nation-building in these countries not only because the framework conditions were more propitious (a stronger international position, for instance, or the dynamism of a rapidly expanding economy), but also because participatory means were used during the process of nation-building. It does make a great difference whether or not popular movements were able to assert themselves against traditionally powerful groups at decisive phases in history. During developments in Austria, the established authorities always remained more powerful (cf. Gerlich/Ucakar 1981). This holds true for a period as far back as the Counter Reformation during which a predominantly Protestant country was forcefully recatholicized, or one could point out how frightened the Hapsburgs were of the popular movement directed against Napoleon and how it was repressed (cf. Heer 1981, p. 171). But the defeat of the revolution of 1848 is the most decisive event in this context, and its repercussions are perhaps still felt today in the lack of political self-confidence on the part of the Austrian middle-classes. One cannot help but have the impression that even today legal circles in Austria are greatly characterized by their desire to realize the values of the Kremsier Constitution which never came into force (cf. Pelinka/Welan 1971, p. 13).

The lack of changes pushed through from below always corresponded to reforms imposed from above. Josephinism, the economic reforms during the period of neo-absolutism, the period at the turn of the century under the cabinets made up of civil servants, and not least the unilateral introduction of universal suffrage by Franz Joseph I (cf., however, Ucakar 1985) can be considered examples of such reforms. This train of thought could be extended—the founding of the Republic in 1918 was determined too greatly by external circumstances to correspond to the needs of Austrians who declared they were part of the German Reich; the transformation of Austria from an agricultural to an industrial country was based on Hitler's investments in arms and carried out by a totalitarian regime (which at this time was already seen as foreign); and finally, the restoration of the Republic and reconstruction after 1945 were desired and controlled by the victorious allied powers.

The Revolution of 1848 was an opportunity not only to fully integrate the German-speaking bourgeoisie into the monarchy, but also to find a solution to the national conflicts in order to develop a Pan-Austrian national identity on this basis. Since this was not possible, Austria remained a mere concept, a "nation of court counselors" ("Hofratsnation")—only the army, bureaucracy and nobility identified fully with the Hapsburg state (Bruckmüller 1984, p. 66ff.). The bourgeoisie was indifferent or advocated a German irredenta. Nor could the masses be integrated into the state. Instead of a convincing national consciousness, a defensive government ideology was developed which was strengthened by the fact that the German Austrians saw themselves as the dominant group in the monarchy and endeavored to retain this position (Bruckmüller 1984, p. 205). The underprivileged nationalities, in particular the Czechs, each developed their own national consciousness which, paradoxically, was initially the result of the efforts of the central state to solve the crisis of penetration, since it had to use and thus promote the language understood by the people. Initially, the Czech movement was supported by the nobility alone, but it then spread to the bourgeoisie and finally, unlike in German-speaking areas of the empire, to the masses (Bruckmüller 1984, p. 106ff.).

An exceptional aspect greatly highlighted by Bruckmüller—which, incidentally, is not easily understood by contemporaries having grown up in Vienna, since the city did not constitute a federal state until relatively late—is that the opportunities to develop an identity were most common in the federal states, because they had traditions of popular participation within the framework of the self-administration of the estates which had never completely died out (Bruckmüller 1984, p. 30ff.). The policies of the political parties after 1918 and 1945 at the level of the federal states actively promoted this state consciousness. Identification with the federal states is thus one element of Austrian consciousness with fragmentary continuity. The same is presumably true of the camps, that is the parties in Austria, although this has seldom been pointed out. They offered their supporters opportunities of identification which were expressed in the "Lager"-mentality, usually described negatively, and which manifested themselves in the amazing continuity of the camps despite the gaps from 1934 and 1938 to 1945 (Wandruszka 1977).

It has often been said that the First Republic was "a state that no one wanted." And indeed, there were almost no signs of an emerging national consciousness. In this context, of course, the catastrophic economic developments and the active promotion of the anschluss idea, within Austria and from abroad, must be taken into account (Kreissler 1984, p. 29ff.).

The desire for unification with the German Reich existed in different forms in the political groups. The phrase about "the second German state" used by the corporate state just goes to prove this, as do the declarations of support for the anschluss by K. Renner (cf. Panzenböck 1985) and cardinal Innitzer after it had taken place. Prominent figures like the Christian Socialist E.K. Winter[6] or the communist A. Klahr who worked for the development of an Austrian national consciousness remained outsiders (cf. Kreissler 1984, p. 41ff.). The intensive political conflicts between the camps were undoubtedly a great obstacle to national integration, as was shown in particular by the events leading up to 1938.

Both this period and the period of Nazi rule beginning in 1938 were chapters in Austrian history which were not dealt with thoroughly after 1945. Even today, as opinion polls demonstrate, they remain widely ignored. Yet it was the anschluss period in particular which in various ways decisively contributed to the emergence of Austrian national consciousness (Kreissler 1984, p. 189ff.). It should certainly, however, not be forgotten that the initial support for the new rulers was substantial (cf. Katzenstein 1976, p. 163ff.). A total of nearly 600,000 Austrians, for instance, were members of the Nazi party (cf. Luza 1984, p. 286)—this corresponds closely to the number of members in the two major democratic parties after 1945, and, compared internationally, this percentage of the total population is considered uncommonly high. Yet even among these Austrians who initially supported Hitler, skepticism soon became widespread as the anti-Austrian measures taken by the authorities who were considered to be characterized by their typically Prussian attitudes began to have an effect. The regime became continuously less popular as the burdens of the wartime era grew. Decisive stimulus for a new start after 1945, however, came from the resistance movement against Hitler in which many groups whose number is often underestimated were active (Luza 1984), as well as from emigrated Austrians who were scattered across many countries (Kreissler 1984, p. 157ff.). After 1945, the accomplishments and sacrifices of both of these movements were by no means given the recognition they deserve.

After the allies had stipulated in the Moscow Declaration that Austria was to be restored (cf. Kreissler 1984, p. 287), Austrian party leaders often rather spontaneously began to commit themselves to the Austrian option, as the future Federal President A. Schärf describes (cf. Bluhm 1973, p. 49), and wide sectors of the population also began to support this idea. After hostilities came to an end, this also permitted the reconstruction of the fabric of the state under difficult conditions in times of need, destruction and occupation.

In comparison with the general acceptance of the need to establish a political consensus among the major camps, thoughts about Austrian national consciousness were, of course, by no means predominant among the dominant political forces. The clearest initial supporters of Austrian national consciousness were above all the communists—who were, however, forced into a minor role during the course of the cold war, and conservative groups in the People's Party (Kreissler 1984, p. 375ff.). The first Socialist Party platforms did not at all deal with the idea of an Austrian nation, for instance. The two major parties increasingly attempted to win the votes of former Nazis and therefore avoided offending them.[7] And, as Kreissler has observed, Social Partnership mostly emphasized social peace alone, which by no means can be equated with the development of national consciousness (Kreissler 1984, p. 493).

Yet the dynamic process of reintegration nevertheless began its sustained advance. It was given decisive stimulus by the signing of the State Treaty in 1955, which restored to Austria its complete independence and freed it from occupation by the Allies, as well as by the effects of social change. The new middle class which began to form in the 1960s at the latest reduced the importance of the "Lager"-mentality and began to develop a new and explicit relationship with its own past and identity. Reactions, even official reactions, to German nationalist activities which had begun to recur became continuously clearer, and one of the ways this was expressed was in the proclamation of the national holiday in 1966. Nevertheless, as was mentioned in the introduction, it becomes obvious time and again that this new national consciousness is burdened by shadows from the past. This is illustrated, for instance, by the problems of the minorities policy. In this context, the "German Carinthians'" resistance to recognizing the attested rights of Austrians of Slovenian origin is not a laudable chapter in contemporary Austrian history (cf. Kreissler 1984, p. 433ff.). In addition, this example demonstrates the effect, albeit negative in this case, of participatory identification which is expressed in the myth of the Carinthians' defensive struggle (Perchinig 1986). The difficulties of the FPÖ—which, from 1983 to 1986, took part for the first time in a coalition government—in choosing between "nationalist" and liberal, or in combining these two elements (cf. Perchinig 1983), not to mention the continued existence of numerous radical right-wing groups, also make it clear that Austrian national consciousness is by no means uniform and that even today it is definitely still very heterogeneous and diverse.

The aim of the following analysis of relevant opinion poll results is to assess these individual tendencies and inconsistencies. By means of this analysis an attempt will be made to portray the present state of Austrian national consciousness, although I am, of course, aware of its limited meaningfulness due to the method on which it is based.

4. Opinion Poll Results

> "Ich glaube, das gute Österreichische
> ist besonders schwer zu verstehen, es
> ist in gewissem Sinne subtiler als alles
> andere und seine Wahrheit ist nie auf
> der Seite der Wahrscheinlichkeit."
>
> *(Ludwig Wittgenstein)*

Public opinion polling on both commercial and political topics has been well established in Austria since the 1960s. Perhaps one of the reasons it is widely popular among Austrian political authorities, and those of the parties in particular, is that it is well adapted to their tendency to want to learn of the wishes of the population without any open participatory conflicts in order to successfully pursue policies which are not participatory in our sense of the word, but rather manipulative in accordance with a Josephinist tradition. In Austria it is even frequently claimed that it is a particularly democratic political instrument, which is a somewhat bizarre confusion of concepts. Public opinion polling has not passed over the question of national consciousness. There is a growing number of surveys dealing with this issue (cf. Wagner 1982, p. 124ff.). One of the most comprehensive and interesting is the study carried out by the Paul Lazarsfeld Gesellschaft in 1980 (Gehmacher 1980). In the following, some of the individual results of this study in particular[8], supplemented by various other survey results—among them are those of a very recent and unpublished survey (Ulram 1987)—will be subjected to a secondary analysis so as to outline the present state of Austrian national consciousness.

In doing so, of course, the limits to this method must not be forgotten. Although a carefully conducted opinion poll certainly does attain representative results, it is not certain whether these reflect true, deeper, perhaps even unconscious opinions or the readiness to act, or whether they are indeed just answers to survey questions (cf. Heer 1981, p. 16). Answers which are offered rather hurriedly in a specific social situation—which an interview is—when the respondent frequently has the impression he should say the right thing, must necessarily remain somewhat superficial.[9] Complementing this method by other methods which delve deeper should, therefore, always be advocated, even though the demands of representativeness are not as easy to fulfill. We have attempted to do this in a study about the general understanding of politics (Gerlich/Ucakar 1981). The findings and results from our study are the basis for the choice of results and my interpretation of them in this secondary analysis. It is essential to appreciate above all that the chances of achieving a realistic understanding of political interrelationships are by no means equal in all strata. People in the upper classes and those with more education are in fact better able to recognize interrelationships and relate them to their own interests—as a means of simplification, only the latter of these two criteria, education, is used in the following interpretations. This group generally has a realistic idea of politics—which can mean they would like to see improvements made and therefore express criticism. Austrians belonging to the middle and lower social and educational strata, by contrast, usually see politics in stereotypes—these stereotypes of Austrian politics are usually positive, but sometimes negative. They find it hard to make concrete connections between politics and the conditions under which they personally live. Their answers are therefore usually less reliable (Gerlich/Ucakar 1981).

The results shown below are from surveys on three issues. First, national consciousness as such is illustrated. Second, this is then compared to the desire for unification with Germany, which indirectly at least qualifies the existence of an Austrian nation. Third, complementary results are given—these are mostly emotional assessments of the federal states or national character, or they deal with national self-image.

Table 10.1

Concepts associated with Austria

(concepts which are appropriate for Austria; chosen by respondents; 1980 opinion poll, values in percent)

	all	compulsory schooling	secondary education	high school university graduates
republic	81	78	87	88
democracy	68	60	74	83
state	40	40	39	36
federal country	35	31	36	35
country	23	28	20	7
a people	19	22	18	13
nation	16	15	17	19

Source: Gehmacher 1980, II, p. 1

What relationship do Austrians have with their nation? As is demonstrated in table 10.1, when given a list to choose from, Austrians seldom associate the concept of "nation" with their country. Presumably, this would be more common in countries with a strong national consciousness. The more educated strata more often choose the correct but complex concepts "republic" and "democracy," the less educated strata "state," "country" and "people." On the whole it can be said that consciousness of Austria as a nation is still low (see table 10.2).

The results differ somewhat when interviewees are asked explicitly whether Austria is a nation. Table 10.2 allows 3 choices—yes, no and, between these, the response "Austria is beginning to see itself as a nation." In 1980, the number of affirmative answers was very high—two-thirds of interviewees—but the fact that there were so many affirmative answers from members of the lower educational strata presumably means that these largely reflect stereotypes. The second choice, however, chosen by about one-fifth of the interviewees, is probably not so much an indication of halting identification with the nation as it is of a realistic point of view. This is made clear by numerous cross-tables not shown here which verify that those expressing this opinion have much clearer and informed ideas about concrete political questions, for instance Austria's international position or the exact date on which the State Treaty was signed (Gehmacher 1980, II, pp. 47 and 49). The third choice, however, the rejection of the Austrian nation, is still preferred by more than one in ten Austrians. They are represented in all strata, and their choice is probably due to one of two causes—either they have a certain nostalgia for the Hapsburg Monarchy or they show remnants of Pan-German consciousness.[10] The latter is confirmed by the large proportion of FPÖ supporters who made this choice, although as a group they are ambivalent, since a larger proportion of them affirm the existence of an Austrian nation than, for example, ÖVP supporters. It is interesting to break down the data according to two other criteria. In the analysis according to age, it can be seen that the young identify less with the nation but are more realistic—this may be related to the gradual process of national identification during the course of a lifetime. The right side of the table gives a disturbingly clear idea of the importance of general economic conditions for national consciousness. Those who judge the economic situation more negatively also identify less with the Austrian nation. Is this indeed just fair-weather national consciousness? (See table 10.2)

This is confirmed to a certain degree by table 10.3 which demonstrates the development of Austrian national consciousness over several decades (it should be noted that the questions were not always exactly comparable). On the one hand, an impressive increase in positive identification can be seen—this confirms that the processes of dynamic nation-building and reintegration mentioned earlier are taking place—but on the other hand a stagnation, or even a slight reversal of this process, at least temporarily, can also be detected, maybe as a reaction to more difficult times. This is paralleled to a certain extent by the erosion of loyalty to the traditional parties (cf. Plasser

1987). Recently, however, Austrian national consciousness has become somewhat stronger, presumably due to the increase in public and private discussions about questions of Austria's past. Without going into detail, it should be mentioned in this context that survey results verify a strong orientation toward the Second Republic (one half of the population considers it to be the most important period in Austrian history), and that nearly two-thirds of those respondents affirming the existence of an Austrian nation declare that it has only developed since 1945 (nearly 80 percent of the "realists") (cf. Gehmacher 1980, II, pp. 6 and 19). This also confirms the assumptions made above about the beginning of the nation-building process and the tendency to repress thoughts about earlier periods in Austrian history.

Table 10.2
National consciousness
(1980 opinion poll, values in percent)

Question: Austria...	all	compulsory schooling	secondary education	high school university graduates
is a nation	67	69	68	57
is becoming a nation	19	16	20	30
is not a nation	11	10	11	14

Question: Austria...	-19	20-29	30-39	40-49	50-59	... 60 and above
is a nation	60	65	69	61	71	70
is becoming a nation	27	21	22	22	17	13
is not a nation	11	12	8	15	9	12

Question: Austria...	SPÖ	ÖVP	FPÖ	yes crisis	no crisis
is a nation	71	64	68	61	69
is becoming a nation	16	22	15	17	19
is not a nation	10	11	17	18	10

Source: Gehmacher 1980, II, p. 15

Table 10.3
Development of national consciousness
(opinion polls, values in percent)

	1956	1965	1972	1980	1987
Austria is a nation	49	48	62	67	75
Austria is beginning to see itself as a nation	-	23	12	19	16
Austria is not a nation	46	15	7	11	5
no answer	5	14	19	3	5

Sources: Kreissler 1984, p. 497; Gehmacher 1980, II, p. 15; Ulram 1987

Next is the second part where we ask the related question—how do Austrians judge the anschluss? Less positively than they do the concept of an Austrian nation, but still more than positively enough! Remnants of German nationalist consciousness are seen to be stronger than would be supposed on the basis of the negative answers to the question about the existence of an Austrian nation. As table 10.4 shows, one-third of the respondents agree, at least from a historical point of view, with an ideological statement clearly formulated in terms used by German nationalists. Agreement to this statement is greater among members of the lower educational strata (which indirectly shows that although they may give an impression of indifference, those with a "realistic" attitude toward the Austrian nation are more sincere!), among older citizens (the repression of certain memories definitely plays a role in this!) and among supporters of the FPÖ (over 50%!). In addition, the relationship with the perception of an economic crisis spoken of above is apparent here too. In any case, it can be seen on the whole that Austrian national consciousness is to some extent qualified.[11] (See table 10.4)

Table 10.5, which is from a different survey, reinforces this impression. This question does not concern the past, but the possibility of an anschluss in the future. Only about one-half of all Austrians can rule out this possibility with certainty—and here again, the tendency to do so is greater in the upper educational strata. In some regions more greatly oriented toward Germany, this proportion even falls below 50%.

Table 10.4
Judgement of the anschluss
(1980 opinion poll, values in percent)

Question: The anschluss at long last brought about national unification with the German people.

	all	compulsory schooling	secondary education	high school university graduates
agree	34	38	33	17
disagree	58	50	61	81
no answer	8	12	6	2

Question: The anschluss at long last brought about national unification with the German people.

	-19	20-29	30-39	40-49	50-59	... 60 and above
agree	25	26	31	36	40	39
disagree	68	65	62	56	55	50
no answer	7	9	6	9	6	11

Question: The anschluss at long last brought about national unification with the German people.

	SPÖ	ÖVP	FPÖ	yes crisis	no crisis
agree	37	33	53	43	33
disagree	57	58	41	49	60
no answer	7	6	6	9	7

<u>Source</u>: Dr. Fessel + GfK 1980, quoted in Lyon, 1985

This orientation toward Germany, however, would presumably have been even greater if this type of survey had been conducted in earlier periods. This is indicated by table 10.6 which demonstrates the orientation of reporting on foreign events in Austria's mass media in three different periods. P. Katzenstein's survey shows that Austria has become increasingly interested in the rest of the world and that our orientation toward our neighbor to the northwest has greatly weakened in the long-term—this too is proof that a process of reintegration is taking place in Austria.

Table 10.5
Anticipation of another anschluss
(1980 opinion poll, values in percent)

Question: Do you personally believe there will be another ... anschluss ... in the distant future?

	definitely not	other answers
all respondents	55	45
compulsory school	47	53
technical school	60	40
high school	73	27
university	78	22
Vienna	66	34
Burgenland, Lower Austria	60	40
Styria, Carinthia	51	49
Upper Austria, Salzburg	49	51
Tirol, Vorarlberg	45	55

Source: Dr. Fessel + GfK 1980, quoted in Lyon 1985, p. 150

Table 10.6
Orientation of reporting on foreign events
(sample survey of two large daily newspapers, percentage of total articles)

	1933-1938	1946-1955	1958-1969
Germany	25	14	10
the Successor States	21	16	8
the rest of Europe	41	35	41
the rest of the world	13	34	41

Source: Katzenstein 1976a, p. 181

Table 10.7 in turn shows that when presented with a long list of countries to choose from, Austria is selected as the most attractive nation by one in three Austrians, although Germany is a close second, being chosen by one in four. It is informative to divide the respondents according their basic attitude toward Austrian national identity. A clear majority of those denying the existence of an Austrian nation prefer Germany; a relatively large proportion of realists coolly and calculatingly select Switzerland which, on the whole, is third.

Table 10.7
Attractiveness of various nations
(1980 opinion poll, values in percent)

Question: Which nation are you most attracted to?

	Austria	Germany	Switzerland
all respondents	33	26	11
Austria is a nation	35	28	11
Austria is becoming a nation	31	21	14
Austria is not a nation	24	30	12

Source: Gehmacher 1980, II, p. 236

If, in summary, the results of the first and second parts of the surveys dealt with here are compared, a process of growing national identification can clearly be seen, yet at the same time German nationalist orientations continue to exist to no small degree—that is, Austrian national consciousness is undergoing dynamic change and distinctions are arising.

Table 10.8
State consciousness
(1980 opinion poll, values in percent)

Question: Which Austrian federal state are you most attracted to?

	all	Vi	LA	B	St	C	UA	S	T	V
Vienna (Vi)	5	17	12	6	16	14	5	12	10	2
Lower Austria (LA)	13	3	49	3	9	7	3	7	13	2
Burgenland (B)	5	1	2	77	2	4	-	5	6	-
Styria (St)	17	1	1	3	69	10	3	3	6	1
Carinthia (C)	14	1	1	2	2	86	-	5	3	2
Upper Austria (UA)	13	1	1	1	3	3	63	12	9	2
Salzburg (S)	11	-	2	-	4	6	9	67	7	-
Tirol (T)	14	1	-	2	3	4	3	7	77	-
Vorarlberg (V)	4	-	2	2	-	4	1	7	15	65

Sources: Gehmacher 1980, I, p. 31 and II, p. 248

In the third part of this analysis of opinion poll results we will first deal with state consciousness, which was already mentioned above with regard to history. Table 10.8 does, in fact, illustrate an enormous inclination to identify with one's own federal state. Vienna is the only exception and it is apparently less commonly identified as a federal state. Several facts support the interpretation that state and national consciousness have a sort of complementary relationship. In some surveys, for instance, Austrian national consciousness is particularly strong in Vienna and Lower Austria (and state consciousness here is relatively weak), whereas the opposite is true for Carinthia, Tirol and Burgenland. The data, however, are not too uniform, nor is the question in table 10.8 explicitly about state consciousness. Other questions not presented here in detail show, furthermore, that in connection with national consciousness, attitudes toward Vienna are unique and ambivalent. On the one hand, 25 percent of all Austrians say Vienna is the federal state they are least attracted to, and on the other hand, 30 percent believe Vienna best embodies Austria's uniqueness—both of these percentages are higher than for any other state (Gehmacher 1980, II, pp. 250 and 252). This reflects a traditional ambiguity which has, by no means, been completely overcome.

The next two questions have to do with the Austrian self-image. What do Austrians consider to be endearing national characteristics? Table 10.9 contains several of these means of strengthening national identification. Austrians are unanimous as to which of these belong at the top of the list: countryside, family, language—that is, aspects of private life are considered particularly important—but also political and social peace. The factors ranked in the middle have, in part, to do with emotional and everyday aspects, and the more educated strata are more reserved in selecting them. Childhood, food and drink are less of a medium of identification for them. People in these groups have primarily rational reasons for their patriotism—as is shown by their answers to other questions. They may therefore superficially appear to be more skeptical, but since their patriotism is based on rational arguments, it is probably more lasting than a profession of love for one's country which is founded merely on the satisfaction of oral needs (see also Strotzka 1980).

This is demonstrated, for example, in table 10.10 which concerns the question of national talents and indicates that the lower educational strata stress music, sports and food as a means of identification, whereas the more educated strata quite realistically emphasize Austrians' not always pleasant social manners. Here too, private and public, emotional and rational forms of identification stand side by side. Table 10.10 clearly shows the importance of music and sports in particular for national identification.

Table 10.9
National characteristics
(1980 opinion poll, values in percent)

Question: There are various reasons for loving a country and enjoying living there. Here is a list of several of them. Now tell me for every characteristic whether it is generally important or generally unimportant for your love of Austria. (percentage answering important)

	all	compulsory schooling	secondary education	high school university graduates
beautiful countryside	97	96	97	96
political and social peace	96	95	97	96
family and friends live here	94	95	93	92
friendly people	94	95	94	90
common language	93	94	94	89
political neutrality	87	85	91	82
this is where I spent my childhood	86	88	86	78
this is where my parents and grandparents lived	82	86	80	69
has produced many good musicians and poets	79	77	80	79
satisfaction with governmental policies	74	78	73	62
good food	74	78	76	53
people's ability to enjoy life	74	73	76	71
unassuming nature of the people	73	74	77	58
good wine and beer	56	59	57	38
low aspiration for achievement	28	29	27	26

Source: Gehmacher 1980, I, p. 26

In 1973, a direct question about national pride was asked (cf. table 10.11). The total percentage of affirmative answers is quite high. What is striking is that national pride grows as age increases—this in turn indicates that the young identify less with Austria—and that, in contrast, it decreases as the educational level rises. As has been shown in the most recent surveys, these tendencies in public opinion have scarcely changed since then (Ulram 1987).

Table 10.10
Austrians' talents
(1980 opinion poll, values in percent)

Question: What are Austrians particularly talented in?

	all	compulsory schooling	secondary education	high school university graduates
playing music and singing	60	62	57	58
sports	49	54	49	23
eating and drinking	47	49	45	46
dealing with people	30	26	31	42
arranging things to their advantage in any situation	27	19	31	51
adapting to any political structure	20	16	23	28
simple, natural life	17	18	16	13
talking	15	16	14	13
helping others	13	15	12	5
art	10	6	11	18
love	4	5	3	2

Source: Gehmacher 1980, I, p. 37

Table 10.11
National pride

Question: Are you proud to be an Austrian?
(values in percent, sample survey)

	all	-29	age 30-49	50 and above	compulsory schooling	secondary/ university education
absolutely	56	38	56	68	65	51
mostly	34	50	34	24	29	37
not really	2	2	2	1	1	2
not at all	1	1	1	1	0	2
undecided	7	9	7	6	5	8

Sources: IMAS survey 1973, Wagner 1982, p. 129

Table 10.12

Nostalgia for Austria in a foreign country
(1980 opinion poll, values in percent)

Question: Imagine you are in a foreign country. Which of these Austrian phenomena would really make you feel nostalgic for your home?

	national anthem	folk music
all respondents	32	22
compulsory schooling	31	30
secondary education	35	16
high school/university graduates	26	6

Source: Gehmacher 1980, II, p. 128

The next three tables deal with further concrete phenomena which produce national pride or national identification. Table 10.12 contains the two phenomena which respondents mentioned most frequently as producing nostalgia for their home when they are abroad—the national anthem and folk music. These relatively inarticulate forms of identification also have a greater effect among the lower educational strata.

Table 10.13, however, shows that each stratum is capable of finding the type of music which suits it. The medium of music (which was chosen for this survey from a wide spectrum of possible things one can be proud of) thus plays an important role in all social strata (cf. also Falk 1980). It would be interesting to investigate in a survey whether something similar is true in countries which are not considered to be as musical as Austria.

Another similar question: "What gives you an uplifting feeling of national pride?" In table 10.14, sports and music, in this case the national anthem, are once again by far the most common answers. Athletic victories seem to emotionally move primarily the lower educational strata, while the national anthem, the officially correct answer, has this effect primarily on the upper strata.

Thus with regard to concrete phenomena which produce national pride, an inclination toward music as a means of identification is common to all social strata, though the type of music does vary—and this is true despite the tendency of the lower strata to otherwise emphasize private and emotional forms of attachment to the national community, and the tendency of the upper strata to emphasize public and rational forms.

Table 10.13
Patriotic pride
(1980 opinion poll, values in percent)

Question: Tell me for every field (listed) ... if you are personally proud of Austrian achievements...

	popular music	classical music
all respondents	81	60
compulsory schooling	81	53
secondary education	84	65
high school/university graduates	75	72

Source: Gehmacher 1980, II, p. 116ff.

Table 10.14
Uplifting feeling of pride in Austria
(1980 opinion poll, values in percent)

Question: On which of these occasions would you as an Austrian be most likely to rightly feel proud?

	Olympic victory of an athlete	national anthem
all respondents	32	30
compulsory schooling	34	27
secondary education	31	32
high school/university graduates	30	35

Source: Gehmacher 1980, II, p. 154

The last question to be discussed attempts to ascertain the potential of national pride to impel people to act. The answers are rather mixed. As table 10.15 illustrates, two-thirds of the total population would react actively to the desecration of the Austrian flag—one third by protesting and one third by fighting. The distribution of the answers among the educational strata is different than might be expected; the more educated would choose the more active response—is this perhaps another indication that their rationally founded national consciousness is stronger than identification based on mere emotions? One in four would react passively—the less educated prefer irony, and a surprisingly large proportion of the more educated would simply turn away. This is again reminiscent of the above-mentioned ambivalence in the upper educational strata, many of whose members apparently have a stronger than average Austrian national consciousness, whereas a relatively large number of them clearly reject this concept—i.e. this strata tends to have strong opinions, both for and against.

Table 10.15
Defending the flag
(1980 opinion poll, values in percent)

Question: If you saw the Austrian flag being torn down by foreigners, what would you do?

	all	compulsory schooling	secondary education	high school university graduates
protest against the desecration of the flag	34	35	35	27
fight them	31	26	33	48
laugh at them	20	32	25	6
not pay any attention	5	3	5	15

Source: Gehmacher 1980, II, p. 157

How can the empirical results presented here be summarized and interpreted on the basis of the theoretical categories discussed above? Austrian national consciousness appears to be greatly characterized by the framework conditions which have prevailed in the Second Republic—it even appears that it has emerged primarily in the Second Republic and that Austrians identify primarily with the Second Republic. Earlier periods play a role only in that there are still certain German nationalist tendencies which hark back to these periods. National consciousness is related to the perception of economic developments and can thus be seen as a positive reaction to propitious economic conditions. It is also dependent on the changed international situation, in particular on Austria's wider range of international interests, and on social changes. With regard to the last factor, we should point out the greater educational opportunities that have definitely led to more "realistic" attitudes.

A majority of the mechanisms of identification, however, are apparently of a private, passive and emotional nature. Music, sports and everyday culture including even eating habits appear to play a greater role than public, active and rational processes. Where the opposite is true, however, and this is the case in the upper educational strata in particular, national consciousness appears more realistic but therefore stronger and more readily activated. A special aspect is the role of the federal states as mediators of identity. State consciousness exists, and it may compete with national consciousness. With regard to this aspect, attitudes in Vienna are unique and ambivalent.

As for the attitudes which constitute Austrian national consciousness, it must in summary once again be emphasized that they are not uniform, so that national consciousness on the whole is somewhat heterogeneous and fragile. Passive identification has definitely increased during the process of reintegration, and, in addition, some sectors of the population, above all the upper educational strata, identify more actively with the nation, and this has greater effects. Passive identification in particular, however, still appears somewhat problematic due to the fact that some people explicitly and others implicitly still reject the concept of Austrian national identity.[12]

Does their developing national consciousness help Austrians to form a social identity? Fundamentally, yes, and as the most recent surveys in particular demonstrate, this is no doubt increasingly so—above all when it is developed actively and rationally. Austrians' discussions of their self-image on the occasion of the 1986 presidential election undoubtedly had this effect. When national consciousness is developed passively or based on mere emotions, it is less able to help people form a social identity, and this identity is weaker and more uncertain. But other mediators of identity, such as state consciousness, can compensate for this. Finally, I would like once again to point out that although there will presumably be a certain continuity in the general survey results, they must be considered relative, because the phenomena dealt with are processes which take place over time.

5. Conclusions

> "Das gemeinsame Erinnern gemeinsamer
> Geschichte schafft Identität...
> Nur partizipatorische Integration
> wirkt identitätsbildend"
>
> *(Ernst Bruckmüller)*

The process of the formation of national identity presupposes open discussion about the past of one's own community, and is to this extent retrospective. This reappraisal, this coming to terms with history, which is necessarily also a sorrowful task, may be postponed, but it is a task Austrians will ultimately have to do. Forming a national identity is, of course, on the other hand, a process which should and must be forward-looking. It serves as a guide in an ever more rapidly changing world, and as a basis for dealing with the world in the growing network of international ties.

It hurts to look back. "History is painful" (F. Heer). Wounds can be torn open in the process—but psychological wounds, unlike physical wounds, can only heal when they are opened. It can be hoped that Austrians may learn from countries with an uninterrupted history of national consciousness. De Gaulle was reportedly once called upon by one of his supporters to do something about the leftist intellectual author Jean-Paul Sartre who was continually criticizing him, the conservative president. He is said to have answered that that would be wholly impossible, for Sartre too was France. The repressed periods of Austrian history too are Austria; the groups on the right and on the left about whom silence has reigned, those serving the Christian corporate state or the Austrian Hitler, those in the resistance and those who emigrated—they too are Austria.

It is above all the task of schools and the mass media as well as the political parties to pass on the relevant knowledge. That is the only way a stronger Austrian national consciousness can be created; that is the only way it will be possible to overcome the fragility of Austrian national consciousness resulting from the numerous remnants of German nationalist consciousness residing in the Austrian soul. Trusting the social peace guaranteed by the Social Partnership will not suffice any more than it will suffice to emphasize national symbols, and emotional speeches held on special occasions, or the empty ceremony of the presentation of Austrian folklore and gastronomic culture by the mass media. In order for it to have a lasting effect, dealing with the past must be done consciously (and no one can honestly doubt that Austrians have a lot to catch up on in this respect), and dealing with the future must be done actively.[13] As was explained above, nation-building is part of the process of modernization, and this process implies not only economic but also cultural development. F. Fürstenberg recently demonstrated that the vast majority of Austrians are still actually attached to the values of an agrarian and feudal-bureaucratic culture (cf. Fürstenberg 1985).

This made possible among other things the success of the system of Social Partnership which, particularly during the phase of reconstruction and rapid economic growth, did a great deal to stabilize the system. The demands of the environment, however, are beginning to change radically. Both the present growth crisis and the crisis of meaning which have now spread to this country demand of Austrians a willingness to change and innovative potential to such an extent that it would be difficult to base these on traditional values. It is necessary to step out of the homely warmth of small, easily comprehensible and secure areas and prove ourselves in the wide world (cf. Mongardini 1985).[14] But for this we need a secure, rationally founded and actively acquired identity. Sentimental, passively acquired orientations no longer suffice.

This also means new demands will be made of schools and the media as well as the bureaucracy and, in particular, politics. Schools will have to devote themselves to political education in the manner consistently stipulated by the relevant decree issued by Sinowatz as Minister of Education in 1978 (which in practice, however, has been mostly ignored)—that is, it should no longer be the mere instruction of civics, but entail participatory learning to convey information, improve understanding and increase commitment. Easily said, not quite so easily decreed, and difficult to accomplish in practice in the hierarchical structures of schools (cf. Gerlich/Müller 1988)! A majority of the media, too, adhere only too willingly to the nearly Josephinist precept of objectivity, and apparently do not believe that viewers are capable of judging for themselves, and thus instead of uncovering controversy, they present an entirely harmonious picture.

In the bureaucracy—the innumerable offices of the federal administration—the individual should no longer be treated as a subject, but as a mature citizen. There are innumerable ways to permit active participation and in doing so to strengthen the sense of belonging to the nation. But how hard it is to break with centuries-old traditions! And finally, the political parties ought to see their task less as offering patronage and creating consensus, and instead as making clear their differences of interest and demonstrating the courage to accept conflict—and not conflict in the sense of personal polemics or unobjective slander, but in the sense of demonstrating the differing alternative proposals for solutions to the problems we face, and consistently stating their positions which should not "anticipate a compromise before a controversy has even arisen" (cf. Gerlich 1984). In this sense politics should be a model for the individual and incite and encourage him to active and dedicated participation. This will have to increase the willingness to go through and accept conflict in order to contribute to the emergence of a strong national consciousness.

It could almost be seen as an ironical turn of history that manipulative attempts to foster the formation of identity, by forcing it upon individuals who themselves were passive, were usually ultimately a failure. Experience in Austria too shows that citizens do not let themselves be constantly manipulated. There have been repeated spontaneous outbursts of anger by the populace which have completely surprised the so well-intentioned functionaries who had so successfully appeased, instructed and indoctrinated the people. In contrast to this, a strong identity is formed when the individual is actively involved, when he is given the opportunity to participate or to rationally found his loyalty. This is demonstrated by both Austrian historical developments and the picture of Austrian national consciousness we gain from opinion polls. An individual manipulated by the system evades this manipulation and feigns loyalty only as long as this serves his interests. Individuals who are actively involved develop a real sense of belonging and identity which motivates them to loyalty in both good times and bad. In this regard Austrians are certainly no exception.

Notes

1. I would like to thank Christian Haerpfer and Peter A. Ulram for giving me access to a large amount of interesting information and material, as well as the participants in my courses at the University of Vienna for considering my hypotheses concerning nation-building with skepticism. My thanks also go to W.C. Müller for his comments and criticism.

2. Cf. Kreissler 1985, p. 462, and the attitude in East Germany toward the question of national identity, which is, to a certain extent, comparable to the question Austrians must deal with.

3. To mention only the most important examples: 1848, 1927, 1950, 1984.

4. An exemplary and particularly frustrating fact which can be pointed out is that a majority of Austrian conscripts have a poorer opinion of the federal army after they finish serving than before they begin. This is a perfect example of a missed opportunity to impart identification through participation. Perhaps, though, as a teacher at a large university (for which there are no comparable studies) one should be careful not to prepare to cast the first stone...

5. Pan-Austrian traditions do definitely, however, continue to have an effect in the sometimes even political discussions about the concept of "Central Europe" ("Mitteleuropa") which are frequently revived.

6. The organization founded by Winter, the "Österreichische Gemeinschaft," still exists today and publishes a magazine called "Die Österreichische Nation." Cf. vol. 4, 1985: 60 Jahre Österreichische Gemeinschaft 1925-1985.

7. Kreissler (1984, p. 414) quotes the Austrian author G. Fritsch on this topic.

8. In this context I would like to especially point out the large volume of data compiled by the Lazarsfeld Gesellschaft during their study (quoted as Gehmacher 1980, II).

9. In this context, the choice and formulation of the questions is, of course, an essential element which can at times influence the results. Falk (1980) is correct in pointing out the basic underlying optimism of the survey questions.

10. Cf. also the similar strata-specific differences in the image people have of Austria in Gerlich 1976.

11. More recent surveys, however, show that the anschluss is judged less positively. On the other hand though, one Austrian in two still believes that Nazism did his country not only harm but also good (Ulram 1987).

12. I would like to add that our political leaders have a disturbingly "pragmatic" attitude—perhaps in reaction to the ambivalence of the population described above. As Bluhm's surveys have shown, they have no doubts themselves about the question of Austrian nationality and therefore consider it to be impertinent and of no interest, so to speak (Bluhm 1972, p. 177ff.).

13. Bruckmüller, who stresses the identity-forming effect of political participation in particular, does admit that there are other types of joint action, such as participation in military conflicts, which may also have this same effect (cf. Bruckmüller 1984, p. 212). There are presumably other examples of this, for instance the community-forming effect of rituals which require participation, e.g. religious rites, mass assemblies in totalitarian countries, or elections in single-party states with but one candidate which are nevertheless significant, or, on another level, the activities which

256   *Gerlich*

take place in male organizations (with respect to the latter, Perçhinig 1986 is interesting).

14. The work by Kuschey (1985b) which reports the experience of a contemporary Austrian commuting between Carinthia and Vienna is a delightful illustration of the commuting between home and the world typical of modern man and described by Mongardini.

Bibliography

Balfour, M., *States and Mind*, London 1953 (Balfour, 1953)

Bluhm, W.T., *Building an Austrian Nation*, New Haven 1973 (Bluhm, 1973)

Bruckmüller, E., *Nation Österreich. Sozialhistorische Aspekte ihrer Entwicklung*, Wien 1984 (Bruckmüller, 1984)

Burghardt, A./Matis, H., *Die Nation-Werdung Österreichs, Historische und soziologische Aspekte*, Berichte des Instituts für Allgemeine Soziologie und Wirtschaftssoziologie der Wirtschaftsuniversität Wien, Heft 13/1976 (Burghardt/Matis, 1976)

Falk, G., *Das "österreichische Selbstgefühl" im Spiegel einer Umfrage*, in: Gehmacher 1980 (Falk, 1980)

Firnberg, H., *Das österreichische Nationalbewußtsein*, Zukunft 1/1986 (Firnberg, 1986)

Fuchs, E., *Rot-Weiß-Rosa, Der Österreicher und seine Nation im Lichte empirischer Untersuchungen*, Aufrisse 1/1985 (Fuchs, 1985)

Fürstenberg, F., *Sozialkulturelle Aspekte der Sozialpartnerschaft*, in: Gerlich/Grande/Müller, 1985 (Fürstenberg, 1985)

Gehmacher, E., *Das österreichische Nationalbewußtsein*, Eine Studie der Paul Lazarsfeld Gesellschaft für Sozialforschung, Wien 1980 (Gehmacher, 1980)

Gerlich, P., *Die latente Krise der Traditionsparteien*, in: Koren, S. u.a. (Hg.), *Politik für die Zukunft*, Wien 1984 (Gerlich, 1984)

Gerlich, P., *Nation Österreich—verspätet aber vorbildlich?*, in: Burghardt/Matis 1976 (Gerlich, 1976)

Gerlich, P., *Zur Analyse des politischen Systems: Entwicklung eines Begriffsrahmens*, ÖZP 1972 (Gerlich, 1972)

Gerlich, P./Müller, W.C., *Das politische Systems Österreichs, Ein Lehrbehelf*, Wien 1988 (Gerlich/Müller, 1988)

Gerlich, P./Müller, W.C. (Hg.), *Sozialpartnerschaft in der Krise*, Wien 1985 (Gerlich/Müller, 1985)

Gerlich, P./Ucakar, K., *Staatsbürger und Volksvertretung, Das Alltagsverständnis von Parlament und Demokratie in Österreich*, Salzburg 1981 (Gerlich/Ucakar, 1981)

Gerschenkron, A., *Economic Backwardness in Historical Perspective*, 4th ed, Cambridge, Mass 1979 (Gerschenkron, 1979)

Heer, F., *Der Kampf um die österreichische Identität*, Wien 1981 (Heer, 1981)

Hintze, O., *Staat und Verfassung*, Göttingen 1962 (Hintze, 1962)

Höchtl, J., *Jugend und österreichische Nation, Gesellschaft und Politik*, 3/1980 (Höchtl, 1980)

Katzenstein, P.J., *Disjoined Partners, Austria and Germany since 1918*, Berkeley 1976 (Katzenstein, 1976)

Katzenstein, P.J., *The Last Old Nation: Austrian National Consciousness Since 1945, Comparative Politics* 2/1977 (Katzenstein, 1977)

Klenner, F., *Erst auf dem Wege zum Nationalbewußtsein, Gesellschaft und Politik, 3/1980* (Klenner, 1980)

Kreissler, F., *Der Österreicher und seine Nation*, Wien 1984 (Kreissler, 1984)

Kuschey, B., *Die österreichische Nation wird ein Thema, Aufrisse, 1/1985* (Kuschey, 1985a)

Kuschey, B., *Geständnisse eines Provinzlers, Aufrisse, 1/1985* (Kuschey, 1985b)

Leser, N., *Die nationale Selbstfindung der Österreicher*, in: Jambor, W. (Hg.), *Der Anteil der Bundesländer an der Nationwerdung Österreichs*, Wien 1971 (Leser, 1971)

Lüer, A., *Die Nationale Frage in Ideologie und Programmatik der politischen Lager Österreichs 1918-1933*, phil. Diss., Wien 1985 (Lüer, 1985)

Luza, R.V., *The Resistance in Austria 1938-1945*, Minneapolis 1984 (Luza, 1984)

Lyon, D. u.a. (Hg.), *Österreich "bewußt" sein—bewußt Österreicher sein*, Materialien zur Entwicklung des Österreichbewußtseins seit 1945, Wien 1985 (Lyon, u.a., 1985)

Massiczek, A. (Hg.), *Die österreichische Nation. Zwischen zwei Nationalismen*, Wien 1967 (Massiczek, 1967)

Mongardini,C., *Heimat, Nostalgie, Politik*, Ms., Rom 1985 (Mongardini, 1985)

Moore, B., *Soziale Ursprünge von Diktatur und Demokratie*, Frankfurt 1969 (Moore, 1969)

Panzenböck, E., *Ein deutscher Traum, Die Anschlußidee und Anschlußpolitik bei Karl Renner und Otto Bauer*, Wien 1985 (Panzenböck, 1985)

Pelinka, A., *Verschweizerung des Bewußtseins*, in: Gehmacher, 1980 (Pelinka, 1980)

Pelinka, A., *Windstille, Klagen über Österreich*, Wien 1985 (Pelinka, 1985)

Pelinka, A./Welan, M., *Demokratie und Verfassung in Österreich*, Wien 1971 (Pelinka/Welan, 1971)

Perchinig, B., *Zur Frage der Kärntner Deutschnationalen*, Phil. Diss., Wien 1986 (Perchinig, 1986)

Perchinig, B., *National oder liberal: Die Freiheitliche Partei Österreichs*, in: Gerlich, P./W.C. Müller (Hg.), *Zwischen Koalition und Konkurrenz, Österreichs Parteien seit 1945*, Wien 1983 (Perchinig, 1983)

Plasser, F., *Parteien unter Stress*, Wien 1987 (Plasser, 1987)

Plasser, F./Ulram, P.A., *Unbehagen im Parteienstaat*, Wien 1982 (Plasser/Ulram, 1982)

Ringel, E., *Die österreichische Seele*, Wien 1984 (Ringel, 1984)

Rose, R., *National Pride: Cross-National Surveys*, Glasgow 1984 (Rose, 1984)

Schulmeister, O., *Identität—Nation—Selbstbestimmung*, in: Gehmacher 1980 (Schulmeister, 1980)

Steiner, K., *Politics in Austria*, Boston 1972 (Steiner, 1972)

Stourzh, G., *Kommentar zur Studie "Österreichbewußtsein"*, in: Gehmacher 1980 (Stourzh, 1980)

Strotzka, H., *Das österreichische Nationalbewußtsein—vom Standpunkt des Psychoanalytikers*, in: Gehmacher, 1980 (Strotzka, 1980)

Ucakar, K., *Demokratie und Wahlrecht in Österreich*, Wien 1985 (Ucakar, 1985)

Ulram, P.A., *Österreichbewußtsein 1987*, Dr. Fessel & GfK, Manuskript, Wien 1987 (Ulram, 1987)

Veiter, Th., *Volk und Nation, Gesellschaft und Politik, 3/1980* (Veiter, 1980)

Wagner, G. (Hg.), *Österreich—Von der Staatsidee zum Nationalbewußtsein*, Wien 1982 (Wagner, 1982)

Wagner, G. (Hg.), *Österreich Zweite Republik*, Thaur 1983 (Wagner, 1983)

Wandruszka, A., *Österreichs politische Struktur*, in: Benedikt, H. (Hg.), *Geschichte der Republik Österreich*, 2. Aufl., Wien 1977 (Wandruszka, 1977)

11

Between Alternative and Established Forms of Political Participation

Young Austrians and the Austrian Party System between 1960 and 1987

HEIDEMARIE A. BUBENDORFER

Introduction

The interest in the relationship between young Austrians[1] and the party system within the framework of political science investigations has increased markedly in the last several years[2].

The results of diverse surveys dealing with younger people, carried out over the past 15 years, present the picture of a group of voters which reacts to daily political events on a very emotional basis, one which indicates extreme instability in its actions and on a short-term basis, is very inconsistant. While the Austrian young people of the 1960s are described as being quiet, maintaining a detached attitude toward politics (Kramer/Kramer 1974) and lacking persons who they can respect and look up to, those of the Seventies are considered involved, radical and rebellious[3]. Toward the latter part of that decade, this age group was seen as being disoriented, disinterested and uninvolved, cloaked in a pronounced "privatistic-individualistic attitude of self-worth," "in the pursuit of individual happiness" (Hansen/Veen 1980), and very willing to accept alternative forms of political participation (Gerlich/Ucakar 1981). Toward the mid-Eighties, this group was deemed critical, performance-oriented (Knapp 1985) and more interested.

These developments, their consequences and influences on the Austrian party system are to be examined and analysed in this report.

Young Austrians and the Party System

For many, being a member of the younger generation means being confronted with conflicts and lack of understanding from the adult world on a daily basis. The social position of a young person lies between two extremes—on the one hand, he no longer wants or is able to occupy the social role of being a child and demands freedom and the opportunity to develop his own ideas without outside interference, and on the other, the status of "adult" and the associated rights are not conceded him by the majority of older persons. This transitional period from the world of the adolescent to the world of the adult contains sufficient inherent crisis potential that it is realized under the catchword "generational conflict." "For the maturing adolescent, the end of childhood means an increase in independence while simultaneously occurring at the expense of his original security. Children enjoy freedoms which are lost to the adolescent. A child is not responsible for his actions; he is always able to fall back on the protection provided by an adult. In contrast, the life of an adolescent is filled with existential problems, ones which must be solved alone without the aid of the older generation" (Peterhoff 1985, p. 125).

Assuming the role of an adult does not only mean fulfilling traditional patterns of expectation but also having the courage to re-think this new role, to adapt oneself to trends and the currents of progress. It is only logical that this means distancing oneself from the older generation, which in turn leads to the development of areas of conflict which can only gradually be overcome. The young person's basic willingness to reject authority and everyday pragmatism[4], triggered by the lack of opportunities to influence one's surroundings and the right of having a voice, becomes the crystallization point of conflicts between young and old.

In the past, conflicts were battled out in different degrees of severity. Over time, a series of ruptures occurred in the relationship of the young person to the adult world, as well as to the established party system. The student movements at the end of the Sixties, which occurred somewhat belatedly and less radically in Austria when compared to those in the Federal Republic of Germany, the United States or the Netherlands, were followed by the an "apparently apolitical consumer paradise of the success generation" phase (Plasser/Ulram 1982, p. 135), and saw their breakthrough in 1976 with the "Arena Movement." Toward the end of the 1970s, a "new," albeit directionally opposite, "march through the institutions" (Küberl 1983, p. 201) began; one witnessed a pulling away from the established political system, one which had "done little to integrate the citizens and voters of the future and to motivate these in a positive manner" (Plasser/Ulram 1981, p. 19) and a detachment from established politics, which were repulsive to many[5].

Table 11.1
The Degree of Severity of the Detachment from Politics (in percent)

Age group:	1980	14-24	1986
... The party now in office has no influence on my life	45		44
... Young people today should stay out of politics	23		18
... I basically don't care whether I live in a democracy or not	9		9

Sources:
1980: Plasser/Ulram, 1982, p. 151
1986: Dr. Fessel + GfK: Staats-, Wirtschafts-, Politik- und Gesellschaftsverständnis der Österreichischen Jugend, 1986

Every fifth young person is of the opinion that politics is nothing for young people. Half of the 14- to 24-year-olds surveyed believe that their lives are not dependent on which party is currently in office or that even if the government were to be in the hands of another party, this would not affect their lives significantly. Nine percent do not even care whether they live in a democratic system or not.

The changing system of social values also brought about a change in the relationship between young people and the established party politics at the beginning of the 1980s. Young Austrians consider the problems of the future as a "magnifying glass of existing problems" (Küberl 1983, p. 202)—ensuring peace, finding alternatives to nuclear energy, hindering the destruction of the forest, supporting environmental protection—and are also willing to participate personally toward their solution. But today's young people have also taken on an emancipated attitude toward the adult world and have developed a new understanding of politics and political culture, without transgressing the limits of the given rules of the democratic game.

Despite the fact that in 1987, still two-thirds of all young people surveyed were basically in agreement with the political opinions and views of their parents, this proportion (see Table 11.2) has dropped by more than 20% over the past 25 years. The least conformity with their parents with regard to political issues was shown in 1984, a year which, with its numerous peace demonstrations and the occupation of the Hainburg Au, made a deep imprint on and played a significant role in the development of the Green Party and the Alternative Movement in Austria.

Table 11.2[6]
Agreement with Parents on Political Issues (in percent)

Age groups:	1959/60 17-21	1973 16-25
Opinions ...		
are identical	47	
		49
show little divergence	21	
show some divergence	16	16
show much divergence	9	
		10
are extremely different	11	

Age groups:	1977 16-29	1980 14-24	1983 20-29	1984 14-24	1986	1987
Agree ...						
usually	57	36	36	23	37	29
sometimes	*	36	35	38	30	40
seldom	*	16	17	23	17	18
(almost) never	*	7	7	11	11	3

	1959/60	1973	1980	1983	1984	1986	1987
Generally agree with parents on political issues	84	65	72	71	61	67	69

* not polled
Sources:
1959/60: Dr. Walter Fessel, Jugendstudie 1959/60
1973: IMAS, Die junge Österreicher, 1973
1977: Gehmacher 1979, p. 297
1980: Dr. Fessel + GfK, Jugendstudie 1980
1983: Dr. Fessel + GfK, Jugend und Politik, May/June 1983
1984: Dr. Fessel + GfK, Jugendstudie spezial, 1984
1986: Dr. Fessel + GfK, Staats-, Wirtschafts-, Politik- und Gesellschaftsverständnis der Österreichischen Jugend, 1986
1987: Dr. Fessel + GfK, Jugend und Politik, 1987

The solidarization of smaller interest groups with the goal of joining forces to fight for peace and environmental protection and the intensified treatment of these issues in the media thus led to the considerable increase in the interest that young people had in politics during the 1970s.

Table 11.3
Young People's Interest in Politics (in percent)

How interested are you in politics?

Age groups:	1959/60 17-21	1980 14-24	1981 16-24	1984 14-24	1986	1987 14-24
Very		5	5	14	5	5
Somewhat	} 30	18	18	31	18	16
Not very		39	38	32	34	45
Very little		20	17	} 19	43	33
Not at all	} 70	18	21		-	-

Sources:
1959/60: Dr. Walter Fessel, Jugendstudie 1959/60
1980: Dr. Fessel + GfK, Jugendstudie, 1980
1981: Dr. Fessel + GfK, Jugendstudie, 1981
1984: Dr. Fessel + GfK, Jugendstudie spezial, 1984
1985: Dr. Fessel + GfK, Innen- und Aussenperspektive des österreichischen Parteiensystems, 1985
1986: Dr. Fessel + GfK, Staats-, Wirtschafts-, Politik- und Gesellschaftsverständnis der Österreichischen Jugend, 1986
1987: Dr. Fessel + GfK, Jugend und Politik, 1987

Where over two-thirds of Austrian young people showed only very little or no interest in politics at the end of the Fifties[7], twenty-five years later, only every eighth declares his lack of interest in the political decision-making process. The young people of the Eighties organize their political activities on their own, e.g. in protest marches against the start-up of a nuclear power plant, peace marches, rallies or podium discussions dealing with environmental protection, independent of party statutes and party platforms. Party youth organizations can step in and offer their assistance. The personal involvement of young people thinking along the same lines, without falling under the "supervision" of party dictates, goes hand in hand with a decline in party membership. In recent years, the number of younger party members (see Table 11.4) has decreased by one half.

Table 11.4
Membership in a Political Party (in percent)

Age groups:	1976 20-29	1980 14-24	1986
Am member	23	11	10
Am not member	77	*	89

* not polled
Sources:
1976: Dr. Fessel + GfK, Grundlagenstudie, Feb.-April, 1976, Vol. III
1980: Dr. Fessel + GfK, Jugendstudie, 1980
1986: Dr. Fessel + GfK, Staats-, Wirtschafts-, Politik- und Gesellschaftsverständnis der Österreichischen Jugend, 1986

The Relationship between Young People and the Established Political Parties

The relationship between younger generation voters and the established political parties can generally be described as remote and redundant. The term "disenchantment with the parties," coined in the early 80s and consistantly applied to the above relationship seems without doubt to be justified, although the attitude certainly existed prior to that time.

Table 11.5
Party Disenchantment: The Attitude of the Younger Generation Toward the Political Parties (in percent)

Age groups:	1959/60 17-21	1984 14-24	1986
The parties do not have anything to offer	52	*	48
One should vote for the person rather than the party	57	*	59
I dislike both the SPÖ and the ÖVP equally	*	36	35
I don't concern myself with politics at all anymore and only look out for myself	*	22	38
At the next election, I'm really going to give the big parties a piece of my mind	*	19	17

* not polled
Sources:
1959/60: Dr. Walter Fessel, Jugendstudie 1959/60 (Continued)

Sources (Cont.)
1984: Dr. Fessel + GfK, Jugendstudie spezial, 1984
1986: Dr. Fessel + GfK, Staats-, Wirtschafts-, Politik- und Gesellschaftsverständnis der Österreichischen Jugend, 1986

As early as the late 50s, over half (52%) of the younger people had already indicated an extremely detached and relatively unopportunistic attitude toward the political parties. In 1960, 57% and in 1986, 59% supported the idea of voting for individuals rather than parties.

The development of western political parties in the direction of vote-maximizing "catchall parties" (Kirchheimer 1969) has also led to a coming together of the party platforms, as well as the everyday politics, of the Austrian political parties.

Table 11.6
Differentiating between the Parliamentary Parties (in percent)

The parties in Parliament can be differentiated ...

Age groups:	1980 14-24		1985 20-29		1986 14-24	
to a great degree	13 }	50	7 }	34	10 }	36
strongly	37 }		27 }		26 }	
little	40 }	47	48 }	64	47 }	60
barely	7 }		16 }		13 }	

Sources:
1980: Dr. Fessel + GfK, Jugendstudie 1980
1984: Dr. Fessel + GfK, Jugendstudie spezial, 1984
1985: Dr. Fessel + GfK, Innen- und Aussenperspektive des österreichischen Parteiensystems, 1985
1986: Dr. Fessel + GfK, Staats-, Wirtschafts-, Politik- und Gesellschaftsverständnis der Österreichischen Jugend, 1986

Almost two-thirds of all young people have difficulties differentiating between the parties represented in Parliament; only every third young person can find a noticeable difference.

The mid-Eighties seemed to mark the nadir of the relationship between the younger generation and the political parties; every fifth young person would like to give the "powerful parties" a piece of his mind at the next elec-

266   *Bubendorfer*

tion. Another fifth is wrought with political apathy; every third young person is disgusted with the large parties. One of the reasons for this increasingly cool relationship between the established parties and the under-30 generation is the parties' inability to pay particular attention to the specific problems of this social group, to present their youth organizations in a sufficiently attractive manner to serve as sub-organizations for the development of future party functionaries[8], and to meet the demands made of them in an even somewhat satisfactory manner.

Table 11.7
The Demands made of the Political Parties by the Younger Generation (in percent)

| | 1969 | | 1975 | |
Age groups:	20-25	25-30	20-24	25-29
A party must be prepared to make the necessary decisions, even if these are unpopular.	91	83	86	91
It is essential that the party be led by men who look forward to making decisions and who have adequate authority.	83	77	*	*
The political parties should view it as their duty to carry out reforms.	*	*	68	79
To be attractive to younger voters, a party must understand young people and give them a chance to take part in the decision-making process.	93	93	*	*
A party must have a clear party line and know what it wants.	87	90	*	*

* not polled
Sources:
1969: IFES, Politische Umfrage, 1969
1975: Gehmacher, p. 295

Here, the demand from 93% of the young people surveyed (late 60s) for understanding and being allowed to have a say was paid the least attention to by the larger parties.

To a far greater extent than the older generation, today's younger generation has emancipated itself from the Lager mentality still so widespread in Austria, and is also regarded as the most critical of all age groups.

Table 11.8
The Problem-Handling Deficits of the Parties (in percent)

"In your opinion, are there issues and problems which are ignored or given insufficient attention by the Austrian political parties?"

Age groups:	1980 14-24	1985 19-29	1986 14-24
Yes	41	62	62
No	57	36	34
Which problems come to mind?			
Social policy	20	*	4
Environmental protection	13	24	17
Job market policies	7	17	23

* not polled
Sources:
1980: Dr. Fessel + GfK, Jugendstudie 1980
1985: Dr. Fessel + GfK, Innen- und Aussenperspektive des österreichischen Parteiensystems, 1985
1986: Dr. Fessel + GfK, Staats-, Wirtschafts-, Politik- und Gesellschaftsverständnis der Österreichischen Jugend, 1986

A major proportion of young people—62% in 1986—conceded that the parties have only limited problem-solving capabilities. The criticism that the big parties are doing too little, even in the fields of "classical" party policy such as job security and social policy, is becoming increasingly loud. The urgent demand that satisfactory measures in environmental protection be taken made of the established parties by the younger generation, a challenge which has become increasingly vocal since the 1984 referendum dealing with the peaceful application of nuclear energy, has only been met to a very limited extent. There are several reasons for this: on the one hand, the existence of stalemated economic-political paradigms and the rigid structures of the closely-knit networks between parties and interest groups, also on the personal level. On the other hand, the immobility of the larger parties prevents them from being able to respond to new demands rapidly enough. The practical consequences of the party dilemma were shown in the public and sometimes brutal confrontation between the police and protesters in December, 1984, at the Stopfenreuther Au near Hainburg, Lower Austria, for which the Minister of the Interior had given the police the order to drive those occupying the river banks off the Au, even with rubber truncheons if necessary. Injuries occurred on both sides.

The compromise made by the Sinowatz government to discontinue clearing the Hainburg Au and to review the plans for building a hydroelectric power plant at that site along the Danube did nothing to color the governing party, the SPÖ, "greener," nor make its environmental policies more credible in the eyes of the younger generation.

Table 11.9
Potential Green Voters among those under 30

"... I am for a Green Party in Parliament."

Age group:	1985 19-29	
Very much pro	18	
		} 60
Somewhat pro	42	
Somewhat against	24	
Very much against	15	

Sources: 1985: Dr. Fessel + GfK, Innen- und Aussenperspektive des österreichischen Parteiensystems, 1985

In 1985, 60 percent of the young people surveyed viewed the politicians offered by the parties represented in Parliament as unsatisfactory, particularly with regard to environmental issues; the group polled supported the idea of an additional party, a "green" party, having parliamentary representation.

The results of the National Council Election on November 23, 1986, fulfilled this wish. Despite heated inner-party debates surrounding party ticket make-up in the weeks preceding the election, the "Green Alternative List—Freda Meissner-Blau," succeeded in winning eight seats and becoming the fourth parliamentary party.

Two decisive factors which led to the "Green" party's election success were primarily the strong feeling of trust which the younger voters placed in that party—59% of the "green" supporters were under 30—and the occurrence of two environmental disasters that year (the reactor accident in Chernobyl and the severe pollution of the Rhine River with chemical wastes from an international pharmacutical firm in Basel) which served to evoke increased sensitivity to environmental issues.

For the SPÖ and the ÖVP, the 1986 election results meant a clear rejection of their parties' policies by the younger voters (39% voted SPÖ, 33% voted ÖVP). Each party lost approximately 60,000 of those voters who had supported the respective party in the 1983 National Council Election[9]. Thus, neither large party was able to gain the support of young and/or first-time voters, nor was either party able to convince these voters of its political competency and problem-solving ability, particularly in environmental issues.

Table 11.10
The 1986 National Council Elections

Votes for ... (in percent)	SPÖ	ÖVP	FPÖ	Greens	Invalid
First-time voters	37	35	14	12	1
Under 30 years in age	39	33	12	11	3
Structure of the electorate					
Under 30 years of age	22	20	31	58	

Source: 1986: Dr. Fessel + GfK, Representative exit poll, n = 2,149.

The Politician–The Image of a Poor Actor

In the eyes of the younger generation, the image of the politician is even worse than that of the political parties.

Table 11.11
The Attributes of the Ideal Politician (in percent)

Age group: Characteristic	absolutely essential very important	1959/60 17-21 important advantageous	unimportant not advantageous
Honesty	89	8	-
Keeping one's word	92	8	-
Being intelligent and clever	78	22	-
Possessing firm principles	38	54	7

Source: Dr. Walter Fessel, Jugendstudie 1959/60

The expections of "honesty" and "keeping one's word" which were re-garded as absolutely essential attributes of the "ideal politician" have evi-dently remained entirely unfulfilled in recent years. In an almost unanimous voice, Austrian politicians are accused of frequently telling untruths and/or primarily acting in their own interests during election campaign periods. Sixty percent of young Austrians believe that politicians are corrupt and open to bribery.

Table 11.12
The Image of Austrian Politicians in the Eyes of the Younger Generation (in percent)

Age groups:	1980	1984 14-24 Agree	1980	1984 14-24 Disagree
Politicians ... do their utmost for their voters	64	42	33	55
generally carry out their jobs quite well	75	38	22	53
primarily place their own interests above everything else	58	72	37	24
are corrupt and open to bribery.	32	60	61	31
behave like poor actors.	35	57	61	39
often utter untruths, particularly in election periods.	74	88	23	9

Sources:
1980: Dr. Fessel + GfK, Jugendstudie 1980
1984: Dr. Fessel + GfK, Jugend und Politik in Österreich 1984

In 1984, only 38 percent of the people between the ages of 14 and 24 confirmed that politicians generally carried out their jobs quite well; four years before, twice as many of those surveyed agreed with this statement.

The Younger Generation's Search for a Different, New Type of Politics

Even though the fears voiced in several sociological studies in the early 1980s, according to which the younger generation of the future would be politically apathetic and disenchanted[10], did not become reality, one can still view 1980 as a sort of turning point in the evolution of Austrian poltical culture.

What Ingelhart described as the "silent revolution" in 1979 (Ingelhart 1979) was clearly evidenced in 1980, for the first time since the political turmoil of 1968, during the student and youth unrests in Zurich. The young people of the Eighties are striving toward change, attempting an "outcry of emotion" (Küberl 1983, p. 201), demanding that politics come from the "head and gut," thus not only pushing for a change in the socio-political system but one in the political culture as well.

Table 11.13
Values of Personal Importance to the Younger Generation (in percent)

Age group:	1973 16-30	
	Male	Female
Good health	78	83
Personal freedom	44	28
A clean, intact environment	22	27
Adequate old-age care	8	29

Anxieties	
Age group:	1976 16-25
Unemployment	47
Destruction of the environment	33
Economic crisis	32
Breakdown of the democratic system	10

Source: Gehmacher 1979, p. 287 and 289

Behind this turnaround is a gradually developing reappraisal, particularly in those areas which have a direct personal influence - environment, freedom and peace.

Other important factors include having a good circle of friends and acquaintances, as well as a sense of security and a guaranteed livelihood. The highest value were thus given to the private sphere, followed by freedom and security. Job anxiety has also contributed to the changes in value priorities.

Post-materialistic values are increasingly gaining preference over material prosperity. "Today's younger generation is far more performance-oriented than that of the mid-Seventies. They want to be paid well for their work, but also to have as much leisure time as possible. They no longer view a change in vocation as a disgrace, in other words, no longer want to work solely in pursuit of a career " (Knapp 1985, p. 4).

The established parties have been unable to meet or heed these demands to any appropriate extent. This fact has been a source of dissatisfaction to many—every third young voter shows actual disappointment in the political parties.

Table 11.14
Degree of Satisfaction with the Political Parties (in percent)

Age group:	1985		1986	
	20-29	All Voters	20-29	All Voters
Am basically satisfied with the political parties	47	53	49	48
Am more or less disappointed in the political parties	31	32	32	34

Sources:
1985: Dr. Fessel + GfK, Innen- und Aussenperspektive des österreichischen Parteiensystems, 1985
1986: Dr. Fessel + GfK, "Wirtschaftspolitisches Monitoring I/86," February—March 1986

The portion of those young voters who declared themselves "generally satisfied" clearly lies below that of the average population, but does serve to indicate the general acceptance of political parties as an integral element of the democratic system. Political parties are tolerated but do not produce a particular urge to become personally involved.

Only the parties' sub-organizations at the university level have succeeded to any substantial extent (though this area also shows a declining tendency) in gaining the interest and involvement of young people in their ideas and organized events[11]. Any fears that the younger generation would withdraw from political life[12] have not been verified; the young person of the Eighties is far from possessing an attitude which many deem "disenchantment with democracy." Most young people possess "a traditional understanding of democracy and parliamentarism, in conjunction with more or less optimistic support of and willingness to cooperate in legal, conventional and also unconventional forms of participation" (Jaide 1980, p. 22).

Table 11.15
Satisfaction with the Political System (in percent)

Age groups:	1985 20-29	1986 20-29
I am ...		
very satisfied	7	7
more or less satisfied	69	70
dissatisfied	22	23

Sources:
1985: Dr. Fessel + GfK, Innen- und Aussenperspektive des österreichischen Parteiensystems, 1985
1986: Dr. Fessel + GfK, "Wirtschaftspolitisches Monitoring I/86," February—March 1986

Despite the fact that every fifth person between the age of 20 and 29 years is dissatisfied with the political system, the overriding majority indicated its agreement with and support of the democratic system.

The prevalent frustration is primarily confined to the big parties' "party-made" politicians and the manner in which these conduct politics. In spite of the reproaches of corruption and/or hypocrisy toward the voter, these politicians continue their attempts unswervingly to "sell" their daily and party policies and those of their party in a convincing and believable manner.

Thus, the attitude of the younger generation toward the democratic system is basically affirmative, though the actual manner in which it functions can be realized tends to be viewed with a large grain of salt. For instance, almost two-thirds of the young voters consider it very important that National Council Elections be held[13].

Three-fourths of all young persons between the ages of 20 and 29 years surveyed in 1985 have an extremely positive attitude toward plebicites and referenda. Therefore, the issue is not the negation of the existing democratic instruments but to a far greater extent, the emphasis of new values using the forms and channels provided by direct democratic elements.

The high level of agreement shown for participation in demonstrations and/or citizens' initiatives does not necessarily entail a corresponding level of political involvement, though it does serve to signal the demand for a direct voice, as well as for a spontaneous and easily grasped democracy that even "grants the smallest unit considerable decision-making competency" (Pelinka 1978, p. 9).

Whenever young people deem it worthwhile and essential to become involved, political actions are also initiated.

Table 11.16
The Importance of the Democratic Instruments (in percent)

Age group:	1980 14-24
I place great weight on being able to vote for National Council members.	60

Age group:	1985 20-29
I feel that referenda and public opinion polls are basically a good thing.	74

Sources:
1980: Gerlich/Ucakar 1981, p. 193
1985: Dr. Fessel + GfK, Innen- und Aussenperspektive des österreichischen Parteiensystems, 1985

Table 11.17
The Potential Political Participation of 16- to 24-year-olds (in percent)

Age group:	1981 16-24	
	Support	Rejection
Participation in citizens initiatives	64	28
Participation in demonstrations	41	52
Blocking traffic with a demonstration	16	79
Participation in an unscheduled strike	5	9

Source: Gehmacher 1981, p. 156

Both the peace movement and the "green" movement are dominated by persons between the age of 20 and 30 who are also willing to become politically active and to assume financial burdens in order to realize their objectives even in face of the established political parties. This is a reaction of a generation whose socialization took place in an environment of progressive economic growth, high levels of employment and materialist lifestyles. The limits of exponential growth have long since been reached, the levels of unemployment among the younger members of society have burst the seams of their tolerance.

Table 11.18
Personal Involvement in Political Actions (in percent)

"... I would be willing to become active myself and/or would be willing to accept a personal financial burden."

Age group:	1979 16-29
Environmental protection	59
Personally protesting the start-up of a nuclear power plant	30

Source: Gehmacher 1979, p. 290

It is only very difficult to forecast future perspectives or make prognoses with regard to how the relationship between the younger generation and the party system will develop. The relationship to the established parties depends on their willingness to accept and focus on the new demands being placed on them and to do more than pay lip service to the young voters in promising to discuss their problems and requests with them during election campaigns.

Notes

1. An attempt to present a more exact definition of the term "young person" will not be made here; see Küberl 1983; Pschierer 1985; Peterhoff 1985; Goppel 1985 and other authors on this subject.
2. See Esser 1979; Piskaty et al. 1980; Gehmacher 1981, Plasser/Ulram 1982; Bonengl/Horak/Lasek 1985; Allerbeck 1985.
3. See discussion of the student movement in Austria by Marina Fischer-Kowalsky in: Heinz Fischer (editor) 1974.
4. See Pschierer 1985, p. 141.
5. See Höchtl 1980, p. 11.
6. Due to the different age groupings and survey questions/possible responses in the individual studies, it was difficult to make a uniform and systematic presentation of the time series; nevertheless, I feel that the arrangement of comparative data is methodologically justified.
7. The reasons for the high level of political disinterest during the Fifties could lie in a) the political experiences of the past and b) in the willingness to consume

which was induced by the "economic wonder," and the associated weakening of the imminent crisis potential.

8. See Plasser/Ulram 1982, p. 170ff.

9. Fritz Plasser 1986, p. 44.

10. See Blecha 1981.

11. The December 1984 occupation of the Hainburger Au was primarily organized and co-financed by the political student organizations, the VSSTÖ and the Aktionsgemeinschaft of the University of Vienna.

12. In 1980, Höchtl established that an above-average number of young and first-time voters withheld their votes at several provincial elections: the 1978 Vienna Provincial Council election: 41%; the 1979 Lower Austrian Provincial Assembly election: 30%; the 1979 Upper Austrian Provincial Assembly election: 20% (see Höchtl 1980).

13. Also see Gerlich/Ucakar 1981, p. 193.

Bibliography

Allerbeck, Klaus/Hoag, Wendy, *Die Jugend ohne Zukunft. Einstellungen, Umwelt, Lebensperspektiven*. München/Zürich 1985 (Allerbeck, 1985)

Blecha, Karl, *Die unberechenbare Generation*, in: *Die Zukunft*, März 1981 (Blecha, 1981)

Bonengl, Leopold/Horak, Roman/Lasek, Wilhelm, *Bewußtseinswandel in der Jugend: Sub-, Gegenkulturen, Alternativbewegung und Rechtsextreminismus in Österreich*, in: *Österreichische Zeitschrift für Politikwissenschaft*, 1985/4 (Bonengl et al., 1985)

Bretschneider, Rudolf, *Politikverdrossenheit—Politikerverständnis der österreichischen Jugend*, in: *Junge ÖVP* (Hg.), Wien 1980 (Bretschneider, 1980)

Dr. Walter Fessel, *Jugendstudie 1959/60* (Dr. Walter Fessel, 1959/60)

Grundlagenstudie Feber-April 1976, Band III, Ausgangsstichprobe: 2000; 20-29J, n=369 (Dr. Fessel + GfK, 1976)

Jugendstudie 1980, 14-24J, n=1100 (Dr. Fessel + GfK, 1980)

Jugenduntersuchung 1981, 16-24J, n=847 (Dr. Fessel + GfK, 1981)

Jugend und Politik 1983, 14-22J, n=1027 (Dr. Fessel + GfK, 1983)

Jugendstudie spezial 1984 (Dr. Fessel + GfK, 1984)

Innen- und Außenperspektive des österreichischen Parteiensystems 1985, Ausgangsstichprobe: 1500, 20-29J, n=289 (Dr. Fessel + GfK, 1985)

"Wirtschaftspolitisches Monitoring I/86", Feber-März 1986, Ausgangsstichprobe: 1.513; 20-29J, n=289 (Dr. Fessel + GfK, 1986)

Staats-, Wirtschafts-, Politik- und Gesellschaftsverständnis der österreichischen Jugend 1986, 14-24J, n=1000 (Dr. Fessel + GfK, 1986)

Repräsentative Wahltagsbefragung, (exit poll), n=2.149 Wähler nach Verlassen des Wahllokals, bundesweite Stichprobe (Dr. Fessel + GfK, 1986)

Dr. Fessel + GfK, *Jugend und Politik*, Jänner 1988 (n=998, 14-24J. (Dr. Fessel + GfK, 1988)

Esser, Johannes (Hg.), *Wohin geht die Jugend?*, Reinbeck 1979 (Esser, 1979)

Fischer-Kowalsky, Marina, *Zur Entwicklung von Universität und Gesellschaft*, in: Heinz Fischer (Hg.): *Das politische System Österreichs*, Wien 1974 (Fischer-Kowalsky, 1974)

Gehmacher, Ernst, *Jugend und Politik*, in: Andreas Khol/Alfred Stirnemann (Hg.): *Österreichisches Jahrbuch für Politik 1979*, München 1980 (Gehmacher, 1979)

Gehmacher, Ernst, *Jugend in Österreich. Die unberechenbare Generation*, Wien 1981 (Gehmacher, 1981)

Gerlich, Peter/Ucakar, Karl, *Staatsbürger und Volksvertretung. Das Alltagsverständnis von Parlament und Demokratie in Österreich*, Salzburg 1981 (Gerlich/Ucakar, 1981)

Goppel, Thomas, *Jugend und Parteien*, in: *Politische Studien*, März-April 1985 (Goppel, 1985)

Hansen, Stephanie/Veen, Hans-Joachim, *Auf der Suche nach dem privaten Glück. Jugend heute*: Ergebnisse repräsentativer Studien zu den Wertorientierungen und der politischen Kultur Jugendlicher, in: *Die Zeit*, Sonderdruck aus Nr. 37, Hamburg 1980 (Hansen/Veen, 1980)

Höchtl, Josef, *Jugend und Politk—ein intaktes oder gestörtes Verhältnis*, in: *Junge ÖVP* (Hg.): *Junge Initiativen*. Beiträge zur Gesellschaftspolitik. Jugend und Politik, Ausblick-Sondernummer 3a/1980 (Höchtl, 1980)

Politische Umfrage, 1969 (IFES, 1969)

Die jungen Österreicher, 1983 (IMAS, 1983)

Inglehart, Ronald, *Wertwandel und politisches Verhalten*, in: Joachim Mattes (Hg.): *Sozialer Wandel in Westeuropa*, Frankfurt/New York, 1979 (Inglehart, 1979)

Kirchheimer, Otto, *Der Wandel des westeuropäischen Parteiensystems*, in: Gilbert Ziebura (Hg.): *Beiträge zur allgemeinen Parteienlehre*, Darmstadt 1969 (Kirchheimer, 1969)

Knapp, Ilan, zitiert in: *Die Presse*: *Wertewandel bei den Jugendlichen. Für Leistung, gegen Schmarotzertum*, 11.12.1985 (Knapp, 1985)

Kramer, Dorit/Kramer, Helmut, *Jugend und Gesellschaft in Österreich*, in: Heinz Fischer (Hg.): *Das politische System Österreichs*, Wien 1974 (Kramer/Kramer, 1974)

Küberl, Franz, *Jugend—Aufforderung zur Veränderung der Gesellschaft*, in: *Österreichische Monatshefte 5/1983* (Küberl, 1983)

Pelinka, Anton, *Bürgerinitiativen—gefährlich oder notwendig?*, Freiburg/Würzburg, 1978 (Pelinka, 1978)

Peterhoff, Klemens A.M., *Ein Generationenkonflikt?*, in: *Politische Studien*, März-April 1985 (Peterhoff, 1985)

Piskaty, Georg/Plasser, Fritz/Spitzenberger, Karl/Ulram, Peter, *Jugend und Politik. Österreichisches Institut für Bildung und Wirtschaft*, Forschungsbericht 23, Wien 1980 (Piskaty et al., 1980)

Plasser, Fritz, *Die Nationalratswahlen 1986: Dokumentation, Analyse und politische Konsequenzen*, in: Österreichische Monatshefte, 8/1986 (Plasser, 1986)

Plasser, Fritz/Ulram, Peter A., *Kommt die Demokratie der Nichtwähler?*, in: Österreichische Monatshefte 1/1981 (Plasser/Ulram, 1981)

Plasser, Fritz/Ulram, Peter A., *Unbehagen im Parteienstaat—Jugend und Politik in Österreich*, Wien/Köln/Graz 1982 (Plasser/Ulram, 1982)

Pschierer, Franz, *Jugendwelt—Erwachsenenwelt*, in: Politische Studien, März-April 1985 (Pschierer, 1985)

12

Reform Tendencies in the Austrian Party System

WOLFGANG MANTL

> To predict the future
> does not force it
> to become reality.
>
> *Franz Blei*[1]

1. Crisis phenomena

Is it intellectual exaggeration to talk about a rising temperature curve of the Republic? Fear of the future, diminished growth, increased burdens, a decrease of "the (common) orientation in life and of value judgements"[2] are no longer foreign concepts for Austria. Feelings of powerlessness, privatism, opportunism appear as well. Cynicism grows on the fields of burnt-down trust in the achievements of the Second Republic. Hopeless contempt and a basic anarchistic desire are the most extreme, even if not yet massively apparent points of departure for turning away from the status quo. As a rule the question is not (yet?) one of disillusionment with politics and democracy in general, but one of disillusionment with politicians mainly directed—and there is a certain amount of unfairness involved—against the functionaries and machinery of the parties[3], and only to a minor degree against the bureaucracy of the state and of associations.

Another frequently overlooked reservation has to be added: If in Europe there is talk about a crisis of the parties and if a bleak future is predicted for them, then in the final analysis not the parties in general are meant —because they will exist as long as democracy with proportional representation exists—but the big parties of the catch-all type in the form of social integration parties, i.e. concretely the social-democratic and Christian-democratic parties. After the Second World War they were considered the epitomy of "modern" parties; first, with a remarkable lead, Christian democracy, which can be regarded as the actual "inventor" of this kind of party. Political science participated in the modernity of these parties, which became one of its most popular objects of analysis, and described the positive characteristics which distinguished them so favorably from the bitter conditions of the interwar period: preservation of the stability and identity of the political system and of the continuity of political actions, a solid ethical system with regard to responsibility, efficiency through a complex organization based on the division of labor, integration of a plurality of opinions, ideas, values, and interests, capability to compromise, and strong decision-making power.

Today not even the apologetic self-presentations of the major parties dare paint such positive pictures; instead, they prefer to show themselves clad in the rough clothes of the repentant sinner. The proud garment of the reconstruction era stays in the closet. How far removed are we from Karl Loewenstein, who in 1964, with regard to the British system, celebrated especially "the invention and development of political parties as the only means of activating and mobilizing the otherwise completely undifferentiated will of the voters in our mass-society"[4]. He placed this cultural achievement next to and even above the development of the principle of representation and the parliamentary system by the British.

Lack of efficiency, democratic deficiencies (in large collective systems the individual's chance to participate is not very high), loss of credibility through unsanctioned cases of corruption, privileges of professional politicians, waste, and bureaucratization of party work, as well as increasing communication problems due to the technical features, based on mass-media, of ritualized and melodramatic politics in the aftermath of the radical change of communication forms brought about by television[5]—all these factors affect social integration parties strongly because for years they have offered themselves as unrivalled guarantors of the common weal, and because due to their size and age it is really true that a lot of negative things can "happen," and because all of this is relentlessly watched under the magnifying glass of former idealizations, promises, and exaggerations.

The major parties are challenged by a number of passive and active forms of behavior ranging from political apathy as an expression of alienation to political activity in new forms for new issues. In practice, this is expressed by voting abstention, invalid votes, long periods of indecision prior to elections, aversion against party membership, the decline of party publications, intra-party opposition, personnel discussions, increasing popularity of citizen initiatives and other parties. Among the latter one can also find new parties fighting for a long time against their solidification as a party, anti-party-parties so to speak, which at least in their focus on Green-alternative problems enjoy—beyond their own voters—a high reputation among young, critical, and intellectual people. This is contrasted by the crumbling reputation of the major parties.

2. The reform scenario

2.1. Points of departure for party reforms

It is not a sufficient reaction of the parties to the crisis phenomena sketched above, if they try to find shelter behind their irreplacability in politics and argue that no practical alternative exists: A universal basis or grass roots democracy would be overstrained, most probably an oligarchy of state bureaucracy and associations would come into existence, and perhaps there would be a decline into the autocracy of a "strong man" and/or that of a strong monopolistic party. There are arguments—beyond that of a ubiquity of parties in Western democracies—in favor of the existence and legitimacy of the big parties: political continuity and consistency, chances to participate and available services, a comprehensive program with the willingness and the capabilty to implement it, a network of services for the socially weak, the "small people," and sensitive receptors for critical intellectuals. These arguments cannot give any reassurance for the simple reason that the real type of the major parties is very often far removed from the ideal type. This is expressed by disillusionment with the parties, possibly amplified or even distorted by the media, but certainly not created by them in the first place, as theorists of conspiracy are so quick to claim.

With regard to the pressure of problems, difficulties, and crises of a political system, whose dangers lie in their accumulation, for instance in the coincidence of lacking efficiency, diminished prosperity, and declining credibility, there are three answers:

a. the adherence to the status quo
b. revolution as the violent, rapid, and complete break with the status quo
c. reform[6] as the middle way of a non-catastrophic change, planned, non-violent improvement, further development and renewal of a system within the framework of its structure of legitimacy and legality

Reforms don't happen by themselves; they need reform pressure, whether brought to bear by public opinion and the citizens' anger or by opposition parties. The public and competition always work as reform generators.

It is humanly only understandable that political agents choose substitutes for reform in order to evade the painful conflicts connected with reform politics. For instance, this may give rise to mere symbolic gestures with the effect

"that concrete political reform proposals and concrete organizational measures are often replaced by highly abstract (and so to speak "metaphysical")
ideological programs"[7] (emphasis in the original). However, at this point a
modifying statement is necessary: Symbolic politics with ideology, symbols
and language do legitimately exist—next to but not instead of factual politics—, something that has to be stressed especially in times of pragmatism,
for instance during grand coalitions.

The agents of party reform are frequently the staff in the organization
centers but also, to an increasing degree, an only loosely affiliated intellectual
elite on the periphery of the parties. Michael Pacher even sees the main importance here: "The real reform center of the political parties lies on the periphery."[8] Parties can be the subject and object of reforms; the subject as the
main factors of the political process and thus the driving force behind the
reform of the state and society; the object—and this is the topic here—as entities that need to be reformed. Therefore party reform can be directed toward the state, society, associations, the media, but also other parties and
most of all one's own party.

Reforms only leave behind the cloudy realm of nice ideas and discussions if there is both the readiness and the capability to reform—Manfred
Prisching has, under the heading "political courage," recently made some
valuable remarks about that[9]—and if measures of implementing and establishing reforms are then taken.

2.2. Latitude for reforms

The question of the latitude for reforms, of the possibilities for action of
reformers is the question of its historically changing limits. At the end of the
80's the following endogenous (a.-c.) and exogenous (d. and e.) restrictions
have to be taken into consideration with regard to the latitude for party reform:

a. Exhaustion of reformism: The fuel for reforms from the two sources of
    Christianity[10] and the Enlightenment[11], which inspite of all tensions are
    quite interlinked, is coming forth a lot less than twenty years ago. This
    affects both reformist party families, social democracy and Christian
    democracy. "Reform abandons its children."[12] Adherence to the status
    quo becomes more attractive; reforms appear as treason or weakness or
    as something that will always fail to live up to unfulfillable expectations.
    The future appears gloomy. Reform dynamics make way for a "con-
    cretist consciousness which focuses on first-hand experiences,"[13] focusses
    on them only and on successful routine. The refusal to see problems,

communication barriers, and suppression support the processes of encapsulation and disrupt the readiness to and capability of reform.

b. Resistance to reform acts as a break or a filter; it can come from one's
own ranks or from other political agents. "Reform politics become impossible when all groups involved are individually too weak to implement the strategies they prefer, but strong enough to block off all the
programs that could burden them."[14] The question whether reforms can
be implemented and established is at stake if the "digestive faculty of the
system"[15] is not evaluated correctly. "Reform programs must be able to
draw the support of the majority."[16] It is only their plausibility which
leads to acceptance.

c. "Core" and "periphery." The major parties' latitude for reform is further
narrowed by the different dispositions of groups at the center and those
on the periphery. The "core" wants politics in "capital letters," wants clear
ideals and simple issues, "a system of values around which everybody can
gather like around an invisible banner."[17] The "periphery" wants differentiated issues, new trends, and intellectual nuances, which more and
more frequently question what the "core" wants.[18] Social and intellectual
conflicts within the major parties increase. Incompatibilities come into
existence which can be softened, bridged, or covered up by the integrative efforts of strong personalities in the party leadership, but which in
any case generate energy-consuming tensions and make reforms more
difficult. Reformers and theorists of reform, mostly coming from the
"periphery," tend to quietly hope that the "core" will accept everything, or
they are ready to sacrifice the "core," or they assume that it is shrinking
away anyway—both, however, at the price of losing the characteristic
feature of a major party.[19] The "core," on the contrary, encapsulates itself
in cognitive dissonances, isolates itself. The fate of the major parties depends on whether they are able to achieve an integrative reconstruction
in the form of a new combination of "core" and "periphery."

d. Technical limitations: Reform politics work efficiently if they are implemented on a medium and long-term basis; they are "long-range politics."[20] The time pressure (for instance brought about by the end of a
functional period, especially that of the central unit of our democracy:
the legislative period) delimits the latitude for reform as does the growing apparatus needed in today's politics (EDP). The latter decreases the
possibilities of political planning especially for small parties and "small"
politicians within the major parties.

e. Economic limitations: It is generally assumed that financial problems
curtail cost-intensive reforms, because they involve institutions and
(major) projects with considerable personnel and material expenses. On
the other hand, it can also be argued that economic restrictions downright generate reform pressure to invent alternatives.

2.3. Reform tendencies

There are critical remarks that party reforms are instrumentalized as public relations instruments or sedatives in order to effect a mobilization and maximization of votes by means of a pronounced style, image corrections, and a demonstrative increase of competence. These remarks lose some of their edge if one realizes that everything that is complained about does after all also belong to the set of legitimate actions within pluralistic democracies. Moreover, behind the "packaging" there are also quite "hard" contents of reform tendencies of an ideological, pragmatic, organizational, or personal kind—which now have to be analyzed. In 1983 Peter Gerlich summarized this decade's demands for party reform in Austria in the following hypotheses[21]:

a. reality instead of ritual
b. politics instead of patronage
c. conflict instead of consociationalism

After this first orientation of the general frame of discussion the question moves to the socio-technical operationalization of reform tendencies, while at the same time the latitude for reform, as sketched above, has to be taken into consideration. A great deal is covered in detail by other essays in this volume.

a. Reform of the electoral law: The effect on the Austrian party system expected through a personalization of the electoral law completely depends on the voters' influence on candidate selection, whether through a (re-)activation of primary elections or through a system of preference votes, etc. The personalization effect aimed at through a new electoral laws furthermore is continued in parliament in the form of the liberal and liberalizing constitutional instrument of the free mandate, which, contrary to the skeptical views of political and legal scientists, has, since the 60's—supported by the jurisdiction of the constitutional court—really shown growing power and should therefore be maintained.

b. Intra-party democracy[22]: Since the turn of the century the parties have had to tolerate the critical question, whether they—so closely connected with the rise of democracy—are themselves structured in a sufficiently democratic way. The problem of intra-party democracy follows the rise of political parties like a shadow. The Federal Republic of Germany still concentrates on what I call the "Fraenkel formula." At the end of the 50's the political scientist from Berlin demanded that the citizens' wishes to participate should be integrated into the parties and not into the governmental process of will formation. The latter should—after the experiences of the Weimar Republic and the challenges regarding party identity posed by the New Left and the Greens—continue to be based on the principle of representation.[23] Switzerland rather tends to upgrade the value of the weak multi-party system by reinforcing, professionalizing, and increasing the organizational density of the parties; in addition, it tries to refine the balance between the government and the people. In Austria participatory democracy is promoted both by the legislative process of governmental bodies and also from within the parties: This ranges from the introduction of plebiscites to the call for the politicalization of party caucuses. The citizens of this country are not satisfied with the "Fraenkel formula."

c. Party financing: The sphere of appropriating funds for the parties, a potential breeding ground for corruption, has led—due to the appearance of large corruption cases—to waves of discussions which produce desiderata that often get stuck a long distance away from a completed reform.

d. Reduction of party power: see chapter 3.

e. Model work: see chapter 4.

3. Reduction of party power

The paradigm of party democracy, namely that modern politics is equatable with the politics of parties (and associations), is not unquestioned any more. An ever increasing number of people wish to break up this convergence and let the borders of politics and party politics diverge. New room is being opened for non-party-political politics. There is, however, an additional sphere which should be kept totally free of politics.[24] In the aftermath of the New Left in the 60's there were especially strong demands for a total politicalization of human life. Every kind of behavior was interpreted as a political event, every social relationship as being based on power. At the present the swing of the pendulum is moving in another direction, that of the reduction of politics in general or at least of party politics.

These demands are nourished by the extensive penetration of state and society by the parties—especially strong in Austria and increasingly felt to be negative—and extremely pompous party activities:

a. Elections campaigns: expensive propaganda (posters, campaign presents, etc.), testimonial advertising through prominent persons in obtrusive parallel election campaigns.

b. Party book system: Patronage, protectionism, intervention with all the problems of equality and justice connected with it and the dangers of a loss of efficiency and corruption.

c. Privileges: The special position of (professional) politicians ranging from income to additional fringe benefits which are increasingly viewed as illegitimate (in a shrinking economy even the self-financed travels of representatives are seen more and more as provocations).

Therefore it is not surprising that the reduction of party power and the party political penetration of the whole system is increasingly demanded: self-restraint, economization, disarmament—a (partial) withdrawal from the economy, from the allocation of jobs and apartments. All of this is also brought about by modern man's consciousness of autonomy, and his educational level. The call for privatization is also fed by doubts as to the meaningfulness of how political-administrative bodies and the parties solve problems. The financial problems of the parties are certainly also a motivation to give up spheres formerly controlled by party politics. Just as in international politics and in private life it is very hard to effect disarmament and economization. It is already hard enough to take measures that produce trust to a degree that a withdrawal can be carried out and also permanently maintained, or that the economization can be successfully completed. All the more difficult is it to attempt "one-sided"[25] disarmament.

What kinds of reforms designed to achieve a reduction of party power are being discussed or in proress? Often the question is only one of signals or small steps. Is it really necessary for polticians to act as an "ornament" at balls, card-playing tournaments, football games and club parties? Should they receive honorary doctorates?[26] Wouldn't it be necessary to give them time to reflect on things in peace, on weekends free of politics, on something like "days of meditation" away from the stress of representatives' conferences? These reforms of form, style, and language can be achieved without big financial expenses.

The institutional reform tendencies can be structured according to the above-mentioned fields of criticism:

a. Election campaigns: Campaign agreements, restriction of campaign expenses. A personalized electoral system with the citizens' influence on candidate selection would also reduce party power.
b. Party book system: Projects of privatization are the farthest removed from party dominance. An improvement of the status quo can, however, at least be achieved by an objectivization and rationalization with regard to the awarding of contracts and subsidies, and with reference to employment and promotion in public service. Within the Austria political culture radical conceptions (for instance total "neutralization" of the public service sector through the prohibition of party political activities on the part of civil servants or through re-staffing of the bureaucracy by means of co-optation) don't have a chance of being implemented. Despite skeptical attitutes with regard to all of that, one must not tire of trying to achieve an improvement with a stronger consideration of the criteria of efficiency and qualification.[27] The explicit introduction of a

"political civil servant" could even build a protective wall against party political intervention in the remainder of the public service sector and thus make work there easier.

c. Privileges: Even if criticism of the social, economic, and juridical status of (professional) politicians might be exaggerated, it is undeniable that their credibility has begun to crumble. Recently introduced measures to reduce privileges will be continued; however, political-cultural efforts and gestures alone will hardly improve the disillusionment of the public.

The reduction of party power also has a positive internal effect for the parties themselves—a revitalization and sound repoliticalization of the parties. This benefits the whole political system, whose capability to take specific interests and values into account, whose capacity to solve problems, and whose potential for innovation will thereby be increased. The democratic hope is that the power freed from the parties will move in the direction of the citizen and not to the bureaucracy of the state and associations.

4. Model work

The revitalization and re-politicalization of the parties in terms of making them more dynamic and regaining more room for action is effected not only by the reduction of party power, but in the last 20 years also by the model work of the parties.[28] New groups, not directly connected with the parties, have come into existence which also contribute to the integrative reconstruction of the "core" and "periphery." Reform tendencies attempt to combine a stable party system with an environment of citizen's activities not organized by the parties into an open capillary system of political interaction. The new model groups form links between politics and party politics and present a further development from the rigid membership party[29] to the "open membership party"[30], something which more closely approaches the participatory ideals of modern democracy with its claims of universality and equality, but also something which might fall short of these ideals.

Model work is political planning by the parties reaching beyond legislative periods and spheres of competence. It is achieved by the unremunerated participation of party functionaries, experts (also young and not yet established persons) and citizens as specialists of everyday routine and actual living conditions, regardless of whether they are party members or not. Model groups see themselves as reform-political groupings—more associated with the parties than actually integrated into them—, which claim for themselves a "free mandate" and develop a corresponding self-confidence. This once more reminds of the liberal trust in the self-organizing power of the citizen.

Model work further develops the categories of counsel and counselling[31] and shows anew "the fundamental importance of the principle of consultation and deliberation for the Western political tradition"[32]—also under modern democratic circumstances. Despite fluid boundaries (for instance regarding the predominantly intellectual brain-trust features of "Action 20," the "1400 Experts," the "Attersee Circle" and the "Austria Model" of the Management Club) model work differs from older consultative bodies and expert commissions through stronger citizen participation and from traditional ways of drafting programs through stronger continuity and stronger orientation on specific issues than on ideological problems. After the start in the 60's in an atmosphere of optimism with regard to progress, science, and planning under the banner of "matter-of-factness" ("Action 20" of the ÖVP and "1400 Experts" of the SPÖ) the "Attersee Circle" of the FPÖ followed in 1970/71. In October 1972 (that is even before the Salzburg Program of the ÖVP) "Model Styria" of the ÖVP was created as the prototype of model work open to participation, which also meant a consolidation, in terms of personnel and platform, of the Styrian People's Party after the death of Josef Krainer in 1971. The development of the model work initially paralleled the reform project of primary elections. It remained relevant, however, even when the efforts connected with primary elections declined.

a. Structure. The construction of model work is simple: full-time management; (small) groups (ideal: upper limit of 40 people) as working groups or associations with a chairperson and a mostly younger reporting secretary. The formation of relatively autonomous sub-systems[33] without external bureaucratic-hierarchical control is quite frequent. One tries to utilize the productivity of the collegial principle to achieve "a highest possible degree of a group dynamic process of opinion formation."[34] Discussion prevails and the written form is only employed in compilation and documentation; then, however, in a highly qualified form (the precise minutes of all group sessions as taken by Barbara Wicha in the Salzburg Commission has rather remained an exception). The chairperson and the reporting secretary of a working group are important as "translators" of the model work for the public and the party—contact persons are most of all the party chairman and the party secretary. The question of how model work is transformed and implemented depends to a great extent on the efficiency, perseverance, and identification of these people. The procedure follows various steps: questioning (not only through the party; again and again, even as a source of conflict, through the model groups themselves)—analysis—formulation of goals—integration into the intra-party political process. Important too is the publication of intermediary results in the form of discussion proposals, which are often far more interesting than the smoothened final reports, which most often are transformed into election programs. Intensive phases (mostly prior to elections) alternate with latent ones. A decisive advantage of model work lies in the fact that it is not subject to time pressure and decision making stress.

b. Function: Model work as political planning serves as problem orientation, as an early warning system, and as a catalog of issues with the aim to suggest solutions inclusive of considerations pertaining to means, aims, and side effects of planned measures. In instances where the competence and energy to evaluate still exist, a certain control function can be exercised with regard to daily politics. Model work is therefore not an esoteric program of and for minorities—even if that aspect should in part also be included—but a solid transition from, in terms of ethics, the "ideological Sunday" to the "responsible weekdays" of political work. Model work also furthers the integration of politics, scientific and artistic knowledge, as well as the citizens' preferences and participatory desires. Furthermore, it exerts an osmotic attraction for as yet politically uncommitted intellectuals and young people searching for direction. Even the inevitably appearing griper is productive because he evokes rationalizing counterarguments and a reconsideration of beaten tracks. It is undoubtedly the case that this also brings about legitimation and a maximization of votes, something much less undesirable in a pluralistic parliamentary democracy than hyper-critical authors tend to stress.[35] Additional products of model work are, almost like an "enlightening message in the bottle," the effects of political education and popularization of scientific methods and artistic experience. Model work means the relativization of existing party structures, evaluated differently by the people concerned, and opens, after certain sectors have died away, new chances of participation without permanent attempts at encirclement.

c. Problems: It would be completely wrong to overlook the problematic aspects of model work. It can't make a big seminar out of politics; it "neither wants to be cognitive perfectionism nor mere speculation."[36] Model work implies a decrease in the importance of the traditional party functionary. It wanders on the narrow brink between a truly participatory process of opening up and a mere rotation of the elite. One problem area is the selection of staff; in practice there are three ways of how one is called upon to paricipate in model work: 1. through the party management, 2. through self-nomination (principle of application) and 3. through co-optation by the model groups. Should politicians and civil servant participate in the first place? I think that this is meaningful, indeed even necessary: Reforms only stand a chance of being implemented if they are an integrated part of the political-administrative system. There is the recurring temptation of producing shows, alibis, and instrumentalization, which is Stockinger's main criticism; Dachs too warns of a "competition of superficialities."[37] The specific value of model work is lost when co-ordination and continuity crumble. Since most contributers to model work are not satisfied with only the production of ideas, the question of how the model is implemented and becomes established—realistically in the form of a modified compromise—is the touchstone of model work.[38]

Despite all these problems, model work increases the complexity and flexibility of political parties, improves their relationship with the environment, and enables, through increased information-input, a more efficient handling of problems when they look for cross-references and new solutions. Model work supplements the pragmatic basis of the bureaucracy of state and associations. As Walter L. Bühl states: "The stronger this micro-variability is, the stronger macro-stability can be" (emphasis in the original).[39] At the same time it has to be stressed that such reform tendencies are in conformity with democracy, since "the principle of safeguarding macro-stability through micro-variability is a genuine basic principle of democracy"[40] (emphasis in the original).

Notes

1. Franz Blei: Menschliche Betrachtungen zur Politik, München 1916, p. 34.

2. Manfred Prisching: Krisen. Eine soziologische Untersuchung. Wien-Köln-Graz 1986, p. 18.

3. Examples from the most recent Austrian literature: Peter Gerlich/Wolfgang C. Müller (eds.): Zwischen Koalition und Konkurrenz. Österreichs Parteien seit 1945. Wien 1983.—Fritz Plasser: Parteien unter Stress. Zur Dynamik der Parteiensysteme in Österreich, der Bundesrepublik Deutschland und den Vereinigten Staaten. Wien-Köln-Graz 1987.—Manfried Welan: Parteien und Verbände in Österreich. Wien 1985.

4. Karl Löwenstein: Der britische Parlamentarismus. Entstehung und Gestalt. Reinbek/Hamburg 1964, p. 12.

5. Fritz Plasser/Peter A. Ulram/Manfred Welan (eds.), Demokratierituale. Zur politischen Kultur der Informationsgesellschaft. Wien-Köln-Graz 1985.

6. It is still the case that science has treated the concept of "reform" much less thoroughly than that of "revolution." Among the best known: Christian Graf v. Krockow: Reform als politisches Prinzip. München 1976. And also: Martin Greiffenhagen (ed.): Zur Theorie der Reform. Entwürfe und Strategien. Karlsruhe 1978.—Stephan Russ-Mohl: Reformkonjunkturen und politisches Krisenmanagement. Opladen 1981.—For Austria: Michael Pacher: Die Reformkapazität einer politischen Partei am Beispiel der "Pläne zur Lebensqualität" (1973-1975). Graz (doctoral thesis in law) 1987, general treatment of the concept of "reform": pp. 13-51.—Manfred Prisching: "Politisierung, Sklerose und Politikcourage. Zu den Bedingungen einer Reformpolitik in Österreich." In: *Österreichisches Jahrbuch für Politik '86*. Wien-München 1987, pp. 269-281.

7. Walter L. Bühl: Krisentheorien. Politik, Wirtschaft und Gesellschaft im Übergang. Darmstadt 1984, p. 145.—Disputes about the feminization of functional titles (chairman/woman), but also the appearance of politicians reciting poetry are examples that belong in this context.

8. Pacher, Reformkapazität, p. 20 (note 6).

9. Prisching, Politisierung, pp. 278-281 (note 6).

10. Christianity "feeds" reformism through its call to make a fresh start (personal repentance and perfecting of man and his world) and with its endeavors—even if they often failed—to improve spiritual and secular circumstances. For a long time these attempts were directed toward a reconstruction of an old situation assumed to be good and ideal (reformatio, regeneratio, restitutio).

11. The Enlightenment, itself an offspring of Christianity, made the concept of reform more dynamic through its philosophy focused on freedom, possibilties of change, and progress, on plan, law, and system, on reason, science, and technology; "the experience of change ceased to be mediated by former analogies of decadence and circular developments; change was understood as "innovation," as new development, as a step into an open future" [Günther Nonnenmacher: "Reform. Schwierigkeiten einer Theorie der Praxis." In: Peter Hauser (ed.): Res Publica. Studien zum Verfassungswesen. Dolf Sternberger zum 70. Geburtstag. München 1977, p. 266.—emphasis in the original].

12. Prisching, Krisen, p. 17 (note 2).

13. Martin Greiffenhagen: "Überlegungen zum Reformbegriff." In: ibid., Theorie, p. 17 (note 6).

14. Prisching, Politisierung, p. 273 (note 6).

15. Greiffenhagen, Überlegungen, p. 23 (note 13).

16. ibid., Überlegungen, p. 26 (note 13).

17. Heinrich Drimmel: "Wer sammelt die 'rechten' Rechten. Letter to the editor." In: *Die Presse*, 11 August 1987, p. 3.

18. Through differentiated activities the parties try to specifically appeal to their "core" and their "periphery." For instance, the Styrian People's Party produced two types of calenders for Christmas 1985—a "beautiful" one by Georg Schmid for the target group "core" and a "critical" one by Manfred Deix for young people. This action indicates the disparity between the two groups and is connected with great deal of brisance for the internal life of the party (especially also because both events simultaneously centered around Christmas).

19. Neither does Fritz Plasser's visionary hope for renewal and reform of the parties as "only a loosely formed voter coalition of change" (*Parteien*, p. 269/note 3) answer the "core"-question of the major parties, which also is a social question as to the political importance of the "little people."

20. Prisching, Politisierung, p. 274 (note 6).

21. Peter Gerlich: "Österreichs Parteien: Ergebnisse und Perspektiven." In: ibid/ Müller: Österreichs Parteien. p. 348 (note 3).

22. Included in the *Österreichische Jahrbuch für Politik '79*. München-Wien 1980 are three important essays: Albrecht K. Konecny: "Innerparteiliche Demokratie in der SPÖ," pp. 377-390.—Alfred Stirnemann: "Die innerparteiliche Demokratie in der ÖVP," pp. 391-433.—Andreas Khol: "Zwischen Technokratie und Demokratie: Die Parteireform der ÖVP 1979/80," pp. 435-468.

23. Ernst Fraenkel: Die repräsentative und die plebiszitäre Komponente im demokratischen Verfassungsstaat. Tübingen 1958: ."... primarily not a problem of the

constitution but one of party statutes. The call for plebiscitary constitutional institutions will remain within politically acceptable limits as long as the voters are of the conviction that their parties are bodies which represent their wishes and opinions to a sufficient degree." (57) The final sentence of this small monography reads: "The state of democracy in a country depends on how democracy within the parties is looked after. Only when the plebiscitary forces within associations and parties are given sufficient room for action can a representative constitution be further developed." (58)

24. In addition to arguments of freedom "in favorem civium," also the viewpoint of efficiency supports this: "Areas free of politics must be regenerated in order to give the federal state, which is in any case overburdened, a chance to concentrate on important matters—there is enough to do even if only the most urgent reform plans are tackled in a determined way" (Prisching, Politisierung, p. 277/note 6).

25. The People's party in Graz tries for the second time to effect a "one-sided" disarmament (with regard to poster advertising) in the campaign for the municipal council election.

26. For instance the planned awarding of an honorary doctorate to Bruno Kreisky did not take place (*Die Presse*, 5 February 1985, p. 1 and p. 4).

27. Such reform steps include: strengthening of the public sphere by improving the methods of how vacancies are advertised, lists of applicants made accessible to the public—structural elements of recruitment in the university system can indeed serve as a model (qualifying exams for professors to teach at a university, appointment); precise description of job and promotion requirements; proof of formal education should not be waived, even if it has the disadvantage of a stereotyped pattern—but it also has the advantage, conform with the idea of equality, to push back other criteria of preference such as origin, protectionism, ideology, and especially party loyalty; at least for once an intensive consideration of a scoring system, (parliamentary) hearings prior to the appointment of top-rank civil servants and high-level judges, rotation of and time limits for the execution of certain functions (this harldy seems to apply to leaders of constitutional services—in their case the permanent establishment of freedom from the chain of command is more relevant), duty to justify personnel decisions, right of competitors to go to court.

28. Herbert Dachs: "Das Modell Salzburg 2000. Dokumentation—Analyse—Kritik." In: *Österreichisches Jahrbuch für Politik '83*. München-Wien 1984, pp. 319-332.—Peter Diem: "Österreich—Modell des Managementclubs des Österreichischen Wirtschaftsbundes." In: *Österreichisches Jahrbuch für Politik '80*. München-Wien 1981, pp. 105-120.—Theodor Faulhaber: "Geerntet haben andere. Ein Rückblick auf den Vorausblick der 'Aktion 20'." In: *Österreichisches Jahrbuch für Politik '81*. München-Wien 1982, pp. 159-179.—Gerhard Hirschmann: "Modell Steiermark." In: *Österreichisches Jahrbuch für Politik '80*. München-Wien 1981, pp. 121-134.—Alberich Klinger: "Wissenschaft als Entscheidungsgrundlage für zukunftsorientierte Landespolitik—am Beispiel der Arbeit des Modells Niederösterreich." In: *Österreichisches Jahrbuch für Politik '84*. München-Wien 1985, pp. 497-510.—Erich Reiter: "Der Atterseekreis innerhalb der Freiheitlichen Partei." In: *Österreichisches Jahrbuch für Politik '82*. München-Wien 1983, pp. 103-124.—Alfred Stockinger: Parteien und Sachverstand. Wissenschaftliche Politikberatungsaktionen als Strategie der image politics am Beispiel der "Aktion 20" der ÖVP und der "1400 Experten" der SPÖ. Wien (Phil. Diss.) 1982.— Ernst E. Veselsky: "Die 1400 Experten der SPÖ." In: *Österreichisches Jahrbuch für Politik '81*. München-Wien 1982, pp. 181-189.—Barbara Wicha: "Die Salzburg-Kom-missionen." In: *Österreichisches Jahrbuch für Politik '79*. München-

Wien 1980, pp. 99-119.—ibid.: "Konfliktfall Politikberatung." In: *Österreichische Monatshefte*, 2. Heft 1982, pp. 67-70.

29. Skeptical with regard to this development: Stirnemann, *Demokratie*, 410f. and p. 426 (note 22) with the criticism of an "unstructured structure" (410) and a "pseudo solution" (411).

30. Welan, Parteien, p. 38 (note 3).

31. In the last 25 years the literature has grown immensely; important examples in chronological sequence: Wilhelm Hennis: "Rat und Beratung im modernen Staat" (1962). In: ibid.: Politik als praktische Wissenschaft. Aufsätze zur politischen Theorie und Regierungslehre. München 1968, pp. 65-80.—Klaus Lompe: Wissenschaftliche Beratung der Politik. Ein Beitrag zur Theorie anwendender Sozialwissenschaften. Göttingen 1966.—Klaus v. Beyme: "Politische Kybernetik? Politik und wissenschaftliche Information der Politiker in modernen Industriegesellschaften." In: *Journal für Sozialforschung*, 24 (1984), pp. 3-16.

32. Hennis, Rat, p. 65 (note 31).

33. Sub-committees, party meetings closed to the public, investigations, hearings, opinion polls, series of articles, activities (social and cultural projects, sport events and parties for the young, contests for photographers and architects, booklets on energy conservation, "market for ideas," model workshops); example and experiment at the same time—with the power to convince but also, however, to disappoint.

34. Veselsky, 1400 Experten, p. 182 (note 28).

35. Stockinger, Parteien, passim (note 28).

36. Lompe, Beratung, p. 102 (note 31.)

37. Dachs, Modell, p. 332 (note 28).

38. In the final analysis the Salzburg committees failed because they were integrated into the Office of the State Government (problems with a bureaucratic-hierarchical environment, limits of competence and responsibility, and official secrecy). The association with a party, as is effected in most cases of model work, allows more freedom. The Salzburg committees then became the "unsought advisors" and wanted through pronounced PR work to "themselves contribute to an active development of politics" (Wicha, Konfliktfall, p. 70/note 28). Between this competitive model work and the one focussing on legitimation only there is, in addition, the standard case of co-operative model work which can achieve success through the persistent work of experts (e.g. in Styria the establishment of a state audit office in 1982 on the basis of model work and a broad range of direct-democratic and participatory instruments in the field of people's legislation in 1986).

39. Bühl, Krisentheorien, p. 213 (note 7): "Macro-structures are the more stable, the higher the statistical number of sub-units and the higher their diversity is" (213f.).

40. ibid., Krisentheorien, p. 214 (note 7)

Bibliography

Beyme, Klaus von, *Politische Kybernetik? Politik und wissenschaftliche Information der Politiker in modernen Industriegesellschaften*, in: *Journal für Sozialforschung 1/1984* (Beyme, 1984)

Blei, Franz, *Menschliche Betrachtungen zur Politik*, München 1916 (Blei, 1916)

Bühl, Walter L., *Krisentheorien. Politik, Wirtschaft und Gesellschaft im Übergang*, Darmstadt 1984 (Bühl, 1984)

Dachs, Herbert, *Das Modell Salzburg 2000. Dokumentation—Analyse—Kritik*, in: *ÖJP 1983* (Dachs, 1983)

Diem, Peter, *Österreich—Modell des Managementclubs des Österreichischen Wirtschaftsbundes*, in: ÖJP 1980 (Diem, 1980)

Faulhaber, Theodor, *Geerntet haben andere. Ein Rückblick auf den Vorausblick der "Aktion 20"*, in: ÖJP 1981 (Faulhaber, 1981)

Gerlich, Peter/Müller, Wolfgang C. (Hg.), *Zwischen Koalition und Konkurrenz. Österreichs Parteien seit 1945*, Wien 1983 (Gerlich/Müller, 1983)

Greiffenhagen, Martin (Hg.), *Zur Theorie der Reform. Entwürfe und Strategien*, Karlsruhe 1978 (Greiffenhagen, 1978)

Hennis, Wilhelm, *Rat und Beratung im modernen Staat (1962)*, in: Ders., Politik als praktische Wissenschaft. Aufsätze zur politischen Theorie und Regierungslehre, München 1968 (Hennis, 1968)

Khol, Andreas, *Zwischen Technokratie und Demokratie: Die Parteireform der ÖVP 1979/80*, in: *ÖJP 1979* (Khol, 1979)

Klinger, Alberich, *Wissenschaft als Entscheidungsgrundlage für zukunftsorientierte Landespolitik—am Beispiel der Arbeit des Modells Niederösterreich*, in: *ÖJP 1984* (Klinger, 1984)

Konecny, Albrecht K., *Innerparteiliche Demokratie in der SPÖ*, in: *ÖJP 1979* (Konecny, 1979)

Krockow, Christian Graf von, *Reform als politisches Prinzip*, München 1976 (Krockow, 1976)

Landfried, Christine, *Politikwissenschaft und Politikberatung*, in: Klaus von Beyme (Hg.), *Politikwissenschaft in der Bundesrepublik Deutschland. Entwicklungsprobleme einer Disziplin*, PVS-Sonderheft 17/1986 (Landfried, 1986)

Lompe, Klaus, *Wissenschaftliche Beratung der Politik. Ein Beitrag zur Theorie anwendender Sozialwissenschaften*, Göttingen 1966 (Lompe, 1966)

Löwenstein, Karl, *Der britische Parlamentarismus. Entstehung und Gestalt*, Reinbeck/Hamburg 1964 (Löwenstein, 1964)

Nonnenmacher, Günther, *Reform. Schwierigkeiten einer Theorie der Praxis*, in: Peter Haungs (Hg.), *Res Publica. Studien zum Verfassungswesen. Dolf Sternberger zum 70. Geburtstag*, München 1977 (Nonnenmacher, 1977)

Pacher, Michael, *Die Reformkapazität einer politischen Partei am Beispiel der "Pläne zur Lebensqualität (1973-1975)"*, Graz (Rechtswiss. Diss.) 1987 (Pacher, 1987)

Plasser, Fritz/Ulram, Peter A./Welan, Manfried (Hg.), *Demokratierituale. Zur politischen Kultur der Informationsgesellschaft*, Wien-Köln-Graz 1985 (Plasser/Ulram/Welan, 1985)

Plasser, Fritz, *Parteien unter Streß. Zur Dynamik der Parteiensysteme in Österreich, der Bundesrepublik Deutschland und den Vereinigten Staaten*, Wien-Köln-Graz 1987 (Plasser, 1987)

Prisching, Manfred, *Politisierung, Sklerose und Politikcourage*, in: *ÖJP 1986* (Prisching, 1986)

Prisching, Manfred, *Krisen. Eine soziologische Untersuchung,* Wien-Köln-Graz 1986 (Prisching, 1986)

Reiter, Erich, *Der Atterseekreis innerhalb der Freiheitlichen Partei,* in: *ÖJP 1982* (Reiter, 1982)

Russ-Mohl, Stephan, *Reformkonjunkturen und politisches Krisenmanagement,* Opladen 1981 (Russ-Mohl, 1981)

Stirnemann, Alfred, *Die innerparteiliche Demokratie in der ÖVP,* in: *ÖJP 1979* (Stirnemann, 1979)

Stockinger, Alfred, *Parteien und Sachverstand. Wissenschaftliche Politikberatungsaktionen als Strategie der image politics am Beispiel der "Aktion 20",* Wien (Phil. Diss.) 1982 (Stockinger, 1982)

Veselsky, Ernst E., *Die 1400 Experten der SPÖ,* in: *ÖJP 1981* (Veselsky, 1981)

Wicha, Barbara, *Die Salzburg-Kommissionen,* in: *ÖJP 1979* (Wicha, 1979)

Wicha, Barbara, *Konfliktfall Politikberatung,* in: *ÖMH 2/1982* (Wicha, 1982)

13

Between Old Symbolic Worlds and New Challenges

A Glance at the Internal Life of the Parties

TONI KOFLER

1. Introductory remarks

If one wants to detect breaks and changes in the organization, value orientation, and political day-to-day routine of the political parties, it is first of all necessary to look for elements of continuity. For Austria it is true that despite all the changes in the party system, which will be described in greater detail, the indicators of stability are in any case quite remarkable.

A first indicator of stability is constituted by the stable voting results. Despite minor formal obstacles for the jump into parliament—in one of the nine constituencies one basic mandate has to be reached, which in the most favorable case can be attained with approximately 2.7% of the votes—only three parties, i.e. ÖVP, SPÖ, FPÖ (formerly VDU), were represented from 1956 onwards in the National Council. Between 1966 and 1983 the total proportion of SPÖ and ÖVP votes amounted to more than 90 percent. That was only changed when in 1986 a fourth party, the Green-Alternative party, won 8 seats in parliament with 4.8% of all votes. This and the exceptionally good election result of the FPÖ caused the proportion of votes for the two major parties to drop to 84.4% (see graph 13.1).

Secondly, the high degree of approval of the established parties can also be seen as an indicator of strong party identification, where party identification is defined as long-term ties of a citizen to a political party. The degree of this identification was in 1976 63%, in 1979 72%, and in 1985 60%, which means that from an overall point of view no dramatic changes can be observed. Subtle erosions can, however, be recognized through the fact that the strength of party ties has changed remarkably. Of those with party ties only 34% continue to feel strongly tied to the party, whereas 58% feel that this is true only to a moderate degree.

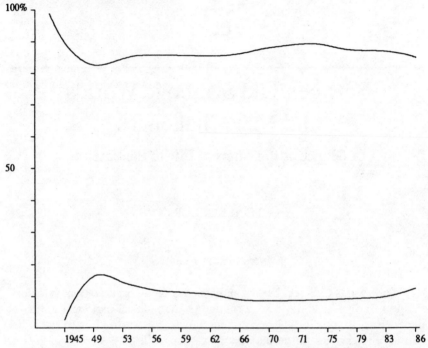

Graph 13.1: Proportion of votes of the two major and the small parties in elections since 1945

Thirdly, in the sphere of organization the number and development of party members is a relevant indicator of political stability. No radical changes occurred here either; the trend in recent years, however, has gone in the direction of a slight decrease in the number of party members.

Fourthly, the programmatic development of the two Austrian major parties has continued to be stable. This kind of stability has to be interpreted as the weakening of rigid camp positions and a tendency in the direction of "catch-all parties." This trend, beginning at the latest in the 60's, is continuously followed, even though it should be clear that this development cannot and will not go as far as to reach a state of convergence. In Austria remnants of "camp mentality" and different positions with regard to certain issues remain unchanged. There are more than enough empirical findings to corroborate this assumption: For instance, in 1985 only 11% thought that the parties differ strongly from one another, while 10 years ago this percentage ranged between 30 and 40%. In 1976 still 19% of all citizens regarded themselves as "left," whereas in 1985 this figure had gone done to 11%. In 1976 26% thought of themselves as "right," while in 1985 this figure decreased to 20% of the population. In 1976 56% of the interviewees labelled the SPÖ as "left"—in 1985 only 47%. In 1976 61% regarded the Austrian People's Party as "right," whereas in 1985 this was the case for only 51%. Thus both with regard to the parties and the population a clear trend toward the "middle" can be observed.

These elements of stability in the Austrian party system, namely a high percentage of votes for the major parties with a high voter turnout, a remarkable degree of party identification, a constantly high degree of organizational density, continuous programmatic development, are consequently interpreted by the representatives of the established parties as signs of the approval and the satisfaction of a silent majority. Skeptics, on the other hand, see the breaks, contradictions, and discontinuities behind this facade—and here this term is to be taken quite literally. The reason for this is that behind long-term and externally clearly visible signs of constancy new problems and challenges appear incessantly which, however, and this is characteristic of new developments, are more difficult to observe. The problem now is that satisfactory argumentation can be based neither on proof of stability nor on that of breaks. Conclusive indicators of an impending collapse of the party system can be deduced as little as the attitude that "everything is okay." This is because a certain relationship of change and stability is an immanent part of every party system, indeed of every social system. This means that the discussion stability or not leads into a blind alley. Therefore the question must read: Does the mixture of change and stability correspond to the changes in society, political culture and individual expectations of politics?

2. The internal structure of the major parties: Quantity counts!

The organizational structure of the major parties lends itself especially well to an analysis of stability and change. Let us first deal with the question of membership.

The number of party members and membership density of the major Austrian parties continues to be impressive. 33% of all SPÖ voters and about 35% of ÖVP voters are party members as well, which means a top position in a European comparison. At the date of survey (October 1987) the SPÖ had 689,000 members. Since 1986 the party has been losing more members than it can balance by newly registered members; in the last decade the number of its members has decreased by 30,000.

For the year 1986 the ÖVP still claimed 1,170,000 members, but this figure is totally unrealistic. My own surveys and other research show that the

ÖVP has approximately between 700,000 and 720,000 members, and even these figures comprise numerous members that only exist on paper.

The following graph 13.2 shows the actual number of voters and members, and thus the organizational density of both major parties since 1980.

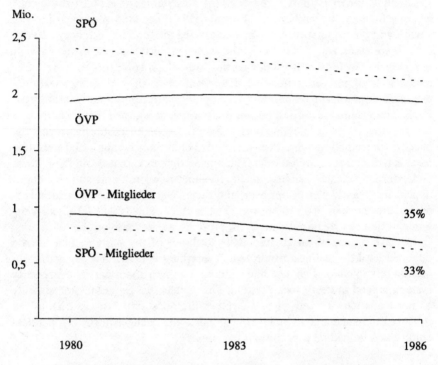

Graph 13.2: Membership density of the major Austrian parties

The membership structure of both major parties, stronger that of the ÖVP, however, shows numerous ludicrous and absurd features. If one adds up the number of members of all organizations which belong to the SPÖ (ranging from automobile associations to socialist fishermen's clubs) in the area of the federal capital of Vienna then the result shows more members than the SPÖ actually has voters. For the ÖVP a regional study, which I conducted, shows a number fetishism which can only be explained socio-psychologically: For instance, out of 34 communities in a certain region there are 15 communities where ÖVP statistics show more members than the party was able to achieve in terms of votes in the 1986 National Council election.

All these crumbling walls behind the facade become all the more visible since the facade itself is losing its glamour. Meanwhile, it has become obvious–not only in political science but also in everyday journalism–that the number of party members is decreasing and can in part only be balanced by

numerous tricks and tremendous effort. The politically unjustifiable significance of a high number of members can only be explained on the basis of a
symbolic world in which members are equated with activists. Today this is
even less the case than formerly, and therefore the anachronistic membership
structure of both major parties is today—if anything—a mixture of an outmoded feudal system and a low esteem for the individual.

Here two points from a study conducted 8 years ago can serve to clarify
this: Research of the motives for joining a party shows that motives like job
advantages, assistance in procuring an apartment, etc. play an important role.
An additional cluster of motives can be found in traditional criteria like "attachment" and "family tradition." Furthermore it is remarkable that those occupational groups that either directly depend on political decisions (employees in public service) or those in which the party has a decisive political influence (agrarian sector) are represented to a far above-average degree among
party members. While, for instance, people still being trained for their job or
housewives are hardly significant as members in political parties, only about
20% of all farmers and 15% of all employees in public service are not members of a party.

It is hardly amazing that in view of these developments—seen from a sociological viewpoint—there is a remarkable shift from membership to "affiliation." A majority of party members is really not inside but also not clearly
outside of the party. The following graph/table 13.1 will illustrate these various forms of membership.

Table 13.1
Types of party membership

care and dependence	low degree	high degree
ideological conception		
low degree	quantitative affiliation	"cared for" affiliation
high degree	qualitative membership	"cared for" membership

The parties tolerate this instable balance, indeed even further it indirectly—which shows lack of willingness to change. At the same time the
membership structure on the whole has become questionable. It belongs to
the old world of symbols with concepts like unity, exclusiveness, unanimity,

all of which have become obsolete. In a fragmented society with diverse interests and mileus a uniform, ritualized membership structure is bound to lose symbolic power. This is a real break, but one that is not accepted by the major parties.

A second aspect of considerable importance for the internal structure is party financing. Financing greatly influences the degree of centralization, the quality of democracy, or the degree to which members can be politically activated. Even a superficial glance at the development of party financing in the last 15 years shows that there can be no question of a break. Quite on the contrary, since 1970 the trend has been increasing, rising limitlessly and exponentially.

According to cautious estimates, about 15 years ago the ÖVP spent approximately 105 million Austrian Schillings (AS), the SPÖ somewhat more. The development since has even surpassed the wildest predictions. Today public subsidies to the major parties by the federal government and the states alone has reached about 900 million AS. Thus it can hardly be doubted any longer that the revenues of each major party are already well in excess of 500 million AS.

At the end of the 70's the parties received about 100 million on the federal level, in 1988 approximately 280 million. In 1979 the nine states subsidized the parties with 300 million, in 1986 already with 600 million. In total this corresponds to about 175 AS which every eligible voters pays to the parties annually. Only a few years ago it was still 90 AS, a figure which internationally is reached by no other country.

Fund raising of the parties has become increasingly more centralistic and thus more and more inimical to participation. Parallel to that the party's own capital funds from membership dues, donations, and party taxes is constantly decreasing. Together with the decrease of the parties' own capital funds the importance of the member declines, while the danger of external influence increases. It is clearly fictional to regard the federal state as by far the most important party financer as something "neutral." The federal state is—in a party society like Austria—not least in the hands of the parties, which means that public financing assumes the character of self-service. A typical example of that was the financial reaction of the major parties to the entry of the Green-Alternative party into the National Council: Immediately the amount was reduced which every party, irrespective of its size, is entitled to. As a consequence the subsidies for the Green-Alternative party were reduced by 60%, while at the same time the financing of the major parties remainded the same—despite a considerable loss of votes. The Austrian party oligarchies continue to ignore the law of decreasing marginal utility, which has already become fully effective. This law states that from a certain point onwards every vote becomes more and more expensive. For instance in the 1986

National Council election the SPÖ spent about 52 AS for one vote, the Green-Alternative party in contrast only 8 AS.

In the parties' financial sphere a break can therefore not be observed at all; on the contrary, the role of money in politics becomes progressively more important. A true break would be the motto "less money, more politics."

As various opinion polls and regional studies show, the internal organizational life of the major parties has become impoverished and rigid. According to cautious estimates the percentage of party members that are in some form active for the parties lies between 5-10% at the most. Meanwhile the number of people who engage themselves politically outside of the major parties is already considerably higher, because the traditional, ritualized participation offers of the parties must appear repulsive to a committed citizen. The fact that the internal organizational life of the major parties "dries up" and becomes desolate is causally connected with the motives for joining a party, which are of a traditional or protectionistic nature. If somewhere in a party activities develop, they are most often triggered by an order from above. Typical examples of this are regular "program discussions," where it is possible, with extensive efforts and expenses, to motivate a few thousand party members—i.e. the real political core—to become active. In the already cited regional study party managers complain that it is more and more difficult to mobilize people for the party. In the region concerned it became obvious that a considerable proportion of party activities could be attributed to internal disputes and "obligatory party events," organized according to party statutes. Thus, there are hardly any public events where the different parties can meet directly. Reality in its complexity is not reflected within the parties; or if it is then mostly in the form of "non-ideological" events. Breaking through the traditional, already long rigidified forms of political participation is neither really desired by the party leadership nor demanded by the average party member. The established parties have stopped the discussion about which framework could make a "lively" participation possible.

This leads us to the topic of intra-party democracy, which offers—from the point of view of internal structure—three interesting aspects:

— First of all, how is information transfer organized from bottom to top and vice versa?
— What are the conditions for decentralized participation?
— Finally, how are diverging opinions dealt with?

At this point it is not possible to consider these questions in great detail. Only so much: The major parties are caught in a fatal vicious circle of weak affective ties with regard to the members, low political expectations, and resulting insufficient organizational and political possibilities of participation. The result: Political apathy is the expression of the "silent majority." The citizens evaluate their influence on politics as more and more insignificant, as is illustrated by the following table.

Table 13.2
Subjective influence on political events (1977 - 1985)

in percent	1977	1981	1983	1985
very strong	17	10	17	9
rather strong	33	30	30	23
rather weak	36	43	39	47
very weak	11	12	10	18
no answer	3	5	3	3

Many politically motivated citizens work more and more outside of the parties or else are integrated into suborganizations or "think-tanks" on the periphery of the classic organization. In view of the numerous sobering facts about the internal life of the major parties it becomes obvious that appeals for democracy and (presumable) democratization strategies are futile if they don't include a basic change in the organizational structure of the parties. This caesura, this change, is hardly felt in the political reality of Austria.

3. Intermediary findings

In order to clarify what has been stated so far, it is noticeable that within the organizational life, financing, membership structure, and in the internal democratic culture of the parties there have been no fundamental breaks. And yet, something that to a certain degree is "new," the parties have learned quickly and developed what one could call a clever mixture of historical relics and new methods out of the societal and socio-psychological trends of the last 15 years. Old foundations are now crowned with the superstructure of "Americanization."

In the sense of an analysis by Leonhard Bauer (1980), which is still important today, one could say: The ÖVP has covered a pre-industrial organization and symbolic world with a modern management structure; the SPÖ has done the same with an industrial organization and symbolic world. It appears as if the SPÖ combination is harder to achieve because the expectations of its core groups are in conflict to a certain extent with elements of a management structure such as efficiency, openness, and flexibility.

However, this change cannot really be regarded as break; it is a process of learning, developed on the basis of survival strategies. The fact that the two fundamental conflicts in our society remain unsolved shows that this is only a forced adaptation. On the one hand, there is the conflict between party system and a post-industrial symbolic world and environment (on the level of issues). On the other hand, there is the conflict between the ritualized world of the parties and a smaller, yet politically active segment of the population (on the level where conflicts take place).

It is a fact that those areas where the established parties have changed, for instance in the spheres of media politics, party management, advertising, or opinion polls, are rather to be seen—from the viewpoint of political science—as measures to calm intra-party conflicts, to reassure voters and supporters, and as simple strategies of need satisfaction. Here, basically, technical solutions are offered to fundamentally political problems. The old question of participation versus efficiency is solved at the cost of participation.

4. New issues, new parties

The Green-Alternative party stands in total contrast—both with regard to its internal structure and its programmatic considerations—to the established party system in Austria. Up until its election success in 1986 the party was in principle not much more than a collection of various decentralized citizen initiatives, primarily from the spheres of ecology, civil rights, peace movements, and feminism. An organization did not actually exist; whoever wanted to participate in discussions and work for the party was considered a member. Financing was based on voluntary donations. Its entry into the National Council and the ensuing pressure of professionalization on the one hand, and federal subsidies to the total extent of approximately 20 million AS, on the other hand, have brought about certain changes: With regard to organization, financing, and membership structure the first efforts to become more professional can be observed. These comprise clear conditions for membership, the establishment of decision-making bodies, and clear internal decision-making procedures. Still, it remains an unchanged fact that the internal life of the Green party is colorful and lively, because only those people become members who are really active in political work. In total, the party at this point has about 2000 members. Additionally, the internal hierarchy is—as a consequence of the small circle of activists—only weakly developed so that the way from bottom to top and vice versa is relatively short. From the theoretical point of view (not at all always from that of political everyday routine) the Green party corresponds largely to conceptions of democratic politics. What is absolutely new about this party, which in many aspects is in striking contrast to the established parties, is its uncompromising rejection of those values that the established parties have long internalized and made taboo. In essence the Greens reject or try to overcome the dominant conception of the economy with its dangerous consequences for nature, people, and the state of democracy in a society.

For the near future the question is whether the Green-Alternative party will be able to strike a balance between its claims in terms of certain issues and the necessary changes which are bound to occur due to its participation in inter-party competition. Here the classic analysis is true: One the one hand, if too few conflicts are openly fought, this will lead to problematic aspects in the form of rigidification. Conversely, if too many conflicts are brought to the surface, this may lead to self-destruction. It seems as if the established parties suppress too many conflicts, while the Green-Alternative party is constantly threatened by exhaustion due to its internal desire to seek conflict.

5. On the polarity of change and stability

In the political system of Austria, which has a tendency to be centralistic and rigid, the two major parties command strong possibilities of influence and penetration. This is connected with the party members, impressive in numbers, yet largely apathetic. Political scientists have largely agreed that Austria is a classic example of rigidified patterns of conflict solution and political apathy. These findings are corroborated by international investigations which indicate that in Austria the potential for participation has a tendency to be weak, whereas the potential for repression is relatively strong. For that reason Kurt Steiner assumed already in 1972 that Austria is on the way to becoming a "depoliticalized democracy"; since then little has changed, with the exception of new forms of protest and new parties. This development, however, takes place outside of the established parties.

Nevertheless, changes do take place. The question is, however, which changes and where will they lead to. The established parties have changed in terms of their organization, their programs, and their financing: They have become more expansive and more efficient from the point of view of political management; they no longer totally helplessly face new—post-industrialist—challenges. Still, it seems as if all these changes do not constitute real breaks but rather more or less forced unpolitical adaptations to a changed environment and new needs.

This means, however, that the parties have gone the way of least resistance. The old structures and symbols, the persistence in pre-industrial or industrial symbolic worlds—whose surpassing raises complicated questions—have in essence remained untouched. Only the facade of the house is renewed in increasingly shorter periods, since this is made necessary by signs of desintegration, conflict, weakening ties, or dissatisfaction, all of which appear in many places. From this point of view, the mixture of stability and change that the established parties have decided on is wrong exactly because any true change has to start with overcoming the rigid internal structure, if it aims at being more than just a new label.

Note

The empirical data stem from my own research and the project "Innen- und Außenperspecktiven des österreichischen Parteiensystems" (1985).

14

The States and the Austrian Party System

RAINER NICK

This book contains much, and that justifiably so, about the change, indeed the "fragility,"[1] of the Austrian party system. The stability premise underlying many previous analyses comes up against the "decomposition" of the voter base of Austria's two big parties, growing voter mobility and the chances of newer, more postmaterialist-oriented groups. The thesis of the "Party Society in Transition" (Kofler 1985), now well proven and often cited, will not and cannot be contradicted here in any way. Nevertheless, when starting an essay on regional aspects of the Austrian states, the viewer is struck first of all by extreme continuities and firmly entrenched factors. To ignore these in the face of the signs of change would constitute a careless disregard of important facts and would confer an inadmissible far-reaching dimension on the prognosis of change. With that in mind, this chapter will purposely examine that part of the Austrian stage that often appears very constant and on which these changes take place.

1. Party System and Federalism in Austria

The Austrian party system is coupled with the Austrian form of federalism in two respects. The organizational make-up of the parties represented in the Austrian National Council and that of most other groups as well reflects the territorial principle, namely the organizational structure of the parties essentially corresponds to the hierarchy of the Austrian state. The fact that most parties must run (and also want to win) in community and state elections affords the party subdivisions possibilities for autonomy from the party leadership and makes them more than mere receivers of orders, in spite of what may be written in the party constitution.[2] "The parties have a double frame of reference at all levels of the political system: in the vertical dimension they constitute one level of party or-ganization, while in the horizontal dimension they account for one aspect of the business of the political system" (Haungs 1975, p. 310).

Correspondingly, in all Austrian states and in the two big parties there are essentially two points of reference for the recruitment of political elites: regional origin and association with an interest group. Most deputies in the state diets as well as in the National Council are the product of a more or less skillful combination of these two factors. In a limited form, this principle also holds true for the members of state and federal governments (cf. Stirnemann 1981). Although the Austrian electoral form of voting by ticket does not provide for a regional distribution of mandates, the parties strive for the widest possible geographic representation of their deputies. The result is a gain in influence for the middle and lower party cadres. In all likelihood, this regional dimension of elite recruitment will not see any change, particularly since the current proposals for electoral reform (regardless from which party) would aim to strengthen the regional ties of deputies, for example by forming smaller election districts. As long as the nomination and ranking of candidates is not effected by binding primaries (either public or inner-party), party organizations at the middle and lower levels will remain a basis of party-internal power. The more members belonging to these middle and lower level organizations, the stronger they are (cf. Kofler 1985).

Austria's federal character, which, internationally seen, is very weak, owes its existence and its continuity over decades to the interests of the Austrian parties. Here lies the second link between the political party system and federalism in Austria. The tie between party interests and federal structure was already evident at the founding of the First Republic and in the constitutional compromise of 1920. The antithesis between Red Vienna and the Christian-Social/conservative majorities in the eight other provinces is undeniably only the visible form of a socially conditioned party political conflict. Austria's weakened federalism was thus a feasible compromise for a party political split that was also manifesting itself geographically. Neither language nor ethnic differences were crucial in deciding between a federalist and a centralist form of government; primarily it was party political considerations.[3] How far Austrian federalism is limited and sustained by party politics is most evident in the constitutional body of the Federal Council, in both its conceptional weakness and in its de facto behavior as a party political appendage to the National Council.[4]

The interrelationship between the Austrian party system and the territorial principle of state organization is a durable one. The historic role of the states and the real power relationships in and between the major parties dispel any need for a discussion of the fundamental advocacy of this form of vertical separation of power. The only question left concerns the shifting of competencies within the states in one vertical direction or the other. While these calls for a shift in competencies may well be veiled with fundamental considerations, they mainly serve to improve the standing of one or the other major party. This is true for the demand for more state competencies (strongly voiced by the ÖVP-led state governments since the SPÖ took over power at the federal level), as well as for its social-democratic response, according to which the rights of communities and districts should be strengthened.

The fact however is, and the proof is evident, that over the last 30 years state decision making has become centralized and that the Austrian social partnership has had a major say in this development.[5] The de facto loss of state competencies was, however, met by the states with forms of symbolic politics intended to create a provincial consciousness within each state. The efforts toward creation of a provincial consciousness range from academic symposiums and publications all the way to promoting certain states as exemplary models and even creating a new state capital city for Lower Austria, because "provincial consciousness is not simply not a transcendental constant but a means of identification deliberately nurtured" (Bruckmueller 1984, p. 62). The fact that no authoritative political group can, nor wants to, shun such politics naturally strengthens the effect of such activities. In spite of an increasing cultural homogenization, particularly through the visual mass media (cf. Blaschke 1986, p. 68), coupled with a dissolution of traditional social milieus and increasing secularization, the creation of a provincial consciousness (kept as vague as possible) seems to be a successful means of evoking a "collective identity" (Weidenfeld 1983, p. 18). It should not be astonishing then that Austrians with great constancy and in overwhelming numbers underscore the differences among their provinces and also want these differences preserved.[6]

The question (admittedly not one free of suggestion), "In your opinion is it true that the Tyroleans, for example, are different from the Viennese or the Carinthians and that the provinces sometimes have quite different interests?" received a "yes" answer from an overwhelming majority (87%). No matter what sex, age, education or province, the affirmative answers to this question were consistently over 80%.

It will not be examined here what it actually means "to be a Carinthian or a Tyrolean," what patriotic feelings make up such a provincial consciousness, what "regional identity" (Koren 1985) means, how strongly federal (i.e. oriented on the borders of the provinces) consciousness is really anchored in the population. In any case, for Austrian political reality it means that practical politics is highly mindful of this (which goes as far as to be reflected in the regional clothing worn by politicians) and attempts to instrumentalize this phenomenon at least through symbolic politics which, without a doubt, can cause it to be strengthened.

Table 14.1
The Heterogeneity of the States

	absolute	true %	not true %	no comment %
Total	1500	87	10	3
Party Preference				
SPÖ	489	84	13	3
ÖVP	439	91	7	2
FPÖ	40	83	17	-
Greens	121	94	4	3
Other/Ambiguous	410	85	12	3
States				
Vienna	316	87	12	1
Lower Austria	285	86	10	5
Burgenland	57	84	7	9
Styria	237	89	8	3
Carinthia	118	84	15	1
Upper Austria	245	89	9	1
Salzburg	83	82	13	5
Tyrol	105	87	9	3
Vorarlberg	53	96	4	-

(For wording of question see text)
Source: Dr. Fessel + GfK, Innen- und Außenperspektive des österreichischen Parteiensystems (1985)

2. Continuity and Stability of State Power Distribution

The continuity of regional party politics in Austria is best evidenced by the fact that for decades there has been no major shift in the balance of power held by the parties at the state level. The fronts staked out between Red Vienna and the other, conservatively governed states, like the entire ideological controversy, have been greatly defused, and the party political relationship between the states has become more balanced.

In addition to Vienna, the SPÖ has since 1945 also established itself as the dominant power in Carinthia (by heeding specific nationalistic interests). In Burgenland, following a structural change, it has occupied the state governor's chair since 1964 (holding the absolute majority since 1968). But 66 years after the party-motivated founding of a federal state, every Austrian state is not equally "open" to the other political camp. An analysis of the state diet elections held since 1949 (when the party landscape was "normalized" through the candidacy of the WdU), permits two types of state to be characterized independent of party political alignment:

— Those states in which the gap between the strongest and the second strongest party in diet elections since 1949, and thus as a long-term average, signals an overwhelming dominance of one party at the state level. This category includes the SPÖ-governed Vienna and Carinthia, and the ÖVP-led Tyrol and Vorarlberg.

— Those provinces in which the electoral margin between the strongest and second strongest party in long-term average is less dramatic, namely those states where, at least at certain times, it appeared possible that the governorship could change party hands or, as in Burgenland, actually did so.

Table 14.2
Margin between Strongest and Second-Strongest Party in State Diet Elections from 1949 to 1986

State	Diet Elections 1949-1986 Margin (%)	Average (%)
Burgenland	12.2 3.6 3.2 1.9 0.9* 3.7 4.6 6.8 10.2	5.23
Styria	5.5 1.0** 2.8 5.4 6.2 3.9 12.0 11.6 8.1 14.1	7.6
Salzburg	10.0 7.7 4.7 4.0 0.3 10.9 6.3 15.1	7.38
Upper Austria	14.2 8.7 9.2 0.8** 4.4 10.2 14.2	8.81
Lower Austria	15.2 9.8 8.6 8.8 5.8 8.2 4.2 13.1	9.21
Carinthia	8.9 19.7 15.4 15.2 16.4 20.6 19.0 22.1 23.3	17.84
Vienna	12.0 19.5 22.0 20.8 29.1 30.8 23.4 20.7	22.29
Vorarlberg	34.3 32.0 25.4 24.0 22.3 29.3 28.5 27.6	27.93
Tyrol	32.4 30.3 28.2 29.5 33.2 26.9 28.7 33.8 39.3	31.37

* The SPÖ replaced the ÖVP in Burgenland as the party with the most votes and diet seats.
** The SPÖ received the most votes in Styria in 1953 and in Upper Austria in 1967.

This categorization is confirmed by the results in the National Council elections. In the first category (Tyrol, Vorarlberg, Vienna, Carinthia) the dominant party remains "ahead" even in "losing" National Council elections, while in the second type the majorities change sides in the same elections. In Vorarlberg and Tyrol the predominance of the ÖVP reaches well into the employee sector, as the ÖVP's absolute majorities in the Vorarlberg and Tyrolean Labor Chambers show. If the gap between the strongest and the second strongest party in state diet elections is observed over time, it is seen to be growing in the second category (Burgenland, Lower Austria, Upper Austria, Salzburg, Styria). This was true for Burgenland up until 1987 as well as for the ÖVP-governed states. And despite the already huge majorities in Tyrol and Carinthia, this gap was seen to widen even further at the last diet election. In Vorarlberg this margin holds at its long-year average. In Vienna at best, the gap is seen to be gradually closing. All in all, in retrospect and in current terms the signs point to a stabilization of the political majority in each particular state. The signs for change in the states, i.e. primarily a change in government in accordance with a parliamentary system, are poor, no matter what party is ahead.

The high concentration of the Austrian party system, repeatedly observed at least until the 1983 National Council election, finds its actual affirmation in state diet elections. It is precisely in regional elections that strongholds of smaller parties are observed and local and regional peculiarities are also expressed in voter turnout. All this, however, is only valid to a limited degree for Austria's states. The average concentration level, i.e. the percentage of votes cast for the two major parties, calculated from the last diet elections in each state is 88.5%. Only two states fall short of this mark: Carinthia (1984) at 79.9% and Vorarlberg (1984) at 75.6%, in each case for SPÖ and ÖVP combined. In both these states, the second strongest party (ÖVP in Carinthia, SPÖ in Vorarlberg) is, and has been for many years, not a major but rather a middle-sized party that at best polls 30% of the vote. In these states, the party spectrum has been enlarged by a traditionally strong third party, the FPÖ, and in Vorarlberg, thanks to this state's special conditions, also by the formation of a green-alternative protest potential (cf. Nick 1986), without, however, detracting from the political predominance of a party consistently polling over 50% of the vote. The KPÖ, well established but also immovable, has successively disappeared from the state parliaments, as has the DFP, that lasted only one term in the Vienna Diet. Apart from Carinthia, the strongholds of the FPÖ are steadily deteriorating. The fact that the ethnic minorities of Slovenes and Croates despite their geographic concentration[7] have never been able to play an independent role in a state diet with their own elected representatives gives food for thought. Austria in its Second Republic has seen no such enrichment of any of its state diets (Carinthia, Burgenland), as, for example, has Schleswig Holstein in the Federal Republic of Germany with the Südschleswigschen Wählerverband (SSW)[8]. In two states (Burgenland from 1968 to 1972 and from 1977 to 1987; Lower Austria continuously since 1959) the big two, SPÖ and ÖVP, are the only parties represented in the statehouse. Neither historically since 1945 nor now (with the exception of Vorarlberg since 1984) have the state diets in any way enjoyed a more colorful spectrum of representatives than has the National Council.

The impression of the party system's concentration and immobility at the state level is reinforced through the form of government by proportional representation anchored in the constitutions of seven Austrian states (Vorarlberg and Vienna excluded). These governments of proportional representation based on the principle of consociational democracy are, however, de facto quite different from a consociational system, such as that of Switzerland, or from the proportional representation system of a Grand Coalition (the model practiced at the national level from 1947 to 1966). Equilibrium and consensus characterize both these proven models. But since Austria's seven state governments of proportional representation are able to operate on a majority principle, they are not coalitions with a mutually agreed respect, control and autonomy of the coalition partners. Rather, in the final analysis, the majority party shapes policy. Representatives of the minority party (or parties, as in Carinthia) holding state portfolios are basically limited to administrative or representative offices. The Vorarlberg example since 1974, in which the SPÖ dropped out of the state government but has not improved its position in the last few years, shows that a strong alternative-oppositional stance does not necessarily lead to success, namely a change of government. The advantages of a visible separation of government and opposition, according to consociational-democratic concepts, primarily lie in the politically more effective means of control and in the clear-cut limits of political responsibility. Contrarily, the form of government by proportional representation practiced in seven Austrian states means an integration of opposition forces, which reduces the minority's possibility to present itself as a political alternative[9].

3. On Provincial Patriarchs, Their Parties and Their Strategy

The integration of opposition forces in state government is undeniably an important stabilizing factor, one could also say a consolidation of existing majority relationships in the states. A good illustration of this is the term of office of Austria's state governors: Wallnöfer in Tyrol from 1963 to 1987, Kessler in Vorarlberg from 1964 to 1987, Kery in Burgenland from 1966 to 1987, Wagner in Carinthia from 1974 to 1988, Haslauer in Salzburg from 1977 to 1989 and Ratzenböck in Upper Austria since 1977. But this is in no way a phenomenon of the current officeholders. Almost all have predecessors with even longer terms of office. A few examples: Wedenig in Carinthia from 1947 to 1965, Maurer in Lower Austria from 1966 to 1981, Gleissner in Upper Austria from 1945 to 1971, Lechner in Salzburg from 1961 to 1977, Ilg in Vorarlberg from 1945 to 1964, Jonas in Vienna from 1951 to 1965 or Josef Krainer Sr. in Styria from 1948 to 1971. Such an accumulation of long-serving heads of government may well be unique to European democracies.

The long term of office commonly enjoyed by the top people in the Austrian states shows that most heads of the state branches of the major parties have reached their career zeniths (whether by personal choice or not) with the office of state governor. There are exceptions such as the former

Salzburg governor, Josef Klaus (ÖVP), who after nearly 12 years as governor switched to national politics and later became Chancellor. But a change from the top jobs at the state to those at the federal level was primarily left to the SPÖ mayors of Vienna (for example mayors Körner and Jonas, who became President and not Chancellor). Provincial patriarchs vying for top positions inside or outside their party (i.e. Chancellor or Chancellor candidate) at the national level are, at most, the exception in Austria and by no means the rule. The following apt quotation from Uwe Thaysen about West German minister presidents does not apply to Austria: "They (the provincial patriarchs) know that it could come to an inner-party change of the top man at the federal level, and that coming from their Land. It could also come to a change of the top man between parties. Those of them with the most ambitious character and platform want to be well prepared for the race. To that end they use the constitutionally guaranteed potentials of their state as well as their party's state organizations, that they take into the election as 'their' potentials" (Thaysen 1985, p. 15). The reasons for the difference in the role of provincial patriarch in the Federal Republic of Germany and in Austria are clear because in at least three central points the Austrian state governors lack the influence of their West German counterparts:

— The fact that the states have less competence than the federal government allows them less room for autonomous politics.
— The lack of an equally powerful parliamentary chamber representing the states means that individual states or groups of states lack veto power. So-called conferences of state governors for the purpose of coordination have nowhere near the same importance.
— In addition to the territorial principle, there is, at least in the case of the two major parties, an organizational interrelationship between the parties and interest groups (suborganizations, unions and chambers) inside and outside the party that limits the influence of the state parties more so than is true for their sister parties in West Germany.

From Austria's long-serving provincial politicians it is also seen that the role of the so-called patriarchs in their own particular state seems to be so important that most of the state governors at least try to portray themselves as a paterpatrias. The undisguised success of the concept of "patriarch" also confirms the thesis of the alleged slavish trust in authority of many Austrians, which is expressed in concrete terms in the "governor's electoral advantage" on election day[10]. Since this phenomenon holds equally for other "authorities" such as chancellor or mayor, on the state level this aspect of political culture above all serves to intensify the provincial consciousness being created. The "patriarch fighting for his state and its children" is excellently suited to gloss over differences in party politics and political interests and to speak and act in the interest of the entire state (which admittedly is not always easy to define). This form of politics is apparent particularly when the acquisition of and (more recently) the prevention of large construction projects and the like are at stake. With such an understanding of politics, the borderline between pragmatic representation of interests and pure populism is often difficult to define.

Against this background it is the state parties (especially the ÖVP), encouraged by the long uninterrupted periods in power, that employ a thoroughly successful concept in assuring the political majority in their particular state: the attempt to create a common identity for their party and their state. This strategy, that Alf Mintzel so thoroughly analyzed for the "most successful" party in the Federal Republic of Germany, the CSU (cf. Mintzel 1978), and that helps ensure the success of the SPD in North Rhine-Westphalia, is supported in the ÖVP state parties by the ÖVP's commitment to federalism and facilitated by a traditional uneven distribution of the ÖVP electorate (for example, West Austria is a stronghold of the ÖVP)[11]. "Identity is experienced as being different, different from others" (Weidenfeld 1983, p. 19). It is therefore totally logical that the state branches of the ÖVP (Austrian People's Party) in Tyrol or Styria, for example, designate themselves as the "Tyrolean" or "Styrian" People's Party and within the party also attempt to create a special image. Styrians depict themselves as "reformers" and Tyrol and Vorarlberg as bulwarks against centralism.

Since a collective finding of identity requires "common convictions, attributes and classifications" and expresses itself "in the manner in which people think as well as in the form of entrenchment of their world view and their social structures" (Weidenfeld 1983, p. 19), different characteristics such as dialects, customs, folk art, regional history (for example, South Tyrol or Carinthia) or even different ethnic background are of great importance in the formation of a provincial consciousness. How much this can be traced to clichés (possibly serving the interests of tourism) must remain open[12]. There is, however, one sociopolitical factor that can be adequately analyzed and that offers a significant possibility for identification: confessional attitude. Once again, the Austrian states differ considerably in this respect (or better, Vienna differs from the other states). In Vienna, the proportion of Catholics is especially low (71.49% as opposed to 84.35% nationwide), and the portion of the population that is nonconfessional is especially high (13.54% as opposed to 5.98% in all of Austria) (Source: Austrian Central Office of Statistics (Ed.): Volkszählung 1981, Wien 1984). This is especially evident in the frequency of church attendance, the aspect that appears best suited as an indicator of religious behavior.

The confessional behavior of the majority of the urban Viennese differs noticeably from that of the population in the other states. More than half of the respondents in Vienna (almost) never go to church, while the same is true for only about a quarter of the respondents in most of the other states.

Deviations among the states and differences in behavior within them primarily appear to depend on the degree of urbanization. For our analysis this means that in rural areas, as Gehmacher/Haerpfer point out in this book, the ÖVP can rely on a still favorable, relatively homogeneous political culture and that regional differences continue in the question of church ties that is central to the value system. Thus, in states such as Tyrol and Vorarlberg there exists a unity of the political system that is not only the product of the hegemony of a party but also of the bourgeois/conservative tendencies in the political culture of the state. The successful emergence of a green-alternative movement in Vorarlberg does not disturb this picture in any way, because in Vorarlberg this tendency extends well into the green-alternative "lager" (cf. Nick 1986). The political culture of metropolitan Vienna (for historic and structural reasons) stands as an antipode to all this.

Table 14.3
Church Attendance According to State and Town Size

	Basis	Several Times per Week	Every Sunday	At Least Once a Month	Several Times a Year (Holidays)	Almost Never	No Reply
		%	%	%	%	%	%
State							
Vienna	316	2	13	9	21	53	1
Burgenland	57	5	25	24	35	11	-
Carinthia	118	4	21	20	27	28	0
Lower Austria	285	3	32	16	24	24	1
Upper Austria	245	3	24	17	19	35	1
Salzburg	83	3	29	13	29	24	2
Styria	237	3	20	25	26	26	-
Tyrol	105	3	32	14	27	22	2
Vorarlberg	53	4	19	26	24	27	-
Town Size							
< 2,000 pop.	322	3	32	26	23	15	1
< 50,000 pop.	672	4	24	18	26	27	1
< 1 million pop.	190	1	20	9	25	44	1
Vienna (1.5 million pop.)	316	2	13	9	21	53	1

Source: Dr. Fessel + GfK, Innen- und Außenperspektive des österreichischen Parteiensystems (1985)

One factor that constitutes an essential contribution to the creation of a provincial consciousness and thus influences various party political orientations can be described as the antithesis of center and periphery. This antithesis is emphasized especially in western Austria, where the "Viennese breed of bureaucratic centralism" is made the scapegoat absolute (Dermutz et al. 1982, p. 162). The usual yardsticks of European regionalism (cf. Lukesch 1981) are not salient because western Austria as a whole is by no means the periphery in the sense of extreme economic disadvantage. Rather, the problems of structural periphery are seen above all within the states themselves, and other (language, ethnic) disadvantages for the majority of the citizens in these states hardly exist. Initiatives such as "Pro Vorarlberg" and "Pro Tyrol" above all reflect the discussion surrounding the distribution of power among the elites at various levels of the federation.[13] Thus, the discussion of regionalism in Austria is laden with party political considerations. In the context of this center-periphery discussion, an antithesis, sometimes artificially heightened (as "Pro Vorarlberg" shows), is noticeable between the "Black West" and "Red Vienna" that is not exhausted in an exchange of clichés. A report by the Information Service for Educational Policy and Research shows 8,300 members of the League of Socialist Academics in Vienna as opposed to not even 500 League members in Vorarlberg and Tyrol together. The extreme disparity in these numbers expresses a party political aspect of social tension in Austria that affects above all the elite (which is the reason for the selection of this example) and not the mass of the population.

The creation of a joint identity of party and state described above is naturally that much easier when the majority party of the state is in opposition to the majority party at the federal level. This is an effect that is not only observed in Austria but also in many other nations, as "off-year elections" show. Nevertheless, the party political constellation in the Austrian states is more than a function of the majority in the National Council, as the successes of, among others, the SPÖ in Carinthia and in Burgenland in the last 15 years show. New majorities in the National Council (i.e. under the given circumstances, a visible participation of the ÖVP in the federal government), could, however, contribute to a weakening of the party-politically motivated front of ÖVP-led states against the federal government. Nor does the success of several ÖVP state parties in establishing the image of a state People's Party make it any less possible to rule out the scenario of a federal government under sole or partial ÖVP leadership, in which a conflict would force the ÖVP state parties to distance themselves from the national party in order to demonstrate their credibility. The reasons for such conflicts easily come to mind: nationalized industry, power plant projects, natural parks, hazardous waste depots etc. The successful strategy of creating a provincial consciousness and the linking of state interests with representation by a party has its price, (as the example of the CDU and CSU shows), namely a growing diversity at the national level including public conflict. The figures in Table 14.4

show that the national parties must also give due consideration to the image their state parties portray.

The fact that agreement to this question is clearly above average in the southern and western states and clearly below average in Vienna (40%) and Lower Austria (49%) confirms the assumption that regional factors are valued differently in metropolitan Vienna, on the one hand, and in the other states, on the other hand, and confirms the existence of a center-periphery attitude. The fact that potential ÖVP voters (62%) more so than SPÖ voters (53%) feel drawn to a party representing regional interests corresponds to the issue base of these parties within the electorate. Even respondents with other or (as yet) no party preference would, according to this survey, greatly enjoy a party focusing on regional interests.[14] (See table 14.4)

4. Is the "Opposition Vacuum" Filling?

The portrait of the Austrian provinces rendered up to this point primarily conveys the impression of great stability and continuity in terms of the party-political balance of power in the individual states. Moving one rung down the ladder of power to the municipalities, the political majorities are seen to be much less consistent. In state capitals such as Graz, Linz, Salzburg or Bregenz, but also Klagenfurt and Innsbruck, the balance of power in the city and town councils does not reflect the dominant position of the particular state's leading party.[15] The Austrian party system is most clearly seen to break open in communal elections in middle and larger cities. Alternative/green groups, citizen lists and sometimes smaller established parties like the FPÖ (in Kufstein, Lustenau and at times Graz) have for years polled electoral successes on the community level.

The communal portrait is thus more heterogeneous, but with the exception of Vorarlberg this trend has yet to successfully break through to the national level. The reasons are evident: on the one hand, the heterogeneity of the green-alternative groups at the state level does not work in their favor (separate candidates and/or integration attempts that bring to light their extreme differences). On the other hand, the sociostructural focal point of new protest groups clearly lies in urban areas. Only where internal differences are pushed into the background by at least having a common candidate for several groups, and where the structurally favorable conditions for new groups are present throughout most of a state, can, as the green-alternative (ALV/VG) example in Vorarlberg shows (cf. Nick 1986), new protest movements hope for success in state diet elections in the foreseeable future. It is precisely the pronounced majorities in the state diets that give new protest groups their chance, because wherever the gap between strongest and second strongest party is especially large, wherever the second strongest party in the state has for years had no strong appeal protest groups can step forward to fill the opposition vacuum.

Table 14.4
Chances for a Regional Party

Question: Would you vote for a party, whose primary aim is to represent the particular interests of your state?

	Basis	Yes %	No %	No Reply %
Total	1500	55	41	4
According to Party Preference:				
SPÖ	489	53	44	3
ÖVP	439	62	34	4
FPÖ	40	62	36	2
Greens	121	46	52	2
Other/Ambiguous	410	52	42	6
According to State:				
Vienna	316	40	58	3
Lower Austria	285	49	45	6
Burgenland	57	63	28	9
Carinthia	118	66	29	5
Upper Austria	245	64	34	2
Salzburg	83	65	34	2
Styria	237	57	38	6
Tyrol	105	64	31	5
Vorarlberg	53	66	34	-

Source: Dr. Fessel + GfK, Innen- und Außenperspektive des österreichischen Parteiensystems (1985)

But the new protest groups are meeting with competition. Internal party opposition is the first to aim to fill this state vacuum (of control and alternative). The hegemony of the Tyrolean People's Party allowed it to articulate deviating concepts (in environmental and international highway traffic problems) in the party periphery and to accomplish political integration semi-directly and publicly in the sphere of the party. The most obvious sign of this are Tyrol's city and town council elections, in which the Tyrolean People's Party campaigns separately in its organizational diversity (as the total party, as a farmer's party, businessman's party, or a party of the youth etc.) but usually with combined forces. Traditional attitudes of party leaders, who view party unity as an important selling point outside the party and an important means of inner-party discipline lead this type of party opening (i.e. through competitive, public primaries) to appear very improbable.[16] But wherever a state party in a dominant position acts as a sort of government party, a flexible and tolerant attitude on its part can help cushion against opposition potential in the electorate.

The voter potential resulting from this opposition vacuum at the state level also awakens the interest of older parties not represented in the power cartel. The Carinthian FPÖ with its populist brand of politics has shown how protest and opposition potential at the state level can be mobilized in favor of a traditional party. These voters (for example in Carinthia) may have completely different values and principles than most sympathizers of new social protest movements, but, on the one hand, the effect of a clearly opposing and controlling power at the state level is a comparable one and, on the other hand, this process is a uniting of various protest groups with sometimes very different political colors, as the genesis of the green-alternative movement in Austria very adequately demonstrates day for day. The uniting of protest potential even from differently motivated groups remains the essential prerequisite for an opposition party (even at the state level) to reach parliamentary strength.

The last means of filling the state opposition vacuum is the direct democracy. When consociational forms of democracy are strongly evidenced both in the constitution and in reality at the level of Austria's federal states,[17] then it is important to bring "direct democracy (into play) as the correlate of consociationalism" (Mantl 1986, p. 35). And in fact, "it was precisely federalism that in the last few years worked to achieve more democracy" (Welan 1986, p. 204), i.e. especially by reinforcing in the state constitutions plebiscitary elements such as the referendum and the popular initiative. In most of Austria's states and communities, the instruments of direct democracy (cf. Welan 1986) are strongly present even though de jure and de facto they primarily function from the top down, namely they are above all instruments in the hands of the parties and other powerful interest groups. The possibility of precisely the provincial patriarchs using these instruments to ensure and support[18] their policies is great and permits this direct democracy in the states to appear more a new set of rules for traditional politics than an opposition alternative. Nevertheless, it is exactly this realistic appraisal of the instruments of direct democracy that can be taken as an indication of a possible development in democracy at the state level, a possible development that means life in the party system of the Austrian states, and more life is what democracy in the Austrian states needs.

5. Epilogue: The Opposition Vacuum Is Starting to Fill!

The diet elections held in Austria's states after conclusion of this manuscript (1986) already appear to answer the question of whether the opposition vacuum is filling. Since the formation of the SPÖ-ÖVP Grand Coalition in early 1987 and ever since the FPÖ consciously took up its oppositional stance under Party Chairman Jörg Haider in late 1986, the background for state diet elections has changed greatly. All diet elections held since the National Council was last elected in 1986 have brought the two big parties losses, in some cases heavy losses, and have seen the ranks of protest voters swell. These voters have above all shifted to the FPÖ, some to the greens (Salzburg, Tyrol) and still others, most spectacularly in Vienna, did not vote at all (election turnout in Vienna was 62.9%).

The predominance of the particular ruling party, whether in Burgenland and Carinthia (SPÖ) or in Lower Austria and Tyrol (ÖVP) declined strongly in comparison to previous elections. The FPÖ, in particular, was able to poll major electoral successes in all state diet elections held since the Grand Coalition came into power (for example, it recently ousted the ÖVP as the second strongest party in Carinthia) and is now represented in the diet of every Austrian state. The formation of the Grand Coalition and the ensuing concentration of power at the national level have undeniably caused many voters to want the opposition vacuum filled at the state level.

Notes

1. See especially the chapter by Fritz Plasser in this book; also other works by this author (for example, Plasser 1987).

2. This is, however, not valid for parties that for whatever reason often seem to withdraw from the rationality of vote maximization. The KPÖ's decline at the state and community level to a purely marginal size is without doubt related to this policy that, in turn, obeys other rationalities (for example, a party discipline dictated by party leaders) (cf. Pelinka 1982, p. 150).

3. "Anmerkungen zu den Gründungstheorien des Bundesstaates" ("Notes on the Theories behind the Founding of the Federal State") see Öhlinger 1981.

4. Even a federalism of a completely different origin and vested with much more extensive competences, such as that in the Federal Republic of Germany, is clearly seen to be laden with party-political considerations (for example, the Federal Council). To pick up on a phrase by former Federal Council President Heinz Kühn (SPD), Uwe Thaysen accurately writes on "Reaching a Political Majority in Federalism": "The provincial patriarchs do not forget that they are party sons" (Thaysen 1985, p. 7).

5. On the loss of competence at the state level and on the discussion surrounding federalism in Austria, see the numerous publications of Institut für Föderalismusforschung in Innsbruck. On the various "Phases of the Discussion Surrounding Federalism in Austria since 1945" see particularly Kreisky, 1981.

6. Older empirical material is given in Kriesky (1981), Zwink (1981), Dermutz et al. (1982), among others.

7. Corresponding data on Austria's ethnic groups can be found in Suppan 1986, p. 79.

8. In Carinthia, things even go so far as to include gerrymandering. In the Carinthian Diet Election Regulations of 1979, the Carinthian Diet drew the borders for the election districts in such a way that these run through the middle of the (relatively) tight-knit Slovenian communities, thereby making the election of a minority list even more difficult.

9. This integration of the opposition as an "ostensible" partner in government with an unchanged balance of power is described in detail by Pelinka (1983) using Tyrol as an example.

10. An interesting illustration of the "governor's electoral advantage" is given by the 1985 Upper Austrian Diet election that fell together with the state's city/town council elections. The Diet election brought the ÖVP 52.1% of the vote, a clearly better result than the 47.9% polled by the ÖVP in the state's combined city/town council elections. See Pointner 1986.

11. See this book's chapter by Ernst Gehmacher and Christian Härpfer on the internal structure of the electorate.

12. See the interesting remarks on Vorarlberg and Tyrol from the British viewpoint by Luther 1985 and 1986.

13. For recent literature on these regional/federal movements see Luther (1985 and 1986). On the power distribution among the elites in the federation see also Kreisky (1981).

14. Considerations from the Green-Alternative lager in Vorarlberg on whether to campaign for the National Council with a regional slate that excluded other groups showed that speculations on such regional parties in Austria are not completely unfounded.

15. See the chapter by Herbert Dachs in this book or also Pelinka (1984).

16. See, for example, this book's chapter by Anton Kofler entitled "Old Product—New Marketing."

17. Here it is important to note the deep entrenchment of Austria's social partnership and the many professional chambers in the states. The consociational mechanisms are particularly evident in the existence of hundreds of corporative institutions in the states.

18. Very good examples of this are the 1986 Anti-Draken Initiative led by Governor Krainer and the Styrian People's Party on basing fighter jets in

Styria that received 243,819 signatures, or the referendum held in Lower Austria at Governor Ludwig's initiative on the establishment of Lower Austria's own capital city.

Bibliography

Blaschke, Jochen, *Der neue Regionalismus in Westeuropa*, in: *Politische Bildung* 2/1986 (Blaschke, 1986)

Bruckmüller, Ernst, *Nation Österreich*, Wien/Köln/Graz 1984 (Bruckmüller, 1984)

Dermutz Susanne et al., *Anders als die Anderen? Politisches System, Demokratie und Massenmedien in Vorarlberg*, Bregenz 1982 (Dermutz et al., 1982)

Haungs, Peter, *Funktionsoptimierende Strukturen lokaler Parteiorganisationen*, in: Konrad Adenauer Stiftung (Hg.): *Strukturprobleme des lokalen Parteiensystems*, Bonn 1975 (Haungs, 1975)

Kofler, Anton, *Parteiengesellschaft im Umbruch*. Wien/Köln/Graz 1985 (Kofler, 1985)

Koren, Hans, *Regionale Identität*, in: Josef Krainer et al. (Hg.): *Nachdenken über Politik*, Graz/Wien/Köln 1985 (Koren, 1985)

Kreisky, Eva, *Thesen zur politischen und sozialen Funktion des Föderalismus in Österreich*, in: *Österreichische Zeitschrift für Politikwissenschaft 3/1981* (Kreisky, 1981)

Lukesch, Robert, *Selbstorganisation und autonome Regionalentwicklung*, in: *Österreichische Zeitschrift für Politikwissenschaft 3/1981* (Lukesch, 1981)

Luther, Kurt R., *The Increasing Salience of the Centre-Periphery Dimension in the Federal Republic of Austria*, Paper prepared for the ECPR Meeting in Barcelona 1985 (Luther, 1985)

Luther, Kurt R., *The Revitalisation of Federalism and Federation in Austria*, in: Michael Burgess (ed.): *Federalism and Federation in Western Europe*, London/Sydney 1986 (Luther, 1986)

Mantl, Wolfgang, *... nach dem Muster der Schweiz?*, in: *politicum* Juni 1986 (Mantl, 1986)

Mintzel, Alf, *Die CSU. Anatomie einer konservativen Partei*, Opladen 1978 (Mintzel, 1978)

Nick, Rainer, *Rahmenbedingungen und Entwicklung der grün-alternativen Szene in Vorarlberg*, in: *Österreichische Zeitschrift für Politikwissenschaft 2/1986* (Nick, 1986)

Öhlinger, Theo, *Anmerkungen zu den Gründungstheorien des Bundesstaates*, in: *Österreichische Zeitschrift für Politikwissenschaft 3/1981* (Öhlinger, 1981)

Pelinka, Anton, *Die KPÖ—Eine Kleinpartei in der Isolierung*, in: Andreas Khol/Alfred Stirnemann (Hg.): *Österreichisches Jahrbuch für Politik 1981*, München/Wien 1982 (Pelinka, 1982)

Pelinka, Anton, *Regierungssystem und Parteiensystem in Tirol*, in: Heinz Fischer/Susanne Preglau-Hämmerle (Hg.): *Heile Welt in der Region? Beiträge zum politischen System Tirols*, Bregenz 1983 (Pelinka, 1983)

Pelinka, Anton, *Zur Dekonzentration kommunaler Parteiensysteme*, in: Andreas Khol/Alfred Stirnemann (Hg.): *Österreichisches Jahrbuch für Politik 1983*, München/Wien 1984 (Pelinka, 1984)

Plasser, Fritz, *Parteien unter Streß. Zur Dynamik der Parteiensysteme in Österreich, der Bundesrepublik Deutschland und den Vereinigten Staaten*, Wien-Köln-Graz 1987 (Plasser, 1987)

Pointner, Hans, *Praktische Wahlforschung in Österreich*, in: *Österreichische Zeitschrift für Politikwissenschaft 2/1986* (Pointner, 1986)

Stirnemann, Alfred, *Innerparteiliche Gruppenbildung am Beispiel der ÖVP*, in: Andreas Khol/Alfred Stirnemann (Hg.): *Österreichisches Jahrbuch für Politik 1980*, München/Wien 1981 (Stirnemann, 1981)

Suppan, Arnold, *Österreichs Volksgruppen im Vergleich*, in: *Politische Bildung 2/1986* (Suppan, 1986)

Thaysen, Uwe, *Mehrheitsfindung im Föderalismus*, in: *Aus Politik und Zeitgeschichte 35/1985* (Thaysen, 1985)

Weidenfeld, Werner, *Die Identität der Deutschen—Fragen, Positionen, Perspektiven*, in: Werner Weidenfeld (Hg.): *Die Identität der Deutschen*, Bonn 1983 (Weidenfeld, 1983)

Welan, Manfried, *Regierungssystem und direkte Demokratie in Österreich*, in: Friedrich Koja/Gerald Stourzh (Hg.): *Schweiz—Österreich. Ähnlichkeiten und Kontraste*, Wien/Köln/Graz 1986 (Welan, 1986)

Zwink, Eberhard (Hg.), *Salzburg Diskussionen*. II. Landes-Symposion, Salzburg 1981 (Zwink, 1981)

15

Party Patronage in Austria

Theoretical Considerations and Empirical Findings

WOLFGANG C. MÜLLER[*]

1. Introduction

The concept of patronage or clientelism[1] covers a broad spectrum of different, but structurally related phenomena[2]. Patronage exists in both traditional and modern societies, under communism and capitalism. Within modern Western democracies, it is found in such differing parties as the French Communist Party and the Italian Christian Democratic Party. In short, patronage is a universal phenomenon; it is encountered—in one form or another—in all political systems (Kaufmann 1974, p. 300; Waterbury 1977, p. 336).

This chapter focuses on "modern" patronage, in which the political parties (or factions) have replaced the "classic" individual patrons (see Weingrod 1968; 1977; Theobald 1983, p. 141ff.). Patronage can be introduced into the party system and within parties for various purposes and the analysis of patronage structures and processes can clarify a number of individual phenomena in party research and, to some extent, connect them with each other. For reasons of space, this chapter is largely limited to the most important aspects of patronage from a political science perspective: voter mobilization, the recruitment of members and activists and the consequences of these uses of patronage at various levels of the party system.

Although party patronage is an important phenomenon in Austrian politics, it has for the most part not been subject to a systematic and theoretically based analysis, although the literature does contain some useful point-

---

[*]   I would like to express my thanks to E. Grande, K. Ucakar, H. Dachs and Delia Meth-Cohn for their critical remarks on this article.

ers[3]. My aim in this work, then, is to develop a theoretical framework for this topic and to present relevant empirical findings. In Section 2, patronage will be discussed within the framework of political motivation structures, in particular in terms of its contribution to solving parties' organizational problems. The third section outlines the spectrum of patronage resources and analyses their respective impact on a party's capacity for control. Sections 4 and 5 present empirical data on the importance of patronage as a source of political motivation and on the patronage activities of Austrian politicians. Finally, in Section 6, we will consider the consequences of patronage from various perspectives and discuss its future importance.

2. Political Motivation Structures and Parties' Organizational Problems

In this section, we will first look at various structures of political motivation, with particular emphasis on that of patronage, and then move on to a more theoretical level to consider the importance of these structures for vote maximization, for maintaining the organizational structure of a party and for dealing with problems of leadership. Some reflections and data on the validity of these theories and hypotheses for Austria then follow in Section 4.

The kinds of loyalty expressed in voting for, membership of, and activity in a party, can stem from a variety of different sources. If the loyalty has a *traditional* or *charismatic* origin, the stimulus for political activity is of a symbolic nature. On the other hand, if a party's political engagement has a rational basis, four different sources of loyalty (at least) can be distinguished. First of all, there is a loyalty based on *overall policy commitments*. In this case, a person supports a particular party because he shares in the values underlying the policies and/or the prospective policies correspond to his own interests. A party is supported then, for example, because it promises to eliminate the death penalty or to lower taxes. In the following two types of loyalty, the incentives are more specific. In the first case, which will here be called *macropatronage*, the incentives for loyalty are of a material nature. The party appeals not to individuals but to a particular collective entity, such as a community, which is not selected on the basis of universal criteria (e.g., the size of the community, its geographic location or structural problems) but rather according to party political advantage. The incentives for the collective entity are indivisible goods; in our example, they are potentially beneficial to the entire community, although they will benefit individual community members to differing degrees.

This source of loyalty is to be distinguished from *micropatronage*, which is directed at individual persons or families, who are given public assets by a party in direct exchange for loyalty (votes, party membership, party activity). Patronage may not violate general standards and an attempt is always made to legitimize patronage deals by such standards, regardless of whether they are applicable or not. Indeed, it is a definitive characteristic of patronage is that it is not universal standards but political exchange relationships that determine the allocation of public assets. Finally, political participation may also be regarded as *rewarding in itself*, whereby we can further distinguish between genuinely political stimuli (fulfillment of civic obligations, etc.) and primarily social stimuli (making friends, contacts, etc.).

In this chapter, we are primarily concerned with micropatronage, although, in practice, macro- and micropatronage are frequently intertwined, the former being in many cases the precondition for the latter (see Zuckermann 1975, p. 19ff.) Both types are of empirical importance in Austria. In the following, patronage will be used to refer to what we have previously defined as micropatronage.

We have already said that patronage can be characterized as an exchange relation; it is, however, to be distinguished from market-type exchange which forms the basis of *exchange theory*[4]. In party patronage, the client no longer faces the classic individual patron but rather the collective patron of the political party. For the client, the party is of course also represented by individuals (members of Parliament, local party functionaries), but they only have access to patronage resources only through the party. From a political science perspective, then, analysis of patronage cannot be limited to the patron-client relationship as in anthropologic research on old-style patronage; it must also deal with the wider context of related macrostructures and processes.

In contrast to earlier patronage forms, party patronage is "democratized" (since patron and client belong to the same horizontal group and the client may, in principle, change his patron). Nevertheless, an *asymmetry in status, power and resources* in favor of the patron exists here as well. The exchange relation is also *informal* and *diffuse*, i.e., the reciprocal relations are not clearly defined as in a contractual agreement. The principle of patronage is to oblige clients to perform favors or services in the future, the precise nature of which is not specified in advance. In contrast to the contract model, the obligation to carry out future favors is not based on technical or legal mechanisms, but instead on the *feeling of personal obligation*. It is not possible to free oneself from such personal obligations (social exchange) by performing particular services or by paying a penalty. Furthermore, the services or favors provided by the party for the individual client are often of existential importance for him and are as a rule more vital for him than his favors are for the party, i.e., the party always retains the upper hand. This kind of patronage relation represents, then, a *particular combination of concrete and generalized exchange*. If the party succeeds in establishing this element of social exchange in its patronage relationships, the client's link to the party is likely to be of a permanent character[5].

Elections are of central significance to political parties. Patronage must then be analyzed in this context in addition to other areas of party life. An empirical example of the use of patronage activities aimed at vote maximization during elections is represented by the "machine party," which attained its classic form in the United States around the turn of the century[6]. This party bound its voters to it using a myriad of patronage deals which symbolized the party's willingness to help the "little man" (Scott 1969, p. 1144). In the organization of its clients, the "machine party" exhibited some features of a party of notables, limiting itself to mobilizing its clients for voting rather than trying to forge a permanent link to the party organization. The empirical evidence for Austria (in this regard rather scanty) indicates that patronage relations, demanding nothing more from the client than appropriate voting behavior during elections, do exist, but the importance of patronage appears to be much greater for membership recruitment, although of course, voting behavior is expected to correspond to this.

Membership recruitment is a particular problem for political parties and structurally related organizations if they limit themselves to those goals which are commonly considered to be the actual purpose of the organization: working out programs and *policies*, propaganda, candidates. These are collective goods, directed at *all* members of a political system, regardless of whether they have contributed to producing them or not. Consequently, the question arises of why rational actors should become party members or activists at all, since they would enjoy the collective goods produced by the party even without spending time and money on party activity. The contribution of any one individual person is, as a rule, so small that the party could easily do its work without him, and the ability of an individual to influence the actual shape of the party's output is too slight to provide a rational basis for active, individual participation (Olson 1965).

Olson's theory of the logic of collective action is based on the premises of new political economics (or neoclassical economics). Although the theory is self-contained and elegant, this comes at the price of screening out empirical phenomena that contradict its premises. It is clear that not all citizens are rational as defined by methodological individualism and there are forms of political behavior that are not compatible with these premises (see the types of loyalty mentioned above). Olson (1965) developed his theory using the example of American interest groups, which are different than European interest groups, and parties in particular, because of their virtual lack of ideology. Parties in Europe have historically resolved problems of mobilization and organization largely through the development of ideologies. Ideologies consist of two components: *first*, a closed system of social, political and economical values, representing nothing less than "a complete theory of the good life for men in society" (Bluhm 1974, p. 4). This closed value system is conducive to action. The second component of ideology is the explanation and interpretation of reality in terms of cause and effect relations (Bluhm 1974, p. 4). To the extent that a party succeeds in presenting its ideology as a secular religion (Bluhm 1974, p. 27), it is able to resolve its problems of mobilization and organization.

However, even if we accept the fundamental premises on which Olson's logic of collective action is based, it is not possible wholeheartedly to accept the theory's applicability to political parties (see Schlesinger 1984, p. 386). In the case of the American interest groups analyzed by Olson, the members' cost-benefit calculation can be carried out within the framework of a monetary evaluation system because of the almost exclusively economic character of the collective goods. For political parties, this is only so in limited areas (economic policy) where the calculation will in any case be considerably more complicated; in other areas (superstructural policy), assessing costs and benefits will be extremely difficult.

These remarks are not intended to deny the validity of Olson's dilemma for political organizations in general and political parties in particular; indeed, as tradition and ideology lose their hold, the dilemma appears all the more clearly. Since it is generally agreed that—apart from a few phases of partial re-ideologization—post-war Austria has seen a considerable de-ideologization of and convergence between the parties (see Kadan/Pelinka 1979; Gerlich/Müller 1983; Gerlich 1987), it follows that the organizational dilemma is of great importance for the Austrian case. Olson himself explained the existence of numerous organizations producing collective goods within his theoretical framework by the fact that there was either a certain *pressure to organize*, or that these organizations, *in addition to their actual organizational purpose* (the production of collective goods), also produced goods that did not have a collective character and that therefore could be distributed exclusively among members of the organization, acting as "selective incentives" to organize. Such private goods serve as compensation for the members' contribution to producing collective goods which benefit everybody. The organization must be able to produce these goods cheaply enough that the main purpose of the organization can still be achieved with the existing resources (which largely come from the members) (see Laver 1981, p. 41).

One way for parties to overcome the organizational dilemma is a patronage strategy. This involves both pressure and incentive or reward elements[7]; the cost of the "selective incentives" is met with public money. An empirical example of the organization of clients as members is the mass clientele or mass patronage party, a type that particularly corresponds to the Italian Christian Democratic Party (DC)[8]. This party type is related to the mass integration party, insofar that as many voters as possible are permanently tied to the party as members. It is distinguished from the classic mass integration party as described by Duverger (1964) by the absence of continuous member activities in local party organizations, by the party leadership's lack of interest in developing political consciousness and consequently in mobilizing members on this basis, and by the party's almost exclusive concern with voter mobilization and the management of power.

The third level on which patronage can be discussed is that of party activists. Their costs are substantially higher than those of (passive) party members, a fact which has given rise to a variety of different conclusions. Some authors conclude from their data that, although the activist begins for (primarily) ideological or *policy-oriented* reasons, with time and the increasing amount of political activity and responsibility, these incentives no longer suffice to maintain their activism and the activists begin to desire personal rewards of a material or social nature[9]. Johnstons's hypothesis goes a step further, arguing that old activists are actually over-compensated because of their earlier activity, costing the party more that their input is worth (Johnston 1979, p. 396). The opposing position to this is that party activists profit less from their involvement in the party than they invest (Rhodes 1984, p. 37ff.). This negative balance is a result of the comparatively low benefits, a heavy workload, and–because of the increasing hostility towards political parties (cf. Fishel 1978; Plasser 1987)–psycho-social pressure. Rhodes (1984; cf. Müller 1984, p. 55) in particular has posited the party organization itself as a charismatic reference point for the activists of a classic machine party. Its incentives are not policy issues and also not exclusively material rewards, but instead the maintenance of the tradition and power of the party itself. The maintenance of the organizational structure of the party is guaranteed by a complex mixture of material and non-material incentives, representing purpose-rational, value-rational and probably also irrational elements (see Weber 1976, p. 12f.).

The observations and interpretations which have been made up to this point apply to the parties of the United States (especially the Democratic Party), as well as to those of Sweden, the Netherlands, India, and the United Kingdom. In the British Labour Party, however, the activists hold far more radical policy positions than the voters and leadership of the party (Steel and Tsurutani 1986, p. 241ff.; Finer 1980, p. 116ff.) and in contrast to activists in the rival parties, maintain their original ideological motivation throughout their activism for the party (Conley and Smith 1983). What incentives in what measure actually determine the recruitment of a given party naturally have consequences for the quality of the party organization[10]. We will discuss this aspect in terms of two dimensions, namely the attempt of activists to influence party policy and their availability for the party.

It can be assumed that party employees and those party activists who are primarily patronage-motivated, provided their compensation is not in jeopardy, will not try to exert any influence on the content of party policy and will leave this to the party leadership. The latter can then rapidly reach decisions and has a free hand to develop policies directed toward marginal voters. If the party activists are primarily socially motivated, the party leadership's options are limited, at least in respect to ways of making policy (to the extent that this impinges on the work of the activists). Party activists who are organized in the party because of their ideological commitments and their policy expectations will, on the other hand, usually try to determine policy positions and concrete party policy according to their views. Party leadership initiatives that are not in agreement with these views will meet with resistance from the activists and will often be watered down or delayed. If *these* party activists are much more radical than the electorate, then the party's chances of maximizing votes in the electoral arena decrease with the increased strength of this group within the party, even if the activists are only able to determine the party's public image and not its actual policy. Party employees and instrumentally motivated activists, as distinguished from ideologically motivated activists, are able to stand for leadership positions regardless of the particular policy content, and are accordingly more multifaceted and flexible party workers (cf. Schlesinger 1964; 1984, p. 388). Their willingness to stand for leadership can be seen in the context of their material dependence on the party and is therefore calculable. In contrast to ideologically motivated party activists, primarily instrumentally motivated party activists will certainly not always be available for their party if rewards are not forthcoming over a period of time or if disadvantages could result from their association.

3. Patronage Resources and the Capacity for Control

In this section, we will first list the most important patronage resources as found in international empirical research on patronage. Since we will assume we are dealing with industrialized nations and party patronage; the classic patronage resources of land and protection from physical violence will not be discussed. As already mentioned, the relation between incentive and compulsion is fluid. The positioning of a particular patronage resource on the continuum between the two poles of incentive and compulsion varies from case to case. For the parties, it is the capacity for control associated with the particular resource that is of interest. We will first deal with these patronage resources in general and then in relation to Austria.

By far the most common patronage resource is *know-how*, especially for dealing with authorities. If the bureaucratic requirements for claiming public services are highly formalized, complicated and tedious, and therefore difficult for the "ordinary" citizen to cope with, the intermediary role of delegates and party functionaries may consist solely of putting through the rightful claims (Chubb 1981, p. 79f.; Higgins 1982). It is also possible, however, for these professional intermediaries, backed up by the power of a party (cf.

Boissevain 1977, p. 90), to expand illicitly the interpretation of the conditions for allocating services. In this case, the patronage resource is no longer know-how concerning access to government services, but the access itself.

During the Italian election campaign of 1958, packages of macaroni were still distributed to "persuade" the recipients (Zuckerman 1975, p. 17); most material patronage resources are, however, rather more subtle. Public money is used in various ways: the allocation of *grants, subsidies* and *government contracts*, and the manipulation of the tax system (*tax incentives, tax relief*). The same goes for the *allocation of credit* by government agencies or those that can be controlled politically[11]. The *distribution of licenses*, for example for practicing certain professions, can be a useful instrument of patronage[12]. *Public housing* is a classic patronage resource in many countries (Higgins 1982, p. 172f.; Chubb 1982, p. 172f.).

The most widespread form of patronage is probably the *allocation of jobs*. These positions are usually in the government administration or in the public sector, but can also be in the private sector and in the party itself. We can distinguish between at least two forms of "job patronage": power patronage and service patronage (Eschenburg 1961, p. 12f.). *Power patronage* refers to the allocation of important positions[13]. The decisive question in selecting personnel is what the client in this position will be able or want to do for the party; consequently, the candidate's party political reliability and his ability to get things done are important criteria. With a consistent power patronage strategy, a party is able to separate its capacity for influence to some extent at least temporarily from electoral success and participation in government, especially where there are no political appointees (i.e., those who are changed with each new government) in addition to the traditional civil service.

The distinctions between power patronage and service patronage are not always clear and may vary over time. From the point of view of voter mobilization and member/activist recruitment, *service or subaltern patronage* (Weber 1976, p. 839) is naturally of greater importance.[14] In this case, the offer of employment in the administration, etc., or the promotion, represents the party's resource in exchange for the client's loyalty *outside of his job*, since the position itself is not political or is of little importance in the decision-making hierarchy.

The coercive character of patronage is perhaps most clearly seen when the exchange consists of waiving *administrative penalties*. Chubb (1981, p. 76f.) used the example of Palermo to show that opportunities for imposing such penalties nearly always exist, and their cumulation can be ruinous especially for small businesses. There is, therefore, always an incentive to get around these penalties by using patronage.

The availability of the individual patronage resources is not fixed but is also, of course, not unlimited. Financial patronage runs into budgetary limitations; it is not possible to allocate more houses than are being built or become vacant, and the same holds true for jobs. The number of licenses could be increased without incurring much cost, but their value would then fall and protests from established license-holders would likely make the strategy counterproductive. Quantitative availability is less of a problem in the waiving of penalties.

Mosca and Pareto differentiated patronage resources according to their capacity for control and considered job patronage more effective in this respect than financial patronage (Zuckerman 1975, p. 17). The efficacy of different forms of patronage is especially problematic where patronage remains a marketlike exchange. If the element of social exchange is anchored in the patronage relationship, then the party's control problem is reduced although it can never be completely ignored. If financial patronage, defined in a broad sense to include all services financed by public money, has a one-off character, then parties are in a relatively weak position vis-a-vis their clients, since they have to hope that they can maintain a sense of gratitude without having the withdrawal of patronage available as a sanction. If there is strong competition between several patronage parties, then the efficacy of financial patronage is not only determined by the client's memory. The possibility of controlling clients is, however, only greater with job patronage than financial patronage under certain conditions, namely when the position is not permanent (tenured) and/or when there are opportunities for advancement. Under these conditions, keeping the job or advancing remains at the patronage party's discretion (at least insofar as it stays in government). As a result of the control problems discussed above, it appears that even job patronage can better serve the formation of a party organization than its continuous operation or its adaptation to new conditions (Johnston 1979, p. 395)—assuming that these last two goals can be achieved through patronage at all (see Section 2). The efficacy of job patronage will also depend on the prevailing economic situation and the degree to which certain occupations are monopolized by the state.

Those resources which involve coercion obviously give patronage parties the greatest capacity for control. But apart from the technical difficulties, the use of coercion also carries the greatest risk that it might provoke resistance which would be counterproductive for the party.

If we apply these experiences and theoretical considerations to Austria, we can see that all the patronage resources listed are available to the governing parties (at federal, state and municipal level). The few investigations into the Austrian administration's attitude towards citizens present a picture that makes it quite plausible to promise party intervention even when "the successful resolution of a problem is barely in doubt" (Konecny 1974, p. 12). The large public sector and the high degree of regulation make it possible to fall back on the material patronage resources mentioned above—from subsidies, to housing and trade concessions. Some "anecdotal material"[15] exists on the actual use of these incentives/rewards in the party interest–their collection and systematic processing would, however, go beyond the scope of this paper. The more prominent the coercive aspect of patronage, the fewer examples one can find of its use.

The potential for job patronage in Austria is also high because of the large public sector. It requires no special research to confirm the political parties' use of this resource. As far as power patronage is concerned, the parties used a large part of the coalition agreements during the time of the first Grand Coalition, to regulate such questions, and even after this form of government was no longer in existence, such agreements were still reached (examples of this kind of negotiation are the Krampus Agreement and the Honolulu Agreement concerning appointments in the central bank). Until recently, these principles were adhered to in the nationalized sector (Dobler 1983; Fehr/Van der Bellen 1982). The extreme federalism of the electricity industry, part of the nationalized sector, is not least a multiplication and federalization of the potential for patronage.

The educational sector is still strongly dominated by job patronage, although more of the service kind (cf. Kok/Morscher 1987). In this field, particularly as regards the appointment of school principals, patronage is used so consistently that even politicians occasionally condemn its use[16]. In one school-teacher association ("Verband der Professoren Österreichs"), a protest organization has been founded explicitly to counteract these practices. There are several forms of job patronage at the regional level, from monopolization of positions by the strongest party with only token participation by the other parties, to a more or less proportional distribution of particular appointments between the two large parties. Where, instead of party settlements, objective procedures for determining appointments have been introduced, this seems in practice to have worked out in favor of the strongest party, which is in a position to lay down criteria for promotion and to prevail in discretionary evaluations[17].

Table 15.1 illustrates certain aspects of job patronage in the ministerial bureaucracy in related positions. The data give some idea of the way the two large parties have used this patronage resource under different political circumstances, since the four reference points mark more or less the end of political eras and the shift in the possibilities for patronage between the parties.

The first election of staff representatives represents the effects of some 20 years of Grand Coalition government. It shows that the party affiliation of the respective minister strongly influences the political ordering of the civil servants in each ministry. The majorities created and/or strengthened at that time have survived all government changes, including thirteen years of single-party government and were found to be changeable only over the long term. The majorities built up in particular ministries under the Grand Coalition were hardly built up further even under single-party governments and thus represent (on the basis of aggregate data) to some extent a peak. Nevertheless, both the SPÖ and the ÖVP have obviously tried to build up their positions during their respective single-party governments, particularly in the ministries previously dominated by the other party. In the absence of better data, the staff elections of 1971 and 1975 are intended to illustrate the changes which took place under the ÖVP single-party government as compared to the Grand Coalition, and under the SPÖ single-party government as compared to the ÖVP single-party government. The election of 1983 illustrates the effects of a long period of single-party government. Table 15.1 indicates that, in each case, the governing party was able to reduce the majority of the other party in their traditionally held ministries or increase their own majorities by some five percentage points in each legislative period. The FPÖ experienced a similar improvement after participating in government (1983-87). It can be assumed that the changes in party political composition are clearer at the leadership position level.

Table 15.1
Ministerial Patronage

ÖVP or SPÖ majorities in staff representation elections in "traditional" ÖVP or SPÖ ministries[a]

Time after ...	ÖVP majority in ÖVP ministries(b)	SPÖ majority in SPÖ ministries(c)
... the Grand Coalition (1967)	74	69
... the sole ÖVP govt. (1971)	74	64
... the first SPÖ govt. (1975)	70	63
... the end of SPÖ govt. (1983)	61	70

a) Only those ministries are included which were always held by the same party at the time of the Grand Coalition and never administered by a party-independent minister.
b) Federal Chancellory, Ministries of Trade, Agriculture, Education, Defense
c) Ministries of the Interior, Social Services and Transport.

The most pertinent example of patronage in the form of waiving penalties is the integration of former National Socialists in both major parties in the immediate post-war period. Former members of the NSDAP who joined the two big parties were "denazified" and did not have to face the consequences of anti-Nazi legislation (cf. Kraus 1988). As voters, this group was interesting for both parties. For the SPÖ, they were particularly important as a source of experts to fill those positions in the nationalized industries that the party was entitled to by the Grand Coalition's agreement on proportional appointment (cf. Secher 1958).

4. Party Patronage from the Client's Perspective

The Austrian parties, for many years at least, have dealt remarkably well with the problems of forming a lasting link with voters and of recruiting members. Voter participation has always been high, fluctuations in voting very small (cf. Haerpfer 1985) and the membership of the parties unusally high (Urban/Zeidner 1983). The degree of organization in the Austrian parties is many times higher than that of comparable parties abroad (Beyme 1985, p. 184f.). Even taking into account the fact that the parties' statistics on membership are probably exaggerated, they still remain high in contrast to international statistics[18]. In the following, we will try to examine the reasons for this phenomenon, in particular, the role of patronage, in terms of the analysis of the motivation structures presented in Section 2. For this purpose, we will rely largely, if not exclusively, on demoscopic investigations. Because of the difficulties with data, emphasis will be placed on the motivations behind party membership, but even in this respect, the existing data base is still thin. Although surveys have been carried out over the past 15 years, their comparability is limited since the interview questions were varied (to a greater or lesser degree) and the given reply categories showed considerable differences, both in form and content. Nevertheless, we can say in advance that patronage is an important motive for joining a party—all existing data support this assessment.

Table 15.2
Motives for Joining a Party, 1969-70 (in percent).

Party members (n = 499) were asked their reasons for joining the party.

Exclusively patronage	Patronage and party goals	Exclusively party goals	Private reasons a)	
19	24	26	32	(= 101)

a)   This mixed category also consists of those who joined the party because of their membership in another organization. Since these organizations also practice patronage, we can assume that at least a proportion of party members in this category also joined for patronage reasons—as G.B. Powell points out.
Source: G.B. Powell 1972, p. 15. Author's calculations.

As Table 15.2 shows, in the period 1969-70 approximately every fifth party member gave patronage as his exclusive reason for joining a party. A further one-fourth of party members mentioned this reason in addition to their commitment to party goals. Consequently, patronage was an important motive for a total of 43% of the interviewees. According to the author of the study (G.B. Powell 1972), however, the number of those members who were motivated to some extent by patronage is actually much higher, perhaps around 50%. This conclusion is reasonable, partly because of the very narrow operationalization of patronage used in this study. A case study of an ÖVP party section in Vienna calculated that 43% of the party members were motivated by patronage (Silberbauer 1968, p. 23).

Table 15.3
Motives for Party Membership, 1980 (in percent)

Party members (n = 582) were asked about their motives for joining a party. Those identified as party members were posed the following question: "I will read you a list of possible reasons for joining a party. Please tell me how important each of these was for you personally. 1 means 'very important,' 5 means 'unimportant'." Column (1) shows the frequency with which the value 1 was mentioned. Column (2) for the values 1 and 2, column (3) for the cumulated frequency of 1, 2 and 3. (Multiple responses possible).

	(1)	(2)	(3)
Patronage			
- career advantage	19	37	49
- obtain housing	13	25	33
Ideology			
- agree with party's general views	35	64	79
Political participation			
- realize own political ideas	17	41	59
Milieu			
- family tradition	32	53	65
- pressure of expectations	13	31	43
Social contacts			
- meet other people	12	32	53
- recommended by friends and acquaintances	9	23	38
- get to know VIPs	7	19	34

Source: Deiser/Winkler 1982, p. 237.

Table 15.3 shows that in 1980, depending on the method of calculation, every fifth or second party member gave career advancement and every eighth or third party member gave the possibility of getting housing as one of his motives for membership. These two reasons do not, of course, cover the

whole spectrum of patronage but they are certainly the most important incentives quantitatively. Because of multiple responses, these numbers cannot
be added together but there is unlikely to be a complete overlap between the
two categories.

Table 15.4:
Motives for Party Membership, 1985 (in percent)

Party members (n = 349) were asked their motives for joining a party. All interviewees were
asked: "For what reasons could you imagine joining or did you join a party? Please tell me for
each point whether you consider it 'very important', 'quite important' or 'unimportant'." Column (1) indicates the response frequency of 'very important' and column (2), the cumulated
frequency of 'very important' and 'important' (multiple responses possible).

	(1)	(2)
Patronage		
- career advantage	24	52
- getting housing/job	22	44
Ideology		
- agree with party's general views	56	87
Political participation		
- realize own political ideas	26	62
Milieu		
- family tradition	41	68
Social contacts		
- meet other people	10	42
- friends and colleagues are members	10	35

Source: Dr. Fessel + GfK-Institute, Innen- und Aussenperspektive des österreichischen
Parteiensystems, 1985.

The reference of the two patronage items in Table 15.3 is certainly clear;
the classification of the other possibilities for reply is, however, debatable.
"Pressure of expectations," for example, could come under patronage as well
a milieu; the same applies to "getting to know VIPs." The reason for putting
the two items under "milieu" and "social contacts" respectively was that these
two motives are only instrumental to a patronage goal and, therefore, on a
different level to the other motives which represent the goal in itself. The
most recent inquiry into reasons for membership (Table 15.4) shows that
between one-fifth and a half of all party membership is to some extent attributable to (expected) patronage. A comparison of Tables 15.3 and 15.4
shows that in 1985, more of the motives were considered "very important"
than in 1980 (etc.). From this we can draw the conclusion that variations in

the data are likely to stem from different ways of measuring and perhaps different interview questions.

Taking the above data together, we can say that the period from 1969-70 to 1985 is characterized by the fact that—depending on the criteria used—between a fifth and a half of party members were motivated (to some extent) by patronage, where patronage is operationalized very narrowly as career advancement. Deiser/Winkler (1982, p. 94ff.; cf. also Eldersveld 1964, p. 281f.) were not satisfied with these data, i.e., with the party members' replies. They confronted the members' own self-portraits with the opinion they had of other party members' motives and came up with considerable discrepancies, with particularly large differences in relation to patronage motives (see Table 15.5). Deiser/Winkler (1982, p. 95f.) have construed this discrepancy as a projection, i.e., one's own socially inacceptable ways of thinking and behaving are attributed to others. These authors "do not doubt" that the "projected statements adequately describe reality." If we accept this appraisal, then at least three-quarters of Austrian party members are motivated to some extent by patronage.

We have already mentioned that, within the period for which we have demoscopic data, there has been no dramatic change in the proportion of party members motivated by patronage, which has remained constantly at a high level. These data do not allow for a more specific picture of the development of mass patronage parties and the importance of patronage motives is not merely a product of the 1950s and 1960s. Numerous sources speak of a general weariness with politics and parties at the beginning of the Second Republic in 1945. Nevertheless, the parties succeeded in rebuilding their organizations to an impressively high level by international standards and in a relatively short period of time. Part of this success, it seems, was due to the importance of patronage as a party function[19], as Hanisch (1985, p. 32ff.) has shown using the example of Salzburg.

Tables 15.2 to 15.5 point to patronage as an important, but definitely not the sole motive for joining a party. Actually existing parties—not mere political science constructs—will always be able to rely on various types of loyalty and will try to set up corresponding incentives (Scott 1969, p. 1147). Of particular relevance in Austria according to response frequency, coming immediately before (self-assessment) or after (projection) patronage, are *general political expectations* (or *ideology*) and *family tradition*. On the whole, however, the motivation structure of party members exhibits features that point in the direction of the mass-patronage party type.

The least-mentioned motive, social contacts, is ranked "very important" by one group which, in size, broadly corresponds to the circle of party activists. Already at the beginning of the 1960s, Kurt Schell (1962, p. 39) reported of the SPÖ activists that party work offered them "a type of club life which to many of them has become a dear habit." Shell conjectured that this system was self-perpetuating.

Table 15.5:
Own and Others' Motives for Party Membership, 1980 (in percent)

Response Frequency of Values 1 and 2 (cf. Table 15.3)	Self-Assessment (1)	Assessment of Others (2)	Difference (2)-(1)
Patronage			
- career advantage	37	78	+41
- obtain housing	25	71	+46
Ideology			
- agree with party's general views	64	61	-3
Political participation			
- realize own political ideas	41	57	+16
Milieu			
- family tradition	53	60	+7
- pressure of expectations	31	36	+5
Social contacts			
- meet other people	32	31	-1
- recommendation of friends and acquaintances	23	32	+9
- meet VIPs	19	30	+11

Source: Deiser/Winkler 1982, p. 74f.

Demoscopic investigations representative of the whole population are obviously not suitable, at least not on statistical grounds, for providing evidence about genuine party activists. Even the group of those members who are only occasionally active in their party comprises only a little over a quarter of the members. This corresponds to some 7% of the electorate, about the same proportion as in the USA or West Germany, where the degree of party organization is about a seventh or a fifth, respectively, of that in Austria (Plasser 1987, p. 130f.). In other words, Austrian party members are extremely inactive.

In the framework of his analysis, G.B. Powell (1972, p. 18) divided party members into his four motivation types (cf. Table 15.2) and their respective activity in election campaigns. He found that an exclusive commitment to party goals resulted in the highest activity in election campaigns, a combination of party goals and patronage to the second highest, patronage alone to the third highest, and "private motives" to the least activity. The efficacy of patronage in promoting activity lies, then, behind that of ideology. These findings are in accordance with those of a local case study of the ÖVP (Silberbauer 1968, p. 32). But participation in party-political educational courses can be seen as partly contradicting this conclusion (Haberson/Szekely 1980, p. 356). White-collar workers and civil servants are strongly over-represented in both parties' courses, that is, precisely those occupational groups, rather than the respective core constituencies of manual workers and farmers, are able to make the most use of patronage in their careers—although, of course, these groups also claim to be more interested in politics (cf. Gerlich/Ucakar 1981, p. 43ff.). Both of these empirical clues point to the fact that not only passive members but also party activists are recruited through patronage. Leser (1973, p. 208) makes the same point about the SPÖ's semi-official activist apparatus (*Vertrauenspersonen*), which he claims is only able to maintain its size of around one-tenth of the members "by using all the opportunities for patronage at the party's disposal and by exploiting all the economic dependencies that have been built up in the various organizations and regions."

We have shown empirically in this section that patronage represents an essential organizational incentive within the Austrian party system and provided some examples of the effectiveness of this mechanism, even for recruiting party activists. This cannot, however, replace a systematic empirical investigation of this aspect of parties, which remains one of the desiderata of research on the Austrian parties, not least because of the parties' unhelpful attitude.

5. Party Patronage from the Politician's Perspective

Another way of looking at the place of patronage in the Austrian party system is to examine the activity of politicians in this area. In the following, we will look at three dimensions: the amount of work devoted to this purpose, the relevance to party politics and the character of patronage deals. As early as 1947, the Lower Austrian section of the Austrian Workers' and Employees' Association (ÖAAB) reported, not without pride, that through its secretariat alone, it had pulled strings for various offices and positions 5529 times in one year[20]. Later accounts are rather more reserved about revealing this kind of information, but this should not lead to the conclusion that the parties have stopped this kind of activity. On the contrary, interviews with delegates reveal that such string-pulling is often one of their most important tasks. In Austria, the term for this is "intervention," which we will use in the following.

In his examination of the Lower Austrian State Diet carried out in 1960, Crane (1961, p. 10f.) established through interviews that, with only a few exceptions, the major task of delegates is in the field of interventions. A series of interviews on this subject with delegates to the Styrian State Diet, carried out in 1961, emphatically confirmed this picture: interventions were carried out by all the delegates, 84% spent most of their time doing this and 16% practically all of their time (Crane 1962, p. 162). The data obtained in 1965 on the activities of Viennese delegates to the Viennese Municipal Council and City Diet show that 40% admitted to interventions in the narrow sense. The authors no doubt correctly speculate that many delegates did not mention this aspect of their activity at all because it does not fit with the theory of democratic representation and would be badly received by the public (Gerlich/Kramer 1969, p. 177).

"This interventionist activity requires a lot of the delegate's time, especially if he takes it seriously," one of the Viennese delegates explained on behalf of his colleagues (Gerlich/Kramer 1969, p. 172). Interviews with delegates to the Upper Austrian State Diet, largely carried out in 1971 (Mayer 1973, pp. 19-22), show an average of 135 interventions per delegate and month with with a total time expenditure of some 34 hours. Two-thirds of the delegates felt themselves to be very heavily or heavily burdened by their interventional activity, merely 15% were not or hardly involved in this kind of work. The latter, which is by no means new for delegates (cf. Gerlich 1974, p. 99), is of great importance at the national level, although this can only be shown by "anecdotal material," there being as yet no investigations. The following profile of the activities of a delegate who had been criticized in the media for his poor showing as a speaker is probably typical for parliamentary backbenchers:

> First of all, I fully represent my district in Vienna; giving speeches is just a side-line. What's most important is that the work is done, that interventions, for example, are carried out.[21]

A parliamentary delegate from western Austria interviewed by me told me about 600 cases of intervention in relation to a single conscription in the army. (The aim of the intervention in the majority of cases was placement in a local unit.)

These pieces of evidence and information are related in a number of ways to the patronage function of political parties. Delegates, of course, always maintain that they do not question citizens who submit intervention requests about their party affiliation. Nevertheless, these contacts serve to expand the party's clientele (cf. Crane 1962, p. 166). Most of the clients, already belong to the delegate's party and interventions represent to a certain extent "claims" that have to be satisfied (Gerlich/Kramer 1969, 179, p. 173). The party dimension of interventions is to some extent confirmed by the investigation in Upper Austria: half of the Upper Austrian delegates regarded their assistance to persons seeking support to be their "most effective party work." There were significant differences among the delegates, depending on their proximity to the actual center of power, the state government: among the government members, for whom the policy option is relatively more available, only one evaluated intervention as the most important aspect of party work, whereas 50% of the frontbench delegates and 60% of the back-benchers viewed the interventionary activities as essential.

From interviews with delegates it also appears that such activities are an important and, at times, even the major vehicle for political competition, as can be seen from the following quotation from an Upper Austrian delegate (Mayer 1973, p. 22). "Since party ideologies are no longer important, delegates have to carry out this kind of activity to remain in the voters's minds." The Styrian delegates also associated the voting behavior of clients with their success in interventions (Crane 1962, p. 162f.), and a Viennese delegate made a similar point (Gerlich/Kramer 1969, p. 172):

What's important for the voter is who got him his apartment, who brings him the most advantage.

An Upper Austrian delegate expressed the situation most clearly (Mayer 1973, p. 21):

The ordinary person doesn't care what a law looks like—he wants help. If he doesn't get it from us, he'll go to the competition.

The usual contacts for politicians who have been requested to intervene are the civil servants, or, if this "direct channel" is not enough, the politicians in the ministries. As already mentioned, politicians with executive functions have at times a rather distant relationship to this kind of activity, being heavily burdened by requests for interventions from both clients and delegates. One long-serving minister with whom I spoke to about interventions in 1985 said he dealt with 3000 to 4000 such cases every year, of which not all were successful. The processing of interventions follows the usual political hierarchy: if the request comes from a fellow minister, the minister responsible will try to resolve it, if the request comes from a delegate, then he is more cautious ("You can experience the most amazing things"). The smallest service that can be done for a delegate whose request has been turned down is to write a letter explaining why the intervention could not be carried out. Such a letter acts as proof for the client, who in principle is success-oriented, of the delegate's attempt and provides an excuse for his lack of success (cf. Crane 1962; Mayer 1973, p. 21).

The delegates interviewed often emphasized that their interventionary activity should not be construed as "protectionism," but rather made up for the clients' or the officials' lack of information (cf. Gerlich/Kramer 1969, p. 172). We mentioned in Section 3 that know-how also represents a patronage resource and that it is sometimes difficult to distinguish between this and protectionism. The resources which the politicians have are multifaceted, vary from region to region and are also subject to change over time (cf. Crane 1962, p. 169; Gerlich/Kramer 1969, p. 173).

In summary, we can say that the patronage function takes up much of the personnel capacity of the Austrian parties and that politicians regard the performance of this function as an important condition for successful political competition.

6. Consequences of Patronage

In this final section, we will first discuss some of the effects of a comprehensive patronage system. We will look at these on three, not always clearly distinguishable, levels: the single party or party system, the society, and state institutions. Finally, we will try to evaluate the effectiveness of a patronage strategy from the perspective of the established Austrian parties and look at what this means for possible future party strategies.

Parties subscribe to a patronage strategy in order to be able to compete with other parties or to secure advantages, particularly in terms of forging a link with voters and recruiting members and activists to the party. A party's patronage strategy does not, however, only have these consequences. In intra-party terms, patronage usually contributes to the stabilization of existing power structures, since the party leadership, if it has access to public resources, naturally allocates these within the party as well (cf. Zuckermann 1975, p. 28f.). According to Graziano (1976, p. 164), this structure-conserving effect of patronage is accompanied by a "total de-ideologization" of any party that adopts such a strategy. On the whole, a patronage system favors a conservative ("reactionary," "populist"–Higgins 1982, p. 134) type of politician. Patronage, then, contributes to the convergence of political parties. Using the example of Italy, which, to be sure, has a very marked institutional structure, it can be seen that in choosing their coalition partners, parties are less concerned with the similarity in policies as with the expected spoils, which in turn contributes further to the instability of coalitions (Zuckerman 1975, p. 64).

Once patronage becomes an acceptable party strategy, it tends to develop a strong dynamic of its own, constantly drawing in new areas until a patronage system exists (cf. Eschenburg 1961, p. 24). Party competition and the ever-increasing importance of patronage over other incentives for loyalty are decisive in this process as is the logic of cooptation, i.e., the integration of all those who could endanger the effectiveness of patronage by building up horizontal structures (Graziano 1976, p. 169). The Italian experience shows that the autonomy of social groups and organizations is gradually undermined and that these become associated in the political power game (Graziano 1973, p. 27ff.). The same kind of situation can also to a great extent be diagnosed in Austria, although it is not solely attributable to patronage, since the penetration of social organizations by the parties originally took place under conditions of ideologically motivated pillarization (Steiniger 1975, p. 195ff.). The maintenance of the parties' omnipresence in social life, even after the disappearance of these conditions, is increasingly a matter of patronage. As already mentioned, the rebuilding of the organizational structure of the parties after the breakdown of national socialism took place, to some extent, through patronage.

It is often argued in the literature that patronage undermines horizontal social relations. Instead of class and status solidarity, the vertical patron-client relationship dominates and clients see other people merely as rivals for patronage benefits[22]. This characterization is most accurate for the classic patron-client relationship (e.g., lord of a manor–peasant), but is also of relevance for "democratized" patronage through parties. In my opinion, the most decisive consequence of the logic of a patronage system, in this respect, is that the "democratization" always remains incomplete and that, in order to maintain the effectiveness of the patronage instrument, the patronage parties have constantly to try and maintain social dependencies and inequalities (Belloni et al. 1979, p. 268ff.).

For state institutions, extensive patronage represents a departure from the ideal of bureaucratic rationality and an undermining of central constitutional principles (cf. Eschenburg 1961; Arnim 1980). Where state activity is determined by patronage, its economic efficiency also suffers; there is often a bloated civil service and the carrying out of inflated patronage expectations–not least because of party competition–leads to an overburdened budget (Cacliagi/Belloni 1981, p. 39ff.). The qualitative dimension of using public money in this way is probably even more important that the quantitative. Positions created or allocated on the basis of patronage are often superfluous and seldom optimally appointed. Public funds distributed (primarily) on these criteria are often of only very limited value in achieving the nominal goal (cf. Scott 1969, p. 1154). A good example of this are the funds supposedly intended for the economic development of Southern Italy but actually primarily used for patronage (cf. for example, Weingrod 1968, 397, p. 400).

There are, however, in the international literature on patronage more positive evaluations of this phenomenon than those previously discussed, deriving partly from structural-functionalist theory but also from concrete historical circumstances. These arguments have some relevance for Austria. Through patronage, for example, the number of people taking part in political life is increased. This can either be seen as burdening the parties with "dead souls" (cf. Leser 1973, p. 206ff.; Stirnemann 1980, p. 425) or, on the other hand, as a chance to raise somewhat the level of political information and to involve people in a country's democratic structures (G.B. Powell 1972; cf. Gerlich/Ucakar 1981, p. 50f.). Patronage has also been characterized as a way of integrating split societies (cf. Scott 1972). In this sense, the proportional patronage (cf. Eschenburg 1961) of the immediate post-war period in Austria undoubtedly contributed to the integration of the 1934 civil war opponents and the re-integration of the former National Socialists in the political system (cf. Hanish 1985)[23]. As already mentioned, within limits, patronage is a very useful way of putting through rightful claims in a remote bureaucracy. Nevertheless, even where patronage strictly observes the law, it is still double-edged, in that a party strategy that concentrates on providing concrete help without pushing for an adminstrative reform that would help everybody, perpetuates existing dependencies (see above).

Although these potentially positive aspects should not be ignored, when they are compared with the negative consequences of patronage[24], we have to reach the conclusion that patronage is a negative phenomenon, at least in the present day. From the perspective of the citizen and in the interest of desirable political reforms, we should be calling for "policy instead of patronage" (Gerlich 1983, p. 348).

But how should patronage be evaluated from the point of view of the established Austrian political parties and what developmental dynamics can we discern? There have been numerous initiatives to cut the web of patronage and to introduce objective procedures, both from the parties and directed at them. Most of these demands, however, are on a superficial level and are aimed at short-term effects on floating voters and the press rather than at a systematic evaluation of the consequences of patronage for the parties. (Moreover, as already mentioned, so-called objective procedures often turn out to be only a more subtle form of patronage). The continuation of extensive patronage activities by the parties is not, on its own, however, a sufficient indicator of the efficiency of this strategy, especially since large organizations are often characterized by inertia and since patronage has a certain dynamism of its own. Indeed, top politicians seem, now and then, to suggest that patronage is not longer efficient. The chairman of the SPÖ at that time, Fred Sinowatz, for example, found it necessary to explain at the 1985 party convention that the SPÖ was not an intervention agency. He argued that the party's *political* work should not be buried. In the same year, the deputy party chairman of the ÖVP, Eduard Busek, maintained in reference to the allocation of jobs and housing by political parties that it was politically more harmful than helpful[25].

This type of politician must, above all, be oriented towards electoral success, since this will directly determine his future political career. The data presented in Section 4 showed that patronage is essential for maintaining the party organization, but the party members recruited in this way are only a small percentage of the electorate. But there is always a protest potential, whose voting behavior will be negatively affected by patronage practices. It appears that the scope and influence of this protest potential is on the increase (cf. Plasser 1987; Müller 1984, p. 70; Plasser/Ulram in this book).

Moreover, there are signs that, under present social conditions, it is increasingly difficult for parties to construe the patron-client relationship as a social exchange. This will mean that an ever larger use of patronage resources will be necessary, while the uncertainty of the clients' voting behavior will increase regardless (cf. Caciagli/Belloni 1981, p. 39f.).

Despite the unquestionably important role of patronage in maintaining the party organization, particularly in terms of financial support (membership dues, donations), its relative weight is now less important; the introduction and the building up of public party funding (Müller/Hartmann 1983; Dachs 1986) have reduced the importance of self-financing through the membership and made the professionalization of party work easier.

From the increasing dysfunctionality of patronage for vote maximization and the increasing dependence of party organizations from the material resources which are received in exchange for patronage, we cannot, however, draw the conclusion that patronage strategies are irrational because they are inefficient. If the established parties, i.e., those that currently have access to patronage resources, renounced the use of patronage, the tendency of the still somewhat disadvantaged segment of the patronage-motivated voters to attach themselves to other political groupings would increase. Even "political abstinence" (not voting) by this group would weaken the established parties, which would not immediately be able to compensate by integrating the protest voters. Perhaps a more important reason for continuing with patronage is the competition among the established parties themselves. Neither party would be advised to hand over the large stock of potential clients to their rival for the questionable possibility of winning those voters, members and activists who are currently put off by patronage. Since party competition is a dynamic process, however, and parties can find themselves in a better or worse situation regarding access to patronage resources, we should not expect both parties to give up their patronage strategies simultaneously without major changes in the overall political situation.

Abandoning patronage would also have consequences for intra-party politics. The ranks of party activists would be reduced by those who were patronage-motivated, while the balance of those who are ideological or policy-oriented would show a sharp increase. It can be assumed that such an internal shift would increase the claim of activists to determine the shape of party policy. At a higher level, the lower ranks of career politicians would be shorn of their previously most important task, carrying out interventions. If they were to devote their extra time to "genuine" politics and took back more of their formal decision-making powers from the party leadership, the latter's hegemony would be endangered and the decision-making process would become much more complex. Whether such a perspective really corresponds to the interests of top politicians, who have the strongest reasons to move away from patronage strategies, is unlikely.

There are, then, a number of barriers to fundamental change in the area of party patronage. As so often, the safest forecast is that there will be no major changes in the forseeable future. The necessary conditions for such a change would be dramatic events (such as election results) and the readiness of party leaders to accept mor intra-party conflicht and greater political risk in the electoral arena.

Notes

1. The concepts of patronage and clientelism are usually used synonymously in the literature. Mühlmann/Llayora 1968, p. 1), regard the concept of "patronage" as referring to the patron's perspective, whereas concepts such as "clientele," etc., imply the client's standpoint.

2. The most important "classic" contributions on this topic are collected in a reader (Schmidt et al. 1977). A particularly good starting point for the subject is provided by three more recent edited volumes (Gelner and Waterbury 1977; Eisenstadt and Lemarchand 1981; Clapham 1982), as well as by a special issue of the International Political Science Review (1983, No. 4). For bibliographies, see Scott 1977a and Roninger 1981.

3. See also Secher 1952; Engelmann 1966, pp. 267, 272; Lehmbruch 1967, p. 26; G.B. Powell 1972; Silberbauer 1968.

4. See Homans 1961; Blau 1964; Waldmann 1972 and Lively 1976.

5. See Graziano 1976, p. 159ff.; Eisenstadt and Roninger 1980, p. 51ff. Also see Mühlmann and Llayora 1968, p. 35 and J.D. Powell 1970, p. 423f.

6. See Ostrogorski 1902, II, pp. 367-440; Merton 1957, pp. 72-82; Sorauf 1980, p. 82ff.; Guterbock 1980.

7. See Flynn 1974, p. 151f.; Scott 1977b, p. 22; Gellner 1977, p. 1; Weingrod 1977.

8. Graziano 1973, p. 24; Belloni et al. 1979; Caciagli and Belloni 1981; Chubb 1972, p. 71ff.. Patronage is, of course, only one of the supporting features of the Italian Christian Democrats (see Pasquino 1980, p. 94ff.).

9. Conway and Feigert 1968, p. 1172f.; Eldersveld 1983; in part, also Conley and Smith 1983.

10. The discussion of the differences among the various types of political activity can take place both under the paradigm of political participation and under that of political competitiveness. The first paradigm, to a certain extent the view "from below," has been applied since Ostrogorski (1902) and Michels (1962) from outside of political science analyses of parties. The normative power of this paradigm should not be denied; however, the competitive paradigm, which to a certain extent represents the view "from above," is more important for explaining actual party decisions.

11. Mühlmann and Llayora 1968, p. 32; Chubb 1981, p. 59ff., 74; 1982, p. 111ff.

12. Mühlmann and Llayora, 1968, p. 32; Chubb, 1981, p. 74; 1982, p. 122ff.

13. For example, see Finer, 1952; Lowi, 1964; Dyson, 1979.

14. See Zuckermann, 1975, p. 17f.; Higgins, 1982, p. 120f.; Chubb, 1981, p. 68ff.

15. Even a systematic analysis of the magazines *Berichte und Informationen*, *Profil* and *Wochenpresse*, and also of the party press in relation to the other parties would probably provide enough examples.

16. The then minister, Helmut Zilk, for example, said of party patronage (Parteibuchwirtschaft): "It makes me puke." (TV Interview, "Pressestunde," June 24, 1984).

17. See, for example, *Wochenpresse*, No. 20, July 10, 1984.

18. Cf. Plasser (1987, p. 115ff.), who does not rely on party statistics but compares membership figures obtained through demoscopic surveys.

19. Also see the contemporary critic, H. A. Kraus, "Die Mißstände in unserem Parteiwesen," in: *Berichte und Informationen* 1947, No. 69ff. (5 parts) and "Die Österreichische Pfründenmentalität," in: Berichte und Informationen 1949, No. 148, as well as Özbudun 1981, p. 265.

20. *Österreichische Monatshefte*, 2nd year (1946-47), p. 379.

21. *Wochenpresse*, No. 29, July 16, 1985.

22. See, for example, Belloni et al. 1979, p. 272; Graziano 1973, p. 5; Higgins 1982, p. 133; Mühlmann and Llayora 1968, p. 38ff.; also Banfield 1958.

23. It is clear from the number of former Nazi party members—more than half a million—that they could not be marginalized for long. Nevertheless, it would have been possible to find more desirable forms of integration.

24. It would be an exaggeration to attribute all these problematic circumstances and developments exclusively to the parties' patronage strategies. It is much more likely that the seeds were already in existence, that the ideal of bureaucratic-legal rationality in state institutions could not have been fully realized in any case, and that clients had the evidence of historical experience behind them to show that it was worth their while to rely on personal contacts rather than on "larger solidarity structures." (Mühlmann and Llayora 1968, p. 42ff.).

25. Fred Sinowatz, "Mutig in die neuen Zeiten," Party Chairman's Speech to the 1985 SPÖ Party Conference, November, November 12, 1985; Eduard Busek, Interview, in: Schwarz-bunter Vogel, Vienna, 1985, p. 230.

Bibliography

Arnim, H.H. v., *Ämterpatronage durch politische Parteien*, Wiesbaden 1980 (Arnim, 1980)

Banfield, E.C., *The Moral Basis of a Backward Society*, New York 1958, (Banfield, 1958)

Belloni, F./Caciagli, M./Mattina, L., *The Mass Clientelism Party: The Christian Democratic Party in Catania and in Southern Italy*, in: *European Journal of Political Research* 7/1979 (Belloni/Caciagli/Mattina, 1979)

Beyme, K. v., *Political Parties in Western Democracies*, Aldershot 1985 (Beyme, 1985)

Blau, P., *Exchange and Power in Social Life*, New York 1964 (Blau, 1964)

Bluhm, W.T., *Ideologies and Attitudes: Modern Political Culture*, Englewood Cliffs, N.J. 1974 (Bluhm, 1974)

Boissevain, J., *When the Saints Go Marching Out: Reflections on the Decline of Patronage in Malta*, in: E. Gellner/J. Waterbury (eds.), *Patrons and Clients in Mediterranean Societies*, London 1977 (Boissevain, 1977)

Burkolter, V., *The Patronage System. Theoretical Remarks, Social Strategies 4*, Basel 1976 (Burkolter, 1976)

Caciagli, M./Belloni, F.P., *The "New" Clientelism in Southern Italy: The Christian Democratic Party in Catania*, in: S.N. Eisenstadt/R. Lemarchand (eds.), *Political Clientelism, Patronage and Development*, Beverly Hills/London 1981 (Caciagli/Belloni, 1981)

Chubb, J., *The Social Bases of an Urban Machine: The Christian Democratic Party in Palermo*, in: S.N. Eisenstadt/R. Lemarchand (eds.), *Political Clientelism, Patronage and Development*, Beverly Hills/London 1981 (Chubb, 1981)

Chubb, J., *Patronage, Power and Poverty in Southern Italy*, Cambridge 1982 (Chubb, 1982)

Clapham, Chr. (Hg.), *Private Patronage and Public Power*, London 1982 (Clapham, 1982)

Conley, M.W./Smith, P.J., *Political Recruitment and Party Activists*, in: *International Political Science Review 4/1983* (Conley/Smith, 1983)

Conway, M.M./Feigert, F.B., *Motivation, Incentive Systems, and the Political Party Organisation*, in: *American Political Science Review 62/1968* (Conway/Feigert, 1968)

Crane, Jr., W., *The Legislature of Lower Austria*, London 1961 (Crane, 1961)

Crane, Jr., W., *The Errand-Running Function of Austrian Legislators*, in: *Parliamentary Affairs 15/1962* (Crane, 1962)

Dachs, H., *Öffentliche Parteienfinanzierung in den österreichischen Bundesländern*, in: *Österreichisches Jahrbuch für Politik 1985*, München/Wien 1986 (Dachs, 1986)

Deiser, R./Winkler, N., *Das politische Handeln der Österreicher*, Wien 1982 (Deiser/ Winkler, 1982)

Dobler, H., *Der persistente Proporz: Parteien und verstaatlichte Industrie*, in: P. Gerlich/W.C. Müller (Hg.), *Zwischen Koalition und Konkurrenz. Österreichs Parteien seit 1945*, Wien 1983 (Dobler, 1983)

Duverger, M., *Political Parties*, London 1964 (Duverger, 1964)

Dyson, K., *Die Westdeutsche "Parteibuch"-Verwaltung*, in: *Die Verwaltung 12/1979* (Dyson, 1979)

Eisenstadt, S.N./Lemarchand, R. (eds.), *Political Clientelism, Patronage and Development*, Beverly Hills/London 1981 (Eisenstadt/Lemarchand, 1981)

Eisenstadt, S.N./Roniger, L., *Patron-Client Relations as a Model of Structuring Social Exchange*, in: *Comparative Studies in Society and History 22/1980* (Eisenstadt/ Roniger, 1980)

Eisenstadt, S.N./Roniger, L., *Patrons, Clients and Friends*, Cambridge 1984 (Eisenstadt/Roniger, 1984)

Eldersveld, S.J., *Political Parties: A Behavioral Analysis*, Chicago 1964 (Eldersveld, 1964)

Eldersveld, S.J., *Motivations for Party Activism*, in: *International Political Science Review 4/1983* (Eldersveld, 1983)

Engelmann, F.C., *Austria: The Pooling of Opposition*, in: R.A. Dahl (ed.), *Political Oppositions in Western Democracies*, New Haven 1966 (Engelmann, 1966)

Eschenburg, Th., *Ämterpatronage*, Stuttgart 1961 (Eschenburg, 1961)

Fehr, E./Van der Bellen, A., *Aufsichtsräte in öffentlichen Unternehmen. Skizzen zur politischen Ökonomie Österreichs*, in: *Zeitschrift für öffentliche und gemeinwirtschaftliche Unternehmen 5/1982* (Fehr/Van der Bellen, 1982)

Finer, S.E., *Patronage and the Public Service*, in: *Public Administration*, 30/1952 (Finer, 1952)

Finer, S. E., *The Changing British Party System, 1945-1979*, Washington D.C. 1980 (Finer, 1980)

Fishel, J. (ed.), *Parties and Elections in an Anti-Party Age*, Bloomington-London 1978 (Fishel, 1978)

Flynn, P., *Class, Clientelism, and Coercion: Some Mechanisms of Internal Dependency and Control*, in: *Journal of Commonwealth and Comparative Politics 12/1974* (Flynn, 1974)

Gellner, E., *Patrons and Clients*, in: E. Gellner/J. Waterbury (eds.), *Patrons and Clients in Mediterranean Societies*, London 1977 (Gellner, 1977)

Gellner, E./Waterbury, J. (eds.), *Patrons and Clients in Mediterranean Societies*, London 1977 (Gellner/Waterbury, 1977)

Gerlich, P., *Funktionen des Parlaments*, in: H. Fischer (Hg.), *Das politische System Österreichs*, Wien 1974 (Gerlich, 1974)

Gerlich, P., *Österreichs Parteien: Ergebnisse und Perspektiven*, in: P. Gerlich/W.C. Müller (Hg.), *Zwischen Koalition und Konkurrenz. Österreichs Parteien seit 1945*, Wien 1983 (Gerlich, 1983)

Gerlich, P., *Consociationalism to Competition: The Austrian Party System since 1945*, in: H. Daalder (ed.), *Party Systems in Denmark, Austria, Switzerland, the Netherlands and Belgium*, London 1987 (Gerlich, 1987)

Gerlich, P./Kramer, H., *Abgeordnete in der Parteiendemokratie*, Wien 1969 (Gerlich/Kramer, 1969)

Gerlich, P./Müller, W.C. (Hg.), *Zwischen Koalition und Konkurrenz. Österreichs Parteien seit 1945*, Wien 1983 (Gerlich/Müller, 1983)

Gerlich, P./Ucakar, K., *Staatsbürger und Volksvertretung*, Salzburg 1981 (Gerlich/Ucakar, 1981)

Graziano, L., *Patron-Client Relationships in Southern Italy*, in: *European Journal of Political Research 4/1976* (Graziano, 1976)

Graziano, L., *A Conceptual Framework for the Study of Clientelistic Behavior*, in: *European Journal of Political Research 4/1983* (Graziano, 1983)

Graziano, L., *Introduction*, in: *International Political Science Review 4/1983* (Graziano, 1983)

Guterbock, Th. M., *Machine Politics in Transition*, Chicago 1980 (Guterbock, 1980)

Haberson, R./Székely, C., *Die politischen Akademien—eine Zwischenbilanz*, in: *Österreichisches Jahrbuch für Politik 1979*, Wien/München 1980 (Haberson/Székely, 1980)

Haerpfer, Chr., *Austria*, in: I. Crewe/D. Denver (eds.), *Electoral Change in Western Democracies*, London 1985 (Haerpfer, 1985)

Hanisch, E., *Zeitgeschichtliche Dimensionen der Politischen Kultur in Salzburg*, in: H. Dachs (Hg.), *Das politische, soziale und wirtschaftliche System im Bundesland Salzburg*, Salzburg 1985 (Hanisch, 1985)

Higgins, M.D., *The Limits of Clientelism: Towards an Assessment of Irish Politics*, in: Chr. Clapham (ed.), *Private Patronage and Public Power*, London 1982 (Higgins, 1982)

Homans, G., *Social Behavior: Its Elementary Forms*, New York 1961 (Homans, 1961)

Johnston, M., *Patrons and Clients, Jobs and Machines: A Case Study of the Uses of Patronage*, in: *American Political Science Review 73/1979* (Johnston, 1979)

Kadan, A./Pelinka, A., *Die Grundsatzprogramme der österreichischen Parteien*, St. Pölten 1979 (Kadan/Pelinka, 1979)

Kaufmann, R.K., *The Patron-Client Concept and Macro-Politics: Prospects and Problems*, in: *Comparative Studies in Society and History 16/1974* (Kaufmann, 1974)

Kok, F./Morscher, I., *Patronage in der Krise: Lehrervereine und parteipolitischer Proporz im Bundesland Salzburg*, in: *Österreichisches Jahrbuch für Politik 1986*, München/Wien 1987 (Kok/Morscher, 1987)

Konecny, A.K., *Politisches Verhalten und öffentliche Meinung in Österreich*, in: *Journal für angewandte Sozialforschung 14/1974* (Konecny, 1974)

Kraus, H., *"Untragbare Objektivität". Politische Erinnerungen 1917 bis 1987*, Wien 1988 (Kraus, 1988)

Landé, C.H., *Political Clientelism in Political Studies: Retrospect and Prospects*, in: *International Political Science Review 4/1983* (Landé, 1983)

Laver, M., *The Politics of Private Desires*, Harmondsworth 1981 (Laver, 1981)

Lehmbruch, G., *Proporzdemokratie*, Tübingen 1967 (Lehmbruch, 1967)

Lemarchand, R., *Comparative Political Clientelism: Structure, Process and Optic*, in: S.N. Eisenstadt/R. Lemarchand (eds.), *Political Clientelism, Patronage and Development*, Beverly Hills/London 1981 (Lemarchand, 1981)

Lemarchand, R./Legg, K., *Political Clientelism and Development: A Preliminary Analysis*, in: *Comparative Politics 4/1972* (Lemarchand/Legg, 1972)

Leser, N., *Gesellschaftsreform ohne Parteireform?*, in: *FS für Eduard März*, Wien 1973 (Leser, 1973)

Lively, J., *The Limits of Exchange Theory*, in: B. Barry (ed.), *Power and Political Theory*, London 1978 (Lively, 1978)

Lowi, Th. J., *At the Pleasure of the Mayor. Patronage and Power in New York City, 1898-1959*, New York 1964 (Lowi, 1964)

Mayer, K., *Landtagsabgeordnete in Oberösterreich,* Forschungsbericht, I. Institut für Soziologie, Hochschule für Sozial- und Wirtschaftswissenschaften, Linz 1973 (Mayer, 1973)

Merton, R.K., *Social Theory and Social Structure,* New York 1957 (Merton, 1967)

Michels, R., *Political Parties,* New York/London 1962 (Michels, 1962)

Mühlmann, W.E./Llaryora, R.J., *Klientschaft, Klientel und Klientelsystem in einer sizilianischen Agro-Stadt,* Tübingen 1968 (Mühlmann/Llaryora, 1968)

Müller, W.C., *Politische Kultur und Parteientransformation in Österreich,* in: *Österreichische Zeitschrift für Politikwissenschaft 13/1984* (Müller, 1984)

Müller, W.C./Hartmann, M., *Finanzen im Dunkeln: Aspekte der Parteienfinanzierung,* in: P. Gerlich/W.C. Müller (Hg.), *Zwischen Koalition und Konkurrenz. Österreichs Parteien seit 1945,* Wien 1983 (Müller/Hartmann, 1983)

Olson, Jr., M., *The Logic of Collective Action,* Cambridge, Mass. 1968 (Olson, 1968)

Ostrogorski, M., *Democracy and the Organization of Political Parties,* 2 Bände, New York 1902 (Ostrogorski, 1902)

Özbudun, E., *Turkey: The Politics of Political Clientelism,* in: S.N. Eisenstadt/R. Lemarchand (eds.), *Political Clientelism, Patronage and Development,* Beverly Hills/London 1981 (Özbudun, 1981)

Pasquino, G., *Italian Christian Democracy: A Party for all Seasons?,* in: P. Lange/S. Tarrow (eds.), *Italy in Transition,* London 1980 (Pasquino, 1980)

Plasser, F., *Parteien unter Streß,* Wien 1987 (Plasser, 1987)

Political Clientelism and Comparative Perspectives, Special Issue, *International Political Science Review 4/1983,* No. 4 (hg. von L. Graziano).

Powell, Jr., G.B., *Incentive Structures and Campaign Participation: Citizenship, Partisanship, Policy, and Patronage in Austria,* Paper prepared for the Conference on Political Participation, Leiden, March 17-22, 1972 (Powell, 1972)

Powell, J.D., *Peasant Society and Clientelist Politics,* in: *American Political Science Review 64/1970* (Powell, 1970)

Rhodes, A.A., *Material and Nonmaterial Incentives in Political Machines,* in: *Archives Européennes de Sociologie 25/1984* (Rhodes, 1984)

Roniger, L., *Clientelism and Patron-Client Relations: A Bibliography,* in: S.N. Eisenstadt/R. Lemarchand (eds.), *Political Clientelism, Patronage and Development,* Beverly Hills/London 1981 (Roniger, 1981)

Schlesinger, J.A., *Political Party Organization,* in: J.G. March (ed.), *Handbook of Organizations,* Chicago 1964 (Schlesinger, 1964)

Schlesinger, J.A., *On the Theory of Party Organization,* in: *Journal of Politics 46/1984* (Schlesinger, 1984)

Schmidt, St.W./Guasti, L./Landé, C.H./Scott, J.C. (eds.), *Friends, Followers and Factions. A Reader in Political Clientelism,* Berkeley 1977 (Schmid et al., 1977)

Scott, J.C., *Corruption, Machine Politics, and Political Change,* in: *American Political Science Review 63/1969* (Scott, 1969)

Scott, J.C., *Comparative Political Corruption,* Englewood Cliffs, N.J. 1972 (Scott, 1972)

Scott, J., *Patronage or Exploitation*, in: E. Gellner/J. Waterbury (eds.), *Patrons and Clients in Mediterranean Societies*, London 1977 (Scott, 1977a)

Scott, J.C., *Political Clientelism: A Bibliography Essay*, in: St.W. Schmidt et al. (eds.), *Friends, Followers and Factions. A Reader in Political Clientelism*, Berkeley 1977 (Scott, 1977b)

Secher, H.P., *Coalition Government: The Case of the Second Republic, American Political Science Review 52/1958* (Secher, 1958)

Shell, K.L., *The Transformation of Austrian Socialism*, New York 1962 (Shell, 1962)

Silberbauer, G., *Probleme der Parteimitgliedschaft in der ÖVP*, Wien 1968 (Silberbauer, 1968)

Sorauf, F.J., *Party Politics in America*, Boston 1980 (Sorauf, 1980)

Steel, B./Tsurutani, T., *From Consensus to Dissensus: A Note on Postindustrial Parties*, in: *Comparative Politics 18/1986* (Steel/Tsurutani, 1986)

Steininger, R., *Polarisierung und Integration*, Meisenheim am Glan 1975 (Steininger, 1975)

Stirnemann, A., *Die innerparteiliche Demokratie in der ÖVP*, in: *Österreichisches Jahrbuch für Politik 1979*, München/Wien 1980 (Stirnemann, 1980)

Theobald, R., *The Decline of Patron-Client Relations in Developed Societies*, in: *Archives Européennes de Sociologie 24/1983* (Theobald, 1983)

Urban, W./Zeidner, E., *Vom Nutzen und Umfang der Parteimitgliedschaft*, in: P. Gerlich/W.C. Müller (Hg.), *Zwischen Koalition und Konkurrenz. Österreichs Parteien seit 1945*, Wien 1983 (Urban/Zeidner, 1983)

Waldman, S.R., *Foundations of Political Action. An Exchange Theory of Politics*, Boston 1972 (Waldman, 1972)

Waterbury, J., *An Attempt to Put Patrons and Clients in Their Place*, in: E. Gellner/J. Waterbury (eds.), *Patrons and Clients in Mediterranean Societies*, London 1977 (Waterbury, 1977)

Weber, M., *Wirtschaft und Gesellschaft*, fünfte revidierte Auflage, Tübingen 1976 (Weber, 1976)

Weingrod, A., *Patrons, Patronage and Political Parties*, in: *Comparative Studies in Society and History 10/1968* (Weingrod, 1968)

Weingrod, A., *Patronage and Power*, in: E. Gellner/J. Waterbury (eds.), *Patrons and Clients in Mediterranean Societies*, London 1977 (Weingrod, 1977)

Zuckerman, A., *Political Clienteles in Power: Party Factions and Cabinet Coalitions in Italy*, Sage Professional Papers in *Comparative Politics 5/1975*, Beverly Hills/London 1975 (Zuckermann, 1975)

16

Party Funding in Austria

BARBARA WICHA

1. Introduction

More than a decade has elapsed since the passage of the "Federal Law Concerning the Duties, Funding and Campaigning of the Political Parties" ("Parties' Law"—Federal Law Gazette 404/1975 as amended) without any success in truly effectively coming to grips with those problems which led to its passage. Then and now, journalists and the public asked the question of the parties' actual worth to the nation. Then and now, complaints were made about the existing lack of transparency of the parties' budgets, the procurement of funds and their use. Then and now, the question was discussed as to what effect access to funds can have on the party landscape (petrification or dynamics) and on the opposition parties. Then and now, the justification of the expenses run up by the parties, particularly in election years, was questioned.

Scholarly attention to the topic has been relatively hesitant in Austria, not because the topic was not explosive enough, but because the most important requirement, the availability of reliable data, is for the most part lacking. Even today, much is based on estimations and projections, despite the stipulations for public accounting of the parties' financial management (cf. also Gerlich 1987, p. 84f.).

The perspectives, however, have changed between 1975 to 1988. If, at the time the Parties' Law was passed, the issue was to finally put an end to the parties' "free" (not constitutionally anchored) legal status, the question today focuses on justifying the extent of public subsidies made at the expense of the general public. Moreover, a documentable increase in voter abstinence in Austria has given more weight to the suspicion that parties financed out of state funds would become even less sensitive to the real problems of the electorate and thus lose an important basis for their very existence, activities and dealings. Thus, a discussion of party funding would lead to a discussion of alienation tendencies between voter and party as well.

One issue which has remained important is to what extent economic influence wielded by individual backers can be transformed into political power. In 1987/88, the matter of equal opportunity for the parties was broadened by that of equal opportunity for individual candidates due to a brief flame-up regarding a new regulation in the electoral law in the SPÖ-ÖVP coalition agreement. The existing proportional and list system was to be supplemented by directly elected candidates and single-member electoral constituencies, with corresponding electoral campaigns.

Control is another issue which has remained constant throughout the years. According to its most recent amendments, the Austrian Parties' Law provides for a public statement of accounts; fulfillment of this stipulation by the parties has, however, remained largely unsatisfactory, as will be shown. Furthermore, in Austria, public discussion in the media is limited by the fact that not only the Austrian Broadcasting Company (ORF) is state-owned (considered a "public responsibility"), but also because the print media landscape consists partly of party newspapers (also subsidized) and independent newspapers that have been partially silenced by government subsidies to the press. Thus, in Austria, even despite all other appeals for thrift, uneasiness about matching subsidies to rising prices has stayed within limits (cf. Naß-macher 1987, p. 118-120). If the parties' rising need for funds is explained by the increase in everyday party expenditures, a significant difference between the majority of European parties (including Austrian) and the North American parties and/or their funding comes to light. While the latter parties generally take "political finance" (or funding) to mean the financing of election campaigns, in most European countries, this term is a synonym for the procurement of funds for the continued operation of an ongoing organization with a permanent staff, permanent departments and its own media, and only secondarily for single political events such as elections.

An Austrian attempt to define "party funding," which should take this diversity into consideration includes, for example, "income in money and money's worth which a party receives as an organization, as well as its periodic and/or election-specific pattern of expenditure" (Kofler 1979, p. 43). Today, the effects of public party funding on the entire party system, its dynamics, transparency and its internal structures, but also on the relationship between party and voter, are central issues of recent comparative studies (cf. Alexander 1980 and 1984; Paltiel 1981; Naßmacher 1987 and Portelli 1988).

2. Justification for Public Party Funding
2.1. Reform of the Parties' Free Legal Status

Words devoted to this topic prior to the passage of the Parties' Law (Federal Law Gazette 404/1975) were marked by the fact that the issue of the legal personality of the political parties in Austria had by no means been clearly answered (cf. on development: Kostelka 1983, p. 37-59) and that consequently, arguments, if not justification, had to be sought for individual funding reforms, especially public funding.

For many authors, the date July 2, 1975, on which the National Assembly passed the "Federal Law Concerning the Duties, Funding and Campaigning of the Political Parties (Parties' Law)," after relatively short preliminary deliberation (Kostelka 1983, p. 40), was significant for two reasons. On the one hand, a basically explosive issue was tabled before a half-empty Parliament, after a discussion which lasted only one hour, and without so much as an attempt at rising public consciousness on a broad scale (cf. also Kofler 1981, p. 364). And yet, the issue was a long overdue reform of a condition unworthy of a democracy. Although it was undisputed that "political parties" de facto play an essential role in the nation, regardless of whether these be designated as such or as "election party" or "campaigning party," or whether as a "parliamentary party, faction, or club" (cf. Wicha 1975, p. 20f.; also Kostelka 1983, p. 40), the Austrian constitution had disregarded or placed minimal weight on this fact. Since 1975, the Parties' Law, and especially the constitutional provisions of Article 1, realize this "long demanded constitutional anchoring of the political parties as defined by their significance for a parliamentarian democracy" (Reports of the Constitutional Committee. 1680 of the enclosures, XIII. GP. 1). The actual significance of the Parties' Law, however, is not in anchoring the parties in the Constitution, but almost exclusively with regard to party funding (cf. also Müller/Hartmann 1983, p. 255).

2.2. The Search for Transparency

Prior to the parties' obtaining constitutional anchoring, the National Council Election Regulation (Art. 46, Section 4, NRWO 1971) already assumed that parties, if they take part in elections, must have funds at their disposal. This law also states that "election parties, at the same time as they submit their election lists, must refund the production costs of the official ballots in the amount of AS 6000.-" (cf. Kostelka 1983, p. 54). The actual issues were, and are, the source(s) of the parties' funds and the associated effects. Also somewhat opaque, both then and now, are the diversity and possible combinations of individual types of fund procurement.

2.2.1. The Diversity of Sources of Income

Large businesses, as the parliamentary parties with their permanent organizations must also be categorized, do not like anyone looking into their
books. Obtaining even a general overview of fund raising and/or the origin of
funds (cf. Müller/Hartmann 1983, p. 262) provides a sense of the difficulties
involved in attempting to determine the actual origin of the parties' budgets
(see graph 16.1 as an example for the year 1984; also Gerlich 1987, p. 85,
provides 1976 as an example).

While the literature does indeed cover one or another accounting system
for the parties' statements of accounts, actual reports are characterized by a
lack of transparency and comparability. The seven main income sources
mentioned by Beyme, namely membership dues, levies on parliamentary
deputies' paychecks, fund-raising drives, proceeds from organized political
events, publications and advertisements, income from party-owned enterprises and assets, donations and public subsidies, (1971, p. 138) are found in
the parties' accounting reports, but they are not truly comparable, as shown
in the examples in the Appendix. If the situation involving the gathering of
individual funding sources on a federal level resembles a puzzle, doing so
would only be half as difficult as tracing fund procurement at the state or
community level, not to mention gathering information about the party-oriented suborganizations which is not even recorded for accounting purposes.

Table 16.1
Party Funding: Fund-Raising

Self-Funding	Direct	Indirect
Self-Funding	Membership dues Party taxes Profits from party-run businesses	Services provided by members Accounting advantages from party-run businesses
Outside funding	Party funding according to the Parties' Law Funding by party clubs Subsidies from States and Municipalities Money Donations	Civic education Press subsidies for party newspapers Surplus payments for advertisements in party newspapers Donations in kind Broadcasting time

(Direct funding = monetary donations to the parties, Indirect funding = non-monetary, expenditure reducing activities which do not go directly to the parties)
(Continued)

Table 16.1 (Cont.)

Party Funding: Origins of Funds

Public Sector	Direct Party funding in accordance with the Parties' Law Club support State support Civic education Press subsidies for party newspapers Subsidies for party-oriented suborganizations Subsidies in kind from the public sector	Indirect Party taxes Share of money donations (tax reductions) Share of donations in kind (tax reductions) Advertisements in party newspapers (tax reductions)
Private Sector	Private money donations Private donations in kind Membership dues	

Graph 16.1
Distribution of the Individual Types of Income among the Parliamentary Parties in 1984

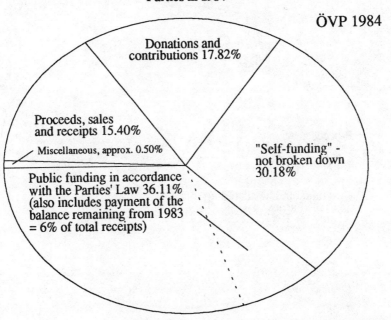

ÖVP 1984

Donations and contributions 17.82%

Proceeds, sales and receipts 15.40%

Miscellaneous, approx. 0.50%

"Self-funding" - not broken down 30.18%

Public funding in accordance with the Parties' Law 36.11% (also includes payment of the balance remaining from 1983 = 6% of total receipts)

362

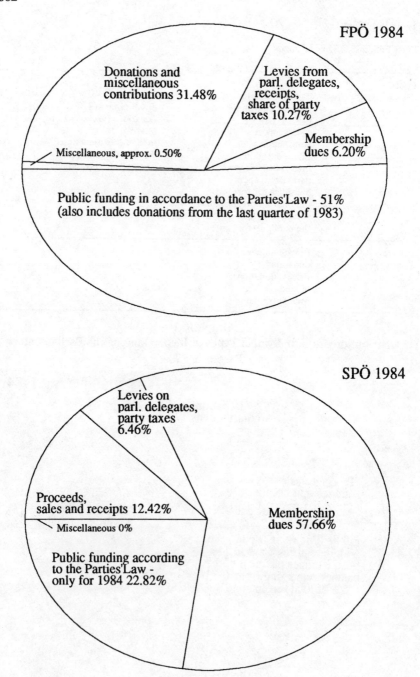

FPÖ 1984

Donations and miscellaneous contributions 31.48%

Levies from parl. delegates, receipts, share of party taxes 10.27%

Membership dues 6.20%

Miscellaneous, approx. 0.50%

Public funding in accordance to the Parties'Law - 51% (also includes donations from the last quarter of 1983)

SPÖ 1984

Levies on parl. delegates, party taxes 6.46%

Proceeds, sales and receipts 12.42%

Miscellaneous 0%

Public funding according to the Parties'Law - only for 1984 22.82%

Membership dues 57.66%

2.2.2 Phases and Forms of Public Funding

While the parties themselves gradually warmed up to the idea of federal party funding, if only for reasons of self-sufficiency (cf. Pelinka/Welan 1971, esp. p. 311-314; also Müller/Hartmann 1983, p. 266-269), the public had to be presented with examples from abroad supporting this model. Long before the passage of the Parties' Law, and even thereafter, sufficient public funds were at the parties' disposal, albeit under various designations. In reality, this is what makes federal funding so opaque and thus suspect (see Tables 198 to 200). The extent of federal grants, as summarized in the federal budget in Class 104, "Press and Party Subsidies," could give rise to the question of cost-performance ratios:

Budget	Total amount in Class 104
1984	217,615.000
1985	310,271.000
1986	319,909.000
1987	265,957.000
1988	244,680.000

By far the most serious problem, and the one least likely to be resolved, is that "the parliamentary parties are simultaneously beneficiaries and makers of the law" (Arnim v. 1983, p. 7). Even one year before final passage of the Parties' Law (cf. Wicha 1975, p. 51-53; see also Wimmer 1975, p. 6f.), they were already receiving the benefits of around AS 114 million (ibid). What the Parties' Law was to bring with it, though not of course with real success, was, at the very least, the public accounting of the types of party income and expenditures.

2.2.2.1 Review of the Development of Public Funding

After a discussion phase around 1963, during which the parliamentary clubs were already receiving their grants (Federal Law Gazette 286/1963), there followed a consolidation phase between 1967 and 1982. In Austria, in accordance with the West German model, public funds were used for the public relations work of the parliamentary factions (1967), aid for educational work by the party academies (1972) and the general funding of the parties and the press. Finally (1982), the members of the Federal Council, the Second Chamber of Parliament, were also included in the calculation of the particular faction's subsidies. A type of adjustment for inflation was achieved in the "Party Club Law," in that the amount of the 1982 grant (Federal Law Gazette 356/1982) was coupled to the incomes of certain income groups in these parliamentary offices; this method has also been applied to the party academies since 1985. Finally, the 1987 amendment to the Parties' Law (Federal Law Gazette 133/1987) provides for the grants to the parties to be adjusted according to the published consumer price index.

Indirectly, the parties are well served by the possibility of utilizing "paid political broadcasts" in the ORF, the Austrian state-owned broadcasting system. Furthermore, various grants to party-affiliated youth, student and research organizations must be included here. Such types of funding do not appear in the parties' accounting statements, while in truth providing a considerable source of relief to the party's coffers. In addition, it had already been a long-time practice in the states to award grants to state parliament clubs for educational work or public relations, but also explicitly as party funding (cf. Wicha 1975, p. 60), before the passage of provincial laws. In Austria, the possibilities of using donations to political parties as tax deductions and tax credits as is done in the U.S. are unknown (cf. Naßmacher 1987, p. 106).

The following is a more detailed presentation of the forms of party funding practiced in Austria.

2.2.2.2 Party Clubs in the National and Federal Councils

The "Party Club Law" (of Nov. 26, 1963, Federal Law Gazette 286/1963, re-published in Federal Law Gazette 156/1985) refers to state monies, initially only for party clubs of the National Council, but now also for those of the Federal Council. According to this law, party clubs generally have a right to reimbursement of costs (for the salaries for four "a" covenanted public officials, wage level 20, and four "d" covenanted public officials, wage level 21). In addition to this basic allowance, National Council and Federal Council clubs were entitled to funds amounting to the gross salaries of one or two covenanted public official(s) "a"/level 20 respectively, corresponding to the club's strength (for each group of 10 delegates started). Ninety percent of the basic allowance and the National Council share are booked for purposes of public relations work, which is defined in the 1985 Party Club Law as follows (Federal Law Gazette 156):

1. Letters and circulars from the representatives to the voters in their constituency;

2.   printed matter and brochures, with which the representative or the parliamentary clubs report on their parliamentary activities;
3.   official enquetes and events in which the public is informed about parliamentary activities.

The 1987 amendment evidently tends to take account of the smaller parties entering Parliament, providing for grants amounting to the annual gross salaries of four "a," wage level 20, covenanted public officials, and specifically due to those clubs that send representatives to committees. Furthermore, for clubs with more than 10 representatives, the grant now increases by two additional salaries of the same classification and wage level per each group of 20 representative started.

2.2.2.3 Subsidies for Political Educational Activities and Political Publications

In the discussion of party business management, the parties in Austria, as in the Federal Republic of Germany laid claim to their right to conduct political educational activities. Party academies were founded on the basis of the law covering subsidies for civic education in the fields of political parties, as well as political publications, and outfitted with public funds (Federal Law Gazette 272/1972 of July 9, 1972). While at that time, the political think tanks of the parliamentary parties obtained a basic allowance (in 1984, each party received AS 4 million) and subsidies corresponding to their proportional representation in Parliament, the Amendment in Federal Law Gazette 538/1984 once again formulated funding in terms of salaries, accordingly making such grants dynamic. "The basic allowance corresponds to the annual gross income of four full Austrian university professors with level 10 salaries, as well as six "b," wage level 20, covenanted public officials ... The club, as a legal entity, receives for each representative of that political party, an additional one-third of the above-mentioned annual gross salary of a full Austrian university professor." Thus, the Renner Institute (SPÖ), The Political Academy (ÖVP) and the Freedom Party's educational organization, were able to divide the following grants over the last few years. In 1972, at the time the law was introduced, the total sum was no more than 28.95 million Austrian shillings.

1984: AS 47.20 million
1985: AS 55.54 million
1986: AS 70.50 million
1987: AS 79.51 million
1988 budget: AS 79.51 million

2.2.2.4 Press Subsidies

Passage of the "Press Subsidy Law" (Federal Law Gazette 405/1975, on funding the press) took place at the same time as that of the Parties' Law. The former regulation was repeatedly the target of the non-party press, because for the most part, it benefits the basically non-profit party media in such a manner that, according to the chief editor of one of the so-called independent Austrian daily newspapers, the "Salzburger Nachrichten," "one (should) possess so much honesty to at least speak openly of party subsidies rather than a press subsidy" (Ritschel, in: the "Salzburger Nachrichten" of Dec. 7, 1984, p. 2). Such a statement is justified, since alone in 1982, party newspapers received around AS 28 million of the AS 77 million press subsidies, as well as a subsidy of AS 7.6 million for political publications (see Müller/Hartmann 1983, p. 259).

	1984	1985	1986	1987	1988 Budget
Press subsidy	80,675	125,675	122,533	58,174	44,437
Political publications	6,840	6,156	6,002	4,180	3,186
Special subsidies				27,160	20,704

2.2.3. The Black Boxes of "Miscellaneous" and "Donations"

To an even lesser extent than they do with public funding do the parties permit disclosure of the diverse patrons from whom they traditionally receive their existence, which is not always without strings attached. It is certainly no wonder that there is wide divergence in the estimates and projections, and that some authors in the course of the years have completely failed to look into this complex issue.

Again, it is not so much the actual amount that is problematic, but rather the uncertainty, the assumptions and conjectures that, to an unknown extent, "economic power can be transformed into political influence by way of contributions or loans to the parties" (Arnim v. 1983, p. 7). There has been absolutely no mention of transparency in the field of private or collective, at any rate non-federal, third-party funding. To what extent the Association of Austrian Industrialists not only provides financial support to the ÖVP, but also the FPÖ, could only be determined indirectly, even by Kofler (1981, p. 379); the degree of estimation necessary here is shown by the figures. "While the Austrian news magazine 'Trend' mentions AS 8 million going to the FPÖ per year, Kofler puts the lower limit at AS 43 million. The latter sum is calculated from the tax payments as determined on the basis of the 1975 amendment to the Austrian Federal Income Tax Law, and also does not appear unrealistic in comparison to older figures" (Müller/Hartmann 1983, p. 256). Similar difficulties, however, were faced by those who wanted to reveal the direct financial interrelationship between the Austrian Trade Union Federation (ÖGB) and the party landscape as well. To investigate the already mentioned third-party in-kind contributions to the political parties is like groping around in the dark; such "donations" (also known as "subsidies in kind") are made in the form of employment contracts, motor vehicles put at a politician's disposal and other "payments" in kind. Especially those funds that flow to the parties in a round-about manner via other organizations are well veiled; here it would also be necessary to include the suborganizations indirectly associated with the parties in the calculations, most of which were only estimates. It is very obvious, contrary to Naßmacher (1987, p. 119), that scandals brought to light by the media did not improve the atmosphere surrounding the parties. In spite of the Parties' Law, with all its controlling regulations, an in-depth look into that portion of the parties' income termed "donations" (in the monetary sense as well in money's worth) still remains hidden from the public eye to a large extent. Indirect fund procurement, whether in the form of "subsidies in kind" or as donations to party-oriented suborganizations, remains extremely difficult to determine. Nor, for obvious reasons, do such sources of income become superfluous after public subsidization of the parties was approved in 1975. "Partial financing with public funds has only increased the financial base of the parties, but still has not basically changed their methods for procuring funds. In conjunction with membership dues, real donations without return and real earnings from the operation of business enterprises, as well as inner-party levies (parliamentary delegates, managers and members of the parties' supervisory boards must contribute a percentage of their income to their party), an extensive indirect funding system had already developed before the 1975 Parties' Law" (Reiter 1981, p. 35). As a means of warding off corruption (or at best, reducing susceptibility to corruption), far more control was called for. So, for example, Pelinka (1981, p. 276) called for the mandatory registration of all individual donations over a certain amount and of all collective donations, independent of their amount, as well as for "round-about funding" (organizations that pass their funds on to parties).

Table 16.2
Direct Funding for Parties as per Article 2a and b of the Parties' Law between 1978 and 1986

	1978	1980	1984	1986
AS per vote	10,715854	11,750535	13,950611	17,389898
	Total No. of Votes 4,554,000. -	Total No. of Votes 4,680,708. -	Total No. of Votes 4,652,126. -	Total No. of Votes detto
ÖVP				
Votes	1,980,374	1,981,286	2,097,808	detto
Basic allowance	4,000,000. -	5,000,000. -	6,000,000. -	14,000,000. -
Party share/vote	21,221,398. -	23,281,171.20	29,265,701. -	36,480,667. -
Total ÖVP	25,221,398. -	23,231,171.20	35,265,701. -	50,480,667. -
SPÖ				
Votes	2,324,309	2,412,778	2,312,529	detto
Basic allowance	4,000,000. -	5,000,000. -	6,000,000. -	14,000,000. -
Party share/vote	24,906,955. -	28,351,432. -	32,261,190. -	40,214,643. -
Total SPÖ	28,906,955. -	33,351,432. -	38,261,190. -	54,214,643. -
FPÖ				
Votes	249,317	286,644	241,789	detto
Basic allowance	4,000,000. -	5,000,000. -	6,000,000. -	14,000,000. -
Party share/vote	2,671,644.50	3,368,220.30	3,373,104. -	4,204,636. -
Total FPÖ	6,671,644.50	8,368,220.30	9,373,104. -	18,204,636. -
Total:				
Basic allowance/Art.2(2)a	12,000,000. -	15,000,000. -	18,000,000. -	42,000,000. -
Difference/Art.2(2)b	48,800,000. -	55,000,800. -	64,900,000. -	80,900,000. -
(rounded)	60,800,000. -	70,000,800. -	82,900,000. -	122,900,000. -

Total: Basic allowance / Art. 2(2)a
Difference / Art. 2(2)b
(rounded)

2.2.4. The Transparency of Party Funds

Opinions clashed about the latter demand, not only due to the long strived for Law for Data Protection; Brünner, for example, felt that donations "up to a reasonable amount (must be) excepted from any mandatory registration requirements" (1981, p. 694). Disclosure of donations automatically necessitates taking into account the differences in how parties raise funds. Increased and stricter registration of donations would be tantamount to preferential treatment of those parties with a large proportion of self-funding. (See graph 16.1).

It is not merely the material basis that gives rise to concern, but also the fact that while government funding is supposed to reduce the discrepancies between the willingness of party sympathizers to help finance their party, and the ability of party leaders to raise funds, in reality, it widens this gap. It must, however, also be mentioned that some inner-party groups which possess particularly advantageous access to funds become increasingly independent of the main party, promoting the tendency to decentralize (and, of course, influencing the degree of inner-party participation).

In accordance with the Amendment published under Federal Law Gazette 538/1984, donations over AS 100,000.- to a party as a whole or to a party-oriented suborganization at the state, county or community level, must be separately listed in an appendix to that party's Statement of Account, whereby this list of donations must be presented to the president of the Federal Audit Office. The call for disclosure of particularly small donations does not stem from accounting practices but rather from a scandal, without which there would hardly have been a demand for individual disclosures of every donation over AS 10,000.- (the SPÖ's Notice of Motion from 1980, II-1474 of the supplements to the stenographic National Council Minutes, NR, XV.GP, 8/21/80, No.75/A). Brünner would only accept the mandatory disclosure of donations over certain amounts if party funding were also subject to stricter controls. He is thus one of the critics of excessive control and of "a complete integration of the political parties into the public sphere, whether through complete government party funding or whether through exaggerated mandatory disclosures and public control" (Brünner 1981, p. 694). When he speaks of a transparency of self-funding by the party, he not only means membership dues and party taxes, but also the income from party-owned businesses. This, then, not only includes "businesses that are managed by, but also those dominated by a party or party-affiliated suborganizations" (Brünner 1981, p. 695). With this species, there would be problems with transparency similar to those with the "private or semi-private enterprises working for and subsidized by the state which are eliminated from the accounts" (ibid). If there is indeed to be control, then the obligation for disclosure would also have to apply to such operations. Thus, Pelinka, from the perspective of obtaining more control and containing potential corruption, logically calls for : "1. Disclosure of the ownership relationships of all firms in which the parties and/or their affiliated suborganizations hold an interest, 2. Prohibiting the granting of public funds to operations that are directly or indirectly, entirely or partially owned by a party, or one of the party-affiliated suborganizations" (1981, p. 276).

2.3. Bringing Color to the Party Landscape

An appeal was made in 1975 for the introduction of a financial "shot in the arm" by the state on the basis of the unequal existential conditions of the individual parties. Thirteen years later, a similar argument was made (cf. Pinto-Duschinsky 1981, p. 4-6): there is an inequality between the individual parties' existential conditions, meaning that the system is basically unfair. In the interest of a living democracy and quasi-equality of instruments, the state would have to make additional resources available, especially to the opposition parties (cf. Wicha 1975, p. 90f.). There is a need for more effective parties, which carry out the duties put to them in a more professional manner and which, as parliamentary factions, manage the bureaucracy more effectively. For this reason, grants would have to be made in accordance with the responsibility, and from the parties' perspective, also sufficiently high. Such public grants could be made in the form of partial funding, i.e., in a reasonable relationship to other sources of income, and could ward off the threat of the parties' dependency on business enterprises, interest groups and lobbies (cf. Wicha 1975, p. 85). Furthermore, positive experience in other countries with such grants have been shown since the 1950s (cf. Wicha 1975, p. 75-82). Proponents of state party funding hoped to have found in it a means to prevent the "petrification" of the political landscape. The opposition argued with warnings of the splintering off and the boundless formation of new parties (cf. Wicha 1975, p. 230). The same argument was used by its supporters; state party funding would improve the start-up conditions for smaller and new groups, and enhance and vitalize the political spectrum. In view of the international experiences already mentioned, additional state funding was offered as a means of changing the status quo (ibid, p. 89) or feared as such, depending on the respective standpoint.

Correspondingly, those who observed a "petrification" of Austrian politics conceded that the Parliament obviously could not turn a deaf ear to these deliberations, and that not only the "established parties," but also those that had been even somewhat successful (1% of the votes in the National Council Election), should receive public grants, at least for the respective election year.

2.4. Increased Petrification?

It is mentioned in passing that practically all the arguments in favor of party funding at least partially with public monies are also used against the idea of state funding (cf. Pinto-Duschinsky 1981, p. 6-10). It has been stated, for example: "There is the danger that certain parties will be privileged and that others be discriminated against. State funding makes access difficult for small and new parties, which only receive public funds after an election, while the established parties already dispose of public funds received in advance of the elections. Thus, the thresholds of access rise in accordance with increased funding levels" (Arnim v. 1982, p. 7). Even if the conditions for the Federal Republic of German and Austria are not completely identical, analogies cannot be denied, either in theory or in practice.

No satisfactory solution has been found for the fact that very different levels of access to public funding exist for the governmental and the opposition parties. It is a fact "that those parties that serve as the power behind the throne have unlimited access to public resources, since funds which have been entrusted to the state organs to carry out public obligations to the public are placed at their disposal. Governmental public relations is the key term, since in this type of work, it is difficult to draw a clear boundary between legitimate information to the citizens on the part of the government and questionable party solicitation with unjustifiable use of public resources; a door is opened to the broad field of problematic financial privileges of the government party or parties" (Brünner 1981, p. 695). To prevent misunderstandings, these statements apply to government parties at the federal as well as state levels.

2.5. Control of Expenditures

The fact that public funds should only be allocated when the parties are also prepared "to keep exact records of how the funds are used" and to make these records available to the public, has been considered restrictive by some.

In the case of election costs, however, not only must accounting be carried out, but it is expected that such costs be kept as low as possible from the start, as provided in Article III of the Parties' Law. The purpose here is "to prevent the election campaign costs of the parties already in the National Council from becoming excessive during the National Council Election, despite an inherent interference in the principle of free election, and to provide a means of limiting and controlling these costs" (Kostelka 1983, p. 54). According to the figures published in the "Official Gazette of the Wiener Zeitung," campaign expenditures did not increase between 1975 and 1983, at least not with regard to the legally required disclosure period of five weeks prior to the election. "Thus, the election campaign costs of all three parties were approx. AS 60 million in 1975, approx. AS 64 million in 1979 and approx. AS 63 million in 1983, at least in the last five weeks prior to the election. This fact, and in some cases, the much higher estimates of actual election campaign costs, necessitate a critical evaluation of the published figures; this in turn implies that the legislator's second intention, namely to decrease campaign costs over the long term, has more or less failed" (Kofler 1985, p. 95). An amendment restricting National Council Election campaign costs according to the Parties' Law was passed in 1986 in the Federal Law Gazette as 553/1986. Deadlines were, however, shortened; a party's total campaign budget had to be made known to the commission five weeks prior to the election and published in the "Official Gazette of the Wiener Zeitung" four weeks before that.

Restrictions and self-limitation—yes or no? Despite everything, on the broad basis thoroughly typical of the Austrian political process, agreement was reached that the now constitutionally recognized parties would receive public funds officially and in accordance with a specific law, and would submit mandatory statements of account that were to be published no later than September 30 of the following year. In the Appendix, samples of the ÖVP, the SPÖ and the FPÖ Statements of Accounts from 1986 show that even after the points to be included in the accounting reports had been defined (in accordance with the amendments to the Parties' Law dated Dec. 16, 1982, Federal Law Gazette 643/1982, Federal Law Gazette 667/1983, and Federal Law Gazette 538/1984), such a report need not be particularly transparent. This lack of transparency is evident despite the fact that the amendment to the Parties' Law which called for the disclosure of donations exceeding AS 30,000.- (Federal Law Gazette 643/1982, Art. 5 and 6) provided hope for more exact accounting. A feasible alternative is provided by Italy, where parties are required to go into far more detail (See Appendix 6.3), thus permitting far better comparison than we now find in Austria (see Statements of Accounts / Party Income and Expenditure Sheets for 1983 and 1984 in the Appendix). We should, however, agree with Naßmacher, when he warns of the short preparation and disclosure time of two to three weeks after the end of the accounting year (cf. Naßmacher 1987, p. 118).

3. The Cost-Benefit Problem

There is hardly an area of society in which the "party as a business enterprise" has not played a role. To a far too great extent, in fact, according to most Austrians. In response to the question as to who should have more or less influence on Austrian politics, the following responses were given (cf. Ucakar 1985, p. 534, Table 5.2.-7):

47%   the voter should have more influence
1%   the voter should have less influence
8%   the parties should have more influence
24%   parties should have less influence
       (remainder undecided)

What is also lacking is obviously the willingness to recognize the legitimacy of the parties (ibid, p. 539). A question which becomes more important is the extent to which the Austrians would be prepared, in the long run, to fund "their" parties with membership dues, the most natural expression of support. On the one hand, there could be a party crisis, or at least partial erosion of the parties (Beyme 1983, p. 250), and on the other, mass parties. It is certainly justified, in view of the unusually high party density in Austria as compared to the rest of Europe, to state that "great importance is to be given this source of funds in Austria" (Pelinka 1981, p. 267). For most authors, however, it was, and is, also a problem to produce a performance structure which is at least partially comparable to quantitatively measurable monetary funds (as provided by the accounting statements). For example, can recruitment or communication functions be sufficiently quantified to express them in monetary terms? If we are only speaking of quantity, can the motives and ulterior motives associated with payment of membership dues be irrelevant to the recipient? Or is the alleged Strauss quotation provided by Beyme true, in which the parties "don't give a hoot why the voters vote for their party" (1983, p. 247)? Can we agree with Beyme, who continues to speak of the growth of the parties' functions, i.e., the power of patronage and the recruitment of elites, "without this being deemed positive by the Left or Right" (1983, p. 250)?

Or is it closer to the truth when Norbert Leser counts patronage among the peculiarities of the Austrian political system? "This means that joining a party establishes the prerequisite for favors to which one actually has a constitutional right as a citizen. ... People are not taught democracy or political consciousness, but in reality, are taught opportunism" (Leser 1985, p. 88f.). The idealistic value of participation, of being able to play a role in creating or developing something, to realize oneself, to experience politics first hand, would indubitably be a reward which would encourage party funding. Beyme takes a very critical standpoint: "The normative right of the transmission paradigms was disclosed in a likable manner, but analytically, disguised in an alarming one. Participation was categorized as one of the productive forces (...), contrary to numerous warnings of realistic democratic and party theories, without a realistic awareness that this commodity would hardly be pursued as emphatically by the majority as would capital, labor or knowledge" (1983, p. 249). The ways and means, however, in which Austrian election campaigns, for example, are managed and funded, also the 1986 Federal Presidential Election, could provide the sceptics food for thought (cf. on the attractiveness of the Green alternatives: Plasser 1985, among others).

Whether the two consequences of public funding listed below (according to Reiter 1981, p. 42f.), in light of what has just been said, are always considered beneficial, desirable or even useful, by the parties, remains to be seen.

— Mandatory disclosure of party funding of the entire party organization, including its holding interest or participating in business enterprises, and
— A certain measure of inner-party democracy which would go beyond the shows of democracy staged at well-prepared party conventions and guarantee the party members' participation in the development of political objectives.

Despite every attempt to promote the parties in a national manner, doubt must be expressed as to the applicability of the cost-benefit arguments. On the one hand, this is because the citizen's benefit from the mere existence of a large party cannot be quantified. On the other hand, it is also very difficult, or even impossible, to try to include non-monetary forms of support in an analysis of expenditures (cf. Kofler 1979, p. 41).

4. Focal Point and Expectation: Fighting Corruption
4.1. A Triple Objective

The Parties' Law and the instrument of a regulated, if possible, balanced mix of party funding, should clearly serve as a catchall for many other topics in political discussions: for an increase in participation, for an increase in involvement and inner-party democracy, for a "clean" political landscape, for better performance of tasks, and for more dynamism in the system. On the one hand, that sounds relatively naive, but nevertheless shows the importance of funding. Even with more emphasis placed on the monetary effects of public subsidies and donations, there are still four objectives to be found in most countries:

"— Prevention (limitation, elimination) of corruption
— Controlling (preventing, disclosing) influence
— Creating equal financial opportunities
— Keeping expenditures under control" (Naßmacher 1982, p. 4).

In Austria, as elsewhere, a (party's) law and a mixed funding system are expected to produce a positive change on three levels simultaneously: in the political culture, in the institutions and institutional rules, and in the duties.

Since the first phases of scholarly concern with party funding in Austria (in chronological order, Pelinka/Welan 1971; Wicha 1975 and 1976; Wimmer

1975; Pelinka 1978; Kofler 1979 and 1981, among others, should be mentioned here), the focal points of the discussion have changed significantly. From the hope of increased participation, the emphasis has shifted to an increase in institutionalized control to suggested measures to combat corruption. Thus, the parties and their funding efforts were no longer placed in the foreground with regard to quantity but rather to quality (cf. also Wicha 1980; Kofler 1981; Khol 1981; Pelinka 1981; Kadan 1981 and Reiter 1981; Müller/ Hartmann 1983; Kofler 1985, and with emphasis on the quantitative, descriptive analysis of the situation in the states, see Dachs 1986, as well as Naßmacher 1987).

4.1.1. Changes in Attitude

Decision-makers were encouraged by the hopes they placed in the effectiveness of legal regulations, even though in retrospect, in light of the scandals which have taken place since the beginning of the Eighties, these expectations may not have been fulfilled that completely. As late as 1979, Widder stated: "The National Council, by legally regulating the financial resources and the flow of money within the parties and having these examined according to the exactly defined criteria of the law, has created a reliable, transparent and controllable environment, which it can control and influence more or less strongly according to need, for example through additional regulations and controls, also via public politics and other means. Thus, the National Council is able to maintain specialized environmental relationships to the political parties in this way, and can devote itself to other problems more objectively because it can assume that it will not be threatened by any additional problems from that side, either in the form of party funding scandals or other blatant or hidden demands for money by the parties ..." (p. 307f.).

What has remained wishful thinking despite all commitments and good intentions is a positive change in the broad but elusive area of political culture. "The brightening of the politician's darkened image and his winning credibility require political-cultural efforts to raise political morale, in addition to the already mentioned political virtues, foresight, perseverance and willingness to take initially unpopular steps, must not be forgotten. A political shot in the arm with a few "unpolitical" politicians (like Dries van Agt in the Netherlands, or Peter Glotz in the Federal Republic of Germany) would be precisely what the doctor ordered for the established Austrian parties—not naive crackpots, but rather (partial) non-conformists with the ability to view their roles in a self-critical manner. But more is needed than an improvement in the political culture. ..." (Mantl 1981, p. 216).

4.2 Institutional Points of Departure
4.2.1 Disclosure of Donations: Strict Becomes Half-Hearted

At the same time and with the same content as the inner-Austrian discussion of constitutional reform, which focus on improved transparency for
the citizen, additional opportunities for control within the political bureaucratic system, and more firmly established game rules, regulations demanding
more disclosure and tranparency are being formulated. Incompatibility rules
are made, a reduction in political immunity is being demanded, as is the disclosure of politicians' financial statements, the reduction in accumulation of
offices and a revision of politicians' incomes and fringe benefits. Why positions are conferred and why they are sought become a matter of interest.
Moreover, one is increasingly sensitive to the motives of private or collective
donors.

In such a climate of mistrust, it is only natural to associate concepts like
bribery, black market money and corruption with catchwords like "party
funding" and "party donations." As a consequence of inner-Austrian turbulence, disclosure regulations should be particularly strict. As late as 1980, all
donations over AS 10,000.- were supposed to be recorded individually. In accordance with the Dec. 16, 1982 amendment to the Parties' Law (Federal
Law Gazette 643/1982), donations in excess of AS 30,000.- and their donors
were to be disclosed in a separate list of donations. The legislators and the
amendment's beneficiaries were one and the same, and thus logically chose
to distance themselves; if a donor refused to allow his name to be published,
the donation would have to be returned. The first report deadline as set by
the law (Federal Law Gazette 643/1982, Art. I, Parag. 7-10 of the amended
Parties' Law and Art. II, Federal Law Gazette 643/1982), went by unheeded.
One-third of the National Council delegates contested the amendment, so
that it was subjected to examination by the Constitutional Court. The deadline for presenting the first statements of account was postponed until 1985
(amendment in Federal Law Gazette 667/1983). Finally, as a constitutional
provision in the amendment to the Parties' Law in Federal Law Gazette
538/1984, the President of the General Auditing Office was delegated the
task of receiving and maintaining donor lists and, at the request of the respective party, publically establishing that everything had been duly declared.
The ceiling, however, over which a declaration has to be made, was raised
tenfold above the initial sum; only for amounts exceeding AS 100,000.- is a
detailed declaration disclosing donor and amount mandatory.

Raising the ceiling in this manner was justified by the fact that no one
would make a donation to a party "if he were then to be pillarized for it.
Protecting the privacy of the donor" (Graff 1985, p. 20) is of the utmost importance, although control is certainly necessary. The donation lists were to

be drawn up for the first time in 1985 (Art. V, Federal Law Gazette 538/1084), whereby their comparability left something to be desired.

4.2.2. No Indication of Limiting Expenditures

With the increasing criticism of the established parties and the skepticism about justification of their involvement in all facets of life, as well as a new positive attitude toward saving, at least propagated in other areas, criticism of the parties' expenditures, particularly those contributed by the taxpayer in the form of government funding, is also on the rise. Federal funding has at least quintupled in relation to the number of eligible voters in Austria since 1970 (according to Kofler 1985, p. 107), and has not decreased in any way, but rather has become much more dynamic with regard to grants to the parliamentary clubs and the party academies. Critics do not view public "subsidies for democracy" (Naßmacher 1982, p. 17) as such as being problematic, but instead, are concerned about the changing relationships among funds, the relationship of funds to performance, and between funds and their intended or coincidental application, for under certain circumstances, even in increase in funds would be supported (see ibid., p. 18).

It looks particularly bad that precisely those laws with which the parties increase the share of public donations to themselves, are passed unanimously, and at best with the comment that democracy and its practice do have their price. If direct payments of public funds to the parties are accepted, then the "development in the direction of state parties" (according to Zundel in Kofler 1985, p. 107) is seen to be moving ahead in leaps and bounds.

When the Parties' Law was passed in 1975, the parliamentary parties each received a basic allowance of AS 4 million. Then, the parties were awarded an additional sum depending on the number of votes polled in the 1975 National Council Election in the following manner: SPÖ–AS 22.5 mil., ÖVP–AS 17 mil., FPÖ–2 mil. In 1978, the basic allowance remained AS 4 million per party. After the 1979 amendment to the Parties' Law (Federal Law Gazette 569/1979), however, this basic allowance was raised to AS 5 million per party, the SPÖ receiving an additional AS 23,804,658, the ÖVP an additional grant of AS 19,386,576 and the FPÖ an additional AS 2,804,767. The amendment in the Federal Law Gazette 356/1982, passed July 1, 1982, increased the basic allowance to AS 6 million, and as of the amendment published in Federal Law Gazette 538/1984, the parties each receive a basic allowance of AS 14 million.

378

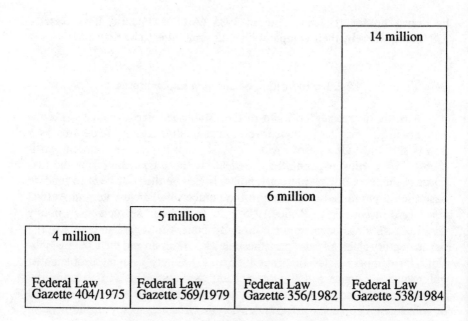

Graph 16.2: The Developments of Direct Public Funding as Foreseen in the
Parties' Law from 1975 to 1986

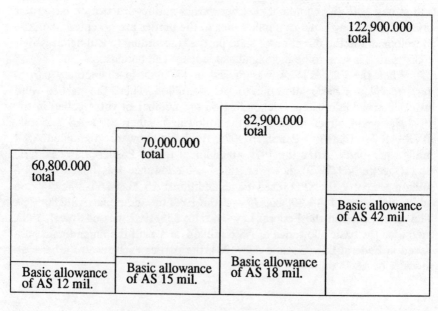

Graph 16.3: Total "Grants to Political Parties"

In the Federal Budget for 1986 (Federal Law Gazette 1/1986) of Dec. 17, 1985, a total of AS 122,900,000 were allocated to the parties under the classification "Grants to Parties" (Class 1043), AS 125,675,000 as "Press Subsidies" (Class 1041), AS 6,156,000 as "Public Relation Subsidies" (Class 1040) and AS 55,540,000 as "Grants for Party Educational Work." An increase in the last named category of AS 14,786,000 over that in 1985 brings up the total amount of grant money available for "Party and Press Subsidies" (Class 104) equal to AS 325,057,000, or about AS 15 mil. more than in 1985. For 1987, this grant complex was budgeted at AS 265,957,000 and for 1988, put at AS 244,680,000.

The grant situation is similar for the states. Even though the amount of party funding may differ significantly among the individual states (according to Dachs, 1986, p. 453), it is possible to determine an overall doubling of grant money in a period of only 6 years. The basis for calculation was the share of public funding per eligible voter between 1979 and 1985. Exceptions to this generalization are provided by Upper Austria, which provided AS 92.80 per voter in 1979 and only somewhat more in 1985 (AS 95.40), and Tyrol, which showed an increase in grants from around AS 50 per voter to AS 60. Vorarlberg showed an even greater discrepancy; there, public funding per eligible voter tripled over the 6-year period (cf. Dachs 1986, p. 452).

4.3. Money and Regulation of Activities

A question posed by many authors, even though truly satisfactory replies are not forthcoming, concerns the possible limitation of the parties' spheres of activity. How much remains from the Leibholz concept today, that "only the parties have the possibility of uniting millions of voters in geographically extensive areas (as opposed to city states) into groups capable of political action" (according to Ucakar 1985, p. 569), and thus become a type of surrogate for direct democracy? The more the traditional parties defend their umbrella purvues, without simultaneously providing a guarantee for truly being able to solve the problems of their constituencies, the more the uneasiness toward the parties grows (cf. Plasser/ Ulram 1982). "An extensive understanding of politics, hypertrophic organizational practices and a history of a servile mentality have led to an exceptionally high degree of political alienation in Austria. The pronounced feeling of helplessness on the part of the voter corresponds to an equally marked distrust of the political system's central institutions" (Plasser 1985, p. 136). The interrelationship of party and economy, without the former really being able to provide solutions to the voters' existential problems (unemployment, environmental crises, etc.), makes the established political groups and organizations even less transparent, and at the same time, less attractive. For these reasons, the voters' willingness to accept alternatives has increased (cf. Plasser/Ulram 1985). It has also been noticed that more and more voters favor an extension of the party spectrum as well (ibid, p. 136f.).

More self-dicipline with regard to taking on tasks on the part of the parties would also be advisable, not solely due to the fact that an excess of activities and duties is driving the parties to the limit of their own capabilities. As viewed from a perspective of democratic theory, it is also problematic that parties justify their needs for funding by citing the tasks which they assign themselves, since it is the parties themselves that approve additional fund allocations.

The Austrian Parties' Law and its amendments do not include anything about the duties or responsibilities of the parties, except that they "are to play a role in the development of political objectives." The prerequisites for fulfilling this task are party platform, personnel and certain rules. The Parties' Law, however, does not seem the least bit interested in such factors. The only disclosure required of the parties is that of funds. Nor is interest shown for the transparency of the inner-party structures and processes, party platform or of options for membership participation. Similarly, there is no mention made that fund allocations would tie into particular inner-party structures. For a very simple reason, one could agree with Kofler when he states that the present form of funding for the large parties has a tendency to be hostile to participation (1985, p. 106). With an already traditional lack of business knowledge common in large segments of the population, for which the school system is not unjustly blamed, and Austrian-style political education did little to improve, only a small circle is familiar with and able to comprehend party funding at all, not to mention the fact that hardly anyone knows their way around the budget, the allocation of funds or around such fine differentiations as "party-owned enterprises." Only in extreme cases, above all those involving blatant corruption (often supported by the media), is the party financial management a subject of discussion, even within the party's rank and file. Here, as elsewhere, the following holds true in putting reforms into effect: wherever pressure from the party rank and file or from "outside" (media, oppositional parties, the public) is lacking, there is no necessity for a change in behavior or procedures. According to the present state of affairs, "party leadership and managers of party-oriented suborganizations unfortunately do not have to consider whether they want to stay with the almost re-privatization of public funds, or whether they should in some respects take a major step and consciously use the instrument of party subsidizing for structural reform and in strengthening the political system's democratic institutions" (Uwe Schleth 1973, after Pelinka 1981, p. 278, Note 30).

5. Is There an Alternative to Resignation?

Almost fifteen years of the Parties' Law, and the first steps toward actually taking the order for transparency and open statements of account truly seriously, cannot disguise the fact that the present situation of the parties is unsatisfactory with regard to the subject of funding. At least once a year, in connection with the drawing up and debate of the budget, the media should take up the topic on a federal and state level, and inquire as to the justification of funds employment, while paying particular attention to the use of public funds.

The negative undertone that is almost always audible does not least of all come from the gap between the use of funding and returns in performance, which is not easy to prove on a quantitative basis, but also from the tense situation produced by the schism between appeals for thrift in all other sectors and the government's indefatigable spending spree in funding the parties.

While the parties are legally and formally obligated to provide statements of account, a limitation to expenditures, including those for election campaigns, is not foreseen. Regulating income (with the corresponding mandatory registration of donations and disclosure of ownership relationships, participation and indirect funding of the parties), only makes sense in connection with control, and above all, in limiting party expenditures. This would also be "desirable from the standpoint of susceptibility to corruption—parties could be innoculated against this disease by limiting their presently boundless financial requirements" (Pelinka 1981, p. 277). What equally upsets the critics is the fact that the allocation of funds is coupled with innumerable rituals and formal conditions (electoral success, etc.), while in reality, no influence is exerted on inner-party democracy or the democratic game rules (cf. Pelinka, ibid.). If the suggestion made by the political parties, particularly during fund-raising drives, holds true, namely that their political success is partially, if not entirely, dependent on the amount of funds available, then the suspicion arises that competition between the parties has, at least to some extent, shifted to the level of fund procurement. Thus, the "meta-level of fund procurement" (Müller/Hartmann 1983, p. 279) occasionally is granted more significance than the preparedness and capabilities of the parties to discover their own limitations and to completely exhaust the present problem-solving capacity with brainpower and manpower.

Studies show that while an increase in federal funding enhances the independence of financially strong groups, it also serves to distance the party leadership even further from the rank and file. This appears to me to be one of the most significant weaknesses of the present funding structure. Ordinary party members become less important for the party budget and party leadership, while party platforms and personnel policy decreasingly turn to the rank and file, instead directing their activities at independent voters or "important" donors. While the last named continue to exert their control over the party budget management (not always recognizable from outside the party), the members have largely waived this right. This eliminates at least one source of pressure acting within the party to strengthen the inner-party formation of political objectives from bottom to top.

Even though a strengthening of identification with the movement or party on the part of the members (through funding) does not prevent some squabbling, limited funds and control from within make the non-established parties more inventive in the search for less cost-intensive strategies. Therefore, the latter parties would be strategically better armed at that moment at which they come into public funding resources.

This article should show that, despite the Parties' Law, the seeds of reform with regard to party funding have not yet come to maturity. Above all, the beginnings are to be continued in their effecting inner-party control and the formulation of political objectives. Theory and practice, however, will not be able to avoid re-focusing their interest from the income side to the expenditure side of the balance sheet. Were it possible to make the income-expenditure statements of the parties and political movements truly comparable, a major step would be taken toward increased transparency, and possibly also toward a more dynamic party landscape.

6. Appendix

Table 16.3
6.1 Income Received by the Parliamentary Parties According to the 1983 and 1984 Statements of Accounts (in absolute figures)

Type of Income	ÖVP 1983	ÖVP 1984	SPÖ 1983	SPÖ 1984	FPÖ 1983	FPÖ 1984
From public funds (acc'd. to Parties' Law)	29,837,228.70	42,665,227.50	34,897,329.20	38,261,192.40	9,043,314.25	11,553,071.25
(Subsidized monthly publications)	37,148.30	38,910.50				
"Self-Funding"	36,655,095.27	35,675,331.87				
Membership dues			93,233,254.65	96,653,537.20	1,108,357.26	1,405,684.52
Levies on parl.delegates					1,992,916.59	2,327,179.45
Returns on assets						
National Council Election Fund or dues received from party organizations and clubs			77,482,700. -	10,400,000. -		
Share of party taxes			658,963.18	440,100. -		
Capital proceeds			1,083,856.74	1,024,439.77		
Proceeds, sales and receipts						
Interest, discounts	4,643,942.56	18,192,546.91	16,534,142.38	20,828,245.84		
Donations / grants	698,207.46	197,193.94	511,850.94	4,674.28		
Miscellaneous income	6,426,669.40	21,054,283.96	269,847.03	21,734. -	2,418,334.10	7,129,744. -
Loans	279,298.57	346,352.13			179,553.38	235,479.85
Reserves					2,190,318.92	
Outside funding	46,506,356.44x)			8,317,543.96	11,540,600.97	
Total income	125,083,946.70xx)	118,169,846.81x)	232,989,488.08	167,633,923.49	28,473,395.47	22,651,159.07

x) Not listed as "Income" on ÖVP Statement of Accounts
xx) According to the Statement, total income only came to AS 78,577,590.26
xxx) Balance of AS 44,488,937.99 for loans and formation of reserve funds
Note: Only the SPÖ listed the annual share of public grants for 1984 without carrying over the remainder from 1983;
ÖVP, 1984 (without remainder): AS 35,265,701.-
FPÖ, 1984 (without remainder): AS 9,373,104.-

384

Table 16.4
6.1.1 Income Received by the Parliamentary Parties According to the 1983 and 1984 Statements of Accounts (in percent)

Type of Income	ÖVP 1983 (Statement)	ÖVP 1983 (Calculation)	ÖVP 1984	SPÖ 1983	SPÖ 1984	FPÖ 1983	FPÖ 1984
From public funds (acc'd. to Parties' Law) Subidized monthly publications	37.97%	23.85%	36.11%	14.98%	22.82%	31.76%	51.00%
"Self-funding"	0.05%	0.03%	0.03%				
Membership dues	46.65%	29.30%	30.18%				
Levies on parl. delegates				40.01%	57.66%	3.89%	6.20%
Returns on assets						7.00%	10.27%
National Council Election Fund				33.25%	6.20%		
Dues from party organizations				0.28%	0.26%		
Share of party taxes Capital proceeds				0.47%	0.61%		
Proceeds, sales and receipts	5.91%	3.71%	15.40%	7.09%	12.42%		
Interest, discounts	0.89%	0.56%	0.16%	0.22%	0.003%		
Donations/grants	8.18%	5.14%	17.82%	0.12%	0.01%	8.49%	31.48%
Miscellaneous	0.36%	0.22%	0.29%			0.63%	1.04%
Loans						7.69%	
Reserves, outside funds		37.18%		3.57%		40.53%	
	100.01%	99.99%	99.99%	99.99%	99.983%	99.99%	99.99%

Remarks:

1) Percentual discrepancies due to rounding up or down

2) Included in the 1983 grants in accordance with the Parties' Law are: Remainder carried over from 1982 and 1st-3rd quarters of 1983 (explicit listing by the ÖVP and the FPÖ!) Included in 1984 grants: Remainder carried over from 1983 and the 1st-4th quarter of 1984 (explicit listing by the FPÖ; the ÖVP Total Amount and Remainder carried over from 1983.

3) To facilitate comparability with the SPÖ and FPÖ figures, the 1983 calculated amounts for the ÖVP including reserves and outside funds were placed in the second column. Column 1 ("Statement") is based on the figures provided in the Statement of Accounts and total income of AS 78,577,590.26.

Table 16.5

6.1.2 Expenditures by the Parliamentary Parties According to the 1983 and 1984 Statements of Accounts

Type of Expenditure	ÖVP		SPÖ		FPÖ	
	1983	1984	1983	1984	1983	1984
Election campaign promotion						
Mar. 21-Apr.24,'83	28,575.731,-	-				
Nat.Council Election						
Campaign grants	63,065,822.01	42,216,622.28	55,151,077.80	49,489,300.27	10,988,094.31	117,036.71
Party activities and events			147,134,376.04	78,183,141.22	227,952.73	1,297,505.79
P.r. costs (without personnel costs) incl. press circulars, monthly					3,652,442.26	4,613,744.6
publications and press conferences				4,197,890.44	3,608,961.64	
Personnel costs	28,447,842.28	25,845,633.77	27,092,448.42	34,508,362.43	5,236,011.94	5,703,607.-
Rents	4,229,360.89	4,557,341.25	2,822,110.91	3,422,234.75	1,440,981.05	1,475,392.65
Personnel and inkind costs for administration minus third-party expenditures						
International activities	765,190.52	1,061,311.52			572,099.36	775,597.37
Miscellaneous expenditures Acquisitions						
Increase to reserve funds or partial coverage of outside funds/loans	-	44,488,937.99 x)	-	1,223,161.31	-	62,187.75
Total expenditures	125,083,946.70	118,169,846.81 x)	232,989,488.08	167,633,923.49	28,473,395.47	22,651,159.07

x)   De facto only AS 73,680,908.82 according to Statement of Accounts; here also including formation of reserves

Bibliography

Arnim, Hans Herbert von, *Aktuelle Probleme der Parteienfinanzierung. Stellungnahme zum Entwurf eines Gesetzes über die Neuordnung der Parteienfinanzierung vom 21.6.1983* (BT-Drucks. 10/183), Wiesbaden 1983 (Arnim, 1983)

Beyme, Klaus von, *Interessengruppen in der Demokratie*, 3. Auflage, München 1971 (Beyme, 1971)

Beyme, Klaus von, *Theoretische Probleme der Parteienforschung*, in: *Politische Vierteljahresschrift 3/1983* (Beyme, 1983)

Brünner, Christian, *Zur Analyse individueller und sozialer Bedingungen von Korruption*, in: Christian Brünner (Hg.), *Korruption und Kontrolle*, Wien 1981 (Brünner, 1981)

Busek, Erhard, *Die Frage nach der Alternative oder: der Zustand der Demokratiekritik in Österreich*, in: *Wort und Wahrheit 3/1973* (Busek, 1973)

Dachs, Herbert, *Öffentliche Finanzierung in den österreichischen Bundesländern*, in: *ÖJP 1985*, München/Wien 1986 (Dachs, 1986)

Graff, Michael, *Überlegungen zur Parteienfinanzierung aus öffentlichen Mitteln*, in: *ÖMH 1/1985* (Graff, 1985)

Kadan, Albert, *Parteienfinanzierung in Österreich und der Bundesrepublik Deutschland*, in: *Sozialwissenschaftliche Schriftenreihe des Instituts für politische Grundlagenforschung 1/1981* (Kadan, 1981)

Khol, Andreas, *Krise der Parteien—Krise der Demokratie*, in: *ÖJP 1980*, München/Wien 1981 (Khol, 1981)

Kofler, Anton, *Parteienfinanzierung und deren Auswirkungen auf innerparteiliche Strukturen, dargestellt am Beispiel der ÖVP*, Diplomarbeit, Universität Innsbruck 1979 (Kofler, 1979)

Kofler, Anton, *Parteienfinanzierung und deren Auswirkungen auf innerparteiliche Strukturen, dargestellt am Beispiel der ÖVP*, in: *ÖJP 1980*, München/Wien 1981 (Kofler, 1981)

Kofler, Anton, *Parteiengesellschaft im Umbruch*, Wien 1985 (Kofler, 1985)

Kostelka, Peter, *Politische Parteien in der österreichischen Rechtsordnung*, in: Oswin Martinek u.a. (Hg.), *Arbeitsrecht und soziale Grundrechte. Festschrift für Hans Floretta zum 60. Geburtstag*, Wien 1983 (Kostelka, 1983)

Leser, Norbert, *Parteienkrise oder Demokratiekrise? Das wachsende Unbehagen: Immer mehr Probleme, immer weniger Lösungen*, in: *Conturen 19A/1985* (Leser, 1985)

Mantl, Wolfgang, *Korruption und Reform im österreichischen politischen System*, in: Christian Brünner (Hg.), *Korruption und Kontrolle*, Wien 1981 (Mantl, 1981)

Müller, Wolfgang C./Hartmann, Martin, *Finanzen im Dunkeln: Aspekte der Parteienfinanzierung*, in: Peter Gerlich/Wolfgang C. Müller (Hg.), *Zwischen Koalition und Konkurrenz. Österreichs Parteien seit 1945*, Wien 1983 (Müller/Hartmann, 1983)

Naßmacher, Karl-Heinz, *Öffentliche Rechenschaft und Parteienfinanzierung. Erfahrungen in Deutschland, Kanada und in den Vereinigten Staaten*, in: *aus politik und zeitgeschichte, 14-15/1982* (Naßmacher, 1982)

Naßmacher, Karl-Heinz, *Öffentliche Parteienfinanzierung in Westeuropa: Implementationsstrategien und Problembestand in der BRD, Italien, Österreich und Schweden*, in: *PVS 1/1987* (Naßmacher, 1987)

Pelinka, Anton, *Der Zustand der Demokratie in Österreich*, in: *Wort und Wahrheit, 3/1973* (Pelinka, 1973)

Pelinka, Anton, *Parteienfinanzierung im Parteienstaat*, in: *ÖJP 1977*, München/Wien 1978 (Pelinka, 1978)

Pelinka, Anton, *Parteienfinanzierung und Korruption*, in: Christian Brünner (Hg.), *Korruption und Kontrolle*, Wien 1981 (Pelinka, 1981)

Pelinka, Anton/Welan, Manfried, *Demokratie und Verfassung in Österreich*, Wien/Frankfurt/Zürich 1971 (Pelinka/Welan, 1971)

Pinto-Duschinsky, Michael, *British Political Finance 1830-1980*, Washington/London 1981 (Pinto-Duschinsky, 1981)

Plasser, Fritz, *Die unsichtbare Fraktion. Struktur und Profil der Grün-Alternativen in Österreich*, in: *ÖJP 1984*, München/Wien 1985 (Plasser, 1985)

Plasser, Fritz/Ulram, Peter A., *Unbehagen im Parteienstaat*, Wien 1982 (Plasser/Ulram, 1982)

Plasser, Fritz/Ulram, Peter A., *Entsteht ein neues Parteiensystem?*, in: *ÖMH 2/1985* (Plasser/Ulram, 1985)

Reiter, Erich, *Vorschläge zur Neuregelung der Parteienfinanzierung in Österreich*, in: *Sozialwissenschaftliche Schriftenreihe des Instituts für politische Grundlagenforschung, 1/1981* (Reiter, 1981)

Ucakar, Karl, *Demokratie und Wahlrecht in Österreich*, Wien 1985 (Ucakar, 1985)

Wicha, Barbara, *Parteienfinanzierung aus öffentlichen Mitteln. Ihre Voraussetzungen und ihre Probleme*, Wien 1975 (Wicha, 1975)

Wicha, Barbara, *Notwendigkeit und Grenzen einer Parteienfinanzierung*, in: Andreas Khol/Robert Prantner/Alfred Stirnemann (Hg.), *Um Parlament und Partei. Alfred Maleta zum 70. Geburtstag*, Graz/Wien/Köln 1976 (Wicha, 1976)

Wicha, Barbara, *Nehmen und Schämen. Nichtmusische Gedanken zu tricoloren Sphärenklängen*, in: *ÖMH 9/1980* (Wicha, 1980)

Widder, Helmut, *Parlamentarische Strukturen im politischen System. Zu Grundlagen und Grundfragen des österreichischen Regierungssystems*, Berlin 1979 (Widder, 1979)

Wimmer, Inge, *Die Parteien und ihre Finanzen. Überlegungen zum Thema Parteienfinanzierung. SWA Rechtsgutachten Nr. 51*, Wien 1975 (Wimmer, 1975)

Zundel, Rolf, *Wieviel Geld für die Parteien?*, in: *Die Zeit 17/1983*, zitiert nach Anton Kofler, *Parteiengesellschaft im Umbruch*, Wien 1985 (Zundel, 1985)

17

The Legal Status of Political Parties

BERNHARD RASCHAUER

1. Introduction

"The Austrian Republic is a creation of the parties".[1] In contrast to our deus creator, who from afar smilingly follows man's doings in the world of his creation, the political parties have set up house in their creation and thoroughly taken possession of it.

The founding, or refounding, of the "parties of the first hour" took place—in April 1945—without any legal basis. Once, however, the Austrian Associations Law was in force after April 1945, these parties simply did not bother to register as required and thus subject themselves to official supervision. In view of their vital role in the Austrian state, no official was willing to order their discontinuation as the law would have required. Solely the FPÖ, that was founded at a later time, was constituted in compliance with the Law Relating to Associations.[2]

Since the parties founded early on thus existed without a legal basis, it was for many years debated whether they could be deemed to have a legal personality at all[3] and, if so, what kind of legal person they were.[4] In the early postwar years though, the courts did not dare question the legal capacity of these political parties (Supreme Court Decision OGH SZ 21/24).

On this unsteady footing, the two big parties forming the Grand Coalition built a parity nest for themselves in innumerable forums[5]: they enacted the laws (for example, in the promotion of economic development, economic controls and school administration) that granted decision-making powers to their representatives and they brought into being those facilities (for example, the executive management of the nationalized industries, the National Bank, the Austrian broadcasting company) that they managed by so-called "proportional" representation. Anton Pelinka's statement that is purposely quoted in its 1974 version is thus formulated in all conceivable generosity of understatement: "The influence of the Austrian parties can be felt in all areas of society, in the economy and in the arts as well as in that area strictly taken as politics. The parties exert a decisive influence that goes beyond Parliament and the Government."[6]

2. The Law Concerning the Political Parties 1975

This statement dating back to 1974 is significant because one year later the following provision was added to Austrian constitutional law: "The existence and diversity of political parties are essential components of the democratic order of the Republic of Austria" (§1, Paragraph 1, of the Law Concerning the Political Parties 1975). Given the prevailing circumstances, this constitutional act must have appeared to historic-political observers less a normative rule than an ominous statement of fact.

This Law Concerning the Political Parties was passed, after lengthy hesitation about the "self-service impression" that it conveyed[7], because of the political parties' financial plight. The "Parties' Law"[8] announced in Federal Law Gazette No. 404 from 1975 primarily contains provisions on financial assistance to big political parties from public funds.[9] The first draft on this subject, drawn up in 1967, did not meet with the necessary majority; however, with the Federal Law on the Promotion of Political Education and Publicity (Federal Law Gazette No. 272/1972) regulating state assistance to the "party academies,"[10] the psychological barriers to supporting political parties out of public funds fell in Austria, too.

Just what does the Parties Law provide for in its preamble? First it declares, as already mentioned, the existence and diversity of political parties to be essential components of the democratic order of the Republic of Austria (§1, Paragraph 1). The normative content of this provision is unclear.[11] A certain plurality in electoral processes and in the make-up of general representative bodies has always been regarded as an integral part of the constitutional principles of "election by proportional representation" (Articles 26, 95, Federal Constitution Act)[12] and of "free" election (Article 8, State Treaty 1955).[13] In this respect the provision is nothing new. On the other hand, it cannot be imputed that in this statement the authors of the constitutional law intended, as an aside, to declare unconstitutional those articles of the election regulations stipulating the requirements of a minimum number of seats and a minimum percentage of the vote that ensure that only "parties of a considerable numerical importance" are represented in the general representative bodies. If, however, Austria were to develop to a two-party system not only in various representative bodies but also structurally and in general terms, the dictate of "diversity" could take on unexpected legal significance.

3. The Founding of Political Parties

One of the goals of the preamble of the Parties Law was to retroactively legitimize the parties' flight from the Associations Law. The constitutional provision contained in §1, Paragraph 3, first sentence, and Paragraph 4 thus specifies: "The founding of political parties is unrestricted, insofar as the Federal Constitution does not provide anything to the contrary. ... The political parties are to adopt statutes, which are to be published in a periodic publication and filed with the Federal Ministry of the Interior. These statutes are especially to show who the party's organs are and which of these are authorized to act on behalf of the party as well as what rights and obligations its members have. The political party acquires legal personality by filing its statutes."

While the original 1967 draft for a Parties Law still stated that "further provisions will be set by federal law," party founding is now conclusively regulated in the Constitution. In general, it must be said of these provisions that they confine themselves to a statement of formal requirements. All in all, numerous questions remain unresolved; Kostelka[14] therefore justly speaks of a "manifest lack of norms".

Moreover, it should be noted that the possibilities for founding a political party, as specified in the Parties Law, do not rule out the fact that associations with a political objective can still be founded according to the Associations Law.

The provision of the Parties Law cited above states the following: The political party—it should more precisely say "the proponent or proponents,"[15] because in this stage the entity giving notice is not yet a political party—is to adopt statutes. The content of these statutes is only defined by law insofar as

a)   there must be at least two organs; in particular those organs authorized to represent and act on behalf of the party must be designated;

b)   the members' rights (for example, to vote) and obligations (for example, to pay membership dues) must be set down.

c)   From this it is also concluded that the statutes must provide for the party to have at least two members; the Parties Law evidently also permits "closed" parties.

d)   From the regulation of legal capacity it also follows that a name, a party designation, must be given. It is not the Minister of the Interior's duty to examine a designation's admissibility: if it is possible to confuse the designation with the name of other parties, bodies or interest groups, these groups are free to take action at civil law (§43, Austrian Civil Code) to have the newly founded party cease and desist; if the given designation violates identification prohibitions under public law (for example, under the Prohibition Law[16]), then it is the Minister of the Interior's duty to notify those authorities with the competence for interdiction or penalty.

e)   Finally, from §1, Paragraph 2, it is concluded that the group must at least indicate that its purpose is to be instrumental in developing political objectives. A more precise definition of its purpose is not required.

If, for example, the sole purpose of the political party is designated as the holding of sports events, the Minister of the Interior is in what appears to be an awkward situation, because according to a (in the author's opinion correct) decision handed down by the Constitutional Court (VfGH B 195/82 of March 1, 1983) he is not empowered to not accept or officially reject the statutes. The very first manifestation of such a "pseudo party" (if the party isn't also permitted under the Associations Law) would, however, suffice to have it prohibited by the security authorities in accordance with the Associations Law.

Similarly, the Minister of the Interior can only acknowledge the fact that a party's statutes lay down its purpose to be the violent overthrow of the state and the constitution; the Minister of the Interior can only notify the district attorney that, in his view, an act preparatory to commission of the criminal offense of treason is given.

This also holds true, despite what many people refuse to admit in the light of the provisions of the Prohibition Law and of Article 9 of the State Treaty of 1955, when, considering all circumstances, the party's given purpose falls under the Prohibition of Resuming National Socialist Activities.

Considering these meager provisions of the Parties Law, it must be noted that there is no requirement to state the types of activities of the political party, to give information on its funding, to precise the requirements for adopting resolutions, the powers and duties of its officers, the arbitration of disputes between members and between members and officers or on the dissolution and liquidation of the party.

Finally, it must be noted that the party's internal structure does not have to be "democratic". The democracy principle of the Federal Constitution only refers to the organization and workings of the nation, and the Parties Law contains no provisions on "inner-party democracy".[17] Thus, the Minister of the Interior also has to acknowledge statutes under which the founder is not elected, is chairman for life and has the exclusive power to make decisions and the authority to act in the name of the party.

The statutes must be published in a periodic publication before they are filed. Consequently, a proponent, who publishes in a small-town or university newspaper or the like "statutes" of just enough lines to meet the minimum requirements described above and then sends these to the Minister of the Interior informing him of their publication, has founded a political party. Whether the statutes sent to him were "adopted" by anyone, as §1, Paragraph 3, of the law would seem to require, is beyond the knowledge of the Minister of the Interior.

Definitions of political parties as being "permanent, organized associations of people, who by joint activity aim to exert extensive influence on the development of state objectives,"[18] state what is typical and customary, but do not address the minimum requirements set forth by law. Legally speaking, a political party can also be founded for the purpose of participating in chamber elections or blocking a new power plant.

> The political party acquires legal personality by filing its statutes (§1, Paragraph 4, Parties Law). The uncommon simplicity of this process has meanwhile given rise to almost 200 "political parties."[19]

Since the Minister of the Interior has no investigative competence, any administrative agency or any court confronted with a "political party" is forced to examine for itself whether this entity meets the minimum requirements and therefore has legal capacity as a political party.—The pointlessness of the Minister of the Interior's "notary function" deserves to be reproved by the General Accounting Office.

4. Legal Nature, Legal Capacity, Capacity to Act

An abstract entity takes on a legal personality by filing its statutes; it thus becomes a "legal person," an independent subject of rights and duties distinct from the persons of its members.

Basically this is a legal person under private law (Supreme Court decision OGH SZ 51/154) since there are no rules that exempt the membership relationship from the "legal concepts defining the private-law rights and duties of the state's inhabitants among themselves" (§1, Austrian Civil Code). This means that disputes between members or between members and officers are ultimately[20] to be decided by a court of civil law (§1 JN[21]). For example, resolutions that unjustly discriminate against individual members can be declared invalid according to §879 of the Austrian Civil Code.

Becoming a legal person is not the same as acquiring capacity to act. If, for instance, a party is founded under the name "Confederation of Austrian Trade Unions (ÖGB)," and is subsequently sued by the original ÖGB to refrain from using this name, a situation can arise in which the new party can indeed be sued, but, as long as it has no legal capacity, a trustee will have to be appointed to safeguard its interests. Many of the mini parties, such as those whose founder is also the sole member, are presumably in this "interim stage".

Legal capacity is acquired through the acts of constitution (for example calling a plenary meeting, electing the first officers, taking of office by those elected) foreseen in the statutes.

Once the party is constituted, the persons holding the offices called upon by the statutes to represent and act on behalf of the party are authorized to act with legal consequence for the political party. An act or omission performed by these persons in the exercise of their official duties is deemed by law to be an act or omission of the legal person. The many questions concerning punishment for offenses and concerning liability, that only begin to come to mind, cannot be dealt with here.

It is significant that, contrary to the Associations Law, there is no obligation to disclose to the authorities the names of the officeholders and functionaries (authorized to act for the party). This and the fact that the statutes do not have to contain any provisions on the adoption of valid resolutions, leaves the door wide open for no end of fighting over who the chairman of a particular political party "really" is. Thus, in conducting legal transactions the question remains whether a certain contract was concluded with "the party".

5. Activities of Political Parties—Election Parties—Clubs

In general, the political parties are allowed to do anything a private individual is allowed to do. They are basically subject to the same rules, permit criteria and prohibitions. Therefore, the political parties are, of course, subject to the prohibitions regarding high treason (§242ff, Austrian Criminal Code) or resumption of national socialist activities (Prohibition Law). The use of the words "in general" and "basically" is meant to show the many exceptions ranging from special fiscal regulations and preferential treatment of public events and advertising of political parties (for example, in laws governing road traffic, commodities duties, supervisory fees, nature preservation, public events and assembly) all the way to specific privileges.

In accordance with the provision of §1, Paragraph 3, Sentence 2 of the Parties Law, the activity of the political parties must "not be subject to restraint by any special legislation". It follows, thus, that no rules are permitted that would restrain political parties in comparison to all other individuals. For this reason, a special law of constitutional character was needed to justify the legal limitation of election campaign costs (Article III, Parties Law), and for this reason it is the author's opinion that party-specific limitations of the freedom to accept donations are unconstitutional. For this reason, a constitutional provision (Art. 147, Paragraph 4, Federal Constitution) was also necessary to stipulate that employees or other functionaries of a political party may not be members of the Constitutional Court. This is, by the way, the only provision of the Austrian Federal Constitution that rules out the influence of party politics.

Preferential treatment of the political parties is allowed by law insofar as under the constitutional principle of equality it is to be seen as "justified by the facts". A legal prohibition against searching "party headquarters" would therefore be unconstitutional. A number of the privileges enjoyed by political parties warrant critical examination in this connection. For instance, why should a nation-wide popular initiative normally require 10,000 signatures, while the same initiative also becomes valid with the signatures of only eight members of the National Council or four members from each of three state diets?

Considered on the basis of its own foundation, a political party is only permitted to perform those activities that conform with the objectives set forth in its statutes. Any actions over and above this can be stopped through legal action on the part of its members or by administrative agencies acting in accordance with relevant police regulations (Associations Law, Assembly Law). Political parties do not, however, forfeit their legal capacity through an ultra vires act.

Matters become difficult to interpret when statutes stipulate only enough to meet the minimum requirements, in that they state that the party will participate in developing political objectives. Is such a party allowed to organize an intramural soccer tournament?

As a rule, one essential function of political parties is the participation in elections, especially elections for the general bodies of representation. It is precisely in this connection that the legal regulations establish a new category, the so-called "election party".

The "election party" is the election proposal or ticket raised to the status of a legal person. This legal person possesses limited rights and duties, particularly in connection with its participation in the electoral process, its share in the campaign costs and with regard to contesting the election.[22] It acquires its legal capacity by filing the election proposal, provided it is not rejected, and maintains its legal personality for the duration of the legislative period of the particular representative body.[23]

This gives rise to curious legal duplications and even multiplications[24]: on the one side are the political parties and on the other the election parties, with various election parties from the same political party for the different federal, state and city or town elections. The election parties, and not the political parties, are entitled to award the seats won in the election.

Thus, election parties, especially those on the national and state level, are creations of expediency serving the purposes of electoral process. Since their name is identical with that of the political parties "behind" them, the voters are absolutely unaware of their separate legal existence. In city and town council elections, however, the special status of the election parties is clearly evident because the lists of candidates for city or town council are often filed under a colorful variety of names. Therefore, it must be noted that these election parties are not political parties in the sense of the Parties Law; they have no rights beyond those that they derive from the election regulations. Thus any election campaigns, rallies or meetings conducted by a "candidate list" that has not acquired a legal personality as a political party are, legally speaking, held by private persons.[25]

"Election parties" running in various chamber and other elections as "factions" are even more removed from the concept of the political party.

Finally, it is noted that the total number of those members of parliament belonging to a certain election party are again granted their own legal personality as a so-called "club" under the provisions of parliament's rules of procedure, according to which such clubs have rights and duties (for example, the right to file motions, nomination duties). In the clubs of green and alternative parties it becomes especially obvious that the failure to provide rules for the validity of club decisions and for the capacity to represent and act on behalf of the club can give rise to practical problems.

The "mandatory faction vote" (parallel voting behavior among the representatives of the same club) is neither ordered nor substantiated by law, but rather by the statutes of the political party behind the club (exclusion being justified by conduct detrimental to the party) and by considerations of courtesy and the division of labor within the club.

6. The Legal End of Political Parties

The Parties Law contains no provisions for the manner in which parties cease to exist, apparently out of concern that the dissolution of parties could be controlled by an act of state.

Any association can resolve to dissolve itself, and there is no apparent reason why this rule should not also apply to political parties. The announcement of such a resolution has, of course, no legal relevance[26] for the Minister of the Interior because, when statutes only meet the minimum requirements prescribed by law, he has absolutely no capacity to examine whether the resolution was adopted by the competent persons and whether the person announcing the resolution is really a party officer authorized to act for the party. To put it simply: just about anybody can come along and say that a certain party was disbanded... Therefore, every administrative agency and every court of law, when confronted with a specific case, is to examine whether the political party in question still exists under law.

A political party is free to resolve to amend its statutes. For lack of any pertinent legal provision, it is, in principle, not necessary for the party to publish an amendment to the statutes in a periodic publication and to make it known to the Minister of the Interior. It could possibly be teleologically argued that at least those amendments to the statutes that touch on the above-mentioned minimum requirements must be published and filed. But then, what can or should be done about the following case: John Doe takes out a paid advertisement in a newspaper to announce that a well known big party has amended its statutes as follows, and forwards a copy of the newspaper to the Minister of the Interior for the latter's information. The Minister of the Interior knows that the announcement is not correct, but since he does not "officially" know this and since the law does not call on him to conduct an investigation, he can do nothing more than put the announcement on file.

In the event that a political party makes known to the Minister of the Interior an amendment to its statutes and even if this amendment touches on the minimum requirements, there is nothing to advocate the assumption that with every such announcement a new legal entity is born.[27] Only in the rather theoretical extreme case that an amendment to the statutes causes one of the mentioned minimum requirements to be dropped without replacement does the political party subsequently forfeit its status as a legal person, because in this case there are no longer any statutes on file with the Minister of the Interior that would suffice to initiate the legal consequence of legal capacity.[28] Whether this is the case is not to be examined by the Minister of the Interior, but by any court or agency on a case to case basis.

And what about the party that "lapses into illegality" through an amendment to its statutes and subsequently professes a violent overthrow of the republic and activities forbidden under the Prohibition Law? Since a democratic orientation is not one of the minimum requirements demanded by the constitutional provisions of the Parties Law for legal capacity, the party cannot, as the Constitutional Court[29] has decided, lose its legal personality through such an amendment of its objectives. The authorities with competence for interdiction and penalty are, however, to put an end to any illegal activity, including unauthorized electoral participation.

It is the nature of legal persons that their legal personality is independent of a change in their members. The theoretical borderline case of a party losing all its members might be a case for a trustee; there is, however, no reason to doubt the legal capacity of the now abstract entity.

With regard to practices prevailing in other countries, it should be noted that no authority in Austria, not even the Constitutional Court, is authorized to dissolve a party by an act of state.[30]

Kostelka[31] points out that the state organ that established the legal capacity of a political party can also abolish it. He thus concludes that a political party can be dissolved by an act of law of constitutional character. Aside from the fundamental problematics of democratic values posed by such a silencing of the minority by the majority, it remains to be legally examined whether, as long as the existence and diversity of political parties are essential elements of the fundamental principle of democracy (§1, Paragraph 1, Parties Law), such a constitutional law does not represent a "total change" of the Constitution and therefore require a referendum in accordance with Article 44, Paragraph 3, of the Austrian Federal Constitution.

Notes

1. Pelinka 1974, p. 31, 48.
2. cf. Schaden 1983, p. 225, 228.
3. cf. especially Ostheim 1964, p. 533, and 1967.
4. cf. Mantl 1971, p. 109f.
5. cf. evidence in Kostelka 1983, p. 37, 49, note 47.
6. Pelinka 1974.
7. cf. in particular Schaden 1983, p. 229f.
8. cf. as first interpretations Berchtold 1976, p. 33; Ermacora 1976, p. 85.
9. On this question, cf. the article by Wicha.
10. The law speaks of "the designated legal entity represented in the National Council by a party".
11. Kostelka 1983, p. 41 speaks of an "interpretive explanation".
12. cf. Oberndorfer/Pernthaler/Winkler 1976.
13. cf. the fundamental article of Merkl in Klecatsky (ed.), Die Republik Österreich, 1968, p. 84.
14. Kostelka 1983, p. 43.
15. In my opinion, this is merely a legistic error. cf., by contrast, Kostelka 1983, p. 46.
16. "Verbotsgesetz," forbidding Nazi activities.
17. cf. Schaden 1983, p. 232ff. with further references.
18. Walter/Mayer 1985, p. 56.
19. In practice, the Federal Ministry of the Interior announces the founding in the official gazette of the Wiener Zeitung.
20. The statutes can, for example, demand that an inner-party board of arbitration be applied to first.
21. "Jurisdictionsnorm," Austrian Court Organization Act.
22. cf. Kostelka 1983, p. 53f.
23. Even such activities qualify for preferential treatment provided broadly formulated statutory criteria (for example, being a "political event") are met, cf. for example §1 Supervisory Fees Act.
24. cf. already Koja 1958, p. 482.
25. This does not mean that such measures do not qualify for preferential treatment on the basis of substance (for example "political events"), cf. for example §1, Supervisory Fees Act.
26. cf. by contrast, Kostelka 1983, p. 52.
27. As Kostelka 1983, p. 45, 52f. seems to presume.
28. So too Kostelka 1983, 52f. apparently.
29. VfGH G 175/84 of November 29, 1985. cf. Nowak 1986, p. 138; Merli 1986, p. 6.
30. Kostelka 1983, p. 50f.
31. Kostelka 1983, p. 49f.

Bibliography

Adamovich, Ludwig, *Handbuch des österreichischen Verfassungsrechts*, 6. Auflage, 1971 (Adamovich, 1971)

Berchtold, Klaus, *Das Parteiengesetz, Österreichisches Verwaltungsarchiv 1976* (Berchtold, 1976)

Ermacora, Felix, *Verfassungsänderungen 1975*, in: *Juristische Blätter 1976* (Ermacora, 1976)

Koja, Friedrich, *Die Rechtsfähigkeit der Wahlpartei und der politischen Partei*, in: *Juristische Blätter 1958* (Koja, 1958)

Kostelka, Peter, *Politische Parteien in der österreichischen Rechtsordnung*, in FS Floretta, 1983 (Kostelka, 1983)

Mantl, Wolfgang, *Der österreichische Parteienstaat*, 1969 (Mantl, 1969)

Merli, Franz, *Österreichische Gemeindezeitung 4/1986* (Merli, 1986)

Nowak, Manfred, *Europäische Grundrechtezeitung*, 1986 (Nowak, 1986)

Oberndorfer/Pernthaler/Winkler, *Verhältniswahlrecht als Verfassungsgrundsatz, 1976* (Oberndorfer/Pernthaler/Winkler, 1976)

Ostheim, Rolf, *Zur Rechtsfähigkeit der politischen Parteien nach bürgerlichem Recht*, in: *Juristische Blätter 1964* (Ostheim, 1964)

Ostheim, Rolf, *Zur Rechtsfähigkeit von Verbänden im österreichischen bürgerlichen Recht*, 1967 (Ostheim, 1967)

Pelinka, Anton, *Struktur und Funktion der politischen Parteien*, in: Heinz Fischer (Hg.), *Das politische System Österreichs*, 1974 (Pelinka, 1974)

Schaden, Michael, *Parteien und Rechtsordnung*, in: Peter Gerlich/Wolfgang C. Müller (Hg.), *Zwischen Koalition und Konkurrenz*, Wien 1983 (Schaden, 1983)

Walter, Robert/Mayer, Heinz, *Grundriß des österreichischen Bundesverfassungsrechts*, 5. Auflage, 1985 (Walter/Mayer, 1985)

18

Recruitment and Recruitment Strategies

ALFRED STIRNEMANN

1. Introduction

The study of political parties[1] considers the recruitment of candidates for the top constitutional offices, alongside the articulation and the aggregation of various interests, as one of the parties' three most important functions within a modern party democracy.[2] It is an undisputed fact in the political science literature[3] dealing with Austria that it is the political parties that select the candidates for all constitutional organs. This is true for all legislative bodies at the national and regional levels, from Parliament to the state diets, as well as for all executive offices from the federal and state governments down to the mayors and portfolio-bearing councilmen in larger communities. In many cases this also applies for the top administrative offices, all the way to the county presidents, and even the courts of public law such as the Constitutional and Administrative Courts. Local government only feels this influence to a very limited degree, particularly in smaller communities, where "candidate lists" are a common occurrence and on the increase.

It is equally undisputed that the make-up of the legislative bodies is mainly decided by candidate nomination and not by the voter casting his ballot.[4] This means that up to three-fourths of all nominations primarily hinge on inner-party decisions. The prevailing, rigid law of electoral lists makes the composition of political bodies largely predictable. Not more than a few crucial seats are actually decided on Election Day.

Despite the established importance of the inner-party selection of candidates, a surprisingly small number of political science studies have been conducted on this subject. While the regulations governing candidate lists have been examined for their formal prerequisites and their impact on the political system, no such study has been made of the actual compilation of lists in the inner-party selection process. With the exception of studies such as that by

Gerlich-Kramer[5] on the Vienna City Council/State Diet, no systematic quantitative analysis of political careers has been undertaken that would show how candidate selection and its problematics can be described. There are indeed a few biographies, particularly of leading politicians, but their concentration on a single person leaves no room for the generalization that would permit further predictions to be made. In most cases topics of this sort have seen journalistic treatment as the subject of political news magazines.[6] A systematic long-term study of political careers employing empirical materials remains to be desired.

A first attempt at such an analysis can be found in K.H. Naßmacher's study of the Austrian system of government[7], but there too no mention is made of how a particular candidate came to be on the slate, how he was politically socialized and made a career for himself, against whom he fought his way up and against whom he lost. In electoral studies,[8] too, the analyst's attention is devoted on the one hand to the campaigning party, its platform, structure, politics, political message and the controversies between parties as well as their issue-setting capacity, and, on the other hand, to the voter, the motives and determinants for his decision. Hardly any mention is made of the candidates and their careers, except in the case of leading candidates.

This self-imposed restriction may find its justification in the fact that, in keeping with Austrian electoral law and its candidate lists, the voter actually does not vote for a candidate but for a party slate. The individual candidate thus remains an unknown quantity for political science study in Austria.

2. Definitions and Problems

Recruitment is the nomination of candidates for public offices to be awarded by general election. This term is therefore not used for those public offices filled by political appointment, such as top administrative or judicial posts.[9] This is by no means intended to infer that these have less import on public life, but merely to indicate that such appointments and careers are governed by other political laws, not to mention the fact that other formal prerequisites prevail here (in the form of education, job requirements, gradual or rapid advancement up a formal career ladder).

This recruitment process consists of various steps, for instance the political socialization of possible candidates, the establishment of formal or informal criteria in staking out potential candidates and finally in the selection of candidates, namely the process in which a potential candidate becomes the official seeker of a particular public office.

Taken from this point of view, recruitment strategies can be understood as the planned as well as systematic and purposeful act of nominating candidates for public office. The subject of the planned application of this strategy can be either the individual (potential) candidate or the campaigning group within whose circle candidate nomination takes place. In the former case, recruitment strategy is understood as the sum of all the advice that a candidate could expect from political science in order to be successfully nominated for public office by a certain In group. Seen from the standpoint of the group campaigning as a whole, recruitment strategy can be construed as the answer to the search for the optimum candidate, i.e. the one with the greatest chance of winning, both with regard to a particular individual and to the type of person sought. In the evaluation of this chance it will be necessary to consider the potential for success both within the group (party) nominating the candidate and in the eyes of the voter.

The formulation of these strategies must take into consideration certain given, formal prerequisites such as the platform, statutes and organizational rules of the parties as well as the election regulations established by law. Both these norms are reciprocal in influence. After all, the election regulations are largely defined by what was purposeful and good in the eyes of those political powers that up to now held or helped constitute the majority. This shaping of the national election regulations by the parties according to their needs is subject to checks and balances dictated by the constitution and the presumed will of the voter. For instance, in its candidate selection process a party can discriminate against certain age groups (senior citizens) or in favor of others (quotas for female candidates), which is generally not permitted under the constitution, and, if so, then usually only the other way around, i.e. by imposing minimum age limits for particular offices (for example, for the office of Federal President). These norms contain provisions on the minimum percentage of votes a campaigning group must receive, namely in the form of an initial seat, a minimum percentage or a majority election system. These provisions are intended not only for efficiency but also to prevent too serious splintering in the thoroughly well-meaning interest of the existing traditional parties in their competition with emerging political powers and groups.

Finally, it is certainly possible to analyze such recruitment strategies from the standpoint of participatory democracy, from a particular view of democracy, in order to develop through political science those strategies that help meet this requirement or bring it a bit closer to being met, or that permit established strategies to be evaluated in the light of this requirement. This study will therefore serve to examine whether the demand for legitimacy (to what extent a particular strategy permits the will of those represented–in the election of legislative representatives–or of those governed–in the election of executive officials–to be expressed best and genuinely) and the demand for effectiveness (whether a particular strategy permits the democratic system to function optimally and to what extent this strategy can provide the political system with personnel suited in character, intellect and ability to serve the particular body politic) are fulfilled.

The scientific literature dealing with the recruitment and selection of candidates in Austria has brought forth three attempts to explain recruitment strategies:

a)   the seniority principle of Karl-Heinz Naßmacher,
b)   the description of technocratic career patterns by Anton Pelinka and
c)   the principle of the permanence of mandates after Heinz Fischer.

But first the basic conditions for recruitment and candidate selection will be examined.

3. Federal Norms for Recruitment

The electoral law of proportional representation with rigid lists that has been in force in Austria since the birth of the republic generally does not allow the voter to cast his vote for a particular candidate, but for a party's list. The lists contain a maximum of twice as many candidates as the number of seats to be awarded in the particular election district (thus 84 candidates for the most heavily populated state Vienna, and 12 candidates for each of the two smallest states Vorarlberg and Burgenland). Since the "Minor Electoral Reform" of 1970[10] under which the present amendment to the National Council Election Regulations was passed, each state constitutes one election district. The Second Republic can be divided into three periods with regard to its election regulations:

1.   The first period ran from 1949 to 1961 and was characterized by the possibility to "rank and strike" nominees. At that time, several options were available to the voter to change the order of preference dictated by a party's list:

a)   change the order of the candidates,
b)   strike individual candidates from the list or
c)   add new names to the party's slate.

The essence of this ranking and striking was that it made it possible to win over a larger number of voters; since no official ballots were provided in those days, large numbers of ballots with candidates' listed in a different order than decided by the party were printed and distributed at the entrance to the polling stations. It was thus possible in at least several cases[11] to get candidates elected to Parliament who were not nominated in party committees.
It is also noteworthy that all successful attempts at ranking and striking always involved ÖVP candidates and always ones from the same league (ÖAAB, Austrian League of Workers and Employees).

Table 18.1
Candidates Elected by "Ranking and Striking"

Election	Election District	Name of Candidate	Advanced from Position to Position	Groups Represented
1949	(21) Styria	Barthold Stürgkh	3 to 1	Large-acred landlords instead of farmers
1953	(22) Styria	Hanns Kottulinsky	6 to 3	Industrialists' Association instead of tradesmen
1956	(14) Upper Austria	Franz Nimmervoll (instead of Alfred Gasperschitz)	4 to 3	Farm and forest workers instead of civil servants
1956	(24) Carinthia	Ludwig Weiss (instead of Adolf Praus)	5 to 4	Catholic Action, Catholic Workers Movement

To be successful, this type of ranking and striking demanded a powerful organization inside or alongside the campaigning group, one that, evidently having been unsuccessful in the inner-party selection of candidates, later circulated the dissenting ballots. Critics of this tactic referred to it as "fraudulent substitution." This criticism is probably deserved since it is likely that very few voters took notice of the lists but instead voted solely according to party. The SPÖ in particular was opposed to this possibility of ranking and striking although not one of its deputies was ever elected through such an attack on strict party discipline. According to a statement[12] by then National Council President Johann Böhm, it was precisely in this party that anxiety ran high that the official party slate could possibly be infiltrated by persons from small groups on the far political left with totalitarian aims.

2. The second period ranged from 1962 to 1971. The ranking and striking option remained, but an official ballot was introduced. This change was sponsored above all by the FPÖ that welcomed the considerable savings brought about by having the authorities now pick up the bill for ballots that had previously been printed at party expense. Since then, a vote cast on anything other than an official ballot has been invalid. Thus, despite the continued possibility to rank and strike candidates, the probability of

a change in the list decided on inside the party had become more or less unlikely. Among the reasons for this was the absence of information and publicity that would have informed the voter of this option[13]. According to actual observations, election officials often omitted the complicated tallying of plus and minus points for candidate preference, and only announced the number of times a candidate was ranked or struck, probably under the tacit assumption held by all the parties represented by polling officials and witnesses that the few times a candidate was struck would not amount to a change in the list anyway and could therefore be disregarded.

3. A third period commenced in 1971 when the disliked and, since the introduction of the official ballot, ineffectual possibility of ranking and striking candidates was eliminated in the "Minor Electoral Reform" and replaced with the (first-)preference vote. This was indeed a simplification and, as its so to speak only "positive" feature, it did not permit an unpopular candidate to be eliminated or ranked down by the voter. A similar effect could nevertheless be achieved by moving a candidate to the top of the list.

This was only put into practice once, namely in the 1983 National Council election when, sanctioned[14] so to speak by the SPÖ party leaders, Josef Cap[15] was called on to set an environmental grassroots-democracy accent as a symbol for red-green voters and thereby prevent them from drifting off to newly emerging green parties. Various election committees (Campaign "Critical Voters," Artists' Committee for Cap, Scientists for Cap) came out with demands for "Cap for Parliament." That was the first time that the mass media took a closer look into the "bizarre mechanism"[16] of preference votes. Even Catholic circles strove, albeit unsuccessfully, to move up the list a candidate (H. Schattovits) who emphasized family issues (see table 18.2).

Cap polled twice as many preference votes as were necessary to get him into Parliament and relegated the mighty union and National Council president Anton Benya to second place. The candidate Schattovits came away with only 13% of the necessary preference votes and thus took a place much further down the list.

Both changes in the election regulations have the common characteristic that they reduce the voter's possibility to influence the list of candidates by a decision made in the voting booth, while steadily strengthening the influence wielded by party forums in the recruitment of candidates. The voter finally has so little say in changing the ticket drawn up by party decision that the latest National Council elections did nothing more than confirm a particular party's will (or led to a party tactical maneuver[17] at the urging of the party leaders). From this it is very clear to see that the particular electoral regulations in force represent a compromise among the different parties on the opportunities the voter is to be given to amend party decisions.

Table 18.2
The Five Candidates with the Most Preference Votes (1983)

	Name/Party/ District	Number of Preference Votes	In % of Electoral Quota	In % of Party Votes in That District
1.	J. Cap (SPÖ, Vienna)	62,457	229.0	11.3
2.	J. Haider (FPÖ, Carinthia)	10,232	38.8	27.8
3.	B. Kreisky (SPÖ, Lower Austria)	4,685	17.0	1.1
4.	A. Mock (ÖVP, Lower Austria)	4,561	16.9	1.0
5.	H. Schattovits (ÖVP, Vienna)	3,563	13.0	1.1

Source: Federal Ministry of the Interior. Records of Electoral Points from the 1983 National Council Election after: Müller 1984, p. 96

4. Candidate Selection within the Parties

This section too will start with a look at the formal procedures for nominating candidates at the federal level. Candidate selection at the state and community level generally takes place according to similar formal regulations contained in the state party statutes.

The importance of inner-party candidate nomination can be seen from the fact that, because of Austrians' extraordinary electoral stability, once the candidate lists have been drawn up the composition of the general legislative bodies is already established with almost 90% certainty.

Organizationally seen, the lists of candidates for the National Council elections are drawn up by all parties as follows:[18]

The county organizations together with the party's town organizations select the candidates, make these known to the state party organization and jockey with the other counties for the best possible placement on the list. The desire to do at least as good as in the last election gives rise to the pattern of "permanence of membership in Parliament" established by H. Fischer. Even after the creation of uniform state election districts, the most important factor for the nomination of candidates remains the county party organization. The state party organization then attempts to draw up the list of candidates for the election district (state) taking into account the counties' recommendations, whereby it must also give due consideration to the wishes of the national party organization. These wishes have grown steadily since the inner-party statutory reforms in the early 1970s.

The SPÖ's new party statutes from 1968[19] state as follows:

"Persons whose election is in the interest of the National Council's work irrespective of their place of residence, are to be nominated to one-fifth of the positions on the list of candidates. In such cases, the national party's executive committee is to reach in good time an agreement with the pertinent organizations on the candidates' rank on the list."

The ÖVP[20] employs a three-step procedure for candidate nomination:

a) The proposal procedure ("primary elections"), in which the county party leaders present to the state party organization their proposals, which are to have been worked out with the participation of all party members, if at all possible, but at any rate with the local party leaders or suborganizations. This procedure thus provides "the opportunity for all party members to assist in candidate nomination," as was indeed the case in numerous actual primary elections held in the 1970s, but does not make such primaries mandatory, with the result that "participation of the local party leaders and suborganizations" can basically be seen as a type of primary election.

b) The nomination procedure, in which the state and national party organizations each have the right to nominate 5% of the total candidates, however at least one candidate, for a National Council election district. In elections for state diets, the state party organization has the exclusive right to nominate 10% of all the candidates. This of course in no way says whether the candidates nominated by the national or state party organization also have to be assigned a position on the list from which they will actually be elected.

c) The ranking procedure, according to which the candidates are alloted their positions by the state party executive committee, that is to make this decision known to the national party leadership no later than 14 days before the deadline for submission. The national party in turn has seven days in which to object to the list's order of preference. The state party executive committee is then bound to comply to the best of its ability with the wishes of the national party leadership, but does not make a final decision. Thus, by trusting in the interplay between the national party's right to make an objection and the state party's decision to persist, flexible possibilities for individual solutions were created.

Remaining seats (those not awarded on the state list but established in the second electoral step) are decided by the national party leadership that draws up proposals for election district collectives. In state elections, it is the executive committee of the state party that draws up the proposal in the event that remaining votes have to be counted. Furthermore, it must be noted that for elections in professional interest groups, it is the ÖVP's suborganization in that particular field that nominates and ranks the list of candidates.

These provisions on the national organization's special rights were reinforced in the new party organization statutes issued by the ÖVP in May 1980[21]. These state that "before a candidate is renominated for the National Council or the Federal Council the state party organizations are obliged to consult the national party chairman and the chairman of the ÖVP parliamentary faction." Furthermore, the national organization's special right to name 5% of the candidates was increased to 10% of the number of seats won by the ÖVP in the previous National Council election, and it was decided that these candidates are "to be assigned a position from which they can be elected." Thus, the right of nomination is passed from the national party's executive committee (National Organization Statutes 1972) to the National Party Chairman (National Organization Statutes 1980).

In the FPÖ, it is the state party organizations that clearly have the most say in nominating candidates since this third party does not win more than one initial seat in any state, which precludes any need for the list's electable candidates to reflect a proportional distribution according to county. The final decision is made by the national party leadership that, in particular, also decides who is to occupy the remaining seats awarded in the second electoral step. Ties are decided not by lot, as in elections of party officials, but by the chairman's vote.

With the statute revisions instituted by the two big parties, the influence of their national party organizations was reinforced. The ÖVP even introduced party evaluation of a legislator's performance and thus made a clear statement against mandates automatically being carried over, as in the "permanence of membership in parliament."

A second possibility held by the party leadership to influence the make-up of its parliamentary faction, over and above that of invoking party necessity or the special rights of the national party, is the right of its top committees to decide who will occupy the seats awarded on the basis of remaining votes. It often happens that the candidate lists for the remainder votes in the two election district collectives East and West are led by those party leaders who are also top candidates on the list of an election district and thus sure to win an initial mandate. By deciding to take either the initial or the remaining mandate, they can influence the membership of their faction just as easily as when the party's executive committee formally decides who is to occupy a remaining seat.

5. The Influence of Political Culture on Candidate Recruitment

It would by far surpass the scope of this chapter to outline more than a few of those characteristics of Austria's[22] political culture[23] that are essential to candidate recruitment. Following that, several thoughts on possibly emerging new political forces and on political mechanisms affecting candidate selection will also be presented.

1. Austria is an advanced party state. Austria's general tendency to strong institutionalization is reflected at the party level by enormous party machines that steadily take over more functions than those originally intended for parties. Particularly the sphere of activity defined as "Bürgerservice" (public service provided by the party for the citizen) is in a state of constant growth. This is probably a consequence of the extensive bureaucratization and the ever more confusing net of incentives and subsidies. The parties thus play the role of guide in the resulting tangle of entitlements. Huge party machines are matched by huge membership figures that by far surpass those of comparable parties in other countries. But the influence exerted by the members on their party is steadily decreasing since, in the transformation of all parties from membership to voter parties, purely formal membership is reduced to insignificance and is devoid of any real influence. The parties are increasingly coming to the conviction that large membership rolls are occasionally not an advantage but an enormous headache. This tendency is further reinforced by the increasing share of government funding for parties, which has the effect of making party leadership also financially independent of the rank and file. A general trend to put the parties' image in a negative light is matched by the ever increasing number of duties they take on, whose discharge, however, leaves more and more to be desired.

2. The parties have developed special-purpose and subsidiary organizations that penetrate the whole fabric of society and further politicize it. Spheres of life not directly influenced by politics in other countries are in Austria the parties' fields of action thanks to their having been totally organized and saturated by party politics and to the tendency to have party representatives preside at important social functions, even in non-political sectors.

3. The quasi total organization of society by the parties has given rise to an almost consummate patronage system. The political parties enjoy the right to make proposals for very many not even indirectly political posts reaching far into the business world. The general acceptance of this phenomenon by society and occasionally exaggerated conceptions of the existing patronage system have the effect of enhancing it, because even those persons who reject the system often do not hesitate to opportunistically exploit it, thereby strengthening it. Moreover, the short period in which the Austrian Freedom Party, traditionally one of the most vehement critics of the patronage and proportion system, served in the Government (1983-1986) saw this party become fully integrated in the proportionate system with proportionate membership of FPÖ candidates in the supervisory boards and boards of directors of state-owned and state-affiliated industries. Important fields in which political patronage is practiced include job appointments, particularly in the school system, as well as housing allocation and government subsidizing.

It is interesting to note that within the parties themselves there is a countermovement against what is viewed as an undignified system of protection, because this form of political patronage is beginning to be counterproductive for the parties, for example in the case of schoolteachers and civil servants. The parties are confronted with the problem that when appointing a new school director, the nine out of ten unsuccessful candidates tend at the very least to discontinue their work in the party, with the result that the damage done inside the party often overshadows the other advantages.

4. Characteristic for Austria is the interrelationship existing between parties and interest organizations. This is illustrated by the fact that, on the one hand, elections in interest organizations, especially those of a public-law nature such as the professional chambers, run according to party factions, with the result that most interest organizations can be clearly defined according to their political sympathies. On the other hand, parties partially or wholly adopt certain interests as their own and also accept the candidates proposed by interest organizations.[24]

With regard to the interest organizations it should also be mentioned that these essentially consider the interests of the population as producers (as farmers, in other self-employed capacities or as employees), but that the interests of the individual person as a consumer, patient, radio listener, TV viewer or as a someone with an interest in a healthy environment are often neglected, both because there are no comprehensive consumer interest organizations and because those organizations that claim to represent these consumer interests often do so in word only and always subordinate to the producers' interests. One of the most flagrant examples of this is the government's appointment of representatives to the consumer interest boards of the Austrian TV and radio broadcasting company (ORF).

Table 18.3
Interrelationship of Parties and Interest Groups (%)

	SPÖ	ÖVP	FPÖ	KPÖ	Other
Chambers of Commerce	10	85	-	-	5
Chambers of Agriculture	10	84	2	-	4
Chambers of Labor	63	29	5	2	1
Trade Union Federation	75	17	-	7	1

Source: Pelinka 1978, p. 418

5. *The Surrender of Long-Held Values*. This general term can be defined as an overall secularization and desacralization of public life that questions the formerly accepted binding character of the traditional values that found their effective ideological expression in *Austria's three political lagers*, each of which grew out of the liberalism of the 19th century, and also in the particular Marxist, Christian or nationalistic concept. The automatic effectiveness of this value system is unsettled and thus no longer serves the parties as an instant identification mechanism in their appeals to members or voters. The tendency to take no longer self-evident truths for granted has declined, thereby liberating a larger number of voters from their party ties. Consequently, the ratio of seats held by the different parties is subject to greater fluctuation and single-issue movements are emerging.

6. The Emergence of Citizens' Initiatives. A growing importance is being accorded to *citizens' initiatives* that give voice to new problems and interests. These are often fundamental interests aimed at alternative or environmental problems and that above all derive from the individual's role as a consumer. These initiatives are seen to question established solutions and means of attacking problems and also to declaim an uncritical submissive mentality and the conviction that public officials always know best.

Whether the traditional parties will be able to articulate and integrate these new interests and problems and, what's more, to enlarge their choice of candidates by recruiting proponents of these new interests and problems, or whether these citizens' initiatives from single-issue move-ments will consolidate as electoral groups and ultimately parties, is one of the most decisive questions facing the Austrian party system and thus also the parties' future recruitment strategies.

7. Finally, the above-mentioned political mechanisms are seen to include an alternation between the preference of "older" and "younger" candi-dates, see-sawing between the idealization of one or the other of these age groups with its repercussions on lowering the age limit for active and passive suffrage and on the introduction or elimination of age limits, and thus an influence on candidate selection.

A second area includes the demand by advocates of women's liberation for a minimum number of female candidates on a party's ticket. To date, this demand has been particularly well met in the unpromising slots of candidate lists, namely in those that were filled to provide "twice the number of candi-dates," and the statistics on party performance thus improved.

A third movement that can be listed under the term mechanism is the grassroots movement, whose aim it is to give the voter a greater opportunity to elect a candidate personally chosen by him and therefore personally ac-countable to him.

6. The Seniority Principle after Naßmacher

In addition to party organizational structure, relationship to interest groups, voter and membership structure and platforms, Karl-Heinz Naß-macher[25] also examined the candidate selection system used by the Austrian parties, whereby he confined himself to illustrating the formal rules for can-didate nomination contained in the statutes and internal rules of the particu-lar parties and in the structural characteristics of the candidates and repre-sentatives according to town of origin, occupation and age. He then meritori-ously attempted for the first time to work out selection patterns by analyzing the safe slots on the tickets of the big parties in several election districts in a comparison of four National Council elections (1956, 1959, 1962, 1966).

Unfortunately, the study makes no mention of the candidates in losing positions nor of those who advanced to safe places on the list. It does, how-ever, formulate a hypothesis on these. Naßmacher examines "the different age structure of members of parliament and of unelected candidates" and ar-rives at a hypothesis on the selection pattern of both parties. He argues: "If the young candidates are primarily assigned losing places and the older can-didates winning slots on the party ticket, then candidates for the National Council must be nominated largely by their advancing up the list. The younger candidates become older and thus grow into the safe slots."[26]

Table 18.4

The ÖVP Ticket in Election District 11 (Viertel unterm Manhartsberg) 1956-1966 Shown According to League Membership

	1956	1959	1962	1966
1	Hartmann ÖBB	Raab ÖWB	Figl ÖBB	Withalm ÖWB
2	Withalm ÖWB	Hartmann ÖBB	Hartmann ÖBB	Prader ÖAAB
3	Mayer ÖBB	Withalm ÖWB	Withalm ÖWB	Fachleutner ÖBB
4	Ehrenfried ÖAAB	Mayer ÖBB	Prader ÖAAB	Minkowitsch ÖBB
5	Ullmann ÖBB	Prader ÖAAB	Fachleutner ÖBB	Gindl ÖBB
6	Hirsch ÖWB	Ullmann ÖBB	Minkowitsch ÖBB	Friedrich ÖAAB
7	Hainisch ÖWB	Schmidt ÖWB		

Source: Naßmacher 1968, p. 69

Table 18.5

Advancement of SPÖ Candidates in Election District 07 (Vienna West)

Election District	Position	1956	1959	1962	1966
07	1	Schärf	Olah	Olah	Broda
	2	Moik	Moik	Broda	Kratky
	3	Slavik	Broda	Kratky	Gratz
	4	Olah	Kysela	Kysela	Hanzlik
	5	Kysela	Slavik	Slavik	Stemmer
	6	Glaser	Kratky	Pfoch	Pfoch
	7	Kratky	Bock	Stemmer	Dinhof

Source: Naßmacher 1968, p. 70

This hypothesis, however, is not validated solely by examination of the top slots alone, not even by including the speculative slots just short of the so-called "safe" positions. He calls this selection pattern the seniority principle, according to which "in both parties a trial period must be absolved in order to advance to the formal upper echelons of the political elite: a seat in the National Council is 'waited out' by campaigning in losing positions."[27]

The author's objection to this attempt to explain candidate selection is twofold. On the one hand it is too formal and does nothing more than explain the peculiarities of a candidate list. It is natural for electoral law to provide for people to move up the ladder to replace others leaving the list through death or political appointment. The fact that this often carries over from one legislative period to the next is a simple matter of probability. The longer and the more persistent someone pursues a nomination, the better his chances are, purely mathematically speaking, of ultimately being nominated. On the other hand, it appears to me that an intermittent factor has been overlooked here and a jump made from a postquam to a propterquam. Prader's mentioned move from the losing slot 8 (1956) to the uncertain rank 5 (1959) and from there to the safe number 4 position (1962) in Election District 11 (Manhartsberg) and Representative Franz Soronics' advance from the losing rank 5 (1956) to the winning slots 3 (1959) and 1 (1962 and 1966) in Election District 25 (Burgenland) probably have more to do with their inner-party careers in the league, where each of them after all was chairman, than with a stated automatic seniority mechanism for candidates originally placed in losing slots.

The second objection to the seniority hypothesis results from a comparison of the candidates in winning and losing positions. Heinz Fischer has namely shown that many "symbolic candidates" never advance to winning slots and leave the list as symbolic candidates, while, conversely, first-time candidates can also run in a winning position. Such symbolic candidates often serve as a cosmetic correction, for instance to have a party's candidate list statistically more closely reflect voter or population structure. An example of this is the fact that the SPÖ's symbolic candidates include more women, more "real" workers, and those of the ÖVP more persons in a "real" self-employed capacity, and, of course, more younger candidates. But these younger candidates alone are not enough to prove Naßmacher's hypothesis. With regard to the specific form of the selection system in the ÖVP and SPÖ, Naßmacher has discovered clearly different recruitment patterns.

Within the ÖVP it has "become customary for certain slots in certain election districts to belong to certain leagues." This pattern of "leagues holding traditional positions on the tickets is relatively rigid." Naßmacher sees the seniority principle in the SPÖ as existing largely in is pure form.

He must, however, grant that this principle "is only broken with for women's rights proponents: as a matter of principle, new candidates start at the end of the line." And "these statements still (provide) no information on how a hitherto losing candidate is assigned a winning position. In this case, the seniority principle is occasionally broken." Nor does the seniority principle, as Naßmacher states, explain the following observation: "Many candidates leap-frog over several slots, others stay in the same place or drop back... This break with the seniority principle opens the door both for initia-

tives within the framework of inner-party democracy as well as for the informal influence of the party's executive committee to affect candidate nomination when already elected representatives leave the list."[28]

Table 18.6
ÖVP Basic Seat in Vienna (1959-1966)
Candidate's Position on Party Slate

Election District	ÖAAB	ÖWB	ÖBB
01	2	1	
02	1	2	
03	1	2, 3	
04	1, 2		
05	1	2 (as of 1962)	2 (until 1959)
06	2	1	
07	1	2	
Number of Seats	8	6-7	1-0

Source: Naßmacher 1968, p. 68

Unfortunately, no further studies have been conducted to date that pick
up on the proposals given in Marvick and Stiefbold's[29] campaign handbook
and empirically take a closer look at candidate careers. If this hypothesis
holds, then candidates from the middle slots must have passed the legislature
by now and the candidates from the losing lower ranks must now be our parliamentary representatives. A prima facie impression, which needless to say
deserves precise examination, does not confirm this hypothesis.

7. Two Technocratic Career Patterns after Pelinka

Anton Pelinka has repeatedly dealt with the recruitment problem, first
in 1970 in "Elitenbildung in den österreichischen Großparteien"[30], then in
"Parteien und Verbände"[31] 1971 and finally in 1974's collective work "Das
politische System Österreichs."[32]

Recruitment proceeds almost exclusively through parties and interest
groups. "Anyone who wants to advance to the functional elite in politics must
pursue a career through and by means of a party."[33]

He sets out from the Naßmacher "Principle of Seniority and Waiting
Out a Seat," but strips it of the idea of an automatic mechanism formulated

by Naßmacher, and cautiously speaks of a "cursus honorum," of certain previous works and waiting periods, that an upwardly-striving candidate must absolve.

This is true for the majority of cases at the local (town or city council), provincial (state diet, state government) and federal levels (federal government, National Council). Often, previous works are rendered at several levels. The "cursus honorum" or career pattern that the candidates must complete on their way up the political ladder also leads through offices in the parties and interest groups. Thus, of the 165 representatives to the eleventh legislative session of the National Council, 140 (84.8%) had held public office (as of January 1, 1968) on leading committees of their parties at the federal, state, county and city/town level. In addition to the career patterns of the ÖVP, where recruitment is conducted by its three leagues often according to a preset pattern that remains constant over several legislative periods, in the SPÖ candidate selection is steered by two sources, namely party activists on the one hand and union stewards and union officials on the other hand, (33 representatives, 44.6%), that only meet up relatively late in the inner-party nomination process. He here sees a further recruitment channel through which experts bypass the customary preliminary stages and waiting periods without "waiting it out" and are put directly on the ticket by the interest groups at work in the economic and social partnership. A third, also technocratic, pattern of career advancement puts "experts, especially those firmly rooted in the administrative sectors of the ministries and interest groups," in leading positions in the government and (or) Parliament. In the ÖVP, these experts are drawn from three sources, namely the chambers of commerce (Business League), the agriculture chambers (Farmers' League) and the higher levels in the federal and provincial administration (ÖAAB, League of Workers and Employees), as well as from the universities.

A further technocratic career pattern concerns the significance of those groups that the author in another publication[34] termed secondary groups of political socialization. Pelinka refers here to the socialist high school and college student organizations VSM and VSSTÖ, to which almost every Socialist member of parliament who attended college belongs, as well as to the "Confederation of (color-bearing) Catholic University Fraternities" (Cartellverband, CV), to which 19 (22.4%) of the 85 ÖVP National Council representatives in the eleventh legislature belonged. The career described here is also a technocratic one because the persons in question launched their political careers on the basis of their expert capacity in addition to their stemming from particular student fraternities. From this it is evident that in individual cases the two technocratic career patterns given above overlap or reinforce each other, for instance when former VSSTÖ members are also labor chamber experts or when CV members come from the ministerial administration.

In both these technocratic recruitment strategies Pelinka sees the stage of increasing personalization of politics, in the form of the federal chancellors and the inclination by the leaders of the two big parties to override their own party machine, as producing far-reaching consequences for inner-party structures. Accordingly, the traditional advancement pattern of waiting one's way into the political elite via previous works and waiting periods will see a decline in importance, while the influence of the vote-oriented party leadership will increase. This trend will cause the traditional membership party with its focus on certain target groups in the electorate to become a voter party. This will strengthen the position of the party leaders at the cost of the parties' lower and middle strata. Traditional concepts of inner-party democracy will steadily decline in real substance. The members of a party, who, according to this concept, should serve the basic function of inner-party democracy, will continue to lose influence.

In an effort to have the parties democratically legitimize the candidates nominated by them according to the two technocratic career patterns, discussions were pursued for some time on inner-party primaries patterned after the primaries in the United States. These efforts, however, brought few results and have meanwhile been dropped by all the parties, in some cases with the feeble excuse that the inner-party nomination of candidates from the county level on up was designed with the name "primary."

Thus, recruitment continues to be possible solely through and by means of the political parties, with the control of access accorded to a small group inside the parties, the party leaders. This is illustrated by the victory of the SPÖ party leaders in the 1968 statute reform, in which §52 of the Organization Statute provides for 20% of the candidates to be nominated by the leaders in response to central party needs.

8. "The Permanence of Membership in Parliament" after Fischer

Heinz Fischer qualified Naßmacher's hypothesis by maintaining instead of a general principle of seniority a "principle of the permanence of membership": "Anyone who is already a member of Parliament has an extremely good chance of being renominated to a sure place on the ticket for the next election and thus of being elected, as long as he:

a) does not reach the age limit,
b) is not appointed to a different office or
c) does not decline a nomination for true personal or medical reasons."[35]

Cases in which a person already holding a seat in Parliament is not re-elected, and which thus represent an exception to the above principle of membership permanence, are rare. "The rate of renewal in the National

Council is essentially a product of the age limits set forth in the party statutes and of the number of appointments to other offices that would conflict with a seat held in the National Council." What's more, the recently created possibility of reclaiming a seat previously given up has made it customary for ministers and state secretaries to resign their seats temporarily and resume them later or run for office in the next election.

Fischer illustrates his permanency principle in the transition from the eleventh (1966-1970) to the twelfth (1970-1971) legislative session. Of the 124 "old" representatives, 120 were reelected and only two representatives from each the ÖVP and SPÖ were not. From the twelfth to the thirteenth (1971-1975) legislature, 148 of the 151 representatives remained in Parliament. One SPÖ candidate was sacrificed for a central necessity, and two ÖVP candidates were victims of the three so-called "nonaligned candidates." Thus, a regularity can be observed here, according to which about a fourth or a fifth of the sure slots on the party tickets are vacated at the end of a legislative period, while the remaining three-fourths or four-fifths of the representatives campaign again, with more than 95% of them retaining their seats.

Of further interest here is the question of what principles govern the nomination of candidates to the vacated places on a ticket. Fischer's study refutes Naßmacher's seniority principle. In general, the next lower candidates replace those who have left the list, but Fischer observed that those candidates who had just missed being elected in the last election do not automatically move up to "electable slots." Nor is the automatic mechanism of the seniority principle seen to apply when a vacated parliamentary seat is filled between elections.

According to Table 18.7 drawn up from the thirteenth legislative period, in only one case did the next-ranked candidate succeed to office (and this was not because he was next on the list, but because the parliamentary faction needed a doctor to speak for public health policy). In one case, all of 42 candidates were passed over.

H. Fischer offers the following principles to explain how vacated slots are filled:

a) the principle of territorial representativity (from a particular county or province),
b) the principle of leagues in the ÖVP, which corresponds to the SPÖ's principle of the union seat,
c) the principle of party necessity (SPÖ)[36] or of the special rights of the national party (ÖVP)[37], that was made still stronger by the reform of party statutes. This principle of party necessity is reinforced by the party leadership's postelection decision on who is to occupy remaining seats. Depending on the election returns, just-missed initial seats can be replaced

by remaining seats and speculative list slots can be turned into definitive seats.

Table 18.7

Deputies Leaving and Moving up the Party List
First Half of 13th Legislative Period (October 10, 1971 to December 31, 1973)

Departing Candidate	State	Rank Held	Replacement Candidate	Rank Held	Positions Skipped Over
Leopold Gratz	Vienna	24	Karl Lausecker	56	32
Erwin Frühbauer	Carin-thia	7	Johann Graden-ecker	13	6
Herta Winkler	Styria	140	Dr. Jolanda ffenbeck	24	10
Hans Mayr	Vienna	24	Dr. Alfred Gisl	66	42
Josef Ortner	Upper Austria	13	Franz Köck	25	12
Peter Schieder	Vienna	24	Dr. Kurt Heindl	35	11
Dr. Johanna Bayer	Styria	12	Wilhelmine Moser	20	8
Fritz Hahn	Vienna	14	Dr. Günther Wiesinger	15	0

Source: Fischer 1982. p. 147

Thus, for the majority of seats, the principle of the permanence of membership in Parliament amounts so to speak to a principle of political stagnancy. The interesting question of recruitment strategy is confined to a fifth or a fourth of the seats to be decided in any election, which, when accumulated over a four- to six-year period entirely renews the composition of the National Council.

In this connection, a study should be conducted to examine why "new candidates" appear, and what new characteristics they possess in comparison to the representatives leaving office. Be that as it may, H. Fischer established that candidates in losing slots do not automatically advance according to a seniority principle.

9. Available Data and Future Fields of Study

Here the attempt will be made to summarize, again confined to the Austrian National Council, what data have been obtained to date through research on the recruitment of elected representatives and where the areas for future study lie, in order to examine proposed hypotheses or evolve new theories to explain the recruitment process.

I. It appears to be undisputed that the political parties hold a universally valid monopoly on the recruitment of candidates. It would seem that there is no way past the parties to a political mandate. Even alternative and environmental groups are forced to bow to the rules and found a party.[38] Not even powerful interest groups can get around this, as the famous anecdote by Julius Raab goes to show: "they (in this case the Association of Austrian Industrialists) want a representative, but they can't even elect a representative's toes!"

Once the party slates are drawn up, the composition of the National Council has been decided with far more than 90% certainty. On Election Day, the voter himself actually decides only very few seats, namely the crucial ones.

Table 18.8
Crucial National Council Seats That Were Actually Decided on Election Day

National Council Election	SPÖ	ÖVP	VdU1) FPÖ2)	KPÖ3) VGÖ4)	Crucial Seats	In % of of All Seats5)
Oct. 9, 1949	-9	-8	+16	+1	17	10
Feb. 22, 1953	+6	-3	-2	-1	6	4
May 13, 1956	+1	+8	-8	-1	9	5
May 10, 1959	+4	-3	+2	-3	6	4
Nov. 18, 1962	-2	+2	0	-	2	1
Mar. 6, 1966	-2	+4	-2	-	4	2
Mar. 1/ Oct. 4, 1970	+7	-7	0	-	7	4
Oct. 10, 1971 arithmetically7)	(+12) +3	(+2) -3	(+4) 0	- -	6) 3	- 2
Oct. 5, 1975	0	0	0	-	0	0
May 6, 1979	+2	-3	+1	-	3	2
Apr. 24, 1983	-5	+4	+1	-	5	3
Nov. 23, 1986	-10	-4	+6	+8	14	7

1)   until 1953
2)   since 1956
3)   until 1959
4)   1986
5)   rounded off
6)   Because of the increase of 18 seats on the National Council from 165 to 183 seats, there were no contested (net) seats

(Cont.)

(Cont.)

7) The new electoral law when applied to the 1970 National Council election would give—according to the calculations for which I am indebted to Dr. Herbert Maurer of the Statistical Service of the State Government in Linz—an (arithmetic) result of 90 SPÖ, 83 ÖVP and 10 FPÖ seats. Thus, there was an arithmetic switch of three seats from the ÖVP to the SPÖ in the 1971 National Council election.

From Table 18.8 it is seen that, aside from the anomaly of the immediate postwar period with the highest percentage of 10%, maximum 2% to 5% of the seats were contested in the postwar period, and that involved double the number of candidates (the winning and the losing candidates). The larger shift to 7% in the last National Council election (1986) comes close to the landslide in the 1949 National Council election triggered by the restoration of suffrage to former Nazi party members and the VdU's campaigning for election. All the other representatives were practically elected when the list was drawn up.[39]

This is naturally a result of the relatively stable voter behavior prevailing in Austria—until the last National Council election in 1986. This situation could change with the emergence of new alternative or environmental voter groups or with an increased protest behavior on the part of the voter, as was already seen in the 1984 Vorarlberg and 1986 Styrian State Diet elections foreshadowing the 1986 National Council election. The voter's direct exertion of influence by concerted use of preference votes for one candidate is not only very difficult and improbable, but can, as W.C. Müller has shown, be carried ad absurdum by the anticipated mobilization of preference votes for the list leaders or representatives of strong lobbies (for example a union, whose members are told to get out the vote for a certain candidate).

II. Selection according to the principle of the permanence of membership in Parliament, that was put forth by H. Fischer and that actually represents a more precise definition of K.H. Naßmacher's earlier seniority principle and A. Pelinka's principle of previous work and waiting out a seat, would appear to be validated in its restriction to the sure, already held mandates. It is, however, not suited to explain the selection of new candidates.

III. There is still no uniform hypothesis on how these first-time candidacies come to be. That this is the fundamental problem in explaining candidate recruitment can indeed be seen from the fact that even those representatives who retain their seats according to the principle of membership permanence were once first-time candidates, for whose nomination no comprehensive hypothesis has yet been offered. We are faced here with numerous specific theses that are neither founded on systematic empiric analysis, nor that have been adequately examined over a longer period of time. The following strives to present the explanations attempted to date and to evolve hypotheses whose validation will have to be subject to later study.

A) The Hypothesis of Territorial Origin within the Election District
What is needed here is a study of how often this principle was broken by the nomination and election of candidates from outside the election district.

B) The Hypothesis of Equal Representation of an Election District's Component Precincts

C) The Hypothesis of Waiting Out a Seat
A study should be conducted of whether this grueling work is still a road to political candidacy today and, if so, in what cases.

D) The Hypothesis of Social Representation
Austrian electoral law appears to be based on the philosophy that the population's representation in the legislative bodies should mirror its social structure. In Austrian political debate, this is one of the most commonly voiced arguments in favor of an electoral law providing for almost pure proportional representation.

E) The Hypothesis of the Replacement of Popular Representatives with Technocratic Representatives
A detailed study of the repeatedly described process, according to which the popular type of representative of interests is replaced by a technocrat, albeit one with contacts to certain interest groups.

F) The Hypothesis of Technocratic Recruitment
This recruitment differs from that of the preceding hypothesis in that experts from ministries and the universities are recruited without having a clear relationship to a certain interest group.

G) The Hypothesis of Recruitment via the Secondary Groups of Political Socialization[40]
In these the individual politician learns the ropes of political work, and from them he takes on value systems, particularly in his very impressionable years from childhood through college. Groups of this type have played a special role in Austrian politics, especially in connection with the formation of lagers that is typical for our country.[41]

H) The Hypothesis of the Growing Percentage of Professional Politicians

I) The Hypothesis of a Parliament of Public Administrators
In contrast to the parliament of prominent citizens of the liberal era that was composed of lawyers, notaries, doctors and clergymen, today's public administrators predominate in influence and numbers.

J) The Hypothesis of the Declining Number of Self-Employed Persons as Candidates

K) The Hypothesis of the Academization of the Political Career
According to this theory, the portion of college (and also high school) graduates is steadily increasing.

L) The Hypothesis of Party Slates Consisting of Predominantly Young or Predominantly Old Candidates

M) The Hypothesis of the Increasing Centralization of Candidate Selection
   Working from the observation that, not least of all due to the influence
   of the mass media (and here, above all, the electronic media, namely
   television), elections to legislative bodies are more or less taking on the
   character of referendums on the Federal Chancellor, but also in view of
   the growing significance of government financing for political parties, it
   is predicted that the position of the party chairman and thus of the party
   leaders and the central apparatus will take on a new strength.

N) Analysis of the Reasons for "Window Dressing" (celebrities recruited
   into politics from other fields)
   The two big parties repeatedly exhibit the tendency to nominate candidates who do not come from their own rank and file, sometimes not
   even from the same "political lager."

O) Analysis of the Effect of the Work Done by the Party Academies
   A comparison of the lists of those who attended party academies as well
   as a survey of new candidates for their reasons for attending inner-party
   education sessions would reveal to what extent these academies have influenced recruitment.

P) Analysis of the Outcome of Quotas for Female Candidates

Q) Considerations of Democratic Theory
   Finally, the results should be examined in a democratic theoretical approach to determine whether

— with regard to legitimacy and
— with regard to the effectiveness of democratic institutions, and democracy in general,

any results can be ascertained and what proposals for improvement can
be made from the standpoint of participatory democracy. In this connection,
precisely the intended reform of the electoral laws announced prior to the
1986 National Council election by the big two as one of the goals of the up-
coming legislative period should be examined for its contribution to participatory democracy. The proposals made by H. Fischer and H. Neisser, particularly those prescribing more emphasis on the person of the candidate supplementary to the existing candidate lists, and any reform concepts resulting
therefrom should also be examined for this aspect of democracy.

Notes

1. For the three functions see: Lipset 1983.
2. Hermens, *Verfassungslehre*, 1968b, p. 169.
3. Naßmacher 1968, Pelinka 1982, Fischer 1982.
4. Pelinka 1982, p. 40.

5. Gerlich/Kramer 1969.
6. Particularly the news magazines "Profil" and "Wochenpresse."
7. Naßmacher 1968, p. 67ff.
8. Stiefbold et al. 1966.
9. cf. the definition by Herzog (1975): "Recruitment of elites as a chain of successive career steps, whereby in the course of their personal, professional and political development people pass through certain phases and jobs that follow each other in succession, each of which positively or negatively influences their further chances for advancement and, to this extent, represent one process." p. 36f.
10. 1970 Electoral Reform: Federal Law dated November 27, 1970, Federal Law Gazette No. 391 on the election of the National Council (NRWO 1971).
11. Müller 1984.
12. Personal communication from Felix Hurdes.
13. cf. "Neues Österreich," "So reiht und streicht man richtig" (March 6, 1966) and the preceding agitation by the "Action for Individual Election" by the student faction "Wahlblock" (Union of Austrian Academics).
14. Bruno Kreisky according to "Wiener Zeitung" of April 14, 1983.
15. Josef Cap held the hopeless number 46 on the party list for the Vienna Election District and number 102 on the list for the Election District Collective East. See W.C. Müller 1984, p. 106.
16. D. Lenhardt, "Die Presse" (February 17, 1983).
17. AZ, (March 22, 1983).
18. Fischer 1982. p. 123.
19. SPÖ Party Statutes (1968).
20. ÖVP National Party Organization Statutes (1972).
21. ÖVP National Party Organization Statutes (1980).
22. On Austrian political culture see Heinz Fischer 1982 and A. Khol/A. Stirnemann (eds.): *Österreichisches Jahrbuch für Politik* (annually since 1977).
23. On political culture see Lehmbruch 1967, where "political culture" is imparted with "generally prevalent value concepts," p. 12.
24. cf. A. Stirnemann 1969 and A. Stirnemann 1981.
25. Naßmacher 1968.
26. Ibid, p. 67.
27. Ibid, p. 67.
28. Ibid, p. 70.
29. Stiefbold et al. 1966.
30. Pelinka 1970.
31. Pelinka 1971.
32. Pelinka 1982, cf. also Pelinka 1979 and Pelinka 1972.
33. Pelinka 1970, p. 535.
34. cf. Stirnemann 1969, and Stirnemann 1981.
35. Quoted after Fischer 1982, p. 121.
36. §22, Paragraph 1 of the SPÖ Party Statutes.
37. §33, Paragraph 1, lit. b, of the ÖVP Party Statutes.
38. This is true for all political levels with the exception of community politics, where name lists and loose voter alliances often campaign.
39. Despite demands for increased observance of the voter's will and for the personal accountability of the elected official that were voiced at public discussions leading up to the 1983 National Council election, two candidates in safe slots were

426   *Stirnemann*

"removed" from the list by party resolution after the election. These were the representatives Erwin Lanc (SPÖ) of Vienna and Agnes Schierhuber (ÖVP) of Lower Austria.

40. cf. Stirnemann 1969 and Stirnemann 1980, Stirnemann 1981.
41. cf. A. Wandruzka 1954.

Bibliography

Fischer, Heinz, *Die parlamentarischen Fraktionen* in Fischer, H. (Hg.): *Das politische System Österreichs*, dritte Auflage, 1982 (Fischer, 1982)

Gerlich, Peter/Kramer, Helmut, *Abgeordnete in der Parteiendemokratie*, Wien 1969 (Gerlich/Kramer, 1969)

Hermens, F.A., *Verfassungslehre*, 2. Auflage, Frankfurt/Main 1968b (Hermens, 1968b)

Herzog, Dietrich, *Politische Karrieren*, Köln-Opladen 1975 (Herzog, 1975)

Lehmbruch, Gerhard, *Proporzdemokratie*, Tübingen 1967 (Lehmbruch, 1967)

Lipset, S.M., *Political Man, The Social Basis of Politics*, Extended Edition, London 1983 (Lipset, 1983)

Müller, Wolfgang C., *Direktwahl und Parteiensystem*, in: Khol, Andreas/Stirnemann, Alfred (Hg.): *Österreichisches Jahrbuch für Politik '83*, S. 83, Wien 1984 (Müller, 1984)

Naßmacher, Karl-Heinz, *Das österreichische Regierungssystem oder alternierende Regierung?*, Köln-Opladen 1968 (Naßmacher, 1968)

ÖVP, *Bundesparteiorganisationsstatut der ÖVP*, beschlossen vom 15. a.o. Bundesparteitag am 1.12.1972 in Salzburg, Wien 1972 (ÖVP, 1972)

ÖVP, *Bundesparteiorganisationsstatut der ÖVP* beschlossen vom 22. o. Bundesparteitag am 29.2., 1.3.1980 in Salzburg, Wien 1980 (ÖVP, 1980)

Pelinka, Anton, *Elitenbildung in den österreichischen Großparteien*, in: *Wort und Wahrheit, Zeitschrift für Religion und Kultur*, Wien 1970, Heft 6, S. 534-541 (Pelinka, 1970)

Pelinka, Anton, *Parlamentarismus in Österreich*, in: Weinzierl, Erika/Skalnik, Kurt, *Österreich—Die Zweite Republik*, Graz 1972, Band 2, S. 9-30 (Pelinka, 1972)

Pelinka, Anton, *Volksvertretung als funktionelle Elite—Der österreichische Nationalrat auf dem Weg zum Arbeitsparlament*, in: Khol, Andreas/Stirnemann, Alfred, *Österreichisches Jahrbuch für Politik '78*, S. 39, Wien 1979 (Pelinka, 1979)

Pelinka, Anton, *Struktur und Funktion der politischen Parteien*, in: Fischer H. (Hg.), *Das politische System Österreichs*, dritte ergänzte Auflage, 1982, Wien, München, Zürich (Pelinka, 1982)

Plasser, Fritz/Ulram, Peter A., *Unbehagen im Parteienstaat*, Wien-Köln-Graz 1982 (Plasser/Ulram, 1982)

SPÖ-*Organisationsstatut*, Stand 1.11.1983, beschlossen am Bundesparteitag am 2.-4.10.1978 (SPÖ, 1978)

Stiefbold, Rodney et al. (Hg.), *Wahlen und Parteien in Österreich*, Wien 1966 (Stiefbold, 1966)

Stirnemann, Alfred, *Interessengegensätze und Gruppenbildungen innerhalb der ÖVP*, Wien (IHS-Forschungsbericht Nr. 39) 1969 (Stirnemann, 1969)

Stirnemann, Alfred, *Innerparteiliche Demokratie in der ÖVP*, in: Khol, Andreas/Stirnemann, Alfred, *Österreichisches Jahrbuch für Politik '79*, Wien 1980, S. 391 (Stirnemann, 1980)

Stirnemann, Alfred, *Innerparteiliche Gruppenbildung am Beispiel der ÖVP*, in: Khol, Andreas/Stirnemann, Alfred, *Österreichisches Jahrbuch für Politik '80*, Wien 1981, S. 415 (Stirnemann, 1981)

Wandruszka, Adam, *Österreichs politische Struktur*, in: Benedikt Heinrich (ed.), *Geschichte der Republik Österreich*. Wien 1954 (Wandruszka, 1954)

19

The Austrian Way?

MELANIE A. SULLY

1. Historical Background

During the years of the Great Coalition a consensus developed on the political goals of the nation and partisan change was a predictable business. Austria was regarded, until recently, as a paradigm of hyperstability, social peace and prosperity. The Kreisky era (1970-83) brought unprecedented affluence, modernisation of the infra-structure and the introduction of advanced social welfare schemes, more consumer durables and increased leisure time. In this period the SPÖ became one of the most successful Social Democratic parties in Western Europe with impressive electoral victories and a large membership.

The Socialists enjoyed the confidence of a broad section of the electorate and broke new ground in winning over salaried employees and civil servants. Amongst the youth and women it was similarly popular as well as forging ahead in its traditional strongholds. In the election of 1979, the SPÖ secured a record 51.03 percent of the vote and won a majority in five of the nine provinces. By contrast, the Opposition parties seemed feeble and forlorn unable to dam the Socialist tide and lacking ideas and initiative. The People's Party sought a change of leadership after every setback in a desperate but vain effort to counter the 'Kreisky effect'. The only result was to give the impression of weakness and instability at elite level compared with the SPÖ. The competing interests of the different leagues in the ÖVP and the strength of the politicians in the provinces further contributed to the apparent paralysis of the party during these years.

The only other parliamentary party, the FPÖ, hardly seemed worthy of serious attention and was frequently ridiculed as a kind of 'taxi party' with which all its deputies could easily arrive at the Nationalrat. These were the years of undisputed dominance by the Socialists but above all by the personality and charisma of Bruno Kreisky. Bridges were built with catholics and liberals and internationally Austria's standing was high. Vienna expanded to include a United Nations complex and the controversial Middle East peace initiatives of the Chancellor earned respect abroad. Austria was portrayed as the 'island of the blessed' which fostered the illusion that the country could be spared the misfortune of economic recession and a high level of political conflict that had become the norm elsewhere (e.g. as in Britain). Much of this fitted admirably into a cosy mythical tradition according to which the Austrian achievement has often been quoted as the ability to convince the World that Beethoven was an Austrian and Hitler a German. Music, mountains and Mozart were part of the package that Austria most liked to export.

2. The Aftermath of the Kreisky Era

Since 1983 the cracks have visibly begun to appear in the neat edifice, which had undermined the self-confidence of Austrians and dented the image of the country abroad. The scandal and accident-prone republic staggered through a series of crises from the 1984 debate on 'December 8' shop opening times, through the disturbing scenes of Hainburg,[1] on to the 'Reder affair', the 1985 wine scandal and the Waldheim election of 1986. The latter in particular and the Reder case, with lingering shadows of the Nazi past, provoked hostility in the Anglo-American world, normally favourably disposed to the serene Alpine republic.

These difficulties occurred in rapid succession after a major change in Austrian politics heralded in by the 1983 election and the resignation of Kreisky as Chancellor.[2] The loss of an absolute majority for the SPÖ was a severe electoral setback for the party and signalled a new mood of change. For the time being the party could console itself with the thought of continuing in office, albeit with a coalition partner in the shape of the FPÖ. Even before the 1983 election, new groups were forming which were beginning to fundamentally question the established basis of the Austrian party system with its famous rigid and all-powerful 'Lager mentality'. The referendum in November 1978 with its narrow majority against nuclear energy was the first stirring of discontent and an indication that 'the time was out of joint' in the state of Austria. Zwentendorf acted as a catalyst for the as yet nebulous and politically inchoate increase in protest. New social movements flourished based in the women's and peace groups and popular with the young and the ecologists.[3] Domestic conflict has since intensified and the potential exists for further unrest. The combined effect of these changes has had a profound destabilising influence on the Austrian party system and previous partisan alignments. New issues, such as a concern for the environment and the quality of life, became more salient. In this respect Austria followed the path of advanced industrial societies where an increase in conflict between materialist and non-materialist goals was already apparent. The political scene has recently been complicated by a shift to the Right as witnessed by Waldheim's election, Vranitzky's emergence for the SPÖ as Chancellor and the appointment of a Benedictine monk, loyal to the Vatican, to succeed Kardinal König. In addition, a revival of old prejudices such as anti-semitism, catholicism and a reassertion of conservative values has been apparent. Unlike the Greens and the feminists, this 'new type' of politics often looks remarkably similar to the older style which has deeper roots in the indigenous political culture.

Against this background came the election of Jörg Haider as leader of the FPÖ at the party's conference in Innsbruck in September, 1986. This precipitated an early dissolution of the 'small' coalition and an election was held in November. The SPÖ claimed that 'liberal' tendencies in the FPÖ had been pushed too far into the background for a continuation of the coalition. Haider's energetic campaigning with its populist style presented a real challenge to the established parties. The FPÖ had, in coalition, become too closely identified with the 'system' to effectively articulate the protest vote, traditionally a vital element of electoral support. Haider, free from the shackles of coalition, could appeal once again to the disgruntled and disaffected and mobilise them for the 'third force' in the party system. Members in the FPÖ had been uneasy at the growth in support for the Greens and ecological groups some of whom, with a middle-class bias, threatened the position of the Freiheitlichen. The party stood on the brink of annihilation and Haider's robust radicalism offered hope at the eleventh hour.

With Kreisky's departure the social-liberal consensus, which he had encouraged, rapidly disintegrated. The SPÖ was open to criticism for intolerance towards intellectual dissidents and the expulsion of Günther Nenning was symptomatic of this attitude. The euphoria of the previous social democratic decade had evaporated and it seemed as though the SPÖ was struggling to develop new ideas and initiatives. From being a party of the oppressed and underprivileged, it had all too frequently become identified with corrupt deals, intrigue and excessive patronage. The patience and discipline of the rank and file and youth movement avoided an open rupture on the question of the nature and direction of Socialism. Undeniable progress had been made in social policies, reform of the penal code, education and health but the Left was painfully aware that despite an absolute majority, no fundamental redistribution of wealth had occurred.[4]

'Die Reformen und Innovationen der siebziger Jahre erfolgten im Kontext einer ausgeprägten Kontinuität der Eigentumsverhältnisse, der institutionellen Gegebenheiten und der sozialökonomischen Arrangements. Vor allem die "Sozialpartnerschaft" funktionierte in ungebroche-

ner Kontinuität und ließ auch die durch den Regierungswechsel bewirk-
te Änderung der Kräfteverhältnisse nur wenig zur Geltung kommen.
Umverteilung hat, wie vermerkt, nicht stattgefunden. "Mitbestimmung"
auf betrieblicher Ebene ist nicht stärker geworden. Die Orientierung auf
das Auslandskapital ist womöglich noch ausgeprägter geworden. Man
war vor allem bestrebt, den kapitalistischen Akkumulationsprozeß in
Gang zu halten, um solcherart die Arbeitsplätze zu sichern bzw. neue zu
schaffen.'[5]

The oil crisis and its repercussions put Social Democrats on the defensive and a concern grew to protect the achievements of the welfare state. This
took priority over further expansion and the SPÖ had to accept less
grandiose goals in this new climate. These trends were slower to take root in
Austria than elsewhere in Western Europe but the country had always been
more 'Eastern' European in displaying such a time-lag. Kreisky probably
hoped that Austria's tardiness would be its salvation and that before the recession started to bite, an international upswing would come to the rescue.
This gamble particularly applied to the policy of full employment which was
to be so costly and lead to a stock-pile of neglected problems in the nationalised industries. The hoped-for economic improvement did not materialise
and Kreisky's Austria too became the victim of cut-backs with prospect of job
losses and youth unemployment.

3. Winds of Change

After the 1983 election the SPÖ suffered a series of defeats in provincial
and Arbeiterkammer elections. It was no longer the indomitable force in the
Austrian party system but as yet no credible challenger had sufficient power
to fill the vacuum. In the Land election in Lower Austria of October 1983,
the SPÖ lost three seats and four percent of the vote. A year later in an election in Vorarlberg its vote dropped from 29 to 24 percent; this was followed
by a further blow in an election in Upper Austria in October 1985 when the
SPÖ vote declined from 41.4 percent to 37.9 percent. The Presidential ballots
in May and June 1986 resulted in further humiliation for the party with the
election, for the first time, of a 'black' Federal President, the controversial
Kurt Waldheim. This unleashed an unashamed positive appraisal of the wartime past of soldiers who had simply 'done their duty' for the Fatherland.
Although provoking international ostracism, this struck a chord domestically
and Haider, well-known for his stance in the Reder-Frischenschlager affair,
was in tune with this new mood. The Liberal International, worried by the
alleged ultra-right putsch at the Innsbruck conference, threatened to expel
the FPÖ and sent observers to monitor the tone of the party's election cam-

paign in 1986. 'Liberal Democracy', as understood in the Anglo-Saxon World, has never had a strong independent presence in Austria and in the Kreisky era was incorporated, to some extent, within the SPÖ. In the 1980s it has become an even weaker force as liberals in the FPÖ were routed by the nationalist 'young Turks' from the western provinces.

The composition of the Austrian party landscape has, in addition to the endemic weakness of liberalism and a fall-off in support for the Socialists, demonstrated in recent years an overpowering inertia in the catholic-conservative camp. The ÖVP's tragic inability to capitalise on the misfortunes of the SPÖ artificially prolonged the leading position of the Socalists. Handicapped by a decentralised federal structure, the ÖVP seemed unable to move forward with unanimous resolution to capture the spoils of office. Success for Conservatism, when it came, was credited to Waldheim, a candidate supported by, but not of, the ÖVP, and to Haider who advanced at the expense of the ÖVP.

By contrast the more tightly-knit social-democratic Lager has displayed some adaptability and a remarkable resilience under pressure. The SPÖ was able to salvage some of its flagging act in 1986 with a swift leadership change after the Waldheim débâcle. Franz Vranitzky, a banker politician, taught the Socialists that privatisation was not, after all, tabu and that redundancies and cut-backs were unavoidable. Kreisky's paternalistic state was no more but it was the SPÖ not the conservatives who had buried it. Vranitzky's 'new Austria' stressed the importance of individual initiative and the Leistungsprinzip and was critical of abuses and waste in the welfare state. In this way the SPÖ neatly responded to the changed political climate while the ÖVP looked on helpless and envious. The SPÖ's answer to difficult times was essentially conservative and pragmatic which made reform initiatives even harder for the People's Party. In power since 1970, the SPÖ felt and acted like a governmental party. Its task in meeting contemporary challenges was incomparably easier than the problems which confronted the British Labour Party, confined to Opposition and isolated from the chief economic centres of power. Thatcherism too benefited from a sensational and jingoistic foreign policy which had no scope in tiny, neutral Austria. Conservatism, to be popular in Austria, had to appeal to different, often very crude, emotions in the domestic arena and it was to be Haider rather than the Biedermeier figure of Alois Mock who was most at home in this milieu.

The party system was placed under extra strain with the emergence of the environmentalist lobby and the burgeoning of several Green groups scoring successes in local and regional politics. Sectarian squabbles spoilt the chance of a breakthrough at national level in 1983 and neither the United Greens with 1.93 percent nor the Alternative List with 1.36 percent won parliamentary representation. The process of building common links and forging a joint electoral strategy was still in its infancy as the 1986 election was abruptly announced. Sympathy for the Greens could be expected following the disaster of Chernobyl earlier in the year but once again fractional feuds damaged their high electoral hopes. The integrative capacity of the SPÖ meant that progress was slower for a take-off of the Greens in Austria compared with West Germany. So long as the SPÖ was in office offering hope of social progress, potential Red/Greens could be persuaded to stay in the fold. In the 1983 election the presence of Josef Cap, the Socialist Youth leader, on the SPÖ list helped to attract the young interested in Alternative policies. Cap was elected to parliament but failed to hold his support and the disillusioned looked elsewhere for solutions. The Left Socialists have since 1945 been muted and tame compared with West Germany and have remained numerically insignificant in a party with 700.000 members. They have failed to penetrate the rank and file and mobilise trade unionists to make any lasting impact. This has helped the SPÖ retain its resilience in a time of party dealignment. As Austria is a non-NATO country, the Left was deprived of a natural and obvious target in foreign affairs and, nearer at home, extensive nationalisation rendered traditional calls for state control superfluous. The post-materialist phase added a challenge from the Greens which, despite internal difficulties, became more important in 1986. The Landtag election in Styria in September 1986 encouraged the VGÖ-AL alliance and produced gloom in the ranks of the Socialists:

Table 19.1
Styrian LTW (Sept. 1986)

	1986 %	1986 Seats	1981 (LTW) %	1981 (LTW) Seats	NRW 1983 % (in Styria)	
ÖVP	51.75	30	50.9	30		42.27
SPÖ	37.6	22	42.7	24		49.45
FPÖ	4.59	2	5.1	2		3.97
KPÖ	1.18	-	1.3	-		0.76
VGÖ-AL	3.73	2	-	-	VGÖ	1.55
					AL	1.82
Others	1.13	-	-	-		0.18

The Green presence constituted a problem for the ÖVP as well as the SPÖ. A survey in 1984 showed that 16 percent of the support for the Greens came from former ÖVP voters compared with 5 percent in the BRD who had formerly voted CDU/CSU and who had changed to the Greens. According to the same poll, 19 percent of the Green-Alternatives were ex-SPÖ voters and 4 percent had come via the FPÖ. The West German Greens could claim similar support from former Social Democrats but had not been able to attract FDP voters.[6]

Much of the appeal of both the Greens and the FPÖ under Haider in the 1986 election can be traced to the negative image of the two big parties who, it was feared, were conniving together to reform the Great coalition. Although in disagreement on other policies, both the Greens and the FPÖ vehemently attacked the abuse of power and the privilege, corruption and bureaucracy which had almost become synonymous with the two party system. By comparison, the ÖVP's professed opposition to the 'party book' had a hollow ring and failed to convince. The keenest recipients of the new teaching were to be the young and first-time voters. The 1986 election demonstrated a further loosening of Lager loyalties and a weakening in party identification which can only be alarming for both the SPÖ and the ÖVP.[7]

The Austrian voter of the 1990s is currently maturing in a profoundly apolitical climate where traditional loyalties are in a process of disintegration. Voting is no longer ritualistic but has become a cavalier act of fancy depending on rational considerations of the maximisation of self-interest. The SPÖ's discussion on the Perspektiven '90 theme and the ÖVP's programmatic debate on the Zukunftsmanifest are unlikely to inspire the electorate of the future. Both the established parties and the media are in danger of becoming increasingly out of touch with the troubles and views of the 'ordinary man in the street'. The small man–the victim of big power politics by cartel management–cannot be dismissed as an insignificant force. The Green 'circus', with its incessant stormy meetings and tempermental displays of sectarian wrath, lost much of the initiative in 1986 to fully exploit this discontent and the opportunity was seized unexpectedly by an old force revamped at the last minute, the FPÖ. It would be premature to predict whether this is a temporary phenomenon or not and the outcome is dependant on the performance of the Greens in parliament and the ability of the big two to win back credibility. The age-structure of the electoral basis for the parties offers little comfort at present for the SPÖ and the ÖVP as can be seen in Table 19.2.

The Austrian party system is more of an enigma for political scientists than in the past but one variable, at least, is consistent and predictable–the inveterate failure of the communists to reduce the Socialist grip on the Left of the political spectrum. The KPÖ made slight gains in 1986 but in a changing party landscape its style of yesteryear seems curiously quaint and anachronistic. Its unpopularity has deprived protest voters on the left of an immediate and obvious alternative. An additional element of continuity has been the importance of personalities in politics. This has continued from the 'Kreisky-who else?' phase through to the 1986 campaign with the total identification of the SPÖ with Vranitzky and the importance of the 'Haider effect'.[8] In other respects the party system has become increasingly mobile and the electorate's behaviour less predictable. For the Socialists a major problem has been mobilisation of the once reliable party faithful. Such voters currently disenchanted with their 'normal' party are abstaining. In the future they could return to the fold or be 'captured' by enemy pieces on the multicoloured chessboard.

Table 19.2
Age profile of voters, 1986

Age	SPÖ	ÖVP	FPÖ	Greens
Up to 29	22	20	31	58
Up to 49	28	25	32	32
Up to 59	23	27	15	6
Up to 69	12	13	10	2
70 plus	15	15	12	3
%	100	100	100	100

Source: Dr. Fessel + GfK-Institut, Repräsentative Wahltagsbefragung (exit poll), N= 2.149 Wähler nach Verlassen des Wahllokales

The growth in aversive attitudes to the main parties was the byproduct of changes in the social structure, a development by no means unique to Austria.[9] An increase in occupational and residential mobility tends to affect patterns of voting behaviour. As industrialised societies mature, agriculture becomes less important and a dramatic shift takes place to the service sector. This process is also accompanied by an erosion of local and institutional loyalties. For both the SPÖ and the ÖVP such developments mean that their traditional clientele vote is being constantly undermined and replaced by an unknown entity-the new middle class. These trends have created a different set of values and a mood more hostile to state expenditure and schemes wasteful of taxpayers' money. This novel scenario is deeply opposed to the Kreiskyism of the 1970s and is critical of the neglect in reforming the nationalised industries as also of the policy of full employment.

Paradoxically it was the SPÖ of the Kreisky era which helped to spawn the 'modern' Austria and overcome the relative backwardness of the country to make it 'europareif'. Social Democracy modernised Austria, introduced new technology into its industry, revolutionised the availability of consumer goods and then aghast looked on in disbelief when the progeny of this new age emerged grumbling and critical. One of the cruelest ironies, for an outside observer of the party scene, is to note the reappraisal of the Kreisky years from positive and glowing gratitude to embittered rejection. Difficulties for the SPÖ are not exclusively an Austrian feature but are typical of a more general trend:

> 'The problems of the Social Democratic parties have been compounded by the fact that the increasing levels of education, information, and political sophistication are resulting in a dramatic shift in the basis of political support from diffuse to specific criteria. Thus the Social Democratic parties cannot assume that they will be able to hold onto their traditional constituencies simply because they are representatives of the working class or because of what they have done for workers in the past. Increasingly, they will have to respond to specific voter demands to maintain their support. The growing emphasis on specific rather than symbolic outputs is, on the one hand, threatening to bankrupt the welfare state and already has led to the tax revolt backlash. On the other hand, the increasing output evaluation orientation of the voters is threatening to split the Social Democrats' traditional constituencies as the result of the rise of a new set of crosscutting issues'[10].

4. Can the Old Mould Survive? The Party System in Flux

At first glance, a reformation of the Great Coalition could give a semblance of normality to the Austrian political scene for this is what most foreign observers associated with the country for two decades until 1966. Even after this date, it was generally assumed that the arrangement lived on by proxy in the guise of a paracoalition of social partnership. Unlike those first decades of the Republic, the big two now have more vociferous opponents in the National Assembly. Yet there are few signs of a fundamental and permanent realignment of partisan forces. The big two could still engineer a comeback, take advantage of a reprieve and devise a viable strategy to counter the new politics. The 1986 election dislodged the system primarily in favour of a parliamentary (and 'established') party viz. the FPÖ. It success was based on the negative mobilisation of voters and not rooted in a basic issue realignment. A full regime change was thwarted by a shifting coalition strategy which maintained an element of continuity in a phase of potential instability.

The task of winning back lost ground is likely to be hard for a demoralised People's Party, more ideologically diffuse and less homogeneously structured than the Socialists. The SPÖ too has become stale after sixteen years in office and seems often to prefer to trust to good luck rather than action to steer it through difficult years. Its complacency was given a jolt by the loss of the Presidency in 1986 and led to an uncharacteristic burst of activity and a new leader. This move, forced on the SPÖ, saved it from a greater disaster in the November general election. Despite this, the result was cold comfort for the Socialists and the trend since 1979, in all Bundesländer, has been unfavourable for the SPÖ as Table 19.3 shows.

Table 19.3
Voting Patterns in general elections since 1979 for the SPÖ (%)

Province	1979	1983	Change	1986	Change	Change since 1979
Burgenland	52.95	51.35	-1.60	49.0	-2.4	-4.0
Carinthia	56.23	52.93	-3.30	47.2	-5.7	-9.0
Lower Austria	48.41	45.88	-2.53	42.4	-3.5	-6.0
Upper Austria	50.25	46.31	-3.94	42.1	-4.2	-8.1
Salzburg	44.93	41.33	-3.60	36.8	-4.5	-8.1
Styria	51.37	49.45	-1.92	44.1	-5.4	-7.3
Tyrol	37.67	34.84	-2.83	29.2	-5.6	-8.4
Vorarlberg	33.42	27.32	-6.10	25.5	-1.8	-7.9
Vienna	60.60	56.57	-4.03	52.4	-4.2	-8.2
Austria	51.03	47.65	-3.38	43.1	-4.6	-8.0

Source: Austrian Statistical Central Office

    To reverse this trend will require a fundamental re-evaluation of the SPÖ's strategy and internal organisation. The ÖVP is similarly on the defensive and is more liable to increased fragmentation in the wake of the disappointing results of the 1986 election. Despite these insidious dangers, the numerical preponderance of the two main parties is impressive (see graph 19.1). The close overlap between the major econnomic interest groups and the SPÖ and the ÖVP further strenthens their position.[11] Social partnership provides an ongoing stabilising element in a fluid party system which has cushioned the demise of the SPÖ and ÖVP. It cannot indefinitely prop up the big two as can be seen in Table 19.4 and graph 19.2. In 1979 for the first time the percentage of votes for the SPÖ and the ÖVP fell slightly, a trend consolidated in 1983 and 1986 through the impact of new parties and the gains of the FPÖ. The Social Partners too have had to concede ground to the new social movements as Zwentendorf and Hainburg testify but in the main continue to diffuse the forces of realignment. They are autonomous actors less suceptible than parties to the dictates of electoral whim and merit close scrutiny to assess the real forces of change operating on the Austrian party system.[12] As the Lager system loosens, so too could the close relationship between parties and interest groups begin to dissolve. Further research in this area could de-

termine the overall continuity in both Austrian politics and, just as importantly, the economic system.

Table 19.4
Distribution of seats in the Nationalrat (%) for the SPÖ/ÖVP compared
with other parties, 1945-86

	SPÖ/ÖVP (%)	Others (%)
1945	97.58	2.42
1949	87.27	12.73
1953	89.09	10.91
1956	94.55	5.45
1959	95.15	4.85
1962	95.15	4.85
1966	96.36	3.64
1970	96.36	3.64
1971	94.54	5.46
1975	94.54	5.46
1979	93.99	6.01
1983	93.44	6.56
1986	85.79	14.21

Valid votes in millions

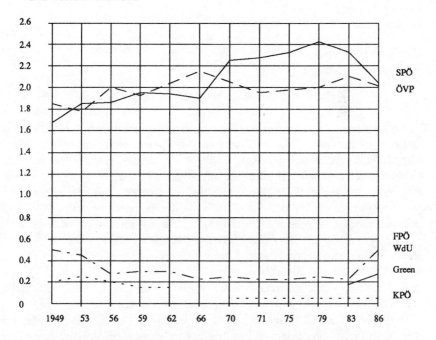

Graph 19.1: Electoral Profile of the Parties since 1949

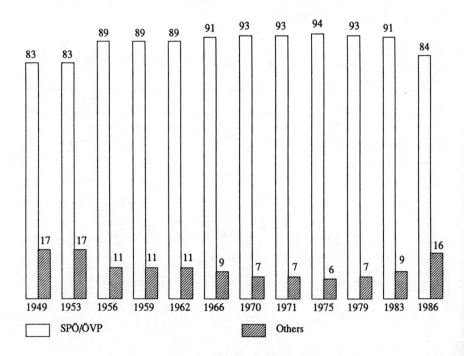

Graph 19.2: Percentage of votes for the SPÖ/ÖVP compared with other parties (1949-1986)

5. Towards a 'New' Democracy?

This current phase of uncertainty is accompanied by a more pessimistic mood than in the Kreisky era. Austrians seem less confident of their own identity and unsure of the future. There is an increasing tendency to reject the economic and political influence of the capital. In these respects, the new politics is rooted in older, more established, cultures and prejudices. The party landscape is in a process of reformation as economic difficulties and political conflict become more familiar. Austria was anxious to catch-up with the rest of modern western industrialised nations but inevitably this introduced stress into the party system which was not so welcome. The postwar mentality showed an inability to tolerate high levels of political conflict. Social partnership and consensus were regarded as guarantors against past tragedies of civil war and foreign occupation. Experiments were regarded with suspicion and ultracaution forced the parties into a rigid mould. Formal democracy had been achieved but had not fully matured. Too much conflict is still considered unhealthy and damaging to social peace. Past memories are too recent to allow for fundamental changes in political outlooks. In February 1984 Austria commemorated the fiftieth anniversary of the civil war relieved that these were the horrors of the past. Developments since have not encouraged Austrians to relax and the violence surrounding the Hainburg occupation towards the end of 1984 was a timely reminder that events could get out of control to threaten social peace. The response of the traditional elites to a proliferation in protest will be crucial in determining the shape of the party system. The SPÖ can no longer rely on the mediocrity of its opponents to disguise its own shortcomings. The 1986 election showed a decline in voter-participation with a turn-out of just over 90 percent. Whilst Lager loyalties may be loosening, substitute self-identification patterns have yet to solidify. The results of the 1986 election demonstrated that the traditional concentration and rigidity of the Austrian party system can no longer be taken for granted. Electoral volatility is on the increase with the young and new middle class particularly prone to switching allegiances. Forecasts on future developments could be complicated by proposed revisions in the electoral system.

A clear opportunity exists to establish a more mature democracy by a greater willingness to accept and respond with more sensitivity to social cleavages. This could liberalise archaic structures particularly in the economic decision-making process, especially if new attitudes also evolve within the ÖGB. Juxtaposed with such trends is the possibility of a relapse into more reactionary politics exploiting the frustration and disillusionment with the status quo:

> 'Ein Teil dieser Proteststimmen kann durchaus auch anderen Gruppierungen zufließen—seien dies mögliche Neugründungen (etwa jeder sechste Österreicher kann sich vorstellen, eine Antisteuerpartei zu wählen, ein weiteres Drittel hielte eine solche zumindest für "nützlich"), sei dies durch die Mobilisierung allgemeiner Antiparteien- und Antiprivilegienresentiments wie im Falle der erfolgreichen Haider-FPÖ in Kärnten: Le Pen, Almirante und Glistrup auf österreichisch sind so unwahrscheinlich nicht.'[13]

Yet even here it is evident that negative attitudes have been integrated into a 'traditional' anti-establishment party viz. the FPÖ. The party book system may be under attack but it is conceivable that voters will cynically accept its formal pay-offs in every day life but switch to parties rejecting the 'Reds' and the 'Blacks' in elections. Future cohorts of voters could be less influenced by party sub-cultures even if they continue to accept multiple membership in their associations to secure career advancement. The continued grip of the Lager on partisanship is currently in question.

The SPÖ and the ÖVP have new challenges to meet in the 1990s if the party system is to retain its historical continuity. This includes the greater toleration of conflict at both inner and intra-party levels. Austria stands at the crossroads between a number of alternatives and it is too early to judge which option will be followed.

Changes at the mass level linked with demographic and attitudinal changes suggested that a break-down of the old Lager structure is under way even here although this does not have to lead to more homogeneity and con-sensus politics. New cleavages related to gender, youth and the ecology open up. Some changes can be expected by the rising challenge presented by ex-cluded groups such as Alternatives/Ecologists amounting to a new kind of sub-culture. This does not mean that chaos will take over; a regeneration could lead to a more mature democracy able ultimately to withstand conflict and endure longer. What it does mean is that models of the future will have to be more complex and sophisticated to reflect these developments.

Inter-segmental elite co-operation characterises the consociational regime. This, in the case of Austria, replaced the sub-cultural hostility of the pre-war period. Elite co-operation offset the persistence of the Lager/ghetto mentality at mass level. Coalescent elite behaviour reinforced by autonomous social partnership (not rooted in constitutional norms) continued even after 1966. Moreover, parties retained a remarkably tight grip on membership and organisation despite the development of a competitive catch-all strategy to cope with electoral volatility. The assumption then was that the political cul-ture would become less fragmented and more homogeneous, thus fulfilling one of the main preconditions for a transition to a depoliticised democracy.

The politics of accommodation was continued by the elites under differ-ent types of government formations, but its hey day was over. A new scenario was emerging which meant the demise of consociationalism. New forms are still evolving which challenge the old stereotypes. Much discussion has taken place recently about the revival of polarisation in Austrian politics, yet this cannot be confused with the Lager conflicts of the 1930s along a simple Left-Right axis. Issues of today cut across the old blocks presenting a more in-triguing mosaic for the political analyst. Similarly the current Red-Black coalition is not a revamp of the pre-'66 model but is a new breed likely to be more ephemeral and shaped by a different Zeitgeist.

The road to a fully competitive party system faces an uncertain future complicated by the reappearance of a Grand Coalition in 1987 and a worsen-ing economic climate. The Austrian "model" has in the past been associated with the Great Coalition and social partnership as powerful interlocking sys-tems and an exemplary level of political stability. These have been the object of admiration, not to say envy, for foreign observers who have often perhaps neglected the price paid in terms of a sacrifice in a participatory democracy. The future could see the social partners more on the defensive but opens up the exciting possibility of greater democracy and participation. Ultimately this could strengthen the foundations of the political system if such a develop-ment is not feared or resisted by the elites.

The Second Republic has become classified as the paradigm for a stable western democracy. However, the term political stability confronts the political scientist with problems since mere "changes" cannot be regarded as promoting instability and systems do change on occasions to maintain stability. The converse may also be true, i.e. that lack of change and rigidity may induce instability, and this is worth bearing in mind in a discussion of Austrian politics. Political stability can be related to the maintenance and durability of government institutions, the social order and political parties over time and in this sense the Second Republic could have a long healthy future.

6. Continuity and Change

The present party system is far more fluid and amorphous than ever before. Today there are no encapsulated camps but rival parties face complex challenges from within their social groups as well as from each other. This could promote the desire for co-operation even if only to reinforce dual hegemony but it is likely to make smooth functioning more difficult. Greater cynicism and frustration is now more detectable which in an extreme form could lead to a legitimacy crisis. In the past high participation but low citizen influence has been the norm but this in the future could give way to lower political engagement. The 1987 Municipal election in Vienna revealed that two-thirds of first-time voters did not vote. The growth of a "new" politics is a manifestation of this discontent and previously minor concerns for Austria, such as the Third World and unilateral disarmament, are having a greater significance as the country's political culture becomes more "Westernised". New social movements start to burgeon (despite powerful economic interest groups) with a more universalist, less insular consciousness. The Austrian tradition of the 'Obrigkeitsstaat' has also to be remembered as a formative psychological influence which has led to the temptation to drift along without active political engagement. Social partnership requires consent but not participation. This has been an essential feature of the Austrian model which may recede in the future.

It is difficult to ascertain whether these changes are fundamental enough to firstly dealign and then to significantly realign Austrian politics.

The election of 1966 showed high volatility and was followed by the "critical" election of 1970 which inaugurated a process of realignment continuing into the 1980s. New patterns of voting behaviour were initiated and both main parties were losing their "Stammwähler" because of socioeconomic and demographic factors. The Kreisky "coalition" cushioned the effect of this, neutralising new trends, and the system remained stable and based on consensus politics. The 1986 election highlighted the continued weakness of the ÖVP and saw a growth in support for small parties on the periphery. The

FPÖ doubled its vote and the Greens entered Parliament. The new mood of greater virulence set by the Presidential election continued. "Parteiverdrossenheit" was on the order of the day as was shown by high abstentions in Vienna and the number of invalid votes. Waldheim and the concomitant troubles were part and parcel of increasing domestic difficulties reflecting a new, less favourable economic outlook.

In 1986, electoral turn-out was the lowest since the war, yet at 90.5%, for a foreign observer, there hardly seems cause to panic. The two-party system is under stress but still numerically preponderant. The SPÖs percentage support is impressive especially if viewed in relationship to other parties. The mass membership of the parties although declining is, taken on a comparative basis, remarkable. The pervasive network of ancillary associations as well as the striking membership-voter ratio further promotes continuity. The two small parties, especially the Greens, lack sociological and ideological coherence and a strongly defined nationwide organisational network.

Despite recent fears, there is relatively little violence in evidence in the political culture. The "Oper" demonstration, with its allegations of police brutality, and increasing student unrest could suggest that Hainburg was not an isolated incident. Yet little inner-city violence, or racial tension exists to place the regime in question. Terrorist and armed attacks are still within respectably low levels compared with elsewhere and there is an absence of any 'Northern Ireland' type conflict.

The high integrative capacity of the SPÖ is helpful in promoting stability and continuity. The loyalty and discipline of the rank and file in the party and unions persist with no competition on the left. Cutbacks and increased social hardship are bound to be accompanied by a rise in protest but this does not necessarily inaugurate an eclipse of the entire system. There is still a high degree of consensus on foreign policy goals and economic performance is by Western European standards creditable.

On balance it would seem that changes are not drastic enough to threaten the continuation of the 'Austrian Way' but some revisions of opinion on the criteria for success may be in order. In the future, conflict may have to be learned to be accepted not as an evil influence signifying failure and verging on Weltuntergang but, within limits, as fulfilling a positive role. This would avoid disillusionment and enhance confidence in an age of uncertainty.

7. Conclusion

The hallmark of the new politics is action, engagement and participation. The established parties seem sympathetic to direct democracy but on their terms and only if controlled. This may not be an entirely adequate response in the long term. To be credible the main parties will have to convert rhetoric into action. Programmatic debate has to be translated into practice e.g. the 25% Quotenregelung for women in the SPÖ. The "open party" lacks conviction and it may already be too late for the SPÖ to retain its integrative role on the Left and with young people. The SPÖ needs to develop channels of communication with youth, foreign workers, women, the unemployed, the underprivileged and those with special needs. This is the task of Social Democracy for the rest of the century and is necessary too for the survival of the Austrian way. A beginning has already been made but working groups and ideas need the needs of government departments. The big parties do not always show an ideal amount of sensitivity in responding to minority interests in practice as witnessed by the Great coalition's self-interested plans to steamroller the economic interests of smaller groups on the question of party finance.

For the ÖVP the new situation poses a problem of survival as it is not so homogeneous as the socialist camp (as witnessed by the Draken dispute) and faces threats from Haider as well as the Greens. Conflicts within the Lager could increase making mutual accommodation more difficult. Yet the big two, like superpowers, have strong vested interests to pull together and an uneasy detente is likely. The model could therefore be in the process of adapting to different times and the initiatives could rest with the parties. The SPÖ went more cleverly on the offensive in this respect stealing some of the conservatives' clothes in the process. The scope for the response from the ÖVP is more limited given the SPÖs pragmatism, particularly under Vranitzky.

Both parties are in need of a large dose of glasnost and a concerted policy of perestroika if the Austrian way is not to be an endangered species. Austria could then continue to serve as an example for others to emulate as it has done in the past.

Notes

1. See Pelinka 1986.
2. Plasser/Ulram 1984.
3. See 'Neue Soziale Bewegungen', *Österreichische Zeitschrift für Politikwissenschaft* 1986.
4. Chaloupek 1978, pp. 191ff.
5. See Prager 1980.
6. Plasser/Ulram 1985.
7. Haerpfer 1985.
8. See Sully 1987.
9. See Ulram 1985, pp. 203-39.
10. Sänkiaho 1984.
11. See Nick/Pelinka 1983.

12. Pelinka 1985, pp. 171-83.
13. Plasser/Ulram 1985, p. 22.

* I wish to acknowledge the assistance of the Leverhulme Trust for making this research possible.

Bibliography

Chaloupek, G., *Die Verteilung der persönlichen Einkommen in Österreich*, in: *Wirtschaft und Gesellschaft* 2/78 (Chaloupek, 1978)

Haerpfer, Christian, *Abschied vom Loyalitätsritual?*, in: Plasser, Fritz/Ulram, Peter/ Welan, Manfried (Hg.): *Demokratierituale*, Wien 1985 (Haerpfer, 1985)

Nick, Rainer/Pelinka, Anton, *Bürgerkrieg-Sozialpartnerschaft*, Wien 1983 (Nick/ Pelinka, 1983)

Pelinka, Anton, *Politische Herrschaftsrituale*, in: Plasser, Fritz/Ulram, Peter/Welan, Manfried (Hg.): *Demokratierituale*, Wien 1985 (Pelinka, 1985)

Pelinka, Anton, *Hainburg—mehr als nur ein Kraftwerk*, in: Khol, A./Ofner, G./Stirnemann, A. (Hg.): *Österreichisches Jahrbuch für Politik '85*, Oldenbourg 1986 (Pelinka, 1986)

Österreichische Zeitschrift für Politikwissenschaft 1986/2 (special issue)

Plasser, Fritz/Ulram, Peter, *Themenwechsel-Machtwechsel?*, in: Koren, Stephan/Pisa, Karl/Waldheim, Kurt (Hg.): *Politik für die Zukunft*, Wien 1984 (Plasser/ Ulram, 1984)

Plasser, Fritz/Ulram, Peter, *Entsteht ein neues Parteiensystem?*, in: *Österreichische Monatshefte 2/1985* (Plasser/Ulram, 1985)

Plasser, Fritz, *Parteien unter Streß*, Wien 1987 (Plasser, 1987)

Prager, T., *Managementwechsel ohne aufregende Folgen*, in: *Wirtschaft und Gesellschaft 2/80* (Prager, 1980)

Sänkiaho, Risto, *Political Remobilisation in Welfare States*, in: Dalton, Russel J./Flanagan, Scott C./Beck, Paul Allen (eds.): *Electoral Change in Advanced Industrial Democracies*. Princeton, New Jersey 1984 (Sänkiaho, 1984)

Sully, Melanie, *Austria at the Crossroads*, in: *The World Today*, Feb. 1987 (Sully, 1987)

Ulram, Peter, *Um die Mehrheit der Mehrheit*, in: Plasser, Fritz/Ulram, Peter/Welan, Manfried (Hg.): *Demokratierituale*, Wien 1985 (Ulram, 1985)

Documentation of Austrian Election Results
1945–1986

Table 20.1
National Council elections 1945-1986

year	eligible voters	cast. voters	voter turnout	valid votes	ÖVP votes	%	SPÖ votes	%	FPÖ (WdU) votes	%	KPÖ (KLS) votes	%	other votes		%
1945	3,449,605	3,253,329	94.3	3,217,354	1,602,227	49.80	1,434,898	44.60			174,257	5.40	5,972		0.18
1949	4,391,815	4,250,616	96.8	4,193,733	1,846,581	44.03	1,623,524	38.71	489,273	11.66	213,066	5.08	21,289		0.50
1953	4,586,870	4,395,519	95.8	4,318,688	1,781,777	41.25	1,818,517	42.10	472,866	10.94	228,195	5.28	17,369		0.40
1956	4,614,464	4,427,711	96.0	4,351,908	1,999,986	45.95	1,873,295	43.04	283,749	6.52	192,438	4.42	2,440		0.05
1959	4,696,603	4,424,658	94.2	4,362,856	1,928,043	44.19	1,953,935	44.78	336,110	7.70	142,578	3.26	2,190		0.05
1962	4,805,351	4,506,007	93.8	4,465,131	2,024,501	45.43	1,960,685	43.99	313,895	7.04	135,520	3.04	21,530		0.48
1966	4,886,818	4,583,970	93.8	4,531,885	2,191,109	48.34	1,928,985	42.56	242,570	5.35	18,636	0.41	150,585	*)	3.38
1970	5,045,841	4,630,851	91.8	4,588,961	2,051,012	44.69	2,221,981	48.42	253,425	5.52	44,750	0.97	17,793		0.38
1971	4,984,448	4,607,616	92.4	4,556,990	1,964,713	43.11	2,280,168	50.03	248,473	5.45	61,762	1.35	1,874		0.04
1975	5,019,277	4,662,684	92.9	4,613,432	1,981,291	42.94	2,326,201	50.42	249,444	5.40	55,032	1.19	1,464		0.03
1979	5,186,735	4,784,173	92.2	4,729,251	1,981,739	41.90	2,413,226	51.02	286,743	6.06	45,280	1.95	2,263		0.05
1983	5,316,436	4,923,019	92.6	4,853,417	2,097,808	43.20	2,312,529	47.60	241,789	4.98	31,912	0.66	169,379	**)	3.50
1986	5,461,291	4,940,243	90.5	4,852,188	2,003,663	41.30	2,092,024	43.12	472,205	9.73	35,104	0.72	249,192	***)	5.10

*)   NCE 1966: DFP (Democratic Progressive Party)

**)

NCE 1983:

	votes	%
VGÖ (United Greens of Austria)	93,798	1.93
ALÖ (Alternative List of Austria)	65,816	1.36
ÖP (Austria Party)	5,851	0.12
AUS (Stop Foreigners Movement)	3,914	0.08

***)

NCE 1986:

	votes	%
The Green-Alternative / List Freda Meissner-Blau / The Green Alternatives / Democratic List (GAL)	234,028	4.82
Carinthian Greens - United Green-Alternatives	6,005	0.12
	1,059	0.02
Mir reicht's (I have had enough)	8,100	0.17

Table 20.2
Federal presidential elections in Austria
The first federal president of the Second Republic, Dr. Karl Renner, was elected by the
Federal Assembly on 20 December 1945

Elections by the people:

1st ballot:

6 May 1951;	eligible voters 4,513,597		voter turnout 97%
Dr. Burghard Breitner	662,502	votes	= 15.41%
Gottlieb Fiala	219,969	"	= 5.12%
Dr. Heinrich Gleißner	1,725,451	"	= 40.14%
Ludovica Hainisch	2,132	"	= 0.05%
Dr. Theodor Körner	1,682,881	"	= 39.15%
Dr. Johannes Ude	5,413	"	= 0.13%

2nd ballot:

27 May 1951		
Dr. Heinrich Gleißner	2,006,332	= 47.94%
Dr. Theodor Körner	2,178,631	= 52.06%
5 May 1957	eligible voters 4,630,997	voter turnout 97.2%
Dr. Wolfgang Denk	2,159,604	= 48.88%
Dr. Adolf Schärf	2,258,255	= 51.12%
28 April 1963	eligible voters 4,869,603	voter turnout 95.6%
Dr. Josef Kimmel	176,646	= 4.0%
Dr. Julius Raab	1,814,125	= 40.6%
Dr. Adolf Schärf	2,473,349	= 55.4%
23 May 1965	eligible voters 4,874,928	voter turnout 96%
Dr. Alfons Gorbach	2,260,888	= 49.3%
Franz Jonas	2,342,436	= 50.7%
25 April 1971	eligible voters 5,023,767	voter turnout 95.3%
Dr. Kurt Waldheim	2,224,809	= 47.2%
Franz Jonas	2,487,239	= 52.8%
23 June 1974	eligible voters 5,031,654	voter turnout 94.1%
DDr. Alois Lugger	2,238,470	= 48.3%
Dr. Rudolf Kirchschläger	2,392,367	= 51.7%
18 May 1980	eligible voters 5,215,894	voter turnout 91.6%
Dr. Norbert Burger	140,741	= 3.2%
Dr. Wilfried Gredler	751,400	= 16.9%
Dr. Rudolf Kirchschläger	3,538,748	= 79.9%

1st ballot:

4 May 1986	eligible voters 5,436,837	voter turnout 89.5%
Dr. Kurt Steyrer	2,061,104	= 43.7%
Dr. Kurt Waldheim	2,343,463	= 49.6%
Dr. Otto Scrinzi	55,724	= 1.2%
Freda Blau-Meissner	259,689	= 5.5%

2nd ballot:

8 June 1986	eligible voters 5,436,837	voter turnout 87.3%
Dr. Kurt Steyrer	2,107,023	= 46.1%
Dr. Kurt Waldheim	2,464,787	= 53.9%

Table 20.3
The popular referendum on 5 November 1978 concerning a federal law about the peaceful use of nuclear energy in Austria

The results of the referendum total and according to states (1978)

State Constituency	eligible voters	voter turn-out in %	cast votes total	cast votes invalid	cast votes valid	yes-votes	valid votes of these %	no-votes	%
Burgenland 1	187,879	68.1	127,897	3,513	124,384	74,377	59.8	50,007	40.2
Carinthia 2	355,219	63.0	223,637	5,726	217,911	117,841	54.1	100,070	45.9
Lawer Austria 3	964,048	71.9	692,756	20,602	672,154	341,831	50.9	330,323	49.1
Upper Austria 4	809,904	68.0	550,776	12,811	537,965	254,337	47.3	283,628	52.7
Salzburg 5	277,141	61.0	169,096	3,573	165,528	71,576	43.2	93,947	56.8
Styria 6	793,746	58.1	461,351	8,928	452,423	238,851	52.8	213,572	47.2
Tyrol 7	355,164	44.8	158,960	2,800	156,160	53,357	34.2	102,803	65.8
Vorarlberg 8	169,065	75.6	128,069	1,290	126,779	19,731	15.6	107,048	84.4
Vienny 9	1,171,613	63.8	746,940	16,753	730,187	404,808	55.4	325,379	44.6
total for Austria	5,083,779	64.1	3,259,482	75,996	3,183,486	1,576,709	49.5	1,606,777	50.5

Table 20.4
Petitions for parliamentary decisions in Austria (1964-1987)

Year	concerning	absolute	% of eligible voters
1964	Austrian broadcasting reform	833.389	17,30
1969	law on working hours	889.659	17,80
1969	discontinuence of the 13th school year	339.407	6,80
1975	protection of human life	896.579	17,90
1980	repeal of the Nuclear Energy Prohibition Act	421.282	8,00
1980	Tightening up of the Nuclear Energy Prohibition Act	147.016	2,80
1982	enactment of a law to economize on the conference in Vienna	1,361.561	25,74
1985	Konrad Lorenz petition Federal Constitutional Law	353.906	6,55
1985	extension of Civil Alternative Service (substitute military service)	196.376	3,63
1985	holding a popular referendum on the buying of interceptor aircraft	121.182	2,23
1987	FPÖ anti-privilege petition	250.435	4,56

Contributors

Franz *Birk*, director of IFES (Institute for Empirical Social Research) in Vienna.

Heidemarie A. *Bubendorfer*, PhD-student in Vienna.

Herbert *Dachs*, professor of political science at the University of Salzburg.

Ernst *Gehmacher*, director of IFES (Institute for Empirical Social Research) in Vienna.

Peter *Gerlich*, professor of political science at the University of Vienna.

Christian *Haerpfer*, vice-director of the Institute for Conflict Research in Vienna.

Anton *Kofler*, coordinator of the Parliamentary Club of the Greens.

Wolfgang *Mantl*, professor of political science and constitutional law at the University of Graz.

Wolfgang C. *Müller*, assistant professor of political science at the University of Vienna.

Rainer *Nick*, assistant professor of political science at the University of Innsbruck.

Günther *Ogris*, a free-lance contributor for IFES in Vienna.

Anton *Pelinka*, professor of political science at the University of Innsbruck.

Fritz *Plasser*, director of the section for fundamental political research in the federal party headquarters of the ÖVP and a lecturer for the Department of Political Science at the University of Innsbruck.

Bernhard *Raschauer*, professor of constitutional and administrative law at the University of Vienna.

Alfred *Stirnemann*, director of the Austrian Institute for Political Education in Mattersburg.

Melanie A. *Sully*, lecturer for the Department of Humanities, North Staffs Polytechnic, U.K.

Kurt *Traar*, director of the IT-Institute in Vienna.

Peter A. *Ulram*, director of Dr. Fessel & Co. (Institute for Public Opinion Research) in Vienna.

Barbara *Wicha*, lecturer for political science at the University of Salzburg.

Index

accommodation, politics of, 442
agenda, political, 205, 212
alienation, political, 6, 57, 216, 261
alignments, political, 312
alignments, stable, 41
alternative parties,
    genesis of, 175
Americanization,
    of party work, 304
anschluss-idea, 2, 14, 23, 224, 243
anti-establishment party, 441
anti-Fascist parties, 23
anti-party-resentiments, 436
antisemitism, 137
apartisans, 50
apathy, political, 303
attitudes, antidemocratic, 225
attitudes, confessional, 317
Austro-facism, 3
autonomy deficit, 191
avant-garde, postmaterialistic, 13

black boxes
    in party financing, 366
bureaucratization,
    of political parties, 280

cadre sections, 42
camp culture, 69, 70
camp loyalties, 75
camp mentality, 9, 24, 41, 69, 118, 298
camps, historical, 42
camps, ideological, 2
campaign research, 78
candidate recruitment,
    influence of political culture, 410
candidate selection, 403, 407
career patterns, 416
catch-all parties, 28, 298
Catholicism, 3, 22, 217
church attendance, 318

citizen movements, 173, 412
civic duty, 274
civic orientations, 135
civil war, 441
cleavages, historical, 22, 69
cleavages, new, 4, 30, 31
cleavages, party founding, 1
cleavages, religious, 48
cleavages, traditional, 201, 213
class parties, 26, 114, 147
classe politica, 11, 211
class voting, 150, 117
class voting,
    decline of, 118
clientelism, traditional, 11, 327
coalition government, 84
coalition, grand, 12, 16, 25, 58, 83, 110, 198,
    315, 323, 336, 389
coalition, small, 431
colonization, party-political, 69
concentration, 5, 21, 29, 314
conflict, generational, 32
consciousness, national, 223, 241
consensus, social-liberal, 198, 431
consociational democracy, 4, 24, 199, 315
consociationalism, 35, 284, 442
contested seats, 421
convergence, 4
corporate state, authoritarian, 23
corruption, 10, 211, 280, 374
crisis, diagnosis of, 53, 279
crisis management,
    state interventionist, 44
cut back management, 44
cynicism political, 443

dealignment, 12, 41, 49, 119, 131, 151, 198, 216
dealignment,
    functional model of, 61
decline of parties, 53, 131
declaration of independence, 23

decomposition, 31, 51, 57, 309
decompression, effect of, 55
deconcentration, 4, 191
de-confessionalization, 48
de-industrialization, 145
democracy, competitive, 4
democracy, intra-party, 284, 303
democracy, new, 440
democracy, post-industrial, 41, 61, 118
democracy, postauthoritarian, 23, 198
democratization, 347
density, behavioral, 62
density, organizational, 299
density, social, 62
diffuse support, 62
disclosure, of donations, 376
discontent, political, 264
dissatisfaction, political, 211
dissolution, 13, 99, 119, 145, 311

ecological parties, 178
educational structures, 147
efficacy, political, 6
election campaigns, funding of, 374
election, critical, 42, 55, 60, 198, 443
election parties, 394
electoral arena, 350
electoral behavior, 60, 73, 93, 117
electoral behavior, determinants of, 126
electoral behavior, factors of, 140
electoral behavior, long-term factors of, 124
electoral behavior, model of, 122
electoral behavior, stable, 70
electoral behavior, trends in, 76
electoral composition, 165
electoral composition, trends in, 167
electoral foundation, 54
electoral law, 284
electoral periods, 41
electoral reform, 404
electoral wavering, 76
elite, hegemonic, 55
environmentalism, 13, 120, 185, 202, 206, 433
erosion, of affective ties, 50
erosion, of party ties, 70
exceptionality, end of Austrian, 69
exchange theory, 329
expenditures, control of, 371
expenditures, limiting of, 377
expenditures,
        by parliamentary parties, 385

Fascist parties, 2
federalism, 309
feminism, 305
floating vote, 43, 112

fragility,
        of the party system, 309
fragmentation, 4, 24, 58, 71, 438
frame-parties, post-industrial, 192
FPÖ electorate, structure of, 162
fund raising, 302, 360
funding system, mixed, 374

golden age,
        of the Austrian party system, 41, 80
grassroots movement, 413
green-alternative parties, 173
green-alternative parties,
        electoral success of, 181
green-alternative parties,
        parliamentarization of, 188
green-alternative parties,
        structure and recruitment of, 181
green parties, history of, 186
green parties, voting for, 130
green voters, potential of, 85
green voters, young, 268

hegemony, socialdemocratic, 55, 198
historical compromise, 198
hyperstability, 5, 42, 216, 429
hypertrophy, organizational, 8

identification, affective, 51
identification, conative, 50
identity, national, 2, 35, 217, 223
ideological conceptualization, 200, 213
ideological voting, decline of, 53
image politics, 61
immobilism, 191
immune-system, of major parties, 48
impotence, political, 7
incentives, 332
independent voters, 151
infrastructure, political, 6, 24
in-kind contributions, 367
interest organizations, 411
interest parties, 43
invalid votes, 76
issues, new, 305
issue orientation, 201
issue voting, 197, 215

job patronage, 336

Kreisky era, 5, 61, 146, 429, 440

laical parties, 2
laicism, 217
lager-mentality, 235, 430, 442
late deciders, 51, 76
law-and-order syndrome, 201

legal status,
  of political parties, 359, 389
legitimacy crisis, 443
legitimacy, of the parties, 373
legitimation, political, 10

machine party, 330
macropatronage, 329
major parties,
  social structure of, 46
mass parties, origin of, 22
materialism, 138
media power, 106
membership dues, 302
membership in parliament,
  permanence of, 418
membership recruitment, 330
micropatronage, 328
milieus, traditional, 58
ministerial patronage, 337
mobilization, appellative, 43
mobilization, political, 8
model work, political, 287
modernization, social, 12, 45, 58
multi-party system, 34, 59, 113

nation-building, 240
national characteristics, 247
national pride, 248
National Socialism, 3, 24
nationalization, 25
nationalized industries, 210
Nazi party, members of, 236
negative voting, 62, 76, 81
neocorporatism, 37
neo-populism, 86
networks, political, 48
neutrality, permanent, 31, 224
nomination, 310, 402
non-voting, 76
normal vote, 42
normalization, 60
notable parties, old-style, 22

occupational structures, 146
opposition, fundamental, 189
opposition,
  political malaise of, 55
opposition vacuum, 320
organizational logic, 43
organizational problems, 328
over-organization, 10, 411
ÖVP electorate, structure of, 155

participation deficit, 191
participation, political, 259
participatory revolution, 70

partisans, strong, 9
partisans, weak, 50
party-book system, 8, 16, 218, 285
party clubs,
  in national and federal councils, 364
party, dominant, 55
party electorates, 145
party elite, 44
party expenditures, 358
party financing, 285, 302
party funding, 357
party funding,
  origins of funds, 360
party identification, 9, 50, 57, 87, 169, 297, 435
party images, 114, 125
party leaders, 321, 328
party leaners, 9
party loyalty, 99
party machine, 15
party management, 288
party members, 8, 54, 21, 264, 299
party members, core, 15
party members, degree of activity, 303, 342
party members, international, 8
party members, registered, 8
party members, social structure of, 149
party membership, density of, 300
party membership, motives, 338
party membership, types of, 301
party, new, 174, 305
party organization, 298
party patronage, 327
party platforms, 4
party platforms, historical, 26
party platforms, post-war, 28
party politics, regional, 312
party power, 285
party press, 366
party, protest, 185
party reform, 16, 279
party reform, latitude for, 282
party reform, scenarios, 281
party reform, tendencies, 284
party, regional, 321
party sections, 61
party shifters, 52, 62, 78
party state, 21, 410
party state, loss of significance, 34
party-superstructure, 60
party system, communal, 320
party system, encapsulated, 52
party system, regional, 309
party system, generation-specific, 59
party transformation, 31, 44, 47
party typology, 26
party work, active, 9
patriarchs, provincial, 315

patriotic pride, 250
patronage, 9, 44, 327
patronage parties, 347
patronage, political, 284
patronage ressources, 333
patronage strategy, 346
peace movement, 31, 191, 305
penetration, organizational, 8
personality-voter, 43, 82
personalization, 43, 72
pillarization, 9, 22, 41, 52, 347
pluralism, 4
polarization, 4
polarization, generational, 32
Political Action Study, 7, 16, 217
political agenda, 45
political clubs, 394
political culture, 5, 223, 318, 443
political education, 365
political efficacy, 15, 57, 135, 304
political finance, 358
political generations, 128
political interest, 263
political motivation, 328
political parties, founding of, 391
political socialization, 128
political trust, 100, 135
politician, ideal, 269
politicians, image of, 213, 270
politics, new, 444
populism, 346, 431
position issues, 125
post-materialism, 13, 120, 141, 213
power, sub-cultural, 47
primaries, 408
problems, strategic, 12
professionalization,
    of staff work, 43, 349
proportional representation, 3, 21, 314
protest culture, 7, 44
protest motives, 138
protest parties, 173
protest parties, new, 44
protest potential, 348
public grants, 370
public funding, forms of, 363

rationality, collective, 60
rational voter, 118
realignment, 41, 52, 60, 437
realignment, potential, 52
recruitment, federal norms, 404
recruitment,
    of political elites, 33, 401
recruitment, theories of, 423
re-education, 337, 348
referendum, 322, 325, 430

regionalism, 1, 309, 319
religious voting, 127
re-politicalization, of the parties, 287
representation deficit, 191
responsiveness, 15
ritualism, democratic, 6

satisfaction, political, 272
secularization, 48, 311, 412
secularization, political, 199, 214
self-image, Austrian, 246
self placement, ideological, 108, 200
semantic, political, 199
silent revolution, 271
single-issue movements, 175
small parties, emergence of, 191
social guaranteeism, 198
social movements, new, 188, 443
social partnership, 237, 438
social structure, politicalized, 42
society, pre-modern, 45
sociopolitical orientations, 203
socio-structural change, 45
SPÖ electorate, structure of, 151
specific support, 16
stability, political, 299, 443
stability, structural, 42
strategy, defensive, 85
strategy-mix, 43
stress, socio-cultural, 44
structure, sub-cultural, 47
subculture, political, 42
subjective political competence, 136
suprastructure, political, 24
symbolic politics, 45, 311
system support, 10

tax issue, 208
taxpayers' money, use of, 210
televization, 43
time of voting decision, 79
trends, electoral, 98
trends, structural, 70
turbulence, political, 57
turn out, 5, 444
two-and-a-half-party system, 4
two-party system, 3, 390
two-party system, bipolar, 59

urban citizen initiative, 176

valence issues, 125
value orientations, 134, 271
value change, 13, 197
volatility, 51, 63, 441
voter coalition, dominant, 55
voter coalitions, loose, 53

voter coalition, reform-oriented, 55
voter coalition, traditional, 41
voter efficacy, 6
voters, first-time, 70
voter market, monopolized, 59
voter, new type of, 43

voter, stationary, 76
voters, traditional, 45, 50, 54
voter typology, 139

welfare state, 44, 201
Weltanschauung parties, 28, 52